WHY PEOPLE KILL THEMSELVES

Third Edition

WHY PEOPLE KILL THEMSELVES

A 1990s Summary of Research Findings on Suicidal Behavior

By

DAVID LESTER, PH.D.
Center for the Study of Suicide
Blackwood, New Jersey

CHARLES C THOMAS • PUBLISHER
Springfield • Illinois • U.S.A.

Published and Distributed Throughout the World by

CHARLES C THOMAS • PUBLISHER
2600 South First Street
Springfield, Illinois 62794-9265

© *1992 by* CHARLES C THOMAS • PUBLISHER

ISBN 0-398-05767-2

Library of Congress Catalog Card Number: 91-34834

First Edition, 1972

Second Edition, 1983

With **THOMAS BOOKS** *careful attention is given to all details of manufacturing
and design. It is the Publisher's desire to present books that are satisfactory as to their
physical qualities and artistic possibilities and appropriate for their particular use.*
THOMAS BOOKS *will be true to those laws of quality that assure a good name
and good will.*

Printed in the United States of America
SC-R-3

Library of Congress Cataloging-in-Publication Data

Lester, David, 1942–
    Why people kill themselves : a 1990s summary of research findings
on suicidal behavior / David Lester. — 3rd ed.
        p.   cm.
    Includes bibliographical references.
    ISBN 0-398-05767-2
    1. Suicide.   2. Suicidal behavior.   I. Title.
HV6545.L43   1992
362.2'82 — dc20   91-34834
                                                                              CIP

PREFACE

In my volume *Why People Kill Themselves* published in 1972 (Lester, 1972), I reviewed all of the literature, both theory and research, published in the English language up to 1970. In the second edition of that volume (Lester, 1983), I reviewed research and theory on suicide published during the 1970s. The present volume reviews theory and research published on suicide in the 1980s.

This review of the 1980s is much longer than the earlier review of the 1970s because the amount written on suicide in the last decade has increased dramatically. In the 1960s, about one thousand articles and books appeared in the English language on suicide, in the 1970s about two thousand articles and books, and in the 1980s about three and a half thousand articles and books in the 1980s.

This increase in the volume of research publications on suicide makes keeping current with the literature quite difficult for the scholar, and I hope that the present review facilitates the task for those wishing to become acquainted with current research and theorizing on suicide.

In the first edition of this series (Lester, 1972) I described the major theories of suicide in detail and subjected them to an extensive critique. The review of the 1970s literature and the current review assume that the reader is aware of the essays in that first volume.

I was also very critical of each individual research study in the first volume of this series. I refrained from critiquing each research study in the second volume, and I continue this stance in the present volume. Almost every study on suicide suffers from methodological flaws, brought about in part by the difficulty in designing adequate research into this topic. It seems redundant to criticize every study for the same basic flaws which are pervasive in all of the research. I have found that it is easy to criticize the research conducted by others but difficult to design and execute better studies. Furthermore, the simple weight of accumulated results from several, admittedly flawed, studies begins to suggest the existence of an important finding which merits future intensive study.

Notwithstanding this, I have in the concluding section of several of the chapters made some general criticisms of the research reviewed and suggested some important issues, often methodological, which ought to be addressed in future research. In the final chapter of the book, I have also singled out some areas of study which seem to me be to characterized by enormous methodological difficulties.

As before, the literature has been filtered through my own idiosyncratic cognitive structures. I have focussed on research and theory and neglected clinical papers. On the other hand, I have tried to broaden my survey of the literature, extending beyond the major abstracting services (*Biological Abstracts, Index Medicus, Psychological Abstracts,* and *Sociological Abstracts*) to include abstracts in the fields of anthropology, criminal justice, history, political science, urban studies, and women's studies. I have also cited research from earlier years which I missed in my two previous reviews.

To facilitate locating literature on suicide, I have written a general guide to finding information on suicide (Lester, et al., 1980).

REFERENCES

Lester, D. *Why People Kill Themselves.* Springfield, IL: Charles C Thomas, 1972.
Lester, D. *Why People Kill Themselves.* Springfield, IL: Charles C Thomas, 1983.
Lester, D., Sell, B. H., & Sell, K. D. *Suicide: A Guide to Information Sources.* Detroit: Gale Research Company, 1980.

CONTENTS

		Page
Preface		v
Chapter 1.	THE INHERITANCE OF SUICIDAL INCLINATIONS	3
	Twin Studies	3
	Studies of Adoptees	3
	Family Studies	4
	Evolution and Suicide	4
	Discussion	5
Chapter 2.	PHYSIOLOGICAL FACTORS IN SUICIDE	7
	The Dexamethasone Suppression Test	7
	Completed Suicide	7
	Attempted Suicide	8
	Conclusion	8
	Cerebrospinal Fluid	8
	5-HIAA	9
	HVA	10
	MHPG	11
	Other Biochemicals	11
	Urine	12
	Norepinephrine	12
	Cortisol	12
	5-HIAA	13
	MHPG	13
	Vanillylmandelic Acid	13
	Plasma	13
	Thyroid-Stimulating Hormone	13
	Cortisol	13
	Monoamine Oxidase Activity	14
	Imipramine Binding	15

Adrenoceptor Binding   15
Serotonin   15
Other Biochemicals   15
Single Case Studies   16
Central Nervous System   16
Serotonin   16
Norepinephrine   16
Dopamine   17
5-HIAA   17
HVA   17
MHPG   17
Tryptophan   17
Other   17
Binding Sites   18
GABA   18
Benzodiazepine   18
Corticotrophin Releasing Factor   18
Muscarinic (Cholinergic)   18
Beta-Adrenergic   18
Serotonergic   18
Other Physiological Variables   19
Biorhythms   19
Blood Type   20
Brain Dysfunction   20
Early Respiratory Distress   20
Ectomorphy   20
Electromagnetic Power Lines   21
Electrodermal Activity   21
Evoked Potentials   21
Eye Color and Tatoos   22
Fluoride   22
Growth Hormone Response   22
Heart Rate   22
Intestinal Activity   22
Phenylthiocarbamide   23
Prolactin Response   23

Sensitivity to Pain   23
Tryptophan Consumption   23
Ventricular Enlargement   24
Viral DNA   24
The Brain's Electrical Activity   24
Discussion   25
Endocrine Systems   26
The Thyroid System   26
The Adrenal System   27
Conclusions   27

Chapter 3.   SEX DIFFERENCES IN SUICIDE   39

The Sex Ratio   39
Attempted Suicide   40
Sex Differences in Suicides   40
Attempted Suicide: Adolescents]   40
Attempted Suicide: Adults   41
Completed Suicide   42
Black Men and Women   43
MMPI Differences   43
Suicidal Females   43
Suicide in Pregnancy   44
Abortion   44
The Suicidal Act   44
The Menstrual Cycle   45
Oral Contraceptives   45
A Physiological Theory of Sex Differences in Suicide   46
Discussion   46

Chapter 4.   CHILDHOOD EXPERIENCES AND SUICIDE   50

Pfeffer's Research   51
Abortions   53
Abuse   53
Abusing Parents   55
Runaways   55
Adoption   56
Birth Order   56
Childhood Loss   57

	Dating	59
	Early Memories	60
	The Family	60
	Family Acceptance of Suicide	62
	Completed Suicides	62
	Perception of the Family	62
	Mothering	63
	Parent Characteristics	63
	Parent's Age	63
	Perinatal Conditions	64
	Puberty	64
	Punishment and Discipline	64
	Sibships	64
	Suicide in the Family and Others	65
	Predicting Later Suicide	67
	Discussion	67
Chapter 5.	SOCIOLOGICAL THEORIES OF SUICIDE	74
	The Classic Theories	74
	Durkheim's Theory of Suicide	74
	Henry and Short	75
	Gibbs and Martin	77
	New Theories	77
	Lester's Critical Mass Theory	77
	Lester's Social Deviance Theory	78
	Lester's Subcultural Theory	78
	Interpersonal Skills and Attempted Suicide	79
	Sociobiology	79
	Criminology-Based Theories of Suicide	80
	A Classical Theory of Suicide	80
	A Positivist Individualistic Theory of Suicide	80
	A Social Structure Theory of Suicide	80
	A Learning Theory of Suicide	81
	A Social Control Theory of Suicide	81
	A Social Reaction Theory of Suicide	81
	A Social Conflict Theory of Suicide	82
	Discussion	82

Chapter 6. THE RELIABILITY AND VALIDITY
            OF SUICIDE RATES   85

        Certification Errors   85
            Studies of Death Certificates/Autopsies   85
            Police Versus Medical Records   85
            Studies of Characteristics of Decedents   85
            Date of Injury and Date of Death   86
            Other Research Designs   86
            Coroners/Medical Examiners   87
        Effect of Legal Changes   87
        Concurrent Validity Studies   88
        Test-Retest Reliability   88
        Immigrants   88
        Discussion   88

Chapter 7. SOCIOLOGICAL CORRELATES OF SUICIDE   91

        Age   91
            Individual Studies   92
            Cultural Patterns   93
        Anomie   93
        Cohort Analyses   93
            Relative Cohort Size   94
            The Uematsue-Lester Cohort Theory   94
        Cultural Evolution   95
            Communism   95
        The Economy   96
            The Depression and the Great Crash   96
            The Wealth of the Region   96
            Strikes   96
            Unemployment: Completed Suicide   97
            Unemployment: Attempted Suicide   98
            Females in the Labor Force   99
            Regional Studies   99
            Time-Series Studies   100
            Seasonality of Suicide and GNP   102
        Education   102
        Era   102

Fertility   103
Health Services   103
The Homeless   103
Immigrants   103
Legal Effects   104
Marital Status   105
Nursing Homes   106
Occupation   106
   Women   107
   Academia   107
   Dentists   108
   Physicians   108
   Police   110
   Farmers   111
   Other Workers   111
Place of Birth and Place of Death   112
Population Change   112
Prison, Jail and Correctional Inmates   112
   The Typical Suicide   113
   Suicides Versus Others   114
   Overcrowding   115
   Attempted Suicide   116
Race/Ethnicity   116
   Australia: Aboriginees   116
   Brazilian Japanese   116
   Fiji   116
   Hungary   117
   Israel   117
   Malaysia   117
   Native Americans/Canadians   117
   Nigeria   118
   Peru   119
   Saudi Arabia   119
   Singapore   119
   South Africa   119
   South Pacific   119

United Kingdom 119
United States 120
United States: Amish 121
United States: Black/White Differences 121
Zimbabwe 122
International Comparisons 122
Religion 122
Miscounting Errors 122
Regional Studies 122
Other Studies 123
Societal Approval of Suicide and
Belief in Life after Death 124
Social Class 124
Urban-Rural 124
Urbanization 125
War 125
War Years 125
Military Draft 126
Servicemen 126
Veterans 127
Civil Violence 127
The Persecuted 128
Civilian Interns 128
A–Bomb Survivors 128
Indices of Pathology and Personality 128
America 128
Cross-National Studies 129
Within-Nation Studies 129
Primitive Societies 129
The Sociology of Attempted Suicide 130
Discussion 130
Chapter 8. THE VARIATION OF SUICIDE OVER TIME 149
Hour of Day 149
Month 149
Completed Suicide 149
Attempted Suicide 152
Presidential Elections 152

Day   152
   Completed Suicide   152
   Attempted Suicide   153
Sports Events   153
Holidays   154
   Completed Suicide   154
   Attempted Suicide   155
The Day of the Month   155
Birthdays and the Birthday Blues Effect   155
Astrological Studies and Month of Birth   155
Effect of Kennedy's Assassination   156
Lunar Phase   156
Temporal Stability   156
Theoretical Speculation   157
Discussion   157

Chapter 9.   MULTIVARIATE TIME SERIES AND REGIONAL STUDIES OF SUICIDE RATES   161

America   161
   Parishes   161
   Census Tracts   161
   Cities   161
   SMSAs   162
   Counties   162
   States   163
Studies of Primitive Societies   164
Studies Over Nations   165
Other Nations   166
   Australia   166
   Belgium   167
   Canada   167
   England   168
   Germany   168
   Hungary   168
   India   168
   Ireland   169
   Japan   169

New Zealand 169
Sri Lanka 169
Time Series 170
Australia 170
Canada 171
England 171
Finland 171
France 171
Israel 171
Norway 172
Sweden 172
Differences between Nations 172
Pockets of Violence 172
Discussion 173
Chapter 10. METEOROLOGICAL CORRELATES OF SUICIDE 178
Weather 178
Time-Series Analyses 178
Regional Studies 179
Day-by-Day Studies 179
Latitude and Longitude 179
Discussion 180
Chapter 11. THE EFFECTS OF SOCIAL RELATIONSHIPS
ON SUICIDE 182
Children 182
Couples 183
Effects of Attempting Suicide
on Social Relationships 184
Family Patterns 184
Hostility in Bystanders and Significant Others 185
Institutional Disruption 185
Interpersonal Conflict 186
Interpersonal Skills 187
Pet Ownership 187
Role Relationships 187
Social Integration 188
Sports Participation 189
Divorce 190

Suicide in Peers 190

Suicide Pacts 191

Survivors of Suicide 191

Discussion 191

Chapter 12. METHODOLOGICAL ISSUES 196

Methodological Problems with Ecological Studies 196

Opportunity-Based Suicide Rates 196

Areas of Research Which Have Been Neglected 196

Discussion 196

Chapter 13. THE SUICIDAL ACT 198

Interrupting the Suicidal Act 198

Intoxication and Suicide 198

The Truly Impulsive Act 199

The Preceding Hours 199

Near-Death Experiences 200

The Location of Suicide 200

The Cathartic Effect of Attempting Suicide 200

Successive Suicidal Actions 201

Intent and Lethality 201

Knowledge of Suicide Prevention Services 203

The Motives for Suicide 203

Recent Stress 204

Completed Suicides 204

Attempted Suicides 205

Suicidal Ideators 207

Adolescents 207

Sex Difference 208

Age Differences 208

Particular Precipitating Events 209

After the Act 209

Suicide Pacts 209

Discussion 210

Chapter 14. THE INCIDENCE OF SUICIDE 216

Community Surveys 216

College Students 218

Children and Adolescents 219

       Preschoolers   221
       Gifted School Students   222
     Other Groups   222
       Psychiatric Patients   222
       Mental Health Agencies   222
       The Elderly   222
       Special Groups   222
     Standardizing Estimates   223
     Discussion   223

Chapter 15.   THE METHOD CHOSEN FOR SUICIDE   227
     Firearms   227
       The Effect of Strict Hangun Control Laws   227
       Attempting to Measure
       The Extent of Firearm Ownership   230
       Actual Firearm Ownership   230
       Time-Series Analyses of
       Firearm Ownership in the USA   230
     Car Exhaust   231
       Detoxifying Car Exhaust   231
       A regional Study of Car Ownership   232
     Domestic Gas   232
     Medications and Poisons   233
     Drowning   235
     Will People Switch Methods?   236
     Association between Methods   236
     How Do People Rate the Different Methods?   237
     The Methods Used By Immigrants   237
     Early Determinants of Choice of Method   237
     Knowledge About Methods   238
     Correlates and Consequences of Choice of Method   238
       Era   239
     Studies of Particular Methods   240
       AIDS   240
       Burning   240
       Car Exhaust   240
       Cutting/Piercing   240
       Drowning   240
       Firearms   241

	Hanging	242
	Jumpers	242
	Medication	243
	Russian Roulette	244
	Self-Cutters	244
	Trains and Subways	245
	Throwing Oneself on a Hand Grenade	245
	Discussion	245
Chapter 16.	THOSE WHO MAKE REPEATED ATTEMPTS AT SUICIDE	253
	Repeaters Versus First-Time Attempters	253
	Adolescents	256
	Follow-Up Studies	256
	Clustered Versus Chronic Repeaters	257
	Subsequent Completed Suicide	258
	Discussion	258
Chapter 17.	COMMUNICATION AND THE SUICIDAL ACT	261
	Who Leaves Notes?	261
	Completed Suicides	261
	Attempted Suicides	261
	The Content of Suicide Notes	262
	Sex Differences	263
	Simulated Versus Genuine Notes	263
	Completers Versus Attempters	264
	Physician (And Other) Contacts	264
	Poetry	265
	Communication of Suicidal Intent	265
	Discussion	266
Chapter 18.	PSYCHIATRIC DISORDER AND SUICIDE	269
	Psychiatric Patients in General	270
	Adolescents	272
	Psychiatric Diagnosis	272
	Depressive Disorder	276
	Suicidal Ideation	276
	Attempted Suicide	276
	Completed Suicide	278

Major Affective Disorder 278
Unipolar Depression 280
Bipolar Disorders 280
Unipolar Versus Bipolar 281
Mania 282
Atypical Depression 282
Endogenous Depression 283
Neurotic Depression 283
Masked Depression 283
Primary/Secondary Affective Disorder 283
Depression with Obsessions 284
Depressive Symptoms 284
Depression Scores 284
Hopelessness 285
Beck's Research 285
Others' Research 285
Social Desirability 288
Schizophrenia 289
Characteristics of
Shizophrenic Completed Suicides 289
Characteristics of
Schizophrenic Attempted Suicides 291
Completed Versus Attempted Suicides 292
Suicidal Ideation 292
Schizoaffective Disorders 293
Atypical Psychoses 293
Personality Disorders 293
Borderline Personality Disorder 294
Deliberate Self-Harm Syndrome 295
Alcoholism 296
Alcohol Abuse in Attempted Suicides 296
Attempted Suicide in Alcoholics 297
Alcohol Versus Drug Abuse 299
Alcoholism in Completed Suicides 299
Completed Suicide in Alcoholics 299
Completed Versus Attempted Suicide 300
Suicidal Ideation 301
Alcohol Abuse as a Predictor of Suicide 301

Drug Abuse   301
  The Relationship between
  Drug Abuse and Suicide   301
  Completed Suicide in Drug Abusers   301
  Drug Abuse in Completed Suicides   302
  Drug Abuse in Attempted Suicides   302
  Attempted Suicide in Drug Abusers   303
  Amphetamine Users   304
  Cigarettes   304
  Cocaine   304
  Glue   304
  Opiates   304
  Steroids   305
Crime and Criminals   305
  Juveniles   305
  Adults   306
  Lesser Conduct Disorders   307
Other Disorders and Syndromes   307
  Eating Disorders   307
  Firesetters   308
  Homosexuality   309
  Hypochondriasis   310
  Mental Retardation   310
  Multiple Personality   310
  Obsessions   311
  Panic Disorder   311
  Phobias   311
  Transsexualism   311
Discussion   311
Chapter 19. MEDICAL ILLNESS   332
General Health   332
  Suicidal Preoccupation   332
  Attempted Suicide   332
  Completed Suicide   333
  AIDS   335
  Amputees   336
  Ankylosing Spondylitis   336

Appendectomies 336

Asthma/Hypertension 336

Cancer 337

Corticosteroid-Induced Psychosis 337

Crohn's Disease 337

Cushing's Syndrome 338

Dermatitis 338

Diabetes 338

Dialysis Patients and Renal Disease 338

Disability 338

Epilepsy 339

Headache 340

Heart Disease Patients 340

The Homebound 341

Huntington's Disease 341

Leprosy 341

Pain 341

Parkinsonism 342

Psychosomatic Disorders 342

Spinal Cord Patients 342

Terminally Ill 343

Transplant Patients 343

Ulcers 343

Correlations Between Illnesses 344

Discussion 344

Chapter 20. SUGGESTION AND SUICIDE 351

Clusters of Suicide 351

Epidemics 352

Statistical Tests of Clustering 352

The Effects of Publicized Suicides 352

Television News 352

Newsworthy Events 354

Television Films 354

Newspaper Coverage 355

Discussion 355

Chapter 21. SUICIDE AND AGGRESSION 359

Anger and Aggression in Suicidal People 359
  Aggression in Completed Suicides 359
  Aggression in Attempted Suicides 359
  The Direction of Aggression 360
  Suicidal Ideation and Aggression 360
  Suicide Attempters Versus Assaultive Persons 361
  Completed Versus Attempted Suicides 362
Murder and Suicide 362
  Studies of Murder-Suicide 362
  Murderers Versus Other Offenders 364
  Murderers Versus Suicides 364
  Sociological Studies 364
Violent Offenders and Patients 365
Discussion 366

Chapter 22. THE PERSONALITY OF SUICIDAL PEOPLE 370

Academic Performance 370
Alexithymia 371
Anhedonia 371
Anomie 371
Anxiety 371
Attitude toward Suicide 372
Baseball Performance 373
Death Concerns 373
Defense Mechanisms 374
Delayed Auditory Feedback 374
Developmental Maturity 374
Extraversion 374
Handedness 375
Hysteroid-Obsessoid 375
Impulsivity 375
Intelligence 375
Jungian Personality Traits 377
Learned Helplessness 377
Learning Disability 377
Locus of Control 377
Loneliness 378

Memory   378
Mood   378
Nervous Habits   379
Neuroticism and Psychoticism   379
Purpose in Life   380
Reasons for Living   380
Religiosity   380
Risk-Taking   380
Self-Concept   381
Separation Anxiety   382
Smoking and Recreation   382
Social Dysfunction   382
Thinking   382
   Problem-Solving Skills   384
Time Perception   385
Type A Personality   386
Understanding of Suicide   386
Withdrawal   386
Personality in General   387
Predicting Suicidal Risk with Psychological Tests   389
   MMPI   389
   Rorschach   391
   Suicide Prediction Scales   392
Discussion   392

Chapter 23.   SUICIDAL TYPES   403

Empirical Analyses   403
   Adolescents   403
   Adults   404
Studies of Different Types   404
Cultural Differences   405
Abstract Typologies   405
Discussion   406

Chapter 24.   OTHER SELF–DESTRUCTIVE BEHAVIORS   408

General Self-Destructiveness   409
Indirect Life-Threatening Behavior   409
Car Crashes   410

	Sociological Studies	411
	Self-Mutilation	411
	Alcoholism	412
	Faking Suicide	412
	Suicides Versus Accidental Deaths	412
	Discussion	413
Chapter 25.	SUICIDAL BEHAVIOR IN LOWER ANIMALS	415
	Completed Suicide	415
	Self-Mutilation	416
	Discussion	416
Chapter 26.	PSYCHOLOGICAL THEORIES OF SUICIDE	418
	Lester's Social Learning Theory of Suicide	418
	Classic Theories of Personality and Suicide	418
	Maris's Pathways Theory	419
	New Psychological Theories of Suicide	419
	Lester's Physiological Theory of Suicide	419
	Lester's Existential Theory of Suicide	420
	A Personality Factor Relevant for Suicide	421
	Lester's Deindividuation Theory of Suicide	422
	Lester's Depression Paradox Theory of Suicide	423
	Lester's Family Process Theory	425
	Lester's Predispositional and Situational Theory	426
	Shneidman's Commonalities of Suicide	427
	The Rationality of Suicide	428
	Lester's Early Events Theory	428
	Discussion	431
Chapter 27.	CONCLUSIONS	435
	Trends in the 1980s	435
	Genetics	435
	Biochemistry	435
	Sex Differences	436
	Childhood Experiences	436
	Sociological Approaches	436
	Social Relationships	436
	Methods for Suicide	436
	Suicide Notes	437

Suggestion and Clusters 437

Personality 437

Animals 437

Indirect Self-Destructive Behavior 437

Psychological Theory 438

Noteworthy Contributions 438

WHY PEOPLE KILL THEMSELVES

Chapter 1

THE INHERITANCE OF SUICIDAL INCLINATIONS

There are only two valid methods for studying the inheritance of behaviors: twin studies and cross-fostering (or studies of adoptees).

Twin Studies

Lester (1986) reviewed research on suicide in identical and nonidentical twins. He concluded that the research did show an increased concordance rate for suicide in monozygotic twins over dizygotic twins. However, no study had yet appeared in which the monozygotic twins were reared apart, a crucial condition for demonstrating a genetic effect. Secondly, none of the studies had controlled for psychiatric diagnosis so that we can tell whether it is suicide *per se* which is inherited or merely psychiatric disorder.

Pritz and Mitterauer (1985) found no evidence for an increased rate of concordance in identical twins over same sex siblings for suicidal ideation, suicide attempts or completed suicide, but their sample sizes for attempted and completed suicide were tiny (one and two respectively).

Studies Of Adoptees

Schulsinger et al. (1979) found a higher rate of suicide in adopted children as compared to non-adopted children. The adopted children who completed suicide had a higher frequency of suicide in their biological relatives than did non-suicidal adopted children, but not in their adoptive relatives. (There were no differences in psychiatric illness in the biological or adoptive relatives.) (The non-adopted suicides did not have more suicides in their relatives than non-adopted nonsuicidal people, but they did have a higher incidence of psychiatric illness in their relatives.)

Kety (1986) analyzed data from this sample further. Comparing depressed and non-depressed adoptees, he found that the depressed adoptees had more biological relatives (but not more adoptive relatives) who had completed suicide. This phenomenon was found for adoptees with affective reactions and bipolar depression and almost reached statistical significance for neurotic and unipolar depressions. Wender et al. (1986) compared adoptees with and without affective disorders. For those with affective disorder, their biological relatives (but not their adoptive relatives) had a higher incidence of completed suicide, unipolar affective disorder and alcohol abuse (but not attempted suicide or neurotic depression). No differences were found for adoptees without psychiatric disturbance.

Family Studies

Egeland and Sussex (1985) studied suicide in the Amish from 1880–1980 and found 26 suicides. Four families accounted for 19 of the suicides. (One family had seven suicides and another five.) The authors concluded that affective disorders were probably genetically transmitted in these families and that the suicides were evidence of this.

Evolution And Suicide

Lester (1988) has proposed an evolutionary theory of suicide. It has long been noticed that animal populations adjust to the size and abundance of nutrients in the environment. When resources are abundant, the population grows; when resources are scarce, the population shrinks. Does the human animal fits this pattern? Many human practices can be viewed as serving to achieve population regulation. Infanticide, geronticide, and murder in general can be seen as reducing the population in times of scarce resources. Social regulations on marriage, taboos on child spacing, and homosexuality can also be seen as ways of controlling population size.

Suicidal behavior fits well into this process. Suicide clearly removes the genes of those individuals from the gene pool and reduces the size of the population. Furthermore, when we look at the kinds of individuals who complete suicide, we find that, typically, suicide rates are highest in those who are older and past child-bearing age, except in the poorest nations of the world where suicide rates are higher among the young and fertile female members of the society (15- to 24-year-olds) than among the older women (Lester, 1982). Thus, it seems that when resources are scarce, as in the poorest nations, it is the fertile who kill themselves at the highest rate, thereby reducing the potential for growth in the population.

The fact that suicide rates are much higher in those who are psychiatrically disturbed can also be seen as genetically useful, for the suicide of these people removes their (possibly defective) genes from the gene pool in the society.

The existence of fatalistic suicide (Durkheim, 1897), in which people kill themselves in conformity to societal pressures, may also be seen as fitting the type of suicide necessary for this evolutionary view better than the suicides of the isolates and the alienated of the society (egoistic and anomic suicides). The ritualistic suicides, for example, suttee in Indian widows and seppuku in Japan, are suicides committed in response to social pressures. Mass suicide too can be seen as satisfying this evolutionary need.

Discussion

Although there is some evidence that monozygotic twins have higher concordance rates for suicide than dizygotic twins, no study has yet studied monozygotic twins reared apart (the critical group for proving the existence of an inherited component to a behavior), and so the inferences from the research must remain tentative. Furthermore, no study has yet disentangled psychiatric disturbance from suicide per se. It may be that psychiatric disturbance is inherited and that this is the reason for the greater incidence of suicide in monozygotic twins or in adoptees from suicidal biological parents.

The studies of adoptees reviewed above were not cross-fostering studies of suicide. To conduct a methodologically sound cross-fostering study of suicide, the adopted children of mothers who completed suicide would have to be compared with the adopted children of non-suicidal mothers for the incidence of suicide, after psychiatric disturbance has been controlled for. The studies of adoptees reviewed above were not of children from suicidal mothers. The research merely documented the stress of adoption and the possible genetic transmission of psychiatric disturbance.

Future research into the inheritance of suicide must endeavor to remedy both of these methodological flaws in past research into this topic.

REFERENCES

Durkheim, E. *Le Suicide.* Paris: Felix Alcan, 1897.

Egeland, J., & Sussex, J. Suicide and family loading for affective disorders. *Journal of the American Medical Association,* 1985, 254, 915–918.

Kety, S. S. Genetic factors in suicide. In A. Roy (Ed.) *Suicide.* Baltimore: Williams & Wilkins, 1986, 41–45.

Lester, D. The distribution of sex and age among completed suicides: a cross-national study. *International Journal of Social Psychiatry,* 1982, 28, 256–260.

Lester, D. Genetics, twin studies and suicide. *Suicide & Life-Threatening Behavior,* 1986, 16, 274–285.

Lester, D. *The Biochemical Basis for Suicide.* Springfield, IL: Charles C Thomas, 1988.

Pritz, W. F., & Mitterauer, B. J. Bipolar mood disorders. *Psychopathology,* 1985, 18, 293–304.

Schulsinger, F., Kety, S. S., Rosenthal, D., & Wender, P. H. A family study of suicide. In M. Schou & E. Stromgren (Eds.) *Origin, Prevention and Treatment of Affective Disorders.* New York: Academic, 1979, 277–287.

Wender, P. H., Kety, S. S., Rosenthal, D., Schulsinger, F., Ortmann, J., & Lunde, I. Psychiatric disorders in the biological and adoptive families of adopted individuals with affective disorders. *Archives of General Psychiatry,* 1986, 43, 923–929.

Chapter 2

PHYSIOLOGICAL FACTORS IN SUICIDE

The 1980s have witnessed a tremendous growth in the number of physiological studies of suicidal individuals. This, of course, is consistent with the general change from a strong preference for experiential explanations of human behavior manifest in the 1960s to the current preference for genetic and physiological explanations. The research conducted on the physiology of suicidal people has been conducted primarily as a means of studying the physiological causes of depression since the majority of suicides are also depressed. It would be preferable to await sound physiological theories of depression (and other disorders such as schizophrenia) before attempting to identify the physiological characteristics of depressed or schizophrenic suicides, but research has proceeded nevertheless.

The Dexamethasone Suppression Test

In the dexamethasone suppression test, the patient is given a dose of dexamethasone (a synthetic corticosteroid), causing the pituitary gland to cease production of the adrenocorticotrophic hormone (ACTH). The resulting plasma cortisol level should remain low for about eighteen hours, but often patients fail to show this suppression in plasma cortisol levels.

Completed Suicide

Four studies have appeared on the dexamethasone suppression test in completed suicides. Two have found an association between non-suppression and completed suicide (Boza, et al., 1988; Coryell and Schlesser, 1981), one suggestive evidence (Clements et al., 1985), and one no association (Yerevanian et al., 1983).

Attempted Suicide

Three studies have found a positive association between non-suppression and attempted suicide (Krishnan et al., 1984; Lopez-Ibor et al. 1985; Targum et al., 1983), and two studies have found a negative association (Robins and Alessi, 1985; Schmidtke et al., 1989 [but only for females]).

In contrast, eleven studies have reported no association (Ayuson-Gutierrez et al., 1987; Banki and Arato, 1983a, 1983b; Banki et al., 1988; Brown et al., 1986; de Leo et al., 1986; Hubain et al., 1986; Kocsis et al., 1986; Modestin and Ruef, 1987; Roy et al., 1986; Schmidtke et al., 1989 [but only for males]).

No association has been found between non-suppression and the method for suicide (Schmidtke et al., 1989) or suicidal ideation (Kocsis et al., 1986; Maes et al., 1989). Agren (1983) reported an association between the lethality of the attempt and non-suppression but found no association in another study (Agren and Wilde, 1982).

Only one study introduced controls for depression (Targum et al., 1983), and this study reported an association between non-suppression and attempting suicide.

Conclusion

The research suggests a possible link between non-suppression and completed suicide, but an association between non-suppression and attempted suicide seems unlikely. More definitive conclusions must await research on larger samples with controls for the level of depression.

Incidentally, two papers have suggested that the DST may cause suicide (Beck-Friis et al., 1981; Kronfol et al., 1982), but Coryell (1982) failed to support this suggestion in a sound research study.

Cerebrospinal Fluid

Brain amines break down as follows: serotonin breaks down into 5-hydroxyindoleacetic acid (5-HIAA), dopamine into homovanillic acid (HVA), and norepinephrine into 3-methoxy-4-hydroxyphenylglycol (MHPG). Many studies have examined the levels of these metabolics products in the cerebrospinal fluid of suicidal and non-suicidal patients.

(1) 5-HIAA

Many studies have reported lower levels of 5-HIAA in attempted suicides (Agren and Niklasson, 1986; Asberg et al., 1984; Banki and Arato, 1983a; Lidberg et al., 1985; Linnoila et al., 1983 for impulsive suicide attempters; Montgomery and Montgomery, 1982; Ninan et al., 1984, 1985; Oreland et al., 1981; Roy et al., 1989a; Traskman et al., 1981 in both depressed and the non-depressed attempted suicides; van Praag, 1983, 1986; Virkkunen et al., 1989). Brown et al. (1982) found lowered levels in suicidal patients, and Edman et al. (1986) and Lopez-Ibor et al. (1985) in mixed groups of ideators and attempters. Arato et al. (1988), however, reported *higher* levels in completed suicides.

Agren (1980) reported a negative correlation between 5-HIAA levels and the seriousness of the most serious suicide attempt ever, and Agren (1983) reported a negative correlation between 5-HIAA levels and the severity and lethality of the previous attempt at suicide and with current and recent suicidal ideation.

Six studies have reported no differences: Banki et al. (1985), Lester (1989b), Roy et al. (1985, 1986), Roy-Byrne et al. (1983) and Secunda et al. (1986). Roy-Byrne et al. (1983) also found no association between 5-HIAA levels and the risk-rescue scores for the suicide attempt or a family history of suicidal behavior.

Several studies have compared those making suicide attempts with violent and non-violent methods: two found no differences (Roy et al., 1985; van Praag, 1983) and three no significant differences for violent attempters (Banki and Arato, 1983a; Edman et al., 1986; and Traskman et al., 1981). Banki et al. (1984), however, found lower levels of 5-HIAA in psychiatric patients who made violent suicide attempts and in those diagnosed as alcoholics who made non-violent suicide attempts.

Linnoila et al. (1983) also found lower levels of 5-HIAA in impulsive violent offenders versus non-impulsive offenders, suggesting that levels of 5-HIAA in the cerebropsinal fluid may be related to impulsivity in general rather than suicide in particular. Asberg et al. (1984) found lower levels of 5-HIAA in murderers who murdered lovers or rivals versus those who murdered other victims. Lidberg et al. (1984) found low levels of 5-HIAA in three people who first murdered their children and then attempted suicide. Lidberg et al. (1985) found low levels of 5-HIAA in alcoholic murderers and murderers who had killed sexual partners. Van Praag (1986) found that depressed patients with low levels of 5-HIAA had made more prior suicide attempts, had more fights with friends and were more hostile when interviewed. However, Lopez-Ibor et al. (1985) found no lowering of 5-HIAA levels in psychiatric inpatients who had major depressions and a history of aggressivity as compared to those without such a history. Rydin et al. (1982) found that depressed and suicidal patients with low levels of 5-HIAA were more anxious, hostile and poorly adjusted (on the Rorschach ink-blot test).

This research does suggest that suicidal persons have lower levels of 5-HIAA in their cerebrospinal fluid. However, several caveats must qualify this conclusion. First, none of the studies matched the suicidal and non-suicidal patients for the level of depression or anxiety or for the severity of their psychological disturbance. Second, low levels of 5-HIAA may be associated with hostility, violence and impulsivity in general. The association with suicidal behavior may be a result of these more basic associations. No study has yet attempted to resolve this dilemma in an adequately designed study. Third, the one study on completed suicides reported the opposite phenomenon.

Finally, the frequent assertion that suicide attempters using violent methods for suicide have lower levels of 5-HIAA in the cerebropsinal fluid than non-violent attempters is simply not borne out by the research results yet.

(2) HVA

Several studies have reported significant associations between suicidal behavior and HVA levels: Montgomery and Montgomery (1982), Roy et al, (1986, 1989a), and Traskman et al. (1981), but for depressed patients attempters only. Agren (1982) found that the seriousness of the most serious suicide attempt ever made was negatively related to the level of HVA in depressed patients, and Agren (1983) replicated this association with the severity and lethality of the most recent suicide attempt and current and recent suicidal ideation.

One study found conflicting results. Banki, et al. (1984) found lower levels of HVA in attempted suicides who used violent methods but higher levels in those who used non-violent methods (but only for the depressed patients in this latter group).

Thirteen studies, however, found no relationship between cerebrospinal levels of HVA and attempted suicide: Agren and Niklasson (1986), Banki and Arato (1983a), Banki et al. (1985), Lester, (1989b), Lidberg et al. (1985), Ninan et al. (1984, 1985), Oreland et al. (1981), Roy et al. (1985),

Secunda et al. (1986), and Virkkunen et al., (1989). Brown et al. (1982) who studied suicidal behavior in patients with personality disorders also found no differences.

The weight of the evidence is, therefore, against lowered levels of HVA in suicidal patients. It is also worth noting that none of the studies reviewed made any attempt to match suicidal and non-suicidal patients for the severity of psychological disturbance, depression, anxiety, etc.

(3) MHPG

Agren (1980, 1983) reported that the level of MHPG was negatively related to the severity and lethality of recent suicide ideation and attempts in depressed psychiatric patients and to the seriousness of the most serious suicide attempt ever. Agren and Niklasson (1986) and Virkkunen et al. (1989) have also reported lower levels in attempted suicides. In contrast, Roy et al. (1989b) found higher levels of MHPG in violent suicide attempters (but not of norepinephrine). Cerebrospinal (and plasma) levels of MHPG (and norepinephrine) did not predict subsequent completed suicide.

Ten studies found no association between the levels of MHPG and suicidal behavior: Banki et al. (1985), Brown et al. (1982), Lester (1989b), Lidberg et al. (1985), Ninan et al. (1984, 1985), Oreland et al. (1981), Roy et al. (1985, 1989b) and Secunda et al. (1986).

These studies seem to indicate that there is no association between suicidal behavior and cerebrospinal levels of MHPG, though again no study matched patients for levels of psychological disturbance, depression, anxiety, etc.

(4) Other Biochemicals

No differences have been found in cortisol levels in the cerebrospinal fluid of attempted suicides or suicidal ideators (Banki et al., 1984, 1985; Kocsis et al., 1986; Secunda et al., 1986; Traskman et al., 1980). While two studies reported lower levels of HVA in attempted suicides (Agren and Niklasson, 1986; Roy et al., 1986), two have reported no differences (Secunda et al., 1986; Virkkunen et al., 1989).

Arato et al. (1988) found no differences in the levels of cortisol, ACTH or beta-endorphins in completed suicides. However, higher levels of the corticotrophin releasing factor have been reported in both attempted suicides (Banki et al., 1988) and completed suicides (Arato et al., 1988). Kavert et al. (1988) reported higher levels of 5-HT in completed suicides but normal levels of dopamine, epinephrine, norepinephrine and 3-methoxy metabolites.

Niklasson and Agren (1984) studied depressed inpatients who had unipolar or bipolar affective disorders and found that their suicidality was negatively related to the cerebrospinal levels of creatinine. Agren and Niklasson (1986) reported lower levels of xanthine, but not hypoxanthine. Agren et al. (1983) also found that suicidal tendencies in patients over time varied with the levels of hypoxanthine and xanthine.

Banki et al. (1985) compared psychiatric patients who had attempted suicide with those who had not and found that the attempted suicides had lower levels of magnesium in the cerebropsinal fluid but no significant differences in calcium.

Urine

Norepinephrine

Dajas et al. (1986) found no differences between depressed psychiatric inpatients and controls in the norepinephrine/epinephrine ratio in the urine. However, for the depressed patients, the norepinephrine/epinephrine ratio was negatively related to the degree of suicidal ideation, as was depressed mood. The absolute levels of norepinephrine and epinephrine were not related to suicidal ideation.

Ostroff et al. (1982) reported on two completed suicides and one attempted suicide who had been in an endocrinological study, all of whom had low norepinephrine/epinephrine ratios in their urine. Ostroff et al. (1985) pursued this finding by studying a sample of psychiatric inpatients with a history of attempted suicide and those without one. They found no differences in the absolute urinary levels of norepinephrine and epinephrine, but the ratio of these biochemicals was significantly lower in the attempted suicides.

Prasad (1985) found a lower norepinephrine/epinephrine ratio in those making violent attempts at suicide (by jumping or hanging) as compared to those who used wrist-slashing.

Cortisol

Ostroff et al. (1982) found three suicidal patients in an endocrinological study, two completed suicides and one attempted suicide. All three had higher urinary cortisol levels.

Agren and Wide (1982) studied patients with major depressions and found that the medical lethality of the most serious ever suicide attempt was negatively related to the level of cortisol in the urine. (Interestingly, urine and plasma cortisol levels were not related.)

Prasad (1985) found higher cortisol levels in those making suicide attempts by jumping or hanging as compared to those slashing their wrists.

5-HIAA

No studies of urinary levels of 5-HIAA of suicidal and non-suicidal patients have appeared, but Bertilson et al. (1982) have reported that there was no association between urinary and cerebrospinal levels of 5-HIAA.

MHPG

Agren (1983) found that urinary levels of MHPG were negatively related with current or recent suicidal ideation in depressed psychiatric patients and with the severity and lethality of previous suicide attempts. Secunda et al. (1986) found lower levels of MHPG in attempted suicides.

Vanillylmandelic Acid

Secunda et al. (1986) found normal levels of VMA in attempted suicides.

Plasma

Thyroid-Stimulating Hormone

Agren and Wide (1982) studied patients with major depressions and found that the medical lethality of their most serious suicide attempt ever was not related to the plasma level of the thyroid-stimulating hormone or the change in the level of the thyroid-stimulating hormone after an injection of the thyroid-releasing hormone.

Cortisol

Kocsis et al. (1986) reported lower levels of cortisol in attempted suicides, but three other studies reported no differences (Ayuson-Gutierrez et al., 1987; Brown et al., 1986; Hubain et al., 1986). In addition, de Leo et al. (1986) found no association between serum cortisol levels and suicidal risk or intent, and Maes et al. (1989) found no association with suicidal ideation.

Meltzer et al. (1983, 1984) gave serotonin orally to manic-depressive patients and found that those who had attempted suicide had a greater serum cortisol response (but the difference was not found between those with prior suicidal ideation and those without.)

Monoamine Oxidase Activity

Monoamine oxidase is one of the enzymes that breaks down the neurotransmitters into their metabolites. Several studies have explored the concentration of monoamine oxidase in the blood.

Agren (1983) found that platelet monoamine oxidase activity was not related to current suicidal ideation or the severity of past suicidal attempts in depressed psychiatric patients. Gottfries et al. (1980) studied patients with affective disorders and found that suicidal ideation was not associated with platelet monoamine oxidase activity. Six patients who had attempted suicide using active methods for suicide had lower monoamine oxidase activity than nine using passive methods and non-suicidal patients. Oreland et al. (1981) studied depressed psychiatric patients and found that those who had attempted suicide did not differ from those who had not attempted suicide in their monoamine oxidase activity. These three studies do not lend much support for an association between plasma levels of monoamine oxidase activity and suicidal behavior.

Sullivan et al. (1979) studied male alcoholics and found that those with low levels of monoamine oxidase activity had a higher incidence of attempted suicide in their first degree relatives (as well as increased rates of alcoholism and psychiatric hospitalization in the relatives and lower levels of monoamine oxidase activity).

Buchsbaum et al. (1976) identified college students with high and low levels of platelet monoamine oxidase activity and found no differences in their history of attempted suicide. However, the students with low levels had a higher incidence of completed and attempted suicides in their families.

Coursey et al. (1982) followed-up college students with high and low levels of platelet monoamine oxidase activity. Those with low levels were more likely to enter a psychiatric hospital but had no greater incidence of attempted suicide in their families.

On the whole, this research does not support a lower level of monoamine oxidase activity in suicidal subjects. The increased incidence of suicide and psychiatric disorders in the relatives of people with low monoamine oxidase activity levels is without controls for the degree of psychiatric disturbance or depression, and can be only tangentially related to suicide.

Imipramine Binding

Although Marazziti et al. (1989a, 1989b) found decreased capacity for binding in attempted suicides (Bmax but not Kd), Roy et al. (1987) and Wagner et al. (1985) found no decrease. In fact, Wagner et al. found increased binding in violent suicide attempters.

Adrenoceptor Binding

Carsten et al. (1988) found no differences in platelet adrenoceptor binding in attempted suicides and psychiatric controls.

Serotonin

Braunig et al., (1989) found lower levels of serotonin in attempted suicides and patients with suicidal ideation, but Modai et al. (1989) found no association between serotonin levels and attempted suicide or suicidal ideation.

Other Biochemicals

Attempted suicide has been shown to be associated with higher levels of testosterone (Roland et al., 1986) melatonin (Beck-Friis et al., 1985), di-homo-gamma-linolenic acid in those using violent methods (Virkkunen et al., 1987), and potassium (Irmis, 1983), and lower levels of norepinephrine (Roy et al., 1989b), zinc (Hronek et al., 1989), calcium (Irmis, 1983), and prostaglandin (2-alpha) (MacMurray and Bozzetti, 1987), especially in those using violent methods. Mendelson et al. (1982) found higher levels of the luteinizing hormone in completed suicides.

Attempted suicide does not appear to be associated with cholesterol (Virkkunen et al., 1987), glucose (Lester, 1989b; Virkkunen et al. 1989), MHPG (Roy et al., 1989b) or the monoacetyldapsone/dapsone ratio (Traskman-Bendz et al., 1988).

Norepinephrine, MHPG and melatonin were not associated with the method for suicide, and norepinephrine and MHPG were not associated with subsequent completed suicide (Beck-Friis et al., 1985; Roy et al., 1989).

Maes, et al. (1989) found no association between suicidal ideation and the levels of the adrenocorticotrophic and thyrotropin-secreting hormones, free thyroxene, L-tryptophan or the L-tryptophan/other amino acids ratio. However, Demling et al. (1988) found that suicide attempters had lower levels of total tryptophan but not free tryptophan. The levels of competing large neutral amino acids was lower only in non-disturbed suicide attempters.

Single Case Studies

Two papers have appeared monitoring cerebrospinal fluid levels of various biochemicals in one person before or after a suicidal action (Braunig et al., 1988; Dent et al., 1986), reporting higher levels of serotonin after a suicide attempt and low levels of 5-HIAA, cortisol, prolactin, and beta-endorphins and high levels of HVA and MHPG before a completed suicide.

Central Nervous System

Serotonin

Korpi et al. (1986) compared the brains of suicides, schizophrenics and controls. The suicides and schizophrenics had *higher* levels of serotonin in the basal ganglia, but the suicides had lower levels of serotonin in the hypothalamus. For the schizophrenics, the brains of those dying from suicide did not differ in the concentration of serotonin from the brains of those dying from other causes. Cheetham, et al. (1989) found less serotonin in the putamen and, in those using violent methods, less in both the putmamen and hippocampus.

However, Arato et al. (1987), Manchon et al. (1987) and Owen et al. (1986) found no differences in the concentration of serotonin in the hippocampus or the cortex.

Norepinephrine

Moses and Robins (1975) found that suicides had higher levels of norepinephrine in some areas of the hypothalamus, and, for the depressed suicides, the hippocampus. Manchon et al. (1987) found higher levels in the hippocampus.

Dopamine

Moses and Robins (1975) and Manchon et al. (1987) found no differences in the dopamine concentrations in the brains of suicides and controls.

5-HIAA

Korpi et al. (1986) compared the brains of suicides, schizophrenics and controls and found higher levels of 5-HIAA in the occipital cortex of the suicides and schizophrenics. For the schizophrenics, those dying of suicide did not differ in 5-HIAA concentrations from those dying of other causes. Owen et al. (1986) found higher concentrations of 5-HIAA in the hippocampus but not in the occipital cortex. Owen et al. (1983) also reported no differences in the frontal cortex.

Arato et al. (1987) and Crow et al. (1984) found no differences in the cortex in the concentration of 5-HIAA of suicides versus controls. Cheetham, et al. (1989) found no differences either except that those using violent methods had more 5-HIAA in the putamen.

HVA

Crow et al. (1984) found no differences in homovanillic acid in the frontal cortex of suicides and controls.

MHPG

Crow et al. (1984) found no differences in the concentration of MHPG in the frontal cortex of suicides and controls.

Tryptophan

Korpi et al. (1986, 1988) compared the brains of suicides, schizophrenics and controls and found no differences in the concentration of tryptophan.

Other

No differences have been found in the levels of monoamine oxidase (Stanley, 1984), decarboxylase activity (Cheetham et al., 1988a), gamma-aminobutyric acid (GABA) (Cross et al., 1988; Korpi et al., 1988; Manchon et al., 1987), somatostatin immunoreactivity (Charlton et al., 1988a), corticotropin-releasing factor immunoreactivity (Charlton et al., 1988b), or taurine, glycine, threonine, glutamate, aspartate, or alanine (Korpi et al. 1988). Completed suicides may have less glutamine in the hypothalamus (Korpi et al., 1988).

Binding Sites

In recent studies, investigators have been examining the concentrations of receptors (or binding sites) at the synapses of the nerve cells in the brain. Neurotransmitters produce their biological effect by interacting with these receptors.

GABA

Completed suicides were found to have more GABA binding sites, but only in the frontal cortex (Cheetham et al., 1988a).

Benzodiazepine

Manchon et al. (1987) found more of some types of benzodiazepine binding sites in the hippocampus region of completed suicides.

Corticotrophin Releasing Factor (CRF)

Nemeroff et al. (1988) found fewer CRF binding sites in the brains of completed suicides.

Muscarinic (Cholinergic)

One study found more muscarinic binding sites in suicides as compared to controls (Meyerson et al., 1982), while two studies have reported no differences (Kaufman et al., 1984; Stanley, 1984).

Beta-Adrenergic

Several studies have found more beta-adrenergic binding sites in suicides (Mann, 1986; Mann et al., 1986a; Meana and Garcia-Sevilla, 1987; Biegon and Israeli, 1988 for beta$_1$ receptors only in some regions), while others have reported no differences (Crow et al., 1984; Meyerson et al., 1982). De Paermentier et al. (1989) reported fewer sites but the particular region with the deficit differed for suicides using violent and nonviolent methods.

Serotonergic

(1) **Imipramine:** One study has reported more imipramine binding sites in the brains of suicides (Meyerson et al., 1982), three have reported

fewer binding sites (Arora and Meltzer, 1989b; Crow et al., 1984; Mann and Stanley, 1984), and two have reported no differences (Owen et al., 1986; Stanley et al., 1982). Arato et al. (1987) found more sites in the left cortex than in the right for suicides and the reverse for the controls. There were no significant differences in the hippocampus. Gross-Iseroff et al. (1989) found more sites in the hippocampus, fewer in the frontoparietal cortex and no differences in other regions (such as the basal ganglia and the prefrontal cortex). Clearly, the situation may be quite complex.

(2) **Ketanserin:** Three studies have reported more binding sites in the brains of suicides (Mann, 1986; Mann et al., 1986a; Stanley and Mann, 1983), while four studies report no differences (Cheetham et al., 1988b; Crow et al., 1984; Owen et al. 1983; Owen et al., 1986).

(3) **Serotonin:** Six studies have found no differences in serotonin binding sites between the brains of suicides and controls (Crow et al., 1984; Lawrence et al., 1989; Mann, 1986; Owen et al., 1983; Owen et al., 1986; Stanley and Mann, 1983). One study found more sites but only for suicides using violent methods (Arora and Meltzer, 1989a).

Meyendorff et al. (1986) gave suicidal patients fenfluramine which they hypopthesized would reduce these binding sites. The suicidal ideation and depression scores of the patients decreased but their psychotic symptoms did not.

Overall, therefore, this research seems exploratory, inconsistent or negative. Furthermore, few of the studies have introduced controls for the psychiatric disturbance of the suicides.

Other Physiological Variables

Biorhythms

D'Andrea et al. (1984) found that more completed suicides occurred on days predicted to be critical than on other days, but they did not use a comparison group of non-suicidal deaths.

Lester (1990) tried to replicate these results using samples of suicides, homicide victims and natural deaths. No variation over the biorhythm cycles was found for the suicides, nor differences from the distribution of homicide victims and natural deaths (save that the distributions of suicides and homicide victims differed for the intellectual cycle). Lester found no increased risk on critical, semicritical or non-critical days.

Linna and Liikkanen (1983) found no differences between completed suicides and heart failure deaths in biorhythms. At the moment, therefore, evidence for a relationship between suicidal deaths and biorhythms remains unproven.

Blood Type

No study has yet appeared that explores the distribution of blood types in samples of attempted or completed suicides. However, Lester (1987a) studied seventeen of the eighteen major industrialized nations and found that suicide rates were higher in those nations with fewer type O people and with more type A, type B, and type AB people. Lester then checked and found that Hungary, the nation with the highest suicide rate, had a lower proportion of type O people than these seventeen nations.

Brain Dysfunction

Kenny et al. (1979) compared adolescent suicide attempters with medical controls for their performance on the Bender-Gestalt Visual Motor Test under normal conditions and with background interference. The suicidal adolescents performed worse, suggesting neurological dysfunction. (They also had more behavior problems at school and had failed a grade more often.)

Robins et al. (1977) compared suicidal and nonsuicidal elderly white male psychiatric patients and found no differences in signs of brain damage. Ellis et al. (1989) found no differences in neuropsychological impairment between suicide attempters and psychiatric inpatients.

Early Respiratory Distress

Salk et al. (1985) compared adolescents who completed suicide with those who had not. The suicides were more likely to have shown respiratory distress in the first hour after birth (and to have had mothers who sought no maternal care in the first twenty weeks of pregnancy and who had had chronic diseases during pregnancy).

Ectomorphy

Lester (1987c) used a simple measure of ectomorphy (height divided by the cube root of the weight) to assess 126 white male completed suicides. He did not have comparison figures for a non-suicidal group, but he did find that those who died by suffocation had higher ectomorphy scores (that is, were thinner) than those using other methods. Thomas and Greenstreet (1973) compared medical students who later killed themselves with controls and found them to have been more underweight, more ectomorphic, more nervously tense, heavier smokers, lighter drinkers, and lower in diastolic blood pressure.

In a cross-cultural study, Lester (1981) calculated ectomorphy ratios for typical infants and children from ten industrialized nations. Those nations with the more ectomorphic one-year-olds had higher male and female suicide rates (though only the association with the male suicide rates was statistically significant). (The ectomorphy scores of the children were not related to the calorie intake, caffeine consumption or gross national product per capita of the nations.) This finding does support Sheldon's hypothesis and is quite remarkable since it relates infant physiques to adult suicidal behavior in the nations. A parallel study on individuals would be most welcome.

Electromagnetic Power Lines

Reichmanis et al. (1979) found that completed suicides were more likely to live near power lines with particular fields (0.10–1.07 and 1.76–2.78 V/m) than were random people in the same area. Overall, the suicides were exposed to stronger magnetic fields (Perry et al., 1981). McDowall (1986), however, failed to confirm the association between completed suicide and living near power lines.

Electrodermal Activity

Thorell (1987; Thorell and D'Elia, 1987, 1988) found that attempted suicides differ in their electrodermal response from controls. In one study the suicidal subjects were more hyporesponsive on the phasic (but not the tonic) stimulus-unrelated response, in a second study generally hyporesponsive and in a third study less responsive but not significantly so. Thus, Thorell's results are inconsistent at present.

Evoked Potentials

Agren et al. (1983) found that the amplitude of evoked potentials in patients with major depressive disorders was not related to the number of prior suicide attempts or their seriousness. However, the slope function was negatively related to the incidence and the seriousness of prior suicide attempts.

Eye Color And Tattoos

Lester (1986) studied samples of white male suicides and natural deaths. The two groups did not differ in the incidence of tattoos or in eye color. (Lester found that males with tattoos were more likely to use guns for their suicide, and males with brown eyes were more likely to use hanging and poison.)

Fluoride

Grandjean et al. (1985) studied a group of cryolite workers who had been employed from 1924 to 1961 and exposed to fluoride. Of the 206 (out of 431 workers) who had died, thirteen (6.3 percent) had died from suicide as compared to an expected number of six.

Stimulated by this finding, Lester (1987b) studied the relationship between mild levels of exposure to fluoride and suicide rates in the states of the USA. He found that states where more people drank fluoridated water had lower suicide rates.

These two studies, of course, have very different methodologies and explore very different levels of exposure to fluoride. However, further research on fluoride may be of interest in the light of these findings.

Growth Hormone Response

Ryan et al. (1988) administered desmethylimipramine to depressed patients, and those with suicidal preoccupation showed less secretion of the growth hormone afterwards.

Heart Rate

Irmis (1982) compared attempted suicides with neurotic patients and found the suicides to have significantly different resting heart frequencies as measured from their EKGs, but he did not describe the direction of the difference. Edman et al. (1986) found no differences between suicide attempters making violent and non-violent attempts in their heart rate or electrodermal response (skin conductance). Those making violent attempts did show faster habituation to tones.

Intestinal Activity

Lechin et al. (1983) found that unipolar depressed patients with a high intestinal tone (motility) were currently more suicidal.

Phenylthiocarbamide

Kimmel and Lester (1987) found no differences in past suicidal ideation and suicide attempts between those who could taste phenylthiocarbamide and those who could not.

Prolactin Response

Coccaro et al. (1989) gave psychiatric patients fenfluramine (a serotonin releasing/uptake inhibiting agent), and the prolactin response was less in patients who had attempted suicide. Freeska et al. (1989) found that reduced prolactin release after intravenous fentanyl predicted subsequent completed suicide.

Sensitivity to Pain

Rosenthal and Rosenthal (1984) found that some children who attempted suicide showed neither pain nor crying in response to their suicide attempt (or to other accidents), and this was especially true for those whose motives were self-punishment and reunion.

Tryptophan Consumption

The synthesis of serotonin (5-hydroxytryptamine) requires the precursor amino acid L-tryptophan which is obtained from our diet, and corn has low levels of tryptophan as compared to other cereals. Lester (1985) found no association for a sample of 38 nations between per capita corn consumption and suicide rates.

Kitahara (1987–1988) noted that the level of serotonin in the brain was not controlled simply by levels of tryptophan. Although the rate of synthesis of serotonin is affected by the availability of tryptophan, a high level of tryptophan does not necessarily mean a high level of serotonin. Other amino acids in the blood (such as tyrosine, phenylalanine, leucine, isoleucine and valine) compete with tryptophan for access to the brain. If the levels of these other amino acids are high, less tryptophan is carried to the brain. Kitahara, therefore, argued that the blood level of tryptophan *relative* to the blood levels of the other amino acids was the important factor. Kitahara took six nations and examined the total dietary intake of the citizens of those nations for the major amino acids. He calculated the tryptophan/other amino acid ratios for each nation based on their total dietary intake. Kitahara found that when the dietary tryptophan ratio is low, suicide rates tended to be high.

In a sample of 32 nations, Kitahara (1986a) found no association between estimated tryptophan intake from the national diet and suicide rates. Lester (1989a) replicated this study, controlling for the level of economic development of the nations, and found no association. In a reduced sample of European nations, the association was negative (Kitahara, 1986b).

Kitahara (1987) then compared the diets of attempted suicides and normal controls. He found that the suicidal people took in less ascorbic acid, but did not differ in their intake of tryptophan, tyrosine, calcium, phosphorus, vitamins A, D and E, thiamine, riboflavin, or niacin.

Cowen and Charig (1987) gave tryptophan intravenously to depressed patients. Suicidal preoccupation was related to changes in the levels of prolactin and the growth hormone and to weight loss.

Ventricular Enlargement

Levy et al. (1984) gave CAT scans to chronic schizophrenics and found that those who had attempted suicide had higher ventricle-brain ratios than those who had not attempted suicide. Those making more violent and dangerous suicide attempts had the highest ratios. In a follow-up study, three schizophrenics who completed or attempted suicide were found to have had high ratios.

Schlegel et al. (1989) found no association between the ventricle-brain ratio and suicidal impulses in depressed patients. Nasrallah et al. (1984a) found that three schizophrenics who completed suicide all had high ventricle-brain ratios. However, in a comparison of manic patients who had attempted suicide in the past with those who had not, no differences in ventricle-brain ratios were found. Nasrallah et al. (1984b) found no association between attempting suicide and the ventricle-brain ratio.

These studies, therefore, show no consistent association between suicide and the ventricle-brain ratio.

Viral DNA

Carter et al. (1987) found no association between the presence of viral DNA in the brain and completed suicide.

The Brain's Electrical Activity

Struve (1983) found no differences between suicidal and non-suicidal psychiatric patients in the incidence of abnormal EEGs. Struve, et al.

(1977) found a higher incidence of paroxysmal EEGs in suicidal ideators and attempters than in other psychiatric patients. There was no increased incidence of six and fourteen per second spiking. The high incidence of paroxysmal EEGs was found for both sexes, in both aggressive and non-aggressive suicidal patients, but not in adolescents. Struve (1983) found no excess incidence of paroxysmal EEGs in completed suicides over comparison groups.

Struve (1983) compared suicidal psychiatric patients with non-paroxysmal EEGs to those with paroxysmal EEGs. The paroxysmal EEG patients with suicidal ideation were more reactive to precipitating events and had more frequent and intense suicidal ideation in the past. For those attempting suicide, the paroxysmal attempters made less lethal attempts, more impulsive attempts, and had more frequent, intense and reactive suicidal ideation in the past.

Struve (1985) studied female psychiatric patients and found that the taking of oral contraceptives was not related to the incidence of attempted suicide in patients with normal EEGs. However, among those patients with paroxysmal EEGs, those patients taking oral contraceptives had a significantly higher incidence of attempted suicide than those not taking oral contraceptives. Struve felt that this association may be a result of the tendency for oral contraceptives to produce depression (and other psychiatric side effects) in some women which is tolerated less well by those with cerebral dysfunction.

Discussion

Struve (1986) has reviewed research on electroencephalograms and suicide and made some important methodological points. He first noted that the research is based on non-invasive scalp EEGs. This technique will miss abnormal electrical activity too weak to be registered on the scalp. Thus, incidences of abnormal electrical activity will be underestimates.

Struve noted that EEG abnormalities, when observed, may assist in the detection of biological (and related psychiatric) illnesses in patients. If these underlying biological illnesses can be cured, the risk of psychiatric disturbance (and accompanying suicidal tendencies) may be reduced. Alternatively, some particular cerebral dysrhythmias may be specifically related to suicidal behavior.

Occasionally, depressive disorders can result from organic causes. Disturbances of mood, including depression, are quite common in endocrine disorders. Occasionally, these endocrine imbalances are associated with abnormal EEGs. Fader and Struve (1972) reported a case of a woman who underwent a thryoidectomy. The amount of replacement thyroid was insufficient, and she developed depression and made two suicide attempts. She showed an abnormal EEG, leading Fader and Struve to increase the amount of replacement thyroid, eliminating her depression.

The hypothetical association between small sharp spikes and suicide, though the evidence is inconsistent, illustrates a similar problem. Small et al. (1975) reported that small sharp spiking could be a marker for manic-depressive disorder. Thus, if small sharp spiking is found to be associated with suicidal behavior, this association may be a by-product of the association between spiking and affective disorders.

Struve in his research, which found that suicidal tendencies were associated with paroxysmal EEGs, also found that assaultive behavior was associated with paroxysmal EEGs. Perhaps there are episodic behavioral disorders (Monroe, 1982), disorders which appear for brief periods of time (hours or days), involving emotional instability, alteration in mood and impulsive acting-out. The cerebral dysfunction may also impede appropriate responses to situational stress.

The lack of specificity of the suicidal behavior/paroxysmal-EEG relationship prevents the formulation of a physiological theory of suicide based on EEG research. At most, the study of EEGs may permit a qualitative description of types of suicidal behavior in those with cerebral dysfunction and those without such dysfunction.

Endocrine Systems

The Thyroid System

Although depressive symptoms often complicate the progress of patients with thyroid disorders, Rich (1986) found no published cases of suicide in these patients. Thus, it was not yet possible to estimate the suicide risk in these patients. However, Fader and Struve (1972) have reported a case of a woman who made two suicide attempts after undergoing a thyroidectomy, even though she had been placed on replacement thyroid. Increasing the dose of the replacement thyroid eliminated the depression, and no more suicidal behavior was observed.

Linkowski et al. (1983) compared women with affective disorders who had attempted suicide with those who had not. They did not differ in their basal thyrotropin levels nor in their response to the thyrotropin-releasing hormone. (In addition, Linkowski classified the attempts at suicide as violent and non-violent and found that the women making the two kinds of attempts did not differ on these measures.) Linkowski followed-up these patients for five years and found that four had completed suicide (three violently). All four had a weak response to injections of the thyrotropin-releasing hormone. However, Linkowski et al. (1984) found less response in women who had attempted suicide and who completed suicide subsequently.

Drummond et al. (1984) studied a sample of 48 completed suicides and found that four had abnormal thyroid functioning. All were female, and their suicides were violent. Thus, perhaps the thyroid hormone system may provide a marker for suicide.

The Adrenal System

Cushing's syndrome is a condition associated with overproduction of adrenal cortical hormones. Cases of suicide in Cushing's syndrome patients have been noted (Spillane, 1951). Cohen (1980) studied 29 patients with Cushing's syndrome and found 25 to be significantly depressed, five with severe depressions. One of these five severely depressed patients had attempted suicide. (There was a family history of depression or suicide in eight of the patients.) However, an exact suicide rate has not been reported for Cushing's syndrome patients.

Adrenal cortical insufficiency is known as Addison's disease, but no cases of suicide in Addison's syndrome have been reported. Dorovini-Zis and Zis (1987) found that completed suicides using violent methods had heavier adrenal glands than non-suicidal deceased persons.

Conclusions

There has obviously been a tremendous amount of research on this topic, but much of the research has been quite poor. The sample sizes are often small, and investigators typically produce several papers without making it clear whether data from *new* subjects are presented in each report.

More importantly, several investigators have reported the influence of confounding variables on the results. For example, in brain studies, age and post-mortem delay affect the results (Mann et al., 1986b) as does the medication taken by the patient (Cheetham et al., 1988b). If the samples sizes were adequate, in the region of hundreds rather than tens, these confounding variables could be taken into consideration in the statistical analyses. Studies of small samples make such procedures impossible.

Finally, the fact that suicides are often depressed or otherwise psychiatrically disturbed makes it essential that the type and severity of psychiatric disturbance be controlled for in this research. This has rarely been done. Combined with the inconsistency of the results, proposing a physiological theory of suicide is not possible at this time. The sole finding with some degree of support is that suicides may be characterized by low levels of 5-HIAA in the cerebrospinal fluid.

It is to be hoped that research into this area in the 1990s will: (1) employ larger samples, (2) employ more sophisticated statistical analyses, and (3) control for the type and severity of psychiatric disturbance.

REFERENCES

Agren, H. Symptom patterns in unipolar and bipolar depression correlating with monoamine metabolites in the cerebrospinal fluid. *Psychiatry Research*, 1980, 3, 225–236.

Agren, H. Life at risk. *Psychiatric Developments*, 1983, 1(1), 87–103.

Agren, H., & Niklasson, F. Suicidal potential in depression. *Psychopharmacology Bulletin*, 1986, 22, 656–660.

Agren, H., Niklasson, F., & Hallgren, R. Brain purinergic activity linked with depressive symptomatology. *Psychiatry Research*, 1983, 9, 179–190.

Agren, H., Osterberg, B., & Franzen, O. Depression and somatosensory evoked potentials. *Biological Psychiatry*, 1983, 18, 651–659.

Agren, H., & Wilde, L. Patterns of depression reflected in pituitary-thyroid and pituitary-adrenal endocrine changes. *Psychoneuroendocrinology*, 1982, 7, 309–327.

Arato, M., Banki, C., Bissette, G., & Nemeroff, C. Elevated CSF CRF in suicide victims. *Biological Psychiatry*, 1989, 25, 355–359.

Arato, M., Falus, A., Sotonyi, P., Somogyi, E., Tothfalusi, L., Magyar, K., Akil, H., & Watson, S. Postmortem neurochemical investigation of suicide. In H. Moller, A. Schmidtke, & R. Welz (Eds.) *Current Issues of Suicidology.* Berlin: Springer-Verlag, 1988, 242–246.

Arato, M., Tekes, K., Tothfalusi, L., Magyar, K., Palkovits, M., Demeter, E., & Falus, A. Serotonergic split brain and suicide. *Psychiatry Research*, 1987, 21, 355–356.

Arora, R., & Meltzer, H. Serotonergic measures in the brains of suicide victims. *American Journal of Psychiatry*, 1989a, 146, 730–736.

Arora, R., & Meltzer, H. ^{3}H-imipramine binding in the frontal cortex of suicides. *Psychiatry Research*, 1989b, 30, 125–135.

Asberg, M., Bertilsson, L., & Martensson, B. CSF monoamine metabolites, depression and suicide. *Advances in Biochemical Psychopharmacology,* 1984, 39, 87–97.

Ayuson-Gutierrez, J., Cabranes, J., Garcia-Camba, E., & Almoguera, I. Pituitary-adrenal disinhibition and suicide attempts in depressed patients. *Biological Psychiatry,* 1987, 22, 1409–1412.

Banki, C. M., & Arato, M. Amine metabolites and neuroendocrine responses related to depression and suicide. *Journal of Affective Disorders,* 1983a, 5, 223–232.

Banki, C. M., & Arato, M. Amine metabolites, neuroendocrine findings and personality dimensions as correlates of suicidal behavior. *Psychiatry Research,* 1983b, 10, 253–261.

Banki, C. M., Arato, M., Papp, Z., & Kurcz, M. Biochemical markers in suicidal patients. *Journal of Affective Disorders,* 1984, 6, 341–350.

Banki, C. M., Bissette, G., Nemeroff, C., & Arato, M. Corticotrophin-releasing factor in depression and suicide. In H. Moller, A. Schmidtke, & R. Welz (Eds.) *Current Issues of Suicidology.* Berlin: Springer-Verlag, 1988, 247–251.

Banki, C. M., Vojnik, M., Papp, Z., Balla, K., & Arato, M. Cerebrospinal fluid magnesium and calcium related to amine metabolites, diagnosis and suicide attempts. *Biological Psychiatry,* 1985, 20, 163–171.

Beck-Friis, J., Asberg, M., Varpila-Hansson, R., Tomba, P., Aminoff, A., Martensson, B., Thoren, P., Traskman-Bendz, L., Eneroth, P., & Astrom, G. Suicidal behavior and the dexamethasone suppression test. *American Journal of Psychiatry,* 1981, 138, 993–994.

Beck-Friis, J., Kjellman, B., Aperia, B., Unden, F., von Rosen, D., Ljunggren, J., & Wetterberg, L. Serum melatonin in relation to clinical variables in patients with major depressive disorder. *Acta Psychiatrica Scandinavica,* 1985, 71, 319–330.

Bertilsson, L., Tybring, G., Braithwaite, R., Traskman-Bendz, L., & Asberg, M. Urinary excretion of 5-HIAA. *Acta Psychiatrica Scandinavica,* 1982, 66, 190–198.

Biegon, A., & Israeli, M. Regionally selective increases in beta-adrenergic receptor density in the brains of suicide victims. *Brain Research,* 1988, 442, 199–203.

Boza, R., Milanes, F., Llorente, M., Reisch, J., Slater, V., & Garrigo, L. The DST and suicide among depressed alcoholic patients. *American Journal of Psychiatry,* 1988, 145, 266–267.

Braunig, P., Pollentier, S., & Rao, M. Increased serotonin after a suicide attempt. *Biological Psychiatry,* 1988, 24, 725–727.

Braunig, P., Rao, M., & Fimmers, R. Blood serotonin levels in suicidal schizophrenic patients. *Acta Psychiatrica Scandinavica,* 1989, 79, 186–189.

Brown, G., Ebert, M., Goyer, P., Jimerson, D., Klein, W., Bunney, W., & Goodwin, F. Aggression, suicide and serotonin. *American Journal of Psychiatry,* 1982, 139, 741–746.

Brown, R., Mason, B., Stoll, P., Brizer, D., Kocsis, J., Stokes, P., & Mann, J. Adrenocortical function and suicidal behavior in depressive disorders. *Psychiatry Research,* 1986, 17, 317–323.

Buchsbaum, M., Coursey, R., & Murphy, D. The biochemical high-risk paradigm. *Science,* 1976, 194, 339–341.

Carsten, M., Engelbrecht, A., Russell, V., van Zyl, A., & Taljaard, J. Biological markers in juvenile depression. *Psychiatry Research*, 1988, 23, 77–88.

Carter, G., Taylor, G., & Crow, T. Search for viral nucleic acid sequences in the postmortem brains of patients with schizophrenia and individuals who have committed suicide. *Journal of Neurology, Neurosurgery & Psychiatry*, 1987, 50, 247–251.

Charlton, B., Wright, C., Leake, A., Ferrier, I., Cheetham, S., Horton, R., Crompton, M., & Katona, C. Somatostatin immunoreactivity in postmortem brain from depressed suicides. *Archives of General Psychiatry*, 1988a, 45, 597–598.

Charlton, B., Cheetham, S., Horton, R., Katona, C., Crompton, M., & Ferrier, I. Corticotropin-releasing factor immunoreactivity in postmortem brain from depressed suicides. *Journal of Psychopharmacology*, 1988b, 2(1), 13–18.

Cheetham, S., Cromptom, M., Czudek, C., Horton, R., Katona, C., & Reynolds, G. Serotonin concentrations and turnover in brains of depressed suicides. *Brain Research*, 1989, 502, 332–340.

Cheetham, S., Cromptom, M., Katona, C., & Horton, R. Brain 5-HT2 receptor binding sites in depressed suicide victims. *Brain Research*, 1988b, 443, 272–280.

Cheetham, S., Cromptom, M., Katona, C., Parker, S., & Horton, R. Brain GABA$_a$/benzodiazepine binding sites and glutamic acid decarboxylase activity in depressed suicide victims. *Brain Research*, 1988a, 460, 114–123.

Chyatte, C., & Smith, V. Brain asymmetry predicts suicide among Navy alcohol abusers. *Military Medicine*, 1981, 146, 277–278.

Clements, C., Bonacci, D., Yerevanian, B., Privitera, M., & Kiehne, L. Assessment of suicide risk in patients with personality disorder and major affective disorder. *Quality Review Bulletin*, 1985, 11(5), 150–154.

Coccaro, E., Siever, L., Klar, H., Maurer, G., Cochrane, K., Cooper, T., Mohs, R., & Davis, K. Serotonergic studies in patients with affective and personality disorders. *Archives of General Psychiatry*, 1989, 46, 587–599.

Cohen, S. I. Cushing's syndrome. *British Journal of Psychiatry*, 1980, 136, 120–124.

Coryell, W. Suicidal behavior and the DST. *American Journal of Psychiatry*, 1982, 139, 1214.

Coryell, W., & Schlesser, M. Suicide and the dexamethasone suppression test in unipolar depression. *American Journal of Psychiatry*, 1981, 138, 1120–1121.

Coursey, R. D., Buchsbaum, M., & Murphy, D. Two-year follow-up of suicides and their families defined as at risk for psychopathology on the basis of platelet MAO activities. *Neuropsychobiology*, 1982, 8, 51–56.

Cowen, P., & Charig, E. Neuroendocrine response to intravenous tryptophan in major depression. *Archives of General Psychiatry*, 1987, 44, 958–966.

Cross, J., Cheetham, S., Crompton, M., Katona, C., & Horton, R. Brain GABA$_B$ binding sites in depressed suicide victims. *Psychiatry Research*, 1988, 26, 119–129.

Crow, T., Cross, T., Cooper, S., Deakin, J., Ferrier, I., Johnson, J., Joseph, M., Owen, F., Poultier, M., Lofthouse, R., Corsellis, J., Chambers, D., Blessed, G., Perry, E., Perry, R., & Tomlinson, B. Neurotransmitter receptors and monoamine metabolites in the brains of patients with Alzheimer-type dementia and depression and suicides. *Neuropharmacology*, 1984, 23, 1561–1569.

Dajas, F., Barbeito, L., & Cervenansky, C. An association between norepinephrine-to-epinephrine ratio and suicidal ideation in depression. *American Journal of Psychiatry,* 1986, 143, 683–684.

D'Andrea, V., Black, D., & Stayrook, N. Relation of the Fliess-Swoboda biorhythm theory to suicide occurrence. *Journal of Nervous & Mental Disease,* 1984, 172, 490–494.

De Leo, D., Pellgrini, C., Serraiotto, L., Magni, G., & de Toni, R. Assessment of severity of suicide attempts. *Psychopathology,* 1986, 19, 186–191.

Demling, J., Langer, K., Stein, W., Holl, R., & Kalb, R. Plasma amino acids and suicidal behavior. In H. Moller, A. Schmidtke, & R. Welz (Eds.) *Current issues of suicidology.* Berlin: Springer-Verlag, 1988, 263–269.

Dent, R., Ghadiran, A., Kusalic, M., & Young, S. Diurnal rhythms of plasma control *Neuropsychobiology,* 1986, 16, 64–67.

De Paermentier, F., Cheetham, S., Crompton, M., Katona, C., & Horton, R. Lower critical beta-adrenoceptor binding sites in postmortem samples from depressed suicide victims. *British Journal of Pharmacology,* 1989, 98, supplement, 818P.

Dorovini-Zis, K., & Zis, A. Increased adrenal weight in victims of violent suicide. *American Journal of Psychiatry,* 1987, 144, 1214–1215.

Drummond, L., Lodrick, M., & Hallstrom, C. Thyroid abnormalities and violent suicide. *British Journal of Psychiatry,* 1984, 144, 213.

Edman, G., Asberg, M., Levander, S., & Schalling, D. Skin conductance habituation and CSF 5-HIAA in suicidal patients. *Archives of General Psychiatry,* 1986, 43, 586–592.

Ellis, T., Berg, R., & Franzen, M. Organic and cognitive deficits in suicidal patients. In D. Lester (Ed.) *Suicide '89.* Denver: AAS, 1989, 291–293.

Fader, B. W., & Struve, F. A. The possible value of the electroencephalogram in detecting subclinical hypothyroidism associated with agitated depression. *Clinical Electroencephalography,* 1972, 3, 94–101.

Freeska, E., Arato, M., Banki, C., Mohari, K., Perenyi, A., Bagdy, G., & Fekete, M. Prolactin response to fentanyl in depression. *Biological Psychiatry,* 1989, 254, 692–696.

Gottfries, C., von Knorring, L., & Oreland, L. Platelet monoamine oxidase activity in mental disorders. *Progress in Neuropsychopharmacology,* 1980, 4, 185–192.

Grandjean, P., Juel, K., & Jensen, O. M. Mortality and cancer morbidity after heavy occupational fluoride exposure. *American Journal of Epidemiology,* 1985, 121, 57–64.

Gross-Isseroff, R., Israeli, M., & Biegon, A. Autoradiographic analysis of tritiated imipramine binding in the human brain postmortem. *Archives of General Psychiatry,* 1989, 46, 237–241.

Hronek, J., Holecek, V., & Kolomaznik, M. Zinc-serum levels in dementia. *Activitas Nervosa Superior,* 1989, 11, 125–126.

Hubain, P., Simonnet, M., & Mendelwicz, J. The dexamethasone test in affective illness and schizophrenia. *Neuropsychobiology,* 1986, 16(2–3), 57–60.

Irmis, F. Higher ECG reaction to orthostasis in neurotic patients. *Activitas Nervosa Superior,* 1982, 24(3), 180–181.

Irmis, F. Serum levels of potassium and calcium in neurotics, suicides and controls. *Activitas Nervosa Superior,* 1983, 25, 213–214.

Kaufman, C. A., Gillin, J., Hill, B., O'Laughlin, T., Phillips, I., Kleinman, J., & Wyatt, R. Muscarinic binding in suicides. *Psychiatry Research,* 1984, 12(1), 47–55.

Kauvert, G., Zucker, T., Gilg, T., & Eisenmenger, W. Measurement of biogenic amines and metabolites in the CSF of suicide victims and nonsuicides. In H. Moller, A. Schmidtke, & R. Welz (Eds.) *Current issues of suicidology.* Berlin: Springer-Verlag, 1988, 252–262.

Kenny, T. J., Rohn, R., Sarles, R. M., Reynolds, B. J., & Heald, F. P. Visual-motor problems of adolescents who attempt suicide. *Perceptual & Motor Skills,* 1979, 48, 599–602.

Kimmel, H. L., & Lester, D. Personalities of those who can taste phenylthiocarbamide. *Psychological Reports,* 1987, 61, 586.

Kitahara, M. Dietary tryptophan ratio and suicide. *International Journal of Biosocial Research,* 1986a, 8(1), 53–60.

Kitahara, M. Tryptophan uptake from diet and the incidence of suicide. *Biology & Society,* 1986b, 3(2), 74–79.

Kitahara, M. Insufficient ascorbic acid uptake from the diet and the tendency for suicide. *Journal of Orthomolecular Medicine,* 1987, 2, 217–218.

Kitahara, M. Dietary tryptophan ratio and suicide in the United Kingdom, Ireland, the United States, Canada, Australia and New Zealand. *Omega,* 1987–1988, 18, 71–76.

Kocsis, J., Kennedy, S., Brown, R., Mann, J., & Mason, B. Suicide and adrenocortical function. *Psychopharmacology Bulletin,* 1986, 22, 650–655.

Korpi, E. R., Kleinman, J., Goodman, S., Phillips, I., DeLisi, L., Linnoila, M., & Wyatt, R. Serotonin and 5-HIAA in brains of suicide victims. *Archives of General Psychiatry,* 1986, 43, 594–600.

Korpi, E. R., Kleinman, J., & Wyatt, R. GABA concentrations in forebrains areas of suicide victims. *Biological Psychiatry,* 1988, 23, 109–114.

Krishnan, K. R., Davidson, J., Rayasam, K., & Shope, F. The dexamethasone suppression test in borderline personality disorder. *Biological Psychiatry,* 1984, 19, 1149–1153.

Kronfol, Z., Greden, J., Gardner, R., & Carroll, B. Suicidal behavior and the DST. *American Journal of Psychiatry,* 1982, 139, 1214–1215.

Lawrence, K., De Paermentier, F., Cheetham, S., Crompton, M., Katona, C., & Horton, R. Brain 5-HT uptake sites. *British Journal of Pharmacology,* 1989, 98, supplement, 812p.

Lechin, F., van der Dijs, B., Acosta, E., Gomez, F., Lechin, E., & Arocha, L. Distal colon motility and clinical parameters in depression. *Journal of Affective Disorders,* 1983, 5, 19–26.

Lester, D. Ectomorphy and suicide. *Journal of Social Psychology,* 1981, 113, 135–136.

Lester, D. Corn consumption, tryptophan and cross-national homicide and suicide rates. *Journal of Orthomolecular Psychiatry,* 1985, 14, 178–179.

Lester, D. Tattoos, eye color and method for suicide. *Activitas Nervosa Superior,* 1986, 28, 239–240.

Lester, D. National distribution of blood groups, personal violence (suicide and homicide), and national character. *Personality & Individual Differences*, 1987a, 8, 575–576.

Lester, D. Suicide and homicide rates and fluoride. *Psychological Reports*, 1987b, 61, 802.

Lester, D. Ectomorphy ratios of completed suicides. *Perceptual & Motor Skills*, 1987c, 64, 86.

Lester, D. Tryptophan uptake and national rates of suicide and homicide. *Journal of Orthomolecular Medicine*, 1989a, 4, 159–160.

Lester, D. Biochemical correlates of suicidal behavior in arsonists. *Psychological Reports*, 1989b, 64, 258.

Lester, D. Biorhythms and the timing of suicide, homicide and natural deaths. *Skeptical Inquirer*, 1990, 14, 410–412.

Levy, A., Kurtz, N., & Kling, A. Association between cerebral ventricular enlargement and suicide attempts in chronic schizophrenia. *American Journal of Psychiatry*, 1984, 141, 438–439.

Lidberg, L., Asberg, M., & Sundqvist-Stensman, U. 5-HIAA levels in attempted suicides who have killed their children. *Lancet*, 1984, 2, 928.

Lidberg, L., Tuck, J., Asberg, M., Scalia-Tomba, G., & Bertilsson, L. Homicide, suicide and CSF 5-HIAA. *Acta Psychiatrica Scandinavica*, 1985, 71, 230–236.

Linkowski, P., van Wettere, J., Kerkhofs, M., Brauman, H., & Mendlewicz, J. Thyrotropin response to thyreostimulin in affectively ill women. *British Journal of Psychiatry*, 1983, 143, 401–405.

Linkowski, P., van Wettere, J., Kerkhofs, M., Gregoire, F., Brauman, H., & Mendelewicz, J. Violent suicidal behavior and the thyrotropin-releasing hormone thyroid-stimulating hormone test. *Neuropsychobiology*, 1984, 12, 19–22.

Linna, M., & Liikkanen, A. The nature of suicide in Finnish Lappland. In J. P. Soubrier & J. Vedrinne (Eds.) *Depression and suicide*. Paris: Pergamon, 1983, 133–137.

Linnoila, M., Virkkunen, M., Scheinin, M., Nuutila, A., Rimon, R., & Goodwin, F. Low cerebrospinal fluid 5-HIAA concentration differentiates impulsive from nonimpulsive violent behavior. *Life Sciences*, 1983, 33, 2609–2614.

Lopez-Ibor, J. J., Saiz-Ruiz, J., & Perez de los Cobos, J. Biological correlates of suicide and aggressivity in major depressions. *Neuropsychobiology*, 1985, 14(2), 67–74.

MacMurray, J., & Bozzetti, L. Prostaglandin synthesis among alcoholic suicide attempters and non-attempters. *Neuropsychobiology*, 1987, 17, 178–181.

Maes, M., Vandewoude, M., Schotte, C., Martin, M., Blockx, P., Scharpe, S., & Cosyns, P. Hypothalamic-pituitary-adrenal and thyroid axis dysfunctions and decrements in the availability of L-tryptophan as biological markers of suicidal ideation in major depressed females. *Acta Psychiatrica Scandinavica*, 1989, 80, 13–17.

Manchon, M., Kopp, N., Rouzioux, J., Lecestre, D., Deluermoz, S., & Miachon, S. Benzodiazepine receptor and neurotransmitter studies in the brain of suicide. *Life Sciences*, 1987, 41, 2623–2630.

Mann, J. J. Increased serotonin-2 and beta-adrenergic receptor binding in the frontal cortices of suicide victims. *Archives of General Psychiatry*, 1986, 43, 954–959.

Mann, J. J., McBride, P., & Stanley, M. Postmortem serotonergic and adrenergic receptor binding to frontal cortex. *Psychopharmacology Bulletin*, 1986a, 22, 647–649.

Mann, J. J., McBride, P., & Stanley, M. Aminergic receptor binding correlates of suicide. *Psycopharmacology Bulletin*, 1986b, 22, 741–743.

Mann, J. J., & Stanley, M. Postmortem monoamine oxidase enzyme kinetics in the frontal cortex of suicide victims and controls. *Acta Psychiatrica Scandinavica*, 1984, 69, 135–139.

Marazziti, D., de Leo, D., & Conti, L. Further evidence supporting the role of the serotonin system in suicidal behavior. *Acta Psychïatrica Scandinavica*, 1989a, 80, 322–324.

Marazziti, D., Placidi, G., Cassano, C., & Akiskal, H. Lack of specificity of reduced platelet imipramine binding in different psychiatric conditions. *Psychiatry Research*, 1989b, 30, 21–29.

McDowall, M. E. Mortality of persons resident in the vicinity of electric transmission facilities. *British Journal of Cancer*, 1986, 53, 271–279.

Meana, J., & Garcia-Sevilla, J. Increased alpha 2-adrenoceptor density in the frontal cortex of depressed suicide victims. *Journal of Neural Transmission*, 1987, 70, 377–381.

Meltzer, H. Y., Uberkoman-Wiita, B., Robertson, A., Tricou, B., & Lowy, M. Enhanced serum cortisol response to 5-hydroxytryptophan in depression and mania. *Life Sciences*, 1983, 33, 2541–2549.

Meltzer, H. Y., Perline, R., Tricou, B., Lowy, M., & Robertson, A. Effect of 5-hydroxytryptophan on serum cortisol levels in major affective disorders. *Archives of General Psychiatry*, 1984, 41, 379–387.

Mendelson, J., Dietz, P., & Ellingboe, J. Postmortem plasma luteinizing hormone levels and antemortem violence. *Pharmacology, Biochemistry, & Behavior*, 1982, 17, 171–173.

Meyendorff, E., Jain, A., Traskman-Bendz, L., Stanley, B., & Stanley, M. The effects of fenfluramine on suicidal behavior. *Psychopharmacology Bulletin*, 1986, 22(1), 155–159.

Meyerson, L., Wennogle, L., Abel, M., Coupet, J., Lippa, A., Raih, C., & Beer, B. Human brain receptor alterations in suicide victims. *Pharmacology, Biochemistry & Behavior*, 1982, 17(1), 159–163.

Modai, I., Apter, A., Meltzer, M., Tyano, S., Walevski, A., & Jerushalmy, Z. Serotonin uptake by platelets of suicidal and aggressive adolescent psychiatric inpatients. *Neuropsychobiology*, 1989, 21, 9–13.

Modestin, J., & Ruef, C. DST in relation to depressive somatic and suicidal manifestations. *Acta Psychiatrica Scandinavica*, 1987, 75, 491–494.

Monroe, R. Limbic ictus and atypical psychoses. *Journal of Nervous & Mental Disease*, 1982, 170. 711–716.

Montgomery, S., & Montgomery, D. Pharmacological prevention of suicidal behavior. *Journal of Affective Disorders*, 1982, 4, 291–298.

Moses, S. G., & Robins, E. Regional distribution of norepinephrine and dopamine in brains of depressive and alcoholic suicides. *Psychopharmacology Communications,* 1975, 1(3), 327–337.

Nasrallah, H. A., McCalley-Whitters, M., & Chapman, S. Cerebral ventricular enlargement and suicide in schizophrenia and mania. *American Journal of Psychiatry,* 1984a, 141, 919.

Nasrallah, H. A., McCalley-Whitters, M., & Pfohl, B. Clinical signs of large cerebral ventricles in manic males. *Psychiatry Research,* 1984b, 13, 151–156.

Nemeroff, C., Owens, M., Bissette, G., Andorn, A., & Stanley, M. Reduced corticotrophin releasing factor binding sites in the frontal cortex of suicide victims. *Archives of General Psychiatry,* 1988, 45, 577–579.

Niklasson, F., & Agren, H. Brain energy metabolism and blood-brain barrier permeability in depressive patients. *Biological Psychiatry,* 1984, 19, 1183–1206.

Ninan, P., van Kammen, D., & Linnoila, M. Reply. *American Journal of Psychiatry,* 1985, 142, 148.

Ninan, P., van Kammen, D., Scheinin, M., Linnoila, M., Bunney, W., & Goodwin, F. CSF 5-HIAA levels in suicidal schizophrenic patients. *American Journal of Psychiatry,* 1984, 141, 566–569.

Oreland, L., Wiberg, A., Asberg, M., Traskman, L., Sjostrand, L., Thoren, P., Bertilsson, L., & Tybring, G. Platelet MAO activity and monoamine metabolites in cerebrospinal fluid in depressed and suicidal patients and in healthy controls. *Psychiatry Research,* 1981, 4(1), 21–29.

Ostroff, R., Giller, E., Bonese, K., Ebersole, E., Harkness, L., & Mason, J. Neuroendocrine risk factors of suicidal behavior. *American Journal of Psychiatry,* 1982, 139, 1323–1325.

Ostroff, R., Giller, E., Harkness, L., & Mason, J. The norepinephrine-to-epinephrine ratio in patients with a history of suicide attempts. *American Journal of Psychiatry,* 1985, 142, 224–227.

Owen, F., Chambers, D., Cooper, S., Crow, T., Johnson, J., Lofthouse, R., & Poulter, M. Serotonergic mechanisms in brains of suicide victims. *Brain Research,* 1986, 362, 185–188.

Owen, F., Cross, A., Crow, T., Deakin, J., Ferrier, I., Lofthouse, R., & Poulter, M. Brain 5-HT2 receptors and suicide. *Lancet,* 1983, 2, 1256.

Perry, C. V., Reichmanis, M., Marino, A., & Becker, R. Environmental powerfrequency magnetic fields and suicide. *Health Physics,* 1981, 41, 267–277.

Prasad, A. J. Neuroendocrine differences between violent and nonviolent parasuicides. *Neuropsychobiology,* 1985, 13, 157–159.

Reichmanis, M., Perry, F., Marino, A., & Becker, R. Relation between suicide and the electromagnetic field of overhead power lines. *Physiological & Chemical Physics,* 1979, 11, 395–403.

Rich, C. L. Endocrinology and suicide. *Suicide & Life-Threatening Behavior,* 1986, 16, 301–311.

Robbins, D., & Alessi, N. Depressive symptoms and suicidal behavior in adolescents. *American Journal of Psychiatry,* 1985, 142, 588–592.

Robins, L. N., West, P. A., & Murphy, G. E. The high rate of suicide in older white men. *Social Psychiatry,* 1977, 12, 1–20.

Roland, B., Morris, J., & Zelhart, P. Proposed relation of testosterone levels to male suicides and sudden deaths. *Psychological Reports,* 1986, 59, 100–102.

Rosenthal, P., & Rosenthal, S. Suicidal behavior by preschool children. *American Journal of Psychiatry,* 1984, 141, 520–525.

Roy, A., Ninan, P., Mazonson, A., & Pickar, D. CSF monoamine metabolites in chronic schizophrenic patients who attempted suicide. *Psychological Medicine,* 1985, 15, 335–340.

Roy, A., Agren, H., Pickar, D., Linnoila, M., Doran, A., Cutler, N., & Paul, S. Reduced CSF concentration of homovanillic acid. *American Journal of Psychiatry,* 1986, 143, 1539–1545.

Roy, A., de Jong, J., & Linnoila, M. Cerebrospinal fluid monoamine metabolites and suicidal behavior in depressed patients. *Archives of General Psychiatry,* 1989a, 46, 609–612.

Roy, A., Everett, D., Pickar, D., & Paul, S. Platelet tritiated imipramine binding and serotonin uptake in depressed patients and controls. *Archives of General Psychiatry,* 1987, 44, 320–327.

Roy, A., Pickar, D., de Jong, J., Karoum, F., & Linnoila, M. Suicidal behavior in depression. *Biological Psychiatry,* 1989b, 25, 341–350.

Roy-Byrne, P., Post, R., Rubinow, D., Linnoila, M., Savard, R., & Davis, D. CSF 5-HIAA and personal and family history of suicide in affectively ill patients. *Psychiatry Research,* 1983, 10, 263–274.

Ryan, N., Puig-Antich, J., Rabinovich, H., Ambrosini, P., Robinson, D., Nelson, B., & Novacenko, H. Growth hormone response to desmethylimipramine in depressed and suicidal adolescents. *Journal of Affective Disorders,* 1988, 15, 323–337.

Rydin, E., Schalling, D., & Asberg, M. Rorschach ratings in depressed and suicidal patients with low levels of 5-HIAA in cerebrospinal fluid. *Psychiatry Research,* 1982, 7, 229–243.

Salk, L., Lipsitt, L., Sturner, W., Reilly, B., & Levat, R. Relationship of maternal and perinatal conditions to eventual adolescent suicide. *Lancet,* 1985, 1, 624–627.

Schlegel, S., Maier, W., Philipp, M., Aldenhoff, J., Heuser, I., Kretzschmar, K., & Benkert, O. Computer tomography in depression. *Psychiatry Research,* 1989, 29, 221–230.

Schmidtke, A., Fleckenstein, P., & Beckmann, H. The dexamethasone suppression test and suicide attempts. *Acta Psychiatrica Scandinavica,* 1989, 79, 276–282.

Secunda, S., Cross, C., Koslow, S., Katz, M., Kocsis, J., Maas, J., & Landis, H. Biochemistry and suicidal behavior in depressed patients. *Biological Psychiatry,* 1986, 21, 756–767.

Small, J., Small, J., Millstein, V., & Moore, D. Familial associations with EEG variants in manic-depressive disease. *Archives of General Psychiatry,* 1975, 32. 43–48.

Spillane, J. D. Nervous and mental disorders in Cushing's syndrome. *Brain,* 1951, 74, 72–94.

Stanley, M. Cholinergic receptor binding in the frontal cortex of suicide victims. *American Journal of Psychiatry,* 1984, 141, 1432–1436.

Stanley, M., & Mann, J. Increased serotonin-2 binding sites in frontal cortex of suicide victims. *Lancet,* 1983, 1, 214–216.

Stanley, M., Virgilio, J., & Hershon, S. Tritiated imipramine binding sites are decreased in the frontal cortex of suicides. *Science,* 1982, 216, 1337–1339.

Struve, F. Electroencephalographic relationships to suicide behavior. *Clinical Electroencephalography,* 1983, 14, 20–26.

Struve, F. Possible potentiation of suicide risk in patients with EEG dysrhythmias taking oral contraceptives. *Clinical Electroencephalography,* 1985, 16, 88–90.

Struve, F. Clinical electroencephalography and the study of suicidal behavior. *Suicide & Life-Threatening Behavior,* 1986, 16, 133–165.

Struve, F., Saraf, K., Arko, R., Klein, D., & Becka, D. Relationship between paroxysmal electroencephalographic dysrhythmia and suicide ideation and attempts in psychiatric patients. In C. Shagass, S. Gershon, & A. Friedhoff (Eds.) *Psychopathology and brain dysfunction.* New York: Raven, 1977, 199–221.

Sullivan, J. L., Cavenar, J., Maltbie, A., Lister, P., & Zung, W. Familial biochemical and chemical correlates of alcoholics with low platelet monoamine oxidase activity. *Biological Psychiatry,* 1979, 14, 385.

Targum, S. D., Rosen, L., & Capodanno, A. The dexamethasone suppression test in suicidal patients with unipolar depression. *American Journal of Psychiatry,* 1983, 140, 877–879.

Thomas, C., & Greenstreet, R. Psychobiological characteristics in youth as predictors of five disease states. *Johns Hopkins Medical Journal,* 1973, 132, 16–43.

Thorell, L. Electrodermal activity in suicidal and nonsuicidal depressed patients and in matched healthy subjects. *Acta Psychiatrica Scandinavica,* 1987, 76, 420–430.

Thorell, L., & D'Elia, G. Electrodermal responsivity and suicide risk. *Archives of General Psychiatry,* 1987, 44, 1112.

Thorell, L., & D'Elia, G. Electrodermal activity in depressive patients in remission and in matched healthy subjects. *Acta Psychiatrica Scandinavica,* 1988, 78, 247–253.

Traskman, L., Asberg, M., Bertilsson, L., & Sjostrand, L. Monoamine metabolites in CSF and suicidal behavior. *Archives of General Psychiatry,* 1981, 38, 631–636.

Traskman, L., Tybring, G., Asberg, M., Bertilsson, L., Lanto, O., & Schalling, D. Cortisol in the CSF of depressed and suicidal patients. *Archives of General Psychiatry,* 1980, 37, 761–767.

Traskman-Bendz, L., Stanley, M., Stanley, B., Matthews, B., & Brown, L. N-acetylation and serotonergic measures in a group of psychiatric patients. *Acta Psychiatrica Scandinavica,* 1988, 77, 736–740.

van Praag, H. M. CSF 5-HIAA and suicide in nondepressed schizophrenics. *Lancet,* 1983, 2, 977–978.

van Praag, H. M. Autoaggression and CSF 5-HIAA in depression and schizophrenia. *Psychopharmacology Bulletin,* 1986, 22, 669–673.

Virkkunen, M., de Jong, J., Bartko, J., & Linnoila, M. Psychological concomitants of history of suicide attempts among violent offenders and impulsive fire setters. *Archives of General Psychiatry,* 1989, 46, 604–606.

Virkkunen, M., Horrobin, D., Jenkins, D., & Manku, M. Plasma phospholipid essential fatty acids and prostaglandins in alcoholic, habitually violent and impulsive offenders. *Biological Psychiatry,* 1987, 22, 1987–1096.

Wagner, A., Aberg-Wistedt, A., Asberg, M., Ekqvist, B., Martensson, B., & Montero, D. Lower tritiated imipramine binding in platelets from untreated depressed patients compared to healthy controls. *Psychiatry Research,* 1985, 16, 131–140.

Yerevanian, B. I., Olafsdottir, H., Milanese, E., Russotto, J., Mallon, P., Baciewicz, G., & Sagi, E. Normalization of the dexamethasone suppression test at discharge from hospital. *Journal of Affective Disorders,* 1983, 5, 191–198.

Chapter 3

SEX DIFFERENCES IN SUICIDE

The basic sex difference in suicide is that men complete suicide more than women while women attempt suicide more than men. Reviews of the research on sex differences have been published by Lester (1984, 1988b).

The Sex Ratio

De Graaf and Kruyt (1976) surveyed the Netherlands for one year in 1970–1971 and tracked down 731 male and 478 female completers and 1,562 male and 2,551 female attempters. Shichor and Bergman (1979) found 452 male and 346 female completed suicides in Israel in 1962–1966, along with 1,241 male and 1,975 female attempted suicides. The sex difference was not found in those 65 years of age or older.

Barraclough (1987) found that the sex ratio was reversed (with a higher female completed suicide rate than male rate) for those aged 5–14 in many nations, particularly in Asian and South American nations. Fuse (1980) and Lester (1982) noted that female completed suicide rate was relatively higher as compared to the male rate in East Asian nations. Lester found, though, that the male/female ratio of completed suicide rates was not related to the gross national product per capita of the nations.

Brown (1986) found a higher female completed suicide rate than male rate among the Aguaruna in the Peruvian Amazon region. Haynes (1984) found a higher rate of completed suicide in Indian women than Indian men in Fiji, but only for those over the age of 30.

In San Diego, Kushner (1985) found that percentage of completed suicides which were male decreased from 1880–1972. The male completed suicide rate decreased while the female rate increased. Little change in the methods used for completed suicide was observed over the period.

Steffensmeier (1984) found no clear trend in the ratio of female to male completed suicide rates from 1960 to 1978 in the USA and so could discern no effect from women's liberation.

Attempted Suicide

Hansen and Wang (1984) found a similar rate of attempted suicide in a Danish town for men and women, though the women attempters were older than the men.

Kessler and McRae (1983) looked at 45 studies on attempted suicides from 1940–1980 and noted that the female/male ratio increased, peaking in 1955–1970, after which there was a decrease. They suggested that this paralleled self-reported psychological stress and rates of overall psychopathology.

Sex Differences in Suicides

Attempted Suicide: Adolescents

Drude (1978) looked at teenagers attempting suicide by drugs and presenting at an emergency room. The whites had a higher proportions of men than did the blacks. The women were more likely to have used multiple drugs and analgesics, whereas the men were more likely to be alcohol abusers and to have used volatile substances (such as paint thinner).

Kotila and Lonnqvist (1988) found that teenage boys who attempted suicide in Helsinki were more likely to have somatic illness, psychiatric disturbance, and indirect self-destructive behavior (such as criminality, violence, and substance abuse). The girls attempted suicide more often at school, with a clear precipitating event, and often out of revenge accompanied by painful affect. The boys and girls did not differ in prior suicide attempts or psychiatric care, psychosis, intent or lethality.

Stelzer et al. (1989) found that suicidal adolescent boys had more positive relationships with their parents than girls, were closer to their mothers, and seemed less impulsive, but had experienced more stressful life events.

In contrast, Bosworth et al. (1989) found no differences between male and female adolescent suicide attempters in age, race, social class, whether living with parents, recent stress, use of alcohol, prior suicide attempts, prior psychiatric treatment, the method used or the total suicidal intent score. The men did plan the suicidal act more. Sherer (1985) found no sex differences in the extent of suicidal ideation (or depression) in college students.

Attempted Suicide: Adults

In Canada, Barnes (1985) found that male suicide attempters were more often living alone, drug abusers, with employment problems and criminal charges, and with a diagnosis of personality disorder or substance abuse (and less often a transient situational disturbance) than the women attempters. The two groups did not differ in stress, illnesses, prior suicidal behavior, prior psychiatric treatment or the circumstances of the act. Ennis, et al. (1989) found that male attempters were more likely to abuse alcohol (while female attempters tended non-significantly to abuse drugs more), but the men and women did not differ in the incidence of a major depressive disorder or depression.

In England, Hawton et al. (1982) found that male attempters were more often alcohol or drug abusers, more often used alcohol before the attempt and were more often epileptics. The rates were 245–314 per 100,000 per year for men and 419–553 for women. Also in England, Morgan (1980) found that women attempters were less likely to have increased their alcohol intake in the prior three months, to have used alcohol before the suicidal act, and to have legal problems.

Frierson (1989) found that women who attempt suicide with firearms were less likely than men to shoot themselves in the head. (They were similar in age but less likely to have been intoxicated. The women were more often alcohol abusers, with a major depressive disorder and with stressful life circumstances whereas the men were more often schizophrenic and drug abusers.) Women who attempted suicide with overdoses were younger than the women using guns and more often had previously attempted suicide. (They did not differ in race or diagnosis.)

Rygnestad (1982) found that male attempters were more often not married and unemployed, with more prior psychiatric hospitalizations, more alcoholism and drug abuse, had more often been in prison, and more often diagnosed as psychotic and less often as neurotic than female attempters. Varadaraj et al. (1986) found no differences between male and female attempters in impulsivity, premeditation, motives or the presence of a suicide note.

Schmidtke and Schaller (1989) found that, after the suicide attempt, women had a more positive self-concept than did men. However, while the men's self-concept improved during the next three weeks, that of the women worsened.

In Sri Lanka, Hettiarachchi and Kodithuwakku (1989) found no differences among male and female self-poisoners in whether they used rat poison or agrochemicals. In Hong Kong, Pan and Lieh-Mak (1989) found that female suicide attempters were more often married, illiterate, not born in the Mainland, and motivated by interpersonal friction (whereas the men were motivated more by financial difficulties and physical and psychiatric illness). They did not differ in psychiatric diagnosis, method used or whether it was the first attempt.

Completed Suicide

In Finland, Nayha (1977) found that male completed suicides were more often from the lower classes while female suicides were more often from the higher classes.

Breed (1972) found that female completed suicides had received more prior psychiatric treatment, more often were diagnosed as passive-dependent personalities and less often abused alcohol than the men. (The sexes did not differ in depression or intropunitiveness.) The women were more impulsive in their suicidal action, were less likely to have delusions of grandeur or dreams of glory and were more often chaotically disorganized. (They did not differ in eight other symptom areas, including homicidal and non-homicidal violence.) Breed proposed five components to the suicidal mentality. The sexes did not differ in commitment, rigidity or shame. The men more often felt that they were failures, their goals had lost meaning and they had lost hope. The women were more often alone with frustrated dependency needs. (The men, however, more often kept their problems to themselves despite their lower social isolation.)

In Sacramento, Bourque et al. (1983) found that male suicides used guns more often, left suicide notes less often, were more often single and less often married/divorced/widowed, were of higher social class, were more often employed, had less of a history of suicide and psychiatric treatment, had more arrests, had less alcohol and barbiturates in their blood, had less often experienced loss/disruption of relationships, and had lived longer in California.

Among completed suicides aged 10–24 in California, Cosand et al. (1982) found that the females had more often attempted suicide, were less often employed, more often married, less often used alcohol, had fewer arrests, and made more visits to doctors/psychiatrists. They did not differ in psychiatric symptoms. Compared to the general population, for those aged 20–24 both sexes were less often employed, the men were less often married and the women more often married.

In San Diego, Rich et al. (1988) found that women suicides were older, used guns less and overdoses more, more often had a diagnosis of a major depression and less often economic stressors. The sexes did not differ in race or substance abuse.

Black Men And Women

Baker (1984) compared black men and women suicide attempters and found the women to be younger and more often diagnosed as having an affective disorder or adjustment reaction while the men were more often diagnosed as psychotic. The groups did not differ in many aspects (including prior attempts, method used, family history of alcohol abuse or psychiatric disorder, or use of alcohol before the attempt).

MMPI Differences

Sendbuehler et al. (1978a, 1978b) found that high scores on the Mf scale of the MMPI were associated with greater seriousness in a group of male suicide attempters, while low scores were associated with greater seriousness in female attempters. Compared to controls, the male attempters had higher Mf scores while the women attempters had lower Mf scores. Different average MMPI profiles were found for men and women attempters (824 and 482 respectively).

Leonard (1977) compared male and female completed suicides who had taken the MMPI. The women had lower scores on the F and Pt scales and higher scores on the Si, Pa and Ma scales, an alcoholism scale and the Goldberg Index. More of the females were diagnosed as schizophrenic. A different set of differences were found for male and female suicidal living patients.

Suicidal Females

Hawton et al. (1985) found that mothers who attempted suicide were more likely to be child abusers than control mothers. The attempters who abused or who were at risk for abuse were younger, were more likely to be intoxicated at the time of the attempt and were more likely to have been in psychiatric care.

Tomlinson-Keasey et al. (1986) identified the female suicides in Terman's sample of gifted children who were examined in childhood in 1920 and who have been followed-up ever since. They found that suicides have worse mental health, more early loss, more stress in the family of origin, poorer physical health, and used alcohol more compared to living controls and controls dead from natural causes. However, their study failed to control for the differences in psychiatric disorder in the three groups.

Suicide In Pregnancy

In Britain, Lewis and Fay (1981) identified six ante-partum completed suicides and eleven post-partum suicides in over 2.3 million births, indicating that suicide is rare at these times. Lester (1987) found that attempted suicide in pregnant women in Hungary was more common in the second trimester. Also, those who admitted attempting suicide were more likely to have an abortion after the attempt than those claiming that the overdose was an accident. Rayburn et al. (1984) found that pregnant women calling a poison control center after an overdose were more likely to be in the first trimester than the second or third trimesters.

Lester and Beck (1988) found that pregnant women who attempted suicide did not differ in depression, hopelessness, suicidal intent or medical lethality of the attempt from non-pregnant women attempters. Eight of the fifteen attempts of the pregnant women were related to the pregnancy, and three themes were identified: prior loss of children (by miscarriage, adoption or death), potential loss of a lover and a desire for an abortion.

Abortion

Mackenzie et al. (1975) found only one attempted suicide in the 18 months after an abortion in 307 women. Tishler (1981) reported two cases of adolescents who had elective abortions, but who attempted suicide on the day the baby was due.

The Suicidal Act

Dicter (1972) reported that alcohol-intoxicated suicide attempts were more common in men whereas drug-intoxicated suicide attempts were more common in women (though he does not define his terms clearly.)

Andress (1976) found that women who completed suicide were more likely to leave a suicide note than men. They also were more likely to shoot themselves in the trunk rather than the head than were men. Gupta et al. (1982) found that men jumping to their death in India jumped from higher heights than women. Harvey and Solomons (1983) found no differences in survival between men and women jumping from a particular high bridge in Australia, though the survivers were younger.

In contrast, Bailey (1981) found no differences in the serum levels of meprobamate between men and women self-poisoners using the drug. Pommereau et al. (1989) found no differences in the severity of physical injury of men and women suicide attempters by jumping.

The Menstrual Cycle

Ekeberg, et al. (1986) found no association between suicidal attempts by overdose (or accidental overdose) and the menstrual cycle. Fourestie et al. (1986) found no variation in suicide attempts over the menstrual cycle for women using oral contraceptives, but suicide attempts peaked on days 1–7 and 28+ for those not using oral contraceptives. These women also more often had low levels of plasma estradiol after their suicide attempt.

McClure et al. (1971) studied female callers to a suicide prevention center. Thirteen out of the 50 reported feeling better rather than worse premenstrually which McClure felt suggested hypomania or a bipolar affective disorder. These women tended to have a higher incidence of suicide in family members, but not significantly.

Hunt et al. (1987) found more suicides than expected among women receiving hormone replacement therapy for menopause.

Oral Contraceptives

Vessey et al. (1985) found that women taking oral contraceptives or with an IUD had a higher attempted suicide rate than women using diaphragms (though the groups did not differ in prior suicide attempts when coming to the family planning clinic for the first time). The rate of attempted suicide was not associated with how many months the women had been taking the pill.

A Physiological Theory Of Sex Differences In Suicide

Skutsch (1981a) proposed a theory of depression based upon high levels of dopamine in the central nervous system, and Lester (1988a, 1988c) has shown how her theory can account for sex differences in suicidal behavior, since brain dopamine levels are affected by estrogen.

Skutsch (1981a) noted that the highest levels of circulating cortisol occur in January and February (in the Northern Hemisphere) whereas aldosterone levels are low in winter and peak in April and May. She suggested that dopamine is sensitive to temperature. The early summer leads to a drop in dopamine levels, which triggers a rise in aldosterone levels. Skutsch (1981b) used this to account for the fact that the suicide rates for women peaked in the spring and the fall, unlike those for men which showed only a spring peak.

Skutsch (1981b) also suggested that the secondary peak in the fall for women might be accounted for by the monthly variation in the levels of circulating estrogens. Estrogens inhibit the output of dopamine which reduces the likelihood of depression. Estrogen levels in women are lowest in the spring and the fall, leading to peaks in the suicide rate at those times.

Discussion

Although the sex difference in suicidal behavior has remained of interest in the 1980s, much of the research has been opportunistic. Investigators with a sample of attempted or completed suicides have simply compared the men and the women for the variables measured in the study. Very little of the research has been stimulated by or relevant to the theories of the sex difference in suicide (Lester, 1988b), and so we are no closer to understanding this sex difference now than we were ten years ago.

REFERENCES

Andress, L. V. R. An epidemiological study of the psychosocial characteristics of suicidal behavior in Riverside County between 1960 and 1974. *Dissertation Abstracts International,* 1976, 37B, 1481.

Bailey, D. N. The present status of meprobamate ingestion. *American Journal of Clinical Pathology,* 1981, 75, 102–106.

Baker, F. M. Black suicide attempters in 1980. *General Hospital Psychiatry*, 1984, 6, 131–137.

Barnes, R. Women and self-injury. *International Journal of Women's Studies*, 1985, 8, 465–474.

Barraclough, B. M. Sex ratio of juvenile suicide. *Journal of the American Academy of Child & Adolescent Psychiatry*, 1987, 26, 434–435.

Bosworth, T., Kurkjian, J., Spirito, A., Dovost, L., Bond, A., & Brown, L. Sex differences among adolescent suicide attempters. In D. Lester (Ed.) *Suicide '89*. Denver: AAS, 1989, 45–46.

Bourque, L. B., Cosand, B., & Kraus, J. Comparison of male and female suicide in a defined community. *Journal of Community Health*, 1983, 9, 7–17.

Breed, W. Five components of a basic suicide syndrome. *Life-Threatening Behavior*, 1972, 2, 3–18.

Brown, M. R. Power, gender, and the social meaning of Agaruna suicide. *Man*, 1986, 21, 311–328.

Cosand, B. J., Bourque, L., & Kraus, J. Suicide among adolescents in Sacramento, California, 1950–1979. *Adolescence*, 1982, 12, 917–930.

De Graaf, A. C., & Kruyt, C. S. Some results of the response to a national survey of suicide and attempted suicide in the Netherlands. In *Suicide and Attempted Suicide in Young People*. Copenhagen: WHO, 1976, 52–58.

Dicter, R. M. Suicidal patients among admissions to Louisville General Hospital. *Journal of the Kentucky Medical Association*, 1972, 70, 773–776.

Drude, K. P. Acute drug ingestions in a children's hospital emergency room. *Journal of Clinical Child Psychology*, 1978, 7, 154–155.

Ekeberg, O., Jacobsen, D., Sorum, Y., & Aass, G. Self-poisoning and the menstrual cycle. *Acta Psychiatrica Scandinavica*, 1986, 73, 239–241.

Ennis, R., Barnes, R. A., Kennedy, S., & Trachtenberg, D. D. Depression in self-harm patients. *British Journal of Psychiatry*, 1989, 154, 41–47.

Fourestie, V., de Lignieres, B., Roudot-Thoraval, F., Fulli-Lemaire, I., Cremniter, D., Nahoul, K., Fournier, S., & Lejonc, J. L. Suicide attempts in hypo-oestrogenic phases of the menstrual cycle. *Lancet*, 1986, 2, 1357–1360.

Frierson, R. L. Women who shoot themselves. *Hospital & Community Psychiatry*, 1989, 40, 841–843.

Fuse, T. To be or not to be. *Stress*, 1980, 1(3), 18–25.

Gupta, S. M., Chandra, J., & Dogra, T. D. Blunt force lesions related to the heights of a fall. *American Journal of Forensic Medicine & Pathology*, 1982, 3, 35–43.

Hansen, W., & Wang, A. G. Suicide attempts in a Danish town. *Social Psychiatry*, 1984, 19, 197–201.

Harvey, P., & Solomons, B. Survival after free falls of 59 metres into water from the Sydney Harbor Bridge. *Medical Journal of Australia*, 1983, 1, 504–511.

Hawton, K., Fagg, J., Marsack, P., & Wells, P. Deliberate self-poisoning and self-injury in the Oxford area. *Social Psychiatry*, 1982, 17, 175–179.

Hawton, K., Roberts, J., & Goodwin, G. The risk of child abuse among mothers who attempt suicide. *British Journal of Psychiatry*, 1985, 146, 486–489.

Haynes, R. Suicide in Fiji. *British Journal of Psychiatry*, 1984, 145, 433–438.

Hettiarachchi, J., & Kodithuwakku, G. C. Self-poisoning in Sri Lanka. *Human Toxicology,* 1989, 8, 507–510.

Hunt, K., Vessey, M., McPherson, K., & Colemen, M. Long-term surveillance of mortality and cancer incidence in women receiving hormone replacement therapy. *British Journal of Obstetrics & Gynecology,* 1987, 94, 620–635.

Kessler, R. C., & McRae, J. Trends in the relationship between sex and attempted suicide. *Journal of Health & Social Behavior,* 1983, 24, 98–110.

Kotila, L., & Lonnqvist, J. Adolescent suicide attempts. *Acta Psychiatrica Scandinavica,* 1988, 77, 264–270.

Kushner, H. I. Women and suicide in historical perspective. *Signs,* 1985, 10, 537–552.

Leonard, C. V. The MMPI as a suicide predictor. *Journal of Consulting & Clinical Psychology,* 1977, 45, 367–377.

Lester, D. The distribution of sex and age among completed suicides. *International Journal of Social Psychiatry,* 1982, 28, 256–260.

Lester, D. Suicide. In C. S. Widom (Ed.) *Sex Roles and Psychopathology.* New York: Plenum, 1984, 145–156.

Lester, D. The timing of attempted suicide during pregnancy. *Acta Paediatrica Hungarica,* 1987, 28, 259–260.

Lester, D. *The Biochemical Basis For Suicide.* Springfield: Thomas, 1988a.

Lester, D. *Why Women Kill Themselves,* 2nd Ed. Springfield: Thomas, 1988b.

Lester, D. A physiological theory of sex differences in suicide. *Medical Hypotheses,* 1988c, 25, 115–117.

Lester, D., & Beck, A. T. Attempted suicide and pregnancy. *American Journal of Obstetrics & Gynecology,* 1988, 158, 1084–1085.

Lewsi, G. J., & Fay, R. Suicide in pregnancy. *British Journal of Clinical Practice,* 1981, 35, 51–53.

Mackenzie, I. Z., & Hillier, K. Delayed morbidity following postglandin-induced abortion. *International Journal of Gynecology & Obstetrics,* 1975, 13, 209–214.

McClure, J. N., Reich, T., & Wetzel, R. D. Premenstrual symptoms as an indicator of bipolar affective disorder. *British Journal of Psychiatry,* 1971, 119, 527–528.

Morgan, H. G. Social correlates of non-fatal deliberate self-harm. In R. Farmer & S. Hirsch (Eds.) *The Suicide Syndrome.* London: Croom Helm, 1980, 90–102.

Nayha, S. Social group and mortality in Finland. *British Journal of Preventive & Social Medicine,* 1977, 31, 231–237.

Pan, P. C., & Lieh-Mak, F. A comparison between male and female parasuicides in Hong Kong. *Social Psychiatry,* 1989, 24, 253–257.

Pommereau, X., Tedo, P., & Penovil, F. Attempted suicide by jumping from a height. In S. D. Platt & N. Kreitman (Eds.) *Current Research on Suicide and Parasuicide.* Edinburgh: University of Edinburgh, 1989, 153–162.

Rayburn, W., Aronow, R., Delancey, B., & Hogan, M. Drug overdose during pregnancy. *Obstetrics & Gynecology,* 1984, 64, 611–614.

Rich, C. L., Ricketts, J. E., Fowler, R. C., & Young, D. Some differences between men and women who complete suicide. *American Journal of Psychiatry,* 1988, 145, 718–722.

Rygnestad, T. K. Prospective study of social and psychiatric aspects in self-poisoned patients. *Acta Psychiatrica Scandinavica,* 1982, 66, 139–153.

Schmidtke, A., & Schaller, S. Sex differences in the metaperspectives of parasuicides. In D. Lester (Ed.) *Suicide '89.* Denver: AAS, 1989, 6–7.

Sendbuehler, J. M., Kincel, R., Beausejour, P., & Nemeth, G. Attempted suicide. *Psychiatric Journal of the University of Ottawa,* 1978a, 3(2), 87–94.

Sendbuehler, J. M., Kincel, R. L., Nemeth, G., & Oertel, J. Dimensions of seriousness in attempted suicide. In V. Aalberg (Ed.) *Proceedings of the 9th International Congress for Suicide Prevention & Crisis Intervention,* Helsinki: Finnish Association for Mental Health, 1978b, 506–522.

Sherer, M. Depression and suicidal ideation in college students. *Psychological Reports,* 1985, 57, 1061–1062.

Shichor, D., & Bergman, S. Patterns of suicide among the elderly in Israel. *Gerontology,* 1979, 19, 487–495.

Skutsch, G. Manic depression. *Medical Hypotheses,* 1981a, 7, 737–746.

Skutsch, G. Sex differences in seasonal variations in suicide rate. *British Journal of Psychiatry,* 1981b, 139, 80–81.

Steffensmeier, R. H. Suicide and the contemporary woman. *Sex Roles,* 1984, 10, 613–631.

Stelzer, J., Inayatulla, M., Cheyne, L., & Elliott, C. Gender differences in teen suicide attempters. In D. Lester (Ed.) *Suicide '89.* Denver: AAS, 1989, 11–13.

Tishler, C. Adolescent suicide attempts following elective abortion. *Pediatrics,* 1981, 68, 670–671.

Tomlinson-Keasey, C., Warren, L. W., & Elliott, J. E. Suicide among gifted women. *Journal of Abnormal Psychology,* 1986, 95, 123–130.

Varadaraj, R., Mendonca, J., & Rauchenberg, P. Motives and intent. *Canadian Journal of Psychiatry,* 1986, 31, 621–624.

Vessey, M. P., McPherson, K., Lawless, M., & Yeates, D. Oral contraception and serious psychiatric illness. *British Journal of Psychiatry,* 1985, 146, 45–49.

Chapter 4

CHILDHOOD EXPERIENCES AND SUICIDE

A number of studies have explored the association between particular childhood experiences and later suicidal behavior. Most have focussed on one or two particular childhood experiences, such as loss of a parent through death or divorce. These will be reviewed below. Occasional studies, however, have explored a wide variety of childhood experiences simultaneously.

For example, Slap et al. (1989) compared a sample of adolescent suicide attempters to adolescents with acute illnesses. The attempters were more often female, with prior psychiatric care and suicide attempts, and had more often run away from home, worse school performance, more stressful life events, more alcohol/drug use, more often a diagnosis of psychopathy, poorer impulse control and worse family relationships. The groups did not differ in parental divorces or death.

This type of study is poorly conceived. The control group is of normal adolescents, and so the differences identified between the attempters and the control group are probably a result of the differences in psychiatric disturbance rather than suicidal behavior. Furthermore, it is impossible in such a study to discern which are the crucial experiential or psychological variables leading to the suicidal behavior. A factor analysis would at least identify clusters of related variables which may or may not be associated with suicidal behavior, and a path analysis might suggest causal links.

Kosky (1983) compared some adolescent suicide attempters with non-suicidal psychiatric patients. He found that the suicide attempters had more experience of violence between parents, loss (of any kind, whether through death or separation and of people, pets or possessions), loss in the prior year, parents on social security, parents with both medical and psychiatric illnesses, and physical abuse from their parents. The parents of the suicide attempters were of lower social class, and the adolescents were more often male, doing less well academically, and less often had been in psychiatric care. The two groups of adolescents did not differ in

50

the number of siblings, birth order, delinquent behavior, behavior problems in school, attempted suicide in their parents, or perinatal difficulties.

In a later study, Kosky et al. (1986) studied depressed children and compared those with suicidal ideation and those with none. The suicidal ideators had more disturbance in their relationships with their father and their siblings and a more hostile family relationship, and had received more persecution, discrimination and abuse. (The groups did not differ in symptoms of emotional disorder or conduct disorder, extrafamilial relationships, or experience of broken homes and loss.)

Pettifor et al. (1983) followed-up adolescents seen at a community mental health center to see which factors predicted completed suicide by age thirty. The suicides had more life-threatening thoughts (but not suicide attempts), residential mobility, parents with marital and life stress, depressed mothers, alcoholic fathers, separations from parents, siblings in trouble at school and with the law, school problems, psychiatric hospitalizations and inconsistent parents, and less parental support and affection. (They did not differ in social class, physical abuse, legal problems, intelligence or whether living with a biological parent.)

Pfeffer's Research

Pfeffer and her colleagues have studied intensively a group of suicidal children in the community. Pfeffer et al. (1980) found that the suicidal children showed more psychomotor activity in the prior six months, had more suicidal parents, and were more preoccupied with death, but did not differ in diagnosis, stressful events, sleep disturbance, depression, anxiety, firesetting, aggression, running away, stealing, parental pathology, marital tensions, defense mechanisms, or intelligence.

Pfeffer et al. (1983) found that suicidality was associated with assaultiveness in these children. The suicidal-only children were more likely to have an affective disorder, the assaultive-only children a specific developmental disorder, while the suicidal-and-assaultive children were more likely to have a borderline personality disorder. The suicidal children were more likely to have suicidal parents and the assaultive children assaultive parents. The suicidal children showed more reality testing, more intellectualization and less compensation in their ego functioning.

Pfeffer et al. (1984) found the suicidal children to have more recent and past depressions, more use of introjection as a defense mechanism, more recent aggression, more parental separations, more parental depression and more parental psychiatric hospitalizations.

Pfeffer et al. (1988b) followed up the sample for two years and found an increase in suicidal ideation. At the time of follow-up, the suicidal children were more depressed, showed more aggressive behavior, general pathology, and the defence mechanisms of denial, projection and reaction formation. (They did not differ in age, sex, race, impulse control, hopelessness or parental depression.)

Pfeffer and her colleagues also studied child and adolescent inpatients. Pfeffer et al. (1988a) found that the suicidal children had experienced more paternal violence and had parents with more recent stressful events (but their parents did not differ in suicidal behavior, maternal violence, substance abuse, or recent psychiatric disturbance). Prior suicidal behavior was associated with a diagnosis of major depression and alcohol abuse in both the boys and girls. Suicidal behavior in the boys was also associated with the absence of delusions, problems with girl friends, family assaultive behavior and suicidal behavior in their siblings. Suicidal behavior in the girls was associated with recent aggression, a borderline personality disorder, sexual abuse, problems with boy friends, sibling drug abuse, parental arguments, and recent deaths and negatively with anorexia/bulimia and schizophrenia. (The suicidal and non-suicidal patients did not differ in race, parental divorces/separations, birth order, number of siblings, or parental psychiatric disorder.)

The suicidal inpatients were more depressed, had shown more recent aggression, had more suicidal mothers, more often diagnosed with a major depressive disorder, an adjustment disorder or a specific developmental disorder (and less often mental retardation or schizophrenia), had higher WISC arithmetic and coding scores, had a greater preoccupation with death, and showed more introjection, displacement and total defensive behavior. (They did not differ in recent stressful events, birth order, parental violence, medical illness, alcoholism, psychiatric hospitalization, school and peer pressures, father's suicidal behavior, age, sexual maturity, history of pregnancy, medical complications at delivery, soft neurological signs, or abnormal EEGs. The mothers of these children had attempted suicide more often whereas the mothers of the community sample had thought of suicide more often (Pfeffer et al., 1986).

The suicidal-only inpatients more often abused alcohol, had been physically and sexually abused, and had a depressive disorder or borderline personality disorder (Pfeffer et al., 1989). The suicidal-assaultive patients had more violence in their homes, had been in more accidents and more often had a borderline personality disorder. However, suicidality and assaultiveness were not associated in these inpatients (Pfeffer et al. 1987).

Abortions

Campbell et al. (1988) found that teenagers who had abortions had less suicidal ideation before the abortion but more suicide attempts after the abortion as compared to older women (but not significantly so). (The statistical analyses in this paper were poor.)

Abuse

Goodwin (1981) studied 201 families with sexual abuse of the child and found that five mothers and eight daughters attempted suicide during the 30-month follow-up.

Briere and Runtz (1986) found that women at a crisis-counseling center who had been sexually abused were more likely to have attempted suicide in the past and be suicidal now. For those women who had been sexually abused, current suicidal ideation was associated with the number of perpetrators and the experience of both physical and sexual abuse (but not with the age at the time of the abuse or whether it was incestuous or involved intercourse). Those abused both physically and sexually had attempted suicide more in the past. Among the women at the center who had attempted suicide, those with a history of sexual abuse attempted suicide at a younger age. Briere et al. (1988) found also that men seen at the center who had been sexually abused were more likely to have attempted suicide in the past.

Van Egmond and Jonker (1987) found a high incidence of physical and sexual abuse in female attempted suicides, and repeaters had experienced more sexual abuse than non-repeaters. Ninety-one percent of the abused women had made their first suicide attempt after the abuse. Plummer et al. (1989) found that adolescent suicide attempters had more experiences of physical and sexual abuse than suicidal ideators and non-suicidal adolescents. They were also more often diagnosed as having an affective disorder but did not differ in substance abuse, family pathology or parental divorce.

Smith and Crawford (1986) found that high school students who had attempted suicide had experienced a greater frequency of physical beating, rape and sexual abuse than the rest of the students. (They were also more depressed.)

Among female psychiatric inpatients, Bryer et al. (1987) found that those who had been abused as children (either physically or sexually) had attempted suicide more in the past and experienced more suicidal ideation. Edwall et al. (1989) found that girls in a drug treatment program who had been sexually abused had a higher incidence of attempted suicide in the previous year (regardless of whether the abuse was extrafamilial or intrafamilial) but no greater probability of prior suicidal ideation.

Herman and Hirschman (1981) compared women in psychotherapy who had experienced overt incest with their fathers with those who had experienced merely seductive fathers. The incest cases had shown a greater incidence of suicide attempts in adolescence.

Hibbard et al. (1988) compared junior high school students who had been abused with those who had not and found more attempted suicide in those who had been sexually or physically abused. The abused children also had abused alcohol more and run away more, but did not differ in self-esteem, depression or anger. Myers et al. (1985) found that acutely suicidal children were more likely to have abusing fathers (and abused mothers) than psychiatric controls.

Kroll et al. (1985) compared alcoholics in treatment who had been abused as children with those who had not been abused. The abused alcoholics were more likely to have made serious suicide attempts (but not suicidal gestures).

Walsh and Rosen (1988) found that adolescent self-mutilators who had attempted suicide were more likely to have experienced sexual abuse than non-attempters, recent loss and peer conflict. The groups did not differ in experience of physical abuse, family violence, childhood illnesses or surgery, or divorce.

In contrast, Asarnow and Guthrie (1989) found no differences between suicidal and nonsuicidal adolescent psychiatric inpatients in their history of sexual or physical abuse. Khan (1987) found no differences in sexual abuse (or peer/family relations and diagnosis) between adolescent suicide attempters and psychiatric controls. Pettifor et al. (1983) found that physical abuse in childhood did not predict completed suicide by age thirty in adolescent patients at a community mental health center. Spirito et al. (1987) found no differences between adolescent suicide attempters and psychiatric controls in physical or sexual abuse (or substance abuse by self or parents, depression, or hopelessness).

Abusing Parents

Roberts and Hawton (1980) found that attempted suicide was more common in both the mothers and fathers of abused/neglected children than in the general population. Those parents who had attempted suicide were more likely to have marital problems, prior psychiatric contacts and repeated abuse. (They did not differ in number of children, mother's age at the birth of her first child, social class, or whether they were guilty of abuse versus neglect.) Roberts and Hawton suggested that perhaps both attempting suicide and abusing children were symptoms of marital conflict.

Oliver (1985) studied families with child abuse in two generations or more. Thirty-three percent of the mothers (both abused and abusing therefore) had attempted suicide and 23 percent of the fathers.

Runaways

In a study of male runaways, Janus et al. (1987) found that those who had been sexually abused tended to have more suicidal ideation than those who had not been abused. Nilson (1981) simply compared runaways with other children referred from county agencies and found more abuse in the backgrounds of the runaways and more suicide attempts (but less suicidal ideation).

Stiffman (1989) found that 30 percent of youth in a shelter had attempted suicide. These attempters were more often females from unstable families with missing parents, had run away before, had more negative life events and behavioral problems, had higher depression scores, more often abused drugs and alcohol, and had more disturbed family members and friends. (They did not differ in race, age, social class, self-esteem or social anxiety.)

Yates et al. (1988) found that runaways were more likely to have attempted suicide than non-runaways seen at an outpatient clinic. They were also younger, more often white and from outside the community. They were more depressed and more likely to be drug abusers. (The non-runaways had more sexually-transmitted diseases and more often wanted family planning help.)

Adoption

Boult (1988) found that 14 of 82 adults adopted as children had attempted in adolescence. Seventy-one percent of the attempters were sensitive about being adopted and 43 percent had been taunted about it. Boult did not, however, study any comparison group.

Birth Order

Haycock (1989) found that prisoners making serious suicide attempts were more likely to be firstborns or only children than those making gestures. In an analysis of cases from the literature of children and adolescents who were completers, attempters or threateners, Husain and Vandiver (1984) found an excess of firstborns over last-borns. In a small sample of adolescent completed suicides, Leblhuber, et al. (1983) found 5 firstborns, 16 middle children and 8 last-borns. Stober (1983) found fewer firstborns and more middle children in suicidal adolescent inpatients as compared to psychiatric controls.

Motto (1984) found that a birth order position of fourth or more predicted subsequent completed suicide in male adolescent depressed inpatients. Odejide et al. (1986) found an excess of first borns over last borns among attempted suicides in Nigeria. Pettifor et al. (1983) claimed that being a middle child predicted completed suicide by age thirty in a sample of community mental health center adolescent patients.

O'Gorman et al. (1975) found no differences in sibling position of attempted suicides in the Australian Army as compared to non-suicidal soldiers. Ishii (1973, 1977) found no differences in sibling position between completed suicides at Kyoto University (Japan) and other students.

Gaines and Richmond (1980) found no differences in birth order between basic trainees in the military who made suicidal gestures and normal controls. Pfeffer (1984) found no differences in birth order between suicidal children and non-suicidal children in a community sample or in a psychiatric sample (Pfeffer et al., 1988c).

Lester and Caffery (1989) found in college students that neither suicidal ideation nor a history of suicidal attempts, threats or ideation were related to sibling position.

Taylor and Stansfeld (1984) found no differences in the birth order of adolescent suicide attempters by overdose and psychiatric controls.

Veeraraghavan (1985) found no differences in the numbers of first versus last-borns in a small sample of attempted suicides in Delhi (India).

Lester (1987) reviewed the research on birth order and combined the statistics from several studies. The composite picture from this large multi-sample was an excess of first and middle-borns for completed suicides and an excess of middle and last-borns for attempted suicides. Lester (1989a) presented the case of a suicide of a middle-born teenager.

Childhood Loss

Rutstein (1971) found that female attempted suicides had a greater experience of both childhood and recent loss than non-suicidal psychiatric patients. Ishii (1973, 1977) found that students at Kyoto University (Japan) who completed suicide had experienced loss of parents more than had other students. (They also had better educated fathers.) Abane et al. (1978) found that attempted suicides had more experience of broken homes and deceased parents than normals.

Hetzel (1971) found that attempted suicides had more often lost both parents as compared to medical casuality controls (but did not differ in the loss of only one parent). The loss was more often due to divorce or separation and less often due to death. The age at loss did not differ, but the attempted suicides more often had a loss of more than five years duration. Repeaters and non-repeaters did not differ in their experience of loss. Experience of loss was not related to the impulsivity of the suicide attempt, seeking help prior to the attempt or the precipitating cause.

Budner and Kumler (1973) found that the parents of college students with suicidal ideation had separated and divorced more than the parents of non-suicidal students (though the age of the student at the time of the breakup did not seem to be critical).

Adam et al. (1980, 1982a) found that attempted suicides had more experience of the death of the father or parents' separation and divorce than general medical patients. Female attempted suicides had experienced more parental loss than male attempters. The loss was especially common for ages 0–5 and 17–20. The suicide attempters also had experienced more unstable and chaotic homes after the loss of the parent than had the general medical patients. Adam et al. (1982b) found that experience of early parent loss was associated with a greater frequency of later suicidal ideation and attempts. Bolger et al. (1989) found that students who had thought about suicide in the past had experienced more parental absences, especially in those who had thought about suicide in preadolescence.

Allebeck et al. (1988) found that Swedish conscripts who later committed suicide had more often experienced an absent parent. Bagley (1989) found that adolescent suicides had more often been in foster/adoptive care and separated from biological parents than matched normal controls. Farmer (1980) found that attempted suicides by self-poisoning (aged 15–30) had experienced more loss of parents and more deaths of siblings than normal controls.

Garfinkel et al. (1982) found that adolescent suicide attempters were more likely to have an absent parent than other emergency room patients, and Grossi (1987) found that adolescents in a residential treatment center who had made prior suicide attempts were more likely to have experienced separation from a parent. Khan (1987) found that adolescent suicide attempters had more experience of parental loss than psychiatric outpatients but not more than psychiatric inpatients.

Iga (1986) found more loss of both parents in Japanese high school and college students who attempted suicide than in non-suicidal students. Stober (1983) found more absent parents in suicidal adolescent inpatients as compared to psychiatric controls. Kerfoot (1988) found that adolescent suicide attempters were more often from broken homes with remarriage than were non-suicidal psychiatric outpatients.

Lester (1989b) presented data from the detailed biographies of thirty famous suicides. He found that sixteen of them had experienced loss in childhood. Most had lost a father, had loss through death, and with the most common age at the time of loss being 6–14.

Murphy (1982) found that suicide attempters by self-poisoning had more often lost parents by death (but not by divorce or separation) than appendicitis patients. The mothers of the attempters were also more often taking medication. Wasserman and Cullberg (1989) found no differences in the experience of early parental loss or suicide in family members in attempted suicide by diagnosis. The drug abusing attempters, however, had experienced more loss between the ages of 15 and 18.

No increase in the incidence of loss was reported by Birtchnell (1981) for female attempted suicides versus non-suicidal psychiatric patients. Gutierrez et al. (1988) found no excess of childhood loss in psychiatric patients who completed suicide and those who did not. Goldney (1981) found that the lethality of the suicide attempts by young women was not related to experience of parental loss or to childhood stress. Those experiencing loss and those not did not differ in depression scores. Haycock (1989) found no differences in childhood parental loss between prisoners making serious suicide attempts versus gestures. Riehl et al. (1988) found no differences in loss of parents by death or divorce between attempted suicides and non-suicidal psychiatric inpatients and surgical patients. Silove et al. (1987) found no differences between attempted suicides and general practitioner patients. Berk (1949) found no differences in parental loss before adolescence between schizophrenics who had previously attempted suicide and those who had not.

In a sample of native Americans at boarding school, Manson et al. (1989) found that attempting suicide was associated with having a friend or relative attempt or complete suicide, having a friend die (but not parent or sibling), and having less social support. The attempters were also more depressed and more often alcohol abusers. A similar pattern of results was found for having suicidal ideation.

Weiss (1980) found that suicidal intent in a sample of attempted suicides was related both to childhood loss and recent loss. The younger attempters had experienced more early loss but not more recent loss.

Levitan (1981) found that 16 percent of women with rheumatoid arthritis had a parent who commited suicide by the time the patient was six, but he did not employ a control group in his study.

In a review of the research studies, Schaller and Schmidtke (1988) estimated that the incidence of broken homes for completed suicides was 40 percent and for attempted suicides 47 percent, but the incidence was also high for drug abusers (43 percent) and delinquents (44 percent). The incidence was lower for psychiatric patients (24 percent) and alcoholics (28 percent) and normals (17 percent).

Dating

Wright (1982) found that teenagers who were not allowed to date early had more recent suicidal ideation than those allowed to date early. They had worse relationships with their mothers, had stricter mothers and were more dependent and unsure, but they abused drugs less.

Early Memories

Monahan (1983) found that children who had attempted suicide had more early memories than non-suicidal controls, but these memories were more unpleasant and the content reflected alienation more.

The Family

Abane et al. (1978) found that attempted suicides had poorer relationships with the parents and siblings than normal controls. Choquet and Davidson (1978) found that young attempted suicides saw their parents more often as either too authoritarian or not authoritarian enough than normal controls, and the same for their parents' interest in the children.

Motanky (1971) compared suicidal adolescents with adolescents in crisis and normal adolescents. The parents of the three groups did not differ in their suicidal ideation. The suicidal adolescents, however, perceived their parents as more suicidal than did the other adolescents. The suicidality of the adolescent was not correlated with that of the parents.

Freidrich et al. (1982) found that suicidal ideation in eighth and ninth graders was predicted by their grades and by their family environment (whether it had organization, independence, cohesion, and an achievement orientation, though they did not specify the direction of these associations). Fritz (1987) found that college students who had thought of suicide were more likely to have experienced early family disruptions.

Gaines and Richmond (1980) found that basic trainees in the military who made suicidal gestures did not differ from normal controls in the job level of their fathers or their parents' education, marital status or psychiatric history.

Goldney (1981) found that young women attempting suicide as compared to controls were more likely to see their parents as controlling, less interested in them and less proud of them. Their homes had more friction with quarrels between the parents and also between the parents and children.

Grossi (1987) found that adolescents in a residential treatment program who had previously attempted suicide had parents with more difficulties in their marriage, job and parenting. The families had also moved more often, and the attempters more often felt that no-one cared about them.

Joffe et al. (1988) found that teenagers in the community who were preoccupied with suicide (attempters and ideators) were more likely to have parents who had been arrested and more family dysfunction (but they did not differ in parental drinking or family income).

Kashani et al. (1989) found that adolescents in the community with current suicidal ideation had parents with greater psychopathology than did non-suicidal children. Kerfoot (1988) found the adolescent suicide attempters had family members with more psychiatric disturbance (especially mothers), attempted suicide and delinquency (but not unemployment or contact with welfare).

In a clinical study of a small sample of suicidal children, Orbach et al. (1981) found that 64 percent of them had a suicidal parent and their families were involved in a major crisis. There were typically demands made on the children to assume responsibilities beyond their capabilities, and they had no satisfying relationships with adults.

Ross et al. (1983) found that suicidal ideators more often had fathers who were more abusive, depriving, punitive and rejecting and less affectionate. Their mothers were more often shaming and rejecting and less often affectionate and tolerant. Both parents were more often guilt-inducing and favored siblings and less often stimulating and favored the subject. Suicidal ideation was also associated with parental death and divorce.

Silove et al. (1987) gave a parental-bonding questionnaire to attempted suicides and general practitioner patients. The groups did not differ in maternal care, maternal protection, paternal care, or in having affectionless and controlling parents. The suicide attempters reported more paternal protection (and more recent interpersonal stress).

Taylor and Stansfeld (1984) found that adolescent suicide attempters by overdose more often had disturbed relationships with their parents than psychiatric controls. (They also had run away from home more, had more psychiatric symptoms, more often had an eating disorder, but less often were phobic. They did not differ in social class or the country of birth of their mother.)

Wright (1985) found that high school students and college students who had recent suicidal ideation had worse relationships with their fathers, parents more often in conflict, depressed and angry, fathers (but not mothers) who more often abused alcohol and, for the college students, more physical abuse by their parents. They did not differ in having a poor relationship with their mothers or in having permissive parents.

In contrast, Borst and Noam (1989) found that adolescent suicide attempters did not differ from psychiatric controls in having a family history of psychiatric disorder, substance abuse or completed suicide or in their parents' marital status. Myers et al. (1985) found that, among acutely suicidal children, the more seriously suicidal children were more likely to be *negative* for a family history of depression.

Family Acceptance of Suicide

May (1989) found that families which showed a greater acceptance of suicide were more likely to have children with suicidal ideation (as well as greater depression and hopelessness).

Completed Suicides

Kaplan and Maldaver (1989) found that adolescents who completed suicide had parents with more pathology (especially in the area of individual attachment) than control families.

Husain and Vandiver (1984) analyzed case studies of suicidal children and adolescents reported in the literature. They found that the completed suicides more often had rejecting fathers than the attempters and threateners. They also were older, more often tall and overweight, with more prior suicide attempts, alcohol or drug abuse, depression as a precipitant and mothers who had completed suicide.

Motto (1984) found that having a psychiatrically disturbed opposite sex parent predicted completed suicide in alcohol-abusing depressed inpatients.

Perception of the Family

Coonelly (1988) found that adolescents who had attempted suicide had a more idealized perception of their family than students who had only thought about suicide or non-suicidal students. Their parents were also seen as the least authoritarian and the least enmeshed.

McIntire and Angle (1981) found that self-poisoning children and adolescents saw their parents less often as exerting little control and having low expectations than comparison adolescents.

McKenry et al. (1982) found that adolescent suicide attempters, as compared with medical patients, enjoyed time spent with their parents less (as did the parents), saw their parents' marriage as less well adjusted (as did the parents), saw their mothers as less interested in them (but not their fathers), felt more parental pressure to do well in school, had fathers who were more depressed and had mothers who were more anxious and who had engaged in more prior suicidal behavior.

Iga (1986) found that high school and college students in Japan who had attempted suicide had a more negative attitude toward both parents than non-suicidal students and more of them contemplated running away from home.

Mothering

Dingman and McGlashan (1986) found that schizoaffective patients who completed suicide had poorer mothering than the average psychiatric patient, while the schizophrenics and unipolar depressives who completed suicide had better mothering.

Goldney (1985) found that female attempted suicides experienced less maternal and paternal care and more maternal and paternal overprotection than did controls from general practitioners.

Triolo et al. (1984) compared adolescent suicide attempters with emergency room controls. For those aged 12–15, the attempters had stricter mothers, who were less patient and who did not enjoy being with the child. For those aged 16–18, the suicide attempters had mothers who disapproved of their friends, and who also were strict, and had parents who spent little quality time with the child. The attempters of both ages were more depressed and had lower self-esteem. Male and female attempters did not differ in these maternal and parental characteristics.

Parent Characteristics

Garfinkel et al. (1982) found that adolescent suicide attempters had more unemployed fathers and employed mothers than other emergency room patients.

Tishler and McKenry (1982) compared the parents of adolescent suicide attempters to those of adolescents with minor injuries. The fathers of the attempters (but not the mothers) had lower self-esteem. The fathers were also more depressed while the mothers had more suicidal ideation and anxiety. Both parents of the attempters used alcohol more.

Parents' Age

Mehr et al. (1981) compared adolescents' attempted suicides with accident victims and other patients and found no differences in the ages of their parents (or their marital and employment status).

Perinatal Conditions

Salk et al. (1985) explored 46 perinatal, birth and maternal variables for their ability to discriminate between adolescent suicides and controls. Three items were significant: respiratory distress in the neonate for more than an hour at birth, no antenatal care in the first twenty weeks of pregnancy, and the mother having a chronic disease during the pregnancy. (Birth weight and maternal age were among the variables not significant.)

Puberty

In a sample of children with major depressive disorders, Ryan et al. (1987) found that prepubertal children made less lethal suicide attempts than postpubertal children, but they did not differ in suicidal intent. Zubrick et al. (1987) claimed that the frequency of suicidal ideation and attempts did not change from pre- to post-puberty (though the rate did increase from eleven-year-olds to twelve-year-olds), but my analysis of the data reveals an effect from puberty for females aged 12–14.

Punishment and Discipline

Yesavage and Widrow (1985) found that male inpatients with major depressive disorder who showed self-destructive behavior in the hospital had fathers who administered extremely severe discipline, mothers who administered mild discipline, and parents who fought and abused alcohol. They had not experienced more childhood loss.

Sibships

O'Gorman et al. (1975) found no differences in the number of siblings in attempted suicides in the Australian Army as compared to non-suicidal soldiers. Lindsay (1973) studied 200 consecutive psychiatric inpatients and 44 completed suicides. More of the suicides and the psychiatric inpatients came from small family groups (sizes of one and two siblings) than expected on the basis of the population of New Zealand. Choquet and Davidson (1978) found that young attempted suicides were less likely to have zero to 2 siblings and more likely to have 4 or more compared to normal controls.

Birtchnell (1981) found that female attempted suicides came more often from large sibships (greater than six) than non-suicidal psychiatric patients. In France, Choquet et al. (1980) found that adolescent suicide attempters came from large sibships (greater than three) more often than the general population. Farmer (1980) found that attempted suicides by self-poisoning (aged 15–30) came from larger sibships than normal controls. Kerfoot (1988) found that adolescent suicide attempters more often had more than two siblings than non-suicidal psychiatric outpatients.

Lester and Caffery (1989) found no association in college students between sibship size and current suicidal ideation or prior suicide attempts and threats. Those who had considered suicide in the past had fewer siblings than those who had not. Wandrei (1985) found that female attempted suicides who later completed suicide more often came from small sibships than those who did not kill themselves.

Taylor and Stansfeld (1984) found no differences in number of siblings between adolescent attempters by overdose and psychiatric controls. Gaines and Richmond (1980) found no differences in the number of siblings of basic trainees in the military who made suicidal gestures and normal controls, Mehr et al. (1981) found no differences between adolescent suicide attempters, accident victims and other patients. Pfeffer (1984) found no differences in the number of siblings of suicidal and non-suicidal children in a community sample or in a psychiatric sample (Pfeffer et al., 1988c).

Suicide In the Family and Others

Abane et al. (1978) found that attempted suicides had experienced more suicidal behavior in their siblings and friends than normal people. (Too few parents had been suicidal for parents to be studied.) The attempters also had more psychiatric illness in their families, especially their parents.

Kopp et al. (1987) in Hungary found in a community sample that attempted suicide was associated with a family history of completed suicide. Coleman et al. (1987) found that runaways with suicidal preoccupation were more likely to a family history of suicide and friends who had attempted or completed suicide than nonsuicidal runaways. They were also more often female and experienced domestic violence at home.

Farberow et al. (1987) found that youths with suicidal ideation in the community were more likely to have had suicidal friends and family members who completed suicide than were non-suicidal youths. Fritz

(1987) found that college students who had thought of suicide were more likely to have had family members who attempted or completed suicide. Garfinkel et al. (1982, 1983) found that adolescent suicide attempters (and, among the attempters, the more serious attempters) were more likely to have a family history of attempted and completed suicide (and medical illness and psychiatric disturbance) than other emergency room patients.

Linkowski et al. (1985) found that a family history of suicide was associated with a higher probability of attempted suicide in female unipolar and bipolar patients and with a higher probability of attempted suicide by violent methods in both male and female patients.

Murphy and Wetzel (1982) found that a family history of suicidal behavior in white male attempted suicides was more common in those with personality disorders, average in those with a primary affective disorder, and least common in those with other or no diagnoses.

Tishler et al. (1981) found that about one fifth of a sample of adolescent suicide attempters had experienced recent suicidal behavior in family members (and the same percentage the recent death of a friend or relative).

Tsuang (1983) found that psychiatric patients had more relatives who had completed suicide than medical patients. In addition, psychiatric patients who completed suicide had more relatives who had also completed suicide than other psychiatric patients. The incidence of completed suicide in relatives was greatest in depressive patients.

In contrast, Bolger et al. (1989) found no association between contact with suicide and thinking about suicide in the past among a sample of students. Gutierrez et al. (1988) found no excess family history of suicide (or psychiatric disturbance and alcoholism) in psychiatric patients who completed suicide as compared to those who did not.

Scheftner et al. (1988) followed-up 955 patients with affective disorders for five and a half years and found that 27 completed suicide. Among their 5,042 relatives, 44 completed suicide, but only one of these was a relative of a suicide in the sample of patients. Attempted suicide in the relatives (the number of attempts and their severity) was not related to which patients in the sample completed suicide.

McIntosh and Kelly (1988) found that students who had survived death by suicide in a significant other did not differ in their acceptance of suicide or in their suicidal preoccupation from those surviving the death by natural or accidental causes in a significant other.

Predicting Later Suicide

Aalberg and Hamalainen (1976) found that sleep disturbances in childhood predicted the number of suicide attempts in young adults. Anxiety, panic reactions, total psychiatric symptoms and family/friendship problems in childhood predicted whether the person would attempt suicide by adulthood.

Discussion

The major findings from this body of research are that suicidal people have experienced more physical and sexual abuse, more loss of parents in childhood and more disturbed family relationships.

However, surprisingly, the research has not typically controlled for the severity of psychiatric disturbance, and so we cannot be sure whether these differences pertain to suicidality per se or simply to psychiatric disturbance.

It is also noteworthy that research in the 1980s has not progressed beyond that in earlier years in moving toward a more detailed examination of the past and present patterns of interaction in suicidal and non-suicidal families.

REFERENCES

Aalberg, V., & Hamalainen, K. On the suicidal behavior of young adults. *Psychiatria Fennica*, 1976, suppl., 169–177.

Abane, M., Buffard, G., Dussuyer, I., Morel, J., Quenard, O., & Vedrinne, J. Some comparative factors of suicidal behavior in young civilians and servicemen. In V. Aalberg (Ed.) *Proceedings of the 9th International Conference for Suicide Prevention & Crisis Intervention.* Helsinki: Finnish Association for Mental Health, 1978, 422–428.

Adam, K. S., Bouckoms, A., & Scarr, G. Attempted suicide in Christchurch. *Australia & New Zealand Journal of Psychiatry*, 1980, 14, 305–314.

Adam, K. S., Bouckoms, A., & Steiner, D. Parental loss and family stability in attempted suicide. *Archives of General Psychiatry*, 1982a, 39, 1081–1085.

Adam, K. S., Lohrenz, J., Harper, D., & Steiner, D. Early parental loss and suicidal ideation in university students. *Canadian Journal of Psychiatry*, 1982b, 27, 275–281.

Allebeck, P., Allgulander, C., & Fisher, L. D. Predictors of completed suicide in a cohort of 50,465 young men. *British Medical Journal*, 1988, 297, 176–178.

Asarnow, J. R., & Guthrie, D. Suicidal behavior, depression and hopelessness in child psychiatric patients. *Journal of Clinical Child Psychology*, 1989, 18, 129–136.

Bagley, C. Profiles of youthful suicide. *Psychological Reports*, 1989, 65, 234.

Berk, N. A personality study of suicidal schizophrenics. Doctoral dissertation, New York University, 1949.

Birtchnell, J. Some familial and clinical characteristics of female suicidal psychiatric patients. *British Journal of Psychiatry,* 1981, 138, 381–390.

Bolger, N., Downey, G., Walker, E., & Steininger, P. The onset of suicidal ideation in childhood and adolescence. *Journal of Youth & Adolescence,* 1989, 18, 175–190.

Borst, S. R., & Noam, G. G. Suicidality and psychopathology in hospitalized children and adolescents. *Acta Paedopsychiatrica,* 1989, 52, 163–175.

Boult, B. E. Suicide attempts among adolescent adoptees. *South African Medical Journal,* 1988, 74, 245–246.

Briere, J., Evans, D., Runtz, M., & Wall, T. Symptomatology in men who were molested as children. *American Journal of Orthopsychiatry,* 1988, 58, 457–461.

Briere, J., & Runtz, M. Suicidal thoughts and behaviours in former sexual abuse victims. *Canadian Journal of Behavioural Science,* 1986, 18, 413–423.

Bryer, J. B., Nelson, B. A., Miller, J. B., & Krol, P. A. Childhood sexual and physical abuse as factors in adult psychiatric illness. *American Journal of Psychiatry,* 1987, 144, 1426–1430.

Budner, S., & Kumler, F. *Correlates of Suicidal Ideation.* American Association of Suicidology, Houston, 1973.

Campbell, N. B., Franco, K., & Jurs, S. Abortion in adolescence. *Adolescence,* 1988, 23, 813–827.

Choquet, M., & Davidson, F. Suicide and family. In H. Z. Winnick & L. Miller (Eds.) *Aspects of Suicide in Modern Civilization.* Jerusalem: Academic, 1978, 174–182.

Choquet, M., Facy, F., & Davidson, F. Suicide and attempted suicide among adolescents in France. In R. F. Farmer & S. Hirsch (Eds.) *The Suicide Syndrome.* London: Croom Helm, 1980, 73–89.

Coleman, L., Brown, S., Stultz, M., & Portinsky, R. The subculture of runaway suicidal youth. In R. Yufit (Ed.) *Proceedings of the 20th Annual Meeting.* Denver: AAS, 1987, 275.

Coonelly, M. The family environment of suicidal and non-suicidal youth. In D. Lester (Ed.) *Suicide '88.* Denver: AAS, 1988, 7–8.

Dingman, C. W., & McGlashan, T. H. Discriminating characteristics of suicides. *Acta Psychiatrica Scandinavica,* 1986, 74, 91–97.

Edwall, G. E., Hoffman, N. G., & Harrison, P. A. Psychological correlates of sexual abuse in adolescent girls in chemical dependency treatment. *Adolescence,* 1989, 24, 279–288.

Farberow, N. L., Litman, R. E., & Nelson, F. L. A survey of youth suicide in California. In R. Yufit (Ed.) *Proceedings of the 20th Annual Conference.* Denver: AAS, 1987, 298–300.

Farmer, R. D. The differences between those who repeat and those who do not. In R. D. Farmer & S. Hirsch (Eds.) *The Suicide Syndrome.* London: Croom Helm, 1980, 187–193.

Freidrich, W., Reams, R., & Jacobs, J. Depression and suicidal ideation in early adolescents. *Journal of Youth & Adolescence,* 1982, 11, 403–407.

Fritz, D. Suicide ideation. In R. Yufit (Ed.) *Proceedings of the 20th Annual Conference.* Denver: AAS, 1987, 285–287.

Gaines, T., & Richmond, L. Assessing suicidal behavior in basic military trainees. *Military Medicine,* 1980, 145, 263–266.

Garfinkel, B. D., Froese, A., & Hood, J. Suicide attempts in children and adolescents. *American Journal of Psychiatry,* 1982, 139, 1257–1261.

Garfinkel, B. D., & Golombek, H. Suicidal behavior in adolescence. In H. Golombek & B. D. Garfinkel (Eds.) *The Adolescent and Mood Disturbance.* New York: International Universities Press, 1983, 189–217.

Goldney, R. D. Parental loss and reported childhood stress in young women who attempted suicide. *Acta Psychiatrica Scandinavica,* 1981, 64, 34–49.

Goldney, R. D. Parental representation in young women who attempted suicide. *Acta Psychiatrica Scandinavica,* 1985, 72, 230–232.

Goodwin, J. Suicide attempts in sexual abuse victims and their mothers. *Child Abuse & Neglect,* 1981, 5, 217–221.

Grossi, V. Deliberate self-harm among adolescents in residential treatment centers. In R. Yufit (Ed.) *Proceedings of the 20th Annual Conference.* Denver: AAS, 1987, 276–277.

Gutierrez, H. O., Russakoff, L. M., & Oldham, J. M. The prediction of suicide. In D. Lester (ed.) *Suicide '88.* Denver: AAS, 1988, 127–128.

Haycock, J. Manipulation and suicide attempts in jails and prisons. *Psychiatric Quarterly,* 1989, 60, 85–98.

Herman, J., & Hirschman, L. Families at risk for father-daughter incest. *American Journal of Psychiatry,* 1981, 138, 967.

Hetzel, B. S. The epidemiology of suicidal behavior in Australia. *Australian and New Zealand Journal of Psychiatry* 1971, 5, 156–166.

Hibbard, R. A., Brack, C. J., Rauch, S., & Orr, D. P. Abuse, feelings, and health behaviors in a student population. *American Journal of Diseases of Children,* 1988, 142, 326–330.

Husain, S. A., & Vandiver, T. *Suicide in children and adolescents.* New York: Spectrum, 1984.

Iga, M. *The Thorn in the Chrysanthemum.* Berkeley: University of California, 1986.

Ishii, K. Backgrounds and suicidal behaviors of committed suicides among Kyoto University students. *Psychologia,* 1973, 16, 85–97.

Ishii, K. Backgrounds and suicidal behaviors of committed suicides among Kyoto University students. *Psychologia,* 1977, 20, 191–205.

Janus, M. D., Burgess, A. W., & McCormack, A. Histories of sexual abuse in adolescent male runaways. *Adolescence,* 1987, 22, 405–417.

Joffe, R. T., Offord, D. R., & Boyle, M. H. Ontario Child Health Study. *American Journal of Psychiatry,* 1988, 145, 1420–1423.

Kaplan, K. J., & Maldaver, M. Parental marital styles and completed adolescent suicides. In D. Lester (Ed.) *Suicide '89.* Denver: AAS, 1989, 83.

Kashani, J. H., Goddard, P., & Reid, J. C. Correlates of suicidal ideation in a community sample of children and adolescents. *Journal of the American Academy of Child & Adolescent Psychiatry,* 1989, 28, 912–917.

Kerfoot, M. Deliberate self-poisoning in childhood and early adolescence. *Journal of Child Psychology & Psychiatry*, 1988, 29, 335–343.

Khan, A. U. Heterogeneity of suicidal adolescents. *Journal of the American Academy of Child & Adolescent Psychiatry*, 1987, 26, 92–96.

Kopp, M. S., Skrabski, A., & Magyar, I. Neurotics at risk and suicidal behavior in the Hungarian population. *Acta Psychiatrica Scandinavica*, 1987, 76, 406–413.

Kosky, R. Childhood suicidal behavior. *Journal of Child Psychology & Psychiatry*, 1983, 24, 457–468.

Kosky, R., Silburn, S., & Zubrick, S. Symptomatic depression and suicidal ideation. *Journal of Nervous & Mental Disease*, 1986, 174, 523–528.

Kroll, P. D., Stock, D. F., & James, M. E. The behavior of adult alcoholic men abused as children. *Journal of Nervous & Mental Disease*, 1985, 173, 689–693.

Leblhuber, F., Schony, W., Fischer, F., Sommereder, M., & Lienbacher, G. Study on suicides committed by adolescents in upper Austria covering a period of three years. In J. P. Soubrier & J. Vedrinne (Eds.) *Depression and Suicide*. Paris: Pergamon, 1983, 652–655.

Lester, D. Suicide and sibling position. *Individual Psychology*, 1987, 43, 390–395.

Lester, D. Suicide in a middle-born child. *Adolescence*, 1989a, 24, 909–914.

Lester, D. Experience of parental loss and later suicide. *Acta Psychiatrica Scandinavica*, 1989b, 79, 450–452.

Lester, D., & Caffery, D. Birth order, depression and suicide. *Psychological Reports*, 1989, 64, 18.

Levitan, H. L. Patterns of hostility revealed in the fantasies and dreams of women with rheumatoid arthritis. *Psychotherapy & Psychosomatics*, 1981, 35(1), 34–43.

Lindsay, J. S. Suicide in the Auckland area. *New Zealand Medical Journal*, 1973, 77, 149–157.

Linkowski, P., de Maertelaer, V., & Mendlewicz, J. Suicidal behavior in major depressive illness. *Acta Psychiatrica Scandinavica*, 1985, 72, 233–238.

Manson, S. M., Beals, J., Dick, R. W., & Duclos, C. Risk factors for suicide among Indian adolescents at a boarding school. *Public Health Reports*, 1989, 104, 600–614.

May, J. Family sanction. In D. Lester (Ed.) *Suicide '89*. Denver: AAS, 1989, 68–70.

McIntire, M. S., & Angle, C. R. The taxonomy of suicide and self-poisoning. In C. F. Wells & I. R. Stuart (Eds.) *Self-Destructive Behavior in Children and Adolescents*. New York: Van Nostrand Reinhold, 1981, 224–249.

McIntosh, J. L., & Kelly, L. D. Survivor's reactions. In D. Lester (Ed.) *Suicide '88*. Denver: AAS, 1988, 89–90.

McKenry, P., Tishler, C., & Kelley, C. Adolescent suicide. *Clinical Pediatrics*, 1982, 21, 266–270.

Mehr, M., Zeltzer, L., & Robinson, R. Continued self-destructive behaviors in adolescent suicide attempters. *Journal of Adolescent Health Care*, 1981, 1, 269–274; 1982, 2, 183–187.

Monahan, R. T. Suicidal children and adolescents' responses to early memories test. *Journal of Personality Assessment*, 1983, 47, 258–264.

Motanky, C. S. The role of acting-out and identification in adolescent suicidal behavior. *Dissertation Abstracts International*, 1971, 31B, 7106.

Motto, J. Suicide risk factors in alcohol abuse. *Suicide & Life-Threatening Behavior,* 1980, 10, 230–238.

Motto, J. Suicide in male adolescents. In H. Sudak, A. B. Ford, & N. B. Rushforth (Eds.) *Suicide in the Young.* Boston: John Wright: 1984, 227–244.

Murphy, D. The self-poisoner. *Public Health,* 1982, 96, 148–154.

Murphy, G. E., & Wetzel, R. Family history of suicidal behavior among suicide attempters. *Journal of Nervous & Mental Disease,* 1982, 170, 86–90.

Myers, K. M., Burke, P., & McCauley, E. Suicidal behavior by hospitalized pre-adolescent children on a psychiatric unit. *Journal of the American Academy of Child Psychiatry,* 1985, 24, 474–480.

Nilson, P. Psychological profiles of runaway children and adolescents. In C. F. Wells & I. R. Stuart (Eds.) *Self-Destructive Behavior in Children and Adolescents.* New York: Van Nostrand Reinhold, 1981, 2–43.

Odejide, A., Williams, A., Ohaeri, J. U., & Ikuesan, B. A. The epidemiology of deliberate self-harm. *British Journal of Psychiatry,* 1986, 149, 734–737.

O'Gorman, J. G., Duncan, D., Salas, R., & Fleming, K. Suicidal behavior in the Australian army. *Australian Psychologist,* 1975, 10(1), 6–12.

Oliver, J. E. Successive generations of child maltreatment. *British Journal of Psychiatry,* 1985, 147, 484–490.

Orbach, I., Gross, Y., & Glaubman, H. Some common characteristics of latency-age suicidal children. *Suicide & Life-Threatening Behavior,* 1981, 11, 180–190.

Pettifor, J., Perry, D., Plowman, B., & Pitcher, S. Risk factors predicting childhood and adolescent suicides. *Journal of Child Care,* 1983, 1(3), 17–49.

Pfeffer, C. Suicidal impulses of normal children. *International Journal of Family Psychiatry,* 1984, 5(2), 139–150.

Pfeffer, C., Adams, D., Weiner, A., & Rosenberg, J. Life event stresses on parents on suicidal children. *International Journal of Family Psychiatry,* 1988a, 9, 341–350.

Pfeffer, C., Conte, H., Plutchik, R., & Jerrett, I. Suicidal behavior in latency-age children. *Journal of the American Academy of Child Psychiatry,* 1980, 19, 703–710.

Pfeffer, C., Lipkins, R., Plutchik, R., & Mizruchi, M. Normal children at risk for suicidal behavior. *Journal of the American Academy of Child & Adolescent Psychiatry,* 1988b, 27, 34–41.

Pfeffer, C., Newcorn, J., Kaplan, G., Mizruchi, M., & Plutchik, R. Suicidal behavior in adolescent psychiatric inpatients. *Journal of the American Academy of Child & Adolescent Psychiatry,* 1988c, 27, 357–361.

Pfeffer, C., Newcorn, J., Kaplan, G., Mizruchi, M., & Plutchik, R. Subtypes of suicidal and assaultive behaviors in adolescent psychiatric inpatients. *Journal of Child Psychology & Psychiatry,* 1989, 30, 151–163.

Pfeffer, C., Plutchik, R., & Mizruchi, M. Suicide and assaultive behavior in children. *American Journal of Psychiatry,* 1983, 140, 154–157.

Pfeffer, C., Solomon, G., Plutchik, R., Mizruchi, M., & Weine, A. Suicidal behavior in latency-age psychiatric inpatients. *Journal of the American Academy of Child Psychiatry,* 1982, 21, 564–569.

Pfeffer, C., Plutchik, R., Mizruchi, M., & Lipkins, R. Suicidal behavior in child psychiatric inpatients and outpatients and in non-patients. *American Journal of Psychiatry,* 1986, 143, 733–738.

Pfeffer, C., Plutchik, R., Mizruchi, M., & Lipkins, R. Assaultive behavior in child psychiatric inpatients, outpatients and non-patients. *Journal of the American Academy of Child & Adolescent Psychiatry,* 1987, 26, 256–261.

Pfeffer, C., Zuckerman, S., Plutchik, R., & Mizruchi, S. Suicidal behavior in normal school children. *Journal of the American Academy of Child Psychiatry,* 1984, 23, 416–423.

Plummer, B., Gispert, M., Hayden, R., Robbins, D., & Seifer, R. Depression, hopelessness, and substance abuse among hospitalized adolescents with suicidal ideation or behavior. Paper presented at the International Association for Suicide Prevention, Brussels, 1989.

Riehl, T., Kurz, A., Torhorst, A., & Moller, H. J. Broken-home-related data from patients following an attempted suicide. In H. J. Moller, A. Schmidtke, & R. Welz (Eds.) *Current Issues of Suicidology,* Berlin: Springer-Verlag, 1988, 296–300.

Roberts, J., & Hawton, K. Child abuse and attempted suicide. *British Journal of Psychiatry,* 1980, 137, 319–323.

Ross, M. W., Clayer, J., & Campbell, R. Parental rearing patterns and suicidal thoughts. *Acta Psychiatrica Scandinavica,* 1983, 67, 429–433.

Rutstein, E. H. The effects of aggressive stimuli on suicidal patients. *Dissertation Abstracts International,* 1971, 31B, 7611.

Ryan, N. D., Puig-Antich, J., Ambrosini, P., Rabinovich, H., Robinson, D., Nelson, B., Iyengar, S., & Twomey, J. The clinical picture of major depression in children and adolescents. *Archives of General Psychiatry,* 1987, 44, 854–861.

Salk, L., Lipsitt, L., Sturner, W., Reilly, B., & Levat, R. Relationship of maternal and perinatal conditions to eventual adolescent suicide. *Lancet,* 1985, 1, 624–627.

Schaller, S., & Schmidtke, A. Broken homes and suicidal behavior. In H. J. Moller, A. Schmidtke, & R. Welz (Eds.) *Current Issues of Suicidology.* Berlin: Springer-Verlag, 1988, 279–295.

Scheftner, W. A., Young, M. A., Endicott, J., Coryell, W., Fogg, L., Clark, D. C., & Fawcett, J. Family history and five-year suicide risk. *British Journal of Psychiatry,* 1988, 153, 805–809.

Silove, D., George, G., & Bhavani-Sankaram, V. Parasuicide. *Australia & New Zealand Journal of Psychiatry,* 1987, 21, 221–228.

Slap, G. B., Vorters, D. F., Chaudhuri, S., & Cantor, R. M. Risk factors for attempted suicide during adolescence. *Pediatrics,* 1989, 84, 762–772.

Smith, K., & Crawford, S. Suicidal behavior among normal high school students. *Suicide & Life-Threatening Behavior,* 1986, 16, 313–325.

Stiffman, A. R. Suicide attempts in runaway youth. *Suicide & Life-Threatening Behavior,* 1989, 19, 147–159.

Stober, B. Social environment and suicidal children and adolescents. In J. P. Soubrier & J. Vedrinne (Eds.) *Depression and Suicide.* Paris: Pergamon, 1983, 608–615.

Taylor, E., & Stansfeld, S. Children who poison themselves. *British Journal of Psychiatry,* 1984, 145, 127–135.

Tishler, C. L., & McKenry, P. Parental negative self and adolescent suicide attempts. *Journal of the American Academy of Child Psychiatry,* 1982, 21, 404–408.

Tishler, C., L., McKenry, P., & Morgan, K. Adolescent suicide attempts. *Suicide & Life-Threatening Behavior,* 1981, 11, 86–92.

Triolo, S. J., McKenry, P., Tishler, C. L., & Blyth, D. Social and psychological discriminators of adolescent suicide. *Journal of Early Adolescence,* 1984, 4, 239–251.

Tsuang, M. T. Risk of suicide in the relatives of schizophrenics, manics, depressives and controls. *Journal of Clinical Psychiatry,* 1983, 44, 396–400.

Van Egmond, M, & Jonker, D. Sexual and physical abuse. In R. Yufit (Ed.) *Proceedings of the 20th Annual Conference.* Denver: AAS, 1987, 124–125.

Veeraraghavan, V. *Suicides and Attempted Suicides in the Union Territory of Delhi.* New Delhi: Concept, 1985.

Walsh, B. W., & Rosen, P. M. *Self-Mutilation.* New York: Guilford, 1988.

Wandrei, K. E. Identifying potential suicides among high-risk women. *Social Work,* 1985, 30, 511–517.

Wasserman, D., & Cullberg, J. Early separation and suicidal behavior in the parental homes of 40 consecutive suicide attempters. *Acta Psychiatrica Scandinavica,* 1989, 79, 296–302.

Weiss, J. The suicidal syndrome. In K. Achte, V. Aalberg & J. Lonnqvist (Eds.) *Psychopathology of depression. Psychiatria Fennica,* 1980, supplement, 269–275.

Wright, L. Parental permission to date and its relationship to drug use and suicidal thoughts among adolescents. *Adolescence,* 1982, 17, 409–418.

Wright, L. Suicidal thoughts and their relationship to family stress and personal problems among high school seniors and college undergraduates. *Adolescence,* 1985, 20, 575–580.

Yates, G. L., MacKenzie, R., Pennbridge, J., & Cohen, E. A risk profile of runaway and non-runaway youth. *American Journal of Public Health,* 1988, 78, 820–821.

Yesavage, J., & Widrow, L. Early parental discipline and adult self-destructive acts. *Journal of Nervous & Mental Disease,* 1985, 173, 74–77.

Zubrick, S., Kosky, R., & Silburn, S. Is suicidal ideation associated with puberty? *Australian & New Zealand Journal of Psychiatry,* 1987, 21, 54–58.

Chapter 5

SOCIOLOGICAL THEORIES OF SUICIDE

The three major sociological theories of suicide were proposed by Durkheim, by Henry and Short and by Gibbs and Martin. These theories have been reviewed and critiqued in depth recently by Lester (1989a). In this chapter we will briefly report research from the 1980s directly relevant to these three theories and review new theories which have been proposed.

The Classic Theories

Durkheim's Theory of Suicide

Besnard (1988) suggested a redefinition of Durkheim's concept of anomie/fatalism as widening or narrowing the field of opportunities. Anomie involves indeterminate goals and unlimited aspirations while fatalism involves closed horizons. Besnard suggested a second dimension— whether there is a chronic structural situation or an acute crisis resulting from a sudden change.

Two tests of Durkheim's theory of suicide appeared in the 1970s. Rootman (1973) tested Durkheim's theory using a sample of non-literate societies. He classified each society as high or low for social regulation and social integration based on indices of social behavior such as the permanency of residence and power vested in a chief. His indices of regulation and integration correlated positively but weakly, suggesting that they were different concepts. Although he did not use statistical tests on his data, his results suggest that suicide rates were highest in three groups of societies: low integration and high regulation, high integration and high regulation, and high integration and moderate regulation. Rootman concluded that integration seemed to be more important than regulation. (He also reported that the suicide rates of the societies were strongly related to an index of the attractiveness of the future life.)

Masumura (1977) also used a sample of non-literate societies and

74

found that group life was positively associated with suicide rates, as was elaboration of ceremony and ritual. (Presence of an organized priest-hood was not related to suicide rates.) Thus, suicide rates were *positively* associated to apparent indices of social integration and regulation, which Masumura saw as contrary to Durkheim's theory.

Lester (1989a) took seven social variables in modern nations which he thought relevant to social integration and social regulation. He factor-analyzed them and extracted two factors which appeared to measure these dimensions. He then classified the 53 nations into low, moderate or high on each of the two factor scores, resulting in a three-by-three array of nations. Durkheim's theory predicts that the nations in the corner cells (with high and/or low scores on the two factors) would have the highest suicide rates and the nations in the center cell (with moderate scores on both factors) would have the lowest suicide rates. In fact the nations with high scores on both factors and with low scores on both factors had the highest suicide rates, and the nations moderate on both had the lowest scores. There was some asymmetry though, with low social regulation and high social integration appearing to be the more power-ful determinants of high suicide rates. In a replication of this study using a different data set, Lester (1989e) failed to replicate the results for the three-by-three cell array. However, suicide rates remained associated with the social integration factor scores but not with the social regulation factor scores.

Lester (1988f) has proposed applying Durkheim's theory of completed suicide to attempted suicide, arguing that attempted suicide should be positively associated with social integration (rather than negatively as in the case of completed suicide), since attempted suicide is more often a way of communicating to and manipulating significant others.

Henry and Short

Lester has argued from Henry and Short's theory that suicide should be less common when there are clear external events to blame for one's misery. Aponte (1970) hypothesized similarly that suicide should be less common during earthquakes, wars, disasters and other tragedies, but he did not test his hypothesis empirically. Lester (1986b) used the theory to account for the low suicide rate in concentration camps during the Second World War, while Lester (1988b) used the theory to explain the increasing rate of teenage suicide in the USA at a time when the conditions for teenagers appear to be improving.

Lester (1981) predicted from Henry and Short's theory that the existence of a free press in nations should be related to the suicide and homicide rates. He found that a free press was associated with a higher homicide rate (once the gross national product per capita was controlled for) but not with the suicide rate.

In support of the theory, Lester (1984) predicted that suicide should be common where the quality of life is higher while homicide should be less common. Data from 43 nations with objective quality of life measures supported this prediction (but, interestingly, not for youth suicide rates [Lester, 1988e] or for only a reduced sample of industrialized nations [Lester and Georges, 1986]). Lester (1985a, 1986b, 1989c) replicated this result using ratings of the quality of life in the American states in 1931 and in 1940 and in American cities in 1930, but a study of SMSAs in 1981 failed to produce the same result (Lester, 1985b) as did a study of the nine regions of the USA (Lester, 1987d). In this latter study, economic conditions were positively associated with suicide rates, but education and crime were negatively associated with suicide rates and the other components of the quality of life index not significantly associated with suicide rates.

Levi (1982) proposed a theory of suicide and homicide that is very similar to Henry and Short's. Levi argued that homicide and suicide are both acts in response to situations in which the individual is socially and politically limited or isolated. Homicide takes place in settings where others are available as victims and accomplices, where the individual is able to victimize others and where policing is weak. In contrast, suicide takes place when a victim is not readily available. This may be the case for several reasons. The antagonist may have departed, the antagonist may be a thing rather than a person (such as the death of a loved one or a disease such as insanity or cancer), the antagonist may be perceived as too powerful and thus not open to attack, or there may be no one around who fits the antagonist's role. Even when potential victims are available, homicide may not be an option if the person has an internal locus of control and so does not blame others, but rather takes responsibility himself. Levi noted that murderers see themselves as superior to others, while suicides see themselves as inferior to others; the murderer as overwhelming others and the suicide as being overwhelmed by others. Finally homicide or suicide must be seen as possible behaviors with few inhibitions against the acts.

Since this theory argues, like Henry and Short, that suicide and homicide are opposed behaviors, Levi sought to show in a cross-national study that variables which correlate in one direction with suicide correlate in the opposite direction with homicide (such as smaller households, a higher percentage of workers in industry, a longer life span, and smaller population growth which correlated positively with suicide rates and negatively with homicide rates). (Population size and the gross national product of the poorest 20% of the population did not correlate with either suicide or homicide rates.)

Gibbs and Martin

Gibbs (1982) found that a composite measure of status integration was significantly associated with the suicide rate over twelve age groups, but the associations with each individual measure of status integration (labor force, marital, and parental) were not significant, though still negative. Gibbs and Martin (1981) examined the association of a very simple measure of status integration (the percent of males aged 15–24 in designated marital statuses) with the suicide rate over selected status groups in British Columbia (Canada) and found some (inconsistent) evidence for an negative association.

Stafford and Gibbs (1985) found that suicide rates and some measures of status integration were *positively* associated over age-by-race-by-sex groups in the USA (for employment, household, marital and simultaneous measures of status integration), but the associations were negative for occupational and residential measures. Stafford and Gibbs (1988) found negative associations between measures of marital and occupational integration and suicide rates over age groups for each race-by-sex group. Lester (1989d) found that changes in nations' status integration from 1950–1960 did not predict 1960 suicide rates or changes in suicide rates from 1950–1960.

Lester (1987e) has applied Gibbs and Martin's theory to homicide, but he found no association between status integration and homicide rates in the USA over age groups.

New Theories

Lester's Critical Mass Theory

Lester (1988d) argued that, when the rate of people committing suicide in a society reaches a high level, then the behavior becomes increasingly

common because, among other reasons, it is seen as socially more acceptable and more people in the society know someone who has committed
suicide.

Lester (1987c, 1988d) found that the suicide rate of nations in 1970 was
associated with the absolute increase (but not the percentage increase)
from 1970 to 1980 (but not for youth suicide rates [Lester, 1988e]). The
effect was greater in those nations with the higher suicide rates, and
the effect reached its maximum after seven years. Lester (1989b) replicated
this result for 1960–1970, but the tendency was no longer statistically
significant. Lester (1988c) failed to find this phenomenon in the states of
the USA from 1970 to 1980.

Lester's Social Deviancy Theory

Lester has proposed that suicide may be more common among people
who find themselves sociologically deviant as compared to the community in which they live. For example, Lester (1986c, 1987b) documented
that the smaller the size of the immigrant group in Australia, the higher
its suicide rate. Lester (1980, 1987b) documented that the suicide rates of
non-whites are higher in those states where there are fewer non-whites,
whereas this is not so for the suicide rate of whites. Lester (1988a) pointed
out, however, that the type of black citizen who lives in those states with
few blacks is very different in education, social class, and household size
than the type of black citizen who lives in states where there are many
blacks.

Related to this theory, Cheetham et al. (1983) studied attempted suicide in Asians in South Africa precipitated by deviating from the culture,
such as marrying outside of the caste. Over half of the attempters had
been cultural deviant, Christians most so and Moslems least so (with
Hindus in between). The culturally deviant attempters were younger,
more often female and more often middle class.

However, Lester (1988g) found that the number of workers in the
major occupational groups or in the major medical specialities were not
related to the suicide rates of these groups.

Lester's Subcultural Theory

Lester has also proposed that subcultures may exist in which suicide in
seen as a more appropriate behavior and in which it is more common. In
line with this, Lester (1986–1987) found that an index of southern subculture was associated with gun ownership and the use of guns for homicide

and suicide. The stronger the southern subculture, the higher the suicide rate by guns and the lower the suicide rate by hanging and other methods. Lester (1987a) documented a cluster of completed suicides in a group of teenagers and made suggestions as to which features of the teenage subculture may be conducive to suicide.

Platt (1985) proposed a subcultural theory of attempted suicide and to explore its usefulness interviewed people (both suicide attempters and controls) living in an area of Edinburgh with a high rate of attempted suicide and others living in an area with a low rate. Contrary to Platt's expectation, the differences between the attempters and the controls were similar in both regions in their attitudes toward attempted suicide. Thus, the high rate of attempted suicide did not seem to have changed people's value orientations or ways of behaving with respect to suicide.

Interpersonal Skills and Attempted Suicide

Lester (1988f) suggested that attempted suicide might be a result of poor interpersonal skills (which forces the individual to use inappropriate methods for communicating distress), combined with low self-esteem and low self-confidence. Lester showed how this could explain the differing rates of attempted suicide in subgroups of the population by sex, education, and age.

Sociobiology

DeCatanzaro (1980) looked at suicide from the perspective of sociobiology. Sociobiology views suicide as aberrant since it does not advance the welfare of the genes. But deCatanzaro argued that (1) suicide may be independent from biological evolution and a result instead of humans' ability to learn, (2) suicide may be pathological and the genes that were once appropriate for the environment in which we lived fail to be useful in our new unusual environment, (3) suicide could be altruistic and benefit others who share our genes, and (4) suicide may be immune to the pressure of natural selection since, after all, it is more common in those with low reproductive success such as the elderly and the isolated. In a research study planned from this perspective, deCatanzaro (1984) found that suicidal ideation was stronger in those with poor health, in those with with unstable heterosexual relationships and in those who felt that their families would be better off without them.

Criminology-Based Theories of Suicide

Lester (1990) proposed a series of theories of suicide, each one based on one of the classic theories of crime and delinquency.

A Classical Theory of Suicide

A classical theory would view suicide as a rational decision made by an individual who weighs the costs and benefits of suicide versus other alternative actions. This viewpoint has rarely been proposed for suicide. However, Yang (1990), an economist, has proposed a cost-benefit and a demand-supply analysis of suicide which is based upon such a viewpoint. In addition, Clarke and Lester (1989) have argued that the choice of a method for suicide is a rational choice based upon the effects of different methods for suicide on the body and on the mind.

A Positivist Individualistic Theory of Suicide

Positivist individualistic theories of suicide include the majority of psychological and psychiatric theories proposed so far to account for suicide. Such theories look for the causes of suicide in the individual's physiological constitution, psychological characteristics and psychiatric state.

A Social Structure Theory of Suicide

Two variants of social structure theory were proposed. In a culture deviance theory, it was suggested that there exist suicidal subcultures, especially in small communities such as schools, psychiatric hospitals and prisons, or native American reservations. These subcultures have different values and attitudes from the mainstream culture.

In addition, more broad subcultural patterns were described, such as the use of guns to solve problems (in both murder and suicide), which characterize whole regions. For example, it has long been true that Hungary has the highest suicide rate of any nation in the world. In addition, Hungarian immigrants to other nations have the highest suicide rates of all immigrant groups. Perhaps Hungarians have a subculture which makes suicide more likely?

Strain theories focus on the emotional experiences of those who have difficulty working toward the culturally-approved goals by socially acceptable means. Those who fail in this task will experience anger, frustration and despair. They become retreatists, to use Robert Merton's (1957) set of types, perhaps episodic retreatists.

A Learning Theory of Suicide

Learning theories of suicide have been proposed in recent years. For example, Lester (1987f) presented a convincing case that learning factors may play a strong role in the appearance of suicide in distressed individuals. Related to learning theories, a neutralization theory of suicide focuses on the ways in which the potential suicide neutralizes the inhibitions against killing himself. Interestingly, very little research has been conducted on this latter issue, and it would appear to merit more intensive study in the future. If we could find how people decrease their inhibitions against committing suicide, we might obtain some ideas as to how these inhibitions might be increased.

A Social Control Theory of Suicide

A social control theory of suicide focuses on the social bonds and internal controls which prevent people from committing suicide. The major sociological theory of suicide, that proposed by Durkheim, fits here. Durkheim proposed that social integration and social regulation, in moderation, both served to make suicide less likely. Thus, increased social bonding should make suicide less likely. Psychological theories of suicide too have recognized the importance of social bonds—good relationships with parents, spouses and lovers, children and friends.

One variant of the social control theories, containment theory, focuses in addition on the internal forces that inhibit the appearance of suicidal behavior, such as strong ego strength and a positive self-image, belief in an internal locus of control, and good frustration tolerance and low impulsivity.

A Social Reaction Theory of Suicide

A social reaction theory of suicide focuses on the ways in which people might be labeled as "suicidal" in the society and how they react to this labeling. Do they reject it or do they accept it and enter the career of being suicidal?

Lester (1990) noted that putting patients on suicide alert in institutions (in order to monitor them more closely so as to prevent suicide) may result in labeling, as might clients deciding to call a suicide prevention center. Suicide education programs may introduce people to the suicidal career and show them how to proceed in the career.

A Social Conflict Theory of Suicide

A social conflict theory of suicide views suicide as the result of oppression of one group in the society by another group. Evidence was produced which suggested the role of suicide in manipulating the power balance in their relationships by oppressed individuals. Possible sexist biases in suicidology were also discussed.

It was suggested that modernization along capitalist lines might increase the risk of suicide, but the evidence for this was not strong yet. However, Hendin (1982) has argued that the oppression resulting from racism and social class may play a role in the high rates of suicide in young urban black males.

Discussion

It can be seen that the three classic theories of suicide have continued to generate research and interest in the 1980s. However, the 1980s have also witnessed the appearance of several new theories of suicide, both of completed suicide and of attempted suicide, which may generate research in the 1990s and which suggest very different strategies for preventing suicide (Lester, 1990).

REFERENCES

Aponte, R. Epidemiological aspects of suicide and attempted suicide in Venezuela. *Proceedings of the 5th International Congress for Suicide Prevention.* Vienna: IASP, 1970, 52–57.

Besnard, P. The true nature of anomie. *Sociological Theory,* 1988, 6(1), 91–95.

Cheetham, R. W., Edwards, S., Naidoo, L., Griffiths, J., & Singh, V. Deculturation as a precipitant of parasuicide in an Asian group. *South African Journal of Medicine,* 1983, 63, 942–945.

Clarke, R. V., & Lester, D. *Suicide: Closing the Exits.* New York: Springer-Verlag, 1989.

deCatanzaro, D. *Suicide and Self-Damaging Behavior.* New York: Academic, 1981.

deCatanzaro, D. Suicidal ideation and the residual capacity to promote inclusive fitness. *Suicide & Life-Threatening Behavior,* 1984, 14, 75–87.

Gibbs, J. P. Testing the theory of status integration and suicide rates. *American Sociological Review,* 1982, 47, 227–237.

Gibbs, J. P., & Martin, W. Still another look at status integration and suicide. *Social Forces,* 1981, 59, 815–823.

Hendin, H. *Suicide in America.* New York: Norton, 1982.

Lester, D. Regional suicide rates and the hazards of minority status. *American Journal of Psychiatry,* 1980, 137, 1469–1470.

Lester, D. Freedom of the press and personal violence. *Journal of Social Psychology,* 1981, 114, 267–269.

Lester, D. The association between the quality of life and suicide and homicide rates. *Journal of Social Psychology,* 1984, 124, 247–248.

Lester, D. The quality of life and suicide. *Journal of Social Psychology,* 1985a, 125, 279–280.

Lester, D. The quality of life in modern America and suicide and homicide rates. *Journal of Social Psychology,* 1985, 125, 779–780.

Lester, D. Suicide. *Israel Journal of Psychiatry,* 1986a, 23, 221–223.

Lester, D. Suicide, homicide and the quality of life. *Suicide & Life-Threatening Behavior,* 1986b, 16, 389–392.

Lester, D. Suicide rates in immigrants to Australia. *Medical Journal of Australia,* 1986c, 144, 280.

Lester, D. Southern subculture, personal violence (suicide and homicide), and firearms. *Omega,* 1986–1987, 17, 183–186.

Lester, D. A subcultural theory of teenage suicide. *Adolescence,* 1987a, 22, 317–320.

Lester, D. Social deviancy and suicide. *Journal of Social Psychology,* 1987b, 127, 339–340.

Lester, D. Indirect evidence for effects of suggestion in suicide *Psychological Reports,* 1987c, 61, 576.

Lester, D. Quality of life and rates of suicide and homicide. *Perceptual & Motor Skills,* 1987d, 64, 94.

Lester, D. Status integration, suicide and homicide. *Psychological Reports,* 1987e, 61, 672.

Lester, D. *Suicide As a Learned Behavior.* Springfield, IL: Charles C Thomas, 1987f,

Lester, D. Demographic attributions related to black suicide. *Journal of Social Psychology,* 1988a, 128, 407–409.

Lester, D. One theory of teenage suicide. *Journal of School Health,* 1988b, 58, 193–194.

Lester, D. The critical mass hypothesis of suicide. *Psychological Reports,* 1988c, 62, 626.

Lester, D. A critical mass theory of national suicide rates. *Suicide & Life-Threatening Behavior,* 1988d, 18, 279–284.

Lester, D. Youth suicide. *Adolescence,* 1988e, 23, 955–958.

Lester, D. Toward a theory of parasuicide. *Corrective & Social Psychiatry,* 1988f, 34(1), 24–26.

Lester, D. Social deviancy and suicide. *Psychological Reports,* 1988g, 63, 968.

Lester, D. *Suicide From a Sociological Perspective.* Springfield, IL: Charles C Thomas, 1989a.

Lester, D. The critical mass hypothesis applied to national suicide rates. *Psychological Reports,* 1989b, 64, 746.

Lester, D. The quality of life and suicide rates in American cities in 1930. *Psychological Reports.* 1989c, 65, 1358.

Lester, D. Association of population growth, technological development and social integration on rates of personal violence (suicide and homicide). *Psychological Reports,* 1989d, 64, 462.

Lester, D. A test of Durkheim's theory of suicide using data from modern nations. *International Journal of Comparative Sociology,* 1989e, 30, 235–238.

Lester, D. *Understanding and Preventing Suicide.* Springfield: Charles C Thomas, 1990.

Lester, D., & Georges, V. C. National character and rates of personal violence (suicide and homicide). *Psychological Reports,* 1986, 58, 186.

Levi, K. Homicide and suicide. *Deviant Behavior,* 1982, 3, 91–115.

Masumura, W. T. Social integration and suicide. *Behavior Science Research,* 1977, 12, 251–269.

Merton, R. *Social theory and social structure.* Glencoe, IL: Free Press, 1957.

Platt, S. D. A subculture of parasuicide. *Human Relations,* 1985, 38, 257–297.

Rootman, I. A cross-cultural note on Durkheim's theory of suicide. *Life-Threatening Behavior,* 1971, 3, 83–94.

Stafford, M. C., & Gibbs, J. P. A major problem with the theory of status integration and suicide. *Social Forces,* 1985, 63, 643–660.

Stafford, M. C., & Gibbs, J. P. Changes in the relation between marital integration and suicide rates. *Social Forces,* 1988, 66, 1060–1079.

Yang, B. Is suicide a rational choice? In D. Lester *Understanding and Preventing Suicide* Springfield, IL: Charles C Thomas, 1990, 15–20.

Chapter 6

THE RELIABILITY AND VALIDITY
OF SUICIDE RATES

C riticism continues to be made about the accuracy of official statistics on suicide which are based on death certificates. There are several studies which have located undercounting of suicides, but other research continues to indicate that these errors may not have much impact on the results of research into suicide.

Certification Errors

Studies of Death Certificates/Autopsies

In Ireland, Clarke-Finnegan and Fahy (1983) examined post-mortem results in Galway County and found a suicide rate of 13.1 (per 100,000 per year) instead of the official rate of 5.8. In Alaska, Hlady and Middaugh (1988) found that suicides of native Americans were more likely to be misrecorded (primarily as a result of delayed determinations and a failure to update records) than those of whites. Others have also documented certification errors: Malla and Hoenig (1983) in Newfoundland, Marshall and Soule (1988) in an Alaskan native American village, Moyer et al. (1989) in Vietnam veterans, Shaw and Sims (1984) in the United Kingdom, and Thorslund and Misfeldt (1989) in Greenland.

Police Versus Medical Records

Williams et al. (1987) noted that in Italy, the police had records of fewer suicides than the medical examiners.

Studies of Characteristics of Decedents

Evenson et al. (1988) looked at former psychiatric patients who had died and found that those whose deaths were classified as undetermined were very similar in diagnosis, age at death, sex and race to the suicides while the unusual accidental deaths were quite different.

They suggested that the undetermined deaths may really have been suicides.

Asencio et al. (1988) in Spain found that the greater the proportion of unnatural deaths for which a magistrate's office ordered a post-mortem, the greater the percentage of suicides identified. In Denmark, Asnaes and Paaske (1980) found that autopsies identified suicides which the police investigation had not revealed.

In Portugal, de Castro et al. (1989) found that "controversial" deaths resembled the suicidal deaths in characteristics, and the rate of controversial cases was almost the same as the suicide rate.

Platt (1988) compared completed suicides and undetermined deaths in Scotland. The suicides were more often men aged 25–64 or women with prior psychiatric contact. The suicides more often used hanging and the undetermined deaths drowning. The groups did not differ in sex, age, social class, marital status or prior psychiatric contact.

For those dying from overdoses of dextropropoxyphene in Copenhagen, Theilade (1989) compared those certified as suicides, undetermined and accidents. The suicides were most often depressed and the accidental deaths least often. More of the accidental deaths were alcohol abusers than the suicides and undetermined, whereas almost all of the drug abusers were certified as accidental deaths. Alcohol was found in the body most often in the accidental deaths, less often in the suicides and least often in the undetermined deaths. Overall, the undetermined deaths resembled the suicides more than the accidental deaths.

Burvill et al. (1982a) found that the increase in undetermined deaths after 1968 in Australia seemed to come from previous classified accidental deaths rather than from suicides.

Date of Injury and Date of Death

Rich et al. (1985) compared the date of the suicidal act and the date of death on the certificate and found them to be the same in only 46 percent of the cases. Phillips and Sanzone (1988) found that 93 percent of the suicides in California occurred within one day of the day of injury, 84 percent on the same day. The proportion dying on the same day as the injury was greater in men than in women and in married people, but age and race had no effect.

Other Research Designs

In the USA, Kleck (1988) simply looked at the number of deaths in undetermined and accidental death categories that could be used to hide suicides and guessed that about 26 percent of suicides were hidden in these other categories. There was no attempt to validate this guess. Kolmos and Bach (1987) claimed that differences in the accidental and undetermined death rates in Scandinavian nations could not account for the differences in the suicide rates but, since they had no way of determining validly how many accidental and undetermined deaths were suicide, their logic is seriously flawed.

Lester (1983) found that monthly variation in suicidal deaths in the USA by poisoning was significantly different from the monthly variation of accidental deaths by poisoning. He thought that this evidence suggested that accidental deaths were not concealed suicides. Over the states of America, Lester (1985) found that the suicidal and accidental death rates from poisons were positively associated as were the two rates of death by firearms. Lester argued that the positive association suggested that accidents were not disguised suicides since then the associations would be negative. Moens (1985) in Belgium found that the suicide rates of the districts were positively associated with the undetermined death rate and accidental death rates from poisons.

Coroners/Medical Examiners

Lester (1986a) compared the behavior of coroners from eight nations certifying a standard set of possibly suicidal deaths with the national suicide rates. The association was not statistically significant.

Pescosolido and Mendelsohn (1986) studied social correlates of county suicide rates in America and found that introducing medical examiner variables into the multiple regressions had only a minimal imapct on the relationships identified.

Effect of Legal Changes

Jennings and Barraclough (1980) found no association from year-to-year in changes in the number of suicide verdicts in England and the numbers of open or accident verdicts. Changes in the law about death certification or High Court decisions also had no discernible effect on the suicide rate. They concluded that legal and administrative influences on the suicide rate were not apparent.

Concurrent Validity Studies

Lester (1986b) compared the different ratings of suicide rates in primitive societies made by different investigators and found that they were positively associated.

Test-Retest Reliability

Lester (1987) found that, although the suicide rates of nations rose from 1875 to 1975, the rates one hundred years apart were positively associated, almost significantly. However, the stability of the suicide rates of counties in England from 1873 to 1973 was zero (Lester, 1988).

Immigrants

Burvill et al. (1982b) confirmed that the suicide rates of immigrant groups in Australia were strongly related to the suicide rates of the home nations for both men and women. Kliewer and Ward (1988) found that the suicide rates of immigrants in Canada of both men and women were correlated with the suicide rates in home nations. Lester (1980) found that the suicide rates of immigrants to the USA and to Australia were in a similar rank order to the suicide rates of the home nations, overall, for both sexes, and for most ages. Lester (1989) also replicated this finding for immigrants to Chicago in 1920.

Discussion

Although research convincingly documents that some suicidal deaths are misclassified and not recorded as suicidal deaths, there is no evidence that this misclassification invalidates the use of societal suicide rates in sociological research. This conclusion is similar to that made after reviewing the research of the 1970s.

REFERENCES

Asencio, A. P., Gomez-Beneyton, M., & Llopis, V. Epidemiology of suicide in Valencia. *Social Psychiatry & Psychiatric Epidemiology,* 1988, 23, 57–59.

Asnaes, S., & Paaske, F. Uncertainty of determining mode of death in medico-legal material without autopsy. *Forensic Science International,* 1980, 15, 3–17.

Burvill, P. W., McCall, M., Stenhouse, N., & Woodings, T. The relationship between suicide, undetermined deaths and accidental deaths in the Australian born and migrants in Australia. *Australia & New Zealand Journal of Psychiatry,* 1982a, 16, 179–184.

Burvill, P. W., Woodings, T., Stenhouse, N., & McCall, M. Suicide during 1961–1970 in migrants in Australia. *Psychological Medicine,* 1982b, 12, 295–308.

Clarke-Finnegan, M., & Fahy, T. Suicide rates in Ireland. *Psychological Medicine,* 1983, 13, 385–391.

de Castro, F. E., Pimenta, F., & Martins, I. The truth about suicide in Portugal. *Acta Psychiatrica Scandinavica,* 1989, 80, 334–339.

Evenson, R. C., Cho, D. W., & Holland, R. Identifying psychiatric suicides for research purposes. *Journal of Clinical Psychology,* 1988, 44, 1029–1032.

Hlady, W. G., & Middaugh, J. P. The underrecording of suicide in state and national records, Alaska, 1983–1984. *Suicide & Life-Threatening Behavior,* 1988, 18, 237–244.

Jennings, C., & Barraclough, B. M. Legal and administrative influences on the English suicide rate since 1900. *Psychological Medicine,* 1980, 10, 407–418.

Kleck, G. Miscounting suicides. *Suicide & Life-Threatening Behavior,* 1988, 18, 219–236.

Kliewer, E. V., & Ward, R. H. Convergence of immigrant suicide rates to those in the destination country. *American Journal of Epidemiology,* 1988, 127, 640–653.

Kolmos, L., & Bach, E. Sources of error in registering suicide. *Acta Psychiatrica Scandinavica,* 1987, 76, supplement 336, 22–43.

Lester, D. The validity of national suicide rates. *British Journal of Psychiatry,* 1980, 136, 107–108.

Lester, D. Monthly variation of suicidal and accidental poisoning deaths. *British Journal of Psychiatry,* 1983, 143, 204–205.

Lester, D. Accidental deaths as disguised suicides. *Psychological Reports,* 1985, 56, 626.

Lester, D. Coroner's decisions and suicide rates. *Psychological Reports,* 1986a, 58, 586.

Lester, D. Reliability of estimates of suicide rates in nonliterate societies. *Psychological Reports,* 1986b, 59, 1214.

Lester, D. The stability of national suicide rates. *Sociology & Social Research,* 1987, 71, 208.

Lester, D. Stability of suicide rates in small areas. *Psychological Reports,* 1988, 62, 368.

Lester, D. Suicide rates in immigrant groups and their countries of origin. *Psychological Reports,* 1989, 65, 818.

Malla, A., & Hoenig, J. Differences in suicide rates. *Canadian Journal of Psychiatry,* 1983, 28, 291–293.

Marshall, D. L., & Soule, S. Accidental deaths and suicides in southwest Alaska. *Alaska Medicine,* 1988, 30(2), 45–52.

Moens, G. F. The reliability of reported suicide mortality statistics. *International Journal of Epidemiology,* 1985, 14, 272–275.

Moyer, L. A., Boyle, C. A., & Pollock, D. A. Validity of death certificates for injury-related causes of death. *American Journal of Epidemiology,* 1989, 130, 1024–1032.

Pescosolido, B. A., & Mendelsohn, R. Social causation or social construction of suicide. *American Sociological Review,* 1986, 51, 80–101.

Phillips, D. P., & Sanzone, A. G. A comparison of injury date and death date in 42,698 suicides. *American Journal of Public Health,* 1988, 78, 541–543.

Platt, S. D., Backett, S., & Kreitman, N. Social construction or causal ascription. *Social Psychiatry & Psychiatric Epidemiology,* 1988, 23, 217–221.

Rich, C., Young, D., Fowler, R., & Rosenfeld, S. The difference between date of suicidal act and recorded death certificate date in 204 consecutive suicides. *American Journal of Public Health,* 1985, 75, 778–779.

Shaw, S., & Sims, A. A survey of unexpected deaths among psychiatric in-patients and ex-patients. *British Journal of Psychiatry,* 1984, 145, 473–476.

Theilade, P. Deaths due to dextropropoxyphene. *Forensic Science International,* 1989, 40, 143–151.

Thorslund, J., & Misfeldt, J. On suicide statistics. *Arctic Medical Research,* 1989, 48, 124–130.

Williams, P., De Salvia, D., & Tansella, M. Suicide and the Italian psychiatric reform. *European Archives of Psychiatry,* 1987, 236, 237–240.

Chapter 7

SOCIOLOGICAL CORRELATES OF SUICIDE

A vast number of studies appear each decade looking at social correlates of suicidal behavior. This chapter makes an effort to summarize the results of much of this research.

Age

The major epidemiological finding of the 1980s has been the rising suicide rate among those aged 15–24 in the USA and some (but not all) nations of the world (Lester, 1988a), so that in the USA the distribution of completed suicide by age is bimodal. This is found in smaller regions too. For example, in Texas in 1980, Lloyd et al. (1987) reported a bimodal distribution of suicide by age, with peaks at 25–29 and 70–74.

Altergott (1988) found different socioeconomic correlates of suicide rates of young adults and old adults over a small sample of nations. On the whole, the social correlates were of opposite sign for the elderly suicide rate than for the total suicide rate. For example, educational level was negatively associated with the overall suicide rate and positively associated with the elderly suicide rate. The time spent by men working, age, the percentage of gross national product spent on pensions and the percentage of elder adults widowed or divorced were positively related to the overall suicide rate and negatively with the elderly suicide rate.

Seiden (1981) noted that the white suicide rate increased monotonically with age in the USA while the black suicide rate peaked early and then declined with age. Seiden suggested the following possible reasons: (1) differential life expectancies between the races means that only the strongest survive, (2) the stress of being a minority is greatest in youth, after which there is less stress, (3) the violent-prone among blacks are screened out early in life, (4) the status of the elderly among blacks increases with age, (5) blacks have more traditional values of respect toward the elderly and toward suicide, and (6) the motives for suicide are stronger among young blacks.

91

From 1934 to 1983, Stafford and Weisheit (1988) found that the age distributions for male and female suicide rates in the USA have become more similar for blacks and less similar for whites.

Individual Studies

Conwell et al. (1989) found that, with increasing age, suicides were more often widowed, more often living alone, more often reacting to physical illness and loss, and less often intoxicated at the time of the act. The middle-aged suicides were more often in treatment for depression. No differences in method were observed.

Maris (1985) compared young completed suicides (in the teens or twenties) with older suicides and found no differences in method used, hopelessness, depression, the number of close friends, or seeing death as an escape. The younger completers were more often female, saw death as a revenge, had more suicidal behavior in their family members, used alcohol more, more often had divorced parents, were more irritable and had lower self-esteem.

Michel (1988) found that suicides in Bern (Switzerland) under the age of 25 more often left a suicide note and had suicidal actions with objectively more suicidal intent. They also tended to be more often male, living with others, with fewer prior suicide attempts, less prior comunication, a lower depression score and less prior medical care.

Vogel and Wolfersdorf (1989) compared elderly and younger completed suicides among hospitalized psychiatric patients. The elderly suicides had more physical diseases, more delusional fears and auditory hallucinations, felt lonelier, had experienced more loss through death and had more interpersonal problems.

Among attempted suicides in England, Morgan (1980) found that the younger attempters (15–25) were more often unemployed and dissatisfied with their jobs whereas the older attempters had more legal problems and had increased their alcohol intake in the prior three months. In Newcastle (England), Wynne et al. (1987) found that elderly suicide attempters by overdose more often had physical and psychiatric precipitants and less often social precipitants. The elderly suicides used analgesics less and benzodiazepines and prescribed medications more. They used multiple drugs less often and less often were intoxicated at the time of the overdose. They did not differ in prior suicide attempts. In a sample of people with adverse drug reactions, Peterson and Thomas

(1975) found that the elderly were more often white and female, but did not differ in the presence of alcohol abuse.

Cultural Patterns

Fuse (1980) looked at national suicide rates by age and found three patterns: Hungarian in which the rise with age is linear, Scandinavian in which the rates peak in middle age, and Japanese in which the rates rise with age except for a secondary peak at age 25–34. Bimodal distributions appeared to be characteristic of underdeveloped countries. Lester (1982c) found that the patterns were not as simple or clear-cut as Fuse described. In addition, Lester found that, whatever the gross national product per capita of the nation, older males have the highest suicide rates but, for females, as the gnp per capita decreased, the peak age for suicide decreased also.

Anomie

Achte et al. (1972) found that suicide attempters from worse social conditions (low social class, lack of education, working incapacity and unsatisfactory living conditions) had a stronger desire to die. Frustrating childhood experiences were not related to the desire to die, but the desire was stronger the more neurotic and the younger the attempter. Achte measured anomie with a combination of variables (divorced/ widowed, imprisoned, unemployed, distant from relatives, etc.), and the men obtained higher scores than the women. The anomic men were mostly 26–44 while the anomic women were mostly under 25.

Cohort Analyses

A number of studies in the 1980s tried to tease out the impact of age, era and cohort on suicide rates. This is impossible since the three variables are not independent of one another, that is, two of these variables determines the third (Kupper et al., 1985; Newman and Dyck, 1988; Wetzel et al., 1987). For example, using a data set of male suicide rates in the USA from 1935 to 1975 for those aged 15–19 to 65–69 (Lester, 1984), I calculated for this volume the Pearson correlation coefficients between the suicide rates and age ($r = 0.89$, $p < .001$), year ($r = -0.17$, $p < .05$) and cohort ($r = -0.80$, $p < .001$). Partial correlation coefficients for each of these controlling for the other two variables reduced the strength of these associations to zero (rs = 0.03, 0.02 and −0.03, respectively).

A number of studies appeared nonetheless: for Australia (Goldney and Katsikitis, 1983), Canada (Barnes et al., 1986; Hellon and Solomon, 1980; Reed et al., 1985; Solomon and Hellon, 1980; Trovato, 1988), England and Wales (Murphy et al., 1986), Germany (Hafner and Schmidtke, 1985), Japan (Tango and Kurashina, 1987), Sweden (Hafner and Schmidtke, 1985; Nordstrom and Asgard, 1986), Switzerland (Hafner and Schmidtke, 1985) and the USA (Murphy and Wetzel, 1980; Wasserman, 1987).

Relative Cohort Size

In the USA from 1948–1977, Ahlburg (1985; Ahlburg and Schaprio, 1984) found that relative size of the 16–29-year old cohort (relative to the cohort aged 30–64) was positively related to the suicide rate of women and young men, but negatively to the suicide rate of middle-age men.

Holinger (1987a, 1987b) found that the suicide rate of 15–24 year-olds in the USA from 1933–1982 and their proportion in their population were positively associated, whereas for those aged 35–44 and 55–64 the association was negative. The positive association for youths was found in Australia, Canada and Italy as well, but not in Hungary or Japan. Moksony (1989) replicated the result also in Hungary.

The Uematsue-Lester Cohort Theory

Lester (1984a) has argued that birth cohorts might have a given number of potentially suicidal people. If a cohort has a relatively high rate of suicide at one point in its life then, it should have relatively low rates of suicide at other points in its life. A test of this hypothesis in the USA confirmed the prediction for female suicide rates, but for male cohorts the suicide rates of each cohort tended to be consistently low, average or high throughout their lifetime. Lester (1988f, 1988k) replicated these results in Canada and Australia. In both nations female suicide rates fitted the theory while male suicide rates did not.

In contrast, Lindesay (1989) repeated the analyses for English data, but first he transformed the suicide rates of each age-by-sex group to z-scores. Now the males fitted the hpyophesis while the females did not. However, Lindesay also noted that the results appeared to be affected greatly by the suicide rates of particular age groups (women aged 35–44 and men aged 15–29). Wetzel et al. (1987) claimed not to have replicated Lester's result using USA data from 1933–1983, but perusal of their paper indicates that their statistical analysis did not match that used by Lester and is not appropriate for the problem being addressed.

Cultural Evolution

Graber (1989) found that the nations with a greater population density had a relatively higher suicide rate/suicide plus homicide rate ratio. He interpreted this to mean that cultural evolution leads to the inhibition of outward aggression and to turning aggression inwards. Of course, this reasoning assumes that the more densely populated nations are more culturally evolved!

Less speculatively, Lester (1981) has shown that the overall suicide rate of nations (but not the suicide rate of teenagers [Lester, 1988a]) is strongly associated with their gross national product per capita. Lester (1984c) found that the more compassionate nations (as measured by objective indices of social programs) had higher suicide rates. After controls for the gross national product per capita, these correlations were much weaker, but still positive.

In contrast, Lester (1987e) found that the suicide rates of nations were not related to a measure of income inequality. Rahav and Ziv (1988) found that an index of net social progress was not related to the suicide rate divided by the suicide plus murder rate in a sample of nations.

Communism

Lester (1984b) noted that Hungary and Czechoslovakia had the highest and third-highest suicide rates of all nations in 1974. He noted, however, that they also had the highest suicides rates back in the 1920s and 1930s and that immigrants from these nations to the USA were also among the highest of all immigrant groups. Thus, the current high suicide rates cannot be attributed to communism. However, over all nations, Lester (1984c) found that suicide rates were positively related to the communist and to the socialist vote and negatively to the capitalist vote. Lester (1989b) showed that the suicide rate dropped in Hungary in 1956 during the year of the Hungarian revolution, but did not change in Czechoslovakia in 1968.

The Economy

The Depression and the Great Crash

Galbraith (1954) noted that although the USA and New York City suicide rates rose during the periods 1925 to 1932, in 1929 the number of suicides in the USA in October and November were the same as in January, February and September of that year and lower than the number in the summer months. Thus, suicide rates may respond to long-term economic trends but not to crises.

Edmondson (1987) documented that the suicide rate in Manhattan from October fifteenth to November thirteenth in 1929 was lower than the previous year. From October twenty-fourth to the end of the year, only eight people jumped to their death, and only two of these were on Wall Street. In fact the US suicide rate peaked in 1932.

During the Depression in the 1920s, Sainsbury (1980) noted that the suicide rates rose in both men and women in almost all nations. For those aged 20–39, male suicide rates increased in 15 of 20 nations studied while female rates rose in 13 of 19 nations (WHO, 1982). The findings were similar for other age groups.

The Wealth of the Region

Baker et al. (1984) found little variation in suicide rate by the income of the region in the USA. Firearm suicide was less common in wealthier areas while suicide by other methods was more common. Nersesian et al. (1985) found no differences in the suicide rates of children and teenagers by family income in Maine.

Strikes

Ahlburg (1985) found no effect from strike duration, size or volume of the suicide rate in the USA from 1948–1977. Female labor force participation was related (positively) only to the suicide rate of those aged 15–24, and real annual income was related to the suicide rate only of those aged 45–64 (negatively for men and positively for women). Unemployment was negatively related to the suicide rate of men aged 45–64.

For eighteen industrialized nations, Lester (1988) found that the volume and duration of strikes (but not the size) were negatively related to the suicide rates.

Unemployment: Completed Suicide

Bluestone et al. (1981) reported that several employees completed suicide after a plant closing in Detroit. Felstein (1981) claimed that suicide was common after plant shutdowns and relocations but provided no data.

Blumenthal et al. (1989) found that psychiatric patients who subsequently completed suicide were more likely to be unemployed or to have job problems. Bagley (1989) found that adolescent suicides were more often unemployed than matched normal controls. In England, Shepherd and Barraclough (1980) found that completed suicides were less often employed full-time and more often unemployed, with many job changes in the last three years and in jobs with a high suicide rate as compared to living controls. (The two groups did not differ in whether working part-time or retired, age at retirement, chronic sickness, private means, or social mobility.) Olsen and Lajer (1979) found that suicides in Denmark among union members were more likely to have been unemployed in the prior five years than those dying of natural deaths.

Bourque et al. (1983) found that suicides aged 20–64 were more often not employed than the general population while suicides over age 65 were more likely to be employed than their peers. Iversen et al. (1987) found that people unemployed in 1970 in Denmark were more likely to die from suicide in the next ten years than expected. Iga (1986) found that the unemployed had higher rates of suicide in Japan (both men and women).

In Turin (Italy) Costa et al. (1989) found a higher suicide rate than expected among unemployed adult men, especially if they were unemployed both in 1976 and 1981 and if they owned their own house. The unemployed had a higher rate than the employed, and the not-working higher than the working (Crepet and Florenzano, 1988). Over time, the suicide and unemployment rates were associated.

Allston (1988) found that, in Georgia, black women who were employed had a higher suicide rate while white women who were employed had a lower suicide rate. In a reanalysis of some old Canadian data, Ornstein (1983) found that employed women in British Columbia had lower suicide rates than the not employed for all marital statuses and ages except single women 65 years of age and older.

On the negative side, Hawton and Fagg (1988) found that unemployment did not predict subsequent completed suicide in a follow-up study of attempted suicides.

Sathyavathi (1977) compared people completing suicide in India because they were unemployed and those having other reasons for suicide. The unemployed suicides were more often male, younger, single and used poisons more and drowning less.

Platt (1984) reviewed the research up to that point, classifying studies as cross-sectional versus longitudinal and individual versus aggregate. For the cross-sectional studies, the regional analyses gave no consistent results but the individual studies did find more unemployment among completed suicides. For the longitudinal research designs, both the individual and aggregate studies found that unemployment was associated with an increase rate of completed suicide (except for aggregate studies in Britain in which the suicide rate was declining during the periods studied).

Unemployed: Attempted Suicide

In London, Fuller et al. (1989) found a high rate of unemployment in men and women attempted suicides aged 16–65 (60 percent and 40 percent respectively), and the unemployed attempters had made more previous suicide attempts.

Hawton et al. (1988) found that the attempted suicide rate was higher in unemployed than in employed women, the longer the unemployment, and in those unemployed who were aged 30–49. The unemployed attempters were more often alcoholics, repeaters, and with prior psychiatric treatment than the employed attempters.

Platt (1984, 1986b) found that cross-sectional studies had identified an association between unemployment and attempted suicide both in individual and aggregate studies. There were too few longitudinal studies to draw reliable conclusions, but Platt reported a positive association in Edinburgh in an aggregate study over time.

Platt (1988a; Platt and Duffy, 1986) compared unemployed versus unemployed first-time male suicide attempters. The unemployed attempters were more often unmarried, not living with their family, manual workers, drug abusers, and with a criminal record. (They did not differ in separation from parents, psychiatric treatment and a family history of attempted suicide or psychiatric treatment.) Thus, the unemployed attempters appeared to be more disturbed and dysfunctional. Platt identified few differences by length of unemployment.

Platt and Dyer (1987) found that the unemployed male attempters had higher depression scores and hopelessness scores and more often were diagnosed as having a personality disorder and less often a depressive disorder. (They did not differ in suicidal intent, prior suicide attempts or marital status.) For the unemployed attempters, suicidal intent was more strongly associated with depression whereas for the employed attempters suicidal intent was more strongly associated with hopelessness.

Over time in Edinburgh, attempted suicide rates were positively associated with unemployment rates (Platt and Kreitman, 1984, 1985), and a similar positive association was found across city wards. The attempted suicide rate was higher in the unemployed, and extremely high if the men had been unemployed for more than one year.

Females in the Labor Force

Newman et al. (1973) found that the percentage of females in the labor force was associated over census tracts in Chicago and in Atlanta with the suicide rate, though in Atlanta the association was found only for census tracts with white residents.

Davis (1981) found that female participation in the labor force (overall and for those married) was associated with the female suicide rate in the USA from 1950–1969 but not with the male rate. The association differed for the two decades, but ten year time periods is too short for meaningful regression analysis.

In a study of the states of the USA, Yang and Lester (1988) found that the participation of married women in the labor market (part-time or full-time) was not associated with the states' male or female suicide rates. (Total female participation in the labor force was positively associated with the states' female suicide rates.) In a later study, Yang and Lester (1989b) found that the participation of married women in the labor force was associated with the suicide rates of married men and women, positive for full-time work and negative for part-time work. The associations were stronger for male suicide rates than for female suicide rates.

Regional Studies

Munson (1968) found that various indices of economic activity (such as per capita retail sales) were negatively related to suicide rates over counties in Ohio. However, suicide did not load significantly on any of the factors identified from a factor analysis of the 113 variables he used.

In Yorkshire (England), Renvoise and Calyden (1989) found no association for men or for women between completed suicide rates and unemployment rates over the seventeen districts. Charlton et al. (1987) found that changes in the long-term unemployment rate in regions in England were not related to changes in the suicide rates of men aged 20–44.

Pritchard (1988) found that from 1975–1986, both completed suicide rates and unemployment rates increased in ten European Community nations. The increase in the suicide rate from 1975–1986 was positively associated with the unemployment rate in 1984.

In England, Forster and Frost (1985) found that attempted suicide rates and unemployment were positively and almost significantly associated over regions. (The attempted suicide rate was associated with the hospital admissions capacity of the regions.)

Time-Series Studies

In a time-series study over months from 1975–1982 in two Californian SMSAs, Dooley et al. (1989) found that the unemployment rate was not associated with the suicide rate. Changes in the employment rate was positively associated with the suicide rate of those aged 34–49 year-olds, but the association was negative for females. A study of wage-earning adults found that unemployment was not associated with suicidal ideation, while retirement was negatively associated with suicidal ideation. Furthermore, job stress was not related to the presence of suicidal ideation in the non-principal wage earners, but working was (though how the sample of non-principal wage earners contained *non-workers* is not clear).

Filby and Eicher (1983) noted that from 1973–1983 in one county in Ohio the curves for suicides and unemployment were parallel, but they did not perform any statistical analyses on the data. Forsyth and Gramling (1988) found that unemployment and suicide rates were negatively associated over time from 1974–1983 in four SMSAs.

Over time in the USA, Holinger (1987a) found that suicide rates were associated with the unemployment rate (but not with the birth rate). Marhsall and Hodge (1981) found that, in general in the USA from 1933–1976, as unemployment rates went up, so did suicide rates (but only for males). Looking at the percentage and absolute yearly stock market price difference, they found that that only the percentage change was significantly associated with suicide rates. As the economy improved, suicide rates went down. However, unemployment had a stronger impact on suicide rates.

Marshall (1978) studied the suicide rate of white males aged 65–74 from 1948–1972 in the USA and found that their suicide rate was positively associated with unemployment in the elderly and negatively with social security income, the percentage of elderly males with income and social security coverage of the labor force. Thus, it appeared that, as the financial status of the elderly improved, the suicide rate decreased, even after controls for divorce rates, war, and unemployment.

In the USA from 1950–1979, South (1984) found that both white and non-white suicide rates were related to the unemployment rates (but only for males). However, the ratio of the median income for non-whites relative to whites was significantly associated with the non-white suicide rate. Thus, as racial income inequality diminished, the suicide rate of non-whites rose (while there was no impact on white suicide rates).

Hamermesh and Soss (1974) predicted that suicide rates would increase with age and decrease with the amount of personal income. They noted that, in 21 industrialized nations, the male suicide rate increased with age in 19 of the nations, with a peak at age 55–64. They also noted that, in the USA, the suicide rate decreased with real income over time except for adults aged 20–24. Looking at eight broad occupational categories, they found that suicide rates and income were negatively related. Finally, looking at cross-sectional data from 38 of the states they found that suicide rates and income were negatively related except for those aged 25–34. Thus, they found a negative relationship between income and suicide rates over time, status categories and regions. Hamermesh (1974) looked at black suicide rates and, in a time series analysis for 1947–1974, found that unemployment and income were not related to suicide rates. However, in a cross-sectional study of the states, both economic variables were positively related to suicide rates. (Changes in these variables presented a different pattern of results.)

In the United Kingdom, Kreitman and Platt (1984) found that male unemployment rates and male suicide rates (by all methods and by methods other than carbon monoxide) were associated over time, even during the period during which domestic gas was detoxified. Brenner (1983) found in England and in Scotland that unemployment (only the rate of young males) and bankruptcies were positively related to suicide rates (as was alcohol consumption), while per capita income was negatively related to suicide rates. However, Crombie (1989) found that increases in the unemployment rate in regions of Scotland were not related to increases in the suicide rate.

In Finland from 1960–1979, Jarventie and Kivela (1986) found that male suicide rates were associated with unemployment, but not female rates and only for those younger than 65. Nayha (1980) found that the suicide rate in Finland from 1910–1972 was associated with the national income per capita (and the consumption of alcohol), but he implies that taking into account the simple time trend eliminated the association.

Norstrom (1988a) found that unemployment rates and suicide rates were positively associated over time in Sweden from 1920–1968 and for the first and latter parts of this period, too. Cormier and Klerman (1985) found a positive association between suicide and unemployment rates in Quebec from 1866–1981.

Boor (1980) correlated suicide and unemployment rates over a fourteen-year period in eight nations. In four the association was positive, in three zero and in one negative. The associations were stronger for young adults.

In Leeds (England), Standish-Barry et al. (1989) found that male unemployment rates and parasuicide rates measured quarterly were positively associated in those aged 44–54, negatively associated for those aged 55–59, and not statistically significant for other age groups. For females the associations were more consistently negative for all age groups.

Seasonality Of Suicide and GNP

Abe et al. (1986) found that in Japan from 1900 to 1982, the magnitude of the seasonal variation in suicide was negatively related to the gross national product per capita. Over eleven nations, the decrease in seasonality from 1955 to 1972 was positively related to the average annual growth in the per capita gross national product.

Education

Gaines and Richmond (1980) found no differences in education or whether the person graduated from high school between basic trainees in the military who made suicidal gestures and those who did not.

Era

Many studies have examined trends over time for completed and attempted suicides in nations. For example, Weiss (1976) noted increased suicide rates for those aged 15 to 44 in all races and both sexes in the USA from 1960 to 1973. But studies on individual nations have little general interest. Sainsbury (1972) examined the suicide rates of nations in 1921 and 1952. For young men and women, the suicide rates decreased during the period, whereas for women over 40 years of age and men over the age of 50 the rates had increased. This multi-national type of study has more general interest for understanding suicide.

Fertility

Yang and Lester (1989a) found that fertility rates were negatively associated with suicide rates over sixteen nations (looking at various years from 1921 to 1965) and also negatively in time-series studies within each nation.

Health Services

Williams et al. (1986) noted that the increase in general hospital beds in Italy in the late 1970s was associated with a lowered suicide rate (but no impact was found from changes in mental health service beds, community psychiatric services, or hostels).

The Homeless

Altrom et al. (1975) found an excess of suicidal deaths among homeless men in Stockholm, but only for those younger than 50.

Immigrants

Burvill (1971–1972) found that male immigrants to Australia had higher rates of attempted suicide than native Australians, while women showed no differences. Burvill et al. (1973) found that the longer immigrants had been in Australia, the higher their suicide rate. Correlations over the ethnic group showed the suicide rates in Australia to be related to motor vehicle deaths in Australia (for men only) but not to other violent deaths.

Hassan (1987) found that immigrants to Australia had higher suicide rates than the native born, especially during the first nine years. Burvill et al. (1983a) found that some immigrant groups to Australia had higher suicide rates than native born Australians while other immigrant groups had lower suicide rates. The same was true for attempted suicide. There was no association between the completed and the attempted suicide rates of the different immigrant groups.

Burvill et al. (1982, 1983b) found that the suicide rates of immigrants from England, Scotland and Ireland were similar in Australia though the suicide rates in the nations of origin were quite different. They also found that the methods used for suicide shifted from the pattern in the nation of origin to the pattern in Australians for some of the immigrant groups.

Rosenman (1983) reported that immigrants were on the whole under-represented among a sample of attempted suicides in Australia. However, group differences did emerge with, for example, fewer Italians and Greeks than expected but more Germans than expected.

Hewitt and Milner (1974) found that the suicide rate by poisoning in the USA states was associated with the proportion of residents born out of state. Kliewer and Ward (1988) found in Canada that for males between the ages of 10 and 64 the completed suicide rate was high in native born Canadians, but for those 65 and older the suicide rate was higher in foreign born. For females the suicide rates of native and foreign born did not differ. By country, the male and female suicide rates in the home nations were more strongly correlated that the male and female suicide rates of the immigrants in Canada. They also noted that the suicide rates of the immigrant groups shifted from the rates in the home nations toward the rates for Canadian native born for both men and women.

Lester (1989c) found that suicide rates in industrialized nations were not related to the long-term immigration rate, and Lester (1988c) found that the rate of emigration from eight Caribbean islands to the USA was not significantly associated with the suicide rate (or the population size) of the island.

Legal Effects

Lester (1988g) found no association between states laws on suicidal behavior and rates of completed suicide. Hingson et al. (1985) could find no changes in the suicide rate of those aged 15–19 in Massachusetts as a result of raising the drinking age from 18 to 20. Lockhart and Baron (1987) documented that, at least in some regions of Great Britain, after the liquor licensing laws were liberalized, more attempted suicides were intoxicated at the time of their act.

Marital Status

Klebba (1970) looked at the USA as a whole and found suicide rates highest in the divorced and then the widowed for both sexes and for whites and non-whites.

Demi (1979) found that the widows of suicides were more often separated from their spouses at the time of the suicide than widows of accidental or sudden death. (The two sets of widows did not differ in their own current suicidal ideation.)

Borg and Staht (1982) found that widowhood predicted completed suicide in psychiatric patients better than symptoms of or precipitants for the psychiatric illness. Helsin et al. (1982) studied the causes of death in widows/widowers versus the married in a county in Maryland and found an excess of suicide only in the widowers. This excess was especially notable in the first six months of widowhood.

Kreitman (1988) in Scotland found that for men, although the divorced had the highest completed suicide rates, standardizing for age led the widowed to having the highest rates. For women, the widowed had the highest suicide rates, and standardizing for age led to divorced and widowed tied for the highest rates. (Standardizing the age rates for marital status had little impact on the relative rankings of the rates by age.) Kreitman and Schreiber (1980) found that among women aged 15–19, the married had higher attempted suicide rates than the single.

In the USA, Smith et al. (1988) confirmed that the divorced and widowed have the highest suicide rates, and this was found for men and women, whites and blacks. Young widows/widowers (aged 15–44) had an especially high suicide rate.

In the USA, Lester (1987d) found that the ratios of the suicide rates of single/married, divorced/married and widowed/married were greater for males than for females for both whites and non-whites, supporting the thesis that marriage protects men better than women from psychiatric disturbance. Cumming and Lazer (1981) found that the ratio of the suicide rates of the single to the married in Canada were lower for women than for men, suggesting similarly that marriage protects men better than women.

Durkheim (1897) predicted that societies with a high divorce rate would have relatively higher suicide rates in married men as compared to single men. However, Lester (1989f) found that the suicide rate ratio of single/married people was not significantly associated with the divorce rate, either for men or for women.

In Japan, Fuse (1980) found the highest suicide rate in the widowed, then the divorced, single, and lowest in the married. In upper Austria, Schony and Grausgruber (1987) found the highest rate in the divorced and the lowest in the widowed.

Russell (1985) compared the social characteristics of completed suicide in Richmond (VA) with the typical person in the census tract in which they lived. The suicides did not differ from the typical person in race or occupation, but they did differ in marital status.

Nursing Homes

Abrams et al. (1988) reported a lower suicide rate for the residents of nursing homes in New York City than in the elderly general population.

Occupation

Conroy (1989) reviewed NIOSH data for suicide in the workplace. By occupation, the military ranked highest with managers and professional lowest. By industry, public administration ranked highest and the whole-sale trade lowest. In Japan, Fuse (1980) found the highest suicide rates in workers in forestry-fishing and mining and the lowest in security guards and managerial ranks. In upper Austria, Schony and Grausgruber (1987) found the highest suicide rates in the unemployed, skilled workers and old-age pensioners and the lowest rates in students, housewives and white-collar workers. Labovitz and Hagedorn (1971) roughly categorized occupations as client-dependent (service-related) or not and found the former to have higher male suicide rates.

Lampert et al. (1984) found that in Sacramento form 1925–1979, suicide rates were higher for farm laborers, general laborers and service workers and, in general, for the lower statuses. Within each occupational class, the suicide rates rose with age. Stack (1980) found the suicide rate in Detroit to be highest for laborers and higher in blue-collar workers than in white-collar workers and high-status workers.

Lester (1987g) found that the prestige of 36 occupations, the median income, educational level and status consistency were not related to the suicide rates of people in those occupations. Marks (1980) found that the social class of 194 occupations was not related to their suicide rate.

Reinhart and Linden (1982) found that the suicide rates of occupational groups and of industries were associated with the relative increase in size of the groups but not to their absolute size.

Women

Allston (1986) found that suicide rates of women in highly traditional occupations were lower than those of women in non-traditional occupations, which in turn were lower than those of women in moderately traditional occupations. Allston (1988) found that black employed women had higher suicide rates if they had clerical jobs and lower suicide rates if they had service jobs. White women had higher suicide rates if they were in service jobs.

Academia

Black (1971) studied 14 universities in the southwest Rocky Mountain states for 1968–1970 and calculated a suicide rate of 10.2 (and an attempted suicide rate of 65) from reports of university administrators. Completed suicide was more common in science/mathematics students and in graduate students. Ishii (1977) found that suicide in Kyoto (Japan) University students was most common in those in the Faculties of Letters and Education and lowest in the Faculties of Engineering, Pharmacy, Economics and Medicine. Humanities students had a higher rate than science students. By year, sophomores and those in their fifth year or more had the higher rates.

Ishii (1985) found a high suicide rate for university students. The suicide rate varied by department with the Faculty of Letters highest. Sophomores and those who postponed graduate studies had higher rates. Compared to controls, the students who completed suicide had experienced more loss of parents, were more often from the upper class and famous schools, and had more educated parents, more physical health problems, and more loss of a significant other. The suicides peaked at the beginning of the year and the end of the terms.

Arnetz et al. (1987b) found that male college/university professors had a lower suicide rate than the general population while female professors had rates similar to the general population.

Heinrichs (1980) found a lower suicide rate for students in South Dakota than in non-students aged 18–24. The students committed suicide more on weekdays but did not differ in age, sex, race, month, locality or method from the non-student suicides. At the University of

Massachusetts, Kraft (1980) found the suicide rate of students to be low. However, the rate was relatively higher in men, graduates, freshmen and juniors, the single and divorced, and foreign students.

Lehtinen et al. (1986) followed-up youths for thirteen years and found no differences in the incidence of suicidal ideation, recently or ever, in those who graduated from university and those who did not.

In Edinburgh, Platt (1987) found that youths aged 15–24 in school or college had lower rates of completed and attempted suicide than non-students. For the attempters, students and non-students did not differ in prior suicide attempts, but the student attempters were more often unmarried, not living with parents, used prescription drugs more, and had no apparent precipitant (the non-students more often had an inter-personal precipitant) and less often had a criminal record, were a victim of violence, or had relatives who had attempted suicide. Attempted suicide in the students peaked in January, February and October, not at exam time. (The non-students showed no monthly variation.)

Schwartz and Reifler (1980) reviewed data for 53 American colleges in the 1970s and found a suicide rate of 7 per 100,000 per year as compared to a national rate for whites aged 20–24 of 17. The rate of student suicide was not associated with the size of the university. Schwartz and Reifler (1988) reviewed all reports since 1928 and found an average rate of suicide from single institution studies and a low rate from multi-institution studies.

Dentists

Arnetz et al. (1987a) found an elevated suicide rate in Swedish male dentists (but not females) as compared to academics but not as compared to the general population. Simpson et al. (1983a) found a high rate of suicide for dentists in Iowa, but only for those aged 24–44 and over 65.

Physicians

Normal rates of suicide have been reported for Finnish male physicians (Asp et al., 1979). Waring (1977) found that doctors in psychiatric treatment as inpatients had made more prior suicide attempts than patients from other occupations, but nurses had not. Lew (1979) reported a high suicide rate for anesthesiologists, and Daubs (1973) for ophthalmologists. Refracting ophthalmologists had a high rate while ophthalmological surgeons had a low rate.

In a review of research, Bedeian (1982) concluded that physicians (particularly women and psychiatrists) and pharmacists had high suicide rates while dentists and nurses had average suicide rates.

In North Carolina, Revicki and May (1985) found average suicide rates for physicians, high rates for pharmacists and for nurses, and low rates for dentists. Rich and Pitts (1980) in the USA found high suicide rates for male and female physicians, but the female rates were higher (41 per 100,000 per year versus 36). For women, there was no relationship to specialty but, for men, psychiatrists had the highest suicide rate. The age distribution of the psychiatrists' suicides was the same as that for all living psychiatrists.

Arnetz et al. (1987b) found that female Swedish physicians had an elevated suicide rate as compared to the general population (but not males). Birmingham and Ward (1985) reported a high suicide rate in anesthesiolog sts, while Bruce (1981) reported that 8 percent of their deaths were due to suicide. Krieger (1981) found a high rate of suicide among psychiatrists in the San Francisco area, and an especially high rate for the female psychiatrists. In Finland, Rimpela et al. (1987) found that doctors (and lawyers) had higher suicide rates than men in other professions but not when compared to all economically active males.

Richings et al. (1986) reported overly high suicide rates for doctors in Britain in both men and women, but especially for women born overseas.

Anon (1987b) found that prior psychiatric disturbance, alcohol and drug abuse, prior suicidal behavior, professional and financial loss, violence toward the spouse, psychiatric problems in relatives, reduced social support and fewer friends all distinguished physicians who completed suicide from those dying from natural deaths.

Bissell and Skorina (1987) found that female alcoholic professionals had a higher incidence of prior attempted suicide than males. The incidence was greater for female physicians, nurses, attorneys and college women and less for social workers. If the women abused narcotics too, the prior incidence of suicide attempts was even greater.

In England, Neil et al. (1987) found a higher suicide rate among anesthesiologists than the general population of similar age and sex (but no higher than for physicians in general). Sakinofsky (1980) reported a higher rate of suicide for both male and female physicians in Britain and also for the wives of doctors. Male doctors who completed suicide appeared to have an excess of the unmarried and divorced.

Pepitone-Arreola-Rockwell et al. (1981) found a normal suicide rate for male medical students but an elevated suicide rate for female medical students.

In contrast, Kono et al. (1988) found a lower suicide rate than expected for Japanese male physicians.

Police

Guralnick (1963) reported a standard mortality ratio for suicide in police in the USA of 176, and Labovitz and Hagedorn (1971) reported that American policemen had the second-highest suicide rate of all occupational groups. Friedman (1967) reported a rate of 22 per 100,000 per year for 1960–1966 and Neiderhoffer (1967) a rate of 23 for 1950–1965 for New York City policemen, slightly higher than the male suicide rate for the USA at the time. Milham (1976) reported a proportionate mortality ratio for suicide in police officers of 113 for 1950–1971 in Washington State. Nelson and Smith (1970) reported a high rate in Wyoming and Richard and Fell (1975) in Tennessee. Danto (1978) found that 25 percent of a sample of police suicides were in fact murder-suicides.

In contrast, Fabricatore and Dash (1977; Dash and Reiser, 1978) found a low suicide rate for police officers in Los Angeles. Heiman (1975) noted that in the 1930s New York City, Chicago and San Francisco had high rates of police suicide, St. Louis about average and Denver below average. In the 1960s New York City had a high rate while London (UK) had an average rate (see also, Anon, 1978).

Reiser (1982) reported a low suicide rate (8.1) for Los Angeles police. Vena et al. (1986) found an average suicide rate for police officers in Buffalo, while Wagner and Bizeczek (1983) found a high rate for police officers in Chicago (51 per 100,000 per year). In Chicago, 60 percent of the suicides were alcohol abusers.

Loo (1986) found a suicide rate for Royal Canadian Mounted Police of only 14 per 100,000 per year, half of the rate for the general population. Aussant (1984) found that Canadian police who committed suicide typically used a gun. Almost half had experienced professional failure or dissatisfaction with work.

In Northern Ireland, Curran et al. (1988) found that the suicide rate of police rose from 12 (per 100,000 per year) in the 1970s to 33 in the 1980s, a very high rate.

Farmers

Ragland and Berman (1987) found that the suicide rates of farmers and foresters were higher than those of truck drivers. For 1980–1985, the suicide rates of farmers were higher in years when the farm economy was in decline.

Other Workers

An average suicide rate has been reported for members of the boiler-makers union in general, though the shopfitters did have a significantly higher suicide rate (Beaumont and Weiss, 1980). Fitzgerald et al. (1989) found no excess of suicides in the three years after exposure to toxic contaminants. Average suicide rates have also been reported for taxi drivers in Singapore (Koh et al., 1988), gasoline service workers in New Hampshire (Schwartz, 1987), and blue-collar workers at a brewery (Dean et al., 1979).

Excess mortality from suicide has been reported in male tobacco industry workers (Blair et al., 1983), Vermont granite workers (Davis et al., 1983), both actors and actresses (Depue et al., 1985), social workers (Dubrow, 1988), forestry workers who had been probably been exposed to herbicides but only for those working less than 15 years (Green, 1987), pathologists (Harrington and Oakes, 1984), possibly in pharmaceutical industry workers though the numbers were quite small (Harrington and Goldblatt, 1986), in RNs, but only those older than 50 (Katz, 1983), highway workers in California (Maizlish et al., 1988), automobile mechanics in New Hampshire (Schwartz, 1987), chrome leather tanners, but only in one of two tanneries (Stern et al., 1987), taxi drivers in Japan, especially those younger than forty (Uehata et al., 1985), municipal workers in Buffalo, except police officers (Vena et al., 1986), female chemists in the USA (who most commonly used cyanide and barbiturates) (Walraith et al., 1985), Finnish seamen and especially the crew (Wickstrom and Leivonniemi, 1985), and male rubber workers (Andjelkovic et al., 1976). Olsen and Sabroe (1979; Olsen and Lajer, 1979) found a higher suicide rate in Danish bricklayers than in carpenters.

In contrast, fewer suicidal deaths than expected have been reported in chemical workers (Bond et al., 1989), law school students (though the rate was highest in the third year) (Hamilton et al., 1983), Roman Catholic priests (Kaplan, 1988), and firefighters (Musk et al., 1978).

Inconsistent results were found by Hoar and Pell (1981) for chemists at

Du Pont. The data differed for standard mortality ratios and proportional mortality ratios and, in addition, differed from earlier studies. Similarly, Walraith and Fraumeni (1983, 1984) found an average suicide rate for embalmers in New York but a higher rate than expected for embalmers in California. Thomas and Decoufle (1979) found a high suicide rate for plant workers in the pharmaceutical industry, while salespeople in the industry had low rates. The suicides used poisons more, and guns about as often, and other methods less than other suicides.

Fasal et al. (1966) found no excess mortality in California veterinarians, but Schurrenberger et al. (1977) found an excess mortality in Illinois veterinarians, as did Blair and Hayes (1980) for veterinarians with both small animal and other practices and Kinlein (1983) for veterinary surgeons.

Place of Birth and Place of Death

Lester (1981) found that the Pacific region of the USA had the highest rate of death from suicide. However, looking at where people were born, those born in the West North Central region of America had the highest suicide rate.

Population Change

Matsubara (1985) found that the suicide rate in Japanese prefectures was higher in those where the rate of population increase was less.

Prison, Jail and Correctional Inmates

Esparza (1973) reported a high rate of completed suicide in six county jails. Hoff (1973) reported higher rates of both completed and attempted suicide in prisoners than in the general population, with hanging and jumping used most by completers and cutting and pills by attempters.

Lester (1982a, 1987f) found that male prisoners in the USA had a suicide rate of 24 to 25 per 100,000 per year and females 8, rates comparable to those for the general population. There was no association between the suicide rates of the states in general and the suicide rates of the prisoners in each state. The suicide rates in federal and state prisons were similar. In contrast, the suicide rate on death row was 146—very high (Lester, 1986e). Ruback and Innes (1988) also reported a higher than expected suicide rate (based on the age, sex and race of inmates) for US state prisons. In the Maryland state prison system, Salive et al. (1989) found a suicide rate of 40 which was higher than expected. Winfree (1987, 1988) found a high completed suicide in American jails. By state, high jail suicide rates were associated in some years with state expenditures per prisoner and the prison population. Frost and Hanzlich (1988) found that 26 percent of deaths in a county jail were from suicide, and all were from hanging.

For juveniles, Flaherty (1983) found that their suicide rate was much higher for those placed in adult jails and lockups than those placed in juvenile detention centers. Memory (1989) corrected errors in the statistics in the earlier reports (length of stay varied in the three types of facilities) but obtained similar results.

In New York City correctional facilities from 1971 to 1976, Novick and Remlinger (1978) found a suicide rate ranging from 79 to 134 per 100,000 per year. The suicides were younger than those dying of other causes, and the peak age was 35–44. In Texas, Stone (1984) reported a jail suicide rate of 137 and a prison suicide rate of 16.

Backett (1987) found that Scottish prisoners had a high suicide rate and that about two-thirds of the suicides occurred during the first month of imprisonment. Danto (1981) reported a suicide rate in Canadian penitentiaries of 96 (per 100,000 per year) compared to 14 for non-inmates. In a prison in Australia, Hurley (1989) found a suicide rate of 266 with about a quarter occurring in the first two months of incarceration. In the Netherlands, Kerkhof (1987) found a completed suicide rate for inmates of jails and prisons of 50 and an attempted suicide rate in the range 1,000–6,000. Three-quarters of the completed and attempted suicides had visited the prison physician in the four weeks prior to their suicidal action.

The Typical Suicide

Heilig (1973) looked at completed suicides in Los Angeles County jails and found that the majority occurred in the first 24 hours of imprisonment, mostly by hanging, and in those who were intoxicated with drugs or alcohol. In contrast, most attempters in jail used cutting. Petrich (1978) found a history of attempted suicide more common in female jail prisoners than in males and in felons more than misdemeanents. Fawcett and Marrs (1973) studied the Cook County Jail and found that whites and hispanics were overrepresented among the suicidal prisoners. They identified two types of suicidal prisoners: (1) young and impulsive, charged with a violent crime, not depressed, and suicidal soon after incarceration, and (2) slightly older, late in their prison term, hopeless and depressed, who had experienced rejection from a significant other on the outside, and more successful in actually killing themselves.

In the Dade County (FL) jail, Copeland (1989a) found that the typical suicide was young, white, male with a psychotic background, and occurred in the first 24 hours of incarceration. In Oklahoma, Jordan et al. (1987) found that the typical jail completed suicide was white, male, intoxicated with alcohol, and took place soon after confinement in the early morning hours.

In two national surveys (Hayes (1983, 1989) found that the typical suicide in jails was white, single, male, in his early twenties, and by hanging within three hours of incarceration. In the early study, Hayes found that Saturday night, September and midnight to 1 A.M. were the most popular times, and that there was usually no history of psychiatric illness or suicide attempts. The relevance of the presence versus absence of prior arrests differed in the two surveys.

Suicides Versus Others

Rieger (1971) reported suicide rates for federal prisons in the 1950s and 1960s. In one federal penitentiary, among those men who had made previous suicide attempts (though it is not clear whether Rieger is referring to previous attempts before prison, in prison or both), the more serious attempts were made by the older prisoners. Race, type of crime and religion were not associated with a history of attempted suicide. Those making serious attempts had experienced loss of a loved one more often (due to death or divorce). Childhood separation from mother was also more common. Those making gestures or serious attempts were more likely to have a history of suicide than those making moderate attempts.

Albanese (1983) found that prison inmates who attempted suicide were more often white, single, and with longer sentences than other inmates. They were less likely to have narcotics violations but more often threatened the life of the president or to destroy government property. They did not differ in sex, age, religion, or education. They were most likely to attempt suicide on the day of admission or during the first week.

Haycock (1989) found that serious attempters versus gestures were more often opiate abusers (but not alcohol abusers), had more often attempted suicide in the past, had experienced more recent family turmoil, were more depressed, hopeless and inwardly hostile, had committed fewer probation violations, and were more intoxicated at the time of the attempt.

Hopes and Shaull (1986) found that inmates in jail who attempted suicide while in jail were more often substance abusers, had more hopelessness, had made more prior suicide attempts and thought about suicide more. Attempts were most common in the week before or following the trial/sentencing.

Anno (1985) found that inmates who killed themselves did not differ in sex or age from the other inmates, but were more often white/hispanic, single/divorced, Catholic and offenders against the person. Burtka et al. (1988) found that completed suicides in the Wayne County Jail were more often male and more often charged with murder/manslaughter than other prisoners. They did not differ in race or age. Kennedy (1984) compared completed suicides among inmates in police custody with the average arrested person and found that the suicides had committed more serious crimes but did not differ in race or age. In the Maryland state prison system, Salive et al. (1989) found higher suicide rates for whites, those aged 25–34, those with life sentences, those in maximum security and those who had committed offenses against persons. In Alaska, Sperbeck and Parlour (1986) found that, among prisoners sent for psychiatric screening, the suicidal prisoners had more secondary stress, that is non-prison and non-legal such as marital and financial stress.

In the Netherlands, Kerkhof (1987) found that prisoners who completed or attempted suicide were more often non-Dutch, sentenced to long-terms and had committed more serious crimes.

Overcrowding

Cox et al. (1984) found that the larger prisons in Texas had higher suicide rates and that as their population increased the suicide rates increased. In Mississippi, when one prison cut its population by 30 percent, the attempted suicide rate dropped.

Innes (1986, 1987) found that state prisons with the higher population density had the higher suicide rates. Also, from 1979 to 1984, the suicide rate of prisoners increased as did the staff, housing space and inmate population. As the system gets larger, the suicide rate appears to increase.

In two Illinois prisons, Paulus (1988) noted that an increase in the population was accompanied by an increase in the suicide rate, but the methodology of this study is poor.

Attempted Suicide

Wilmotte and Plat-Mendlewicz (1973) found a history of attempted suicide in 8.4 percent of prisoners in Belgium. These prisoners did not differ in age from the others, but were more often French and less often Spanish/Moroccans. The attempted suicides had experienced marital disruption more and were less often married or with children. Attempted suicide was more common in those charged with possession and use of drugs and theft with violence and less common in those charged with fraud and outrages on decency. There were no differences between newcomers versus recidivists.

Power and Spencer (1987) found that young offenders who made suicide attempts, typically lacerated their wrists, and over 90 percent of them reported minimal intent and made attempts of minimal lethality.

Race/Ethnicity

Australia: Aboriginees

Eastwell (1988) found a low suicide rate (about 2 per 100,000 per year) among the Yolngu of the Northern Territory. Jones (1972) reported that completed suicide was absent in full-blooded Australian aboriginess, but Burvill (1971–1972) reported a higher rate of attempted suicide than in other Australians.

Brazilian Japanese

Tsugane et al. (1989) found that first-generation Japanese in Sao Paulo had an average suicide rate as compared to the total population of Sao Paulo but a lower rate as compared to Japanese living in Japan.

Fiji

Lal (1985) found that Indian immigrants to Fiji in 1824–1925, mainly indentured laborers, had a higher suicide rate than in India. The rate increased after 1900, with the suicides having a modal age of 21–30 and mainly being single males. The rate was higher for the first six months after arrival, in Hindus, those of high caste, and Southern (darker) Indians (Dravidians). There were very few Indian women in Fiji at the time, and Lal felt that sexual frustration was an important factor in the high suicide rate.

Haynes (1987) found that suicide was more common among Indians than native Fijians in Fiji.

Hungary

Zonda (1989) found that gypsies in Hungary had higher rates of attempted suicide but lower rates of completed suicide than the general population. The gypsy attempters were younger and less educated than other attempters but did not differ in their history of suicide attempts.

Israel

In Israel, Levav and Aisenberg (1989) found that the suicide rates of Jews were higher than those of non-Jews. Among the Jews, the suicide rate was higher in European Jews than in North African and Asian Jews. Among non-Jews, the suicide rates were highest in the Druze, then Christian Arabs, and lowest in moslem Arabs. However, standardizing the rates for age made Jewish and Druze rates the highest for men and Jewish and Christian Arab rates the highest for women. In a sample of Israeli Jews, Levav et al. (1988) found that suicidal ideation and attempts were less common in the Jews from Europe and the USA as compared to African and Asian Jews.

Malaysia

In one region, Maniam (1988) reported the highest completed suicide rate among Indians, then Chinese and the lowest rate among Malays. The rate of attempted suicide followed a similar pattern.

Native Americans/Canadians

Kraus and Buffler (1976, 1978) reported both a high completed suicide rate and a high attempted suicide rate for Alaskan natives. May (1987) noted that native Americans had a higher suicide rate than the general American population in 1980–1982. This was especially notable among youths. Some native American groups, such as the Apache, had very high suicide rates.

Bagley et al. (1987) found that native Canadians living on reserves had a very high suicide rate. The reserves with the highest suicide rates were poorer, more Northern and more isolated.

Forbes and van der Hyde (1988) found that suicide rates in Alaskan natives had risen markedly since 1965, especially among those aged 15–29. Fox et al. (1984) found a high rate of suicide for native Canadians on one reservation. Garro (1988) found that the more isolated northern groups of native Canadians in Manitoba had lower suicides rates than the southern groups (and had less alcoholism too). Hislop et al. (1987) documented a higher suicide rate in native Canadians in British Columbia, significant for males and females, and for those aged 0–65 (but not for those aged 65+). Jarvis and Boldt (1982) found that native Canadians had a greater proportion of deaths due to suicide in Alberta than whites. The native Canadians had a high incidence of alcohol in their blood and alcohol abuse problems.

Spaulding (1985–1986) found a very high rate of suicide in ten bands of Ojibwa in Ontario, higher than the overall Indian suicide rate and that for Inuits. The modal suicide was a young male using a gun.

Hlady and Middaugh (1987) documented a higher suicide rate in native Americans in Alaska than in whites. The native Americans had a higher suicide rate in rural areas than in urban areas, but not so for whites. The native suicides were younger and more often drunk but did not differ in marital or employment status. Simpson et al. (1983b) reported high rates of attempted and completed suicide among the Hopi.

Kost-Grant (1983) noted a higher suicide rate in Alaskan natives over non-natives, a higher suicide rate by firearms and a higher accidental death rate by firearms. The different native groups (Eskimos, Indians and Aleuts) did not differ in these rates.

Travis (1984) compared two groups of Inupiat Eskimos, one in an economic depression and one with economic growth. The suicide rate of the group in the economic depression rose from zero in 1960 to 106 per 100,000 per year in 1980 while the suicide rate of the other group remained steady in the twenties. (The two groups were similar in education, marital status, household size, and females in the labor force.)

Van Winkle and May (1986) found that suicide rates in New Mexico were highest in the Apache and lowest in the Navaho with the rates of the Pueblo in between. The Navaho rates were similar to the population as a whole. For the Pueblo, the suicide rates were lowest in the traditional tribes and highest in the most acculturated.

Nigeria

Odejide et al. (1986) found a higher proportion of Christians among suicide attempters in Nigeria than expected and fewer Muslims.

Peru

Mezzich and Raab (1980) found that Mestizo and Indian psychiatric outpatients with depressive disorders in Peru had less suicidal ideation and had attempted suicide less often than white psychiatric inpatients with depressive disorders in the USA.

Saudi Arabia

In Saudi Arabia, Daradkeh and Al-Zayer (1988) reported a higher rate of attempted suicide in non-Saudis than in Saudis.

Singapore

Kok (1988) and Tsoi and Kua (1987) found that attempted suicide was most common in Indians in Singapore, then in Chinese and least common in Malays for both sexes. Kua and Tsoi (1985) and Tan (1986) found a similar pattern in rates of completed suicide.

South Africa

Breetzke (1988) found that whites and coloreds in Cape Town, South Africa, had higher suicide rates than blacks. The colored suicides were younger and the white suicides older. The colored suicides used hanging and overdoses more while the whites used firearms more. Lester (1989c) also documented that the black/white differences in suicide rates in South Africa mirrored the American pattern. Suicide rates were highest in whites, then Asian, coloreds and blacks. Wyndham (1986) confirmed this and noted that the peak ages for suicide rates were 45–54 in whites, 35–44 in coloreds, 55–64 in Asians and 25–34 in blacks.

Thomson (1980) reported a low suicide rate (3.1 per 100,000 per year) in the Xhosa, one of the two major black ethnic groups in South Africa.

South Pacific

Hezel (1984) reported a high suicide rate in the Trukese, especially among males aged 15–30.

United Kingdom

Glover et al. (1989) noted a high rate of attempted suicide in London among teenage Asian females (mainly from Bangladesh). Merrill and Owens (1986, 1987, 1988) noted that the female attempted suicide rate in Birmingham was highest in Scots immigrants, then Irish and Asian, then the native English and lowest in the West Indians. For males, the Scots again had the highest rate and West Indians the lowest rate.

For West Indians, those born in the West Indies had a lower rate for attempting suicide than those born in England. West Indian attempters as compared to white attempters were more often female and younger, more often single, less often psychiatrically disturbed, more often separated from parents in childhood, more often pregnant as teenagers, less often an alcohol abuser and less often with prior suicide attempts.

Asian attempters as compared to white attempters, were more often female, young, married, and with fewer prior attempts and prior psychiatric treatment.

United States

In the USA as a whole, Yu et al. (1989) found that the suicide rate of white males was higher than that of Asian-American males. For women the rates were higher for Asian-Americans than for whites. Among the Asian-Americans, the suicide rate was higher in those born in Asia than for those born in the USA.

Among the elderly (age 65 and over) in America, McIntosh and Santos (1981) found the suicide rates of whites, Chinese, Japanese, and Filipino to be higher than the rates of younger people, the rates in blacks to be the same, and the rates in native Americans to be lower.

In Miami, Copeland (1989b) found the highest suicide rates in black-Hispanics, next in native Americans, with the rates of blacks and Haitians much lower. Shai and Rosenwake (1988) found that Cuban-born and Puerto Rican-born Americans had higher suicide rates than white Americans who had higher rates than Mexican-born Americans. For women, the white Americans had higher suicide rates, then, much lower and in order, Cuban-born, Puerto Rican-born and Mexican-born. The Cuban, Puerto Rican and Mexican-born Americans had peaks in their suicide rates at age 30 and 70 plus.

Smith, et al. (1989) found that Hispanic-Americans in five southwestern states had a lower suicide rate than Anglo-Americans. The Hispanic suicide rate peaked for those aged 20–24 and the Anglo suicide rate for those over age 70.

Hoppe and Martin (1986) studied one county in Texas and found that the Mexican-American suicide rates for both males and females were less than the corresponding suicide rates for Anglos. The Anglo suicides were older with a peak at age 65 and over whereas the Mexican-American suicides peaked at ages 15–24 and age 65 and over.

Danto and Danto (1983) found that the Jewish suicide rate in Michigan was lower than the non-Jewish rate. The Jewish suicides were older, more often female, and used poisons more and guns less than non-Jewish suicides. The men were more often married and the women widowed.

United States: Amish

Kraybill et al. (1986) found that Amish and other Mennonites in Pennsylvania had lower suicide rates than the general population and Pennsylvanians of other religious affiliations. However, the Amish suicide rate had been much higher thirty years previously and had only recently dropped to a low rate. The Amish suicides tended to more often be married than non-Amish suicides and to use hanging more. They did not differ in sex or age.

Shaw (1986) found that the suicide rates of the Amish, Mennonite and other churched groups in Lancaster County (PA) were all lower than for the non-churched groups.

United States: Black/White Differences

Bush (1978) compared black and white private psychiatric patients who were suicidal. For the blacks, a recent loss or threatened loss of a significant other was more common as a precipitant, whereas for whites chronic problems were more common. The blacks had closer ties to their families, and over half had conflicts in values with their families.

Kirk and Zucker (1979) compared black males who had attempted suicide with controls. The attempters were more anomic and had a lesser sense of black consciousness. They did not differ in alienation or depression/hostility/anxiety on an adjective checklist. They were more depressed on the MMPI and came from homes lower in socioeconomic status.

Hickman (1984) compared black and white suicide attempters and found the blacks to be younger, more often single or separated, to use overdoses more and more violent methods less, and to more often have problems with their lover. The groups did not differ in psychiatric diagnosis. Key (1986) found black attempters to use different methods for suicide (poisons and walking into traffic more and cutting, gas, firearms and jumping less), but did not differ in age, sex, marital and employment status, diagnosis, prior hospitalizations and precipitants. Politano et al. (1986) found that black adolescent psychiatric inpatients were less suicidal than whites on the Children's Depression Inventory.

Zimbabwe

Lester and Wilson (1988) found that the suicide rates by race in Zimbabwe mirrored those in South Africa with whites having the highest rates, coloreds/asians moderate rates and blacks the lowest rates. They noted that the different races used different methods, with car exhaust used almost exclusively by whites. Soldiers and police officers used mainly guns. They also noted a growing trend for young females in the capital (Harare) to use self-immolation.

International Comparisons

Kitamura (1983–1985) compared adolescent suicide attempters seen in Germany and Japan. The Japanese were less likely to come from broken homes, more often the firstborn, more often psychotic, less often a substance abuser, more often used wrist-slashing and less often drug poisoning, more often had school problems and less often family problems, were relatively less often male, and more often left suicide notes. For completed suicides, similar differences were found for method, precipitants, broken homes and suicide notes. The Japanese suicide rate for teenagers peaked in April with a trough in December, whereas for Germany the peak was in October/November and the trough in February.

Religion

Miscounting Errors

Day (1987) looked at data from Europe from 1860–1904 and found that suicide rates were lower in districts with a higher proportion (both overall and for those married) of Roman Catholics. However, accidental and unknown-cause death rates were higher in these districts, suggesting misrecording of suicide in Roman Catholic districts.

Regional Studies

Faupel et al. (1987) found that suicide was negatively related to the proportion of Roman Catholics in USA counties, but only for moderately and highly urbanized counties, not for rural counties.

Girard (1988) found that church membership was not significantly associated with the suicide rates of the states once the percentage of blacks was placed into the regression equation and the divorce measure used was a proportion of those over 14 years of age.

Lester (1987a) found that the proportion of the population that was Roman Catholic was negatively associated with suicide rates over the US, but this association did not survive controls for other social variables such as divorce, migration and the proportion of elderly. Lester (1987b) found no association between the percentage of Roman Catholics and the suicide rate over nations. However, Lester (1987c) found that the higher the percentage of church attendance in a state the lower the suicide rate, but again the inclusion of other social variables in the regression analysis eliminated the significant effect of church attendance.

Templer and Veleber (1980) found that the suicide rates of the states were not associated with the percentage of Catholics in the US unless they controlled for the percentage of blacks in a multiple regression analysis. In response to this, Lester (1988j) confirmed his earlier research showing that the suicide rate in the US was related to church attendance and not to the percentage of Roman Catholics.

Martin (1984) correlated suicide rates and rates of church attendance in the USA over sixteen categories (four years by two sexes by two races) and found a negative association (the less church attendance, the higher the suicide rate).

Pescosolido and Georgiana (1989) found that the suicide rate of American counties was related to the proportion of Seventh-Day Adventists and Episcopalians, and negatively to the proportion of Evangelical Baptists and Catholics. Suicide rates were higher the more liberal, ecumenical and Presbyterian church members, and the researchers concluded that church participation was a crucial factor in these relationships.

Pope and Danigelis (1981) found that Catholic countries had lower suicide rates than Protestant countries, but only after the Second World War. However, that war saw a change in which type of country was more developed (from Catholic countries before the war to Protestant countries after the war).

Other Studies

Nelson (1977) reported that highly religious elderly VA patients were less likely to show indirect self-destructive behavior than nonreligious patients.

Budner and Kumler (1973) found that college students with suicidal ideation were more likely to be Jewish, to have deserted religion, to attend church rarely and to see religious beliefs as unimportant. Neal (1981) found no differences in England between attempted suicides and psychiatric patients in church attendance, denomination or belief in God.

Jasperse (1976) found that the suicide rate of Catholics in the Netherlands rose from 1961 to 1970 while the suicide rate of non-Catholics stayed steady.

Societal Approval Of Suicide and Belief in Life After Death

Lester (1983, 1988h, 1989d) found that the suicide rate of the nine major regions of the USA was not associated with estimates from polls of the societal approval of suicide in the regions. Lester (1989j) found no association between the suicide rates of the regions and belief in life after death.

Social Class

Adam et al. (1980) found that attempted suicides were of lower social class than general medical patients in New Zealand. Sendbuehler et al. (1978) found that a sample of attempted suicides had the same distribution of social class as the general population. Those attempters from the lower classes made less serious attempts and were less often judged psychotic. The upper class attempters had an MMPI profile of psychotic depression with paranoid and schizoid features, whereas the lower class attempters had a profile indicating a personality disorder, aggressive type. The upper class attempters seemed to be responding more to intrapsychic problems, whereas the lower class attempters seemed to be reacting more to external pressures. The middle class attempters had an MMPI profile of a depressive reaction, with passive-aggressive features.

Urban-Rural

Alexander et al. (1982) found no urban-rural differences in the suicide rate in South Carolina. Barton et al. (1980) found that suicide rates had increased more from 1967–1973 in Minnesota in the small urban areas than in the metropolitan or rural areas. Pasewark and Fleer (1981) found a higher urban suicide rate in Wyoming. Beratis (1986) found a higher rural suicide rate (for men only) in southwestern Greece, and Fuse (1980) found a higher rural rate in Japan (for both sexes).

In contrast, in eleven Californian counties, Gausche et al. (1989) found no differences in the suicide rate of those aged 18 or younger in the urban versus the rural counties. In Alaska, Hlady and Middaugh (1987) found a higher rural suicide rate in native Americans but not in whites. Jarosz (1978) reported no urban/rural difference in completed suicide in communist nations.

In Italy, Micciolo et al. (1988) found no urban/rural difference in suicide rates in the north/central parts, but in the South the rural suicide rate was higher than the urban rate. Sayil (1987) reported higher suicide rates in urban areas than in rural areas in Turkey.

In the USA as a whole, Baker et al. (1984) found that suicide was less common in rural areas by jumping, poisoning, hanging and cutting but more common by firearms. The use of motor vehicle exhaust peaked in smaller cities. In England, Hughes (1983) found no differences between urban and rural suicide attempters in the drug taken or the psychiatric diagnosis.

Urbanization

Hetzel (1971) noted that the suicide rate in Melbourne from 1947–1966 was greater than in the rest of the area, so that by 1966 the metropolitan rate was higher than the non-metropolitan rate, but Krupinski (1979) found no trend for Australia as a whole from 1970–1980 between urbanization and suicide.

War

War Years

Marshall (1981) studied the suicide rates of adult whites aged 25–65 US from 1933–1976. For World War II, the suicide rate decreased only for males aged 25–34. The Korean War had no impact on suicide rates, while the Vietnam War lowered only the suicide rate of females aged 55–64. In a multiple regression analyses, Wasserman (1983, 1989) found no impact of the First World War on American suicide rates, using both yearly data and monthly data. In addition, he found no impact of the Korean and Vietnam war on American suicides rates using monthly data.

Sainsbury (1980) noted that during the Second World War, suicide rates declined on the whole in both belligerent and non-belligerent nations and in both sexes. From 1938 to 1944, male suicide rates dropped in 22 of 23 nations studied and female suicide rates in 16 of 22 nations, including neutral nations (WHO, 1982). Rojcewicz (1971) compared Sweden (neutral), Denmark (gave in) and Norway (resisted) during the Second World War. He noted that the suicide rate dropped in all three nations both for natives and aliens and for civilians and those in the military.

The Military Draft

Hearst et al. (1986) studied those eligible for the draft lottery in 1970–1972 in California and Pennsylvania and, regardless of whether they served, found that they had an elevated suicide rate. The proportion of deaths due to suicide was higher in veterans than in non-veterans.

Servicemen

Chaffee (1982) reported suicide rates of 7.2 (per 100,000 per year) for Navy personnel and 15.2 for Marines. Enlisted men had a higher suicide rate than officers but used similar methods. The Navy suicides were older than expected but the Marine suicides were younger than expected. The Marines used firearms more for their suicides. Kawahara et al. (1989) found a low suicide rate for Navy personnel (6.6). The rate was higher in older personnel, females, whites, apprentices/recruits and blue collar workers.

Datel et al. (1981) found a suicide rate for women in the Army as high as that for men. The rate was higher in female officers than enlisted women whereas the opposite was true for men. The suicide rates were higher in whites than blacks and in grades E1, E2 and E8 (though a later report [Datel and Jones, 1982] found the highest rate in grade E6).

In the Air Force, McDowell and Wright (1988) found that the suicide rate was lower than in the American population. The suicide rate was higher in whites than in blacks, for those stationed in the US, in some occupations (such as structural/munitions and weapons maintenance), and some ranks (such as majors).

In the Navy, Moldeven (1988) found that the black and white suicide rates were similar while in the Marines the black suicide rate was higher. Enlisted men had higher rates than officers, and the suicide rate differed by job (with torpedo mates and hull technicians having the highest rates and hospital corpsmen and aviation structural mechanics the lowest rates). Overall, the Marines had higher suicide rates than the Navy, Army and Air Force.

Rock (1988) found that suicide attempters in the US Army were younger, more often female and more often enlisted than suicide completers (but did not differ in race). Rothberg and McDowell (1988) found that the suicide rate in the US Air Force was higher in whites, enlisted men, those aged 25–29, and the divorced. There was no sex difference. In the US Army, Rothberg et al. (1988) found the suicide rate to be higher in whites, enlisted men and those divorced. Again, there was no sex difference.

In the German Army, Flach (1983) found that completed suicide was equally common in officers, non-commissioned officers and enlisted men. Attempted suicides as compared to normal controls had less social support and more negative life experiences (but not fewer positive life experiences).

In the Nordic nations, the suicide rate of Norwegian servicemen men was higher but that of Finnish and Swedish servicemen lower than the general population of young males (Hytten and Weisaeth, 1989).

Veterans

Adena et al. (1985) found no excess mortality from suicide in Australian Vietnam veterans as compared to other veterans. Anon (1987a) found that American Vietnam veterans had a high suicide rate in the first five years after discharge, but lower rates after that. Overall, their suicide rate was average. Baker (1984) found a relative excess of suicides among Vietnam and Korean veterans and peacetime veterans and a relative deficit among World War Two veterans. Boyle and Decoufle (1987) found no excess of suicide in Vietnam-era veterans regardless of whether they served in Vietnam or elsewhere.

Breslin et al. (1988) found that Army Vietnam veterans had fewer suicides than expected, but not so Marine veterans. Veterans who had been in combat had fewer suicides than noncombatant veterans.

Civil Violence

Loughrey et al. (1988) examined victims of the civil violence in Northern Ireland. Those who had post-traumatic stress disorder were more likely to attempt suicide (and to have marital disharmony) but did not differ in substance abuse, impulsive behavior or explosive behavior.

The Persecuted

Lingens (1972) reported that the suicide rate in the Jewish community in Vienna rose after the Nazis took over the country and rose still higher after the deportations began. Roden (1982) noted that concentration camp inmates in the Second World War had a low suicide rate. Kwiet (1984) documented that Jews in Austria and Germany had average suicide rates in the 1920s but had very high rates during the persecution in the 1930s. There are fewer data on the concentration camps, but Kwiet agreed with others in asserting that the suicide rate was low. The majority of suicides during the persecution and in the camps were elderly and in those not strongly religious.

Civilian Interns

Bloom and Halsema (1983) reported a low suicide rate among civilians interned by the Japanese in the Philippines during World War II.

A–Bomb Survivors

Sorahan (1988) found that survivors of Hiroshima and Nagasakai had expected suicide rates except for those with the most radiation exposure who had lower rates than expected. (It may be, of course, that the potentially suicidal individuals died early from the effects of radiation before they became suicidal.)

Indices of Pathology and Personality

America

Lester (1980a, 1989m) found that the per capita consumption of alcohol was related to the suicide rate over the states of the USA, but not over time in the USA or over nations. Alcohol consumption was loaded on a factor which seemed to tap social disintegration. Norstrom (1988b) found that alcohol consumption and suicide rates were positively related over time in Norway and Sweden but not in Denmark or Finland.

Tabachnick and Klugman (1967) suggested that the amount of death instinct in regions of the country is constant. In contrast to the prediction from this hypothesis of negative correlations between different indices of the death instinct, Lester (1989g) found that the suicide rates of the states were positively related to deaths from cirrhosis of the liver and from motor vehicle accidents. Lester and Frank (1987) found no association between youth suicide rates in the US and the birth rates either for single young women or non-single young women.

Over time in the US, Lester (1988d) found that the suicide rate in election years was related to the need to achieve expressed in the president's inaugural address (but not to the need for power or affiliation). Lester (1989k) found that suicide rates were higher in years when the violence in best-selling novels was less. (No cross-national association was found, however, between the level of violence in movies and suicide rates.)

Cross-National Studies

Lester (1989e) found that the sex ratio for the incidence of depressive disorders in eleven nations was positively related to the sex ratio of completed suicide rates.

Lester (1982b) found that suicide rates of nations were not related to estimates from national samples of the conformity of the nations. However, suicide rates were positively related to measures of independence. Lester (1988b) found the suicide rates of nations were related to measures obtained from samples of individualism (but not power distance, uncertainty avoidance or masculinity). Using objective indices, suicide rates were related to national measures of anxiety but not extraversion. Lester and Georges (1986) found that the suicide rates of industrialized nations were related to objective indices of extraversion, but not to indices of anxiety, compassion or gross national product per capita.

Lester (1986b) found the level of depression in samples in eight nations on a standardized inventory were positively but not significantly associated with the nations suicide rates. Lester (1989i) found the suicide rate of youths in seven nations were weakly associated with measures of the self-esteem of teenagers in those nations.

Lester (1988m) found the extent of pet ownership in industrialized nations was not related to the national suicide rates.

Within-Nation Studies

In India, Lester (1986a) found that a measure of folk-tale aggression in seven provinces was not associated with the suicide rates in those provinces.

Primitive Societies

Lester (1980b, 1986d) found that suicide rates of primitive societies were not related to the incidence of wife-beating or to the custom of twin infanticide. Lester (1986c) found that infant-rearing techniques in primitive societies (such as inflicting pain and overall indulgence) were not related to suicide rates with one exception—consistency in reducing the infant's desires was negatively associated with suicide rates. Lester (1989h) found that suicide rates in primitive societies were not related to ratings of parental warmth, hostility, indifference or control.

Shulman (1989) found that female suicide rates were higher in patrilineal primitive societies while male suicide rates were higher in matrilineal and bilineal primitive societies.

The Sociology of Attempted Suicide

There are fewer studies of the social correlates of attempted suicide since most regions do not count attempters accurately. In Britain, the regional treatment facilities handle most of the attempters (at least by overdoses) permitting more accurate accounting. Platt et al. (1988) found the attempted suicide rate in Edinburgh and Oxford to be higher in women than men (with a peak in women at age 15–19 and in men 20–34), in the lower classes, in the unemployed and the divorced (followed by the single and then the married/widowed).

Discussion

It is impossible to summarize this review of several hundred studies. However, some general comments can be made. First, many of the areas of study have produced inconsistent results, such as those on urban-rural differences. It would be of great interest to see research in the future which proposes alternative theories to account for these inconsistencies and tests the validity of these theories.

Second, it is important in the future to move the research from a simple documentation of correlates of suicidal behavior to finding whether and how these correlates fit into the more comprehensive theories of suicide, both sociological and psychological, which have been proposed.

REFERENCES

Abe, K., Egashira, K., & Suzuki, T. Suicide seasonality and economic growth. *Stress Medicine*, 1986, 2, 79–81.

Abrams, R. C., Young, R. C., Holt, J. H., & Alexopoulos, G. S. Suicide in New York City nursing homes. *American Journal of Psychiatry,* 1988, 145, 1487–1488.

Achte, K. A., Lonnqvist, J., Niskanen, P., Ginman, L., & Karlson, M. Attempted suicides by poisoning and eight-year follow-up. *Psychiatria Fennica,* 1972, 321–340.

Adam, K. S., Bouckoms, A., & Scarr, G. Attempted suicide in Christchurch. *Australian & New Zealand Journal of Psychiatry,* 1980, 14, 305–314.

Adena, M. A., Cobbin, D., Fett, M., Forcier, L. Hudson, H., Long, A., Nairn, J., & O'Toole, B. Mortality among Vietnam veterans compared with non-veterans and the Australian population. *Medical Journal of Australia,* 1985, 143, 541–544.

Ahlburg, D. A. The effects of strikes on suicide. *Sociological Focus,* 1985, 18, 29–36.

Ahlburg, D., & Schapiro, M. Socioeconomic ramifications of changing cohort size. *Demography,* 1984, 21, 97–108.

Albanese, J. S. Preventing inmate suicides. *Federal Probation,* 1983, 46(2), 65–69.

Alexander, G., Gibbs, T., Massey, R., & Altekruse, J. South Carolina's suicide mortality in the 1970s. *Public Health Reports,* 1982, 97, 476–482.

Allston, M. H. Occupation and suicide among women. *Issues in Mental Health Nursing,* 1986, 8, 109–119.

Allston, M. H. Occupational correlates of suicide in black and other non-white Women. In D. Lester (Ed.) *Suicide '88.* Denver: AAS, 1988, 206.

Alstrom, C., Lindelius, R., & Salum, I. Mortality among homeless men. *British Journal of Addiction,* 1975, 70, 245–252.

Altergott, K. Qualities of daily life and suicide in old age. *Journal of Cross-Cultural Gerontology,* 1988, 3, 361–376.

Andjelkovic, D., Taulbee, J., & Symons, M. Mortality experience of a cohort of rubber workers. *Journal of Occupational Medicine,* 1976, 18, 387–394.

Anno, B. J. Patterns of suicide in the Texas Department of Corrections. *Journal of Prison & Jail Health,* 1985, 5(2), 82–93.

Anon. *Decennial Supplement on Occupational Mortality for 1971.* Series DS No. 1, February 9th, 1978. London: Registrar General. 1978.

Anon. Post-service mortality among Vietnam veterans. *Journal of the American Medical Association,* 1987a, 257, 790–795.

Anon. Results and implications of the AMA–APA physician mortality project. *Journal of the American Medical Association,* 1987b, 257, 2949–2953.

Arnetz, B. B., Horte, L. G., Hedberg, A., & Malker, H. Suicide among Swedish dentists. *Scandinavian Journal of Social Medicine,* 1987a, 15, 243–246.

Arnetz, B. B., Horte, L. G., Hedberg, A., Theorell, T., Allander, E., & Malker, H. Suicide patterns among physicians related to other academics as well as to the general population. *Acta Psychiatrica Scandinavica,* 1987b, 75, 139–143.

Asp, S., Hernberg, S., & Collan, Y. Mortality among Finnish doctors. *Scandinavian Journal of Social Medicine,* 1979, 7, 55–62.

Aussant, G. Police suicide. *International Criminal Police Review,* 1984, 39(380), 179–188.

Backett, S. S. Suicide in Scottish prisons. *British Journal of Psychiatry,* 1987, 151, 218–221.

Bagley, C. Profiles of youthful suicide. *Psychological Reports,* 1989, 65, 234.

Bagley, C., Wood, M., & Khumar, H. Suicide and careless death in young males. In R. Yufit (Ed.) *Proceedings of the 20th Annual Meeting.* Denver: AAS, 1987, 31–32.

Baker, J. E. Monitoring of suicidal behavior among patients in the VA health care system. *Psychiatric Annals,* 1984, 14, 277.

Baker, S. P., O'Neill, B. & Karpf, R. S. *The Injury Fact Book.* Lexington: Heath, 1984.

Barnes, R. A., Ennis, J., & Schober, R. Cohort analysis of Ontario's suicide rates 1877–1976. *Canadian Journal of Psychiatry,* 1986, 31, 208–213.

Barton, S. M., Coombs, D., & Mukherjee, D. Urban-rural suicide differentials in Minnesota 1967–1973. *Minnesota Medicine,* 1980, 63, 415–418.

Beaumont, J. J., & Weiss, N. S. Mortality of welders, shopfitters, and other metal trade workers in boilermakers local no. 104, AFL–CIO. *American Journal of Epidemiology,* 1980, 112, 775–786.

Bedeian, A. Suicide and occupation. *Journal of Vocational Behavior,* 1982, 21, 206–223.

Beratis, S. Suicide in southwestern Greece. *Acta Psychiatrica Scandinavica,* 1986, 74, 433–439.

Birmingham, P., & Ward, R. A high risk suicide group. *American Journal of Psychiatry,* 1985, 142, 1225–1226.

Bissell, L., & Skorina, J. K. One hundred alcoholic women in medicine. *Journal of the American Medical Association,* 1987, 257, 2939–2944.

Black, K. A descriptive survey of student suicide in higher education within the southwestern Rocky Mountain states. *Dissertation Abstracts International,* 1971, 32A, 3015.

Blair, A., Berney, B. W., Heid, M. F., & White, D. W. Causes of death among workers in the tobacco industry. *Archives of Environmental Health,* 1983, 38, 223–228.

Blair, A., & Hayes, H. M. Mortality patterns among US veterinarians. *International Journal of Epidemiology,* 1982, 11, 391–397.

Bloom, M., & Halsema, J. Survival in extreme conditions. *Suicide & Life-Threatening Behavior,* 1983, 13, 195–206.

Bluestone, B., Harrison, B., & Baker, L. *Corporate Flight.* Washington, DC: Progressive Alliance, 1981.

Blumenthal, S., Bell, V., Neumann, N. V., Schutter, R., & Vogel, R. Mortality and rate of suicide of first admission psychiatric patients. *Psychopathology,* 1989, 22, 50–56.

Bond, G. G., Lipps, T. E., & Cook, R. R. Mortality comparisons of chemical workers hired before, during and after World War II. *American Journal of Industrial Medicine,* 1989, 15, 335–342.

Boor, M. Relationship between unemployment rates and suicide rates in eight countries. *Psychological Reports,* 1980, 47, 1095–1101.

Borg, S. E., & Staht, M. Prediction of suicide. *Acta Psychiatrica Scandinavica,* 1982, 65, 221–232.

Bourque, L. B., Cosan, B., & Kraus, J. Comparison of male and female suicides in a defined community. *Journal of Community Health,* 1983, 9, 7–17.

Boyle, C. A., & Decoufle, P. Postdischarge mortality from suicide and motor-vehicle injuries among Vietnam-era veterans. *New England Journal of Medicine,* 1987, 317, 506–507.

Breetzke, K. A. Suicide in Cape Town. *South African Medical Journal,* 1988, 73(1), 19–23.

Brenner, M. H. Mortality and economic instability. *International Journal of Health Services,* 1983, 13, 563–620.

Breslin, P., Kang, H. K., Lee, Y., Burt, V., & Shepard, B. M. Proportional mortality study of US Army and US Marine Corps veterans of the Vietnam War. *Journal of Occupational Medicine,* 1988, 30, 412–419.

Bruce, D. Central nervous system depression. *International Anesthesia Clinics,* 1981, 19(4), 121–130.

Budner, S., & Kumler, F. *Correlates of Suicidal Ideation.* American Association of Suicidology, Houston, 1973.

Burtka, G. J., Durand, C. J., & Smith, J. W. Completed suicides in Detroit's Wayne County Jail. In D. Lester (Ed.) *Suicide '88.* Denver: AAS, 1988, 163–164.

Burvill, P. W. Attempted suicide in the Perth statistical division 1971–1972. *Australian & New Zealand Journal Psychiatry,* 1975, 9, 272–279.

Burvill, P. W., Armstrong, B., & Carlson, D. Attempted suicide and immigration in Perth, Western Australia. *Acta Psychiatrica Scandinavica,* 1983a, 68, 89–99.

Burvill, P. W., McCall, M. G., Stenhouse, N. S., & Reid, T. A. Deaths from suicide, motor vehicle accidents and all forms of violent deaths among migrants in Australia 1962–1966. *Acta Psychiatrica Scandinavica,* 1973, 49, 28–50.

Burvill, P. W., McCall, M., Woodings, T., & Stenhouse, N. Comparison of suicide rates and methods in English, Scots and Irish immigrants in Australia. *Social Science & Medicine,* 1983b, 17, 705–708.

Burvill, P. W., Woodings, T., Stenhouse, N., & McCall, M. Suicide during 1961–1970 migrants in Australia. *Psychological Medicine,* 1982, 12, 295–308.

Bush, J. A. Similarities and differences in precipitating events between black and anglo suicide attempts. *Suicide & Life-Threatening Behavior,* 1978, 8, 243–249.

Chaffee, R. B. Completed suicide in the Navy and Marine Corps. *US Naval Health Research Center Reports,* 1982, #82–17.

Charlton, J. R., Bauer, R., Thakhore, A., Silver, R., & Aristidou, M. Unemployment and mortality. *Journal of Epidemiology & Community Health,* 1987, 41, 107–113.

Controy, C. Suicide in the workplace. *Journal of Occupational Medicine,* 1989, 31, 847–851.

Conwell, V., Rotenberg, M., & Caine, E. D. Late life suicide in Monroe County. In D. Lester (Ed.) *Suicide '89.* Denver: AAS, 1989, 247–249.

Cooley, D., Catalano, R., Rook, K., & Serxner, S. Economic stress and suicide. *Suicide & Life-Threatening Behavior,* 1989, 19, 321–336, 337–351.

Copeland, A. R. Fatal suicidal hangings among prisoners in jail. *Medicine, Science & the Law,* 1989a, 29, 341–345.

Copeland, A. R. Suicide among non-whites. *American Journal of Forensic Medicine & Pathology,* 1989b, 10, 10–13.

Cormier, H. J., & Klerman, G. L. Unemployment and male-female labor force participation as determinants of changing suicide rates of males and females in Quebec. *Social Psychiatry,* 1985, 20, 109–114.

Costa, G., Crepet, P., & Florenzano, F. Unemployment and mortality in Italy. In S.

D. Platt & N. Kreitman (Eds.) *Current Research on Suicide and Parasuicide.* Edinburgh: University of Edinburgh, 1989, 40–46.

Cox, V., Paulus, P., & McCain, G. Prison crowding research. *American Psychologist,* 1984, 39, 1148–1160.

Crepet, P., & Florenzano, F. Suicide and unemployment in Italy. In H. J. Moller, A. Schmidtke, & R. Welz (Eds.) *Current issues of suicidology.* Berlin: Springer-Verlag, 1988, 356–363.

Crombie, I. K. Trends in suicide and unemployment in Scotland, 1976–1986. *British Medical Journal,* 1989, 298, 782–784.

Cumming, E., & Lazer, C. Kinship structure and suicide. *Canadian Review of Sociology & Anthropology,* 1981, 18, 271–282.

Curran, P. S., Finlay, R. J., & McGarry, P. J. Trends in suicide. *Irish Journal of Psychological Medicine,* 1988, 5(2), 98–102.

Danto, B. L. Police suicide. *Police Stress,* 1978, 1(1), 32–40.

Danto, B. L. *Crisis behind bars.* Warren, MI: Dale Corporation, 1981.

Danto, B. L., & Danto, J Jewish and non-Jewish suicide in Oakland County, Michigan. In J. P. Soubrier & J. Vedrinne (Eds.) *Depression and Suicide.* Paris: Pergamon, 1983, 267–291.

Daradkeh, T. K., & Al-Zayer, N. Parasuicide in an Arab industrial community. *Acta Psychiatrica Scandinavica,* 1988, 77, 707–711.

Dash, J., & Reiser, M. Suicide among police in urban law enforcement agencies. *Journal of Police Science & Administration,* 1978, 6, 18–21.

Datel, W. E., & Jones, F. Suicide in US Army personnel 1979–1980. *Military Medicine,* 1982, 147, 843–847.

Datel, W. E., Jones, F., & Esposito, M. Suicide in US Army personnel. *Military Medicine,* 1981, 146, 387–392.

Daubs, J. The mental health crisis in ophthalmology. *American Journal of Optometry,* 1973, 50, 816–822.

Davis, L. K., Wegman, D. H., Monson, R. R., & Froines, J. Mortality experience of Vermont granite workers. *American Journal of Industrial Medicine,* 1983, 4, 705–724.

Davies, R. Female labor force participation, status integration and suicide, 1950–1969. *Suicide & Life-Threatening Behavior,* 1981, 11, 111–123.

Day, L. Durkheim on religion and suicide. *Sociology,* 1987, 21, 449–461.

Dean, G., MacLennan, R., McLoughlin, H., & Shelley, E. Causes of death of blue-collar workers at a Dublin brewery. *British Journal of Cancer,* 1979, 40, 581–589.

Demi, A. Mental health of widows after sudden death. *Proceedings of the 10th International Congress for Suicide Prevention.* Ottawa: IASP, 1979, 230–237.

Depue, R. H., Kagey, B. T., & Heid, M. F. A proportional mortality study of the acting profession. *American Journal of Industrial Medicine,* 1985, 8, 57–66.

Dubrow, R. Suicide among social workers in Rhode Island. *Journal of Occupational Medicine,* 1988, 30, 211–213.

Durkheim, E. *Le Suicide.* Paris: Felix Alcan, 1897.

Eastwell, H. D. The low risk of suicide among the Yolngu of the Northern Territory. *Medical Journal of Australia,* 1988, 148, 338–340.

Edmondson, B. Dying for dollars. *American Demographer,* 1987, 9(10), 14–15.

Esparza, R. Attempted and committed suicide in county jails. In B. Danto (Ed.) *Jail house Blues.* Orchard Lake, MI: Epic, 1973, 27–46.

Fabricatore, J. M., & Dash, J. Suicide, divorce and psychological health among police officers. *Essence,* 1977, 1(4), 225–231.

Fasal, E., Jackson, E. W., & Klauber, M. R. Mortality in California veterinarians. *Journal of Chronic Diseases,* 1966, 19, 293–306.

Faupel, C. E., Kowalski, G. S., & Starr, P. D. Sociology's one law. *Journal for the Scientific Study of Religion,* 1987, 26, 523–534.

Fawcett, J., & Marrs, B. Suicide at the county jail. In B. Danto (Ed.) *Jail house Blues.* Orchard Lake, MI: Epic, 1973, 83–106.

Felstein, G. F. Current considerations in plant shutdowns and relocations. *Personnel Journal,* 1981, 60, 369–372.

Filby, R. G., & Eicher, G. M. Unemployment and the suicide rate. *Ohio State Medical Journal,* 1983, 79, 837–848.

Fitzgerald, E. F., Weinstein, A. L., Youngblood, L. G., Standfast, S. J., & Melius, J. M. Health effects three years after potential exposure to the toxic contaminants of an electrical transformer fire. *Archives of Environmental Health,* 1989, 44, 214–221.

Flach, H. A socio-psychological investigation on suicide attempts in a military population. *Crisis,* 1983, 4(1), 16–32.

Flaherty, M. The national incidence of juvenile suicide in adult jails and juvenile detention centers. *Suicide & Life-Threatening Behavior,* 1983, 13, 85–94.

Forbes, N., & van der Hyde, V. Suicide in Alaska from 1978 to 1985. *American Indian & Alaskan Native Mental Health Research,* 1988, 1(3), 36–55.

Forsyth, C. J., & Gramling, R. Suicide, unemployment, dirty work and the underground economy. *International Review of Modern Sociology,* 1988, 18, 175–181.

Forster, D., & Frost, C. Medicinal self-poisoning and prescription frequency. *Acta Psychiatrica Scandinavica,* 1985, 71, 567–574.

Fox, J., Mantowabi, D., & Ward, J. An Indian community with a high suicide rate. *Canadian Journal of Psychiatry,* 1984, 29, 425–427.

Friedman, P. Suicide among police. In E. S. Shneidman (Ed.) *Essays in Self-Destruction.* New York: Science House, 1967, 414–449.

Frost, R., & Hanzlick, R. Deaths in custody. *American Journal of Forensic Medicine & Pathology,* 1988, 9, 207–211.

Fuller, G. N., Rea, A. J., Payne, J. F., & Lant, A. F. Parasuicide in central London. *Journal of the Royal Society of Medicine,* 1989, 82, 653–656.

Fuse, T. To be or not to be. *Stress,* 1980, 1(3), 18–25.

Gaines, T., & Richmond, L. Assessing suicidal behavior in basic military trainees. *Military Medicine,* 1980, 145, 263–266.

Galbraith, J. K. *The Great Crash 1929.* Boston: Houghton-Mifflin, 1954.

Garro, L. C. Suicides by status Indians in Manitoba. *Arctic Medical Research,* 1988, 47, suppl. 1, 590–592.

Gausche, M., Seidel, J. S., Henderson, D. P., Ness, B., Ward, P. M., Wayland, B. W., & Almeida, B. Violent death in the pediatric age group. *Pediatric Emergency Care,* 1989, 5(1), 64–67.

Girard, C. Church membership and suicide reconsidered. *American Journal of Sociology,* 1988, 93, 1471–1479.

Glover, G., Marks, F., & Nowers, M. Parasuicide in young Asian women. *British Journal of Psychiatry,* 1989, 154, 271–272.

Goldney, R., & Katsikitis, M. Cohort analysis of suicide rates in Australia. *Archives of General Psychiatry,* 1983, 40, 71–74.

Graber, R. B. Cultural evolution and the introversion of aggression. *Connecticut Review,* 1989, 11(2), 105–112.

Green, L. M. Suicide and exposure to phenoxy acid herbicides. *Scandinavian Journal of Work, Environment, & Health,* 1987, 13, 460.

Guralnick, L. Mortality by occupation and cause of death among men aged 20–64 years of age. *Vital Statistics, Special Reports,* 1963, 53, #3.

Hafner, H., & Schmidtke, A. Do cohort effects influence suicide rates? *Archives of General Psychiatry,* 1985, 42, 926–927.

Hamermesh, D. S. The economics of black suicide. *Southern Economic Journal,* 1974, 41, 188–199.

Hamermesh, D., & Soss, N. An economic theory of suicide. *Journal of Political Economy,* 1974, 82, 83–98.

Hamilton, M. J., Pepitone-Arreola-Rockwell, F., Rockwell, D., & Whitlow, C. 35 law student suicides. *Journal of Psychiatry & the Law,* 1983, 11, 335–344

Harrington, J. M., & Goldblatt, P. Census based mortality study of pharmaceutical industry workers. *British Journal of Industrial Medicine,* 1986, 43, 206–211.

Harrington, J. M., & Oakes, D. Mortality study of British pathologists. *British Journal of Industrial Medicine,* 1984, 41, 188–191.

Hassan, R. Suicide in Australia. In R. Yufit (Ed.) *Proceedings of the 20th Annual Conference.* Denver: AAS, 1987, 16–17.

Hawton, K., & Fagg, J. Suicide and other causes of death following attempted suicide. *British Journal of Psychiatry,* 1988, 152, 359–366.

Hawton, K., Fagg, J., & Simkin, S. Female unemployment and attempted suicide. *British Journal of Psychiatry,* 1988, 152, 632–637.

Haycock, J. Manipulation and suicide attempts in jails and prisons. *Psychiatric Quarterly,* 1989, 60, 85–98.

Hayes, L. M. And darkness closes in. *Criminal Justice & Behavior,* 1983, 10, 461–484.

Hayes, L. M. National study of jail suicides. *Psychiatric Quarterly,* 1989, 60, 7–29.

Haynes, R. H. Suicide and social response in Fiji. *British Journal of Psychiatry,* 1987, 151, 21–26.

Hearst, N., Newman, T. B., & Hulley, S. B. Delayed effect of the military draft on mortality. *New England Journal of Medicine,* 1986, 314, 620–624.

Heilig, S. Suicide in jails. In B. Danto (Ed.) *Jailhouse Blues.* Orchard Lake, MI: Epic, 1973, 47–55.

Heiman, M. F. Police suicides revisited. *Suicide,* 1975, 5, 5–20.

Heinrichs, E. H. Suicide in the young. *Journal of the American College Health Association,* 1980, 28, 236–237.

Hellon, C. P., & Solomon, M. Suicide and age in Alberta, Canada, 1951–1977. *Archives of General Psychiatry,* 1980, 37, 505–510.

Helsing, K. J., Comstock, G. W., & Szklo, M. Causes of death in a widowed population. *American Journal of Epidemiology*, 1982, 116, 524–532.

Hetzel, B. S. The epidemiology of suicidal behavior in Australia. *Australian & New Zealand Journal of Psychiatry*, 1971, 5, 156–166.

Hewitt, D., & Milner, J. Drug-related deaths in the United States. *Health Services Reports*, 1974, 89, 211–218.

Hezel, F. X. Cultural patterns in Trukese suicide. *Ethnology*, 1984, 23, 193–206.

Hickman, L. C. Descriptive differences between black and white suicide attempters. *Issues in Mental Health Nursing*, 1984, 6, 293–310.

Hingson, R., Merrigan, D., & Heeren, T. Effects of Massachusetts raising its legal drinking age from 18 to 20 on deaths from teenage homicide, suicide and nontraffic accidents. *Pediatric Clinics of North America*, 1985, 32, 221–232.

Hislop, T. G., Threlfall, W. J., Gallagher, R. P., & Band, P. R. Accidental and intentional violent death among British Columbian native Indians. *Canadian Journal of Public Health*, 1987, 78, 271–274.

Hlady, W. G., & Middaugh, J. P. The epidemiology of suicide in Alaska. *Alaska Medicine*, 1987, 29(5), 158–164.

Hoar, S. K., & Pell, S. A retrospective cohort study of mortality and cancer incidence among chemists. *Journal of Occupational Medicine*, 1981, 23, 485–494.

Hoff, H. Prevention of suicide among prisoners. In B. Danto (Ed.) *Jailhouse Blues.* Orchard Lake, MI: Epic, 1973, 203–214.

Holinger, P. C. *Violent Deaths in the United States.* New York: Guilford, 1987a.

Holinger, P. C. Suicide and population shifts. In R. Yufit (Ed.) *Proceedings of the 20th Annual Conference.* Denver: AAS, 1987b, 59.

Hopes, B., & Shaull, R. Jail suicide prevention. *Corrections Today*, 1986, 48(8), 64–70.

Hoppe, S. K., & Martin, H. W. Patterns of suicide among Mexican-Americans and Anglos, 1960–1980. *Social Psychiatry*, 1986, 21(2), 83–88.

Hughes, G. W. Rural versus urban parasuicide. *Journal of the Royal College of General Practitioners*, 1983, 33, 637–640.

Hurley, W. Suicide by prisoners. *Medical Journal of Australia*, 1989, 151, 188–190.

Hytten, K., & Weisaeth, L. Suicide among soldiers and young men in the Nordic countries 1977–1984. *Acta Psychiatrica Scandinavica*, 1989, 79, 224–228.

Iga, M. *The thorn in the chrysanthemum.* Berkeley: University of California, 1986.

Innes, C. A. Population density in state prisons. *Bureau of Justice Special Report*, 1986, December.

Innes, C. A. The effects of prison density on prisoners. *Criminal Justice & Information Network*, 1987, Spring, 1–3.

Ishii, K. Backgrounds and suicidal behaviors of committed suicides among Kyoto University students. *Psychologia*, 1977, 20, 191–205.

Ishii, K. Backgrounds of higher suicide rates among name university students. *Suicide & Life-Threatening Behavior*, 1985, 15, 56–68.

Iversen, L., Andersen, O., Andersen, P. K., Christoffersen, K., & Keiding, N. Unemployment and mortality in Denmark, 1970–1980. *British Medical Journal*, 1987, 295, 879–884.

Jarosz, M. Suicides in Poland. *Polish Sociological Bulletin*, 1978, 2(42), 87–100.

Jarventie, I., & Kivela, S. L. Suicide mortality among the elderly Finnish population. *Public Health*, 1986, 100, 373–384.

Jarvis, G. K., & Boldt, M. Death styles among Canada's Indians. *Social Science & Medicine*, 1982, 16, 1345–1352.

Jasperse, C. W. Self-destruction and suicide. *Mental Health & Society*, 1976, 3(3–4), 154–168.

Jones, I. H. Psychiatric disorders among aboriginees of the Australian western desert. *Social Science & Medicine*, 1972, 6, 263–267.

Jordan, F. B., Schmeckpeper, K., & Strope, M. Jail suicides by hanging. *American Journal of Forensic Medicine & Pathology*, 1987, 8(1), 27–31.

Kaplan, S. D. Retrospective cohort mortality study of Roman Catholic priests. *Preventive Medicine*, 1988, 17, 335–343.

Katz, R. M. Causes of death among RNs. *Journal of Occupational Medicine*, 1983, 25, 760–762.

Kawahara, Y., Palinkas, L. A., Burr, R. A., & Coben, P. Suicides in active duty enlisted Navy personnel. *US Naval Health Research Center Reports*, 1989, #89–34.

Kennedy, D. M. A theory of suicide while in police custody. *Journal of Police Science & Administration*, 1984, 12, 191–200.

Kerkhof, A. J. Suicidal behavior in jails and prisons in the Netherlands. In R. Yufit (Ed.) *Proceedings of the 20th Annual Conference*. Denver: AAS, 1987, 11–13.

Key, L. J. Clinical comparison of black and white suicide attempters. In R. Cohen-Sandler (ed.) *Proceedings of the 19th Annual Meeting*. Denver: AAS, 1986, 78–80.

Kinlein, L. J. Mortality among British veterinary surgeons. *British Medical Journal*, 1983, 287, 1017–1019.

Kirk, A. R., & Zucker, R. A. Some socio-psychological factors in attempted suicide among urban black males. *Suicide & Life-Threatening Behavior*, 1979, 9, 76–86.

Kitamura, A. Suicide and attempted suicide among children and adolescents. *Pediatrician*, 1983–1985, 12(1), 73–79.

Klebba, A. J. Mortality from selected causes by marital status. *Vital & Health Statistics*, 1970, Series 20, #8.

Kliewer, E. V., & Ward, R. H. Convergence of immigrant suicide rates to those in the destination country. *American Journal of Epidemiology*, 1988, 127, 640–653.

Koh, D., Chua, S. G., & Ong, C. N. A study of the mortality patterns of taxi drivers in Singapore. *Annals of the Academy of Medicine of Singapore*, 1988, 17, 579–582.

Kok, L. P. Race, religion and female suicide attempters in Singapore. *Social Psychiatry & Psychiatric Epidemiology*, 1988, 23, 236–239.

Kono, S., Ikeda, M., Tokudome, S., Nashizumi, M., & Kuratsune, M. Cause-specific mortality among male Japanese physicians. *Asian Medical Journal*, 1988, 31, 453–461.

Kost-Grant, B. Self-inflicted gunshot wounds among Alaska natives. *Public Health Reports*, 1983, 98, 72–78.

Kraft, D. P. Student suicides during a twenty-year period at a state university campus. *Journal of the American College Health Association*, 1980, 28, 258–262.

Kraus, R., & Buffler, P. Suicide in Alaskan natives. In R. J. Shephard & S. Itoh (Eds.) *Circumpolar Health*. Toronto: University of Toronto, 1976, 565–557.

Kraybill, D. B., Hostetler, J. A., & Shaw, D. G. Suicide patterns in a religious subculture. *International Journal of Moral & Social Studies,* 1986, 1, 249–263.

Kreitman, N. Suicide, age and marital status. *Psychological Medicine,* 1988, 18, 121–128.

Kreitman, N., & Platt, S. Suicide, unemployment and domestic gas detoxification in Britain. *Journal of Epidemiology & Community Health,* 1984, 38, 1–6.

Kreitman, N., & Schreiber, M. Parasuicide in young Edinburgh women. In R. Farmer & S. Hirsch (Eds.) *The Suicide Syndrome.* London: Croom Helm, 1980, 54–72.

Krieger, G. Psychiatrists who committed suicide. *Journal of Psychiatric Training & Evaluation,* 1981, 3, 271–273.

Krupinski, J. Urbanization and mental health. *Australian & New Zealand Journal of Psychiatry,* 1979, 13(2), 139–145.

Kua, E. H., & Tsoi, W. F. Suicide in the island of Singapore. *Acta Psychiatrica Scandinavica,* 1985, 71, 227–229.

Kupper, L., Janis, J., Karmous, A., & Greenberg, B. Statistical age-period-cohort analysis. *Journal of Chronic Disease,* 1985, 38, 811–830.

Kwiet, K. The ultimate refuge. *Leo Baeck Institute Yearbook,* 1984, 29, 135–168.

Labovitz, S., & Hagedorn, R. An analysis of suicide rates among occupational categories. *Sociological Inquiry,* 1971, 41, 67–72.

Lal, B. V. Veil of dishonor. *Journal of Pacific History,* 1985, 20, 135–155.

Lampert, D., Bourque, L., & Kraus, J. Occupational status and suicide. *Suicide & Life-Threatening Behavior,* 1984, 14, 254–269.

Lehtinen, V., Holmstrom, R., & Vauhkonen, K. Life situation and mental health of individuals with university education. *Psychiatria Fennica,* 1986, 17, 29–39.

Lester, D. Alcohol and suicide and homicide. *Journal of Studies on Alcohol,* 1980a, 41, 1220–1223.

Lester, D. A cross-culture study of wife abuse. *Aggressive Behavior,* 1980b, 6, 361–364.

Lester, D. Freedom of the press and personal violence. *Journal of Social Psychology,* 1981, 114, 267–269.

Lester, D. Suicide and homicide in US prisons. *American Journal of Psychiatry,* 1982a, 139, 1527–1528.

Lester, D. Conformity, suicide and homicide. *Behavior Science Research,* 1982b, 17, 24–30.

Lester, D. The distribution of sex and age among completed suicides. *International Journal of Social Psychiatry,* 1982c, 28, 256–260.

Lester, D. Societal approval of suicide. *Australian & New Zealand Journal of Psychiatry,* 1983, 17, 293.

Lester, D. Suicide risk by birth cohort. *Suicide & Life-Threatening Behavior,* 1984a, 14, 132–136.

Lester, D. Suicide in communist Europe. *Psychological Reports,* 1984b, 54, 628.

Lester, D. The Compassion of nations and its relationship to personal violence (suicide and homicide). *Peace Research,* 1984c, 16(3), 50–53.

Lester, D. Aggression in Indian folktales and personal violence (suicide and homicide). *Psychological Reports,* 1986a, 58, 974.

Lester, D. Level of depression in nations and their suicide rate. *Psychological Reports,* 1986b, 58, 930.

Lester, D. Somatosensory theory and personal violence (suicide and homicide). *Journal of Social Psychology,* 1986c, 126, 681–683.

Lester, D. The relation of twin infanticide to status of women, societal aggression and material well-being. *Journal of Social Psychology,* 1986d, 126, 57–59.

Lester, D. Suicide and homicide on death row. *American Journal of Psychiatry,* 1986e, 143, 559–560.

Lester, D. Religion, suicide and homicide. *Social Psychiatry,* 1987a, 22, 99–101.

Lester, D. Cross-national correlations among religion, suicide and homicide. *Sociology & Social Research,* 1987b, 71, 103–104.

Lester, D. Religiosity and personal violence. *Journal of Social Psychology,* 1987c, 127, 685–686.

Lester, D. Benefits of marriage for reducing risk of violent death from suicide and homicide for white and non-white persons. *Psychological Reports,* 1987d, 61, 198.

Lester, D. Relation of income inequality to suicide and homicide rates. *Journal of Social Psychology,* 1987e, 127, 101–102.

Lester, D. Suicide and homicide in USA prisons. *Psychological Reports,* 1987f, 61, 126.

Lester, D. Occupational prestige and rates of suicide and homicide. *Perceptual & Motor Skills,* 1987g, 64, 398.

Lester, D. Youth suicide. *Adolescence,* 1988a, 23, 955–958.

Lester, D. National character and rates of personal violence (suicide and homicide). *Personality & Individual Differences,* 1988b, 9, 423.

Lester, D. Emigration rates and personal violence indicated by suicide and homicide rates. *Psychological Reports,* 1988c, 62, 610.

Lester, D. Expressed motives in elected President's addresses and rates of personal violence (suicide and homicide) in USA election years. *Perceptual & Motor Skills,* 1988d, 66, 770.

Lester, D. Strikes, suicide and homicide. *International Journal of Contemporary Sociology,* 1988e, 25, 9–14.

Lester, D. An analysis of the suicide rates of birth cohorts in Canada. *Suicide & Life-Threatening Behavior,* 1988f, 18, 372–378.

Lester, D. State laws on suicide and suicide rates. *Psychological Reports,* 1988g, 62, 134.

Lester, D. Societal approval of suicide. *Psychological Reports,* 1988h, 62, 958.

Lester, D. Religion and personal violence (homicide and suicide) in the USA. *Psychological Reports,* 1988j, 62, 618.

Lester, D. Suicide rates in birth cohorts in Australia. *Psychological Reports,* 1988k, 62, 922.

Lester, D. Suicide rates by region of death and place of birth. *Perceptual & Motor Skills,* 1988l, 67, 942.

Lester, D. Attitudes toward animals and personal violence (suicide and homicide). *Psychological Reports,* 1988m, 63, 810.

Lester, D. Personal violence (suicide and homicide) in South Africa. *Acta Psychiatrica Scandinavica,* 1989a, 79, 235–237.

Lester, D. Suicide and homicide rates in Hungary and Czechoslovakia during the suppression of dissent. *Psychological Reports,* 1989b, 64, 666.

Lester, D. Immigration and rates of personal violence (suicide and homicide). *Psychological Reports,* 1989c, 65, 1298.

Lester, D. Social approval of suicide and suicide rates. *Psychological Reports,* 1989d, 65, 1150.

Lester, D. Sex differences in rates of depressive disorders and suicide. *Psychological Reports,* 1989e, 65, 642.

Lester, D. Effect of divorce on the suicide rates of single and married men. *Psychological Reports,* 1989f, 65, 658.

Lester, D. Is the amount of death instinct constant from region to region? *Perceptual & Motor Skills,* 1989g, 69, 810.

Lester, D. Family style and suicide. *Psychological Reports,* 1989h, 65, 514.

Lester, D. The self-image of teenagers and suicide rates. *Perceptual & Motor Skills,* 1989i, 69, 590.

Lester, D. Belief in life after death and suicide rates by region. *Perceptual & Motor Skills,* 1989j, 69, 1090.

Lester, D. Media violence and suicide and homicide rates. *Perceptual & Motor Skills,* 1989k, 69, 894.

Lester, D. Alcohol consumption and rates of personal violence (suicide and homicide). *Activitas Nervosa Superior,* 1989m, 31, 248–251.

Lester, D., & Frank, M. L. Youth suicide and illegitimacy rates. *Psychological Reports,* 1987, 61, 954.

Lester, D., & Georges, V. C. National character and rates of personal violence (suicide and homicide). *Psychological Reports,* 1986, 58, 186.

Lester, D., & Wilson, C. Suicide in Zimbabwe. *Central African Journal of Medicine,* 1988, 34, 147–149.

Levav, I., & Aisenberg, E. Suicide in Israel. *Acta Psychiatrica Scandinavica,* 1989, 79, 468–473.

Levav, I., Magnus, J., Aisenberg, E., & Rosenblum, I. Sociodemographic correlates of suicidal ideation and reported attempts. *Israel Journal of Psychiatry,* 1988, 25, 38–45.

Lew, E. A. Mortality experience among anesthesiologists. *Anesthesiology,* 1979, 51, 195–199.

Lindesay, J. Age, sex and suicide rates within birth cohorts. *Social Psychiatry,* 1989, 24, 249–252.

Lingens, E. Suicide in extreme situations. In J. Waldenstrom, T. Larsson & N. Ljungstedt (Eds.) *Suicide and Attempted Suicide.* Stockholm: Nordiska Bokhandelns Forlag, 1972, 114–121.

Lloyd, L., Armour, P. K., & Smith, R. J. Suicide in Texas. *Suicide & Life-Threatening Behavior,* 1987, 17, 205–217.

Lockart, S. P., & Baron, J. H. Association between liberalization of Scotland's liquor licensing laws and admissions for self-poisoning. *British Medical Journal,* 1987, 294, 116–117.

Loo, R. Suicide among police in a federal force. *Suicide & Life-Threatening Behavior,* 1986, 16, 379–388.

Loughrey, G. C., Bell, P., Kee, M., Roddy, R. J., & Curran, P. S. Post-traumatic stress disorder and civil violence in Northern Ireland. *British Journal of Psychiatry,* 1988, 153, 554–560.

Maizlish, N., Beaumont, J., & Singleton, J. Mortality among California highway workers. *American Journal of Industrial Medicine,* 1988, 13, 363–380.

Maniam, T. Suicide and parasuicide in a hill resort in Malaysia. *British Journal of Psychiatry,* 1988, 153, 222–225.

Maris, R. The adolescent suicide problem. *Suicide & Life-Threatening Behavior,* 1985, 15, 91–109.

Marks, A. Socioeconomic status and suicide in the state of Washington. *Psychological Reports,* 1980, 46, 924–926.

Marshall, J. R. Changes in aged white male suicide. *Journal of Gerontology,* 1978, 33, 763–768.

Marshall, J. R. Political integration and the effect of war on suicide. *Social Forces,* 1981, 59, 771–785.

Marshall, J. R., & Hodge, R. Durkheim and Pierce on suicide and economic change. *Social Science Research,* 1981, 10, 101–114.

Martin, W. T. Religiosity and US suicide rates 1972–1978. *Journal of Clinical Psychology,* 1984, 40, 1166–1169.

Matsubara, T. Mental health of the aged in the depopulated areas of Japan. *Folia Psychiatrica et Neurologica Japonica,* 1985, 39, 465–472.

May, P. A. Suicide and self-destruction among American Indian youths. *American Indian & Alaskan Native Mental Health Research,* 1987, 1(1), 52–69.

McDowell, C. P., & Wright, A. M. Suicide among active duty USAF members. In M. Moldeven (Ed.) *Suicide Prevention Programs in the Department of Defense.* Del Mar, CA: Moldeven, 1988, 3/6–3/70.

McIntosh, J., & Santos, J. Suicide among minority elderly. *Suicide & Life-Threatening Behavior,* 1981, 11, 151–166.

Memory, J. M. Juvenile suicides in secure detention facilities. *Death Studies,* 1989, 13, 455–463.

Merrill, J., & Owens, J Ethnic differences in self-poisoning. *British Journal of Psychiatry,* 1986, 148, 708–712.

Merrill, J., & Owens, J. Ethnic differences in self-poisoning. *British Journal of Psychiatry,* 1987, 150, 765–768.

Merrill, J., & Owens, J. Self-poisoning among four immigrant groups. *Acta Psychiatrica Scandinavia,* 1988, 77, 77–80.

Mezzich, J. E., & Raab, E. S. Depressive symptomatology across the Americas. *Archives of General Psychiatry,* 1980, 37, 181–823.

Micciolo, R., Zimmerman-Tansella, C., Williams, P., & Tansella, M. Geographic variation in the seasonality of suicide. *Journal of Affective Disorders,* 1988, 15, 163–168.

Michel, K. Suicide in young people is different. *Crisis,* 1988, 9, 135–145.

Milham, S. *Occupational Mortality in Washington State.* Washington, DC: NIOSH, 1976, #76–175.

Moksony, F. Aging and suicide in Hungary. Unpublished, 1989.

Moldeven, M. *Suicide Prevention Programs in the Department of Defense.* Del Mar, CA: Moldeven, 1988.

Morgan, H. G. Social correlates of non-fatal deliberate self-harm. In R. Farmer & S. Hirsch (Eds.) *The Suicide Syndrome.* London: Croom Helm, 1980, 90–102.

Munson, B. E. Relationship between economic activity and critical community dimensions. *American Journal of Economics & Sociology,* 1968, 27, 225–237.

Murphy, E., Lindesay, J., & Grundy, E. Sixty years of suicide in England and Wales. *Archives of General Psychiatry,* 1986, 43, 969–976.

Murphy, G. E., & Wetzel, R. Suicide risk by birth cohort in the United States 1949–1974. *Archives of General Psychiatry,* 1980, 37, 519–523.

Musk, A., Monson, R., Peters, J., & Peters, R. Mortality among Boston firefighters. *British Journal of Industrial Medicine,* 1978, 35, 104–108.

Nayha, S. Short and medium-term variations in mortality in Finland. *Scandinavian Journal of Social Medicine,* 1980, 21, supplement, 1–102.

Neal, C. Religion and self-poisoning. *International Journal of Social Psychiatry,* 1981, 27, 257–260.

Neil, H. A., Fairer, J. G., Coleman, M. P., Thurston, A., & Vessey, M. P. Mortality among male anaesthesiologists in the United Kingdom, 1957–1983. *British Medical Journal,* 1987, 295, 360–362.

Nelson, F. L. Religiosity and self-destructive crises in the institutionalized elderly. *Suicide & Life-Threatening Behavior,* 1977, 7, 67–74.

Nelson, Z., & Smith, W. The law enforcement profession. *Omega,* 1970, 1, 293–299.

Nersesian, W. S., Petit, M. R., Shaper, R., Lemieux, D., & Naor, E. Childhood deaths and poverty. *Pediatrics,* 1985, 75, 41–50.

Newman, J., Whittemore, K., & Newman, H. Women in the labor force and suicide. *Social Problems,* 1973, 21, 220–230.

Newman, S. C., & Dyck, R. J. On the age-period-cohort analysis of suicide rates. *Psychological Medicine,* 1988, 18, 677–681.

Niederhoffer, A. *Behind the Shield.* New York: Doubleday, 1967.

Nordstrom, P., & Asgard, U. Suicide risk by age and birth cohort in Sweden. *Crisis,* 1986, 7(2), 75–80.

Norstrom, T. Deriving relative risks from aggregate data. *Journal of Epidemiology & Community Health,* 1988a, 42, 336–340.

Norstrom, T. Alcohol and suicide in Scandinavia. *British Journal of Addiction,* 1988b, 83, 553–559.

Novick, L. F., & Remlinger, E. Study of 128 deaths in New York City correctional facilities. *Medical Care,* 1978, 16, 749–756.

Odejide, A., Williams, A., Ohaeri, J. U., & Ikuesan, B. A. The epidemiology of deliberate self-harm. *British Journal of Psychiatry,* 1986, 149, 734–737.

Olsen, J., & Lajer, M. Violent death and unemployment in two trade unions in Denmark. *Social Psychiatry,* 1979, 14, 139–145.

Olsen, J., & Sabroe, S. Mortality among bricklayers and carpenters/cabinet makers. *Scandinavian Journal of Social Medicine,* 1979, 7, 49–54.

Ornstein, M. D. The impact of marital status, age, and employment on female suicide in British Columbia. *Canadian Review of Sociology & Anthropology,* 1983, 20-, 96–100.

Pasewark, R. A., & Fleer, J. L. Suicide in Wyoming, 1960–1975. *Journal of Rural Community Psychology,* 1981, 2(1), 39–41.

Paulus, P. B. *Prison Crowding.* New York: Springer-Verlag, 1988.

Pepitone-Arreola-Rockwell, F., Rockwell, D., & Core, N. 52 medical student suicides. *American Journal of Psychiatry,* 1981, 138, 198–201.

Pescosolido, B. A., & Georgiana, S. Durkheim, suicide and religion. *American Sociological Review,* 1989, 54, 33–48.

Peterson, D., & Thomas, C. Acute drug reactions among the elderly. *Journal of Gerontology,* 1975, 30, 552–556.

Petrich, J. Metropolitan jail psychiatric clinic. *Journal of Clinical Psychiatry,* 1978, 39, 191–195.

Platt, S. D. Unemployment and suicidal behavior. *Social Science & Medicine,* 1984, 19, 93–115.

Platt, S. D. Clinical and social characteristics of male parasuicides. *Acta Psychiatrica Scandinavica,* 1986a, 74, 24–31.

Platt, S. D. Parasuicide and unemployment. *British Journal of Psychiatry,* 1986b, 149, 401–405.

Platt, S. D. Suicide and parasuicide among further education students in Edinburgh. *British Journal of Psychiatry,* 1987, 150, 183–188.

Platt, S. D., & Duffy, J. C. Social and clinical correlates of unemployment in two cohorts of male parasuicides. *Social Psychiatry,* 1986, 21, 17–24.

Platt, S. D., & Dyer, J. Psychological correlates of unemployment among male parasuicides in Edinburgh. *British Journal of Psychiatry,* 1987, 151, 27–32.

Platt, S. D., Hawton, K., Kreitman, N., Fagg, J., & Foster, J. Recent clinical and epidemiological trends in parasuicide in Edinburgh and Oxford. *Psychological Medicine,* 1988, 18, 405–418.

Platt, S. D., & Kreitman, N. Trends in parasuicide and unemployment among men in Edinburgh 1968–1982. *British Medical Journal,* 1984, 289, 1029–1032.

Platt, S. D., & Kreitman, N. Parasuicide and unemployment among men in Edinburgh 1968–1982. *Psychological Medicine,* 1985, 15, 113–123.

Politano, P. M., Nelson, W. M., Evans, H. E., Sorenson, S. B., & Zeman, D. J. Factor analytic evaluation of differences between black and caucasian emotionally disturbed children on the Children's Depression Inventory. *Journal of Psychopathology & Behavioral Assessment,* 1986, 8(1), 1–8.

Pope, W., & Danigelis, N. Sociology's "one law." *Social Forces,* 1981, 60, 495–516.

Power, K. G., & Spencer, A. P. Parasuicidal behaviour of detained Scottish young offenders. *International Journal of Offender Therapy,* 1987, 31, 227–235.

Pritchard, C. Suicide, unemployment and gender in the British Isles and EEC. *Social Psychiatry & Psychiatric Epidemiology,* 1988, 23, 85–89.

Ragland, J. D., & Berman, A. L. Farm crisis and suicide. In R. Yufit (Ed.) *Proceedings of the 20th Annual Conference.* Denver: AAS, 1987, 102–103.

Rahav, G., & Ziv, L. External restraints and suicide and homicide rates. *Psychological Reports,* 1988, 62, 317–318.

Reed, J., Camus, J., & Last, J. Suicide in Canada. *Canadian Journal of Public Health,* 1985, 76, 43–47.

Reinhart, G., & Linden, L. Suicide by industry and occupation. *Suicide & Life-Threatening Behavior,* 1982, 12, 34–45.

Reiser, M. *Police Psychology.* Los Angeles: LEHI Publications, 1982.

Renvoise, E., & Clayden, D. Suicide and unemployment. *British Medical Journal,* 1989, 298, 1180.

Revicki, D. A., & May, H. J. Physician suicide in North Carolina. *Southern Medical Journal,* 1985, 78, 1205–1207.

Rich, C. L., & Pitts, F. Suicide by psychiatrists. *Journal of Clinical Psychiatry,* 1980, 41, 261–263.

Richard, W., Fell, R. Health factors in police job stress. In W. Kroes & J. Hurrell (Eds.) *Job Stress and the Police Officer.* Washington, DC: NIOSH, 1975, 73–84.

Richings, J. C., Khara, G. S., & McDowell, M. Suicide in young doctors. *British Journal of Psychiatry,* 1986, 149, 475–478.

Rieger, W. Suicide attempts in a Federal prison. *Archives of General Psychiatry,* 1971, 24, 532–535.

Rimpela, A. H., Nurminen, M. M., Pulkkinen, P. O., Rimpela, M. K., & Valkonen, T. Mortality of doctors. *Lancet,* 1987, 1, 84–86.

Robins, L. N., West, P. A., & Murphy, G. E. The high rate of suicide in older white men. *Social Psychiatry,* 1977, 12, 1–20.

Rock, N. L. Suicide and suicide attempts in the Army. *Military Medicine,* 1988, 153, 67–69.

Roden, R. G. Suicide and holocaust survivors. *Israel Journal of Psychiatry,* 1982, 19, 129–135.

Rojcewicz, S. War and suicide. *Life-Threatening Behavior,* 1971, 1, 46–54.

Rosenman, S. J. Subsequent deaths after attempted suicide by drug overdose in the western region of Adelaide 1976. *Medical Journal of Australia,* 1983, 2, 496–499.

Rothberg, J. M., & McDowell, C. P. Suicide in US Air Force personnel, 1981–1985. *Military Medicine,* 1988, 153, 645–648.

Rothberg, J. M., Rock, N. L., Shaw, J., & Jones, F. D. Suicide in US Army personnel 1983–1984. *Military Medicine,* 1988, 153, 61–64.

Ruback, R. B., & Innes, C. A. The relevance and irrelevance of psychological research. *American Psychologist,* 1988, 43, 683–693.

Russell, L. G. Psychosocial characteristics of homicide and suicide victims. *Legal Medicine,* 1985, 20–33.

Sakinofsky, I. Suicide in doctors and their wives. *British Medical Journal,* 1980, 2, 386–387.

Sainsbury, P. The social relations of suicide. *Social Science & Medicine,* 1972, 6, 189–198.

Sainsbury, P., Jenkins, J., & Levey, A. The social correlates of suicide in Europe. In R. Farmer & S. Hirsch (Eds.) *The Suicide Syndrome.* London: Croom Helm, 1980, 38–53.

Salive, M. E., Smith, G. S., & Brewer, T. F. Suicide mortality in the Maryland state prison system. *Journal of the American Medical Association,* 1989, 262, 365–369.

Sathyavathi, K. Suicides among unemployed persons in Bangalore. *Indian Journal of Social Work,* 1977, 37, 385–392.

Sayil, I. Statistical Data on Suicide in Turkey. In R. Yufit (Ed.) *Proceedings of the 20th Annual Conference.* Denver: AAS, 1987, 48–49.

Schony, W., & Grausgruber, A. Epidemiological data on suicide in Upper-Austria 1977–1984. *Crisis,* 1987, 8(1), 45–52.

Schurrenberger, P. R., Martin, R. J., & Walker, J. F. Mortality in Illinois veterinarians. *Journal of the American Veterinarian Medical Association,* 1977, 170, 1071–1075.

Schwartz, A. J., & Reifler, C. B. Suicide among American college and university students from 1970–1971 through 1975–1976. *Journal of the American College Health Association,* 1980, 28, 205–210.

Schwartz, A. J., & Reifler, C. B. College student suicide in the US. *Journal of American College Health,* 1988, 37(2), 53–59.

Schwartz, E. Proportionate mortality ratio analysis of automobile mechanics and gasoline service station workers in New Hampshire. *American Journal of Industrial Medicine,* 1987, 12(1), 91–99.

Seiden, R. H. Mellowing with age. *International Journal of Aging & Human Development,* 1981, 13, 265–284.

Sendbuehler, J. M., Bernstein, J., Nemeth, G., Kincel, R. L., & Sarwer-Forer, G. J. Attempted suicide and social class. *Psychiatric Journal of the University of Ottawa,* 1978, 3(2), 95–98.

Shai, D., & Rosenwake, I. Violent deaths among Mexican, Puerto Rican and Cuban-born migrants in the US. *Social Science & Medicine,* 1988, 26, 269–276.

Shaw, D. G. Suicide and social integration in Lancaster County. *Sociological Viewpoints,* 1986, 2(1), 15–30.

Shepherd, D. M., & Barraclough, B. M. Work and suicide. *British Journal of Psychiatry,* 1980, 136, 469–478.

Shulman, E. Cross-cultural analysis of young female suicide. In D. Lester (Ed.) *Suicide '89.* Denver: AAS, 1989, 22–24.

Simpson, R., Jakobsen, J., Beck, J., & Simpson, J. Suicide statistics of dentists in Iowa 1968–1980. *Journal of the American Dental Association,* 1983a, 107, 441–443.

Simpson, S. G., Reid, R., Baker, S. P., & Teret, S. Injuries among the Hopi Indians. *Journal of the American Medical Association,* 1983, 249, 1873–1876.

Smith, J. C., Mercy, J. A., & Conn, J. M. Marital status and the risk of suicide. *American Journal of Public Health,* 1988, 78, 78–80.

Smith, J. C., Mercy, J. A., & Rosenberg, M. L. Hispanic Suicide in the Southwest, 1980–1982. *ADAMHA Report of the Secretary's Task Force on Youth Suicide,* Washington, DC: US Government Printing Office, 1989, 3, 196–205.

Solomon, M. I., & Hellon, C. Suicide and age in Alberta, Canada, 1951 to 1977. *Archives of General Psychiatry,* 1980, 37, 511–513.

Sorahan, T. Suicide, selection, and A-bomb survivors. *Lancet,* 1988, 1, 1110–1111.

South, S. J. Racial differences in suicide. *Social Science Quarterly,* 1984, 65, 172–180.

Spaulding, J. M. Recent suicide rates among ten Ojibwa Indian bands in Northwestern Ontario. *Omega,* 1985–1986, 16, 347–354.

Sperbeck, D. J., & Parlour, R. R. Screening suicidal prisoners. *Corrective & Social Psychiatry,* 1986, 32(3), 95–98.

Stack, S. Occupational status and suicide. *Aggressive Behavior,* 1980, 6, 233–234.

Stafford, M. C., & Weisheit, R. A. Changing age patterns of US male and female suicide rate. *Suicide & Life-Threatening Behavior,* 1988, 18, 149–163.

Standish-Barry, H. M., Clayden, A., & Sims, A. Age, unemployment and parasuicide in Leeds. *International Journal of Social Psychiatry,* 1989, 35, 303–312.

Stern, F. B., Beaumont, J., Halperin, W., Murthy, L., Hills, B., & Fajen, J. Mortality of chronic leather tannery workers and chemical exposures in tanneries. *Scandinavian Journal of Work Environment & Health,* 1987, 13, 108–117.

Stone, W. E. Jail suicide. *Corrections Today,* 1984, 46(6), 84–87.

Tabachnick, N. D., & Klugman, D. J. Suicide research and the death instinct. *Yale Scientific Magazine,* 1967, 6, 12–15.

Tan, C. T. Suicide trends in Singapore. *Medicine, Science & the Law,* 1986, 26, 238–242.

Tango, T., & Kurashina, S. Age, period and cohort analysis of trends in mortality from major diseases in Japan, 1955 to 1979. *Statistics in Medicine,* 1987, 6, 709–726.

Templer, D., & Veleber, D. Suicide rate and religion within the US. *Psychological Reports,* 1980, 47, 898.

Thomas, T., & Decoufle, P. Mortality among workers employed in the pharmaceutical industry. *Journal of Occupational Medicine,* 1979, 21, 619–623.

Thomson, I. G. Homicide and suicide in Africa and England. *Medicine, Science & the Law,* 1980, 20, 99–103.

Travis, R. Suicide and economic development among the Inupiat Eskimos. *White Cloud Journal,* 1984, 3(3), 14–21.

Trovato, F. Suicide in Canada. *Canadian Journal of Public Health,* 1988, 79, 37–44.

Tsoi, W. F., & Kua, E. H. Suicide following parasuicide in Singapore. *British Journal of Psychiatry,* 1987, 151, 543–545.

Tsugane, S., Gotlieb, S., Laurenti, R., Souza, J., & Watanabe, S. Mortality and cause of death among first-generation Japanese in Sao Paulo, Brazil. *International Journal of Epidemiology,* 1989, 18, 647–651.

Uehata, J., Abe, M., Chida, T., Matsuoka, T., Ogawa, S., & Furumi, K. A study on mortality and cause of death among cab drivers. *Japanese Journal of Traumatology & Occupational Medicine,* 1985, 33, 91–97.

Van Winkle, N. W., & May, P. A. Native American suicide in New Mexico, 1957–1979. *Human Organization,* 1986, 45, 296–309.

Vena, J., Violanti, J., Marshall, J., & Fiedler, R. Mortality of a municipal worker cohort. *American Journal of Industrial Medicine,* 1986, 10, 383–397.

Vogel, R., & Wolfersdorf, M. Suicide and mental illness in the elderly. *Psychopathology,* 1989, 22, 202–207.

Wagner, M., & Bizeczek, R. Alcoholism and suicide. *FBI Law Enforcement Bulletin,* 1983, 52(8), 8–15.

Walraith, J., & Fraumeni, J. Mortality patterns among embalmers. *International Journal of Cancer,* 1983, 31, 407–411.

Walraith, J., & Fraumeni, J. Cancer and other causes of death among embalmers. *Cancer Research,* 1984, 44, 4638–4641.

Walraith, J., Li, F., Hoar, S., Mead, M., & Fraumeni, J. Causes of death among chemists. *American Journal of Public Health,* 1985, 75, 883–885.

Waring, E. M. Medical professionals with emotional illness. *Psychiatric Journal of the University of Ottawa,* 1977, 2(4), 161–164.

Wasserman, I. Political business cycles, presidential elections and suicide and mortality patterns. *American Sociological Review,* 1983, 48, 711–720.

Wasserman, I. Cohort, age, and period effects in the analysis of US suicide patterns. *Suicide & Life-Threatening Behavior,* 1987, 17, 179–193.

Wasserman, I. The effects of war and alcohol consumption patterns on suicide. *Social Forces,* 1989, 68, 513–530.

Weiss, N. Recent trends in violent deaths among young adults in the US. *American Journal of Epidemiology,* 1976, 103, 416–422.

Wetzel, R. D., Reich, T., Murphy, G., Province, M., & Miller, J. The changing relationship between age and suicide rates. *Psychiatric Developments,* 1987, 5(3), 179–218.

WHO. Changing patterns in suicidal behaviour. *Euro Reports & Studies,* #74. Copenhagen: World Health Organization, 1982.

Wickstrom, G., & Leivonniemi, A. Suicide among male Finnish seafarers. *Acta Psychiatrica Scandinavica,* 1985, 71, 575–580.

Williams, P., De Salvia, D., & Tansella, M. Suicide psychiatric reform and the provision of psychiatric services in Italy. *Social Psychiatry,* 1986, 21, 89–95.

Wilmotte, J. N., & Plat-Mendlewicz, J. Epidemiology of suicidal behavior in 1000 Belgium prisoners. In B. Danto (Ed.) *Jailhouse Blues.* Orchard Lake, MI: Epic, 1973, 57–82.

Winfree, T. L. Toward understanding state-level jail mortality. *Justice Quarterly,* 1987, 4, 51–71.

Winfree, T. L. Rethinking American jail death rates. *Policy Studies Review,* 1988, 7, 641–659.

Wyndham, C. H. Cause and age-specific mortality rates from accidents, poisoning and violence. *South African Medical Journal,* 1986, 69, 559–562.

Wynne, H., Bateman, D., Hasanyeh, F., Rawlins, M., & Woodhouse, K. Age and self-poisoning. *Human Toxicology,* 1987, 6, 511–515.

Yang, B., & Lester, D. The participation of females in the labor force and rates of personal violence (suicide and homicide). *Suicide & Life-Threatening Behavior,* 1988, 18, 270–278.

Yang, B., & Lester, D. Fertility rates and suicide. *Psychological Reports,* 1989a, 64, 676.

Yang, B., & Lester, D. The Association Between Working and Personal Violence (Suicide and Homicide) in Married Men and Women. *Proceedings of the Annual Meeting of the Pennsylvania Economic Association.* University Park: Pennsylvania State University, 1989b, 343–350.

Yu, E., Chang, C., Liu, W., & Fernandez, M. Suicide Among Asian American Youth. *Report of the Secretary's Task Force on Youth Suicide,* 3, 157–176. Washington, DC: ADAMHA, 1989.

Zonda, T. On suicide of the gypsies. Brussels: Congress of the International Association for Suicide Prevention 1989.

Chapter 8

THE VARIATION OF SUICIDE OVER TIME

Massing and Angermeyer (1985) reviewed research from different nations on the variation of suicide over time and concluded that there was generally a spring peak, usually in May, though March and June were found, too. The monthly distribution of suicide tended to be bimodal for women, for younger suicides and in recent times. There was also agreement for a peak on Mondays, and this daily variation was stronger in men and in recent times. Let us see how the research of the 1980s supports these general conclusions.

Hour Of Day

Goodman et al. (1989) found in Oklahoma that completed suicide was most common between 3 P.M. and 6 P.M. In Italy, for a sample of suicide attempters, De Maio et al. (1982) found a peak at 4:30 P.M. to 6:00 P.M. Also in Italy, Williams and Tansella (1987) found an excess of completed suicides between 6 A.M. and 4 P.M.

Month

Completed Suicide

Bollen (1983) confirmed the results of an earlier paper by Lester (1979) by noting peaks of completed suicide in the US in April/May and September. Bollen found that the September peak was found for women only. The variation was found for whites but not for non-whites and was clearer for older adults. MacMahon (1983) also confirmed Lester's (1979) results, reporting an April/May peak in the US (with a minor peak in August/September). Warren et al. (1983) found that suicides in the US had a major peak in spring and a minor peak in September and was consistent with a two-harmonic pattern. For adolescent suicides in the US, Wallenstein et al. (1989) reported an early spring peak (January-March).

149

For adults in the US in 1977, Phillips (1984) found that suicide varied over the months for adults and for teenagers (though the peak in teenagers was different from that for the adults, winter rather spring). In California, Phillips and Carstensen (1988) found that only females had a spring peak. In the US Army, suicides peaked in January and June (Rothberg and Jones, 1987).

In Erie County (NY) from 1973 to 1983, Abel et al. (1987) found no variation in the number of suicides by month. Lewis (1978) found that suicide by asphyxiation in Cleveland peaked in different months for different sections of the city. For example, the peak month was June for center city and winter west of the city center. Eastwood and Peacocke (1976) found that suicide rates peaked in May and October for men in Ontario and March and October for women. (Psychiatric admissions for depression showed similar peaks, whereas admissions for neuroses and schizophrenia showed no seasonal variation.) Jones and Jones (1977) found no monthly variation in completed suicides in Cuyahoga County (Ohio).

Lester (1983, 1985b) found that the monthly variation in completed suicide in the US varied by method. For example, suicides by gas peaked in February and March, while suicides by hanging peaked in April, May and June.

Frank and Lester (1988) found that older suicides (age 35 and over) had an April/May peak and fewer suicides on national holidays, but the youth suicides did not show these variations.

Araki et al. (1986) found in Japan that the peak for male suicide was March and for females February and November, though this difference was not statistically significant. The seasonal variation of suicide varied with the method (significantly so for men) but not by age. In another study, Araki and Murata (1987) found an April/May peak for both sexes. Also in Japan, Abe et al. (1986) found that women showed a greater seasonal variation in suicide rates than did men. The degree of seasonality in the suicide rates was negatively related to the gross national product per capita.

Lester and Frank (1988a, 1988b) found in the US that men and women did not differ in the monthly distribution of their completed suicides. Both sexes had two peaks, regardless of method. However, observation of the data showed different peaks by method. For example, males using poisons peaked in the spring while those using hanging peaked in the spring and fall. The monthly distribution did not vary by region, but the seasonal variation was found only for whites. The peak months also differed by age, with the peak for those suicides aged 15–34 in the latter half of the year and the peak for older suicides in the spring and fall.

In England, Meares et al. (1981) found that male suicides peaked in April/May (and the monthly distribution could be represented by a single one-year sinusoidal curve), whereas female suicides peaked in March/April and October/November (and the monthly distribution fitted best two sinusoidal waves with a one year period and a six month period). Micciolo et al. (1989) found a similar pattern in Italy, with the male peak in May and the female peak in May and October/November. In a harmonic analysis, the males had one cycle, the females two. Micciolo et al. (1988) also reported that the seasonal variation was stronger in the north/central part of Italy than in the South and stronger in urban areas. In urban areas the peak was in May, in rural areas June.

In France, Souetre et al. (1987) found that suicides peaked in May with a minor peak in September. The distribution was bimodal in those younger than 25 and unimodal in those 65 and older. Two harmonics described the monthly distribution best.

For completed suicides aged 10–24 in Ontario (Canada), Garfinkel and Golombek (1983) found peaks in fall and winter. In Stockholm, Hjortsjo (1984) found that completed suicide peaked in April. The sexes differed, with males peaking in January and April while women peaked in April and May.

Massing and Angermeyer (1985) in Lower Saxony found a spring peak (April for men and June for women). They also found that the monthly distribution of suicides varied by method. In upper Austria, Schony and Grausgruber (1987) found a May peak.

Nayha (1980, 1982, 1983) found that the peak month for suicide in Finland varied by sex (both sexes had a spring peak and females had a fall peak too), age (the fall peak was apparent only in younger suicides), social class, and marital status (the fall peak was found in those separated and divorced).

In New South Wales (Australia), Parker and Walter (1982) found no seasonal variation in male suicides, while females had a peak in May and a subsidiary peak in November. In Ireland, Reid et al. (1980) found no monthly variation in suicide, overall or for either sex.

Caffee and Coben (1983) in a sample of 542 Navy completed suicides found no variation by month or season. For a small sample of attempted suicides in Ireland, Daly et al. (1986) found peaks in May and September.

Kevan (1980) reviewed research on this topic and concluded that all countries have a spring peak (in April, May and/or June), and this was true for both sexes. Kevan felt that there were too few studies to explore the effects of urban/rural, age, and era and for attempted suicide to draw any conclusions.

Attempted Suicide

In a small sample of adolescent suicide attempters, Christoffel et al. (1988) found no variation by month. In Ontario (Canada), Garfinkel and Golombek (1983) found peaks in October and April for 10–24-year-old suicide attempters. In England, Hawton and Goldacre (1982) found that adolescent attempts at suicide peaked in the first quarter among those aged 12–15 (but not for those aged 16–20). In Italy, De Maio et al. (1982) found a February/March peak for men and a May/June peak for women.

Wenz (1977) found that attempted suicides in the winter and spring had higher scores on a test of social isolation than attempters in other seasons, but did not differ in their expectations of future isolation.

Presidential Elections

Wasserman (1984) found no differences in the completed suicide rate in the Septembers and Octobers before Presidential elections as compared to other years. Boor (1981, 1982) found that the number of completed suicides drops during the month of presidential elections in America and in the two months leading up to the election. In Edinburgh, Masterson and Platt (1989) found that the number of attempted suicides did not drop before general elections. However, afterwards the number rose after a Conservative victory and decreased after a Labor victory.

Day

Completed Suicide

Bollen (1983) confirmed the results of an earlier paper by Lester (1979) by noting a Monday peak in suicide in the US. The Monday peak (and the decrease on national holidays) was stronger for men. This effect was found for whites but not for non-whites and was clearer for older adults. MacMahon (1983) also found a peak on Mondays.

For adults in the US in 1977, Phillips (1984) found that suicide varied over the days of the week for adults, but not for teenagers. For teenagers the number of suicides on a day was negatively associated with the number on the two following days, but this phenomenon was not found for adults. Frank and Lester (1988) found that 15–24-year-olds had peaks for suicide in the US in 1980 on Sunday, whereas those aged 35 and over had a peak on Monday.

In California, Phillips and Carstensen (1988) found that suicide peaks on Mondays for both sexes. In the US Army, Rothberg and Jones (1987) found that suicides peaked on Mondays. Jones and Jones found no day of week variation in completed suicide in Cuyahoga County (Ohio). Caffee and Coben (1983) in a sample of 542 Navy completed suicides found no variation by day of week.

In Stockholm, Hjortsjo (1984) found that completed suicide showed a trough on Tuesday. The sexes differed, with males showing only a Tuesday trough, while women peaked on Mondays and Wednesdays. Nayha (1980, 1982, 1983) failed to find a Monday peak in Finland. In Erie County (NY) from 1973 to 1983, Abel et al. (1987) also found no variation in the number of suicides by day of week.

Attempted Suicide

In Hong Kong, Chiu (1988) found that attempted suicides clustered on Sunday only for housewives. Other women and men did not show a daily variation. In England, Hawton and Goldacre (1982) found that adolescent attempts at suicide peaked on Monday. In Italy, De Maio et al. (1982) found that men showed no variation while the peak for women varied by age (Thursday and Friday for those aged 14–22, Tuesday for those aged 23–40 and Wednesday for those 40 or older).

Sports Events

Curtis et al. (1983) found that, though suicide decreased on major national holidays, there was no drop on Superbowl Sunday or on the day of the last game of the baseball World Series. Lester (1988a) extended the period studied and also found no excess or deficit of suicides in the USA on Superbowl Sunday or the seventh game of the baseball World Series.

Masterson and Strachan (1987) found that rates of attempted suicide fell in Scotland in four years during the period when Scotland was in the

World Cup for soccer. The drop was found in both sexes and for four weeks after the matches.

Holidays

Completed Suicide

Lester (1985a) found no increase in the completed suicide on Christmas day in the US, but there was a higher suicide rate on New Year's Day. In general, suicide rates increased from December eighteenth to January eighth. Lester (1987a) found no excess or deficit of completed suicides at Easter in the US or on Friday the thirteenth (Lester, 1988b). Phillips and Wills (1987) confirmed the drop in suicide rates on national holidays in the US for all groups (except white teenagers) and for all methods of suicide. After Memorial Day, Thanksgiving Day and Christmas Day the decline continues, but after New Year's Day, Independence Day and Labor Day the suicide rates increase. Lester (1987c) published exact suicide rates in the US for each major national holiday during the 1970s.

In Pennsylvania, Sparhawk (1987) found more suicides in the week before Easter but fewer in the weeks before and centered around Christmas. No deficit or excess was found before Independence Day or Thanksgiving. Over all the major holidays, there were fewer suicides in the week before and on the holiday and more in the week afterwards. Caffee and Coben (1983) in a sample of 542 Navy completed suicides found no deviation from chance on national holidays.

Bollen (1983) noted lower rates on national holidays in the US, and this decrease on national holidays was stronger for men. This effect was found for whites but not for non-whites and was clearer for older adults. For adults in the US in 1977, Phillips (1984) found that suicide decreased on national holidays for adults, but not for teenagers.

In California, Phillips and Carstensen (1988) found that suicides declined on major holidays for both sexes. (They noted that suicides seemed to increase *after* New Year's Day and Labor Day.) Jones and Jones (1977) found no difference from chance expectations in completed suicides on major national holidays in Cuyahoga County (Ohio).

Nayha (1980, 1982, 1983) found an excess of suicides on or around national holidays in Finland which is opposite to what is found in the US.

Attempted Suicide

In a small sample of adolescent suicide attempters, Christoffel et al. (1988) found an excess on and around major holidays.

The Day of the Month

Lester and Frank (1987) found more suicides than expected on the fourth–sixth of each month. More detailed analyses showed that this was so only for those older than 35 and only for males.

MacMahon (1983) found a peak at the beginning of the month (around the fifth) with a trough at the end (on the twenty-ninth) for the US. In the US Army, Rothberg and Jones (1987) found that suicides peaked on the fourth–seventh and twenty-second of each month.

In Stockholm, Hjortsjo (1984) found that completed suicides peaked in the first ten days of the month. The sexes differed, with males peaking on days 1–10 and 21+ of the month, while women peaked on days 1–10 of the month.

Birthdays and the Birthday Blues Effect

Hagnell and Rorsman (1980) found no relationship between the date of the completed suicide and the suicides' birthdays. Lester (1986, 1988c) found no evidence for a tendency to commit suicide at or around the time of one's birthday using a sample of completed suicides from Philadelphia, neither for the overall sample nor for either sex. In a small sample of adolescent suicide attempters, Christoffel et al. (1988) found an excess on and around birthdays.

Danneel (1977) explored in West Germany in 1971 to 1972 for those born in the years 1894 to 1953 whether some days of the year had more suicides with their birthday on those days than chance would predict? The answer was no.

Astrological Studies and Month of Birth

Lester (1987b) found no association between the month of births (or the astrological sun sign) and completing suicide, and no differences in these respects between suicides, homicides and natural deaths. Kettle et al. (1988) found that Alaskan natives who completed suicide had an excess of births in April to June. No such phenomenon was found for a much larger sample of Pennsylvanian completed suicides.

Press (1978) studied suicides in New York City and controls born in the same year and living in the same borough and used a computer program to look for astrological chart differences. No significant differences were found. Of eighteen astrologers looking at the charts, only one performed better than chance in identifying the suicides.

Effects of Kennedy's Assassination

Biller (1977) found fewer suicides in the nine days after John Kennedy's assassination than in neighboring years on the same dates.

Lunar Phase

MacMahon (1983) confirmed an earlier paper by Lester (1979) in finding no lunar association in the US as a whole for completed suicide. Lieber (1978) found no lunar variation in completed suicide in Dade County, and Andress (1976) found no association in a county in California. Ossenkopp and Ossenkopp (1973) combined small samples of attempted suicides and accidental self-poisoners and found no lunar variation.

Oderda and Klein-Schwartz (1983) found an excess of unintentional overdose calls to a poison-control center in the five days around the full moon and an excess of suicidal overdose calls around the new moon.

Jones and Jones (1977) found an excess of completed suicides at the time of the new moon in Cuyahoga County (Ohio) but no excess at the time of the full moon. De Voge and Mikawa (1977) found an excess of suicide threat calls at a suicide prevention center during the first quarter and new moon phase (but no excess in general crisis calls).

Temporal Stability

In North Carolina, Grimson (1980) found that suicides (as well as homicides) varied much less from year to year than deaths due to motor vehicle accidents, indicating a greater temporal stability for suicide.

Theoretical Speculations

Gabenneech (1988) hypothesized that suicide would be more common when an event induces a positive anticipation which contrasts with the unpleasant reality when the day arrives. Thus, suicide should be more common, he argued, in the spring, on weekends, and on holidays. It is clear that the data do not fit his predictions. Nevertheless, no other theorist has attempted to propose an alternative explanation of the temporal phenomena associated with suicide.

Discussion

The basic results of this research are clear. In general, completed suicide is more common on Mondays and in the spring and in the fall. Suicide rates are lower on major national holidays and higher at the beginning of the month. There is no lunar effect and no astrological correlates. Not enough studies have been conducted on attempted suicides for reliable conclusions to be drawn.

However, detailed examination indicates that this temporal variation can be affected by sex, age, race, marital status, social class, rural/urban residence and method of suicide. The reasons for this are far from clear.

Little progress has been made on the formulation of theories to account for this temporal variation, and this lacuna should be an important focus for scholars in the 1990s.

REFERENCES

Abe, K., Egashira, K., & Suzuki, T. Suicide seasonality and economic growth. *Stress Medicine,* 1986, 2, 79–81.

Abel, E. L., & Welker, J. W. Temporal variation in violent death in Erie County, NY 1973–1983. *American Journal of Forensic Medicine & Pathology,* 1987, 8, 107–111.

Andress, L. V. R. An epidemiological study of the psychosocial characteristics of suicidal behavior in Riverside County between 1960 and 1974. *Dissertation Abstracts International,* 1976, 37B, 1481.

Araki, S., Aono, H., Murata, K., Shikata, I., & Mitsukuni, Y. Seasonal variation in suicide rates by cause and sex. *Journal of Biosocial Science,* 1986, 18, 471–478.

Araki, S., & Murata, K. Suicide in Japan. *Suicide & Life-Threatening Behavior,* 1987, 17, 64–71.

Biller, O. A. Suicide related to the assassination of President John F. Kennedy. *Suicide & Life-Threatening Behavior,* 1977, 7, 40–44.

Bollen, K. Temporal variations in mortality. *Demography,* 1983, 20, 45–49.

Boor, M. Effects of US presidential elections on suicide and other causes of death. *American Sociological Review,* 1981, 46, 616–618.

Boor, M. Reduction in deaths by suicide, accidents and homicide prior to US presidential elections. *Journal of Social Psychology,* 1982, 118, 135–136.

Chaffee, R. B., & Coben, P. Temporal Variation in Completed Suicide. *US Naval Health Research Center Report,* 1983, No. 83–9.

Chiu, L. P. Do weather, day of week and address affect the rate of attempted suicide in Hong Kong? *Social Psychiatry & Psychiatric Epidemiology,* 1988, 23, 229–235.

Christoffel, K. K., Marcus, D., Sageman, S., & Bennett, S. Adolescent suicide and suicide attempts. *Pediatric Emergency Care,* 1988, 4(1), 32–40.

Curtis, J., Loy, J., & Karnilowicz, W. A comparison of suicide dip effects of major sports events and civil holidays. *Sociology of Sports Journal,* 1983, 3(1), 1–14.

Daly, M., Conway, M., & Kelleher, M. J. Social determinants of self-poisoning. *British Journal of Psychiatry,* 1986, 148, 406–413.

Danneel, R. Haufigkeitsverteilung der Gweburtstage von Selbsmorden. *Archiv fur Psychiatrie Nervenkrankheiten,* 1977, 224, 23–25.

De Maio, D., Carpenter, F., & Riva, C. Evaluation of circadian, circsepten and circannual periodicity of attempted suicides. *Chronobiologia,* 1982, 9, 185–193.

De Voge, S. D., & Mikawa, J. K. Moon phases and crisis calls. *Psychological Reports,* 1977, 40, 387–390.

Eastwood, M. R., & Peacocke, J. Seasonal patterns of suicide, depression and electroconvulsive therapy. *British Journal of Psychiatry,* 1976, 129, 472–475.

Frank, M. L., & Lester, D. Temporal variation of suicide in teens and young adults. *Perceptual & Motor Skills,* 1988, 67, 586.

Gabenneech, H. When promises fail. *Social Forces,* 1988, 67, 129–145.

Garfinkel, B., & Golombek, H. Suicidal behavior in adolescence. In H. Golombek & B. Garfinkel (Eds.) *The Adolescent and Mood Disturbance.* New York: International Universities Press, 1983, 189–217.

Goodman, R. A., Herndon, J. L., Istre, G. R., Jordan, F. B., & Kelaghan, J. Fatal injuries in Oklahoma. *Southern Medical Journal,* 1989, 82, 1128–1134.

Grimson, R. C. A standardized ratio for measuring the suddenness of events. *Social Biology,* 1980, 27, 286–293.

Hagnell, O., & Rorsman, B. Suicide in the Lundby study. *Neuropsychobiology,* 1980, 6, 319–332.

Hawton, K., & Goldacre, M. Hospital admissions for adverse effects of medicinal agents among adolescents in the Oxford region. *British Journal of Psychiatry,* 1982, 141, 166–170.

Hjortsjo, T. The frequency of suicide and chronological parameters. *Crisis,* 1984, 5(2), 65–90.

Jones, P. K., & Jones, S. L. Lunar association with suicide. *Suicide & Life-Threatening Behavior,* 1977, 7, 31–39.

Kettl, P. A., Collins, T., & Bixler, E. O. Season of birth and suicide. In D. Lester (Ed.) *Suicide '88.* Denver: AAS, 1988, 207–208.

Kevan, S. M. Perspective of season of suicide. *Social Science & Medicine,* 1980, 14D, 369–378.

Lester, D. Temporal variation in suicide and homicide. *American Journal of Epidemiology,* 1979, 109, 517–520.

Lester, D. Monthly variation of suicidal and accidental poisoning deaths. *British Journal of Psychiatry,* 1983, 143, 204–205.

Lester, D. Suicide at Christmas. *American Journal of Psychiatry,* 1985a, 142, 782.

Lester, D. Seasonal variation in suicidal deaths by each method. *Psychological Reports,* 1985b, 56, 650.

Lester, D. The birthday blues revisited. *Acta Psychiatrica Scandinavica,* 1986, 73, 322–323.

Lester, D. Suicide and homicide at Easter. *Psychological Reports,* 1987a, 61, 224.

Lester, D. Month of birth of suicides, homicides and natural deaths. *Psychological Reports,* 1987b, 60, 1310.

Lester, D. Suicide and homicide rates on national holidays. *Psychological Reports,* 1987c, 60, 414.

Lester, D. Suicide and homicide during major sports events 1972–1984. *Sociology of Sports Journal,* 1988a, 5, 285.

Lester, D. Personal violence (suicide and homicide) on Friday the 13th. *Psychological Reports,* 1988b, 62, 433.

Lester, D. The birthday blues for males and females. *Psychological Reports,* 1988c, 62, 638.

Lester, D., & Frank, M. L. Sex differences in the seasonal distribution of suicides. *British Journal of Psychiatry,* 1988a, 153, 115–117.

Lester, D., & Frank, M. L. Seasonal variation in suicide rates in the US. *Journal of Clinical Psychiatry,* 1988b, 49, 371.

Lewis, M. S. Hypersurface analysis of communities. *Multivariate Behavior Research,* 1978, 13, 229–236.

Lieber, A. L. Human aggression and the lunar synodic cycles. *Journal of Clinical Psychiatry,* 1978, 39, 385–392.

MacMahon, K. Short-term temporal cycles in the frequency of suicide. *American Journal of Epidemiology,* 1983, 117, 744–750.

Massing, W., & Angermeyer, M. C. The monthly and weekly distribution of suicide. *Social Science & Medicine,* 1985, 21, 433–441.

Masterson, G., & Platt, S. Parasuicide and general elections. *British Medical Journal,* 1989, 298, 803–804.

Masterson, G., & Strachan, J. A. Parasuicide, Scotland and the World Cup. *British Medical Journal,* 1987, 295, 368.

Meares, R., Mendelsohn, F., & Milgrom-Friedman, J. A sex difference in the seasonal variation of suicide rates. *British Journal of Psychiatry,* 1981, 138, 321–325.

Micciolo, R., Zimmerman-Tansella, C., Williams, P., & Tansella, M. Geographic variation in the seasonality of suicide. *Journal of Affective Disorders,* 1988, 15, 163–168.

Miccioolo, R., Zimmerman-Tansella, C., Williams, P., & Tansella, M. Seasonal variation in suicide. *Psychological Medicine,* 1989, 19, 199–203.

Nayha, S. Short and medium-term variations in mortality in Finland. *Scandinavian Journal of Social Medicine,* 1980, 21, supplement, 1–102.

Nayha, S. Autumn incidence of suicides. *British Journal of Psychiatry,* 1982, 141, 512–517.

Nayha, S. The bi-seasonal incidence of some suicides. *Acta Psychiatrica Scandinavica,* 1983, 67, 32–42.

Oderda, G. M., & Klein-Schwartz, W. Lunar cycle and poison center calls. *Clinical Toxicology,* 1983, 20, 487–496.

Ossenkopp, K., & Ossenkopp, M. Self-inflicted injuries and the lunar cycle. *Journal of Interdisciplinary Cycle Research,* 1973, 4, 337–348.

Parker, G., & Walter, S. Seasonal variation in depressive disorders and suicidal deaths in New South Wales. *British Journal of Psychiatry,* 1982, 140, 626–632.

Phillips, D. P. Teenage and adult temporal fluctuations in suicide and auto fatalities. In H. Sudak, A. Ford, & N. Rushforth (Eds.) *Suicide in the Young.* Boston: John Wright, 1984, 69–80.

Phillips, D. P., & Carstensen, L. L. The effect of suicide stories on various demographic groups 1968–1985. *Suicide & Life-Threatening Behavior,* 1988, 18, 100–114.

Phillips, D. P., & Wills, J. S. A drop in suicides around major national holidays. *Suicide & Life-Threatening Behavior,* 1987, 17, 1–12.

Press, N. The New York suicide study. *Journal of Geocosmic Research,* 1978, 2(2), 23–33.

Reid, P., Smith, H., & Greene, S. Seasonal variation in Irish suicidal deaths. *Psychological Reports,* 1980, 46, 306.

Rothberg, J. M., & Jones, F. D. Suicide in the US Army. *Suicide & Life-Threatening Behavior,* 1987, 17, 119–132.

Schony, W., & Grausgruber, A. Epidemiological data on suicide in Upper-Austria 1977–1984. *Crisis,* 1987, 8(1), 45–52.

Souetre, E., Salvati, E., Belugov, J. L., Dovillet, P., Braccini, T., & Darcourt, G. Seasonality of suicides. *Journal of Affective Disorders,* 1987, 13, 215–225.

Sparhawk, T. G. Traditional holidays and suicide. *Psychological Reports,* 1987, 60, 245–246.

Wallenstein, S., Weinberg, C., & Gould, M. Testing for a pulse in seasonal event data. *Biometrics,* 1989, 45, 817–830.

Warren, C., Smith, J., & Tyler, C. Seasonal variation in suicide and homicide. *Journal of Biosocial Science,* 1983, 15, 349–356.

Wasserman, I. The nonreduction of suicide levels prior to Presidential elections. *Journal of Social Psychology,* 1984, 124, 123–125.

Wenz, F. V. Effects of seasons and social isolation on suicidal behavior. *Public Health Reports,* 1977, 92, 233–239.

Williams, P., & Tansella, M. The time for suicide. *Acta Psychiatrica Scandinavica,* 1987, 75, 532–535.

Chapter 9

MULTIVARIATE TIME SERIES AND REGIONAL STUDIES OF SUICIDE RATES

Many researchers interested in the social correlates of suicide rates study the effects of many variables simultaneously, usually using multiple regression and occasionally factor analysis. In these studies, the results often depend upon which social variables are placed into the analysis, and there is no consistency among the different researchers. In this chapter I will review the many studies conducted using this methodology.

America

Parishes

Bankston et al. (1983) studied the association between a number of sociological variables and suicide over parishes in Louisiana. The percentage of Roman Catholics, blacks, French-speaking, urban and living alone people and a poverty index all contributed to the prediction of the suicide rate in a multiple regression.

Census Tracts

Wenz (1977) studied self-injurious behavior in census tracts in Flint (Michigan). The tracts with high rates had more lower class persons, less educated persons, more blue collar workers, and more non-whites and foreign born.

Cities

Porterfield and Talbert (1948) found that suicide and homicide rates were not related over the major cities of the US. Social defectiveness (by which they meant overcrowding, high infant mortality, voting percentage, etc.) was positively related to homicide rates but not to suicide rates.

Gove and Hughes (1980) found that unemployment, living alone and the population density were associated with the suicide rates of cities while median age, percentage of non-whites, percentage poor education, percentage of low income and the population size were not.

SMSAs

Bainbridge (1989) correlated several variables with suicide rates over 75 SMSAs in the US. In the multiple regression, church membership was negatively associated with suicide rates. South (1987) found that suicide rates were associated with in and out migration, the population and population density, and the percentage of older persons in the SMSAs. Stark et al. (1983) found that church membership and changes in the population size, but not the percentage of Catholics, were associated with suicide rates. For the sixty largest SMSAs, both church membership and migration were significantly associated with suicide rates.

Counties

DeGrove (1977) found that the best correlates of white suicide rates in a sample of Florida counties were age, alcoholism death rates, admission rate to psychiatric facilities and the crime rate.

Kowalski et al. (1987) correlated a large set of social variables with suicide rates over the counties of the US. A large number of associations were observed, including divorce, living alone, migration, income inequality, education, family income, and urbanization. They then discovered that these associations were strong in the urban counties but not statistically significant for the rural counties.

In Wyoming, Pasewark and Fleer (1981) found that the counties' suicide rates were not associated with the population shift, rate of state hospital admissions, aid to families or unemployment rates, but the precise methodology used in this study is not clearly defined.

In Texas, Saenz (1989) found that no social variable predicted suicide rates in both metropolitan and non-metropolitan counties in both 1970 and 1980. The most consistent social correlates were the percentage of minorities, the population, and the suicide rate ten years earlier.

Pescosolido and Mendelsohn (1986) examined social correlates of suicide rates over the counties of America. The regression results varied by sex and age, but the divorce rate was a consistent positive correlate of the suicide rates. The effects of income, education, age, marital status, and intercounty migration varied with the age/sex group.

In a study of counties in the Northeastern part of the US, Wilkinson and Israel (1984) found that suicide rates were related to rurality, the proportion of elderly, the sex composition, poverty, divorce and migration.

Abbiati (1977) interviewed people in Maine counties with a high suicide rate and in counties with a low rate. The people in the high rate counties had less hope for the future, felt that succorance was less available to them, felt more of a demand for interpersonal giving, a greater demand for competence and a greater toleration of suicide. Thus, the general population in the high rate areas seems to have more of a suicidal personality.

States

Porterfield and Talbert (1948) found that suicide and homicide rates were negatively associated over the US. Suicide rates were positively correlated with the incidence of alcoholism and to an index of social well-being.

Li (1974) studied changes in the suicide rates in the US from 1950 to 1960 and found them to be negatively associated with changes in the percentage of blacks, and positively with changes in the percentages of broken families and unemployed.

Breault (1986) correlated several social variables with suicide rates over states and over counties. Per capita income, unemployment, the percentage of urban population, and females in the labor force were not associated with suicide in either counties or states. In contrast, divorce rates and church membership were associated with suicide rates in the same direction in both states and counties. At the county level, counties with a higher percentage of Roman Catholics had a lower suicide rate.

Sauer (1980) correlated a large number of social and mortality variables with suicide rates for those aged 35–74 over states and state economic areas, also taking into account race and sex. Suicide rates were positively and consistently associated with a number of mortality rates (for example, stomach cancer and chronic respiratory diseases) and elevation above sea level (for states only).

Medoff and Magaddino (1983) found that a number of variables were associated with the states' suicide rates, including the Roman Catholic proportion, unemployment, longitude, income, age, social class, and gun control laws. Zimmerman (1987a, 1987b) found that suicide rates in the states were associated with divorce, migration and population change, but not state expenditures on public welfare or for other purposes.

Lester (1986) found that the suicide rates of the states were associated with the divorce rate, the percentage of elderly, the percentage of blacks and interstate migration. These associations held up even after controls for the other variables using partial correlation coefficients. Baker and Lester (1986) found that the suicide rates in the states was not associated with the May/November birth ratio.

Sivak (1983) found that suicide rates in the states were associated with a number of variables, such as the cars-per-capita, alcohol consumption, and the accidental death rate. Lester (1988c) took these state data on traffic fatalities and examined the data set with suicide as the dependent variable. A factor analysis identified three factors of variables, two of which were correlated with suicide rates (age of drivers and per capita alcohol consumption) while one was not (traffic fatalities).

Davis (1980) examined just the states with many black residents. Their suicide rate was related to high rates of black immigrants, blacks living alone, blacks aged 20–34, and blacks with low education.

Stack has conducted a number of multiple regression studies of suicide over the states. Stack (1980a) found that suicide rates were associated with Catholicism and the divorce rate, but in the multiple regression the effect of Catholicism became negligible. Stack (1980b) found that divorce, percentage of blacks and income were significant predictors of suicide rates, while Stack (1980c) found that the percentage of black and interstate migration were significant. It is clear that the results depend upon which variables are placed into the multiple regression analysis.

Lester (1988b) tried to deal with the problem of the large number of social variables used in these studies by subjecting some two dozen of them to a factor analysis. He identified seven factors, two of which correlated with the suicide rate: social disintegration (with loadings from divorce, migration, alcohol consumption and church attendance) and east/west.

Studies Of Primitive Societies

Smith and Hackathorn (1982) found that the prevalence of suicide in primitive societies was associated with the importance of pride and shame, the expression of emotions, and the size of the community, as well as family, political, and economic integration (but not religious integration). Suicide was more common in societies with a stable agricultural pattern, restrained or open expression of emotions, and where shame and pride were important.

Studies Over Nations

Hass (1969) factor-analyzed 46 causes of death and socioeconomic variables for 72 nations in 1960. He found that one factor had suicide positively loaded and homicide negatively loaded on it, along with social variables which appear to measure economic development.

Vigderhous and Fishman (1977) found that the female suicide rate of nations was positively associated with the percentage of females in the labor force and the divorce rate and negatively with the birth rate and the male/female occupational similarity. (Associations with the female rate of higher education and female participation in professional occupations were not significant.) A path analysis showed that the divorce rate was the mediating factor in the associations of suicide rate with social variables. (The ratio of the male/female suicide rates and the male/female ratio for labor force participation over time were not consistently related in eleven nations studied.)

Breault and Barkey (1982) found that measures of religiosity (such as the percentage of books published which are religious), divorce and deaths due to political violence were associated with national suicide rates.

Conklin and Simpson (1987) found many social correlates of suicide rates over the nations of the world, including female participation in the labor force, the infant mortality rate, and urbanization. In a factor-analysis, they identified two clusters of variables which correlated with suicide rates (Islam and economic development) and two which did not (Christianity and the Eastern bloc).

Sainsbury et al. (1980) studied the social correlates of suicide rates in 1962 and also how changes in those social variables were related to changes in the suicide rates in the next ten years. Suicide rates were associated with the proportion of young people, the divorce rate, illegitimacy rates, female labor force participation, the murder rate and road accident mortality. Changes in the suicide rate in the next decade were associated with the levels of unemployment, divorce and the proportion of young people at the beginning of the period. Changes in the suicide rate were also associated with changes in most of the variables studied.

Lester (1989c) found that energy consumption and recent changes in status integration were not related to the suicide rates of nations, while population growth and changes in the distribution of occupations were.

None of these variables, however, predicted recent changes in the nations' suicide rates.

Rotton (1986) found that suicide rates in nations of the world were associated with the temperature, rainfall, life expectancy, literacy and energy consumption (but not Roman Catholicism). In the multiple regression analysis, temperature was still significantly associated with suicide rates.

Stack has reported several multiple regression analyses of suicide rates over samples of nations and identified significant correlates: the birth rate and female participation in the labor force (Stack, 1980d), immigration, percentage of elderly and female participation in the labor force (Stack, 1981a), divorce and the GNP per capita (Stack, 1981b), strike volume and size (but not duration) and female participation in the labor force (Stack, 1982a), percentage of elderly and GNP per capita (Stack, 1982b), GNP per capita and female participation in the labor force but not religious book production (Stack, 1983a), and religious book production, gender equality in the labor force and GNP per capita (Stack, 1983b).

Lester (1987b) found that suicide rates were associated with economic sex-equality over a sample of industrialized nations, but not with religious book production, the percentage of Roman Catholics, the gross national product per capita, or the divorce rate. In the same sample of nations, Lester (1988c) found that suicide rates were associated with the birth rate and females in the labor force, but not the gross national product per capita, the percentage of elderly, the percentage of urban and the population density. Lester (1989a) looked at seventeen social variables in eighteen nations of the world. He identified five factors and found that suicide rates were higher in nations with more elderly and with greater female economic equality. No social indicator in 1970 predicted the *absolute* increase in suicide rates by 1980, but scores on Factor V (rural/religious) predicted the *percentage* increase by 1980.

Other Nations

Australia

Burnley and McGlashan (1980) studied statistical divisions in Australia and found that the female suicide rate was higher where the proportion of adult males was higher, the ratio of married males lower and the proportion of apartments higher.

Burnley (1978) looked at correlates of suicide rates over local government areas in Sydney (Australia). Suicide rates were higher where the number of divorced persons was higher and where the proportion of married and widowed persons was lower. The suicide rates were positively related to the percentage of rented dwellings, but not to the proportion of unskilled or semi-skilled workers.

Koller and Cotgrove (1976) found that the attempted suicide rate in the districts of Hobart (Australia) was negatively associated with the percentage of white-collar workers and positively with the sex ratio and percentage of Australian-born residents. Attempted suicide rates were higher in general where there were fewer established families and more from the lower social classes (but were not associated with new families or ethnicity).

Belgium

Moens et al. (1988) correlated the suicide rate of 15–24-year-olds over the districts of Belgium and identified many correlates including emigration, immigration, illegitimacy, population density, older housing, divorce, and living alone (positively) and population growth, persons per room, no telephone, no running water, and larger households (negatively).

Canada

Jarvis et al. (1982) studied a large number of social correlates and found that rates of attempted suicide over census tracts in London (Canada) were associated with living arrangements and socioeconomic status, but not with blue-collarism and mobility. Jarvis et al. (1976) also studied self-injury in census tracts in London (Ontario). Self-injury rates were higher in the core areas of the city, where there many lower class people and the fewest owner-occupied dwellings.

Trovato (1986a) found that inter-region migration and education were related to suicide rates of the Canadian provinces, but not the percentage of Catholics. However, Trovato (1986b) found that the percentage of Catholics, divorce, and education, but not inter-region migration, were related to the provincial suicide rates. The results of multiple regressions obviously depend upon the variables placed in the analysis.

England

In England, Morgan (1980) correlated rates of attempted suicide with social variables over the electoral wards of Bristol. The attempted suicide rate was associated with overcrowding, immigrants, and lack of amenities. Morgan then interviewed attempted suicides and found that more did live in overcrowded quarters but they did not contain a larger proportion of immigrants. Morgan found that the suicide attempters from the central area of the city, as compared to those from other areas, were younger, lived more in bedsitters and crowded quarters away from relatives and had been in residence for less than six months. This study is unusual in combining a sociological and a psychological component in the research design.

Germany

In Heidelberg, Becker et al. (1987) found that attempted suicide by overdose was associated with the divorce rate and foreign residents (positively) and older residents and wage earners (negatively).

In Mannheim, Hafner et al. (1988) identified each attempted suicide by the street in which he or she lived and identified which streets had the highest rates. On two streets, one in 14 people attempted suicide in a ten-year period.

Hungary

Lester and Moksony (1989) compared social correlates of suicide rates over regions in both the US and Hungary. Of the variables examined, only divorce rates were associated with suicide rates in the same direction in both nations. Crime rates, education, and the sex ratio in the population were significantly associated with suicide in the US but not in Hungary.

India

Pandey (1986) presented data which I have analyzed to show that the suicide rate in Indian provinces was associated with population density and literacy but not with population, urbanization, poverty or per capita income (Lester and Agarwal, 1990). The proportion of men among the suicides was negatively associated with the population density.

Ireland

Daly et al. (1986, 1988) found that rates of attempted suicide in the electoral wards of Cork varied with overcrowding, renting from the government, and calls to community care services of all kinds, alcoholism, child neglect and housing difficulties (but not debts).

Japan

Arati and Murata (1986a, 1986b) studied the association of 22 social variables over 46 prefectures in Japan. No variable was associated with the female suicide rate both in 1970 and 1975. For the male suicide rate, only urban-rural residence was significant in both years. By age, rural residence predicted the male suicide rate for those aged 55–64, low income those aged 35–54, and age distribution for those aged 15–24.

New Zealand

In New Zealand, Collette et al. (1979) found that suicide and alcoholism had different social correlates over urban areas. Suicide rates were associated with a high incidence of living in temporary dwellings and the percentage of foreign born. They suggested that suicide rates were higher in areas where what they called normative integration was higher (such as the proportion living in temporary dwellings and the proportion of foreign-born) but were not associated with functional integration (population size, population density and the division of labor).

Sri Lanka

In Sri Lanka, Kearney and Miller (1983, 1985, 1988) found that the suicide rate of the districts was associated with population growth, migration, the sex ratio, and the percentage of Tamils. The female suicide rate was associated with the age at marriage of women. Over time, from 1955–1974, the suicide rate rose about 300 percent, and there was also rapid population growth, an expansion of education, growing unemployment, a later age for marriage and considerable internal migration.

Lester (1989b) compared his data for the states of America with the above data for Sri Lanka. He found similar correlates of suicide rates in both nations (birth rate, migration, and population density). Even the factor analyses of the social variables in the two nations gave similar results. Lester concluded that his earlier findings from the US did have some cross-national generality.

Time Series

In the US from 1933–1970 Lester (1987a) found that the suicide rate was associated with the birth rate, the unemployment rate and the divorce rate.

Stack has carried out several multiple regression studies on the suicide rate in the US and, among the correlates identified, are: unemployment, divorce and birth rates (Stack, 1981c) though divorce was less important before World War II, church attendance, unemployment and the size of the military (Stack, 1983c), church attendance, divorce and mothers' participation in the labor force (Stack, 1985a), divorce and mothers' participation in the labor force (Stack, 1987), and divorce and duration of unemployment (Stack and Haas, 1984).

Using time-series analyses over years, but for the period 1910–1931, Wasserman (1989) found significant effects from alcohol consumption, a business index and the previous year's suicide rates, but not from war. In a mixed design (yearly data for twenty states over an eleven year period) he also found an impact from a business index and the enactment of Prohibition but not from war.

Stewart (1980) found that black suicide rates in the US were predicted by riots and the rate of black females on public assistance times the black female birth rate (but not by demonstrations or black illegitimacy rates).

Wasserman (1983, 1984a, 1984b) carried out time-series analyses of the American suicide rate by month. He found a seasonal effect and significant effects from divorce, war, a business index and unemployment, but Presidential elections and the Korean and Vietnam wars had no impact on the suicide rates.

Australia

Hassan and Tan (1989) studied Australia from 1901–1985 and found that the male/female suicide rate ratio was predicted by urbanization, unemployment and, whichever was placed in the multiple regression, female participation in the labor force or the divorce/marriage ratio. War was not significant in the multiple regression. For the female suicide rate, urbanization and divorce/marriage were significant predictors while war and unemployment were not. For the male suicide rate, unemployment alone was a significant predictor.

Canada

Trovato (1986c) found that neither unemployment, immigration nor the percentage of elderly predicted Canadian suicide rates over time. However, Trovato (1987) found that divorce rates were significant predictors of the suicide rate, while unemployment, divorce and female participation in the labor force were not. Trovato (1987; Trovato and Jarvis, 1986) noted that the results differed for different sex-by-age groups and for different immigrant groups.

England

In England, Low et al. (1981) found in a multiple regression that the *number* of suicides from 1876–1975 was associated with the population size, volume of toxic gas produced, unemployment, the size of the armed forces and the consumption of spirits.

Finland

In Finland, Poikolainen (1983) found that suicide correlated with some measures of heavy alcohol use in a monthly time-series analysis, including alcoholic psychosis for both sexes, alcohol poisoning and pancreatitis (for males), but not alcoholism or liver cirrhosis for either sex.

France

In France, Souetre et al. (1987) found that the monthly suicide rate varied with unemployment, the birth rate, and weather variables (including daylight, sunlight and mean temperature).

Israel

In Israel from 1950–1981, Landau and Raveh (1987) found that the suicide rate was associated with many social variables—including, the marriage rate, divorce rate, homicide rate, psychiatric hospitalization rate, consumer price index, per capita income, and also the year (time trend). Once the time trend was controlled for by means of partial correlation coefficients, all of the significant associations disappeared.

Landau and Rahav (1989) then obtained monthly data on stress from surveys of the concern in Israelis about such things as the economy, security, terrorists and politics. They correlated these indices with monthly rates of male and female completed and attempted suicide. Completed suicides correlated positively with the stress index for men and negatively for women. Attempted suicide rates were not associated with stress for men or women.

Norway

Stack (1989) found that divorce (but not unemployment or religiosity) was associated with the suicide rate in Norway from 1951–1980.

Sweden

In Sweden, Hjortsjo (1987) correlated teenage suicide rates with various indices over time. The most consistent correlates were alcohol consumption in the population as a whole and unemployment in those aged 15–24. Criminality, abortion, and gonorrhea in those aged 15–24 were not associated with suicide rates in teenagers.

Differences Between Nations

Stack (1985b) found that the association between industrialization and suicide was inconsistent over eighteen nations. However, the correlation between the beta coefficient and the percentage of Protestants was positive indicating that in Protestant nations industrialization is positively associated with suicide rates. Stack and Danigelis (1985) found that the male/female suicide rate ratio correlated over time with modernization (that is, urbanization, industrialization and education) in fourteen of seventeen nations and increased during the Great Depression in eleven nations (versus decreasing in only one nation).

Pockets Of Violence

A different methodology was used by Lester (1985). He divided cities in the US according to whether they had high or low suicide rates and high or low homicide rates, giving four types of cities: violent, non-violent, outwardly violent and inwardly violent. He then explored the different social characteristics of each of these types of cities. Lester (1988a) carried out a similar study on the states of America.

Discussion

Obviously a great deal of research has been conducted using multivariate research designs. The results, however, seem to depend on the variables included in the analysis, whether the design is regional or time-series, which statistical techniques are used in the analysis (such as logarithmic transformation of the data), which units are used (nations, cities, etc.), and which time periods are chosen, among other factors. It is important, therefore, in the future to identify which correlates of suicide rates have generality, for it is the general results which will have most import for theories of suicide.

In seeking to make some sense of the complex results possible with multivariate analyses, Lester has gone against the trend and suggested the usefulness of factor-analysis (rather than multiple regression), for factor analysis groups the social indicators form into clusters (or, more accurately, factors) reducing the number of independent social variables in the analysis without researcher bias. Lester has found also that this technique eliminates some of the inconsistencies between the different studies, for correlations between suicide rates and factors remain more stable than correlations between suicide rates and individual social indicators.

REFERENCES

Abbiati, D. L. Suicide in Maine. *Suicide & Life-Threatening Behavior,* 1977, 7, 80–91.

Araki, S., & Murata, K. Social life factors affecting suicide in Japanese men and women. *Suicide & Life-Threatening Behavior,* 1986a, 16, 458–468.

Araki, S., & Murata, K. Factors affecting suicide in young, middle-aged and elderly men. *Journal of Biosocial Science,* 1986b, 18, 103–108.

Bainbridge, W. S. The religious ecology of deviance. *American Sociological Review,* 1989, 54, 288–295.

Baker, G., & Lester, D. Seasonal births, academic achievement and psychopathology (suicide and homicide) *Psychological Reports,* 1986, 59, 742.

Bankston, W. B., Allen, H. D., & Cunningham, D. S. Religion and suicide. *Social Forces,* 1983, 62, 521–528.

Becker, U., Bohmek, K., Breitmaier, J., Drisch, D., Schaefer, D. O., Kulessa, C. H., & Wahl, P. Self-poisoning in Heidelberg. *Crisis,* 1987, 8, 103–111.

Breault, K. D. Suicide in America. *American Journal of Sociology,* 1986, 92, 628–656.

Breault, K. D., & Barkey, K. A comparative analysis of Durkheim's theory of egoistic suicide. *Sociological Quarterly,* 1982, 23, 321–331.

Burnley, I. H. The ecology of suicide in an Australian metropolis. *Australian Journal of Social Issues,* 1978, 13(2), 91–103.

Burnley, I. H., & McGlashan, N. Variations of suicide within Australia. *Social Science & Medicine,* 1980, 14D, 215–224.

Collette, J., Webb, S. D., & Smith, D. L. Suicide, alcoholism and types of social integration. *Sociology & Social Research,* 1979, 63, 699–721.

Conklin, G. H., & Simpson, M. E. The family, socioeconomic development and suicide. *Journal of Comparative Family Studies,* 1987, 18, 99–111.

Daly, M., Conway, M., & Kelleher, M. J. Social determinants of self-poisoning. *British Journal of Psychiatry,* 1986, 148, 406–413.

Daly, M., Kelleher, M. J., Keohane, B., Linehan, C., & Lorenz, W. Deliberate self-poisoning. In S. D. Platt & N. Kreitman (Eds.) *Current Research on Suicide and Parasuicide.* Edinburgh: University of Edinburgh, 1989, 100–109.

Davis, R. Black suicide and the relational system. *Research in Race & Ethnic Relations,* 1980, 2, 43–71.

DeGrove, W. An assessment of community suicide risk. *Suicide & Life-Threatening Behavior,* 1977, 7, 100–109.

Gove, W. R., & Hughes, M. Re-examining the ecological fallacy. *Social Forces,* 1980, 58, 1157–1177.

Hafner, H., Veiel, H., & Welz, R. Epidemiology of suicide and attempted suicide. *Psychiatria Fennica,* 1988, 103–113.

Hass, M. Toward the study of biopolitics. *Behavioral Science,* 1969, 14, 257–280.

Hassan, R., & Tan, G. Suicide trends in Australia, 1901–1985. *Suicide & Life-Threatening Behavior,* 1989, 19, 362–380.

Hjortsjo, T. Suicide among children and young adults during the period 1961–1981. *Crisis,* 1987, 8(1), 30–36.

Jarvis, G. K., Ferrence, R. G., Johnson, F. G., & Whitehead, P. C. Sex and age patterns in self-injury. *Journal of Health & Social Behavior,* 1976, 17, 145–154.

Jarvis, G., Ferrence, R., Whitehead, P., & Johnson, F. The ecology of self-injury. *Suicide & Life-Threatening Behavior,* 1982, 12, 90–102.

Kearney, R. N., & Miller, B. D. Sex-differential patterns of internal migration in Sri Lanka. *Peasant Studies,* 1983, 10, 223–250.

Kearney, R. N., & Miller, B. D. The spiral of suicide and social change in Sri Lanka. *Journal of Asian Studies,* 1985, 45, 81–101.

Kearney, R. N., & Miller, B. D. Suicide and internal migration in Sri Lanka. *Journal of Asian & African Studies,* 1988, 23, 287–304.

Koller, K. M., & Cotgrove, R. C. Social geography of suicidal behavior in Hobart. *Australia & New Zealand Journal of Psychiatry,* 1976, 10, 237–242.

Kowalski, G. S., Faupel, C. E., & Starr, P. D. Urbanism and suicide. *Social Forces,* 1987, 66, 85–101.

Landau, S. F., & Raveh, A. Stress factors, social support and violence in Israeli society. *Aggressive Behavior,* 1987, 13, 67–85.

Landau, S. F., & Rahav, G. Suicide and attempted suicide. *Genetic, Social & General Psychology Monographs,* 1989, 115, 273–294.

Lester, D. Regional variation in suicide and homicide. *Suicide & Life-Threatening Behavior,* 1985, 15, 110–116.

Lester, D. The interaction of divorce, suicide and homicide. *Journal of Divorce,* 1986, 9, 103–109.

Lester, D. Social integration, economic hardship and rates of personal violence (suicide and homicide). *Psychological Reports,* 1987a, 60, 1306.

Lester, D. Cross-national correlations among religion, suicide and homicide. *Sociology & Social Research,* 1987b, 71, 103–104.

Lester, D. Pockets of violence. *Acta Psychiatrica Belgica,* 1988a, 88, 394–399.

Lester, D. A regional analysis of suicide and homicide rates in the USA. *Social Psychiatry & Psychiatric Epidemiology,* 1988b, 23, 202–205.

Lester, D. Rates of personal violence (suicide and homicide), traffic fatalities and alcohol consumption. *Psychological Reports,* 1988c, 63, 570.

Lester, D. Economic factors and suicide. *Journal of Social Psychology,* 1988d, 128, 245–248.

Lester, D. National suicide and homicide rates. *Social Science & Medicine,* 1989a, 29, 1249–1252.

Lester, D. A regional analysis of suicide. *Social Psychiatry & Psychiatric Epidemiology,* 1989b, 24, 143–145.

Lester, D. Association of population growth, technological development and social integration on rates of personal violence (suicide and homicide). *Psychological Reports,* 1989c, 64, 462.

Lester, D., & Agarwal, K. Ecological correlates of suicide and homicide in India and the USA. *Psychological Reports,* 1990, 67, 1374.

Lester, D., & Moksony, F. Ecological correlates of suicide in the US and Hungary. *Acta Psychiatrica Scandinavica,* 1989, 79, 498–499.

Li, W. L. Structural interpretation of suicide. *Sociological Focus,* 1974, 7(2), 89–100.

Low, A., Farmer, R., Jones, D., & Rhode, J. Suicide in England and Wales. *Psychological Medicine,* 1981, 11, 359–368.

Medoff, M. H., & Magaddino, J. P. Suicide and firearm control laws. *Evaluation Review,* 1983, 7, 357–372.

Moens, G. F., Haenen, W., & van de Voorde, H. Epidemiological aspects of suicide among the young in selected European countries. *Journal of Epidemiology & Community Health,* 1988, 42, 279–285.

Morgan, H. G. Social correlates of non-fatal deliberate self-harm. In R. Farmer & S. Hirsch (Eds.) *The Suicide Syndrome.* London: Croom Helm, 1980, 90–102.

Pandey, R. Suicide and social structure in India. *Social Defense,* 1986, 21(83), 5–29.

Pasewark, R. A., & Fleer, J. L. Suicide in Wyoming, 1960–1975. *Journal of Rural Community Psychology,* 1981, 2(1), 39–41.

Pescosolido, B., & Mendelsohn, R. Social causation or social construction of suicide? *American Sociological Review,* 1986, 51, 80–101.

Poikolainen, K. Heavy alcohol use and seasonal variation of suicide rates. *Psychiatria Fennica,* 1983, supplement, 93–96.

Porterfield, A. L., & Talbert, R. H. *Crime, suicide and social well-being in your state and city.* Fort Worth: Leo Potisham Foundation, 1948.

Rotton, J. Determinism redux. *Environment & Behavior,* 1986, 18, 346–368.

Saenz, R. Suicide and net migration in Texas counties 1970 and 1980. *Social Biology,* 1989, 36, 32–44.

Sainsbury, P., Jenkins, J., & Levey, A. The social correlates of suicide in Europe. In R. Farmer & S. Hirsch (Eds.) *The Suicide Syndrome.* London: Croom Helm, 1980, 38–53.

Sauer, H. I. Geographic patterns in the risk of dying and associated factors, ages 35–74 years. *Vital & Health Statistics,* 1980, series 3, #18 (PHS 80-1402).

Simpson, M. E., & Conklin, G. H. Socioeconomic development, suicide and religion. *Social Forces,* 1989, 67, 945–964.

Sivak, M. Society's aggression level as a predictor of traffic fatality rate. *Journal of Safety Research,* 1983, 14(3), 93–99.

Smith, D., & Hachathorn, L. Some social and psychological factors related to suicide in primitive societies. *Suicide & Life-Threatening Behavior,* 1982, 12, 195–211.

Souetre, E., Salvati, E., Belugov, J. L., Dovillet, P., Braccini, T., & Darcourt, G. Seasonality of suicides. *Journal of Affective Disorders,* 1987, 13, 215–225.

South, S. J. Metropolitan migration and social problems. *Social Science Quarterly,* 1987, 68, 3–18.

Stack, S. Religion and suicide. *Social Psychiatry,* 1980a, 15, 65–70.

Stack, S. The effects of marital dissolution on suicide. *Journal of Marriage & the Family,* 1980b, 42, 83–91.

Stack, S. The effects of interstate migration on suicide. *International Journal of Social Psychiatry,* 1980c, 26(1), 17–25.

Stack, S. Domestic integration and the rate of suicide. *Journal of Comparative Family Studies,* 1980d, 11, 249–260.

Stack, S. The effect of immigration on suicide. *Basic & Applied Social Psychology,* 1981a, 2, 205–218.

Stack, S. Suicide and religion. *Sociological Focus,* 1981b, 14, 207–220.

Stack, S. Divorce and suicide. *Journal of Family Issues,* 1981c, 2, 77–90.

Stack, S. The effect of strikes on suicide. *Sociological Focus,* 1982a, 15, 135–146.

Stack, S. Aging and suicide. *International Journal of Contemporary Sociology,* 1982b, 19(3/4), 125–138.

Stack, S. A comparative analysis of suicide and religiosity. *Journal of Social Psychology,* 1983a, 119, 285–286.

Stack, S. The effect of religious commitment on suicide. *Journal of Health & Social Behavior,* 1983b, 24, 362–374.

Stack, S. The effect of the decline in institutionalized religion on suicide. *Journal for the Scientific Study of Religion,* 1983c, 22, 239–252.

Stack, S. The effect of domestic/religious individualism on suicide. *Journal of Marriage & the Family,* 1985a, 47, 431–447.

Stack, S. Economic development, religion and lethal aggression. *Deviant Behavior,* 1985b, 6, 233–236.

Stack, S. The effects of female participation in the labor force on suicide. *Sociological Forum,* 1987, 2, 257–277.

Stack, S. The impact of divorce on suicide in Norway. *Journal of Marriage & the Family,* 1989, 51, 229–238.

Stack, S., & Danigelis, N. Modernization and the sex differential in suicide. *Comparative Social Research,* 1985, 8, 203–216.

Stack, S., & Haas, A. The effect of unemployment duration on national suicide rates. *Sociological Focus,* 1984, 17, 17–29.

Stark, R., Doyle, D., & Rushing, J. Beyond Durkheim. *Journal for the Scientific Study of Religion,* 1983, 22, 120–131.

Stewart, J. B. The political economy of black male suicides. *Journal of Black Studies,* 1980, 11, 249–261.

Trovato, F. Interprovincal migration and suicide in Canada, 1971–1978. *International Journal of Social Psychiatry,* 1986a, 32(1), 14–21.

Trovato, F. The relationship between marital dissolution and suicide. *Journal of Marriage & the Family,* 1986b, 48, 341–348.

Trovato, F. A time-series analysis of international migration and suicide mortality in Canada. *International Journal of Social Psychiatry,* 1986c, 32(2), 38–40.

Trovato, F. A longitudinal analysis of divorce and suicide in Canada. *Journal of Marriage & the Family,* 1987, 49, 193–203.

Trovato, F., & Jarvis, G. K. Immigrant suicide in Canada. *Social Forces,* 1986, 65, 433–457.

Vigderhous, G., & Fishman, G. Sociometric determinants of female suicide rates. *International Review of Modern Sociology,* 1977, 7, 199–211.

Wasserman, I. Political business cycles, Presidential elections and suicide and mortality patterns. *American Sociological Review,* 1983, 48, 711–720.

Wasserman, I. A longitudinal analysis of the linkage between suicide, unemployment and marital dissolution. *Journal of Marriage & the Family,* 1984a, 46, 853–859.

Wasserman, I. The influence of economic business cycles on US suicide rates. *Suicide & Life-Threatening Behavior,* 1984b, 14, 143–156.

Wasserman, I. The effects of war and alcohol consumption patterns on suicide. *Social Forces,* 1989, 68, 513–530.

Wenz, F. V. Ecological variation in self-injury behavior. *Suicide & Life-Threatening Behavior,* 1977, 7, 92–99.

Wilkinson, K., & Israel, G. Suicide and rurality in urban society. *Suicide & Life-Threatening Behavior,* 1984, 14, 187–200.

Zimmerman, S. L. States' public welfare expenditures as predictors of state suicide rates. *Suicide & Life-Threatening Behavior,* 1987a, 17, 271–287.

Zimmerman, S. L. State-level public policy as a predictor of individual and family well-being. *Women & Health,* 1987b, 12, 161–188.

Chapter 10

METEOROLOGICAL CORRELATES OF SUICIDAL BEHAVIOR

The 1990s witnessed very little research on the influence of weather on suicide rates, and the little research which did appear has not moved forward in methodological sophistication.

Weather

Time-Series Analyses

Dixon and Shulman (1983) found that the number of suicides per day in New York City from 1974 to 1979 was not predicted in a multiple regression analysis by the diurnal temperature, the hours of precipitation, the cloudiness, frontal passages, the departure of the temperature from normal or the change in temperature from the previous day.

In a study of completed suicide by month in two Californian SMSAs, Dooley et al. (1989) found no association between the mean temperature and the suicide rate. However, in a study of attempted suicides by month in prison inmates, Ganjavi et al. (1985) found that attempted suicides were more common in months when there were more geomagnetic disturbances (and less consistently with other atmospheric variables). (The incidence of attempted suicide was not related to the rate of assault on inmates.) In Hong Kong, Chiu (1988) found no association between the number of suicide attempts per month and the weather of the month (temperature, humidity, rainfall or sunshine).

Sanborn et al. (1970) found no association between the number of completed suicides and the average barometric pressure over 52 seasons. (The number of suicides was positively related to the number of psychiatric hospital admissions but not to the number of all other deaths.)

In a multiple regression analysis with many social variables included, Brenner (1983) found no association in England from 1954–1976 between the temperature in February and the suicide rate.

178

Regional Studies

Robbins et al. (1972) found that primitive societies living in colder climates had a higher suicide rate. Similarly, in modern nations the mean annual temperature and the suicide rate were negatively related. However, Lester (1988) found that annual temperature, precipitation, and sunshine were not related to suicides in fifteen industrialized nations.

In twelve European nations Thorson and Kasworm (1984) found that the amount of sunshine (but not the annual rainfall) in the capital was negatively associated with the national suicide rate.

Lester (1986b) found that the association between the suicide rates of American SMSAs and temperature (positive) and rainfall (negative) did not survive controls for latitude and longitude.

Day-By-Day Studies

Breuer et al. (1986) looked at the weather on days on which suicide attempts by poison occurred in Dusseldorf (Germany). They found that the incidence of suicide attempts was positively associated with stable and labile upslides, fog and thunderstorms, and warm air/upslides/drier weather and negatively associated with low pressure/toughs and subsidence/downside motions. The attempts were also more common in spring and less common in winter.

Latitude And Longitude

Lester (1980a) found that suicide rates were higher in the West of the USA for both sexes and almost all ages. Suicide rates were also higher in the North, but this was statistically significant only for the overall suicide rate and those aged 65–84. Lester (1980b) found that white suicide rates were higher in the West but that there was no significant North-South variation. Nonwhite suicide rates were higher in the North but there was no East-West variation. Lester (1987a) found that the variation of suicide rates over the country varied by method. Suicide by hanging was higher in the North while suicide by poisons and guns was higher in the West.

Looking at SMSAs, Lester (1986b, 1987b) found that the association between suicide rates and longitude (but not latitude) survived controls for the weather and for southernness.

Stanger et al. (1986) claimed that the suicide rates of American cities were lowest in the middle of the country but, using a complete sample of American cities, Lester (1986a) found no U-shaped distribution by longitude, but rather a westward increase.

In Australia Lester (1985) found that suicide rates were higher in the North but showed no East-West variation. In Canada, suicide rates were higher in the North and West as in the US.

Seiden (1984) found that youth suicide rates were higher in the less dense and the western states and that these states had also seen a greater rise in youth suicide rates from 1964 to 1978.

Discussion

As can be seen from this review, little research has appeared on the influence of meteorological variables on suicide, and our understanding of any association, if it exists, has not advanced at all.

REFERENCES

Brenner, M. H. Mortality and economic instability. *International Journal of Health Services,* 1983, 13, 563–620.

Breuer, W. M., Breuer, J., & Fischbach-Breuer, B. R. Social, toxicological and meteorological data on suicide attempts. *European Archives of Psychiatry & Neurological Sciences,* 1986, 235, 367–370.

Chiu, L. P. Do weather, day of week and address affect the rate of attempted suicide in Hong Kong? *Social Psychiatry & Psychiatric Epidemiology,* 1988, 23, 229–235.

Dixon, K. W., & Shulman, M. A statistical investigation into the relationship between meteorological parameters and suicide. *International Journal of Biometeorology,* 1983, 27, 93–105.

Dooley, D., Catalano, R., Rook, K., & Serxner, S. Economic stress and suicide. *Suicide & Life-Threatening Behavior,* 1989, 19, 321–336.

Ganjavi, O., Schell, B., Cachon, J. C., & Porporino, F. Impact of atmospheric conditions on occurrences of individual violence among Canadian penitentiary populations. *Perceptual & Motor Skills,* 1985, 61, 259–275.

Lester, D. Variation of suicide and homicide by latitude and longitude. *Perceptual & Motor Skills,* 1980a, 51, 1346.

Lester, D. Regional suicide rates and the hazards of minority status. *American Journal of Psychiatry,* 1980b, 137, 1469–1470.

Lester, D. Variation in suicide and homicide rates by latitude and longitude in the US, Canada and Australia. *American Journal of Psychiatry,* 1985, 142, 523–524.

Lester, D. Failure to find a U-shaped distribution of suicide rates of USA cities as a function of their longitude. *Psychological Reports,* 1986a, 59, 310.

Lester, D. Suicide and homicide rates. *Suicide & Life-Threatening Behavior*, 1986, 16, 356–359.

Lester, D. Regional variation of suicide and homicide rates by different methods. *Perceptual & Motor Skills*, 1987a, 64, 1074.

Lester, D. Regional variation in suicide and homicide. *Perceptual & Motor Skills*, 1987b, 64, 430.

Lester, D. Climate and personal violence (suicide and homicide). *Perceptual & Motor Skills*, 1988, 66, 602.

Robbins, M. C., DeWalt, B. R., & Pelto, P. J. Climate and behavior. *Journal of Cross-Cultural Psychology*, 1972, 3, 331–344.

Sanborn, D. E., Casey, T. M., & Niswander, G. D. Suicide. *Diseases of the Nervous System*, 1970, 31, 702–704.

Seiden, R. H. Death in the West. *Western Journal of Medicine*, 1984, 140, 969–973.

Stanger, S. R., Cullinane, J. M., & Hicks, R. A. Longitude and suicide rates of certain US cities. *Psychological Reports*, 1986, 58, 598.

Thorson, J. A., & Kasworm, C. Sunshine and suicide. *Death Education*, 1984, 8, supplement, 125–136.

Chapter 11

THE EFFECTS OF
SOCIAL RELATIONSHIPS ON SUICIDE

Since suicidal behavior typically takes place in an interpersonal context, the study of the social relationships of the suicidal person should be an important area of study. This chapter reviews recent research on this topic.

Children

Kozak and Gibbs (1979) found that completed suicides were less likely to have dependent children than the general population. The suicide rate for married people with dependent children was less than the rate for married people without dependent children, especially for those 35 and older. If very young children were present (0–6 years of age), the suicide rates were highest for those aged 14–24 and age 45 and over, (that is, deviant in age). However, married suicides were found to have more overall dependents than the average household.

Wenz (1979) studied families in which one parent was suicidal. The suicidal parents with more children under the age of 18 and with a higher children/adult ratio were rated as less suicidal. The spacing of the children was not related to the parents' suicidality.

Birtchnell (1981) found that females who attempted suicides more often had more than three children (especially if they had experienced early loss)—more often than non-suicidal psychiatric patients. In Portugal, de Castro and Martins (1987) found that women with children had a lower suicide rate than childless women. The suicide rate in women with more than five children was lower than the suicide rate for those with five or fewer children.

Linehan et al. (1983) found that psychiatric patients who had attempted suicide had fewer children than those who had only suicidal ideation.

Wenz (1982, 1984) found that the degree of suicidal preoccupation in parents who had attempted suicide was negatively related to the number of children but not related to the spacing between the children. A history of suicidal ideation in heads of households was positively related both to the household density and loneliness scale scores.

In contrast, Adam et al. (1980) found that attempted suicides and general medical patients had a similar number of children.

Couples

Bonnar and McGee (1977) looked at married couples in which the wife had attempted or threatened suicide and couples in which the wife was non-suicidal. The more seriously suicidal the wife, the poorer the marital communication as measured by an inventory and by an interview.

Canetto et al. (1989) found that, in couples where one had attempted suicide, the suicidal person was the more disturbed of the two. The suicidal partner did not differ from the non-suicidal partner on a measure of mutuality from the Rorschach ink-blot test, but the couples as a whole scored worse than the norms for a test of marital communication.

Balck and Reimer (1985) found that couples in which one member had attempted suicide had more destructive conflicts than comparison couples. They were more likely, for example, to avoid discussion, came to agreement less often, and often fled from the home. After the suicide attempt, 40 percent of the couples separated and a further 25 percent experienced a worsened relationship.

Birtchnell (1981) found that female attempted suicides more often had very bad marital relationships (with much quarreling, one partner drinking heavily, and an unfaithful husband) than non-suicidal psychiatric patients. The suicide attempters were also more dependent, immature, aggressive, and diagnosed as depressed or alcohol abusers.

Effects of Attempting Suicide on Social Relationships

Van Tol (1978) found that attempted suicides showed a reduction in loneliness in follow-up more often than an increase, and a similar beneficial effect in their relationship with their partner.

Family Patterns

Williams and Lyons (1976) compared normal families with families having an adolescent female attempted suicide. The normal families showed less conflict when discussing a problem and showed more effective talking, a better final consensus, and more specificity in their communications (that is, talking to a specific person). The normal families made more positive supporting statements and fewer non-supportive statements.

Abraham (1978) studied families with a teenager who had attempted suicide, had a psychosomatic disorder or was normal. In laboratory tasks, the suicidal families showed less spontaneous agreement, especially between the father and others, and the father's opinion carried less weight. The suicidal families described themselves on a family description questionnaire as less effective, with a greater discrepancy between their description of their real family and the ideal family. However, the suicidal families did not show more rejection of their teenager or a tendency to make more negative or positive statements about each other.

Keitner et al. (1987) gave the family members of depressed patients who had previously attempted suicide and those who had not done so, a family assessment device which assessed six areas of family functioning (such as problem solving, affective responsiveness, and roles). The two groups of family members did not differ. When the patients were given the test, the suicide attempters rated their families as worse on problem-solving, roles, and general functioning. Thus, the suicide attempters perceive their families as functioning worse, but the other family members do not.

In Yugoslavia, Pancic et al. (1983) found that the families of suicide attempters were less cohesive than the families of completed suicides and non-suicides. Both types of suicides had families that were less warm and accepting as compared to the families of non-suicides.

Wood and Wassenaar (1989) found that Indian suicide attempters in South Africa scored worse on all scales of the Family Assessment Device as compared to medical patients (matched only for age, sex and social class), including problem-solving, communication, role difficulties, affective involvement, behavior control and general functioning. For the attempters, their suicidal intent was not related to scores on the test.

Hostility in Bystanders and Significant Others

Mann (1981) found fifteen cases where a crowd was present when a suicide was about to jump off a building. In four cases, the crowd baited the jumper. In a further sample of twenty-one cases, ten involved the crowd baiting the jumper. Those situations involving baiting tended to be more often in the summer, with a large crowd, at night, when the episode continued for a long time and when the jumper was below the twelfth floor.

Wasserman (1989) interviewed the significant others of attempted suicides and found that 20 had expressed death wishes verbally to the patient, another 27 percent expressed such wishes to others, 20 percent simply turned away from the patient (by not going home, for example), and 5 percent gave orders not to resuscitate the patient. Thus, a great deal of hostility was evident in these significant others.

Institutional Disruption

Clements et al. (1985) found that, of nine suicides among psychiatric patients, six had their therapist on vacation or recently transferred, thereby interrupting the therapeutic relationship, and four were about to be discharged.

Gorenc (1985; Gorenc and Bruner, 1985) studied ten hospitals in Bavaria during two eras and found that the completed suicide rate was associated with the size of the hospital, the physician/patient ratio and forced admissions for at least one of the periods. In one report, the rate of attempted suicide was associated with the size of the hospital and the number of patient admissions. In the other report that rate of attempted suicide was associated with the physician-patient ratio, the nurse-patient ratio and forced admissions. (The more staff, the higher the rate of attempted suicide.)

Interpersonal Conflict

Krauss and Tesser (1971) classified suicides in primitive societies as precipitated by impersonal causes (such as sickness) or by interpersonal frustrations. Interpersonal-frustration suicide rates in primitive societies correlated with four components of Naroll's thwarting disorientation— frequency of warfare, incidence of wife beating, men's divorce freedom and defiant homicide. The impersonal suicide rate was correlated only with men's divorce freedom. (Krauss and Krauss [1968] reported that primitive societies with high levels of thwarting disorientation in general had higher suicide rates overall.)

Riger (1971) studied prisoners who had attempted suicide. Those experiencing more recent loss (by death or divorce) made more severe attempts. (The earlier their separation from mother, the less severe the suicide attempt.)

Griffiths et al. (1986) found that adolescent suicide attempters had experienced more interpersonal conflict and stressful events and shown more problem behavior than medical controls, but no more than patients in outpatient counseling. However, the suicide attempters did have the most intrapsychic problems. Compared to the counseling group, the suicide attempters showed more problem behaviors in the area of drug and alcohol use and missing class (but not anger), more intrapsychic problems such as blaming others more, feeling more hopeless, fear, and low self-worth, and having a more negative attitude toward life, and more interpersonal problems with their father and with harmony/love in the home.

Wasserman (1988) found that attempted suicides had experienced more separations from their partners (but not deaths of significant others) and more relationship problems than other psychiatric patients (but they did not differ in psychiatric diagnosis or prior psychiatric care).

Aldridge and Dallos (1986) found that in families coming for family therapy, if a member of the family was suicidal, there was more likely to be someone about to leave the family and the family was more likely to have a tradition of symptoms at times of conflict and to prevent breakups.

Fieldsend and Lowenstein (1981) found that women attempted suicide more often after quarrels and infidelity in the preceding two days while men attempted more after separation. Interpersonal events were less common in the older attempters (over 36 years of age) as was prior inpatient psychiatric treatment. The attempts of the older people seemed to be, therefore, less interpersonally motivated.

Hanigan (1987) studied college students who had experienced the breakup of a romance in the last nine months. Those who had suicidal thoughts had been involved with the lover for a longer period, the attachment was stronger and the breakup was not initiated by them. They had fewer family members as significant others and more conflict in their families, confided in friends less (especially because of a fear of rejection), and found their support less helpful. They did not differ in the number of friends or whether they found their friendships satisfying.

Interpersonal Skills

Asarnow et al. (1987) found that adolescent suicide attempters did not differ from non-suicidal inpatients in interpersonal skills.

Pet Ownership

Helsing and Monk (1985) found no differences in pet ownership between suicides, those dying of other causes and living controls.

Role Relationships

Palmer and Humphrey (1977) compared male completed suicides, murderers and psychiatric patients for role reciprocity and role loss. The suicides had high role reciprocity and high role loss. The murderers had low role reciprocity. The psychiatric patients had high role reciprocity but low role loss.

Social Integration

Bille-Brahe and Wang (1985) found that attempted suicides were less well socially integrated (in their community, their work and their family/friends) than the general population.

Dooley et al. (1989) found that the extent of social supports was negatively related to the presence of suicidal ideation in community samples of both wage earners and non-principal wage earners. Harter and Marold (1987) found that sixth, seventh and eighth graders with suicidal ideation had less social support than non-suicidal students.

Lyons (1985) compared attempted suicides with non-suicidal citizens and found them to belong to fewer organizations and to have less help available to them in times of crisis. They also had more negative and less positive affect, felt less satisfaction in their personal and financial situation (but not in the areas of time, family, government and physical environment), and were of lower social class.

Topol and Reznikoff (1982) found that adolescent suicide attempters reported more total, family and peer problems than psychiatric and normal controls and also that they were less likely to have a confidant.

Hafner et al. (1988) found that attempted suicide had smaller social networks than did normal controls, and received less crisis support and psychological support from their network. The groups did not differ in contact frequency or everyday support. The attempters had not experienced more suicide attempts in their social networks overall, but they did experience more in their kin while the normal controls experienced more in non-kin.

Hart et al. (1988) found that attempted suicides (with or without a psychiatric diagnosis) had less adequate social integration and availability of attachments (and life satisfaction) as compared to normal controls. Thus, their social networks were impaired. After a six-week follow-up period, the social networks of the disturbed attempters had not improved while those of the non-disturbed attempters had improved.

Tousignaut and Hanigan (1986) found that students who had been seriously suicidal recently had social support networks with more aggravating people and fewer family members in them than non-suicidal students. (They did not differ in having college friends in their networks.) The groups did not differ in having best friends, confidants, or the amount of social support received (except from mothers). The suicidal students reported more dissatisfaction with their social networks, particularly because they desired more to cope with their problems by themselves.

Mullis and Byers (1987), however, found no differences between attempted suicides and non-suicidal psychiatric controls in recent loss, total social network, or functional support. The suicide attempters were less active religiously.

Jarvis et al. (1976) hypothesized that stress led to conformity if the person was subject to strong and internal social controls, but deviance if social and internal controls were weak. If the person was socially well integrated, then innovative strategies (such as neurosis or attempted suicide) were more likely to be tried. If the person was poorly integrated socially, then completed suicide, psychosis or drug abuse was more likely.

Pattison et al. (1979) studied social networks and found that the average person had 22 people in his or her network. Psychiatric patients had 15, and suicide attempters about 14. The suicide attempters appeared to be especially deficient in relatives and co-workers, but less so in family and friends.

Budner and Kumler (1973) found that college students with suicidal ideation had fewer friends who were interested in their problems, were more sociable, and saw themselves as more capable of making friends. They had more difficulty talking to their parents however.

For elderly suicides, Barraclough (1971) found that they were more often living alone than the general elderly population. Furthermore, the suicide rate of the elderly in English boroughs was related to the incidence of the elderly living alone. Bock and Webber (1972) found that the elderly male suicide rate was higher in the unmarried, those with absent relatives, those with no organizational memberships, and those who were lower class.

McIntire et al. (1977) found that suicidal adolescents who improved with time were more likely to have experienced an improved family life (due to finding a good foster home or having parents understand them better).

Sports Participation

Juhasz and Matuzsinka (1978) found that attempted suicides and neurotics both participated less in club sports than control subjects. The attempted suicides participated less often in individual sports and club sports (and in less aggressive sports) than the neurotics, but more in social sports. When they did participate, the attempters were motivated more by desires for interpersonal relationships while the neurotics had more desire for physical training. (The groups did not differ in participation in school gymnastics.)

Divorce

Jacobson and Portuges (1978) studied a group of people seen at a crisis service and found that those who were separated were more suicidal. Suicidal ideation was related to the recency of the separation, but not to merely discussing a future separation. For those recently separated, suicidal ideation was stronger in those who were vacillating and whose spouses were attacking them verbally, but not to emotional dependence, realistic dependence or events increasing the likelihood of divorce.

Suicide in Peers

Overholser et al. (1989) surveyed high school students and found that 27 percent of the boys and 50 percent of the girls knew a student who had attempted suicide, and 21 percent of the boys and 48 percent of the girls knew a student who had talked about suicide. Angst et al. (1979) found that 2.8 percent of the deceased first-degree relatives of schizoaffective patients were suicides.

Dunner et al. (1976) compared unipolar and bipolar affective disorder patients and found no significant differences in the incidence of completed suicide in first-degree relatives. Rao (1973) found no differences in unipolar and bipolar patients in the incidence of suicide in their parents. Marks and Riley (1976) found no association in students between knowing someone who had attempted suicide and having suicidal ideation. In contrast, Budner and Kumler (1973) found that college students who had suicidal ideation had more relatives and friends who had completed or attempted suicide. Reynolds et al. (1975) surveyed residents in Los Angeles and found no differences by ethnic group in personal encounters with suicide in friends and relatives.

Rao (1973) found that psychiatric patients with recurrent episodes of endogenous depression more often had parents who had completed suicide than had patients with single episodes of depression, but no differences were found for suicide in their siblings.

Haberman and Baden (1978) studied suicides and homicide victims in New York and claimed to find that suicides ran in families and that homicides ran in families.

Suicide Pacts

Fishbain and Aldrich (1985; Fishbain et al., 1984) found that 0.0068% of suicides in Dade County (FL) involved suicide pacts. Those involved in the suicide pacts were most often spouses, more often unemployed males, less depressed, with less recent loss or financial problems, more often left suicide notes, more often were found by strangers, with the suicidal act in the early hours of the days, more often under the influence of alcohol, less often in the home, older with the children gone from the home, and with a suicide note which mentions guilt and depression less often. Compared to the pacts involving spouses, the pacts involving lovers were more often of younger people, with a lesser history of depression, with more often love given as the reason for the suicide in the note, and took place less often in the home.

Wickett (1989) documented 97 cases of double suicides involving spouses in the US from 1980–1987. Two-thirds of these were mercy killings followed by suicide and one-third double suicides. In the typical cases, the wife or both were suffering and the husband was the instigator. The couple was typically not living with children and pets were also killed. The method used was firearms, and the couple felt exhausted and helpless and had a fear of parting and institutionalization. It was very rare for the wife to be the instigator, and usually the husband could not bear his wife's suffering or life without her. In the double suicides, the decision was more mutual and less impulsive, and there was less despondency. The couples were more often middle class and left a suicide note.

Survivors of Suicides

Demi (1979) found that widows of suicides had a higher incidence of past suicidal behavior compared to widows of accident and sudden death victims. They did not differ in their current suicidal ideation, however.

Discussion

The research into the social relationships of the suicidal individual has been disappointing. There has not been as much attention given to this topic as there has to other topics, such as the biochemistry of suicide or the association of psychiatric disturbance with suicide. Yet, there has been an increasing focus on the dysfunctional family in general in recent years, especially among psychotherapists, and this perspective merits greater attention in the study of suicide. Given that the suicidal individual may be psychiatrically disturbed, the statistically rare decision to complete suicide will probably be affected by the interpersonal relationships of the individual and his or her pattern of interpersonal functioning.

REFERENCES

Abraham, Y. Patterns of communication versus rejection in families of suicidal adolescents. *Dissertation Abstracts International,* 1978, 38A, 4669.

Adam, K. S., Bouckoms, A., & Scarr, G. Attempted suicide in Christchurch. *Australian & New Zealand Journal of Psychiatry,* 1980, 14, 305–314.

Aldridge, D., & Dallos, R. Distinguishing families where suicidal behavior is present from families where suicidal behavior is absent. *Journal of Family Therapy,* 1986, 8, 243–252.

Angst, J., Felder, W., & Lohmeyer, B. Schizoaffective disorder. *Journal of Affective Disorders,* 1979, 1, 139–153.

Asarnow, J. R., Carlson, G. A., & Guthrie, D. Coping strategies, self-perceptions, hopelessness, and perceived family environments in depressed and suicidal children. *Journal of Consulting & Clinical Psychology,* 1987, 55, 361–366.

Balck, F. B., & Reimer, C. C. Suicide and partnership. In P. Pichot, P. Berner, R. Wolf, & K. Thau (Eds.) *Psychiatry: The State of the Art, Volume 1.* New York: Plenum, 1985, 981–986.

Barraclough, B. M. Suicide in the elderly. In D. W. P. Kay & A. Walk (Eds.) *Recent Developments in Psychogeriatrics.* London: RMPA, 1971, 87–97.

Bille-Brahe, U., & Wang, A. G. Attempted suicide in Denmark. *Social Psychiatry,* 1985, 20, 163–170.

Birtchnell, J. Some familial and clinical characteristics of female suicidal psychiatric patients. *British Journal of Psychiatry,* 1981, 138, 381–390.

Bock, E. W., & Webber, I. Social status and relational system of elderly suicides. *Life-Threatening Behavior,* 1972, 2, 145–159.

Bonnar, J. W., & McGee, R. K. Suicidal behavior as a form of communication in married couples. *Suicide & Life-Threatening Behavior,* 1977, 7, 7–16.

Budner, S., & Kumler, F. Correlates of suicidal ideation. American Association of Suicidology, Houston, 1973.

Canetto, S. S., Feldman, L. B., & Lupei, R. L. Suicidal persons and their partners. *Suicide & Life-Threatening Behavior,* 1989, 19, 237–248.

Clements, C., Bonacci, D., Yerevanian, B., Privitera, M., & Kiehne, L. Assessment of suicide risk in patients with personality disorder and major affective disorder. *Quality Review Bulletin,* 1985, 11(5), 150–154.

de Castro, E. F., & Martins, I. The role of female autonomy in suicide among Portugese women. *Acta Psychiatrica Scandinavica,* 1987, 75, 337–343.

Demi, A. Mental health of widows after sudden death. *Proceedings of the 10th International Congress for Suicide Prevention.* Ottawa: IASP, 1979, 230–237.

Dooley, D., Catalano, R., Rook, K., & Serxner, S. Economic stress and suicide. *Suicide & Life-Threatening Behavior,* 1989, 19, 337–351.

Dunner, D., Gershon, E., & Goodwin, F. Heritable factors in the severity of affective illness. *Biological Psychiatry,* 1976, 11, 31–42.

Fieldsend, R., & Lowenstein, E. Quarrels, separations and infidelity in the two days preceding self-poisoning episodes. *British Journal of Medical Psychology,* 1981, 54, 349–352.

Fishbain, D. A., & Aldrich, T. E. Suicide pacts. *Journal of Clinical Psychiatry,* 1985, 46, 11–15.

Fishbain, D., D'Achilee, L., Barsky, S., & Aldrich, T. A controlled study of suicidal pacts. *Journal of Clinical Psychiatry,* 1984, 45, 154–157.

Gorenc, K. D. Attempted suicide in Bavarian mental hospitals. In P. Pichot, P. Berner, R. Wolf, & K. Thau (Eds.) *Psychiatry: The State of the Art, Volume 1.* New York: Plenum, 1985, 933–938.

Gorenc, K. D., & Bruner, C. Suicidal behavior among patients in Bavarian mental hospitals. *Acta Psychiatrica Scandinavica,* 1985, 71, 468–478.

Griffiths, J. K., Farley, O. W., & Fraser, M. W. Indices of adolescent suicide. *Journal of Independent Social Work,* 1986, 1(1), 49–63.

Haberman, P. W., & Baden, M. M. *Alcohol, Other Drugs and Violent Death.* New York: Oxford University Press, 1978.

Hafner, H., Veiel, H., & Welz, R. Epidemiology of suicide and suicide attempts. *Psychiatria Fennica,* 1988, 103–123.

Hanigan, D. Social networks and social support in a group of young adults with serious suicidal thoughts. In R. Yufit (Ed.) *Proceedings of the 20th Annual Conference.* Denver: AAS, 1987, 176–178.

Hart, E. E., Williams, C. L., & Davidson, J. A. Suicidal behavior, social networks and psychiatric diagnosis. *Social Psychiatry & Psychiatric Epidemiology,* 1988, 23, 222–228.

Harter, S., & Marold, B. Familial values and adolescent suicidal ideation. In R. Yufit (Ed.) *Proceedings of the 20th Annual Conference.* Denver: AAS, 1987, 288–290.

Helsin, K. J., & Monk, M. Dog and cat ownership among suicide and matched controls. *American Journal of Public Health,* 1985, 75, 1223–1224.

Jacobson, G. F., & Portuges, S. H. Relation of marital separation and divorce to suicide. *Suicide & Life-Threatening Behavior,* 1978, 8, 217–224.

Jarvis, G. K., Ferrence, R. G., Johnson, F. G., & Whitehead, P. C. Sex and age patterns in self-injury. *Journal of Health & Social Behavior,* 1976, 17, 145–154.

Juhasz, P., & Matuzsinka, F. Practice of sports in suicide prevention. In V. Aalberg (Ed.) *Proceedings of the 9th International Congress for Suicide Prevention.* Helsinki: Finnish Association for Mental Health, 1978, 435–438.

Keitner, G. I., Miller, I. W., Fruzzetti, A. E., Epstein, N. B., Bishop, D. S., & Norman, W. H. Family functioning and suicidal behaviors in psychiatric inpatients with major depression. *Psychiatry,* 1987, 50, 242–255.

Kozak, C. M., & Gibbs, J. O. Dependent children and suicide of married parents. *Suicide & Life-Threatening Behavior,* 1979, 9, 67–75.

Krauss, H. H., & Krauss, B. J. Cross-cultural study of the thwarting-disorientation theory of suicide. *Journal of Abnormal Psychology,* 1968, 73, 353–357.

Krauss, H. H., & Tesser, A. Social contexts of suicide. *Journal of Abnormal Psychology,* 1971, 78, 222–228.

Linehan, M. M., Goodstein, J., Nielsen, S., & Chiles, J. Reasons for staying alive when you're thinking of killing yourself. *Journal of Consulting & Clinical Psychology,* 1983, 51, 276–286.

Lyons, M. Observable and subjective factors associated with attempted suicide in later life. *Suicide & Life-Threatening Behavior,* 1985, 15, 168–183.

Mann, L. The baiting crowd in episodes of threatened suicide. *Journal of Personality & Social Psychology,* 1981, 41, 703–709.

Marks, A., & Riley, C. Test of Goffman's hypothesis of familiarity and deviance. *Psychological Reports,* 1976, 39, 420–422.

McIntire, M., Angle, C., Wikoff, R., & Schlicht, M. Recurrent adolescent suicidal behavior. *Pediatrics,* 1977, 60, 605–608.

Mullis, M. R., & Byers, P. H. Social support in suicidal inpatients. *Journal of Psychosocial Nursing,* 1987, 25(4), 16–19.

Overholser, J. C., Hemstreet, A. H., Spirito, A., & Vyse, S. Suicide awareness programs in the schools. *Journal of the American Academy of Child & Adolescent Psychiatry,* 1989, 28, 925–930.

Palmer, S., & Humphrey, J. Suicide and homicide. *Omega,* 1977, 8, 45–58.

Pancic, I., Skenderovic, F., & Unger, P. Is the suicidal bringing up the social peculiarity of the most suicidal town of Yugoslavia? In J. P. Soubrier & J. Vedrinne (Eds.) *Depression and Suicide.* Paris, Pergamon, 1983, 183–188.

Pattison, E. M., Llamas, R., & Hurd, G. Social network mediation of anxiety. *Psychiatric Annals,* 1979, 9(9), 56–67.

Rao, A. V. Affective illness in first degree relatives, parental loss and family jointness in depressive disorders. *British Journal of Psychiatry,* 1973, 122, 601–602.

Reynolds, D. K., Kalish, R., & Farberow, N. L. A cross-ethnic study of suicide attitudes and expectations in the US. In N. L. Farberow (Ed.) *Suicide in Different Cultures.* Baltimore: University Park Press, 1975, 35–50.

Rieger, W. Suicide attempts in a Federal prison. *Archives of General Psychiatry,* 1971, 24, 532–535.

Topol, P., & Reznikoff, M. Perceived peer and family relationships, hopelessness and loss of control as factors in adolescent suicide attempts. *Suicide & Life-Threatening Behavior,* 1982, 12, 141–150.

Tousignaut, M., & Hanigan, D. Social network and social support of suicidal young adults. In R. Cohen-Sandler (Ed.) *Proceedings of the 19th Annual Meeting.* Denver: AAS, 1986, 66–68.

Van Tol, D. The influence of the suicide attempt on emotional relationships. In H. Z. Winnick & L. Miller (Eds.) *Aspects of Suicide in Modern Civilization.* Jerusalem: Academic, 1978, 168–172.

Wasserman, D. Separations. *Crisis,* 1988, 9, 49–63.

Wasserman, D. Passive euthanasia in response to attempted suicide. *Acta Psychiatrica Scandinavica,* 1989, 79, 460–467.

Wenz, F. Family constellation factors, depression, and parent suicidal potential. *American Journal of Orthopsychiatry,* 1979, 49, 164–167.

Wenz, F. Family constellation factors and parent suicide potential. *Journal of Nervous & Mental Disease,* 1982, 170, 270–274.

Wenz, F. Household crowding, loneliness and suicide ideation. *Psychology,* 1984, 21(2), 25–29.

Wickett, A. *Double exit.* Eugene, OR: Hemlock Society, 1989.

Williams, C., & Lyons, C. M. Family interaction and adolescent suicidal behavior. *Australian & New Zealand Journal of Psychiatry,* 1976, 10, 243–252.

Wood, N., & Wassenaar, D. R. Family characteristics of Indian parasuicide patients. *South African Journal of Psychology,* 1989, 19, 172–184.

Chapter 12

METHODOLOGICAL ISSUES

Little attention was paid in the 1980s to general methodological issues in suicide research. The major problem raised was concerned with the validity of sociological studies of regional variations in suicide rates.

Methodological Problems with Ecological Studies

Odland (1988) noted that studies of regions fail to take into account the fact that social variables in neighboring regions are similar because of their geographic proximity. Therefore, regression analyses, which are based on an assumption of independence of the data points, are invalid. Lester (1989) showed that, indeed, suicide rates across the states of the US are spatially autocorrelated.

Lester and Stack (1989) explored the effect of the method for choosing nations for cross-national studies. They found that the gross national product per capita and the quality of life were associated with suicide rates of nations for a total national sample of all those with available data and for a random sample from each region of the world where each region provided the appropriate proportion of nations given the number of nations in each region. However, for European nations and for the industrialized nations of the world, neither variable was significantly associated with the suicide rates of the nations. Thus, the critical dimension here appears to be whether a world sample (chosen by any means) or a reduced sample of developed nations is chosen.

Opportunity-Based Suicide Rates

Drawing an analogy from criminology where the use of opportunity-based crime rates has been proposed, Lester (1988) suggested basing suicide rates on opportunities. For example, suicide rates using firearms could be expressed as suicides per gun rather than per capita of the population.

Areas of Research Which Have Been Neglected

Lester (1981–1982) suggested that suicidologists have neglected the more speculative areas of research, such as those involving life after death. Suicidologists might investigate suicide through mediums or, more importantly, though near-death experiences.

Discussion

In the 1970s, the validity of using attempted suicides as a means for finding out about completed suicides was debated (Lester, 1983). This debate disappeared in the 1980s, but it is far from clear whether there was a general consensus reached and what the consensus was. Perhaps the debate will resurface in the 1990s?

REFERENCES

Lester, D. Spiritualism and suicide. *Omega,* 1981–1982, 12, 45–49.

Lester, D. Opportunity-based suicide rates. *Psychological Reports,* 1988, 63, 984.

Lester, D. The spatial autocorrelation of states' suicide and homicide rates. *Perceptual & Motor Skills,* 1989, 68, 218.

Lester, D., & Stack, S. Bias resulting from the choice of sample and results of cross-national analyses of suicide rates. *Quality & Quantity,* 1989, 23, 221–223.

Odland, J. *Spatial Autocorrelation.* Beverly Hills: Sage, 1988.

Chapter 13

THE SUICIDAL ACT

S everal studies have explored the circumstances of the suicidal act and the events in the days and weeks leading up to it.

Interrupting the Suicidal Act

Steer et al. (1987) found that attempted suicides who were interrupted during the act were more likely to complete suicide subsequently than those not interrupted. The interrupted attempters had taken fewer precautions against discovery and were more often non-white and non-single, but they did not differ in sex, age, overall suicidal intent, education, substance abuse, suicide in relatives, or diagnosis.

Intoxication and Suicide

Honkanen and Visuri (1976) found that attempted suicides had higher levels of blood alcohol than other injury victims. Hawton et al. (1989) found that men, those aged 26–50 and alcoholic attempters were more likely to be intoxicated at the time of the attempt than female, older and non-alcoholic attempters. Virkkunen and Alha (1971) found that alcohol was involved in 15 percent of Finnish completed suicides. Those intoxicated were more likely to be male, less likely to be widowed, and less often used hanging. Owens and Jones (1988) found that male suicide attempters were more likely to have drunk alcohol before the act than women (and also were less likely to attempt suicide during working hours). Smith et al. (1989) found that completed suicides were less likely to have alcohol in their blood than homicide victims but more likely than victims of natural deaths.

In contrast, Cattell (1988) found that the elderly dying from suicide versus accidental causes did not differ in blood alcohol levels. Crompton (1985) found that those dying from accidents were more likely to have positive blood alcohol levels than suicides.

198

Welte et al. (1988) found that 33 percent of a sample of completed suicides in Erie County (NY) had alcohol in their blood. Those with alcohol in the blood were more often male, 21–60, left no suicide note, with no prior attempt, with tranquilizers in the body, committed suicide in the evening or at night, used a firearm, and were found in their car. Welte thought that the results suggested greater impulsivity in the suicides with alcohol in their blood.

Goldney (1981a) found that female suicide attempters who made highly lethal attempts were less likely to be intoxicated with alcohol at the time of the attempt than low lethality attempters. The use of alcohol was not associated with depression scores. Peterson et al. (1985) found that suicide attempters using guns who were intoxicated within 24 hours of their attempt did not differ from those who were sober in age, marital status or the wound location. In the United Kingdom, Varadaraj and Mendonca (1987) found that 41 percent of attempted suicides were intoxicated at the time of the attempt. Intoxication was more common in men, older attempters, and attempts taking place on weekends. Rangno et al. (1982) found that alcohol ingestion by suicide attempters using an overdose was not associated with falling into a coma, impaired vital signs or mortality.

The Truly Impulsive Act

Williams et al. (1980) found that 40 percent of a sample of attempted suicides premeditated the act for less than five minutes. These impulsive attempters more often informed someone of the impending act in the prior thirty minutes, were more often observed during the act, thought they would survive, and felt less tension after the act. They did not differ in sex, prior suicide attempts, ingestion of alcohol or whether they used tablets in bottles versus foil.

The Preceding Hours

Chiles et al. (1986) found that newly admitted psychiatric patients who had attempted suicide had more often used alcohol or marihuana in the preceding 24 hours and unsuccessfully sought a social contact than non-suicidal patients. They did not differ in depression, anger, anxiety or antisocial behavior. Clements et al. (1985) noted that staff felt that the depression was lifting in seven of nine psychiatric patients who completed suicide, but the patients themselves did not report an improvement in mood.

Hawton and Fagg (1988) found that attempted suicides who subsequently completed suicide were less likely to have had a major row in the 48 hours prior to their suicide attempt (and less likely to have experienced a breakup with their partner in the prior year). Bowen (1982) found that 49 percent of a groups of suicides by hanging had empty stomachs and an additional 34 percent had stomachs less than half full.

Robins (1986) estimated that 19 percent of a sample of completed suicides were psychotic at the time of their suicidal act. Lester and Smith (1989) presented evidence to suggest that the individual prior to suicide goes through the same emotional stages as the dying person: denial, anger, bargaining, depression and acceptance.

Near-Death Experiences

Ring and Franklin (1981–1982) found that 47 percent of attempted suicides had near death experiences (with out-of-body, dark void and other-world experiences), a proportion comparable to other persons who were near death. Male attempters were more likely to have such an experience than female attempters, and all found the experience positive.

The Location Of Suicide

Hanzlick and Ross (1987) studied eleven white male suicides found dead in hotels/motels within a day of checking in. Most left a note and had loved ones within a day's drive of the hotel. Modestin and Emmenegger (1988) found that 3.8 percent of suicides died far from home in Berne (Switzerland). These distant suicides were younger, more often single and professionals, less often housewives, and used car exhaust and "other" methods more. (They did not differ in sex, season, and the size of the town in which they lived.)

The Cathartic Effect of Attempting Suicide

Van Praag and Plutchik (1985) had psychiatrists, significant others and patients fill out a depression scale *after* their suicide attempt for how the patient felt *before* and *after* the attempt. All three types of raters indicated a decrease in depression after the attempt (whereas control patients showed no change). However, these ratings were not, of course, made blind and so may have been biased.

Successive Suicidal Actions

Clark et al. (1989) studied suicide attempts in a sample of depressed psychiatric patients and found that their suicide attempts fitted a model in which the risk of attempted suicide was higher in some people (a trait hypothesis) better than a model in which the risk of suicide is greater if there has been a prior suicide attempt (a crescendo hypothesis). This held for both sexes. Patients who subsequently completed suicide had the same incidence of suicide attempts as those who did not.

Eyman and Smith (1986) examined the lethality of successive suicidal actions of completed suicides who had previously attempted suicide. For those making up to four previous suicide attempts, the lethality of the actions increased linearly. However, for those making more than five previous attempts, there was no linear trend in lethality.

Fawcett et al. (1987) found that the lethality of prior suicide attempts did not predict subsequent completed suicide within four years for patients with a major affective disorder. Lehtinen and Jokinen (1983) found a similar lack of an association between the seriousness of the suicide attempt and the risk of subsequent completed suicide.

Pierce (1981, 1984) found that the suicidal intent of successive suicide attempts increased from the first to the second attempt and, in those who subsequently completed suicide, from the first to the penultimate attempt. Pierce found that those whose intent increased in subsequent attempts were younger and more likely to subsequently complete suicide. (They did not differ in sex, alcohol abuse, antisocial behavior, social isolation, physical illness, prior psychiatric treatment, bereavement or the time between suicide attempts.)

Intent and Lethality

Eaton and Reynolds (1985) found that the objectively measured objective suicidal intent in attempted suicides was related to the lethality of their action, while the subjective suicidal intent was not. Goldney (1981b) found that the lethality of attempts at suicide by young women was related to their suicidal intent (and to hopelessness). Lethality was not related to marital status, the source of the overdose, depression, death anxiety, prior attempts at suicide, drug abuse, a family history of psychiatric treatment, contact with other suicide attempters or completers, a history of parental loss, a history of violence, social class, or psychiatric diagnosis (depression versus other disorders or endogenous versus non-endogenous depression).

Gorenc et al. (1983) and Lonnqvist (1985) found that the medical lethality of the suicide attempt and the intent to die were related in samples of attempted suicides. Lonnqvist found that the attempts of older people were more lethal and had higher intent. The attempts of those who used antidepressants for their attempt were more lethal and with more intent, and the attempts of those using neuroleptics and hypnotics were also made with more intent. Lonnqvist and Ostramo (1987) found that the more lethal attempters were more likely to subsequently complete suicide. In contrast, Plutchik et al. (1989) found the self-rated or physician-rated lethality and suicidal intent were not related in samples of attempted suicides.

In Sri Lanka, Hettiarachchi and Kodithuwakku (1989) found that attempted suicides using self-poisoning who wished to die more often knew what a lethal dose was and, for women, more often bought the poison rather than finding it already in the home.

Power et al. (1985) compared attempted suicides of high and low lethality and found no differences in total life stress in the prior six months, psychiatric disturbance, alcohol abuse or prior suicide attempts. Suicidal intent was not related to prior suicide attempts or being intoxicated at the time of the act. However, suicidal intent was associated positively with psychiatric disturbance and life stress and negatively associated with alcohol abuse.

James and Hawton (1985) found that suicidal intent in a sample of self-poisoners was not related to the significant other feeling sympathy or guilt. Pallis and Pierce (1979) found that suicidal intent in a sample of attempted suicides was not related to having made prior attempts.

In a study of paraquat ingestion in Surinam, Perriens et al. (1989) found that death was more common if the act was suicidal, in males and in older persons. Ethnicity was not related to fatality, but Hindus were represented more often than in the general population.

Friedman et al. (1984) found no differences in the seriousness of the suicide attempt of adolescent and adult depressed inpatients. Gispert et al. (1985) found that the medical lethality of adolescent suicide attempts was not related to the patient's perceived risk of dying. In a group of elderly suicide attempters, Pierce (1987) found no age differences, but males had higher intent than females.

Knowledge of Suicide Prevention Services

Seager and Oram (1979) found that attempted suicides were as aware of the existence of suicide prevention centers as the general public but less informed as to how to locate and contact them. The attempters had contacted the Samaritans more than the general public (14 percent versus 2 percent).

The Motives for Suicide

Murphy (undated) classified the motives for suicide as follows:

(1) Altruistic
       sacrifice
(2) Magic murder and crime
       killing the world
       killing the parent or leader
       killing the tormentor
       killing a hostile inner plot
(3) Unconscious flight
       killing the defeated self
       escape from guilt
       avoidance of sexual inadequacy feelings
       withdrawal from reality
(4) Pathic
       boredom
       loss of internal and external control
       incurable disease
       cheating the gallows
(5) Conscious flight
       to escape a slow death
       the world is unbearable
       fear of punishment
       escape from rejection
(6) Magic revival
       death and rebirth fantasy

acquiring love after death
regression in order to regenerate
search for a rescuer
(7) Magically being killed
self-offer to the Gods
being one's own judge
homosexual panic
obeying a magic verdict of death
(8) Communication
panic
call for help in distress
powerless transfer of hostility
(9) Revenge
ritualistic duty (hara-kiri)
my death will haunt you
suicide as a gigantic blame

Loughrey and Kerr (1989) asked attempted suicides to choose from nine reasons for their action. The reason chosen was not associated with sex, age, making prior attempts, or method. Those choosing "to die" did have more suicidal intent.

Recent Stress

Completed Suicides

Hagnell and Rorsman (1980) found that completed suicides had experienced more critical events in the week prior to the suicide (especially humiliating events and acute psychiatric episodes) than those dying of natural deaths and had experienced more stressful events in the prior year.

Rich et al. (1986, 1988) found that substance abusers who completed suicides had experienced more recent interpersonal conflict and more stress of all kinds than suicides with affective disorders. Younger suicides had experienced more recent stress (especially in the prior week) and more interpersonal loss or conflict (but less illness). (The younger suicides were also more likely to be substance abusers.) Younger suicides also had more legal troubles and were more often unemployed. Warstadt et al. (1987) in the same sample found that those aged 10–39 had stress from separations and conflict more (and legal problems), those aged 40–49 more economic stress, those aged 50–59 more economic and separation/conflict stress and those older than 60 more stress from illness. Males had more economic stress than did women. Litman (1989) found that completed suicides (as compared to accidental deaths) had experienced more recent stress, loss and deaths of significant others, and prior mental illness. They had also made efforts to obtain the method needed for their suicide.

In a study of Canadian psychiatric patients Kubacki (1985) found that completed suicides had experienced more recent stressful events than attempted suicides.

Attempted Suicides

Zimmerman et al. (1985) found that depressed inpatients who had experienced more psychosocial stressors had also attempted suicide more.

Sonneck et al. (1976) compared attempted suicides with depressed patients with and without suicidal ideation. The attempters had experienced more stress with their partner whereas the depressed patients had experienced more stress from illness.

O'Brien and Farmer (1980) found that first time suicide attempters and repeaters both had experienced more stressful life events than general practice controls. However, during the next year, 66 percent of the attempters experienced a decrease in stress event scores. Farmer and Creed (1989) found that attempted suicides by self-poisoning had experienced an increase in stressful events in the three weeks prior to their suicide attempt, and this was especially true of the non-depressed attempters. Compared to normal controls, the attempters had experienced more severely stressful events but no more mildly stressful events. Experience of stressful events was not related to suicidal intent in the suicide attempt. Extrapunitive attempters had experienced more severe events and more legal events, while intropunitive attempters had experienced fewer severe events and more job loss.

Harder et al. (1980) found that the seriousness of suicide attempts was related to the severity of stressful events in the prior month and the prior year, but not to changes in the stress level. Katschnig (1980) found that there was an increase in life stress from 7–12 months before the suicide attempt to 0–6 months, and especially in the prior month.

Lester (1988) found that college students who were currently thinking about suicide or who had previously threatened or attempted suicide had experienced more stressful events in the prior year than non-suicidal college students. The association with a history of attempted and threatened suicide was still found after controls for the level of current depression.

Linehan et al. (1986) found that, while suicide attempters, ideators and non-suicidal patients did not differ in total life stress (or depression scores), the most important problems facing the attempters were more often interpersonal.

Luscomb et al. (1980) compared attempted suicides with psychiatric controls (who were older, more often psychotic and less often depressed). The attempters had experienced more recent stressful events (but significantly so only for the older subjects), more highly stressful events, and more exits (for the middle-aged and older subjects).

McIntire and Angle (1981) found that the extent of the precipitating stress in a sample of self-poisoners increased with age from 6–10 year-olds to 17–18 year-olds (as did the suicidal intent). Parker (1988) found higher stressful life event scores in adolescent suicide attempters than in accident victims, medical patients or normals, but they also had families with more psychiatric problems, were more often female, and had fathers with less education.

Paykel (1980) found more stressful life events in the prior six months for attempted suicides than for depressives, schizophrenics and normal controls, especially illnesses, arguments, a new person in home and court appearances. The difference was found also for undesirable events, entrances, major upsets and uncontrollable events in the prior month.

Pomerantz and Carter (1987) found that adolescent suicide attempters had experienced more of some kinds of recent family problems (depression of family members, suicide in the family, and the adolescent attacked) than had suicidal ideators and non-suicidal adolescents. The attempters and ideators had more often experienced the death of a sibling or friend, remarriage of parents, an illness or a family member attacked.

Slater and Depue (1981) compared primary depressive patients who had attempted suicide with non-suicidal depressive patients and found that the suicide attempters had more external stressful events, events not caused by their depression, and more events after the onset of the depression than the non-suicidal patients (but no difference in total stressful events). The attempters also had less social support, especially because of a recent exit.

Tegeler and Platzek (1988) found that suicide attempters had experienced more recent stressful life events than schizophrenics, endogenous depressives and the general population, but not neurotic depressives. The attempters showed no peaking in stressful events prior to the attempt.

Thomssen and Moller (1988) found that both mild and serious suicide attempters had experienced more stressful life events than surgical patients. The serious attempters also had fewer social supports than the mild attempters and surgical patients. Welz (1988) reported that suicide attempters had experienced more stressful life events than members of general population, especially in the areas of personal relationships, general well-being, and problems with authority (but not in the areas of work, education or everyday life).

Papa (1980), however, found no relationship between suicidal intent and recent stress in a sample of attempted suicides.

Suicidal Ideators

Bonner and Rich (1987, 1988) found that suicidal students had experienced more recent stress than non-suicidal students, including stress over exams. Bonner and Rich (1989) also found a higher level of jail stress in suicidal prisoners than in non-suicidal prisoners. Kirkpatrick-Smith, et al. (1989) also found life stress to be related to suicidal ideation in school students. Schotte and Clum (1982, 1987) found that negative (but not positive) life events were associated with suicidal ideation in both college and psychiatric patient samples.

In contrast, Carson and Johnson (1985) found recent stress unrelated to the presence of suicidal ideation in college students.

Adolescents

Cohen-Sandler et al. (1982a, 1982b) found that suicidal children who were psychiatric inpatients had experienced more stress in later childhood and in the preceding year (but not in infancy, in pre-school years, or in early childhood) than non-suicidal inpatients. The groups did not differ in their history of psychiatric treatment or the presence of suicide and psychiatric disturbance in their families. The suicidal patients had experienced more stress involving parents, including separation from parents and the divorce and remarriage of parents, more deaths of grandparents, and more psychological trauma. The groups did not differ in post-hospitalization stress. There was a suggestion that the repeaters had experienced more post-discharge stress.

Ferguson (1981) found that gifted ninth graders had experienced fewer recent stressful events than non-gifted adolescents, but for both groups the stress scores was positively related to suicidal ideation and drug or alcohol use.

In high school students, Garrison et al. (1988) found that recent stress events, depression and prior suicidal ideation all predicted suicidal ideation in subsequent years (as did sex and race). Gispert et al. (1985) found that stressful events in the prior year (but not the prior month or lifetime) were related to the rated suicide risk of a group of adolescent suicide attempters (as was depression too).

Myers et al. (1985) found that acutely suicidal children had experienced more recent stress than psychiatric controls. Reynolds (1988) found that suicidal ideation was associated with recent stressful events in adolescents, and with hassles and less social support (and also social class and sex, but not race).

Rubenstein et al. (1989) found that attempting suicide in the past year was asociated with stressful life events in high school students. The attempters had experienced more family and peer loss, problems in family cohesion, suicidal behavior in family and friends, achievement pressure and problems with sexuality. The attempters showed more acting-out behavior and worsened school performance.

Sex Differences

Jennings and Lunn (1962) found that male completed suicides had more often lost a spouse through divorce/separation while the women had more often lost a spouse through death. Furthermore, suicide after loss (or social isolation and miscellaneous worries) was more common in those without physical or mental illness. (Sixty-one percent had a physical illness and 29 percent a mental illness.)

Hamblin and Jones (1972) reanalyzed data from an earlier study by Maris and found that attempted suicide in women followed upon stigmatization, drug abuse, sexual deviation and (negatively) narcissism. In contrast, completed suicide followed negatively upon sexual deviation, drug abuse, and reactive depression. They suggested that a reactive depression may inhibit completed suicide in women with a deviant career pattern.

Age Differences

Eisele et al. (1987) found that teen completed suicides more often had family and school precipitants whereas adult suicides more often had mental illness and medical illness precipitants. The teens and adults did not differ in sex, race, method used, isolation for the suicidal act, alcohol or drug use at the time of the act, prior communications or prior suicide attempts. Husain and Vandiver (1984) found that children below the age of 15 were suicidal more often as a result of rejection or hostility toward them, whereas those aged 16–20 more often were reacting to depression.

Particular Precipitating Events

Dahl (1989) found a high incidence of suicidal ideation after rape or attempted rape (34 percent with moderate intensity together with 29 percent with high intensity). Ellis et al. (1982) found that multiple-incident victims of sexual assault had attempted suicide more in the past than single-incident victims (and had more often received psychiatric treatment and were more often loners and of lower social class).

Wild (1988) reported incidents of completed and attempted suicide in the alleged perpetrators after investigation and prosecution for sexual child abuse. Lester and Baker (1989) documented cases of suicide occurring soon after the arrest of ordinary citizens for buying child pornography through the mail in a government sting operation.

Kaprio et al. (1987) found that completed suicide was more common than expected after bereavement, especially in the first year.

After the Act

Rabin et al. (1984) found in depressed patients that suicidal ideation decreased after one week of treatment while self-image and fatigue were much slower to show improvement.

In a sample of female suicide attempters, Stephens (1987) found that those who were single and had made no prior attempts reported more positive changes after the attempt.

Suicide Pacts

Rosenbaum (1983) reviewed six cases of suicide pacts with a survivor. The instigator was typically deceased, male, psychiatrically depressed and with a history of attempted suicide. The survivor was usually female and not psychiatrically disturbed or with a history of attempted suicide. The instigators resembled non-criminal murderers and murder-suicides. For more research on suicide pacts, see Chapter 11.

Discussion

The research has found, in general, that suicidal individuals have experienced noticeably more stressful events prior to their suicidal action than have non-suicidal individuals. The role of alcohol intoxication at the time of the suicidal act also seems well documented. These, as well as the less well-documented results reviewed above, merit further exploration in the 1990s.

REFERENCES

Bonner, R. L., & Rich, A. R. Toward a predictive model of suicidal ideation and behavior. *Suicide & Life-Threatening Behavior,* 1987, 17, 50–63.

Bonner, R. L., & Rich, A. R. A prospective investigation of suicidal ideation in college students. *Suicide & Life-Threatening Behavior,* 1988, 18, 245–258.

Bonner, R. L., & Rich, A. R. Risk factors of suicide intention in a jail population. In D. Lester (Ed.) *Suicide '89.* Denver: AAS, 1989, 233–234.

Bowen, D. A. Hanging. *Forensic Science International,* 1982, 20, 247–249.

Carson, N. D., & Johnson, R. E. Suicidal thoughts and problem-solving preparation among college students. *Journal of College Student Personnel,* 1985, 26, 484–487.

Cattell, H. R. Elderly suicide in London. *International Journal of Geriatric Psychiatry,* 1988, 3, 252–261.

Chiles, J., Strosaht, K., Cowden, L., Graham, R., & Linehan, M. The 24 hours before hospitalization. *Suicide & Life-Threatening Behavior,* 1986, 16, 335–342.

Clark, D. C., Gibbons, R. D., Fawcett, J., & Scheftner, W. A. What is the mechanism by which suicide attempts predispose to later suicide attempts? *Journal of Abnormal Psychology,* 1989, 98, 42–49.

Clements, C., Bonacci, D., Yerevanian, B., Privitera, M., & Kiehne, L. Assessment of suicide risk in patients with personality disorder and major affective disorder. *Quality Review Bulletin,* 1985, 11(5), 150–154.

Cohen-Sandler, R., Berman, A., & King, R. Life stress and symptomatology. *Journal of the American Academy of Child Psychiatry,* 1982a, 21, 178–186.

Cohen-Sandler, R., Berman, A., & King, R. A follow-up study of hospitalized suicidal children. *Journal of the American Academy of Child Psychiatry,* 1982b, 21, 398–403.

Crompton, M. R. Alcohol and violent accidental and suicidal death. *Medicine, Science & the Law,* 1985, 25(1), 59–62.

Dahl, S. Acute response to rape. *Acta Psychiatrica Scandinavica,* 1989, suppl. 355, 56–62.

Eaton, P., & Reynolds, P. Suicide attempters presenting at an emergency department. *Canadian Journal of Psychiatry,* 1985, 30, 582–585.

Eisele, J. W., Frisino, J., Haglund, W., & Reay, D. T. Teenage suicide in King County, Washington. *American Journal of Forensic Medicine & Pathology,* 1987, 8, 208–216.

Ellis, E. M., Atkeson, B. M., & Calhoun, K. S. An examination of differences between multiple and single-incident victims of sexual assault. *Journal of Abnormal Psychology,* 1982, 91, 221–224.

Eyman, J. R., & Smith, E. K. Lethality trends in multiple suicide attempts. In R. Cohen-Sandler (Ed.) *Proceedings of the 19th Annual Meeting.* Denver: AAS, 1986, 75–77.

Farmer, R., & Creed, F. Life events and hostility in self-poisoning. *British Journal of Psychiatry,* 1989, 154, 390–395.

Fawcett, J., Scheftner, W., Clark, D., Hedeker, D., Gibbons, R., & Coryell, W. Clinical predictors of suicide in patients with major affective disorders. *American Journal of Psychiatry,* 1987, 144, 35–40.

Ferguson, W. E. Gifted adolescents, stress and life changes. *Adolescence,* 1981, 16, 973–985.

Friedman, R. C., Corn, R., Aronoff, M., Hurt, S., & Clarkin, J. The seriously suicidal adolescent. In H. S. Sudak, A. B. Ford, & Rushforth, N. B. (Eds.) *Suicide in the Young.* Boston: John Wright, 1984, 209–226.

Garrison, C. Z., Jackson, K. L., Schluchter, M. D., Geller, B., Marsteller, F., Tse, J., & Hallman, M. Prediction of Suicidal Ideation in Adolescents. In D. Lester (Ed.) *Suicide '88.* Denver: AAS, 1988, 11–12.

Gispert, M., Wheeler, K., March, L., & Davis, M. Suicidal adolescents. *Adolescence,* 1985, 20, 753–762.

Goldney, R. D. Alcohol in association with suicide and attempted suicide in young women. *Medical Journal of Australia,* 1981a, 2, 195–197.

Goldney, R. D. Attempted suicide in young women. *British Journal of Psychiatry,* 1981b, 139, 382–390.

Gorenc, K. D., Kleff, F., & Welz, R. Intentionality and seriousness of suicide attempts in relation to depression. *Boletin de Estudios Medicos y Biologicos,* 1983, 32, 233–247.

Hagnell, O., & Rorsman, B. Suicide in the Lundby study. *Neuropsychobiology,* 1980, 6, 319–332.

Hamblin, R. L., & Jacobsen, R. B. Suicide and pseudocide. *Journal of Health & Social Behavior,* 1972, 13, 99–109.

Hanzlick, R. L., & Ross, W. K. Suicide far from home. *Journal of Forensic Sciences,* 1987, 32, 189–191.

Harder, D. W., Strauss, J. S., Kokes, R. F., Ritiler, B. A., & Gift, T. E. Life events and psychopathology severity among first psychiatric admissions. *Journal of Abnormal Psychology,* 1980, 89, 165–180.

Hawton, K., & Fagg, J. Suicide and other causes of death following attempted suicide. *British Journal of Psychiatry,* 1988, 152, 359–366.

Hawton, K., Fagg, J., & McKeown, S. P. Alcoholism, alcohol and attempted suicide. *Alcohol & Alcoholism,* 1989, 24(1), 3–9.

Hettiarachchi, J., & Kodithuwakku, G. C. Self-poisoning in Sri Lanka. *Human Toxicology,* 1989, 8, 507–510.

Honkanen, J., & Visuri, T. Blood alcohol levels in a series of injured patients with special reference to accident and type of injury. *Annales Chirurgiae et Gynaecologiae,* 1976, 65, 287–294.

Husain, S. A., & Vandiver, T. *Suicide in Children and Adolescents.* New York: Spectrum, 1984.

James, D., & Hawton, K. Overdoses. *British Journal of Psychiatry,* 1985, 146, 481–485.

Jennings, H. C., & Lunn, J. E. A study of suicide in a northern industrial town. *Medical Officer,* 1962, 108, 397–399.

Kaprio, J., Koskenvuo, M., & Rita, H. Mortality after bereavement. *American Journal of Public Health,* 1987, 77, 283–287.

Katschnig, K. Measuring life stress. In R. Farmer & S. Hirsch (Eds.) *The Suicide Syndrome.* London: Croom Helm, 1980, 116–123.

Kirkpatrick-Smith, K., Rich, A., Bonner, R., & Jans, F. Substance abuse and suicidal ideation among adolescents. In D. Lester (Ed.) *Suicide '89.* Denver: AAS, 1989, 90–91.

Kubacki, A. Life events and self-harm. In R. Cohen-Sandler (Ed.) *Proceedings of the 18th Annual Meeting.* Denver: AAS, 1985, 7–9.

Lehtinen, V., & Jokinen, K. Subsequent self-destructive behavior of suicide attempters treated on medical wards in a general hospital. In J. P. Soubrier & J. Vedrinne (Eds.) *Depression and Suicide.* Paris: Pergamon, 1983, 479–483.

Lester, D. Stress and suicidal ideation. *Perceptual & Motor Skills,* 1988, 66, 182.

Lester, D., & Baker, G. Suicide after legal arrest. *Medicine, Science & the Law,* 1989, 29(1), 78.

Lester, D., & Smith, B. Application of Kubler-Ross's stages of dying to the suicidal individual. *Psychological Reports,* 1989, 64, 609–610.

Linehan, M. M., Chiles, J. A., Egan, K. J., Devine, R. H., & Laffaw, J. A. Presenting problems of parasuicides versus suicide ideators and nonsuicidal psychiatric patients. *Journal of Consulting & Clinical Psychology,* 1986, 54, 880–881.

Litman, R. E. 500 psychological autopsies. *Journal of Forensic Sciences,* 1989, 34, 638–646.

Lonnqvist, J. A six-year prospective study on influence of psychiatric consultation on the outcome of attempted suicide in a general hospital. *Psychiatria Fennica,* 1985, 16, 123–131.

Lonnqvist, J., & Ostramo, A. Suicide mortality after the first suicide attempt. In R. Yufit (Ed.) *Proceedings of the 20th Annual Conference.* Denver: AAS, 1987, 179–181.

Loughrey, G., & Kerr, A. Motivation in deliberate self-harm. *Ulster Medical Journal,* 1989, 58(1), 46–50.

Luscomb, R., Clum, G., & Patsiokas, A. Mediating factors in the relationship between life stress and suicide attempting. *Journal of Nervous & Mental Disease,* 1980, 168, 644–650.

McIntire, M. S., & Angle, C. R. The taxonomy of suicide and self-poisoning. In C. F. Wells & I. R. Stuart (Eds.) *Self-Destructive Behavior in Children and Adolescents.* New York: Van Nostrand Reinhold, 1981, 224–249.

Modestin, J., & Emmenegger, P. A. Distant suicide. *Crisis,* 1988, 9, 7–12.

Murphy, K. B. Motives for suicide. Unpublished, undated.

Myers, K. M., Burke, P., & McCauley, E. Suicidal behavior by hospitalized preadolescent children on a psychiatric unit. *Journal of the American Academy of Child Psychiatry,* 1985, 24, 474–480.

O'Brien, S. E., & Farmer, R. D. The role of life events in the aetiology of episodes of self-poisoning. In R. D. Farmer & S. Hirsch (Eds.) *The Suicide Syndrome.* London: Croom Helm, 1980, 124–130.

Owens, D. W., & Jones, S. J. The accidental and emergency department management of deliberate self-poisoning. *British Journal of Psychiatry,* 1988, 152, 830–833.

Pallis, D., & Pierce, D. Recognizing the suicidal overdose. *Journal of the Royal Society of Medicine,* 1979, 72, 565–571.

Papa, L. Responses to life events as predictors of suicidal behavior. *Nursing Research,* 1980, 29, 362–369.

Parker, S. D. Accident or suicide? *Journal of Psychosocial Nursing,* 1988, 26(6), 15–19.

Paykel, E. S. Recent life events and attempted suicide. In R. Farmer & S. Hirsch (Eds.) *The Suicide Syndrome.* London: Croom Helm, 1980, 105–115.

Perriens, J., van der Stuyft, P., Chee, H., & Benimadho, S. The epidemiology of paraquat intoxications in Surinam. *Tropical and Geographic Medicine,* 1989, 41, 266–269.

Peterson, L., Peterson, M., O'Shanick, G., & Swann, A. Self-inflicted gunshot wounds. *American Journal of Psychiatry,* 1985, 142, 228–231.

Pierce, D. The predictive validation of a suicide intent scale. *British Journal of Psychiatry,* 1981, 139, 391–396.

Pierce, D. Suicidal intent and repeated self-harm. *Psychological Medicine,* 1984, 14, 655–659.

Pierce, D. Deliberate self-harm in the elderly. *International Journal of Geriatric Psychiatry,* 1987, 2(2), 105–110.

Plutchik, R., van Praag, H., Picard, S., Conte, H., & Korn, M. Is there a relation between the seriousness of suicidal intent and the lethality of the suicide attempt? *Psychiatry Research,* 1989, 27, 71–79.

Pomerantz, S. C., & Carter, B. F. Troubled youth. In R. Yufit (Ed.) *Proceedings of the 20th Annual Conference.* Denver: AAS, 1987, 270–271.

Power, K. G., Cooke, D. J., & Brooks, D. N. Life stress, medical lethality and suicidal intent. *British Journal of Psychiatry,* 1985, 147, 655–659.

Rabin, A. S., Kaslow, N. J., & Rehm, L. P. Changes in symptoms of depression during the course of therapy. *Cognitive Therapy & Research,* 1984, 8, 479–488.

Rangno, R., Dumont, C., & Sitar, D. Effect of ethanol ingestion on outcome of drug overdose. *Critical Care Medicine,* 1982, 10, 1801–85.

Reynolds, W. M. *Suicidal Ideation Questionnaire.* Odessa, FL: Psychological Assessment Resources, 1988.

Rich, C. L., Fowler, R. C., Fogarty, L. A., & Young, D. San Diego suicide study. *Archives of General Psychiatry,* 1988, 45, 589–592.

Rich, C. L., Young, D., & Fowler, R. C. San Diego suicide study. *Archives of General Psychiatry,* 1986, 43, 577–582.

Ring, K., & Franklin, S. Do suicide survivors report near-death experiences? *Omega,* 1981–1982, 12, 191–208.

Robins, E. Psychosis and suicide. *Biological Psychiatry,* 1986, 21, 665–672.

Rosenbaum, M. Crime and punishment. *Archives of General Psychiatry,* 1983, 40, 979–982.

Rubenstein, J. L., Heeren, T., Housman, D., Rubin, C., & Stechler, G. Suicidal behavior in normal adolescents. *American Journal of Orthopsychiatry,* 1989, 59, 59–71.

Schotte, D., & Clum, G. Suicidal ideation in a college population. *Journal of Consulting & Clinical Psychology,* 1982, 50, 690–696.

Schotte, D., & Clum, G. Problem-solving skills in suicidal psychiatric patients. *Journal of Consulting & Clinical Psychology,* 1987, 55, 49–56.

Seager, C. P., & Oram, J. E. Samaritan contact among parasuicide patients. *British Journal of Psychiatry,* 1979, 135, 587–588.

Slater, J., & Depue, R. The contribution of environmental events and social support to serious suicide attempts in primary depressive disorder. *Journal of Abnormal Psychology,* 1981, 90, 275–285.

Smith, S. M., Goodman, R., Thacker, S., Burton, A., Parsons, J., & Hudson, P. Alcohol and fatal injuries. *American Journal of Preventive Medicine,* 1989, 5, 296–302.

Sonneck, G., Grunberger, J., & Ringel, E. Experimental contribution to the evaluation of the suicidal risk of depressive patients. *Psychiatria Clinica,* 1976, 9(2), 84–96.

Steer, R. A., Beck, A. T., Garrison, B., & Lester, D. Eventual suicide in interrupted and uninterrupted attempters. *Suicide & Life-Threatening Behavior,* 1988, 18, 119–128.

Stephens, B. J. The pseudocidal female. In R. Yufit (Ed.) *Proceedings of the 20th Annual Conference.* Denver: AAS, 1987, 19–20.

Tegeler, J., & Platzek, M. Recent life events and suicide attempts. In H. Moller, A. Schmidtke, & R. Welz (Eds.) *Current Issues of Suicidology.* Berlin: Springer-Verlag, 1988, 311–315.

Thomssen, C., & Moller, H. J. A description of behavioral patterns of coping with life events in suicidal patients. In H. Moller, A. Schmidtke, & R. Welz (Eds.) *Current Issues of Suicidology.* Berlin: Springer-Verlag, 1988, 316–321.

Van Praag, H., & Plutchik, R. An empirical study of the cathartic effect of attempted suicide. *Psychiatry Research,* 1985, 16, 123–130.

Varadaraj, R., & Mendonca, J. A survey of blood alcohol levels in self-poisoning cases. *Advances in Alcohol and Substance Abuse,* 1987, 7(1), 63–69.

Virkkunen, M., & Alha, A. On suicides committed under the influence of alcohol in Finland in 1967. *British Journal of Addiction,* 1971, 65, 317–323.

Warstadt, G., Rich, C., Nemiroff, R., Fowler, R., & Young, D. Suicide, stressors and the life cycle. In R. Yufit (Ed.) *Proceedings of the 20th Annual Conference.* Denver: AAS, 1987, 160–161.

Welte, J., Abel, E., & Wieczorek, W. The role of alcohol in suicides in Erie County, NY, 1972–1984. *Public Health Reports,* 1988, 103, 648–652.

Welz, R. Life events, current social stressors, and risk of attempted suicide. In H. Moller, A. Schmidtke & R. Welz (Eds.) *Current Issues of Suicidology.* Berlin: Springer-Verlag, 1988, 301–310.

Wild, N. J. Suicide of perpetrators after disclosure of child sexual abuse. *Child Abuse & Neglect,* 1988, 12, 119–121.

Williams, C., Davidson, J., & Montgomery, I. Impulsive suicidal behavior. *Journal of Clinical Psychology,* 1980, 36, 90–04.

Zimmerman, M., Pfohl, B., Stangle, D., & Coryell, W. The validity of DSM–III Axis IV. *American Journal of Psychiatry,* 1985, 142, 1437–1441.

Chapter 14

THE INCIDENCE OF SUICIDE

A large number of studies have surveyed various groups to ascertain the incidence of suicidal behaviors and the possible correlates of such behaviors.

Community Surveys

Diekstra and van de Loo (1978) carried out a community survey in the Netherlands and found that 4 percent had attempted suicide and 11 percent considered suicide in the past. Respondents with prior suicidal attempts/ideation had a more positive attitude toward suicide.

In Canada, Bagley (1985) found that 10 percent of a community had previously attempted suicide and over half had thought of suicide. Ramsay and Bagley (1985) reported a lifetime incidence of suicide attempts of 10.1 percent (2.1 percent in the last year) and a lifetime incidence of suicidal ideation of 51.2 percent (9.9 percent in the last year). Some 22.6 percent of the sample had a family member who engaged in suicidal behavior and 63.0 percent a personal acquaintance.

Dyck et al. (1988) found a lifetime prevalence of attempted suicide of 3.6 percent, with the rate higher in females, the young (aged 25–34), and divorced. The attempters were more likely to be unemployed, violent to their families, guilty of child neglect or abuse, psychiatrically disturbed and substance abusers. The risk was greatest for those with schizophrenia, mania and personality disorder.

In Israel, Levav et al. (1988) surveyed a sample of adult Jews and found a previous year incidence of suicidal ideation of 2.7 percent and a lifetime incidence of 7.9 percent. Suicidal ideation did not vary with sex or age, but the less educated, African and Asian Jews, the unemployed, those with low incomes and the non-married reported more. The lifetime incidence of attempted suicide was 1.4 percent, but this incidence did not vary with sex, age, education, marital status, occupation, or

216

income. African and Asian Jews were more likely to have attempted suicide.

Bell et al. (1978) surveyed a community and found that 5.6 percent reported suicidal ideation in the previous year. The incidence was not related to race, sex or social class. Younger people and those single/divorced/separated reported a higher incidence. The suicidal ideators were more depressed, and suicidal ideation was more common in light and heavy drinkers as compared to moderate drinkers and abstainers. Two-and-one-half percent had attempted suicide in the past. The incidence of attempts was not related to marital status, age or social class. The incidence was highest in white females and lowest in white males. A history of attempts was associated with a history of ideation.

Cameron (1972) surveyed people in the community and found no sex or age differences in the desire to die, consideration of suicide or attempted suicide. The lower class respondents had more desire to die, but did not differ in ideation or attempts. Both the young and men had more knowledge about how to commit suicide.

Vandivort and Locker (1979) surveyed residents in two cities and found an incidence of suicidal ideation in the prior month of 5.4 percent. The incidence was higher in the young, the more educated (for men only), the single/separated/divorced, and students. There were no differences by sex or race.

Whitehead et al. (1972) tried to track down every attempted suicide in Ontario and found a male rate of 718 and a female rate of 734. (The inclusion of jails seemed to be responsible for raising the male rate.)

Callahan (1989) found a lifetime incidence of 3.5 percent for attempted suicide, with a higher incidence in women but no variation by age or church attendance. Those attempting suicide had more often received psychiatric treatment. The lifetime incidence for having a relative attempt suicide was 24 percent and for having a relative complete suicide 11 percent.

Goldberg (1981) found that 10 percent of 18–24-year-olds in the community had thought about suicide in the prior months. Suicidal ideation was more common in students but unrelated to age, sex, education and marital status.

In a community sample in Hungary, Kopp et al. (1987) found a lifetime incidence of attempted suicide of 2 percent (2.3 percent in women and 1.7 percent in men).

Lonnqvist et al. (1980) surveyed women working in banks and found that 11.9 percent had thought about suicide in the past year. The suicidal ideators were younger, had experienced more psychiatric symptoms both in the prior three days and in their lifetime, and felt more depression, anxiety and anger. (They did not differ in marital status, education or occupational status.) Suicidal ideation was more strongly associated with depression than anxiety or hyper-irritability.

Moscicki et al. (1988) surveyed five areas in the US and found a lifetime incidence of attempted suicide of 2.9 percent (and 10.7 percent for suicidal ideation). Attempting suicide was most common in Los Angeles (and least common in New Haven), females, those aged 25–44, whites/Hispanics, the separated/divorced, the not-employed, the lower social classes, and those with a psychiatric diagnosis.

Sorenson and Golding (1988a, 1988b) found that Hispanic-Americans in Los Angeles were less likely to have attempted or thought about suicide than whites, and this was so for both sexes. Suicidal preoccupation was greater in the more educated, the younger, the divorced/separated, and those with psychiatric disorders (especially affective disorders). Mexican-Americans who were born in Mexico had a lower incidence than Mexican-Americans born in the US. Acculturation was not related to a history of suicidal preoccupation, but Catholics and church attenders had less suicidal preoccupation.

Wenz (1980, 1983) found greater suicidal preoccupation in a community sample in Michigan in those aged 15–34 and over 75 years of age and in those from the lower social class census tracts.

College Students

Rudd (1989) found that 44 percent of college students had thought about suicide in the previous year and 5.5 percent had attempted suicide. The suicidal students came from disrupted families more, had less educated mothers, were more liberal, and had received more past psychiatric treatment. Wellman and Wellman (1988) found that 6 percent of college students had attempted suicide and 55 percent had thought about suicide. There were no sex differences, and those who were the more seriously suicidal were more likely to know someone who had attempted or completed suicide (most often a friend) and were more accepting of suicide. Westefeld and Furr (1987) found that 5 percent of college students had attempted suicide and 32 percent had considered it. Wright (1985) found that 10.6 percent of high school seniors and 6.4

percent of college students had thought of suicide in the prior six months. Suicidal ideation was associated with an unhappier childhood, alcohol and drug abuse and self-reported delinquent acts.

In Britain, Salmons and Harrington (1984) found a lifetime incidence of suicidal ideation of 55 percent in college students as compared to 45 percent in patients of general practitioners. For the students, females and those born overseas were more likely to report suicidal ideation (but religion did not play a role though the authors claim otherwise). For the patient sample, married individuals were less likely to report having thought about suicide, but sex and religious belief were not associated with a history of suicidal ideation.

Fritz (1987) found that 50 percent of Alsakan college students had thought about suicide, 31 percent had made a suicidal gesture, and 7 percent had made a suicide attempt.

In Egypt, Okasha et al. (1981) found that 0.6 percent of medical students had attempted suicide in the prior year and 2.5 percent had thought about it. The suicidal students were more often female, psychiatrically upset, with physical illness and stressful life events.

Children and Adolescents

Domino et al. (1986–1987) found that about twenty percent of junior high school students had experienced serious thoughts about suicide in the past, and about a quarter knew a completed suicide personally. Having thought about suicide was, however, not related to knowing a suicide or having a family member complete suicide.

Bolger et al. (1989) asked students whether they had first thought of suicide before the age of 13 or after. Seventy-five percent of the students had thought about suicide, and 25 percent during preadolescence. The incidence increased sharply at age eleven. Those who thought about suicide in preadolescence were more likely to have experienced parental absences and to have a family-caused precipitant.

Dubow et al. (1989) surveyed junior high school students and found that 36 percent had thought of suicide in the past and 7 percent had attempted suicide. Suicide attempts and ideation were more common in girls, those of lower social class, and those with more negative life events, less family support, more antisocial behavior and worse academic achievement.

Friedman et al. (1987) found that 53 percent of high school students had thought about suicide and 9 percent attempted suicide. Suicidal preoccupation was not related to grade level, race, religion or age. Those with previous suicidal involvement were more often female and more often had suicidal family members and peers. Of the suicidal ideators, the girls more often had a plan and were more persistent. The oriental-Americans were also more persistent.

Guyer et al. (1989) found that the rates of (non-lethal) self-injury in children in fourteen small Massachusetts communities were 0.02 (per 100,000 per year) for those aged 0–9, 0.51 for those 10–14 and 2.54 for those aged 15–19. Angle et al. (1983) followed up adolescent suicide attempters and found that the peak age was 14–15 and none of the sample attempted suicide after the age of 22.

Pfeffer (1984) interviewed children aged 6–12 and their mothers in the community and found that 12 percent of the children had thought, threatened or attempted suicide in the past versus 26 percent of their mothers (and an estimated 6 percent of their fathers). The presence of suicidality in the children was associated with suicidality in their mothers (but not fathers). The suicidal children had more psychiatric pathology, more depression, more suicidal mothers and lower social class. (They did not differ in the number of siblings, birth order, intelligence, school achievement, physical illness in their parents, impulse control, pregnancy complications at their birth, seizure disorder or having a psychiatric diagnosis.)

In Ontario, Joffe et al. (1988) found that about 4 percent of 12–13 year-olds in the community had attempted suicide in the prior six months and 7 percent had thought about suicide. The percentages for 14–16 year-olds were higher, primarily accounted for by a steep increase in suicidal behavior among girls which offset a decrease in suicidal behavior among boys. No urban/rural differences in incidence were found.

Kashani et al. (1989) found an incidence of current suicidal ideation in community children and adolescents of 6.6 percent. The incidence rose from 8 year-olds to 17 year-olds. Riggs and Cheng (1988) reported that 12 percent of children in grades 9 through 12 had previously attempted suicide.

For teenagers attending free medical clinics, Robins (1989) found a lifetime incidence of attempted suicide of 8 percent (4 percent in the last year). A history of attempted suicide was more common those who came for psychiatric reasons, whites, females, aged 15–18, not living with biological parents, parents skilled or white collar (rather than unskilled), and if more adverse family factors, psychiatric symptoms, prior suicide attempts, drug use, behavior problems, chronic illness, rape, venereal disease, police contact, and school failure.

Smith and Crawford (1986) found that 8.4 percent of high school students had attempted suicide and 62.6 percent had thought about suicide. The attempters had more physical beatings, rape and sexual abuse, friends (but not family) who had attempted or completed suicide, and had a bad relationship with both parents. They did not differ in drug or alcohol use, television viewing, having an intact family, arrest record or inhibition of feelings.

Velez and Cohen (1988) found that the incidence of current suicidal ideation in children in a sample from two counties in New York State ranged from 7 percent to 26 percent depending upon the definition used. The lifetime incidence of attempted suicide was 3.5 percent with the rate highest in 13–14 year-olds. The suicide attempters were more often female, less often from an intact family, and showed more behavioral and emotional problems including drug problems and depression. (They did not differ in race, religion, age, or problems with alcohol.)

Bagley (1975) found that 9.4 percent of 14 year-old girls and 4.5 percent of boys had considered suicide in the past. Besozzi (1972) studied high school and college students in Cologne and found that 5.5 percent had attempted suicide (with the high school students having the higher incidence), 18.1 percent had contemplated suicide, and 7.6 percent were currently suicidal. Berman (1975) found that 2.3 percent of a sample aged 13 to 30 had previously attempted suicide.

In Saipan, Mayer and Bauman (1986) found that 28 percent of ninth to twelfth graders had experienced suicidal thoughts, and there were no differences between boys and girls in this incidence.

In an eleven-year follow-up of teenagers, Smith (1986) found that 14 percent had thought of suicide and 4 percent had attempted suicide. Suicidal preoccupation was associated with dysphoric mood, psychiatric disturbance (anxiety, hostilty, psychoticism, etc.), and weakly with the use of cigarettes, marijuana and cocaine (but not alcohol).

Preschoolers

Pfeffer and Trad (1988) documented that explicit suicidal threats and attempts can occur in children three to six years old. Rosenthal and Rosenthal (1984) found that suicidal preschoolers ran away from home more and showed more non-suicidal self-aggression. They were less impulsive and showed less pain and crying after injuries. They were also more often unwanted, abused and neglected.

Gifted School Students

Harkavy and Asnis (1985) found that 9 percent of the students in a high school for the gifted had attempted suicide. Metha (1987) found that 15 percent of gifted seventh and eighth graders had thought of suicide in the past year as compared to 21 percent of non-gifted.

Other Groups

Psychiatric Patients

Tardiff et al. (1981) examined nearly nine thousand psychiatric inpatients and found that suicidal preoccupation was present in 13 percent of the white male patients, 23 percent of the white females, 8 percent of the black males and 12 percent of the black females. Suicidal preoccupation was more common in the separated/divorced (women only), Catholics (men only) and those with depression.

Mental Health Agencies

Weissman et al. (1973) surveyed a population of married educated women at a job counseling center on campus and found that 12 percent had considered suicide in the prior two weeks, though none said that the thoughts were serious. McClure et al. (1972) found that the lifetime incidence of suicidal thought and attempts in volunteers working on a youth line were 12 percent and 2 percent respectively, and for workers at a crisis and suicide prevention service 35 percent and 8 percent.

The Elderly

Abrahams and Patterson (1978–1979) interviewed people over the age of 65 in a New England town and found that 2 percent reported feeling suicidal in the previous three years.

Special Groups

Feifel and Nagy (1980) found that alcoholics, drug addicts and prisoners were more likely to have experienced suicidal ideation and to have made more suicide attempts than deputy sheriffs and normal people.

In the United Kingdom, Bowen (1972) found that 10 percent of the deaths of crew members of boats were from suicide versus 3.6 percent of passenger deaths.

Standardizing Estimates

One way of standardizing estimates of suicidal preoccupation was suggested by Knight (1984) who gave the percentages of people in the community in New Zealand, giving the different answers to the current suicidal ideation item of the Beck Depression inventory (item 9): 0.2 percent level 3, 0.5 percent level 2 and 1.6 percent level 1. Since this test is widely given, it would be relatively easy to compare estimates from different nations and different groups.

Discussion

Although the incidence of suicidal behaviors in the community is of minor interest, the potential of the studies reviewed in this chapter is for the study of suicidal behaviors in community samples rather than psychologically disturbed groups. The study of suicide in the average person (rather than in the disturbed person) may reveal different correlates and suggest different theories.

Disappointingly, however, the studies on incidence rarely seek to test theoretical ideas proposed for suicide. Having estimated the incidence of suicidal behaviors, the research then typically analyzes the associations of this incidence with the standard, general, and typically simple demographic and social variables common to standardized interview schedules. It is to be hoped that future research of this type will be more theoretically oriented.

REFERENCES

Abrahams, R., & Patterson, R. D. Psychological distress among the community elderly. *International Journal of Aging,* 1978–1979, 9, 1–18.

Angle, C. R., O'Brien, T., & McIntire, M. Adolescent self-poisoning. *Journal of Developmental & Behavioral Pediatrics,* 1983, 4(2), 83–87.

Bagley, C. Suicidal behavior and suicidal ideation in adolescents. *British Journal of Guidance & Counseling,* 1975, 3, 190–208.

Bagley, C. Psychosocial correlates of suicidal behaviors in an urban population. *Crisis,* 1985, 6(2), 63–77.

Bell, R. A., Lin, E., Ice, J., & Bell, R. J. Drinking patterns and suicidal ideation and behavior in a general population. *Currents in Alcoholism*, 1978, 5, 317–332.

Berman, A. L. The epidemiology of life-threatening events. *Suicide*, 1975, 5, 67–77.

Besozzi, C. On the epidemiology of suicidal thoughts of students. In *Proceedings of the 6th International Congress on Suicide Prevention.* Vienna: IASP, 1972, 216–221.

Bolger, N., Downey, G., Walker, E., & Steininger, P. The onset of suicidal ideation in childhood and adolescence. *Journal of Youth & Adolescence*, 1989, 18, 175–190.

Bowen, D. Homicide at sea. *Medicine Science & the Law*, 1972, 12, 184–187.

Callahan, J. Epidemiology of suicide attempts and of survivors. In D. Lester (Ed.) *Suicide '89.* Denver: AAS, 1989, 294–296.

Cameron, P. Suicide and the generation gap. *Life-Threatening Behavior*, 1972, 2, 194–208.

Diekstra, R. F. W., & van de Loo, K. J. M. Attitudes toward suicide and incidence of suicidal behavior in a general population. In H. Z. Winnick & L. Miller (Eds.) *Aspects of Suicide in Modern Civilization.* Jerusalem: Academic, 1978, 79–85.

Domino, G., Domino, V., & Berry, T. Children's attitudes toward suicide. *Omega*, 1986–1987, 17, 279–287.

Dubow, E. F., Kausch, D. F., Blum, M. C., & Reed, J. Correlates of suicidal ideation and attempts in a community sample of junior high and high school students. *Journal of Clinical Child Psychology*, 1989, 18, 158–166.

Dyck, R. J., Bland, R. C., Newman, S. C., & Orn, H. Suicide attempts and psychiatric disorders in Edmonton. *Acta Psychiatrica Scandinavica*, 1988, suppl. 338, 64–71.

Feifel, H., & Nagy, V. Death orientation and life-threatening behavior. *Journal of Abnormal Psychology*, 1980, 89, 38–45.

Friedman, J. M., Asnis, G. M., Boeck, M., & DiFore, J. Prevalence of specific suicidal behaviors in a high school sample. *American Journal of Psychiatry*, 1987, 144, 1203–1206.

Fritz, D. Suicide ideation. In R. Yufit (Ed.) *Proceedings of the 20th Annual Conference.* Denver: AAS, 1987, 285–287.

Goldberg, E. Depression and suicidal ideation in the young adult. *American Journal of Psychiatry*, 1981, 138, 35–40.

Guyer, B., Leschoier, I., Gallagher, S. S., Hausman, A., & Azzara, C. V. Intentional injuries among children and adolescents in Massachusetts. *New England Journal of Medicine*, 1989, 321, 1584–1585.

Harkavy, J. M., & Asnis, G. Suicide attempts in adolescence. *New England Journal of Medicine*, 1985, 313, 1290–1291.

Joffe, R. T., Offord, D. R., & Boyle, M. H. Ontario Child Health Study. *American Journal of Psychiatry*, 1988, 145, 1420–1423.

Kashani, J. H., Goddard, P., & Reid, J. C. Correlates of suicidal ideation in a community sample of children and adolescents. *Journal of the American Academy of Child & Adolescent Psychiatry*, 1989, 28, 912–917.

Knight, R. G. Some general population norms for the short form BDI. *Journal of Clinical Psychology*, 1984, 40, 751–753.

Kopp, M. S., Skrabski, A., & Magyar, I. Neurotics at risk and suicidal behavior in the Hungarian population. *Acta Psychiatrica Scandinavica*, 1987, 76, 406–413.

Levav, I., Magnes, J., Aisenberg, E., & Rosenblum, I. Sociodemographic correlates of suicidal ideation and reported attempts. *Israel Journal of Psychiatry,* 1988, 25, 38–45.

Lonnqvist, J., Niskanen, P., & Sarna, S. Suicidal thoughts and depression in a normal female population. In K. Achte, V. Aalberg, & J. Lonnqvist (Eds.) *Psychopathology of Depression.* Helsinki: Psychiatria Fennica Supplement, 1980, 277–285.

Mayer, P. A., & Bauman, K. A. Health practices, problems and needs in a population of Micronesian adolescents. *Journal of Adolescent Health Care,* 1986, 7, 338–341.

McClure, J., Wetzel, R., Flannigan, T., McCabe, M., & Murphy, G. Volunteers in a suicide prevention program. In *Proceedings of the 6th International Congress for Suicide Prevention.* Vienna: IASP, 1972, 321–329.

Metha, A. Suicidal ideation among gifted adolescents. In R. Yufit (Ed.) *Proceedings of the 20th Annual Conference.* Denver: AAS, 1987, 278–279.

Moscicki, E. K., O'Carroll, P., Rae, D. S., Locke, B. Z., Roy, A., & Regier, D. A. Suicide attempts in the Epdidemiological Catchment Area Study. *Yale Journal of Biology & Medicine,* 1988, 61, 259–268.

Okasha, A., Lotaif, F., & Sadek, A. Prevalence of suicidal feelings in a sample of non-consulting medical students. *Acta Psychiatrica Scandinavica,* 1981, 63, 409–415.

Pfeffer, C. Suicidal impulses of normal children. *International Journal of Family Psychiatry,* 1984, 5(2), 139–150.

Pfeffer, C., & Trad, P. V. Sadness and suicidal tendencies in preschool children. *Journal of Developmental and Behavioral Pediatrics,* 1988, 9(2), 86–88.

Ramsay, R., & Bagley, C. The prevalence of suicidal behaviors, attempts and associated social experiences in an urban population. *Suicide & Life-Threatening Behavior,* 1985, 15, 151–167.

Riggs, S., & Cheng, T. Adolescents' willingness to use a school-based clinic in view of expressed health concern. *Journal of Adolescent Health Care,* 1988, 9, 208–213.

Robins, L. N. Suicide attempts in teen-aged medical patients. In *ADAMHA Report of the Secretary's Task Force on Youth Suicide.* Washington, DC: US Government Printing Office, 1989, 4, 94–114.

Rosenthal, P., & Rosenthal, S. Suicidal behavior by preschool children. *American Journal of Psychiatry,* 1984, 141, 520–525.

Rudd, M. D. The prevalence of suicidal ideation among college students. *Suicide & Life-Threatening Behavior,* 1989, 19, 173–183.

Salmons, P. H., & Harrington, R. Suicidal ideation in university students and other groups. *International Journal of Social Psychiatry,* 1984, 30, 201–205.

Smith, G. M. Interrelations among measures of depressive symptomatology, other measures of psychological distress, and young adult substance abuse. In. G. L. Klerman (Ed.) *Suicide and Depression Among Adolescents and Young Adults.* Washington, DC: American Psychiatric Press, 1986, 301–315.

Smith, K., & Crawford, S. Suicidal behavior among normal high school students. *Suicide & Life-Threatening Behavior,* 1986, 16, 313–325.

Sorenson, S. B., & Golding, J. M. Suicidal ideation and attempts in Hispanics and non-Hispanic whites. *Suicide & Life-Threatening Behavior,* 1988a, 18, 205–218.

Sorenson, S. B., & Golding, J. M. Prevalence of suicide attempts in a Mexican-American population. *Suicide & Life-Threatening Behavior,* 1988b, 18, 322–333.

Tardiff, K., Sweillam, A., & Jacque, C. Suicide and race. *Journal of Psychiatric Treatment & Evaluation,* 1981, 3, 275–278.

Vandivort, D. S., & Locker, B. Z. Suicide ideation. *Suicide & Life-Threatening Behavior,* 1979, 9, 205–218.

Velez, C. N., & Cohen, P. Suicidal behavior and ideation in a community sample of children. *Journal of the American Academy of Child & Adolescent Psychiatry,* 1988, 27, 349–356.

Weissman, M., Pincus, C., Radding, N., Laurence, R., & Siegel, R. The educated housewife. *American Journal of Orthopsychiatry,* 1973, 43, 565.

Wellman, R. J., & Wellman, M. M. Correlates of suicidal ideation in a college population. *Social Psychiatry & Psychiatric Epidemiology,* 1988, 23, 90–95.

Wenz, F. Aging and suicide? *International Journal of Aging & Human Development,* 1980, 11, 297–305.

Wenz, F. The epidemiology of suicidal ideations and behavior and depression in social area populations. In J. P. Soubrier & J. Vedrinne (Eds.) *Depression and Suicide.* Paris: Pergamon, 1983, 292–299.

Westefeld, J., & Furr, S. Suicide and depression among college students. *Professional Psychology,* 1987, 18, 119–127.

Whitehead, P. C., Johnson, F., & Ferrence, R. Measuring the incidence of self-injury. In *Proceedings of the 6th International Congress for Suicide Prevention.* Vienna: IASP, 1972, 274–284.

Wright, L. Suicidal thoughts and their relationship to family stress and personal problems among high school seniors and college undergraduates. *Adolescence,* 1985, 20, 575–580.

Chapter 15

THE METHOD CHOSEN FOR SUICIDE

In recent years, a great deal of research has appeared on the methods used for suicide. In particular, a third major method for preventing suicide (in addition to psychiatric/psychological treatment and suicide prevention centers) has been proposed, namely, preventing access to lethal methods for suicide. The first part of this chapter reviews the evidence for the effectiveness of the strategy (see also Clarke and Lester, 1989).

Firearms

The Effect of Strict Handgun Control Laws

Each of the 50 states of America is permitted to pass its own laws on the control of firearms. Bakal (1968) examined the handgun control laws of each state and coded them for the presence of various characteristics, such as whether a licence is required to sell handguns at retail stores, whether sales are reported to the police, and whether a permit is required to purchase a handgun.

Lester and Murrell (1980) created a Guttman scale of strictness for the 48 continental states of the US from these codings and found that states with the strictest handgun control laws had the lowest firearm suicide rates and the lowest overall suicide rates both in 1960 and 1970. Those states with the stricter handgun control laws did not have higher suicide rates by poisons or hanging/strangulation, though the suicide rate by "other" methods was higher. Thus, Lester and Murrell concluded that switching to an alternative method for suicide did not occur to any great extent in states in which the handgun control laws were stricter.

Further analysis of the data (Lester, 1984) showed that the restrictions on the selling and purchasing of handguns were the most critical characteristics of the laws in the association with lower firearm suicide rates. Restrictions on carrying were unrelated to firearm suicide rates. Finally,

227

controls for social variables (such as percent of blacks and percent of males in each state) did not eliminate these associations. Lester (1983) also found the preventive effect of strict gun control laws for each age group.

Lester (1987b) examined the power of the strictness of handgun control laws and the moral attitude toward suicide in explaining the suicide rates of the continental states. The strictness of the handgun control laws and the percentage of citizens attending church (the operational measure of moral attitudes toward suicide) were both highly correlated with the states' suicide rates, giving a multiple correlation of 0.68, thereby accounting for 46 percent of the variation in the states' suicide rates.

Lester and Frank (1988) looked at data for the 33 percent of gun suicides in 1980 for whom the government had data on the type of gun used. The percentage of handguns used in the states was negatively related to the strictness of the states' handgun control laws. Lester (1988i) examined changes in the proportion of suicides using guns in three states which strengthened their gun control laws and found no consistent changes.

Maxwell et al. (1984) placed the gun control statutes of the states into a multiple regression with socioeconomic variables such as the divorce and unemployment rates and found that only restrictions about the mentally ill buying guns was related to the states' suicide rates by firearms. Medoff and Magaddino (1983) rated six states as having strict gun control and placed this dummy variable into a multiple regression along with several social variables. They found that this dummy variable, as well as the particular requirements of a license to purchase and/or a waiting period, played significant roles in the multiple regression. Sommers (1984) also placed gun control variables in a multiple regression analysis with social variables and found that the suicide rate by firearms over the states in 1970 was significantly associated with only the requirement of a license to carry in addition to unemployment and divorce rates. He found differences in the regression results by sex and by race.

In Toronto, Rich and Young (1988) found that, after a gun control law was passed, the percentage of suicides using guns dropped (only for men) and the percentage using jumping (especially in front of trains) increased. There was no change in the overall suicide rate.

Attempting to Measure the Extent of Firearm Ownership

There are no measures of firearm ownership for each state of the US. However, several indirect measures are available — the accidental death rate from firearms and the percentage of firearms used for crimes such as murder.

Linden and Hale (1972) found that accidental death rates from firearms in the states were associated with the suicidal death rate from firearms, but this was not true for poisons. Lester (1985) found that the percentage of suicides committed with guns in US cities was associated with the percentage of homicides, robbery and assults with guns.

Lester (1987c, 1989) examined the relationship between the accidental death rate from firearms in each state and the percent of homicides committed using firearms with the suicide rate. The accidental death rate using firearms was positively associated with the firearm suicide rate, but not with the overall suicide rate. Similar associations were found for the percent of homicides committed with firearms. (The strictness of the handgun control laws was negatively associated with with overall suicide rate.) Lester and Agarwal (1989) found a similar result for suicidal and accidental death rates from firearms over the regions of India.

Lester (1989a) has also explored the use of per capita subscriptions to three firearm magazines in the states of the US as measures of firearm ownership. Per capita subscription rates to the three magazines were positively correlated with the firearm suicide rate and with the overall suicide rate.

For 1970, Lester (1988a) compared all of these indirect measures of firearm ownership using the states of the US. The firearm suicide rate was significantly associated with the percentage of suicides using firearms, the percentage of homicides using firearms, the accidental death rate from firearms, handgun control law strictness, and subscriptions to *Shooting Times* and *Guns & Ammo.* The suicide rate from all other methods gave correlations indicative of switching for the percentage of suicides by firearms, the percentage of homicides by firearms, the accidental death rate from firearms, and for subscriptions to *Shooting Times,* but not for the strictness of handgun control laws or subscriptions to *Guns & Ammo.* For the nine major regions of the US, the firearm suicide rate was associated with the percentages of suicides and homicides by firearms, the accidental death rate from firearms, the two magazine subscription rates and estimates of gun ownership, and four of the six correlations were statistically significant. The suicide rate by all other methods showed evidence of switching for all the measures except subscriptions to *Guns & Ammo.*

Incidentally, in a study of families seen at a pediatrics outpatient department, Patterson and Smith (1987) found that 38 percent of the families had at least one gun at home and, of these, 55 percent said it was loaded. Half of these said also that the gun was not locked away. Thus, guns may be quite freely available in some homes.

Actual Firearm Ownership

Measures of actual firearm ownership are available for the nine major regions of the continental US (but not for the 48 individual states). Lester (1988b) found that this measure was positively associated with the firearm suicide rate, but not with the overall suicide rate. Markush and Bartolucci (1984) found that estimates of gun ownership in the nine regions of America were associated with the total suicide rate and the suicide rate by firearms, but not with the non-firearm suicide rate. Lester (1988c) compared these results for the US with results from an analysis of data from Australian states. In Australia too the per capita ownership of firearms in the states was positively related to the firearm suicide rate but not to the overall suicide rate.

Time-Series Analyses of Firearm Ownership in the US

The previous studies were regional studies. Clarke and Jones (1989) obtained data on the household ownership of firearms in the US as a whole from 1959 to 1984 using data from national polls. Their time-series analysis indicated that the ownership of handguns was associated with the firearm suicide rate and with the overall suicide rate. Yang and Lester (1989) found, however, that changes in the estimate of handgun ownership from year to year were not associated in these data with changes in the firearm suicide rate.

Boor (1981) found that from 1962–1975 in the US, as domestic production and importing of firearms increased, so did the suicide rate using firearms. Wintemute (1988) found that the number of domestically produced handguns each year from 1946 to 1985 was positively associated with the firearm suicide rate.

Car Exhaust

Detoxifying Car Exhaust

In 1968, the US began to impose emission controls for motor vehicles in order to improve air quality. The result was that the carbon monoxide content in car exhaust dropped from 8.5 percent to 0.05 percent by 1980. This has made suicide more difficult to commit using car exhaust. Death from simple suffocation (elimination of oxygen) takes much longer than poisoning by carbon monoxide.

Clarke and Lester (1987) explored the effects of the reduced toxicity of car exhaust on the use of car exhaust for suicide in the US, and they compared this trend with the same period in England and Wales where emission controls had not been imposed on motor vehicles. They found that the use of car exhaust for suicide in the US leveled off and perhaps declined slightly in the US after 1968. (It must be remembered that older, more toxic cars are still in use and that the emission control system can be disconnected to permit gas richer in carbon monoxide to fill the car or garage.) In contrast, in England and Wales, the use of car exhaust for suicide has risen dramatically since 1970. In regression analyses, Lester and Clarke (1988) found that from 1968 to 1984 the number of suicides in the US using car exhaust increased slightly, while the percentage of suicides using car exhaust decreased.

Lester (1989d) found that in the US from 1950 to 1984, the use of car exhaust for suicide by men was related to the toxicity index of the cars (the per capita ownership of cars weighted by the emission controls in force when they were built), whereas the use of car exhaust for suicide by women was related to the per capita ownership of cars. Lester (1989g) found that the introduction of emission controls on American cars had different effects of the use of car exhaust for suicide by men and women. The male rate dropped immediately, whereas the female rate rose for another eight years before it began to decline.

Lester and Abe (1989c) examined the effects of the increasing ownership of cars in Japan on the suicide rate using car exhaust. Suicide by car exhaust rose from less than 0.02 per 100,000 per year in 1965 to over 1.33 in 1982. Meanwhile, suicide by all other methods rose from about 14.68 per 100,000 per year in 1965 to over 16.18 in 1982. Thus, the proportion of suicides using car exhaust increased dramatically during the period, from 0.1 to 7.6 percent. The ownership of cars increased almost linearly from 1965 to 1982. Along with this change, the suicide rate using car exhaust rose dramatically, with an especially steep increase from 1973 to 1975. However, after 1975, the suicide rate using car exhaust levelled off. Because of weak emission controls, car exhaust was less toxic after 1975 but still capable of killing. Nonetheless, the results appear to indicate that the tightening of emission controls on car exhaust may have inhibited its increasing use for suicide.

The suicide rate by all methods other than car exhaust rose up to 1973, along with the increasing suicide rate by car exhaust. This period, therefore, shows little evidence of switching. As suicide by car exhaust became more common, so did suicide by other methods.

A Regional Study of Car Ownership and Suicide

Lester and Frank (1989) explored the relationship between a simple measure of overall car ownership in the states of the US (regardless of the year in which the car was made) and the use of car exhaust for suicide. They found that the per capita ownership of cars was related to the suicide rate using car exhaust but not to the overall suicide rate. Thus, the more cars are available in a state, the more they are used for suicide.

Domestic Gas

Clarke and Mayhew (1988) have documented accurately the gradual detoxification of domestic gas in England and Wales and the declining suicide rate using domestic gas and overall. They showed that the two curves follow each other extremely closely. In 1958, there were 2637 suicides using domestic gas out of 5298 suicides comprising 49.8 percent of the total number of suicides. By 1977, there were 8 suicides using domestic gas out of 3944, comprising only 0.2 percent of the suicides. Surtees and Duffy (1989) argued that the effect of the detoxification of domestic gas on suicide in general was clearer in men than in women.

Clarke and Mayhew (1989) then explored why Scotland and the Netherlands did not experience an overall decline in their suicide rate as domestic gas was detoxified. They presented evidence to show that the suicide rates were rising in those two nations when domestic gas was detoxified, and they argued that this rising suicide rate masked the effect of the detoxification of domestic gas on the overall suicide rate.

However, in this context, the data presented by Clarke and Lester

(1987) become relevant. Their data show that the use of car exhaust has been rising dramatically in England and Wales in recent years. It may be that those who might have used domestic gas if it were still toxic are now turning to car exhaust. Thus, perhaps people will switch to a similar method to their preferred method if their preferred method is unavailable. However, the rise in the use of car exhaust for suicide has taken place many years after the detoxification of domestic gas, and so there has been a net savings of many lives in the interim period.

Arguing against the hypothesis that limiting access to lethal methods for suicide will decrease the use of those methods for suicide, Sainsbury (1986) claimed that cities in England and the Netherlands with toxic and non-toxic domestic gas in 1967 did not differ in changes in their suicide rate, but his sample sizes were small and the data presentation was inadequate.

Yamasawa et al. (1980) noted that suicide by domestic gas declined in Japan after detoxification of the gas. Lester and Abe (1989a) studied the effects of the detoxification of domestic gas on suicide in Japan from 1969 to 1982. They found that the suicide rate by domestic gas and the production of toxic gas showed a similar pattern. Both increased until the early 1970s, whereupon both showed a dramatic decrease. It appears, therefore, that as the availability of toxic domestic gas was decreased, the use of domestic gas for suicide also decreased. What about the suicide rate by all other methods? Lester and Abe showed that the suicide rate by all other methods rose during this period. The slope of the linear regression line for this plot from 1969 to 1975 was 455.25 and for 1975 to 1982 was 114.18. Thus, it appears that use of all other methods for suicide rose at a lower rate during the latter part of the period under study than in the first part of the period. As toxic gas became less available, the increasing suicide rate by all other methods rose at a *slower* pace. Thus, it is clear that displacement to other methods for suicide did not take place (for then the suicide rate by all other methods would have risen at a faster pace).

Medication and Poisons

Lester (1989c) reported evidence from Clark (1985) to show that, when prescriptions were required for opiates in England in the early 1900s, the use of opiates for suicide declined. Lester also found data which indicated that when sedatives were restricted in Australia in the 1960s, their use for suicide declined without there being an increase in the use of other methods.

In the US from 1960 to 1974, Lester (1989f) found that the suicide rate using barbiturates was associated with the annual sales of barbiturates and with the accidental death rate from barbiturates. In contrast, Sainsbury (1986) claimed (without presenting data) that as barbiturate prescribing fell in Britain, the use of barbiturates for suicide rose! However, in Sweden, as the prescribing of barbiturates fell, so also did their use for suicide.

In Japan prior to 1961 barbiturates were available over the counter without a prescription. From February first, 1961, the Pharmacy Act S.49 required prescriptions for both barbiturates and meprobamate. Yamasawa et al. (1980) noted that the use of hypnotics for suicide declined after these restrictions. Lester and Abe (1989b) examined the use of sedatives and hypnotics for suicide prior to and after the implementation of the Pharmacy Act of 1961. The suicide rate using sedatives and hypnotics peaked at 7.05 per 100,000 per year in 1958. Thereafter, the suicide rate by sedatives and hypnotics declined consistently. Thus, at the time when the Pharmacy Act was implemented in 1961, the suicide rate using sedatives and hypnotics was already declining. The slope of the declining regression line did increase a little after the implementation of the Pharmacy Act. The suicide rate by all other methods was examined for the same time period. The suicide rate by all other methods began declining even earlier, after 1955 in fact, and continued to decline until 1965. Thus, there is no evidence that people switched methods for suicide once prescriptions were required for sedatives and hypnotics.

Lester (1989b) found that the accidental death rates from poisoning by solids/liquids and by gases were positively associated over the states of America with the suicide rates by these two methods. Lester and Agarwal (1989) found a similar association for poisoning in general over the regions of India.

Ekeberg et al. (1987) examined the impact of restrictions in Oslo on barbiturates. The use of barbiturates for attempted suicide decreased significantly, but the use of antidepressants and neuroleptics increased significantly. The sources of the drugs used also changed, with fewer from new doctors and more from psychiatrists (and no changes in non-medical sources and family doctors).

More informally, Adelstein and Mardon (1975) noted that in the 1960s in England, the number of prescriptions for barbiturates decreased, and there was an accompanying decrease in their use for suicide. However, the suicide rate using poisons stayed constant during this period, suggesting that people switched medications. Brewer and Farmer (1985) noted that, after 1976 in the United Kingdom, prescriptions for hypnotics and tranquilizers decreased in number and so did completed and attempted suicide by poisons/overdoses. Forster and Frost (1985) found that from 1968 to 1978 in England the prescription rate for psychotropic drugs and the rate of attempted suicide by medications were positively related. This positive association was also found in a correlation over regions. They estimated that 1,000 fewer prescriptions resulted in 3.8 fewer suicide attempts.

McMurray et al. (1987) noted that the Scottish prescription rates for mefenamic acid and for distalgesic paralleled the admission rate for attempted suicide using these medications to one hospital for the overall period of 1971 to 1985, but they noted that the trends appeared to be diverging for the last four years of the period. Whyte et al. (1989) noted that the use of different benzodiazepine agents for attempting suicide in Victoria (Australia) roughly matched the prescription rates for them.

Moens and van de Voorde (1989) plotted the suicide rate in Belgium from 1971 to 1984 and the prescription rates for various drugs and claimed to "see" no association. However, they did not carry out any statistical analyses of the data.

Several authors have noted that the newer antidepressants have fewer deaths per prescription (Beaumont, 1989; Cassidy and Henry, 1987; Farmer and Pinder, 1989; Henry, 1989; Leonard, 1988). Medications also differ in the amount needed for death. For example, a lethal dose of lithium is 40 tablets or 12 grams while a lethal dose of carbamazepine is 300 tablets or 60 grams (Pary et al., 1987). Farmer and Pinder suggested that patients given different antidepressants may differ in their willingness to comply with the recommended doses. Montgomery et al. (1989) suggested that the medications may differ in toxicity, that some of the drugs may induce suicide, that perhaps too low doses are given of some of the drugs, and that some drugs may be given more often to suicidal and more seriously disturbed patients.

Drowning

Lester (1989e) found that American states adjoining the oceans or the Great Lakes had higher suicide rates by drowning, lower rates by firearms, but similar rates by all other methods.

Will People Switch Methods?

Jennings and Lunn (1962) found that 24 completed suicides out of a sample of 271 had a prior attempt recorded. Nineteen of the 24 used poisoning by pills or gas for their first attempt and 12 used this method for their completed suicide. Robinson and Duffy (1989) found that suicide attempters by overdose were more method-specific in their prior attempts than those using other methods of self-injury, though only the minority were method-specific.

Lester (1989i) looked at college students who rated guns or pills as very acceptable as methods for suicide. Those rating guns as very acceptable rated ten other methods for suicide as more acceptable than those who rated pills as very acceptable. Lester suggested that this might indicate that those who would choose guns for suicide might be more likely to switch than those choosing pills if their preferred method was not available.

Lester et al. (1989) found that 47 percent of psychiatric patients who had attempted suicide were repeaters. Of the repeaters, 32 percent switched methods. Those who switched did not differ from those who did not switch in sex, age or marital status, but they were less often schizophrenic.

Lindesay (1986) noted that restricting access to lethal methods for suicide may have a greater impact on suicide in the elderly since they are less able to aggressively search out alternative methods for suicide if their preferred method is less available.

Association Between Methods

Lester (1987d) found that the suicide rates by poisons, hanging and other methods were positively associated over the states of America and that these rates were negatively associated with the suicide rate by firearms. He suggested that these formed two alternative groups of methods for suicide.

Over time in the US, Lester (1988g) found that the use of poisons and firearms were associated as were the use of hanging and other methods. These results differed from those obtained in the United Kingdom.

How Do People Rate the Different Methods?

Lester (1988d) asked college students to choose their preferred methods for suicide. Men chose guns more often and medications less often. In terms of which qualities of the methods appealed to them, women focussed more on the pain and disfigurement involved and less on the availability. Men and women did not differ in their focussing on the quickness of the method. Lester (1988f) had students rate the acceptability of different methods for suicide and identified two factors: (1) pills versus all other methods. Females gave a four factor solution and males a two factor solution, suggesting that females view the methods in a more complex way than males and may be less likely to switch methods if one is unavailable. Lester (1988h) confirmed on a Semantic Differential type of inventory that guns and pills are viewed very differently. However, on this questionnaire there were virtually no sex differences in perception and no effect from one's own preferred method.

Lester (1988e) had students read a case of suicide, and he varied the method used by the protagonist (pills versus gun). The rated psychiatric disturbance of the protagonist was the same for both methods of suicide.

The Methods Used By Immigrants

Burvill et al. (1983) found that the methods used by English, Scottish, and Irish immigrants to Australia shifted from the pattern in their home nations to the Australian pattern over time.

Early Determinants of Choice of Method

Grof (1985) speculated that early memories affect the choice of method for suicide. The choice of non-violent methods is made by inhibited depressives who desire to eliminate pain by going back to an inter-uterine existence. The choice of violent methods for suicide is made by agitated depressives who want to intensify suffering to speed liberation and who seek to recreate the birth process.

Jacobson et al. (1987) found that those who chose asphyxia for suicide (hanging, strangulation, drowning or gas) were more likely to have experienced asphyxia at birth. Those choosing violent methods for suicide (hanging, strangulation, jumping, and firearms) were more likely to have been twins or to have experienced mechanical birth trauma.

Anesthesia for the mother was not associated with choice of method for suicide. Compared to drug addicts, the suicides less often had a mother given opiates or barbiturates during delivery.

Knowledge About Methods

Carlson et al. (1987) found that pre-adolescents (normals and psychiatric patients) had less realistic awareness of the methods of suicide, the irreversibility of death and the reasons for committing suicide than did adolescents (14 years and older).

Correlates and Consequences of Choice of Method

It is, by now, a trivial observation that choice of method varies with sex, race, and region, but this has been re-reported by Taylor and Wicks (1980). Tonkon (1984) studied adolescent suicides in British Columbia (Canada) and reported that native Indians, rural people and boys tended to use guns more for suicide than non-natives, urban dwellers and girls respectively. Garfinkel and Golombek (1983) in Ontario (Canada) found that female youth tended to use guns for suicide more often over time from 1970–1978. Youths in rural areas used guns and car exhaust more while youths in urban areas used jumping and overdoses more. Gatter and Bowen (1980) found no differences in the proportions with physical disease of those choosing different methods for suicide. Those choosing carbon monoxide less often had a mental disease than those choosing overdoses or other methods.

McIntosh and Santos (1985–1986) found that the elderly in the US do use different methods, but that the race and sex also play a role in this. For example, for blacks and for white males, the elderly use guns and hanging more than the young, but for white females the elderly use guns and hanging less than the young. In Belgium, Moens et al. (1988) found that the geographical pattern of suicide differed for each method.

Husain and Vandiver (1984) found that children used running into traffic and jumping more for suicidal actions while adolescents used poisoning and wrist cutting more. Girls used poisons and wrist-cutting more while boys used shooting and gas more.

Lester (1988j) found no differences between completed suicides using firearms and those using overdoses on whether they scored high on the excitor or the inhibitor scales of the MMPI. Lester and Beck (1980–1981) compared attempted suicides who used cutting with those who use coma-producing drugs. The cutters had less suicidal intent, were more often male and single, had more often recently experienced legal problems and less often recent medical care, interpersonal friction or school failure, and more often had psychosis, alcohol abuse and severe psychiatric disturbance.

In a region of France, Maurice et al. (1989) found that about a quarter to one third of attempted suicides using overdoses, cutting, hanging and drowning had attempted suicide in the last year as compared to zero percent of those using firearms. O'Brien et al. (1987) found no association between the method used by suicide attempters and their suicidal intent scale score or depression scale score.

Peck (1985–1986, 1987) found that teenage completed suicides used hanging more while young adults used guns more. Females used pills more and guns and hanging less often than males. Those with prior suicidal behavior used pills more and carbon monoxide less often. Those who left suicide notes used pills and carbon monoxide more and hanging less. Social class was not related to choice of method. In San Diego, Rich and Young (1988) found that psychotics used guns less often for completed suicide and hanging/jumping more often.

Van Praag and Plutchik (1984) compared non-psychotic depressives who made violent and non-violent suicide attempts. The groups did not differ in their objective depression score, and there was no difference in the proportions of unipolars and bipolars. However, the violent attempters were more often diagnosed as having the vital type of depression.

Era

Moscicki and Boyd (1983–1985) noted that the use of firearms for suicide rose in the US from 1935–1980, so that by the 1980s, two thirds of suicides used guns. Among youths, men and women used guns equally often.

Gist and Welch (1989) noted that teenagers in the US increasingly used guns for suicide from 1955–1979. Up to 1966, the use of guns for suicide was paralleled by a decrease in the accidental death rate using guns, but after 1967 less so. Thus, the increase in the use of guns by teenage suicides up to 1966 could simply be the results of a change in death certification practices, but this is probably not so after 1967.

Studies of Particular Methods

AIDS

Cases have been reported of people trying to commit suicide by contracting AIDS (Flavin et al., 1986).

Burning

Copeland (1985) found that suicide by burning in Miami was mostly used by whites, those older than 50 and females and more often took place at home. Hammond et al. (1988) found that attempted suicide by burning was especially common in Latin women in the Miami area.

In England, those using incineration for completed or attempted suicide were younger, more often unemployed, more often arsonists, psychiatric patients and suicide attempters in the past, more often diagnosed as having a personality disorder and less often as alcoholic, and had attempted suicide more often in the presence of an authority figure (Jacobson et al., 1986).

Parks et al. (1989) found that men tended more to pour the liquid on themselves and light it while women tended more often to light the fire and enter it.

Car Exhaust

Drinker (1938) noted that the use of motor vehicle exhaust for suicide was more common in rural areas than in urban areas.

Cutting/Piercing

Karlsson et al. (1988) compared completed suicides and homicide victims by cutting/piercing and found that the suicides less often had alcohol in their body but more often had drugs. The suicides were pierced more often in areas of exposed skin.

Makela and Honkanen (1984) found that suicide attempters using cutting were younger than those using other methods, used alcohol more, died less often, and were less often diagnosed as psychotic and more often as alcohol abusers. They did not differ in sex or prior psychiatric hospitalizations. However, in a five-year follow-up, a greater proportion of the cutters were dead and a greater proportion were dead from suicide. Minnaar et al. (1980) noted also in South Africa that suicide attempters using wrist cutting were younger than those using poisons or gas.

Takeuchi et al. (1986) identified three types of wrist-cutters:

(1) females with conversion disorder/symptoms who cut to free themselves from pain and frustration and who are depressed, irritable, and dissociated. They tend to repeat and cut delicately.
(2) depressed people who have suicidal ideation, who use other methods for attempting suicide also and cut deeply.
(3) adolescents with behavior disorders, often with high IQ scores, menstrual disturbances and self-hate (perhaps with bulimia) who cut delicately but repeatedly.

Drowning

Copeland (1987) found that suicides by drowning in Miami were mostly older, white, males, sober, depressed over health, without a suicide note and at home.

Firearms

Andress (1976) found that women using guns for suicide were less likely to shoot themselves in the head than were men. Chynoweth (1977) found that completed suicides using guns were more likely to leave suicide notes than those using other methods. Brent et al. (1987) found that youths who used firearms for completed suicide were more often intoxicated than those using other methods. In Houston, Texas, Peterson et al. (1985, 1989) found that suicide attempters using guns were more often male, aged 25–34 and white than those using other methods, but did not differ in marital status. Older attempters were more likely to shoot themselves in the head than in the chest or abdomen, but men and women did not differ in this.

Di Maio (1985) reviewed research on the site of suicidal gunshot wounds. The head and neck was most common for handgun deaths and rifles (about 80 percent), whereas only about 50 percent of shotgun deaths involved the head. The chest was the next most common region of the body, with the abdomen the least common site. In one study on this, Eisele et al. (1981) found that 74 percent of firearm completed suicides shot themselves in the head, 18 percent in the chest, 4 percent in the neck and 4 percent in the abdomen. Those using handguns were most likely to aim for the head (82 percent), then rifles (67 percent) and then shotguns (47 percent). The head wounds were mainly parietal and temporal. All left-handed people inflicted left-side wounds and 91 percent of the right-handed people shot themselves on the right side. Hudson (1981) found that 58 of 3522 suicides by firearms used two or more shots, presumably because the first shot did not kill them. In Alaska, Hlady and Middaugh (1987) found that those using firearms for suicide tended more often to be drunk at the time of death.

Lester (1989h) studied all of the gun deaths in the US in May, 1989. Suicides used handguns less often than murderers. The use of handguns by suicides was not related to their sex and age. In addition, male and female suicides did not differ in whether they shot themselves in the face versus the rest of the body. Wintemute et al. (1988) found that handguns were the firearm of choice for completed suicides in Sacramento regardless of sex or age. However, males were more likely to use long guns for suicide than females. For the 33 percent of suicides using firearms in 1980 in America for whom the government knew the types of guns, Lester and Frank (1988) found that females used handguns more for suicide than males, as did non-whites, those older than 25, and those not single. Selden et al. (1988) found that the caliber of the gun used by suicides to shoot themselves in the head was not related to mortality.

McNeil and Binder (1987) examined psychiatric emergency patients and found that 4 percent of them were carrying guns with them. These patients did not differ from the rest in suicidal behavior in the prior two weeks.

Hanging

Guarner and Hanzlick (1987) found that suicides by hanging in Atlanta were younger and more often white and male. They committed suicide indoors more, in home or a jail, and used a rope or belt.

Jumpers

Seiden (1978) followed up those who survived a jump off the Golden Gate Bridge and a general sample of suicide attempters. Fewer of the jumpers were dead at the time of follow-up, but more of the deaths were suicidal. (The groups, however, differed in sex and time to follow-up.) Simonsen (1983) studied nine suicides jumping from a bridge 35–37 metres high. Six died from drowning and three from the traumatic injuries (with no sex differences in the cause of death).

Cantor et al. (1989) found that those who were stopped from jumping off bridges differed from those who died in being more often alcohol abusers and intoxicated, having more often attempted suicide and been psychiatrically hospitalized in the past, and being more often diagnosed as having a personality disorder. The completed suicides were more often schizophrenic and never married and, if hospitalized for psychiatric reasons, had stayed longer.

Pommereau et al. (1989) compared attempted suicides by jumping and overdoses. The jumpers were more often older, single, psychotic and formerly in psychiatric treatment whereas the overdosers were more often divorced, unemployed, with prior suicide attempts and diagnosed with a reactive disorder. (The groups did not differ in sex and subsequent completed suicide.)

In Athens, Kontaxakis et al. (1988) found that attempted suicides by jumping as compared to those using overdoses were more often male, psychiatrically disturbed, with physical disease, and married/widowed and older.

Seiden and Spence (1983–1984) found that the Golden Gate Bridge was much more popular as a suicide venue in San Francisco than the Bay Bridge, even after allowing for the fact that the Golden Gate Bridge permits pedestrians. The authors documented many cases of people driving across the Bay Bridge in order to jump from the Golden Gate Bridge but not vice versa. Out-of-state jumpers also preferred the Golden Gate Bridge. Imitation/suggestion and the symbolism of the Golden Gate Bridge perhaps account for its popularity as a suicide venue.

Medication

Bancroft et al. (1976) found that the strength of the wish to die in attempted suicides was unrelated to the drug used for the attempt. (A wish to die was more commonly reported in those who were unconscious when admitted to the hospital.)

Charnov and Sturner (1985) compared suicides by different medications and found that men used tranquilizers more while women used antidepressants more. They found that those using tranquilizers were more often intoxicated, less often left a suicide note, less often had been in psychiatric treatment and less often had previously attempted suicide, but they omitted to control for sex in these analyses.

In London, Fuller et al. (1989) found that 51 percent of those attempting suicide by overdose took more than one agent. The mean number of agents taken was 2.4. Thirty-three percent also ingested alcohol. Robinson and Duffy (1989) compared suicide attempters using overdoses with those using other forms of self-injury in Edinburgh (Scotland). The overdosers were older, more often female, of higher social class, less often drunk at the time, less often alcohol abusers or with a psychiatric history, more often depressed and less often violent to others, a victim of violence or with a criminal record.

In emergency room overdose patients, Shader and Anglin (1982) reported that suicide attempters were more often female and younger than patients who were "high." Both suicide attempters and those who claimed accidental overdose of medications used diazepam more and prescription medications more.

In New Zealand, Large et al. (1980) found that 67 percent of suicide attempters with medications used drugs from their own prescription, 15 percent the drugs from others' prescriptions, and 12 percent purchased the drug legitimately (with 6 percent using other sources). Those using their own prescriptions had made more prior suicide attempts, were more often depressed patients, and more often on medication. Turner (1980) found that suicide attempters who sought help prior to their attempt were more likely to have used prescribed drugs for their attempt while those who did not seek help were more likely to use non-prescribed drugs.

Russian Roulette

Fishbain et al. (1987) compared suicides by Russian Roulette with other gun suicides and found them more often to be single, students, in good health, black or latino, Roman Catholic, non-citizens, intoxicated, and alcohol or drug abusers and less often depressed. They did not differ in recent losses, belligerence and hostility, or prior psychiatric illness/attempted suicide.

Self-Cutters

Simpson (1975) compared wrist-cutters with self-poisoners. The wrist-cutters were less depressed but showed more tension and feelings of emptiness. The wrist-cutters more often had an eating disorder, substance abuse, sexual disturbances (such as promiscuity), a negative reaction to menarche and menstruation, a history of early surgery and hospitalization, broken homes, and a diagnosis of personality disorder. They did not differ in homosexuality or prior suicide attempts.

Jones et al. (1979) argued that self-cutters feel tense before the act and relief of tension afterwards, whereas self-poisoners feel depressed and lonely before the act.

Trains and Subways

Guggenheim and Weisman (1974) studied people completing suicide in the subway system. Jumpers and prostrators more often had a history of violence (including military combat and self-directed violence) than those merely touching the live rail. Cocks (1989) found that 43 percent of suicidal acts in the London subway resulted in death, while Johnston and Waddell (1984) found a fatality rate in Toronto of 48 percent. In Toronto the modal age was 20–30 and the modal time 10 A.M. to 5 P.M.

Lindekilde and Wang (1985) found that suicides from trains in one Danish county were younger than other suicides, more often psychiatrically disturbed and more often psychotic. Symonds (1985) found that suicides on the railway were younger, more often female, more often of higher social class, more often non-single, and more often psychiatric patients than accidental deaths on the railways.

Throwing Oneself on a Hand Grenade

Blake (1978) found that this behavior in soldiers awarded the Medal of Honor was more common in enlisted men than in officers and in men from elite squads than ordinary squads.

Discussion

The growth of interest in the methods used for suicide during the 1980s is quite impressive. The research by Lester and his colleagues has been important in exploring fully the possibilities for preventing suicide by restricting access to lethal methods for suicide. Although the efficacy of this strategy is not yet proven, it has provided a third option for suicide prevention (other than psychiatric treatment and crisis intervention services), and it is hoped that the strategy will be examined further by others in the 1990s.

REFERENCES

Adelstein, A., & Mardon, C. Suicides, 1961–1974. *Population Trends,* 1975, 2(Winter), 13–18.

Andress, L. V. An epidemiological study of the psychosocial characteristics of suicidal behavior in Riverside County between 1960 and 1974. *Dissertation Abstracts International,* 1976, 37B, 1481.

Bakal, C. *No Right to Bear Arms.* New York: Paperback Library, 1968.

Bancroft, J. H., Skrimshire, A., & Simkin, S. The reasons people give for taking overdoses. *British Journal of Psychiatry,* 1976, 128, 538–548.

Beaumont, G. The toxicity of antidepressants. *British Journal of Psychiatry,* 1989, 154, 454–458.

Blake, J. A. Death by hand grenade. *Suicide & Life-Threatening Behavior,* 1978, 8, 46–59.

Boor, M. Methods of suicide and implications for suicide prevention. *Journal of Clinical Psychology,* 1981, 37, 70–75.

Brent, D. A., Perper, J. A., & Allman, J. Alcohol, firearms, and suicide among youth. *Journal of the American Medical Association,* 1987, 257, 3369–3372.

Brewer, C., & Farmer, R. Self-poisoning in 1984. *British Medical Journal,* 1985, 290, 391.

Burvill, P., McCall, M., Woodings, T., & Stenhouse, N. Comparison of suicide rates and methods in English, Scots and Irish immigrants in Australia. *Social Science & Medicine,* 1983, 17, 705–708.

Cantor, C. H., Hill, M. A., & McLachlan, E. K. Suicide and related behavior from river bridges. *British Journal of Psychiatry,* 1989, 155, 829–835.

Carlson, G. A., Asarnow, J. R., & Orbach, I. Developmental aspects of suicidal behavior in children. *Journal of the American Academy of Child & Adolescent Psychiatry,* 1987, 26, 186–192.

Cassidy, S., & Henry, J. Fatal toxicity of antidepressant drugs in overdose. *British Medical Journal,* 1987, 295, 1021–1024.

Charnov, J. H., & Sturner, W. Q. Psychotropic drug-related suicides. *American Journal of Forensic Medicine & Pathology,* 1985, 6, 312–318.

Chynoweth, R. The significance of suicide notes. *Australian & New Zealand Journal of Psychiatry,* 1977, 11, 197–200.

Clark, M. J. Suicides by opium and its derivatives in England and Wales. *Psychological Medicine,* 1985, 15, 237–242.

Clarke, R. V., & Jones, P. R. Suicide and the increased availability of handguns. *Social Science & Medicine,* 1989, 28, 805–809.

Clarke, R. V., & Lester, D. Toxicity of car exhausts and opportunity for suicide. *Journal of Epidemiology & Community Health,* 1987, 41, 114–120.

Clarke, R. V., & Lester, D. *Suicide: Closing the Exits.* New York: Springer, 1989.

Clarke, R. V., & Mayhew, P. The British gas suicide story and its criminological implications. *Crime & Justice,* 1988, 10, 79–116.

Clarke, R. V., & Mayhew, P. Crime as opportunity. *British Journal of Criminology,* 1989, 29, 35–46.

Cocks, R. A. Trauma in the Tube. *Stress Medicine,* 1989, 5, 93–97.

Copeland, A. R. Suicidal fire deaths revisited. *Zeitschrift fur Rechtsmedizin,* 1985, 95(1), 51–57.

Copeland, A. R. Suicide by drowning. *American Journal of Forensic Medicine & Pathology,* 1987, 8(1), 18–22.

Di Maio, V. J. *Gunshot Wounds.* New York: Elsevier, 1985.

Drinker, C. W. *Carbon Monoxide Asphyxia.* New York: Oxford University, 1938.

Eisele, J. W., Reay, D., & Cook, A. Sites of suicidal gunshot wounds. *Journal of Forensic Sciences,* 1981, 26, 480–485.

Ekeberg, O., Jacobsen, D., Flaaten, B., & Mack, A. Effect of regulatory withdrawal of drugs and prescription recommendations on the pattern of self-poisoning in Oslo. *Acta Medica Scandinanvica,* 1987, 221, 483–487.

Farmer, R. D., & Pinder, R. M. Why do overdose rates vary between antidepressants? *Acta Psychiatrica Scandinavica,* 1989, suppl. 354, 25–35.

Fishbain, D. A., Fletcher, J. R., Aldrich, T. E., & Davis, J. H. Relationship between Russian roulette deaths and risk-taking behavior. *American Journal of Psychiatry,* 1987, 144, 563–567.

Flavin, D. K., Franklin, J. E., & Frances, R. J. The AIDS and suicidal behavior in alcohol-dependent homosexual men. *American Journal of Psychiatry,* 1986, 143, 1440–1442.

Forster, D., & Frost, C. Medicinal self-poisoning and prescription frequency. *Acta Psychiatrica Scandinavica,* 1985, 71, 567–574.

Fuller, G. N., Rea, A. J., Payne, J. F., & Lant, A. F. Parasuicide in central London. *Journal of the Royal Society of Medicine,* 1989, 82, 653–656.

Garfinkel, B., & Golombek, H. Suicidal behavior in adolescence. In H. Golombek & B. Garfinkel (Eds.) *The Adolescent and Mood Disturbance.* New York: International Universities Press, 1983, 189–217.

Gatter, K., & Bowen, D. A study of suicide autopsies 1957–1977. *Medicine, Science & the Law,* 1980, 20, 37–42.

Gist, R., & Welch, Q. B. Certification change versus actual behavior change in teenage suicide rates, 1955–1979. *Suicide & Life-Threatening Behavior,* 1989, 19, 277–288.

Grof, S. *Beyond the Brain.* Albany: State University of New York, 1985.

Guarner, J., & Hanzlick, R. Suicide by hanging. *American Journal of Forensic Medicine & Pathology,* 1987, 8(1), 23–26.

Guggenheim, F. G., & Weisman, A. Suicide in the subway. *Life-Threatening Behavior,* 1974, 4, 43–53.

Hammond, J. S., Ward, C. G., & Pereira, E. Self-inflicted burns. *Journal of Burn Care & Rehabilitation,* 1988, 9(2), 178–179.

Henry, J. A. A fatal toxicity index for antidepressant poisoning. *Acta Psychiatrica Scandinavica,* 1989, supplement 354, 37–45.

Hlady, W. G., & Middaugh, J. P. The epidemiology of suicide in Alaska. *Alaska Medicine,* 1987, 29(5), 158–164.

Hudson, P. Multishot firearm suicide. *American Journal of Forensic Medicine & Pathology,* 1981, 2, 239–242.

Husain, S. A., & Vandiver, T. *Suicide in Children and Adolescents.* New York: Spectrum, 1984.

Jacobson, B., Eklund, G., Hamberger, L., Linnarson, D., Sedvall, G., & Valverius, M. Perinatal origin of adult self-destructive behavior. *Acta Psychiatrica Scandinavica,* 1987, 76, 364–371.

Jacobson, R., Jackson, M., & Berelowitz, M. Self-incineration. *Psychological Medicine,* 1986, 16, 107–116.

Jennings, H. C., & Lunn, J. E. A study of suicide in a northern industrial town. *Medical Officer,* 1962, 108, 397–399.

Jones, I. H., Congiu, L., Stevenson, J., Strauss, N., & Frei, D. Z. A biological approach to two forms of human self-injury. *Journal of Nervous & Mental Disease,* 1979, 167, 74–78.

Johnston, D. W., & Waddell, J. P. Death and injury patterns, Toronto subway system. *Journal of Trauma,* 1984, 24, 619–622.

Karlsson, T., Ormstad, K., & Rajas, J. Patterns in sharp force fatalities. *Journal of Forensic Sciences,* 1988, 33, 448–461.

Kontaxakis, V., Markidis, M., Vaslamatzis, G., Ioannidis, H., & Stefanis, C. Attempted suicide by jumping. *Acta Psychiatrica Scandinavica,* 1988, 77, 435–437.

Kreitman, N. Some research aspects of suicide and attempted suicide (parasuicide) with special reference to young people. In *Suicide and Attempted Suicide in Young People.* Copenhagen: WHO, 1976, 41–51.

Large, R. G., Epston, A., Kirker, J., & Kydd, R. Self-poisoning. *New Zealand Medical Journal,* 1980, 91, 218–221.

Leonard, B. E. Cost benefit analysis of tricyclic antidepressant overdosage. In B. E. Leonard & S. W. Parker (Eds.) *Risk/Benefits of Antidepressants.* Southampton: Duphar Laboratories, 1988, 1–12.

Lester, D. Preventive effect of strict handgun control laws on suicide rates. *American Journal of Psychiatry,* 1983, 140, 1259.

Lester, D. *Gun Control.* Springfield, IL: Charles C Thomas, 1984.

Lester, D. The use of firearms in violent crime. *Journal of Crime & Justice,* 1985, 8, 115–120.

Lester, D. Preventing suicide. In J. Morgan (Ed.) *Suicide.* London, Ont.: King's College, 1987a, 69–78.

Lester, D. An availability-acceptability theory of suicide. *Activitas Nervosa Superior,* 1987b, 19, 164–166.

Lester, D. Availability of guns and the likelihood of suicide. *Sociology & Social Research,* 1987c, 71, 287–288.

Lester, D. Substitution of method in suicide and homicide. *Psychological Reports,* 1987d, 60, 278.

Lester, D. Firearm availability and the incidence of suicide and homicide. *Acta Psychiatrica Belgica,* 1988a, 88, 387–393.

Lester, D. Gun control, gun ownership and suicide prevention. *Suicide & Life-Threatening Behavior,* 1988b, 18, 176–180.

Lester, D. Restricting the availability of guns as a strategy for suicide prevention. *Biology & Society,* 1988c, 5, 127–129.

Lester, D. Why do people choose particular methods for suicide? *Activitas Nervosa Superior,* 1988d, 30, 312–314.

Lester, D. Effect of method of suicide on perception of the suicidal person. *Perceptual & Motor Skills,* 1988e, 66, 578.

Lester, D. The perception of different methods for suicide. *Perceptual & Motor Skills,* 1988f, 67, 530.

Lester, D. Suicide rates by different methods over time in the UK and the USA. *Psychological Reports,* 1988g, 62, 946.

Lester, D. The perception of different methods of suicide. *Journal of General Psychology,* 1988h, 115, 215–217.

Lester, D. Effect of changes in handgun control laws on suicide rates. *Psychological Reports,* 1988i, 62, 298.

Lester, D. Excitor-inhibitor scales of the MMPI and choice of method for suicide. *Perceptual & Motor Skills,* 1988j, 66, 218.

Lester, D. Gun ownership and suicide in the United States. *Psychological Medicine,* 1989a, 19, 519–521.

Lester, D. Specific agents of accidental and suicidal death. *Sociology & Social Research,* 1989b, 73, 182–184.

Lester, D. Restricting methods for suicide as a means of preventing suicide. *Perceptual & Motor Skills,* 1989c, 68, 273–274.

Lester, D. Suicide by car exhaust. *Perceptual & Motor Skills,* 1989d, 68, 442.

Lester, D. The suicide rate by drowning and the presence of oceans. *Perceptual & Motor Skills,* 1989e, 69, 304.

Lester, D. Barbiturate sales and their use for suicide. *Perceptual & Motor Skills,* 1989f, 69, 442.

Lester, D. Changing rates of suicide by car exhaust in men and women in the United States after car exhaust was detoxified. *Crisis,* 1989g, 10, 164–168.

Lester, D. Use of handguns and long guns in suicide and homicide. *Psychological Reports,* 1989h, 65, 938.

Lester, D. Are those who choose guns for suicide more intent on dying? *Perceptual & Motor Skills,* 1989i, 69, 922.

Lester, D., & Abe, K. The effect of restricting access to lethal methods for suicide. *Acta Psychiatrica Scandinavica,* 1989a, 80, 180–182.

Lester, D., & Abe, K. The effect of controls on sedatives and hypnotics and their use for suicide. *Clinical Toxicology,* 1989b, 27, 299–303.

Lester, D., & Abe, K. Car availability, exhaust toxicity, and suicide. *Annals of Clinical Psychiatry,* 1989c, 1, 247–250.

Lester, D., & Agarwal, K. S. Accidental death rates as a measure of the availability of a method for suicide. *Perceptual & Motor Skills,* 1989, 68, 66.

Lester, D., & Beck, A. T. What the suicide's choice of method signifies. *Omega,* 1980–1981, 11, 271–277.

Lester, D., & Clarke, R. V. Effects of reduced toxicity of car exhaust. *American Journal of Public Health,* 1988, 78, 594.

Lester, D., Fong, C. A., & D'Angelo, A. A. Chronic suicide attempters who switch methods and those who do not. *Perceptual & Motor Skills,* 1989, 69, 1390.

Lester, D., & Frank, M. L. Handguns, long guns and suicide. *Psychological Reports,* 1988, 63, 606.

Lester, D., & Frank, M. L. The use of motor vehicle exhaust for suicide and the availability of cars. *Acta Psychiatrica Scandinavica,* 1989, 79, 238–240.

Lester, D., & Murrell, M. E. The influence of gun control laws on suicidal behavior. *American Journal of Psychiatry,* 1980, 137, 121–122.

Lindekilde, K., & Wang, A. G. Train suicide in the county of Fyn 1979–1982. *Acta Psychiatrica Scandinavica*, 1985, 72, 150–154.

Linden, L., & Hale, B. E. The choice of suicidal methods. In R. Litman (Ed.) *Proceedings of the 6th International Congress for Suicide Prevention.* Ann Arbor: Edward Brothers, 1972, 176–170.

Lindesay, J. Trends in self-poisoning in the elderly 1974–1983. *International Journal of Geriatric Psychiatry,* 1986, 1(1), 37–44.

McMurray, J. J., Northridge, D. B., Abernethy, V. A., & Lawson, A. A. Trends in analgesic self-poisoning in West Fife 1971–1985. *Quarterly Journal of Medicine,* 1987, 65, 835–843.

Makela, R., & Honkanen, R. Attempted suicides treated at a casualty department. *Psychiatria Fennica,* 1984, 15, 127–134.

Markush, R. E., & Bartolucci, A. Firearms and suicide in the United States. *American Journal of Public Health,* 1984, 74, 123–127.

Maurice, S., Pommereau, X., Pueyo, S., Toulouse, C., Tilly, B., Dabis, F., Garros, B., & Salamon, R. Epidemiological surveillance of suicides and attempted suicides in Aquitaine. *Journal of Epidemiology & Community Health,* 1989, 43, 290–292.

Maxwell, S., Stolensky, D., Goodman, N., Sommers, P., & Boyd, J. Suicide by firearms. *New England Journal of Medicine,* 1984, 310, 46–49.

McIntosh, J. L., & Santos, J. F. Methods of suicide by age. *International Journal of Aging & Human Development,* 1985–1986, 22, 123–139.

McNeil, D. E., & Binder, R. L. Patients who bring weapons to the psychiatric emergency room. *Journal of Clinical Psychiatry,* 19876, 48, 230–233.

Medoff, M. H., & Magaddino, J. P. Suicides and firearm control laws. *Evaluation Review,* 1983, 7, 357–372.

Minnaar, G. K., Schlebusch, L., & Levin, A. A current study of parasuicide in Durban. *South African Medical Journal,* 1980, 57, 204–207.

Moens, G. F., Loysch, M. J., & van de Voorde, H. The geographical pattern of methods of suicide in Belgium. *Acta Psychiatrica Scandinavica,* 1988, 77, 320–327.

Moens, G. F., & van de Voorde, H. Availability of psychotropic drugs and suicidal self-poisoning mortality in Belgium from 1971–1984. *Acta Psychiatrica Scandinavica,* 1989, 79, 444–449.

Montgomery, S. A., Baldwin, D., & Green, M. Why do amitriptyline and dothiepin appear to be so dangerous in overdose? *Acta Psychiatrica Scandinavica,* 1989, supplement 354, 47–53.

Moscicki, E. K., & Boyd, J. H. Epidemiological trends in firearm suicides among adolescents. *Pediatrician,* 1983–1985, 12(1), 52–62.

O'Brien, G., Holton, A. R., Hurren, K., Watt, L., & Hassanyeh, F. Deliberate self-harm. *Acta Psychiatrica Scandinavica,* 1987, 75, 474–477.

Parks, J. G., Noguchi, T. T., & Klatt, E. C. The epidemiology of fatal burn injuries. *Journal of Forensic Sciences,* 1989, 34, 399–406.

Pary, R., Lippman, S., Turns, D. M., & Tobias, C. R. Drug selection after overdose recovery. *Journal of the Kentucky Medical Association,* 1987, 85(1), 21–23.

Patterson, P. J., & Smith, L. R. Firearms in the home and child safety. *American Journal of Diseases of Children.* 1987, 141, 221–222.

Peck, D. Completed suicides. *Omega,* 1985–1986, 16, 309–323.

Peck, D. Social-psychological correlates of adolescent and youthful suicide. *Adolescence,* 1987, 22, 863–878.

Peterson, L., Bongar, B., & Netoski, M. Regional use of violent suicide methods. *American Journal of Emergency Medicine,* 1989, 7(1), 21–27.

Peterson, L., Peterson, M., O'Shanick, G., & Swann, A. Self-inflicted gunshot wounds. *American Journal of Psychiatry,* 1985, 142, 228–231.

Pommereau, X., Tedo, P., & Penovil, F. Attempted suicide by jumping from a height. In S. D. Platt & N. Kreitman (Eds.) *Current Research on Suicide and Parasuicide.* Edinburgh: University of Edinburgh, 1989, 153–162.

Rich, C. L., & Young, J. G. Guns and suicide. In D. Lester (Ed.) *Suicide '88.* Denver: AAS, 1988, 156.

Robinson, A. D., & Duffy, J. C. A comparison of self-injury and self-poisoning from the Regional Treatment Center, Edinburgh. *Acta Psychiatrica Scandinavica,* 1989, 80, 272–279.

Sainsbury, P. The epidemiology of suicide. In A. Roy (Ed.) *Suicide.* Baltimore: Williams & Wilkins, 1986, 17–40.

Seiden, R. H. Where are they now? *Suicide & Life Threatening Behavior,* 1978, 8, 203–216.

Seiden, R. H., & Spence, M. A tale of two bridges. *Omega,* 1983–1984, 14, 201–209.

Selden, B. S., Goodman, J. M., Cordell, W., Rodman, G. H., & Schnitzer, P. G. Outcome of self-inflicted gunshot wounds of the brain. *Annals of Emergency Medicine,* 1988, 17, 247–253.

Shader, R. I., & Anglin, C. L. Emergency room study of seductive-hypnotic overdosage. *NIDA Treatment Research Monograph Series,* 1982, ADM82-1118.

Simonsen, J. Injuries sustained from high-velocity impact with water after jumping from high bridges. *American Journal of Forensic Medicine & Pathology,* 1983, 4, 139–142.

Simpson, M. A. The phenomenology of self-mutilation in a general hospital setting. *Canadian Psychiatric Association Journal,* 1975, 20, 429–434.

Sommers, P. The effect of gun control laws on suicide rates. *Atlantic Economic Journal,* 1984, 12(1), 67–69.

Surtees, P. G., & Duffy, J. C. Suicide in England and Wales 1946–1985. *Acta Psychiatrica Scandinavica,* 1989, 79, 216–223.

Symonds, R. L. Psychiatric aspects of railway fatalities. *Psychological Medicine,* 1985, 15, 609–621.

Takeuchi, T., Koizumi, J., Kotsuki, H., Shimazaki, M., Miyamoto, M., & Sumazaki,K. A clinical study of 30 wrist cutters. *Japanese Journal of Psychiatry & Neurology,* 1986, 40, 571–581.

Taylor, M., & Wicks, J. The choice of weapons. *Suicide & Life-Threatening Behavior,* 1980, 10, 142–149.

Tonkin, R. S. Suicide methods in British Columbia adolescents. *Journal of Adolescent Health Care,* 1984, 5, 172–177.

Turner, R. J. The use of health services prior to non-fatal deliberate self-harm. In

R. Farmer & S. Hirsch (Eds.) *The Suicide Syndrome.* London: Croom Helm, 1980, 173–186.

Van Praag, H., & Plutchik, R. Depression type and depression severity in relation to risk of violent suicide attempt. *Psychiatry Research,* 1984, 12, 333–338.

Whyte, I., Dawson, A., & Henry, D. Deliberate self-poisoning. *Medical Journal of Australia,* 1989, 150, 726–727.

Wintemute, G. J. Handgun availability and firearm mortality. *Lancet,* 1988, 2, 1136–1137.

Wintemute, G. J., Teret, S., Krauss, J., & Wright, M. The choice of weapons in firearm suicides. *American Journal of Public Health,* 1988, 78, 824–826.

Yamasawa, K., Nishimukai, H., Ohbora, Y., & Inoue, K. A statistical study of suicide through intoxication. *Acta Medicinae Legalis et Socialis,* 1980, 30, 187–192.

Yang, B., & Lester, D. Suicides rates and handgun ownership in the United States 1958–1984. *Social Science & Medicine,* 1989, 29, 1143.

Chapter 16

THOSE WHO MAKE
REPEATED ATTEMPTS AT SUICIDE

In studies of those who make repeated suicide attempts with those who make only one, two research designs are commonly used, retrospective and prospective. In the first, a group of suicide attempters is asked about previous attempts, and the first-timers compared to the repeaters. In the second design, a group of suicide attempters is followed up, and those who repeat an attempt subsequently compared with those who do not.

Repeaters Versus First-Time Attempters

Achte et al. (1972) found that repeaters were more likely to have had a previous psychiatric disturbance, a family history of suicide (attempted and completed), and other differences not clearly specified in the report.

Davidson and Choquet (1978) compared repeaters and first-time attempters among a sample of young attempters. The repeaters were more often unemployed, had less education, had more school difficulties, and came from larger families. The repeaters more often had alcoholic parents, had more hostile or indifferent parents, and more domineering fathers. They were more anxious and bored and had less steadfastness of purpose. They were more often given a psychiatric diagnosis, especially psychosis or personality disorder, whereas the first timers were more often judged to have a situational disturbance. (They did not differ in sex, age, nationality, broken homes, the occupation of their parents, or a family history of psychiatric illness or suicide.)

Mayo (1973) classified patients who had taken drug overdoses as episodic (one episode), phasic (many overdoses) and continuous. Mayo found that continuous dysfunction was more common in men, the drug dependent and schizophrenics, phasic dysfunction in patients with neurotic depression, personality disorder and schizophrenia, and episodic dysfunction in those with neurotic depression, adjustment reactions, and other psychoses. Denial of suicidal intent decreased with age, while impulsivity peaked in patients aged 16 to 34.

Hetzel (1971) compared repeaters and non-repeaters and found no differences in experience of parent loss, sex, marital status, or pattern of help-seeking, but the repeaters were more often in the low twenties in age and had more prior psychiatric care. Tarter et al. (1975) found that repeaters and first-time attempters did not differ on risk-rescue measures.

Adam et al. (1981, 1983) found no differences between repeaters and non-repeaters in sex, the severity of the previous attempt or the motives for the attempt. Repeaters were more likely to have been diagnosed as psychotic or with a personality disorder and less likely as neurotic.

Bille-Brahe (1982) found that repeaters were more often clients of Public Assistance in Denmark, but did not differ in age, sex, diagnosis or precipitating factors.

In English suicide attempters of West Indian or Asia (mainly Indian and Pakistani) descent, Burke (1980) found that the repeaters were more likely to be Asian males, West Indian females, from minority religions, geographically mobile and making their attempts after drinking.

Barnes (1986) found that repeaters had more chronic health problems, more prior psychiatric hospitalization, more alcohol abuse, and more family stress than the non-repeaters. The female repeaters were younger, had more legal charges and more often had a personality disorder than non-repeaters. The males repeaters were less educated. The groups did not differ in marital status, race, employment, income, social class, living arrangements, the circumstances of the suicidal act or suicidal intent.

Farmer (1980) found that first-time self-poisoners (aged 15–30) and repeaters did not differ in sibship size, sibling position or loss of parents by age 15. The mothers of the repeaters were younger at the birth of the patient. Farmer and Creed (1986) found that repeaters had more intro-punitiveness (but no more extrapunitiveness) than non-repeaters, a greater urge to act out their hostility and more suicidal intent in their suicidal actions.

Stephens (1987) compared women who had made many attempts with first-timers. The repeaters used more violent methods and more often multiple methods. They had more relatives who had attempted or completed suicide, who were substance abusers, and who were psychiatrically disturbed, and they came more often from broken homes. They were less often working class, had more often completed college, and were younger at their first suicide attempt.

In Israel, Katz-Sheiban (1989) found that repeaters were more often male, young, Asian-African, single, precipitated by depression or psychiatric illness and more prone to subsequent completed suicide.

Kreitman and Casey (1988) found in Scotland that repeaters who had made more than five previous attempts were more often middle aged (rather than adolescent or elderly), less often married (and more often divorced or separated), lower class, with a personality disorder, a substance abuser, and with prior psychiatric treatment. Repeaters in general had more often experienced early separation from a parent, had a family history of attempted suicide (but not completed suicide), were living alone, had engaged in violence in the past five years (both as assaulter and as victim), were unemployed and had a criminal record.

Peterson and Bongar (1988) found that repeaters were older, more often diagnosed as schizophrenic or with a personality disorder, living alone, and with prior suicide attempts and prior psychiatric hospitalizations. They did not differ in substance abuse or the presence of an affective disorder.

In Brittany (France), Philippe et al. (1989) found that repeaters were less educated, more likely to be alcoholics, to have had psychiatric care, a mental illness or alcoholism in their relatives, and depressive symptoms and more likely to have been rendered unconscious by their overdose.

Reynolds and Eaton (1986) found that repeaters had higher suicidal intent and lethality, more chronicity, poorer coping strategies, a positive family history for suicide, more alcohol/drug abuse, more depression (but not hopelessness), and less impulsiveness than first-timers.

Sakinofsky (1988) found that repeaters had more problems, were younger, had higher external locus of control scores, lower self-esteem and stronger feelings of powerlessness. At a three-month follow-up, the repeaters had more internal hostility, more depression, better self-esteem and more isolation. At the time of the follow-up, those who had resolved their problems had experienced their problems for a shorter period, had made fewer prior attempts, felt less powerlessness and less internally directed hostility, and had experienced less new stress. Those who had resolved their problems did not, however, repeat suicide attempts less often in the follow-up period.

Ulmanen (1983) found that repeaters were more often male, young, non-married, alcohol abusers and with more prior psychiatric care.

In Edinburgh (Scotland), Wilkinson and Smeeton (1987) found that first-time attempters were younger, but did not differ in sex from repeaters. In a follow-up study, the first-timers and the older attempters were less likely to repeat.

Adolescents

Gispert et al. (1987) found that adolescent repeaters had been less successful in school and absent more from school, had more hostility, depression and life stress, and had more serious suicidal intent than first-time attempters. (They did not differ in social class, age or sex.) Goldacre and Hawton (1985) found that subsequent repeated attempts were more common in adolescents who take overdoses among males aged 16–20 and females aged 12–15. Grossi (1987) found that adolescents in residential treatment centers who had made more than four prior attempts had shown more violence toward their peers than those making only one to three previous attempts.

Kotila and Lonnqvist (1987a, 1987b) found that teenage repeaters as compared to first-timers were older, had more prior psychiatric care, were more often unemployed, came from a worse family situation, had poorer adaptive functioning, had engaged in more criminal behavior, and were more likely to have abused alcohol, medicines, and drugs. They did not differ in sex, social class, loss of a parent through death or divorce, or the presence of psychosis. Poor overall functioning in general in the attempters and the presence of psychosis was associated with greater suicidal intent (but not medical lethality). Suicidal intent was associated with lethality, and intoxication was associated with less suicidal intent (but not with medical lethality).

Follow-Up Studies

In a follow-up of a sample of attempted suicides, those who rated the hospital negatively had a greater likelihood of repeating within three months after release than those rating the hospital positively (Miller and Goldman, 1970). Wenz (1978) followed up a sample of attempters and found no differences in self-concept scores between those who repeated and those who did not.

Hassanyeh and Fairbairn (1985; Hassanyeh et al., 1989) found that the number of prior suicide attempts predicted future suicide attempts after eighteen months while the use of psychotropic drugs (as opposed to analgesic drugs), depression, multiple stresses and intoxication during the act predicted repeating after nine months. Among the variables which did not predict repeating were impulsiveness, anxiety, suicidal intent, sex, marital status, unemployment, parental loss, family psychiatric history, and premenstrual tension.

Pierce (1986) found that attempters who repeated within one year more often perceived their significant others as unsympathetic (rather than sympathetic or neutral), but did not differ in their view of the treatment staff.

Stern et al. (1984) followed up suicide attempters and found that the repeaters had more prior attempts and prior psychiatric treatment. They did not differ in demographic variables, psychiatric evaluation variables, or medical history.

Suleiman et al. (1989) followed up suicide attempters in Kuwait. Those who repeated were more likely to be housewives, but did not differ in age, sex, nationality, marital status, education, religion, of the presence of suicide in their relatives. At the index attempt, the repeaters were more depressed, with more prior depressions and suicide attempts, used self-poisoning with prescribed medications more, and were precipitated more often by family problems. The repeaters showed worse social readjustment during the follow-up period.

Wang et al. (1985) found that suicide attempters who repeated attempts had more often made prior attempts, but did not differ from non-repeaters in attempted or completed suicide in relatives or friends. (Attempters who subsequently completed suicide were older and more often female!)

Clustered Versus Chronic Repeaters

Smeeton and Wilkinson (1988) identified 31 suicide attempters who had made prior attempts and who repeated in the next two years. Eight of these showed clusters, that is, at least four episodes in a three month period, and these tended more to be in their twenties. The remaining 23 were chronic, that is, made five or more attempts spread over the two years, and these tended more to be in their teens and thirties. The two types did not differ in sex.

Subsequent Completed Suicide

Pallis and Barraclough (1977–1978) reanalyzed data from Card (1974) and found that the more lethal methods used for the attempt the more likely later completed suicide. From their own data they found that the earlier attempts of completed suicides were medically more serious than those of attempted suicides.

Discussion

It is not easy to summarize all of these studies, but in general repeaters appear to be more psychiatrically disturbed and more deviant (in terms of substance abuse and criminal behavior). Lester (1987) suggested that repeaters are less well socialized than the one-time attempter and perhaps fit into a learning theory of suicide.

REFERENCES

Achte, K. A., Lonnqvist, J., Niskanen, P., Ginman, L., & Karlsson, M. Attempted suicides by poison and eight-year follow-up. *Psychiatria Fennica*, 1972, 321–340.

Adam, K. S., Isherwood, J., Taylor, G., Scarr, G., & Streiner, D. Attempted suicide in Christchurch. *New Zealand Medical Journal*, 1981, 93, 376–381.

Adam, K. S., Valentine, J., Scarr, G., & Striner, D. Follow-up of attempted suicides in Christchurch. *Australian & New Zealand Journal of Psychiatry*, 1983, 17, 18–26.

Barnes, R. A. The recurrent self-harm patient. *Suicide & Life-Threatening Behavior*, 1986, 16, 399–408.

Bille-Brahe, U. Persons attempting suicide as clients in the Danish welfare system. *Social Psychiatry*, 1982, 17, 181–187.

Burke, A. W. Classification of attempted suicide from hospital admission data. *International Journal of Social Psychiatry*, 1980, 26, 27–34.

Davidson, F., & Choquet, M. Identification of factors of risk which are predictive of repeated suicide. In V. Aalberg (Ed.) *Proceedings of the 9th International Congress for Suicide Prevention*. Helsinki: Finnish Association for Mental Health, 1978, 182–188.

Farmer, R. D. The differences between those who repeat and those who do not. In R. D. Farmer & S. Hirsch (Eds.) *The Suicide Syndrome*. London: Croom Helm, 1980, 187–193.

Farmer, R. D. & Creed, F. Hostility and deliberate self-poisoning. *British Journal of Medical Psychology*, 1986, 59, 311–316.

Gispert, M., Davis, M., Marsh, L., & Wheeler, K. Predictive factors in repeated suicide attempts by adolescents. *Hospital & Community Psychiatry*, 1987, 38, 390–393.

Goldacre, M., & Hawton, K. Repetition of self-poisoning and subsequent death in adolescents who take overdoses. *British Journal of Psychiatry,* 1985, 146, 395–398.

Grossi, V. Deliberate self-harm among adolescents in residential treatment centers. In R. Yufit (Ed.) *Proceedings of the 20th Annual Conference.* Denver: AAS, 1987, 276–277.

Hassanyeh, F., & Fairbairn, A. Repeat self-poisoning. *Practitioner,* 1985, 229, 177–181.

Hassanyeh, F., O'Brien, G., Holton, A. R., Hurren, K., & Watt, L. Repeat self-harm. *Acta Psychiatrica Scandinavica,* 1989, 79, 265–267.

Hetzel, B. S. The epidemiology of suicidal behavior in Australia. *Australian & New Zealand Journal of Psychiatry,* 1971, 5, 156–166.

Katz-Sheiban, B. Suicidal repetition. In D. Lester (Ed.) *Suicide '89.* Denver: AAS, 1989, 273–276.

Kotila, L., & Lonnqvist, J. Adolescent suicide attempts 1973–1982 in the Helsinki area. *Acta Psychiatrica Scandinavica,* 1987a, 76, 346–354.

Kotila, L., & Lonnqvist, J. Adolescents who make suicide attempts repeatedly. *Acta Psychiatrica Scandinavica,* 1987b, 76, 386–393.

Kreitman, N., & Casey, P. Repetition of parasuicide. *British Journal of Psychiatry,* 1988, 153, 792–800.

Lester, D. *Suicide As a Learned Behavior.* Springfield, IL: Charles C Thomas, 1987.

Mayo, J. Psychopharmacological roulette. American Association of Suicidology, Houston, 1973.

Miller, D. H., & Goldman, D. Predicting post-release risk among hospitalized suicide attempters. *Omega,* 1970, 1, 71–84.

Pallis, D., & Barraclough, B. M. Seriousness of suicide attempt and future risk of suicide. *Omega,* 1977–1978, 8, 141–149.

Peterson, L. G., & Bongar, B. Repeaters versus one-timers in the emergency room. In D. Lester (Ed.) *Suicide '88.* Denver: AAS, 1988, 201.

Philippe, A., Gautier, J. Y., & Verron, M. Outcome of suicide attempters with respect to repetition. In S. D. Platt & N. Kreitman (Eds.) *Current Research on Suicide and Parasuicide.* Edinburgh: University of Edinburgh, 1989, 173–179.

Pierce, D. Deliberate self-harm. *British Journal of Psychiatry,* 1986, 149, 624–626.

Reynolds, P., & Eaton, P. Multiple attempters of suicide presenting at an emergency department. *Canadian Journal of Psychiatry,* 1986, 31, 328–330.

Sakinofsky, I. Why do parasuicide repeat despite resolving their problems? In D. Lester (Ed.) *Suicide '88.* Denver: AAS, 1988, 199–200.

Smeeton, N., & Wilkinson, G. The identification of clustering in parasuicide. *British Journal of Psychiatry,* 1988, 153, 218–221.

Stephens, B. J. The characteristics of female single and multiple suicide attempters. *International Journal of Family Psychiatry,* 1987, 8, 231–242.

Stern, T. A., Mulley, A., & Thibault, G. Life-threatening drug overdose. *Journal of the American Medical Association,* 1984, 251, 1983–1985.

Suleiman, M. A., Moussa, M., & El-Islam, M. The profile of parasuicide repeaters in Kuwait. *International Journal of Social Psychiatry,* 1989, 35, 146–155.

Tarter, R. E., Templer, D. I., & Perley, R. L. Social role orientation and pathological factors in suicide attempts of varying lethality. *Journal of Consulting Psychology,* 1975, 3, 295–299.

Ulmanen, I. Self-poisoning patients with several suicide attempts. *Psychiatria Fennica,* 1983, supplement, 115–118.

Wang, A., Nielsen, B., Bille-Brahe, U., Hansen, W., & Kolmos, L. Attempted suicide in Denmark. *Acta Psychiatrica Scandinavica,* 1985, 72, 389–394.

Wenz, F. V. Multiple suicide attempts and informal labelling. *Suicide & Life-Threatening Behavior,* 1978, 8, 3–13.

Wilkinson, G., & Smeeton, N. The repetition of parasuicide in Edinburgh 1980–1981. *Social Psychiatry,* 1987, 22, 14–19.

Chapter 17

COMMUNICATION AND THE SUICIDAL ACT

The major way in which suicidal individuals communicate to others is via a suicide note, and this remains a major research focus for suicidologists.

Who Leaves Notes?

Completed Suicides

Batten and Hicks (1988) found a slight tendency for depressed suicides to leave a suicide note more often than the mentally ill or non-mentally ill suicides. Copeland (1987) found that 47 percent of elderly suicides in Miami left notes, a high percentage. Women have been found to leave a suicide note more often than men (Andress, 1976; Bourque et al., 1983).

Chynoweth (1977) found that completed suicides who left notes were more likely to use guns for their suicidal act. (No differences were found between note leavers and those who did not in sex, age or marital status.) Peck (1985–1986) found that youthful completed suicides who left notes used pills and carbon monoxide more often and guns and hanging less often.

Posener et al. (1989) found that adolescents who left notes were more likely to have used guns than those who did not leave notes but did not differ in age or sex. Wrobleski and McIntosh (1986) found that suicides who left notes gave prior clues to suicide as often as those who did not leave notes.

Attempted Suicides

Eaton and Reynolds (1989) found that adolescent attempted suicides were less likely to leave a suicide note than adult attempters. Garfinkel et al. (1982) found than the more serious adolescent suicide attempters were more likely to leave notes than the less serious attempters.

The Content of Suicide Notes

Peck (1980–1981) argued that suicide was a result of the person failing to achieve desired goals while engaging in conforming behavior, which leads to fatalism. He thought this orientation would be associated also with an external locus of control. He studied suicide notes of those under the age of 35 and classified them as fatalistic versus not fatalistic. The notes of younger suicides were more fatalistic, as were those from the upper classes. (Fatalism in suicide notes was not associated with sex, race, religion, employment status, number of children, marital status, whether living alone, sociability, prior suicidal behavior or experience of broken and strained relationships.)

Leenaars (1987a, 1987b) specified Shneidman's theory of suicide into 50 statements. He found age differences, with notes from younger suicides (18–25 years old) showing more perturbance, dyadic problems, self-criticism, and dichotomous thinking. Balance et al. (1988) found that genuine notes contained more of the statements derived from Aaron Beck's theory of suicide than Henry Murray's theory of suicide.

In a more general study, Leenaars (1989) found that the suicide notes of those aged 18–25 had more disturbed interpersonal relationships, less ability to adjust, more indirect expression of ideas, more identification-egression, and a worse functioning ego than the notes of older adults. Leenaars and Balance (1984) found that the suicide notes of younger suicides had more statements derived from Freud's theory of suicide than notes of older suicides. Lester and Hummel (1980) found that the suicide notes of older people expressed less depression/guilt but did not differ in the desire to die or in anger. They found no differences in these motives for suicide by method of suicide or by living arrangements. Lester and Reeve (1982) found that older suicides were less explicit about their suicidal intentions and used fewer verbs of feeling (versus verbs of action).

Leenaars and Lester (1988–1989) found no differences between the suicide notes of those using active versus passive methods for 49 statements. Those using active methods did have more references to rejection but this was not replicated on a new sample of notes.

In a study of adolescent suicides, Posener et al. (1989) found that older teenagers wrote notes that were more often concrete, unaddressed, with instructions and with no reasons. Those using violent methods wrote notes that were less concrete and with less inward-directed aggression.

Sex Differences

Black (1989) found that the suicide notes of women had more indications of depression, self-hostility, confusion and despondency over the death of others. Leenaars (1987b, 1988a, 1988b) found no differences between the suicide notes of men or women for a variety of content items. Lester and Hummel (1980) and Lester (1989a) found no differences in the notes of men and women in Menninger's three motives for suicide (to die, to kill and to be killed). Lester and Reeve (1982) found that notes written by men contained more negative emotions but were less disorganized.

Simulated Versus Genuine Notes

Henken (1976) compared genuine suicide notes, simulated suicide notes and notes written by people about to die using a computer content analysis. The genuine notes were more concrete, constricted and concerned with interpersonal relationships (especially those with the opposite sex). Edelman and Renshaw (1982) also compared genuine and simulated notes by computer analysis and found the genuine notes to be longer with fewer positive modifiers. The genuine notes had more negative existential density (e.g., "not"), more negative authority (e.g., proper nouns), more negative audience (e.g., "you"), more modified nouns, more modified verbs, more negative generalized others (e.g., third-person pronouns), more cognizance of objects (concrete objects), more modification of objects and actions, more negative modification, more negative modification of known people and positive modification of unknown people, more static action, and less reference to future time.

Lester (1989b) found that the genuine notes more often had content reflecting the desire to kill but did not differ in the desires to be killed and to die.

Leenaars has specified several theories of suicide into several statements and examined the presence of these statements in genuine and simulated suicide notes. Using 50 statements derived from Shneidman's theory of suicide, Leenaars (1987a) found that genuine notes had significantly more of nine but not of the other 41 statements. Leenaars and Balance (1981) found that the genuine notes had more statements derived from Freud, but not from the theories of George Kelly or Binswanger. Leenaars (1988b) found that the genuine notes had more statements derived from Gregory Zilboorg's theory and to a lesser extent, Henry

Murray and Harry Sullivan, but not for the theories of Alfred Adler or Carl Jung. Balance and Leenaars (1986) found that the genuine and simulated notes had different frequencies of statements derived from Aaron Beck's theory of suicide. The genuine notes had more magnification, minimization and overgeneralization, while the simulated notes had more hopelessness, suffering and desire for escape. Lester and Leenaars (1988) found that the genuine notes contained more direct accusations and wills/testaments and fewer conventional "first-form" notes.

McLister and Leenaars (1988; Leenaars et al., 1989) found more signs of unconscious forces at play in the genuine notes than in the simulated notes (as well as more mention of spouses and fathers).

Lester and Leenaars (1987) compared the genuine notes of each pair which naive subjects could easily identify correctly with those which were hard to identify. The protocol sentences used by Leenaars in his research failed to differentiate these two sets of genuine notes.

Lester (1988) has criticized the study of simulated versus genuine notes, arguing that it tells us only about how well non-suicidal people can fake a suicide note. He suggested that simulated notes can be used to provide clues to popular conceptions about suicide. He found that women more often addressed their simulated note to someone than did men, apologized and asked forgiveness, stated that they were unhappy, and said that others would be better off with them dead.

Completers Versus Attempters

Valente (1989) found that completed suicides made more communications (both written and spoken) than did attempted suicides. Livermore (1985) compared suicide from completed suicides with those from attempted suicides. The notes of completers were more often addressed to someone, contained information about whom to contact, said sorry/ forgive me more, said I love you/darling more, and mentioned depression and financial problems more. The completers also more often left multiple notes. The groups did not differ in their use of "first-form" (conventional explanation/forgive me) notes.

Physician (and Other) Contacts

Murphy (1972) compared completed suicides who used ingestion of solids or liquids and those using other methods and found no differences in their contacting of physicians in the previous six months.

Crockett (1987) found that English attempted suicides had consulted more often with their physicians in the prior week, year and five years than normal controls. In the Netherlands, Diekstra et al. (1984) found that 47 percent of a sample of attempted suicides had contacted their general practitioner in the prior two months (and 64 percent used drugs prescribed during the last visit). Diekstra and van Edmond (1989) found that a similar percentage of completed suicides had also made contact with their general practitioner. About a fifth of both completers and attempters had visited their doctor in the prior week.

Deykin (1989) found that adolescent suicide attempters (but not ideators) had more prior contact with the Department of Social Services than medical controls, but she did not note how long prior to the suicidal action.

Petrie (1989) found that 32 percent of a sample of suicide attempters in New Zealand had visited their general practitioner in the previous week and 73 percent in the previous three months. Of this latter group only a third mentioned depression or suicide, however.

Poetry

Sharlin and Shenhar-Alroy (1987) compared the poetry of two Israeli teenage completed suicides and two normal teenagers. The two samples did not differ in the wordage of their poems, but the suicides had more emotionally loaded content, death-related words and words concerned with bad situations.

Communications Of Suicidal Intent

Wolk-Wasserman (1986) found that most suicide attempters had communicated their suicidal intent (92 percent). The neurotics and psychotics most often made indirect and verbal communications while the substance abusers direct verbal and indirect verbal communications. Wolk-Wasserman noted that the significant others were most commonly ambivalent or hostile toward the attempter.

Wrobleski and McIntosh (1986) talked to survivors of suicides and found that 94 percent could recall one or more of thirteen possible clues to suicide in the deceased. Most common, in order, were statements about hopelessness, helplessness, suicide and death. The number of clues given was not related to the sex of the suicide or the presence of a suicide note. Older suicides gave more clues, especially worthlessness and helplessness.

Discussion

The noteworthy advance in the study of suicide in the 1980s was made by Leenaars. In his research, he not only made the research theory-based, an important advance over earlier research, but he also set suicide in the context of the classic theories of personality, such as Freud, Murray and Sullivan. His results are of interest, and his methodology should prove stimulating to others in the 1990s.

REFERENCES

Andress, L. An epidemiological study of the psychosocial characteristics of suicidal behavior in Riverside County between 1960 and 1974. *Dissertation Abstracts International,* 1976, 37B, 1481.

Balance, W. D., & Leenaars, A. A. A predictive approach to Aaron Beck's formulations regarding suicide. In R. Cohen-Sandler (Ed.) *Proceedings of the 19th Annual Meeting.* Denver: AAS, 1986, 51.

Balance, W. D., Plotnick, S. G., & Leenaars, A. A. Significance of content frequencies in suicide notes. In D. Lester (Ed.) *Suicide '88.* Denver: AAS, 1988, 144–145.

Batten, P. J., & Hicks, L. J. The use of mental status in death certification of suicide. *American Journal of Forensic Medicine & Pathology,* 1988, 9, 203–206.

Black, S. T. Gender differences in the content of genuine and simulated suicide notes. In D. Lester (Ed.) *Suicide '89.* Denver: AAS, 1989, 8.

Bourque, L. B., Cosand, B., & Kraus, J. Comparison of male and female suicide in a defined community. *Journal of Community Health,* 1983, 9, 7–17.

Chynoweth, R. The significance of suicide notes. *Australian & New Zealand Journal of Psychiatry,* 1977, 11, 197–200.

Copeland, A. R. Suicide among the elderly. *Medicine, Science & the Law,* 1987, 27(1), 32–36.

Crockett, A. W. Patterns of consultation and parasuicide. *British Medical Journal,* 1987, 295, 476–478.

Deykin, E. Y. The utility of emergency room data for record linkage in the study of adolescent suicidal behavior. *Suicide & Life-Threatening Behavior,* 1989, 19, 90–98.

Diekstra, R. F. W., de Graaf, A. C., & van Egmond, M. On the epidemiology of attempted suicide. *Crisis,* 1984, 5, 108–118.

Diekstra, R. F. W., & van Edmond, M. Suicide and attempted suicide in general practice, 1979–1986. *Acta Psychiatrica Scandinavica,* 1989, 79, 268–275.

Eaton, P., & Reynolds, P. A comparison of adolescent and adult suicide attempters. In D. Lester (Ed.) *Suicide '89.* Denver: AAS, 1989, 80–82.

Edelman, A., & Renshaw, S. Genuine versus simulated suicide notes. *Suicide & Life-Threatening Behavior,* 1982, 12, 103–113.

Garfinkel, B. D., Froese, A., & Hood, J. Suicide attempts in children and adolescents. *American Journal of Psychiatry,* 1982, 139, 1257–1261.

Henken, V. Banality revisited. *Suicide & Life-Threatening Behavior,* 1976, 6, 36–43.

Leenaars, A. A. Protocol analysis studies of Shneidman's formulation regarding suicide. In J. Morgan (Ed.) *Suicide.* London, Ont.: King's College, 1987a, 37–60.

Leenaars, A. A. An empirical investigation of Shneidman's formulations regarding suicide. *Suicide & Life-Threatening Behavior,* 1987b, 17, 233–250.

Leenaars, A. A. Are women's suicide really different from men's? *Women & Health,* 1988a, 14(1), 17–33.

Leenaars, A. A. *Suicide Notes.* New York: Human Sciences, 1988b.

Leenaars, A. A. Are young adults' suicides psychologically different from those of other adults? *Suicide & Life-Threatening Behavior,* 1989, 19, 249–263.

Leenaars, A. A., & Balance, W. A predictive approach to the study of manifest content in suicide notes. *Journal of Clinical Psychology,* 1981, 37, 50–52.

Leenaars, A. A., & Balance, W. A predictive approach to suicide notes of young and old suicides from Freud's formulations regarding suicide. *Journal of Clinical Psychology,* 1984, 40, 1362–1364.

Leenaars, A. A., & Lester, D. The significance of the method chosen for suicide in understanding the psychodynamics of the suicidal individual. *Omega,* 1988–1989, 19, 311–314.

Leenaars, A. A., McLister, D., & Balance, W. An empirical investigation of the latent content of suicide notes. In D. Lester (Ed.) *Suicide '89.* Denver: AAS, 1989, 282–283.

Lester, D. What does the study of simulated suicide notes tell us? *Psychological Reports,* 1988, 62, 962.

Lester, D. Sex differences in the motives expressed in suicide notes. *Perceptual & Motor Skills,* 1989a, 69, 642.

Lester, D. Menninger's motives for suicide in genuine and simulated suicide notes. *Perceptual & Motor Skills,* 1989b, 69, 850.

Lester, D., & Hummel, H. Motives for suicide in elderly people. *Psychological Reports,* 1980, 47, 870.

Lester, D., & Leenaars, A. A. Differentiation of genuine suicide notes. *Psychological Reports,* 1987, 61, 70.

Lester, D., & Leenaars, A. A. The moral justification of suicide in suicide notes. *Psychological Reports,* 1988, 63, 106.

Lester, D., & Reeve, C. The suicide notes of young and old people. *Psychological Reports,* 1982, 50, 334.

Livermore, A. Forty suicide notes. In R. Cohen-Sandler (Ed.) *Proceedings of the 18th Annual Meeting.* Denver: AAS, 1985, 47–49.

McLister, B., & Leenaars, A. A. An empirical investigation of the latent content of suicide notes. *Psychological Reports,* 1988, 63, 238.

Murphy, G. The physician's failure in suicide prevention. *Proceedings of the 6th International Congress for Suicide Prevention,* Vienna: IASP, 1972, 393–399.

Peck, D. Towards a theory of suicide. *Omega,* 1980–1981, 11, 1–14.

Peck, D. Completed suicides. *Omega,* 1985–1986, 16, 309–323.

Petrie, K. Recent general practice contacts of hospitalized suicide attempters. *New Zealand Medical Journal,* 1989, 102, 130–131.

Posener, J. A., La Haye, A., & Cheifelz, P. N. Suicide notes in adolescence. *Canadian Journal of Psychiatry,* 1989, 34, 171–176.

Sharlin, S. A., & Shenhar-Alroy, A. *On Adolescent Suicide and Poetry.* King George, VA: American Foster Care Resources, 1987.

Valente, S. Suicide messages of psychiatric patients. In D. Lester (Ed.) *Suicide '89.* Denver: AAS, 1989, 265–267.

Wolk-Wasserman, D. Suicidal communication of persons attempting suicide and response of significant others. *Acta Psychiatrica Scandinavica,* 1986, 73, 481–499.

Wrobleski, A., & McIntosh, J. L. Clues to suicide and suicide survivors. In R. Cohen-Sandler (Ed.) *Proceedings of the 19th Annual meeting.* Denver: AAS, 1986, 144–146.

Chapter 18

PSYCHIATRIC DISORDER AND SUICIDE

Many studies find that suicides are more disturbed in general than non-suicides. This finding is so common and so expected that the studies hardly merit citing. However, some of the more interesting studies on this topic are noted below.

Briere and Corne (1985) found that callers to a crisis service who had just attempted suicide were more likely to have been hospitalized for psychiatric reasons than those who were only threatening or thinking about suicide. Linehan and Laffaw (1982) found that patients at a psychological clinic had thought about suicide more than a sample from the general population, but they had not attempted suicide more.

Brent et al. (1986) found that the more suicidal adolescent psychiatric patients were more depressed, abused alcohol more and showed more conduct disorder. Brent et al. (1987) found that the lethality of the suicide attempt in adolescents was associated with affective disorder, substance abuse, a family history of affective disorder, and suicidal intent (but not with family abuse or recent stressful life events). Brent et al. (1988) found that adolescent completed suicides more often were intoxicated and less often had a major depressive disorder than suicidal psychiatric patients. Suicidal intent was associated with bipolar affective disorder and substance abuse. (Suicidal intent was not related to recent interpersonal loss, external stressors and living with one's biological parents.)

Kuperman et al. (1988) followed up adolescent psychiatric patients and found that completed suicide was predicted by more severe psychiatric disturbance, an IQ greater than 90, a diagnosis of schizophrenia or organic mental disorder (but not neurosis, affective disorder, substance abuse or anorexia), and having a medical problem. Morrison (1984) found that suicide rates for ex-psychiatric patients peaked for those aged 25–34.

Munley et al. (1977) found that a previous history of suicidal behavior predicted the length of psychiatric hospitalization in VA psychiatric

269

patients. A recent suicide attempt (in the last month) predicted readmission. Thus, suicidality seemed to be associated with a more chronic psychiatric illness.

Evenson (1983) examined the community adjustment of psychiatric patients prior to their commitment and found that those who had threatened suicide were less well adjusted than those who had attempted suicide.

Psychiatric Patients in General

Evenson et al. (1982) found that the suicide rate for psychiatric inpatients was higher than that for outpatients which in turn was higher than that for the general population. Schwartz and Eisen (1984) found that psychiatric patients hospitalized out of state had a higher rate of suicide than those hospitalized in-state, but only for patients under the age of thirty. Out-of-state and in-state patients did not differ in the severity of their disturbance. In a review of research, Nicholson (1986) found no differences in the suicidal behavior or danger to self of patients with voluntary versus involuntary commitment.

Gibbens and Robertson (1983) found that the percentage of deaths due to suicide among mentally ill offenders was greater for those aged less than 50 than for the older offenders. Black (1989) reported higher subsequent SMRs for suicide in female psychiatric inpatients than in male, for the younger patients and for the first two years of follow-up.

Hagnell and Rorsman (1978, 1979) found that 93 percent of the completed suicides in the Lundby Study had received prior psychiatric diagnoses. Compared to controls (living people and those dying from organic diseases), the suicides also more often had a psychiatric illness in the prior year, more depressive illnesses, less organic brain syndromes, more psychiatric treatment, and were more negative toward medical help.

Blumenthal et al. (1989) found that subsequent completed suicide in psychiatric patients was predicted by unemployment and job problems, a short hospital stay and more symptoms before hospitalization.

Burke (1983) compared psychiatric patients who subsequently completed suicide with those who died natural deaths. The suicides more often had received a diagnosis of personality disorder or drug abuse (and less often alcohol abuse) but did not differ in the incidence of depressive disorder in their relatives. The suicides were more likely to have an abnormal premorbid personality.

Fernando and Storm (1984) found that psychiatric patients who completed suicide were more likely to be first-time disturbed, inpatients, men and middle-aged. They had experienced more losses, had previously attempted suicide more often, and were less often schizophrenic. They did not differ in alcohol abuse or physical illness.

Gale et al. (1980) looked at which kinds of psychiatric patients complete suicide and identified two types: (1) male paranoid schizophrenics, with a prior history of attempted suicide, involuntarily committed, with an acute psychosis, who hang themselves in the first few weeks, and (2) chronic undifferentiated schizophrenics with an affective component who are improving and complete suicide by jumping after about a month while out on a pass. Suicides were more often young Puerto Rican males, whites, better educated females, involuntarily committed and schizophrenic and affective disorder patients.

Hoffman and Modestin (1987) found that suicide in psychiatric patients was predicted by less criminal history and more prior suicide attempts (especially by active methods) but not by being childless, coming from a broken home or psychiatric diagnosis. Janofsky et al. (1988) found that suicidal preoccupation in psychiatric inpatients was predicted by the presence of a personality disorder or substance abuse disorder.

Modestin et al. (1986) found that psychiatric inpatients who were judged to be "problems" were more often suicidal than the other patients. Modestin and Hoffman (1989) compared psychiatric inpatients who killed themselves in the hospital with former patients who completed suicide. The former group were less often married and more often living with parents, disabled, with a record of delinquency and schizophrenia (and less often substance abuse), had been psychiatrically ill for a longer time, had been admitted more often, and were less often unemployed and downwardly mobile. Modestin and Kopp (1988a) compared these suicides while in the hospital with other inpatients and found that they had been admitted more often, had more suicide in their families, had experienced more social stress (especially exits), were more disabled and were more downwardly mobile.

In Missouri, Nuttall et al. (1980) found that ex-psychiatric patients who completed suicide were younger and more often female than those who did not. Among the suicides, the men were more often alcoholics and less often diagnosed with an affective psychosis or depressive neurosis.

Roy (1982b) found that psychiatric patients who completed suicide were more often diagnosed as schizophrenic or with an affective disorder (and less often as alcoholic, personality disorder, or situational disturbance). The suicides were younger, more often unmarried, unemployed, living alone, and depressed and had received more prior psychiatric treatment. They did not differ in their experience of loss, children, physical disease, or psychiatric illness and suicide in their family.

Roy (1983b) found that psychiatric patients with a family history of completed suicide were more likely to have attempted suicide. (It did not matter whether the suicidal family member was a first or second degree relative.) Attempted suicide was especially likely if the parent had completed suicide before the patient was eleven years old. Roy (1983c) reported that psychiatric patients who had attempted suicide were less often married, more often unemployed and living alone, had received more prior psychiatric treatment, had attempted suicide more often in the past and were more often diagnosed with depression or schizophrenia. (They did not differ in parental loss, substance abuse, physical disease or completed suicide in first-degree relatives.)

Adolescents

Friedman et al. (1984a) found that adolescents with affective disorder were more likely to have a history of suicide attempts than those with other diagnoses (such as schizophrenia).

In a sample of teenage suicide attempters, Kotila and Lonnqvist (1989) found that psychosis, as well as male sex and serious suicidal intent (but not medical lethality) predicted subsequent completed suicide.

Shafii et al. (1985, 1988) compared a sample of teenage completed suicides with their friends. The suicides more often had a psychiatric disorder, more often two or more disorders, especially depression and substance abuse, more psychosocial stressors, more antisocial/delinquent behavior, a more inhibited personality, more friends/siblings who had attempted or completed suicide (but not parents or relatives), and more emotional problems and more absence of and emotional abuse from their parents.

Psychiatric Diagnosis

Hagnell and Rorsman (1978, 1979) found that 93 percent of the completed suicides in the Lundby Study had received prior psychiatric diagnoses. Compared to controls (living people and those dying from organic diseases), the suicides also more often had a psychiatric illness in the prior year, more depressive illnesses, less organic brain syndromes, more psychiatric treatment, and were more negative toward medical help.

Tsuang and Woolson (1978) looked at psychiatric patients who had subsequently died and found that 9 percent of the deaths of schizophrenics and of the manic patients were from suicide, 8 percent of the deaths of depressed patients, but only 2 percent of the control subjects. Taussigova et al. (1975) found no differences in the incidence of completed or attempted suicide in psychotic patients by diagnosis (schizophrenic, schizoaffective or manic-depressive) or by age.

Babigan et al. (1985) reported an increased mortality rate from suicide in former psychiatric patients diagnosed as schizophrenic, affective disorder, alcoholism, and neurotic depression, but Babigan et al. (1986) reported a lower suicide rate for male former psychiatric patients in general. Tsuang et al. (1980) found an excess in suicides among schizophrenics, manics and depressives as compared to surgical controls.

Barner-Rasmussen et al. (1986) calculated rates for men and women with different psychiatric disorders in Denmark. Those with manic-depressive psychoses had the highest rates, while those with organic disorders had the lowest rates. Black et al. (1985a) found that the subsequent suicide risk in psychiatric patients was greater for schizophrenics, affective disorders, and substance abusers.

Batten (1989) found the highest suicide rate in forensic psychiatric patients, then state hospital patients and correctional inmates and lowest in the institutionalized mentally retarded. Copas and Robin (1982) found that the suicide rate in psychiatric inpatients was greater for those diagnosed as depressive psychotics and psychoneurotics.

Allebeck et al. (1988) found that Swedish conscripts with a diagnosis of personality disorder had a higher rate of subsequent suicide than those diagnosed with a neurotic disorder. Angst and Clayton (1986) compared suicides in unipolar depressives, bipolar depressives, schizophrenics and sociopaths. The unipolar depressives and sociopaths smoked more, but the groups did not differ in drug abuse. The groups differed on some personality traits, with the unipolar depressives being high on aggression, autonomic lability, the schizophrenics on autonomic lability and the sociopaths on aggression, autonomic lability and dominance.

Apter et al. (1988) found that suicidality (as measured by the K–SADS) was greatest in adolescent psychiatric inpatients with conduct disorders, then major depressive disorders and least in schizophrenics. Suicidality was not related to the presence of mania, hallucinations and delusions or thought disorder.

Dingman and McGlashan (1986, 1988) found that psychiatric patients who subsequently completed suicide were more often diagnosed as schizoaffective or unipolar depression and less often as borderline personality disorder. They were more psychiatrically disturbed in the first study, but had better functioning after discharge and with less self-mutilation in the second study. A history of suicidal preoccupation was more common in those diagnosed as borderline and schizotypal personality disorders and schizoaffective.

Evenson et al. (1982) found that the subsequent suicide rate was highest for patients with affective disorders and lowest for those with organic brain syndrome.

Hagnell et al. (1981; Rorsman et al., 1983) found an increased rate of completed suicide in persons with psychiatric disorder and a very high rate in those diagnosed as depressives. Hillard et al. (1983) followed up emergency room psychiatric patients and found the highest suicide rate in those with drug abuse and next in those with affective disorders.

Lonnqvist et al. (1983) followed up male psychiatric patients and found that subsequent completed suicide was most common in those with schizophrenia, affective disorders and neurotic depressions and less common (though still more than for controls) in alcoholics and narcomanics.

Pokorny (1983) followed up VA inpatients and found higher suicide rates in those with affective disorders and schizophrenia and lower suicide rates in those with alcohol or drug abuse in general, though older alcoholics and younger drug addicts also had high suicide rates.

Morrison (1982) followed up patients in private practice and found that highest completed suicide rates for those diagnosed with schizophrenia, followed by those with bipolar affective disorder. The lowest rates were found for those with unipolar affective disorder and conversion disorders.

De Leo et al. (1986) found that attempted suicides with a diagnosis of schizophrenia, major depression or dysthymic disorder had higher suicidal intent on an objective scale than those with a diagnosis of adjustment disorder.

In a sample of completed suicides, Carlson (1984) found that older suicides were more often diagnosed with an affective disorder and less often as alcoholics. The older suicides had less of a history of violence and impulsivity.

Rich et al. (1988) found that psychotic completed suicides were younger than non-psychotic suicides but had as many depressive symptoms as depressed suicides. They did not differ in use of bizarre methods for suicide or in suicidal communications. In the sample of suicides as a whole, the younger suicides (younger than 30) were less often married or living alone, were more often diagnosed as having an antisocial personality disorder or drug abuse (and less often as having an affective disorder or an organic brain syndrome), used hanging more, and had more legal problems, unemployment and separations as precipitating incidents (Rich et al., 1985). Delga et al. (1989) found that psychotic and non-psychotic adolescent inpatients did not differ in their history of suicidal or violent behaviors.

In a review of research, Coryell (1988) concluded that patients with panic disorder had a relatively high rate of completed suicide. Coryell et al. (1982) found as high a suicide rate in a sample of patients with panic disorders as in patients with a primary unipolar depression. A study of anxiety neurotics appeared to suggest a high suicide rate, but the sample size was very small (Coryell, 1986).

Coryell (1981a, 1981b) found relatively fewer prior suicide attempts and subsequent completed suicides in patients with conversion disorder or obsessive-compulsive disorder than in patients with primary unipolar depression.

Looking at inpatients who completed suicide in the hospital, Swart (1987) found that those with personality disorders, neuroses and schizophrenia were younger (modal age 20–39) while those with affective psychoses were older (modal age 50 and older). Those with substance abuse and neurosis committed suicide earlier in their stay (most often in the first week) while those with schizophrenia and affective psychoses committed suicide more often in the second and third months.

Of course, not every study finds a difference. For example, Borst and Noam (1989) found no difference in diagnosis between adolescent psychiatric patients who had attempted suicide and those who had not.

Depressive Disorder

Suicidal Ideation

Jablensky et al. (1981) compared depressed psychiatric patients in different nations and found suicidal ideation more common in Basle, Montreal and Nagasaki than in Tehran and Tokyo. Overall and Rhoades (1982) found that not all depressive symptoms were associated with suicidal ideation. In a cluster analysis of items from the Hamilton Rating Scale for depression, they identified five independent clusters of symptoms: anxious depression, somatizing depression, vegetative depression, paranoid depression and suicidal depression.

Angst and Dobler-Mikola (1985) found that patients with a diagnosis of extensive depression or recurrent brief depression had more suicidal ideation (and higher depression scores) than patients diagnosed with non-recurrent depression. Zetin et al. (1984) found no sex differences in current suicidal ideation in inpatients with major depressive disorders.

Vandivort and Locker (1979) surveyed urban residents and found that those reporting recent suicidal ideation were more depressed. Altman et al. (1971) found that the presence of suicidal thoughts in psychiatric patients was associated with the presence of depression (and a sad facial expression, guilt feelings, delusions of worthlessness and slower speech), a diagnosis of neurosis, homicidal ideas, and being a first admission.

Leonard (1974) had staff rate psychiatric patients in the degree of suicidality. Suicidality was not related to self-rated depression as a whole but was related with the items related to physiological disequilibrium (such as eating disturbance, insomnia and energy level). Suicidality was not related to a diagnosis of depression, drug or alcohol use, nor to the MMPI scale scores of ego-strength, Megargee's overt hostility scores or the Goldberg Index. Suicidality was related to elevated D and Si scale scores and repression-sensitization scores.

Attempted Suicide

Asarnow and Guthrie (1989) found that adolescent psychiatric inpatients who had attempted suicide were more often diagnosed as having a major depressive disorder than the non-suicidal patients. Chabrol and Moron (1988) found that 81 percent of a sample of adolescent suicide attempters had a major depressive disorder and an additional 10 percent a dysthymic disorder. Poldinger (1972) found that the presence of a history of attempted suicide in depressed patients was associated with higher levels of anxiety, age, diagnosis, and sleep disturbance.

Bronisch and Hecht (1987) found that depressed inpatients who had attempted suicide had more psychiatric disturbance/attempted suicide/alcoholism in the first degree relatives than patients who had not attempted suicide. They also more often had divorced parents. The groups did not differ in social functioning or social support, stressful events, frustration tolerance, extraversion, schizoid tendencies or self-reliance.

Clarkin et al. (1984) found no differences between attempters with depressed mood who were adolescents and those who were young adults in diagnosis, type of depression, prior attempts or the lethality of the suicide attempt.

Goldney et al. (1981) found that women who attempted suicide by overdose in four countries had similar depression scores and the same proportion of endogenous depressions.

Gorenc et al. (1983) compared depressed and non-depressed attempted suicides and found that the depressed attempters were younger, less often single, more intent on dying, and made more lethal attempts (but did not differ in sex or prior suicide attempts). The seriousness of the suicidal act (both intent and lethality) was greater in males, the older attempters, the married, the unemployed, those with prior suicide attempts, and those using more active methods for suicide.

Hecht and Bronisch (1988) found no differences between depressive patients who had attempted suicide and those who had not in paranoid ideation or overall complaints. The suicide attempters tended to be less impaired in their functioning, however.

Roy-Byrne et al. (1988) found no differences between affective disorder patients who had attempted suicide and those who had not in the course of the illness, prior psychiatric illness or bipolar versus unipolar (though the attempters were more often female).

Spalt (1980) found that college student psychiatric patients who had a diagnosis of affective disorder had made more suicidal threats and attempts and had had more suicidal ideation. The incidence of suicidal preoccupation did not vary with the type of affective disorder. A later study (Spalt, 1983) found that attempted suicides in non-patient college students who had attempted suicide (10.5 percent of the sample) were more likely to have bipolar disorders (but not unipolar), secondary affective disorders (as well as antisocial personality disorder and somatization disorder, but not alcoholism, drug abuse or homosexuality).

Van Praag and Plutchik (1988) studied depressed inpatients and found that the rate of depressions (expressed as episodes per year since the age of 15) were positively related to the rate of attempting suicide (expressed as episodes per year since the age of 15). The association was higher for patients diagnosed as dysthymic than those with a major depressive disorder. (The association was not statistically significant using the absolute number of episodes.) Older patients had lower rates of both depressions and suicide attempts than the younger patients.

Completed Suicide

Achte (1986) reviewed follow-up studies of depressed psychiatric patients. The longer the follow-up the more subjects had died, and the percentage of deaths due to suicide approached 15 percent as the follow-up period increased.

Berglund and Nilsson (1987) reported an excess of completed suicide in depressed inpatients. They reported that depressed inpatients who subsequently completed suicide had more marital problems, an acute onset and were more brittle/sensitive. They did not differ in poverty or the presence of delusions. Berglund and Smith (1988) found that subsequent suicide was also predicted by a serial color word test and a metacontrast test (which required the suppression of tachistoscopically presented pictures).

Chynoweth et al. (1980) found that depressed suicides as compared to living depressed patients had more guilt, a longer illness, more alcohol abuse, more previous suicide attempts, and more hallucinations, whereas the living depressed had more weight loss, loss of concentration, tension and anxiety, and a family history of psychiatric treatment.

Major Affective Disorder

Fawcett (1988; Fawcett et al., 1987) found that patients with a major affective disorder who completed suicide within four years of admission more often had cycling moods (from depression to mania), panic attacks, depressive turmoil (depression, anger and anxiety) and alcohol abuse, were less likely to have young children at home and had fewer adolescent friendships. The suicides were also more depressed and hopeless, had fewer prior depressive episodes, more often had delusions of grandeur and mindreading, but did not differ in prior suicide attempts or the type of affective disorder. The lethality of earlier suicide attempts did not predict subsequent completed suicide.

Flynn and McMahon (1983) found that psychotic depression and dysthymia as measured by the Millon Clinical Multiaxial Inventory were associated with prior suicidal ideation in a sample of drug abusers in treatment but not with a history of suicide attempts.

Friedman et al. (1983, 1984a) found that among adolescents and young adults with an Axis I diagnosis of depression (or any affective disorder), those with a borderline personality disorder had a higher incidence of suicide attempts (and, in particular, lethal suicide attempts).

Garvey et al. (1986) found that prior attempts at suicide were more common in patients with chronic primary major depressive disorder than in those with episodic primary major depressive disorder (yet the two types of depressive patients did not differ in the level of depression).

Garvey et al. (1983) found that affective disorder patients who had attempted suicide were younger at the age of onset, abused alcohol more and had poorer social functioning than those who had not attempted suicide. The groups did not differ in sex, the affective polarity, the duration of affective episodes, whether the depression was psychotic or the family history of affective disorder.

Kivela et al. (1989) found that suicidal ideation was more common in patients with a major depressive disorder than in those with an atypical depressive disorder or a dysthymic disorder.

Modestin and Kopp (1988b) compared depressed inpatients who completed suicide in the hospital or while on leave with non-suicidal patients. The suicides more often had a bipolar disorder and less often a minor depressive disorder. Six variables discriminated the suicides: broken homes, more prior hospitalizations, suicidal during the hospitalization and at admission, and more stressful events (exits).

Perugi et al. (1988) found that a history of attempted suicide in depressive disorder patients was associated with being female, single, more prior hospitalizations, a longer illness, an earlier age of onset and bipolar type I diagnosis (but not with education, employment status, chronicity of the depressive illness, stressors, the presence of hypomania, depression scale scores or psychotic experiences).

Pfohl et al. (1984) found that psychiatric patients with a major depression were more likely to make frequent non-serious attempts at suicide if they also had a borderline personality disorder (but they also had higher depression inventory scores).

Roy (1983a) found that suicides with a major depressive episode had had more prior depressions, psychiatric admissions and suicide attempts than suicides with a neurotic depression. They did not differ in family members in psychiatric treatment. Roy (1985a) found that affective disorder patients who had attempted suicide had experienced a longer illness and an earlier age of onset.

Steer et al. (1987) found that outpatients with recurrent major depressive disorders were currently more suicidal than patients with dysthymic disorder.

Winokur and Black (1987) found that psychiatric inpatients who had completed suicide more often had been diagnosed as having an affective disorder (especially a unipolar depression) and less often a personality disorder (but the groups did not differ in medical diagnosis).

Unipolar Depression

Fowler et al. (1979) followed-up unipolar depressive patients and found that those with a history of suicidal ideation or attempts were more likely to complete suicide.

Brown et al. (1984) found no differences in suicidal preoccupation in inpatients with unipolar endogenous depressions for whom the onset was before or after the age of fifty. Coryell and Tsuang (1982) found no association between the presence of delusion in unipolar patients and the rate of subsequent suicide.

McGlashen (1987) found that patients with unipolar affective disorders had a higher subsequent rate of completed suicide than patients with borderline personality disorder, but patients with both disorders had the highest suicide rate of all.

Among unipolar inpatients, Miller and Chabrier (1987) found that the presence of delusions per se was not associated with an increased rate of prior suicide attempts, but the presence of delusions of guilt in combination with persecution was associated with an increased rate. Roose et al. (1983) found that delusions were more common among unipolar patients who completed suicide while in the hospital than in non-suicidal controls.

Bipolar Disorders

Nurnberger et al. (1979) found that bipolar patients with only manic episodes had made fewer previous suicide attempts than those with depressed episodes. Dunner et al. (1976) found that bipolar patients who had been hospitalized in the past only for depression were more likely to complete suicide after discharge than other affective disorder patients.

Goldring and Fieve (1984) found that manic-depressive patients who had attempted suicide were younger, had shown the disorder at a younger age and were more often female. Roy (1984) found that manic-depressive patients who completed suicide had experienced more early parental loss, had a shorter illness and had made more prior suicide attempts than nonsuicidal patients. They did not differ in the presence of suicide in relatives. Weeke (1979) reported an excess mortality from suicide in manic-depressive patients, especially for those aged 60 or more.

Unipolar Versus Bipolar

Black (1989) found no differences in subsequent mortality from suicide in bipolar and unipolar depressive patients. Ramos-Brieva and Cordero-Villafafila (1989) found no differences between unipolar and bipolar patients in the incidence of prior attempted suicide or suicidal ideation. The suicide attempters did have a longer current depression.

Till and Kapamadzija (1983) found no differences in the incidence of attempted suicide in unipolar and bipolar depressives. (Women had made more attempts than men, but age was not related to a history of attempts.) Weeke and Vaeth (1986; Weeke et al., 1987) found no differences in the rate of suicide in bipolar and unipolar patients, though both had excess mortality from suicide in the 1950s and in the 1970s.

Coryell et al. (1987) found that bipolar depressives made more serious suicide attempts than unipolar depressives. Black et al. (1987b) found that primary unipolar depressives had fewer suicidal attempts prior to and after hospitalization than secondary unipolar depressives. On the other hand, patients with a major depression did not differ from bipolar patients in subsequent completed suicide (Black et al. 1988c). Dunner et al. (1976) found that unipolar patients (whether hospitalized in the past for mania or depression) had less often attempted suicide in the past than bipolar patients.

Linkowski et al. (1985) found that female unipolar patients had made more prior suicide attempts than had female bipolar patients, but the difference for men was not statistically significant. However, though the female bipolar patients made fewer prior suicide attempts, there was a higher risk of their prior attempts involving violent methods.

Roy (1985b) found that unipolar and bipolar manic-depressive patients did not differ in how many first or second degree relatives had completed suicide. Coryell et al. (1985) found the relatives of bipolar (type I) patients had made more suicide attempts than the relatives of unipolar patients.

Stallone et al. (1980) found that attempted suicide was most common in bipolar II patients (hypomanic), non-suicidal involvement in bipolar I patients (manic), suicidal ideation in other bipolar patients, and an average amount of suicidal involvement in unipolar patients. Incidentally, the suicidal patients more often had suicide in their relatives, were more social isolated and more often were female but did not differ in age or work impairment.

The results of this research are rather inconsistent, and we can draw no reliable conclusions about the relative incidence of suicidality in unipolar and bipolar patients.

Mania

Black et al. (1988a) found that manic patients with other secondary diagnoses were more likely to have a history of suicide attempts than simple manic patients. Bipolar manic patients had a better immediate improvement if they were less suicidal at admission, but the immediate improvement was not related to subsequent suicidal behavior (Black et al., 1988b). The manic patients had a lower percentage of deaths from suicide than other bipolar depressives and unipolar patients (Black et al., 1987a).

In a study of adolescents who made serious suicide attempts, Friedman (1984b) found that they had a manic episode at an earlier age than non-suicidal psychiatric inpatients. They also were more likely to have had parents with a chronic psychiatric illness before the patient was fourteen years old. (There were no differences in the age at the first depressive episode or the lifetime incidence of psychiatric disorder in their families.)

Mitteraure et al. (1988) found that manic-depressive patients with a family history of manic-depression and completed suicide more often attempted suicide and had suicidal tendencies than those with a family history of only manic-depression.

Atypical Depression

Davidson et al. (1982) claimed (with little supporting data) that patients with atypical depression (with accompanying anxiety or with atypical vegetative symptoms such as increased appetite) were less likely to attempt suicide.

Endogenous Depression

Davis (1989) compared a sample of attempted suicides with non-suicidal psychiatric patients and found that the attempted suicides were more often diagnosed as having nonendogenous depression while the controls were more often diagnosed as having endogenous depression.

Kiloh et al. (1988) followed up inpatients with a primary depressive disorder and found the subsequent completed suicide rate to be the same in those with endogenous and neurotic depressions.

Winokur et al. (1987) found that endogenous depressives were less likely to have attempted suicide than neurotic depressives, less likely to have suicidal ideation on admission, and less likely to attempt suicide after admission or release, but did not differ in subsequent completed suicide.

Wolfersdorf et al. (1987) found that patients with endogenous depressions who had delusions were less often suicidal at admission but had attempted suicide more in the past. They did not complete suicide more often in a follow-up study, however.

Neurotic Depression

Zimmerman et al. (1987) found that patients with neurotic depression were more likely to have made non-serious suicide attempts in the past than patients with non-neurotic depressive disorders, but this finding probably developed because a prior non-serious suicide attempt was part of the criteria for diagnosing a neurotic depression!

Masked Depression

Cadlouski et al. (1983) found that psychiatric patients with masked depression were no less likely to have attempted suicide than patients with ordinary depression but were less likely to have serious suicidal ideation.

Primary/Secondary Affective Disorder

Brim et al. (1984) found that psychiatric inpatients diagnosed as having a secondary affective disorder had more suicidal ideation and more severe ideation than patients with a primary affective disorder.

Morrison and Herbstein (1988) found more prior suicidal ideation and attempts in patients with somatization disorder with secondary depression than in primary affective disorder patients. Reveley and

Reveley (1981) found more prior suicide attempts in secondary depressives than in primary depressive, and the two groups did not differ in depression inventory scores (though the secondary depressives had a longer current episode).

Winokur et al. (1988) studied a group of patients with secondary depression and found prior suicide attempts and subsequent completed suicide to be more common in those also diagnosed as substance abusers than in those also diagnosed as anxiety disorder or personality disorder or with only a medical illness.

Depression with Obsessions

Videbech (1975) found that endogenous depressed patients with and without obsessions did not differ in attempted suicide, completed suicide or suicidal ideation. Among the anacastic depressed patients, the presence of aggressive obsessions was not associated with attempted suicide.

Depressive Symptoms

Wold and Tabachnick (1974) compared the depressive symptoms of suicide prevention center patients who completed suicide and those who did not. The suicides had higher levels of somatic symptoms, somewhat higher levels of affective and social symptoms, but a similar duration of depression. They then classified the suicides into types (such as old-and-stable or chaotic-psychotic-borderline) and found differences for each group. For example, all types had higher levels of somatic symptoms of depression. The discarded-stable and old-and-stable had higher levels of affective symptoms while the down-and-out suicides had lower levels.

Depression Scores

Apter et al. (1988) found that suicidality was higher in adolescent psychiatric inpatients who were more depressed. Bagley (1985) found that depression was associated with a history of attempted suicide in a community sample of adults. Bonner and Rich (1987, 1988, 1989) found that suicidal students and inmates were more depressed than non-suicidal persons. Carlson and Cantwell (1982) found that adolescent psychiatric patients with more serious suicidal ideation were more depressed (and had more disturbed family members), and those who had attempted suicide were most depressed. Cattell (1988) found that elderly suicides were more depressed (but less confused and demented) than elderly accidental deaths. Overholser et al. (1987) found that non-psychotic depressed inpatients who were suicidal did not differ in depression scores from the non-suicidal patients at admission, but they were more depressed ten months after discharge. Steer et al. (1983) found that attempting suicide and depression were associated in alcoholics.

In contrast, Chlewinski (1984) found that suicide attempters were less depressed than non-suicidal psychiatric patients.

Hopelessness

Beck's Research

Beck has continued to explore the relationship between his hopelessness scale and suicidal behavior. Beck et al. (1989a, 1989b) found that clinical and objective scale ratings of hopelessness predicted subsequent suicide in a group of psychiatric inpatients and a group of outpatients. Beck et al. (1985) found that hopelessness predicted subsequent suicide in a group of suicidal ideators, while depression scores did not. Beck et al. (1982) found that both hopelessness and depression predicted past suicide attempts in a group of outpatient alcoholics, while Beck et al. (1989c) found that neither scale (nor a DSM III diagnosis of depressive disorder) predicted subsequent completed suicide in alcohol abusers who had previously attempted suicide. Emery et al. (1981) found that suicidal ideation was associated with hopelessness but not with depression in a sample of heroin addicts.

Others' Research

Adam et al. (1980) found that attempted suicides were more depressed and more hopeless (and had higher levels of state anxiety) than general medical patients. Asarnow and Guthrie (1989) found that adolescent psychiatric inpatients who had attempted suicide had more hopelessness (but not more depression) than non-suicidal patients. Biro and Lazic (1988) found that hopelessness differentiated between completed and attempted suicides. Cole (1988) found that hopelessness was associated with suicidal history in university counseling clients (even after controls for social desirability) but not in the general population of students. Cole (1989) found that hopelessness and suicidality were associated in high school students and that the association remained statistically significant even with controls for depression. He also replicated the association in a sample of male juvenile delinquents. Dyer and Kreitman (1984) found that hopelessness was a stronger predictor of suicidal intent in a sample of attempted suicides than was depression.

Bonner and Rich (1987) found that suicidal students obtained higher hopelessness scores than non-suicidal students, as did Evans et al. (1985) (but only for males), and replicated this result with high school children (Rich et al., 1989) and for self-predicted future suicide risk in college students (Rich and Bonner, 1987). Reynolds (1988) found that suicidal ideation was associated with hopelessness and depression in adolescents.

Goldney et al. (1989) found that suicidal ideation was associated with both depression and hopelessness in young adults. Gutierrez et al. (1988) found greater hopelessness in psychiatric patients in the two weeks before they completed suicide than in matched controls (but no differences in depression, hostility or somatization). Nekanda-Trepka et al. (1983) found that hopelessness and, to a lesser extent, depression were associated with the wish to die in psychiatric outpatients.

Holden et al. (1985) found that hopelessness was associated with the desire for suicide in suicidal ideators but not with making preparations to commit suicide.

In a community sample of depressed elderly, Hill et al. (1988) found that the giving up items of Beck's hopeless scale were associated with suicidal preoccupation, but not the hope or the future-anticipation items. Depression, hopelessness and health all predicted suicidal preoccupation.

In a community sample of adolescents, Kashani et al. (1989) found that current suicidal ideation and hopelessness were associated. Kazdin et al. (1983) studied inpatient disturbed children and found that those who had attempted suicide were more depressed and had lower self-esteem than other children. Those who had attempted suicide or thought about suicide were more hopeless and more depressed than the non-suicidal children. Kirkpatrick-Smith et al. (1989) found that both depression and hopelessness were associated with suicidal ideation in school students. Papa (1980) found that hopelessness correlated with suicidal intent in a sample of attempted suicides.

Petrie et al. (1988) found that hopelessness predicted suicidal ideation, prior suicide attempts and future suicide attempts in a sample of attempted suicides in a multiple regression with depression, self-esteem and other psychological test scores.

Wetzel et al. (1980) found that suicidal intent in psychiatric patients was associated with hopelessness scores even with controls for depression scores, but not vice versa. Wetzel and Reich (1989) correlated suicidal intent and hopelessness over days for a sample of psychiatric patients and found that the overall correlation was positive (as was the association between suicidal intent and self-esteem). This latter result would have been more valid if they had considered each patient separately in the correlational analysis over days.

Rubenstein et al. (1989) found that both depression and hopelessness differentiated high school students who had made a suicide attempt in the previous year from those who had not. Schotte and Clum (1982, 1987) found that depression and hopelessness predicted suicidal ideation in a college population, but depression was the strongest predictor. In a psychiatric patient sample, however, only hopelessness predicted suicidal ideation. Topol and Reznikoff (1982) found that adolescent suicide attempters were more hopeless than both psychiatric and normal controls.

Westefeld and Furr (1987) found that suicidal preoccupation in college students was associated with hopelessness, helplessness, depression, loneliness and problems with parents.

Obayuwana et al. (1982) constructed a hope index scale whose scores correlated strongly with those from Beck's scale. Suicide attempters obtained higher scores on both scales than depressed patients.

On the other hand, Asarnow and Carlson (1988) found that family support but not depression or hopelessness discriminated between adolescent attempted suicides and non-suicidal inpatients. However, in another report, Asarnow et al. (1987) found that the attempted suicides were more hopeless and depressed and had less family support than the non-suicidal inpatients. Chabon and Robins (1986) found that suicidal intent was not related to hopelessness or depression in a sample of depressed or suicidal drug abusers. Dietzfelbinger et al. (1989) found that hopelessness did not predict subsequent suicide attempts in a sample of suicide attempters. Ellis et al. (1989) found no differences in psychiatric inpatients between those who had attempted suicide and those who had not in either hopelessness or depression, though Ellis and Ratliff (1986) reported that suicidal inpatients (attempters and ideators) were more hopeless and depressed.

Eaton and Reynolds (1989) found that adolescent suicide attempters were less depressed and hopeless than adult attempters (and made less lethal attempts with less suicidal intent and had less of a suicidal history). The adolescents also were more likely to have psychiatrically disturbed relatives and were less likely to be male and married.

McLeavey et al. (1987) found that self-poisoners did not differ from non-suicidal psychiatric patients in hopelessness. Plummer et al. (1989) found no differences in hopelessness between adolescent suicide attempters, suicidal ideators and non-suicidal adolescents. Ranieri et al. (1987) found that hopelessness was associated with suicidal ideation in psychiatric patients but, in a multiple regression analysis with depression scores, was no longer statistically significant.

Spirito et al. (1987, 1988c) reported that adolescent suicide attempters were more hopeless than psychiatric outpatients or normal high school students but that they did not differ for adolescents hospitalized for a psychiatric consultation. Among the attempters, chronic and acutely suicidal patients did not differ in hopelessness and neither did the more versus less lethal attempters.

Rotheram-Borus and Trautman (1988) found that minority female adolescents who had attempted suicide did not differ in depression or hopelessness from outpatient psychiatric controls (though both of these groups obtained higher scores than normal girls). For the attempted suicides, depression and hopelessness were not associated with suicidal intent. Trenteseau et al. (1989) found that depression, but not hopelessness, was associated with past and present suicidal preoccupation in psycho-geriatric inpatients.

Social Desirability

Linehan and Nielsen (1981, 1983) found that hopelessness scorers were associated with scores on a measure of the tendency to give socially desirable answers. They found that controls for social desirability scores eliminated the association between hopelessness and a history of attempted suicide while controls for hopelessness did *not* eliminate the association between social desirability scores and a history of attempted suicide. However, ratings of the probability of future suicide were not eliminated by controls for social desirability. Mendonca et al. (1983) also found that controlling for scores on a social desirability scale eliminated differences in hopelessness between suicide attempters and ideators and controls.

However, Ellis (1985) found that suicidal ideation was associated with hopelessness (and depression) even after controlling for social desirability. Similarly, Holden et al. (1989) found that hopelessness predicted suicidal ideation in crisis patients and the suicidal intent in the prior suicide attempts of prisoners even after controls for social desirability, and Petrie and Chamberlain (1983) found that hopelessness and suicidality in a sample of attempted suicides were positively associated after controls for depression and social desirability.

Finally, Strosahl et al. (1984) found that *both* hopelessness and social desirability scale scores contributed to the prediction of past suicidal behavior.

Schizophrenia

Book and Modrzewska (1982) found a high rate of death from suicide in schizophrenics in a remote region of Sweden, as did Masterson and O'Shea (1984) in Great Britain. In a ten-year follow-up study of discharged schizophrenic patients, Allebeck et al. (1986) found that 7.8 percent of the deaths were from suicide. Suicide was more common in the younger ex-patients (aged 20–39) while accidents were more common in the older ex-patients. Their suicide rate was higher than expected (Allebeck and Wistedt, 1986).

Cosyns et al. (1987) found the percentage of deaths due to suicide were higher in schizophrenics with a diagnosis of schizoaffective disorder and who were disorganized and paranoid and lower in those with schizoptyal personality disorder and catatonic, residual, and undifferentiated schizophrenia. Black et al. (1985b) found that the most of the suicides in schizophrenics after release occurred in the first two years.

In contrast, Buda et al. (1988) found an excess of suicide not in schizophrenics but in those with a diagnosis of atypical psychosis.

Gulyamov and Bessonov (1986) found that paranoid schizophrenics with Kandinsky's syndrome were more likely to attempt or complete suicide than those without the syndrome.

Roy (1986) reviewed research on suicide in schizophrenics and found that an average of 33 percent had attempted suicide during their illness and, after an average follow-up period of 19 years, 8 percent of the patients had completed suicide. The suicides had a mean age of 31, 74 percent were male, 28 percent were inpatients at the time of their suicidal death, 51 percent had previously attempted suicide and 63 percent were depressed.

Characteristics Of Schizophrenic Completed Suicides

Drake et al. (1985) reviewed research on controlled studies of schizophrenics who had completed suicide and concluded that the suicides tended to be younger, male, better educated, more often unemployed and unmarried, and with a chronic course (with exacerbations). The risk of suicide was greatest in the early years of the illness (the first ten years) and during remissions. The suicides often occurred while on pass or after discharge (that is, after clinical improvement) or in the first six months of hospitalization. There was usually a lack of family support, agitation prior to the suicide and greater depression. The suicides did not differ in loss, prior suicidal behavior, drug and alcohol abuse or hallucinations.

Black and Winokur (1988) found that schizophrenic patients who subsequently completed suicide were younger than affective disorder patients, and the chronic schizophrenic suicides were younger than the acute schizophrenic suicides.

Allebeck et al. (1987) compared schizophrenics who killed themselves with those who did not and found that the suicides had abused alcohol more (for the males only), had more prior attempts at suicide and had more suicidal ideation (for the females only). The groups did not differ in sex, age or the duration of the disorder.

Breier and Astrachan (1984) compared schizophrenics who completed suicide with non-suicidal schizophrenics and non-schizophrenics who completed suicide. The schizophrenic suicides were younger, more often male and white, and less often married. The schizophrenic suicides used more lethal methods for suicide, verbalized their suicidal preoccupation less, and had experienced fewer recent stressors. The groups did not differ in the chronicity of their psychiatric illness.

Drake et al. (1984, 1986) found that schizophrenics who completed suicide were more often depressed and hopeless, had a fear of mental disintegration, lived alone and were college educated more often than living controls or attempted suicides. They did not differ in prior suicide attempts, suicidal behavior in their families, substance abuse, delusions, hallucinations, physical health history of violence or recent interpersonal loss.

Nyman and Jonsson (1986) found that schizophrenics who subsequently completed suicide differed from the rest in being more often male, with prior suicide attempts, having more suicidal ideation, a more chronic regressive course, more subjective social isolation, more often living with their parents and less often financially self-supporting.

Roy (1982a) found that schizophrenics who completed suicide were more often chronic cases with acute exacerbation and had more prior depressive episodes. (They did not differ in most other personal background variables.) The male suicides were more often chronic and un-differentiated schizophrenics while the female suicides were more often paranoid. The male suicides had an earlier onset of the schizophrenia.

Wolfersdorf et al. (1989) found that schizophrenics who completed suicide in the hospital had a longer hospital stay, quicker re-admission, worsened over time, had changed therapists, treatments and wards more, and were more suicidal in the past than alive schizophrenics. They had hallucinations and delusions less often and less often abused drugs or alcohol, but did not differ in children, unemployment, schizophrenia or suicidal behavior in relatives or early childhood developmental disorders. Compared to depressive patients who completed suicide, the schizophrenic suicides were younger, lived alone or in institutions more, were more often unemployed, had improved less, had been admitted more often, and were more often continuously ill. The depressive suicides had more prior and recent suicide attempts, were more suicidal on admission, but did not differ in the duration of their illness. The schizophrenics killed themselves more while out on a pass or after escaping while the depressives killed themselves more often while on vacation or at home. The groups did not differ in the method used for suicide.

Characteristics of Schizophrenic Attempted Suicides

Hauser et al. (1985) found no differences in age at admission, prior hospitalizations and the social relationships of schizophrenics who had attempted suicide previously and those who had not.

Landmark et al. (1987) found that schizophrenics who attempted suicide had moved residence more, been hospitalized more and had poorer work performance than non-suicidal schizophrenics. Those with weaker suicidal tendencies had also moved more, been hospitalized more, and also abused marijuana more than the non-suicidal patients.

Nyman and Jonsson (1986) compared schizophrenics who subsequently attempted suicide with the rest and found than to be more depressed, with diffuse anxiety, with more prior suicidal thoughts and attempts, more often with feelings of depersonalization and a subjectively unhappy childhood, clumsy and gauche, and good as adolescents. Suicide attempts were most common in the female non-regressed schizophrenics.

Prasad (1986; Prasad and Kellner, 1988; Prasad and Kumar, 1988) found that hospitalized and non-hospitalized schizophrenics with a history of attempted suicide were more depressed and more likely to be male. The non-hospitalized schizophrenics who had attempted suicide were also younger, with more family members psychiatrically disturbed.

Rohde et al. (1989a) found that schizophrenic inpatients who had attempted or thought about suicide hardly differed from those who had not (in age, marital status, social class, broken homes, psychiatric illness or suicide in the family, employment, hallucinations, delusions or incoherence). The suicidal schizophrenics were more often female and had more recent stressful life events.

Roy et al. (1984) found that chronic schizophrenics who had previously attempted suicide had more depressive episodes and more prior psychiatric admissions. They did not differ in most personal history variables from the non-suicidal schizophrenics. In a follow-up study, Roy et al. (1986) found that the more subsequent admissions, the more likely future suicide attempts. However, future completed suicide was not predicted by prior suicide attempts (or early onset of the disorder, past depression or multiple admissions).

Wilkinson and Bacon (1984) found that schizophrenics who had attempted suicide were more often employed, had fewer prior admissions for schizophrenia, were less likely to be in treatment at the time and more often had auditory hallucinations. (They did not differ in whether the schizophrenia was acute or recurrent.) In a follow-up study, those who completed suicide had more prior admissions and had made more prior suicide attempts.

Completed Versus Attempted Suicides

Tejedor et al. (1987) found that schizophrenics who completed suicide were younger, used more violent methods and were more often chronic schizophrenics than those who attempted suicide.

Suicidal Ideation

Berk (1949) took a group of schizophrenics who were currently suicidal and who also had previously attempted suicide and compared them with the next schizophrenic in the record file. The suicidal schizophrenics had more often shown overt homosexuality and had been more assaultive in their lives, but the groups did not differ in parental loss before adolescence or alcohol abuse. Few differences were found on projective tests (the Rorschach, the TAT, the Rosenzweig Picture-Frustration Study or the Draw-A–Person Test).

Tejedor et al. (1987) found that suicidal schizophrenics were more depressed and had experienced more stressful life events and more loss in recent months than the non-suicidal schizophrenic patients.

Schizoaffective Disorders

Marneros et al. (1988, 1989) found that unipolar schizoaffective patients attempted suicide more and had more suicidal preoccupation than bipolar schizoaffective patients. Rohde et al. (1989b) found that schizoaffective inpatients who had attempted or thought about suicide more often had auditory hallucinations and delusions, had more schizoaffective episodes but fewer depressive, manic and schizophrenic episodes. (They were also more often married and female.) Angst et al. (1979) found that 22 percent of the deaths of schizoaffective patients were due to suicide at a 12–16-year follow-up.

Atypical Psychoses

Rich et al. (1986b) compared schizophrenic suicides to suicides with atypical psychoses and found the latter to more often abuse drugs and to have an antisocial personality disorder and atypical depressions.

Personality Disorders

Bornstein et al. (1988) found that psychiatric patients with a schizotypal personality disorder were more likely to have a history of prior suicide attempts than other patients. Casey (1989) found that the most common personality disorder in a sample of attempted suicides was explosive (54 percent in men and 33 percent in women) with normal close second (25 percent in men and 44 percent in women). Suicidal intent was not related to the presence or type of personality disorder. The men were more often diagnosed as sociopathic than the women, but did not differ in the other types of personality disorder.

Lester et al. (1989) found that unsocialized suicide attempters (those with an antisocial personality disorder or substance abuse) did not differ in depression, hopelessness or medical lethality of their attempt from depressive disorder attempters, but they did have less suicidal intent and more prior suicide attempts. The attempters with antisocial personality disorder did have lower depression scores than the depressive disorder attempters.

Modestin (1989) compared psychiatric patients with personality disorder who subsequently completed suicide with those who did not. The suicides were older, more often had occupational difficulties, more often lived dependent on others, had made more prior suicide attempts, and showed more suicidal behavior in the hospital. Compared to other completed suicides who did not have a personality disorder, those with a personality disorder who killed themselves had experienced more stressful life events.

Raczek et al. (1989) found that both attempted suicides and suicidal ideators had higher scores on a test of borderline personality traits than non-suicidal patients, the attempters had higher scores on avoidant personality traits, while the groups did not differ on compulsive personality traits.

Borderline Personality Disorder

Fyer et al. (1988) found a high incidence of suicide attempts in patients with a diagnosis of borderline personality disorder, especially if they also were substance abusers or had an affective disorder. Among a sample of delinquent females, Gibbs (1981) found the highest incidence of prior suicide attempts among those with borderline personality disorder, next most among those with antisocial or neurotic personality disorder and least among the socialized delinquents.

Kullgren (1986) found that patients with borderline personality disorder who completed suicide had more often made suicide attempts and been psychiatrically hospitalized, but did not differ in age, sex, age at first psychiatric contact, or health-sickness rating scale scores. Kullgren et al. (1986) found no differences between the borderline suicides and other suicides among psychiatric patients except that the borderline suicides were younger.

Nace et al. (1983) compared inpatients alcoholics with a diagnosis of borderline personality disorder with the other alcoholics. The borderline patients were younger, abused drugs more, had attempted suicide more and had been in more accidents. (They did not differ in social activities or their history of alcoholism.)

Montgomery et al. (1989) studied a group of repeat suicide attempters mainly diagnosed as borderline personality disorder without a major depression. They monitored the patients for up to six months and found that they had brief recurrent depressive episodes, with a median length of three days and an inter-episode interval of eighteen days. They suggested that the suicide attempts may have occurred during these brief depressive episodes.

Paris et al. (1987, 1988, 1989) found a high percentage of completed suicides in a follow-up study of those with borderline personality disorder (7.3 percent of patients and 57.1 percent of deaths). The suicides had experienced fewer problems with their mothers and less separation in the first five years of life than the living patients. They less often had a psychosis but they had attempted suicide more in the past. (They did not differ in social adaptation, impulsiveness, interpersonal relationships, self-mutilation, drug abuse, or the presence of an affective disorder).

Rippetoe et al. (1986) found that prior suicide attempts were more common in patients with borderline personality disorder if they were also depressed or dysthymic.

Shearer et al. (1988) found that the suicidal intent of the most serious prior suicide attempt in a sample of female patients with borderline personality disorder was associated with age, the presence of an eating disorder, the number of prior attempts, a secondary diagnosis of psychosis or anxiety disorder and affective disorder in the parents.

Snyder et al. (1986) found that psychiatric patients with a higher score on a scale to measure borderline personality disorder had made more prior suicide attempts (and at an earlier age) and were more violent both in and out of the hospital. Wade (1987) found that adolescent girls who had attempted suicide obtained higher scores on a test of borderline disorder than non-suicidal girls. Joffe and Regan (1989) found that unipolar nonpsychotic depressive patients who attempted suicide during the present illness scored higher on a test of borderline personality (but did not receive an Axis II diagnosis of borderline personality more often).

In contrast, Weiner and Pfeffer (1986) found no association between borderline personality disorder and suicidal ideation in preadolescent psychiatric inpatients, but suicidal ideation was associated with the presence of major depressive disorder.

Deliberate Self-Harm Syndrome

Pattison and Kahan (1983) argued that a new DSM category was needed for deliberate self-harm. This syndrome has its onset in late adolescence and is characterized by multiple episodes of low lethality, despair, anxiety, anger, cognitive constriction, lack of social support, substance abuse, and depression.

Alcoholism

Kendall (1983) reviewed four theories about the connection between alcoholism and suicide: (1) alcohol abuse may lead to social decline (in the area of work and marriage) and isolation which increases the risk of suicide, (2) alcohol abuse may lead to loss of self-esteem and depression which may increase the risk of suicide, (3) alcohol abuse may be secondary to depression, and (4) alcohol abuse may make any drugs used more lethal. Kendall's review of research concluded that alcoholics do have a high completed suicide rate and retrospective studies on completed suicides discover high rates of alcoholism.

Alcohol Abuse in Attempted Suicides

Adam et al. (1980) found that attempted suicides had a higher incidence of alcoholism than general medical patients. Fernandez-Pol (1986) found that Puerto Rican suicide attempters who lived alone were more likely to abuse alcohol.

Hawton et al. (1989) found that 7.9 percent of a sample of suicide attempters had a diagnosis of alcoholism, 14.6 percent of the men and 4.2 percent of the women. The percentage of alcoholics was greater in those aged 51–69 and in those unemployed. The alcoholic attempters used overdoses less often but, if they did use overdoses, used tranquilizers and sedatives more and non-opiate analgesics less. The alcoholic attempters were more often repeaters.

Kinkel et al. (1989) found that adolescents in school who had attempted suicide were more likely to use alcohol and, for the girls, use drugs than the non-suicidal students. (The suicide attempters were also more often female, 14–16 years old, non-white, from rural/farm areas, with less life satisfaction and more pessimism.) Kirkpatrick-Smith et al. (1989) found that high school adolescents with suicidal ideation were more likely to abuse alcohol and drugs and that substance abuse added significantly to the multiple regression prediction of suicidal ideation.

Among adolescent suicide attempters, Kotila (1989) found that the lethality of the attempt was associated with alcohol abuse (while the suicidal intent was associated with illegal drug use). No such associations were found, however, for young adult attempters. Lester and Math (1988) found that attempting suicide in the past in college men was associated with more cigarette and cocaine use but less alcohol use. Threatening suicide was associated with less use of beer and hard liquor. For women, those who had attempted suicide drank cocktails less while those who had considered suicide drank wine more. The use of marijuana was not associated with prior suicidal preoccupation.

Czeizel et al. (1984) found that suicide attempters who abused alcohol were more likely to repeat their attempts than non-abusers.

Attempted Suicide in Alcoholics

Bascue and Epstein (1980) found that male alcoholics had a very high incidence of prior suicidal attempts (25 percent) and ideation (67 percent). Beck et al. (1982b) found that if depression preceded the alcoholism then alcoholics were less likely to have attempted suicide. Black et al. (1986) found that alcoholics with a history of attempted suicide were younger, more depressed, and had more serious alcoholism symptoms (such as blackouts and binge drinking).

Blankfield (1989) found that female alcohol abusers who had attempted suicide were more likely to have used prescribed psychotropic medications in the past than non-suicidal alcohol abusers. Buydens-Branchey et al. (1989) found that male alcoholics with the onset in adolescence more often had a history of suicidal attempts and depression (but not suicidal ideation) than late onset alcoholics.

Gomberg (1989) found that women in treatment for alcohol problems had a high rate of prior suicide attempts (40 percent). The alcoholic women who had attempted suicide reported more tension, anxiety, nervousness, indecisiveness, dizziness, headaches, hand trembling, paternal alcoholism (but not maternal alcoholism), and abuse of other drugs (including nicotine, valium, cocaine, stimulants, heroin and marijuana).

Hasin et al. (1988) compared alcoholics in treatment who had attempted suicide with those who had not. The attempters were younger, more often drug abusers, with a greater frequency of panic attacks and childhood and adult antisocial behavior, with more severe alcoholism (such as more seizures, DTs and violence when drunk). The groups did not differ in sex, marital status, education or the presence of a major depressive disorder.

Hesselbrock et al. (1988) found a higher incidence of prior suicide attempts in female alcoholics than in male alcoholics. The alcoholics who had attempted suicide were younger (men only), less often married (men only), more often had alcoholic parents (the mothers of the men and the fathers of the women), more often had a major depressive disorder (men only), more often abused drugs, had more severe alcoholism and for a longer time, had more severe psychopathology, and showed more antisocial personality disorder, obsessive compulsive disorder, panic disorder and phobias.

Lesch et al. (1988) followed up chronic alcoholics who had attempted suicide and those who had not. They found that the suicide attempters were more likely to complete suicide, were more often quiet as children, not in church groups, unemployed and deteriorating in social status, with more prior psychiatric care, a poorer relationship with their partner, more severe depression, more gamma and mixed type alcoholics and fewer delta types, and more likely to have had a fluctuating course of alcoholism.

Schuckit (1986) found that male primary alcoholics who had attempted suicide were more likely to have abused drugs, been psychiatrically hospitalized, behaved antisocially when young (for example, been suspended from school or arrested), had more disturbed first-degree relatives, and drank more (resulting in more firings and separations/divorces).

Selakovic et al. (1983) compared alcoholic and non-alcoholic suicide attempters in Yugoslavia. The alcoholics were more often men, in their thirties (and less often teenagers), widows, with suicidal relatives, organic brain syndromes (and less often psychotic) and a higher risk-rescue ratio. They did not differ in the incidence of broken homes, chronic organic disease or prior suicide attempts. (Alcoholic completed suicides were also more often male than non-alcoholic completed suicides but differed in age and method used.)

Vaglum and Vaglum (1987) found that, among female psychiatric patients, the alcoholics were more likely to have made multiple suicide attempts while the non-alcoholics were more likely to have made no attempts.

Wolk-Wasserman (1987) compared suicide attempters who were alcohol and drug abusers with those who had neuroses. The substance abusers had experienced more early loss (but not more recent loss). They had less support from family and friends, and their significant others more often had death wishes for the patient and desires to have someone else to take over the care of the patient. The substance abusers had been in psychiatric care more and had attempted suicide more in the past.

Weissman et al. (1980) found that alcoholics in the community were more likely to have attempted suicide than community residents with other diagnoses, but this excess was a result of the very high incidence of attempts in those with both alcoholism and another psychiatric disorder.

Whitters et al. (1985, 1987) compared alcoholic inpatients who had attempted suicide with those who had not. The attempters more often had symptoms of depression, a major depression, abused drugs, and multiple diagnoses. They did not differ in drinking history, age or marital status. Restricting the sample to patients with a diagnosis of antisocial personality disorder, the attempters had worse alcohol abuse, more symptoms of violence and depression, more often abused drugs, and more often had a conduct disorder prior to the age of 15.

Fowler et al. (1980) found that alcoholics with secondary depressions were more likely to have made suicide attempts in the past than alcoholics without depressions.

Alcohol Versus Drug Abuse

Battegay and Haenel (1985) found that alcoholic suicide attempters were older than heroin-dependent attempters.

Alcoholism in Completed Suicides

Allebeck et al. (1988) found that Swedish conscripts who later completed suicide more often abused alcohol and had alcohol-abusing fathers. In Sweden, Wihelmsen et al. (1983) found that completed suicides were more likely than controls to have abused alcohol and to have arrests for drunkness (but did not have more arrests and convictions in general or other social problems).

Completed Suicide in Alcoholics

In studies from the 1970s missed in my previous volume, eight studies reported a higher rate of suicide in alcoholics than controls (Dahlegren and Myrhed, 1977; Friberg et al., 1973; Nicholls et al., 1974; Robinette et al., 1979; Schmidt and de Lint, 1972; Schuckit and Gunderson, 1974; Thorarinsson, 1979; Virkkunen, 1971). Robinnette et al. reported the excess only for alcoholics given disability separations or returned to duty and not for those given administrative separations from the service. Thorarinsson found the rate to be highest in the younger and active alcoholics. Nicholls et al. for the rate highest in the four years after intake. Ross (1971) found no difference in the history of attempted suicide in alcoholics in hospitals and in prisons.

However, a study by Haberman and Baden (1974, 1978) of unnatural deaths found that alcoholics had relatively fewer suicides (as compared to homicides) than non-abusers, and that suicides had a lower incidence of alcoholics than homicide victims, accident victims and natural deaths.

Gips (1978) reviewed eleven studies on suicide in alcoholics and found an excess mortality from suicide of about 400 percent. Goodwin (1973), also reviewing research, found that both completed and attempted suicides had higher rates of alcoholism than the general population and that alcoholics complete suicide a higher rate than the general population.

Agren and Jakobsson (1987) found an excess mortality from suicide among alcoholics as did Barr et al. (1984), Lindberg and Agren (1988), and O'Hara et al. (1989).

Kapamadzija et al. (1978) compared alcoholic and non-alcoholic suicides in Yugoslavia and found that the alcoholics were more often male, married, from a broken home, with prior attempts at suicide, and with a worse financial and marital situation. The non-alcoholic suicides were more often judged to be psychiatrically ill (especially with a psychosis) and to have worse physical health. They did not differ in age, method of suicide or a history of suicide in their families.

Beck et al. (1989c) found that a higher suicidal intent in the specific area of taking precautions against discovery in an earlier suicide attempt predicted subsequent suicide in a sample of alcohol abusers who had attempted suicide (while depression, hopelessness, sex, race, and a diagnosis of depression did not).

Berglund (1984) found that alcoholics who later completed suicide more often had peptic ulcers, depression, dysphoria and labile or explosive affect, were more often married and were more brittle/sensitive. They did not differ in sleep disturbances, prior suicide attempts, anxiety, psychopathology or the presence of DTs.

Engelbrecht (1983) found that alcoholic completed suicides had made fewer prior suicide attempts than non-alcoholic completed suicides.

Niskanen et al. (1976) found that alcoholism predicted subsequent completed suicide in psychiatric patients who had previously attempted suicide and in those who had not. (Attempting suicide in the hospital and doing so by hanging rather than prior to hospitalization predicted subsequent suicide in those patients who had attempted suicide.)

Completed Versus Attempted Suicide

Biro and Lazic (1988) found that alcoholism differentiated between completed and attempted suicides, and in an earlier report Kapamadzija et al. (1983) found that a sample of completed suicides contained a higher proportion of alcoholics (and depressives) than a sample of attempted suicides. Depression and alcoholism were not associated in either the completed suicides or the attempted suicides.

Suicidal Ideation

Dukes and Lorch (1989) found that suicidal ideation in school children was associated with alcohol use (but not drug use). Farberow et al. (1987) found that suicidal ideation in California youth was associated with both alcohol and drug use (and the suicidal ideators were more depressed). Robbins and Alessi (1985) found that alcohol (and drug) abuse was associated with current suicidality in a sample of adolescent inpatients.

Alcohol Abuse as a Predictor Of Suicide

Beck and Steer (1989) found that alcoholism but not drug abuse predicted subsequent completed suicide in a sample of attempted suicides (as did unemployment and taking precautions in the index suicide attempt). Cullberg et al. (1988) found that attempted suicides who abused alcohol were more likely to subsequently complete suicide than those who did not.

Drug Abuse

The Relationship Between Drug Abuse and Suicide

Inciardi et al. (1978) noted three theories: (1) drug abuse is self-destructive and causes suicidal behavior, (2) drug abuse causes suicide (though confusional states, psychosocial stress, etc.), and (3) they are alternate and separate behaviors with a common cause such as anomie or psychopathology.

Completed Suicide in Drug Abusers

Substance abuse was found to be more common in adolescent completed suicides by Bagley (1989) than in non-suicides. Cullberg et al. (1988) found that attempted suicides who abused drugs were more likely to subsequently complete suicide than those who did not. In contrast, Barr et al. (1984) did not find an excess of deaths from suicide in a follow-up study of drug addicts.

Tunving (1988) compared young drug addicts who had completed suicide at follow up with those who had not. The suicides had abused alcohol more, used drugs intravenously less, had spent more time in prison and had more parents and siblings who were psychiatrically disturbed. They did not differ in the drug abused.

Drug Abuse in Completed Suicides

Allebeck et al. (1988) found that Swedish conscripts who later completed suicide more often abused narcotics.

In a study of a sample of completed suicides, Rich et al. (1989) found more drug abusers in those under the age of 30 and in gay men and more in those with personality disorders than in psychotics. There were no differences in the incidence of alcohol abuse by these variables. Rich et al. (1985) found that if the drug abusers were also depressed, then a history of prior suicide attempts (and psychiatric treatment as well) were more common.

Drug Abuse in Attempted Suicides

Hankoff and Einsidler (1976) found that attempted suicides who were drug abusers had attempted suicide more both in the past and subsequently than attempters who did not abuse drugs.

Gaines and Richmond (1980) found that basic trainees in the military who made suicidal gestures had more prior drug use (but not alcohol use or arrests) than normal controls. Garfinkel and Golombek (1982) found that adolescent suicide attempters were more likely to use drugs than emergency room controls (and were more psychiatrically disturbed).

Eaton and Reynolds (1989) found that adolescent suicide attempters used prescription drugs less (and alcohol too) and street drugs more than adult suicide attempters. McKenry et al. (1983) found that adolescent suicide attempters used drugs more than medical patients, including stimulants, depressants, marijuana, and alcohol. (Their parents used only alcohol more.)

Levy and Deykin (1989) found that, though depression was associated with a history of suicidal ideation and attempts in college students of both sexes, substance abuse was significantly associated with suicidal ideation and attempts in men even after controls for depression.

Fernandez-Pol (1986) found that younger Puerto Rican suicide attempters were more likely to abuse drugs than older attempters.

Attempted Suicide in Drug Abusers

Harris et al. (1979) compared drug addicts who had attempted suicide while addicts with those who had not done so. The attempters had used LSD, alcohol and cocaine more, were more likely to have had black-outs from drug use and found drug use to be less relaxing. The attempters were also more psychiatrically disturbed (on scales of depression, anxiety, anger, obsessive-compulsive tendencies, somatization and social dysfunction).

Davidson (1978) found that 17 percent of a sample of drug abusers had previously attempted suicide. The attempters more often abused four or more drugs and mixed alcohol and drugs. They used hashish and heroin less often and were more often judged to be drug-dependent. They were more often judged to be psychiatrically disturbed and to be from broken homes.

Saxon et al. (1980) found that 37 percent of female drug abusers had attempted suicide as compared to only 11 percent of male drug abusers. The figures for having thought about suicide were 66 percent and 36 percent, respectively. The men, however, had been in more car accidents in which they were the driver, but the men and women did not differ in non-suicidal overdoses.

Ward and Schuckit (1980) studied a sample of polydrug abusers and compared those who had made serious suicide attempts with those making mild attempts or no attempts. The serious attempters were more often diagnosed as sociopaths, used opiates and depressants more, had been psychiatrically hospitalized more in the past, were more likely to have been hyperactive in the past and were more likely to have a mother with an affective disorder. The mild attempters were younger, used CPC more often, and had fewer arrests in the past. Overall, the attempters (serious and mild) were more often female, white and used barbiturates.

Moise et al. (1982) found that white women in drug treatment programs had attempted suicide more in the past than black women in the programs. (They also differed in other personal characteristics.)

Berman and Schwartz (1989) compared adolescent drug abusers who had attempted suicide with those who had not. The suicide attempters were more depressed, more often had learning disabilities, temper tantrums, accidents, illnesses and parent conflicts, and were more lonely.

Cavaiola (1988) found that adolescent drug abusers who had attempted suicide were more psychiatrically disturbed (for example, with depression, anxiety and somatic complaints) than non-suicidal drug abusers.

Harrison (1989) found that the younger among a sample of female drug abusers in treatment were more likely to have attempted suicide.

Ryser (1983) found that female drug abusers seen at emergency rooms in the U.S. more often reported suicidal motivation than males. Suicidal motivation was associated with a greater likelihood of ingestion of aspirin, diazepam and alcohol.

Amphetamine Users

Derlet et al. (1989) found that 12 percent of cases of amphetamine toxicity seen at an emergency room had suicidal ideation.

Cigarettes

In a time-series multiple regression analysis, Brenner (1983) found no association between cigarette consumption in England from 1954–1976 and suicide rates. Czeizel et al. (1984) found that attempted suicides who smoked were more likely to repeat their attempts than non-smokers.

Cocaine

Tardiff et al. (1989) found that 7 percent of the deaths of those dying with cocaine in their body were from suicide.

Glue

D'Amanda et al. (1977) found that heroin addicts who had also sniffed glue did not differ in depression scores but had attempted suicide more and were more currently suicidal than heroin addicts who had never sniffed glue.

Opiates

Watterson et al. (1975) found an increased rate of suicide in opoid addicts in treatment. O'Donnell (1969) followed up narcotic addicts admitted to a federal treatment center and found that 4.7 percent of their deaths were from suicide (more than expected).

Moore et al. (1979) found that opiate addicts on methadone maintenance had higher scores on a scale of suicidal potential than normal people in general, but similar scores to normal people who had previously attempted suicide.

In a study of unnatural deaths, Haberman and Baden (1978) found that narcotic abusers had fewer suicides (as compared to homicides) than non-abusers.

Kosten and Rounsaville (1988) found that 17 percent of opoid addicts in treatment had attempted suicide in the past, more so among the women and whites. In a follow-up study, the attempters functioned worse. Of the addicts who had not attempted suicide in the past, 5.5 percent attempted suicide in the next two-and-one-half years, more among the women and those who were depressed.

Murphy et al. (1983) found that 17 percent of opiate addicts in treatment had attempted suicide in the past (versus 4 percent of community residents). Among the addicts, the attempters more often came from foster homes and orphanages, were physically abused by their parents, had a father mentally ill and siblings alcoholic or depressed, used amphetamines, barbiturates and sedatives and inhalants more, used marijuana less, were more psychiatrically disturbed, had higher addiction severity scores, were more depressed, neurotic and introverted, and had worse social functioning. They did not differ in intelligence, separation from parents, or criminal history.

Steroids

Brower et al. (1989) claimed that steroid use can lead to suicide but could point only to possible cases.

Crime and Criminals

Juveniles

Among incarcerated delinquents, Alessi et al (1984) found more serious suicidal behavior among those diagnosed with an affective disorder or borderline personality disorder than among those with thought disorders. Battle and Battle (1989) found a higher incidence of suicidal behaviors in adolescents before a juvenile court than in a residential treatment school or in outpatient psychotherapy. Allebeck et al. (1988) found that Swedish conscripts who later completed suicide had shown more misconduct in school, ran away more, and had more contact with police and child welfare authorities.

Bettes and Walker (1986) found that antisocial behavior in black psychiatric patients was more common in non-suicidal boys girls and in girls who both had suicidal ideation and had made suicide attempts. The depressed suicide attempters and the angry non-suicidal children had fewer internalizing, psychotic and somatic symptoms than the depressed suicidal ideators. However, Dukes and Lorch (1989) found that delinquency was not associated with the presence of suicidal ideation in school children.

Miller et al. (1982) compared delinquents who had attempted suicide with those who had not, and the attempters had more suicidal ideation, more depression, were more often female, had more conflict with their parents, abused drugs and alcohol more, had lower self-esteem and were more hyperactive. They did not differ in having parents absent or in acting out.

Adults

In a sample of female felons, a history of prior suicide attempts was associated with depression but not alcohol abuse (Martin et al., 1985). Robertson (1987) found excessively high completed suicide rates for mentally abnormal offenders in England.

Modestin and Emmenegger (1986) found that completed suicides in Switzerland had similar criminal records (offenses, convictions, and recidivism) as controls. The suicides had committed more traffic offenses and fewer property crimes than the controls. Adam et al. (1980) found that attempted suicides had more trouble with the police than general medical patients.

Heller et al. (1985) found that defendants examined for pre-trial competency had attempted suicide more in the past than defendants examined for pre-sentence evaluations. For the pre-trial competency defendants, those found incompetent versus competent did not differ in their suicidal history. Those whose victims were dead had attempted suicide less. A history of attempted suicide was not related to the sex of the victim, the relationship to the victims, whether the victim was child, whether the crime was violent or non-violent or the diagnosis. For the pre-sentence defendants, the psychotics and those who injured someone they knew were more likely to have attempted suicide. A history of attempted suicide was not related to whether the crime was violent or non-violent, whether the victim was a child, the sex of the victim, or the severity of injury to the victim.

Lesser Conduct Disorders

Bagley (1989) found that adolescent completed suicides were more often school dropouts or failures than matched normal controls.

Joffe et al. (1988) found that teenagers in the community who had attempted or thought about suicide were more likely to have both conduct and emotional disorders and to be hyperactive (girls only). Kerfoot (1988) found adolescent suicide attempters had more often had school problems (with work and behavior), run away from home, and been delinquent than non-suicidal psychiatric outpatients. (They also had attempted suicide more in the past and more often been in psychiatric care.) Rosenstock (1985) reported that adolescent inpatients who had attempted suicide had more problems in school and showed more uncooperative behavior while those with suicidal ideation showed more disruptive behavior (but did not differ in depression).

Wasileski and Kelly (1982) compared Marine recruits who had attempted suicide with those referred for disciplinary or administrative problems. The attempters were more socially deviant: they had completed less high school, more often been suspended or expelled from school, been arrested more, and run away from home more. They were more depressed and had attempted suicide more as civilians. Rosenberg (1967) found no association between going AWOL and attempted suicide in psychiatric inpatients.

Other Disorders and Symptoms

Eating Disorders

In a review of research studies, Gardner and Rich (1988) found that in studies before 1970, 9.3 percent of patients with eating disorders died, including 1.5 percent from suicide. After 1970, the percentage dying dropped to 5.2 percent but the percent completing suicide remained at 1.5 percent. Achimovich (1985) found that six anorexics in a sample of fifteen had suicidal thoughts. Eight of the fathers, four of the mothers and two of the siblings were also depressed or suicidal.

Dukes and Lorch (1989) found that eating disorders were associated with the presence of suicidal ideation in school children. Shearer et al. (1988) found that the presence of an eating disorder was associated with greater suicidal intent and lethality in the suicide attempts of females diagnosed with a borderline personality disorder. Taylor and Stansfeld

(1984) found that adolescent suicide attempters by overdose were more likely to have an eating disorder than psychiatric controls.

Tolstrup et al. (1985) followed-up anorexics for twelve years and found that 6 percent had died and that two-thirds of the deaths were from suicide. The mean age at contact had been 20 and the mean age at death 27.

Arroyo and Tonkin (1985) compared bulimic and non-bulimic adolescents with eating disorders. The bulimics were older, had been ill for longer, were heavier, vomited more and threatened suicide more often. Halsukami et al. (1986) found that a history of attempted suicide was more common among bulimics if they also had a diagnosis of affective disorder or substance abuse.

Weiss and Ebert (1983) found a greater incidence of attempted suicide in bulimics as compared to non-bulimic girls, but they were also more psychiatrically disturbed. Mitchell et al. (1987) found late onset bulimics (after the age of thirty) were more likely to have attempted suicide than early onset bulimics (and more often had an affective disorder, current depression and drug dependency). Yates et al. (1989) found that patients with bulimia nervosa were more likely to have attempted suicide in the past if they were also diagnosed as having a personality disorder.

Viesselman and Roig (1985) found that bulimarexics were more likely to have been suicidal sometime in the past, but did not differ from bulimics or anorexics in current suicidal ideation, prior suicide attempts, or suicidal behavior in their first-degree relatives.

Walsh and Rosen (1988), however, compared adolescent girls, all of whom were self-mutilators, and found that those who had attempted suicide did not differ from those who had not in the presence of an eating disorder (nor in drug or alcohol abuse or alcoholism in family members).

Firesetters

O'Sullivan and Kelleher (1987) found a high incidence of prior self-mutilation (39 percent) and attempted suicide (54 percent) in psychiatric patients and prisoners who set fires in the community or in the institution, and several of the fires set by patients (19 percent) were meant to be suicide attempts (all of which were set in the hospital).

Homosexuality

Motto et al. (1985) found that being inactively homosexual or actively bisexual predicted subsequent completed suicide in a sample of depressed psychiatric inpatients. However, Wandrei (1985) followed up women who had attempted suicide and found that those who completed suicide did not differ from those who did not in homosexuality (or criminal behavior, substance abuse, or psychiatric disturbance and suicide in family members). Spalt (1983) found no association among college students between having attempted suicide and being homosexual.

Schneider et al. (1989) found that gay college male students were more likely to have thought of suicide than were heterosexual college men, but no more likely to have attempted suicide. Compared to the non-suicidal gay men, more of the suicidal gay men's family members had attempted suicide and more of their siblings abused drugs. Suicidal gay youths were more often from minorities, had fathers who abused alcohol and physically abused them, had social supports which were more rejecting of suicide, were younger when they became aware of the homosexuality, and made their first suicide attempts in the context of their struggle to adjust to their homosexuality.

Shachar et al. (1983) studied the reasons for referral of psychiatric patients who had a diagnosis of homosexuality or sexual orientation disturbance. The women gave depression as the reason more often than men, and the men gave suicidal preoccupations as the reason more often than women.

Rich et al. (1986a) compared homosexual suicides with heterosexual male suicides and found no differences (for example, in substance abuse, police trouble, prior suicide attempts or psychiatric treatment, living alone or relationship difficulties). Wandrei (1987) compared lesbian suicide attempters with heterosexual attempters and found that the lesbians more often came from broken homes, were younger, had moved more, were more educated and more often employed, abused drugs and alcohol more, had made more prior suicide attempts and been psychiatrically hospitalized more often, but did not differ in subsequent death from suicide.

Harry (1983) found that homosexual males who had attempted suicide more often were loners as adolescents, showed childhood cross-gendering, and had negative feelings about their incipient homosexuality. (All variables but the childhood cross-gendering were also significant for women.)

Saunders and Valente (1987) reviewed research on attempted suicide in homosexuals and concluded that the rate was higher than expected. They suggested that this higher rate might be due to excessive alcohol and drug abuse and to interrupted social ties, but they made no test of these hypotheses. Harry (1989) also reviewed research on suicide in homosexuals and found evidence for a higher rate of attempted suicide and completed suicide in homosexuals than in heterosexuals.

Hypochondriasis

De Alarcon (1964) interviewed depressed patients and found that 25 percent of those with hypochondriasis had previously attempted suicide as compared to 7 percent of those with no hypochondriasis.

Chiu and Rimon (1988) found that Chinese psychiatric patients who showed hypochondriasis were more often depressed than those showing paranoia. However, if depressed, the hypochondiacal patients were less likely to be suicidal than the paranoid patients.

Mental Retardation

Sternlicht et al. (1970) found no case of completed suicide in a school for the retarded, but the incidence of attempted suicide was 0.9 percent. Males attempted suicide more than females and the adults more than the adolescents.

Benson and Laman (1988) compared mentally retarded adults who had attempted or thought about suicide with those who had not and found no differences on psychiatric or demographic characteristics (including substance abuse, family pathology or psychiatric problems).

Multiple Personality

Putnam et al. (1986) found that two-thirds of patients with multiple personality had suicidal preoccupation. Ross and Norton (1989) reported that multiple personality patients who had attempted suicide had been more often physically abused (but not sexually abused), raped, treated in the psychiatric system, and diagnosed with affective disorders, schizophrenia, substance abuse and somatization disorder. They also had more personalities after treatment but not before.

Obsessions

Bagley (1985) found that obsessions were associated with a history of attempted suicide in a community sample of adults.

Panic Disorder

Weissman et al. (1989) found that suicidal ideation and attempts were more common in community residents who reported panic disorders than in those reporting panic attacks, other psychiatric disorders or no disorder. (Suicidal preoccupation was not associated with agoraphobia or major depression.)

Phobias

Bianchi (1971) studied psychiatric patients with a fear of disease and found them to have less suicidal ideation and prior attempts than other psychiatric patients.

Transsexualism

Langevin et al. (1977) found that transsexuals had more suicidal ideation and attempts than homosexuals and heterosexuals. Asscheman et al. (1989) found a higher suicide rate than expected in male transsexuals but not in female transsexuals.

Discussion

As in previous chapters it is not easy to summarize the multitude of research findings in such a chapter. However, several broad trends can be noted. Suicidal behavior has been found in general to be more common in those with psychiatric disturbance, in those with psychosis, and in those with affective disorders and schizophrenia. Suicide appears also to be more common in those who abuse drugs and alcohol, in those who have borderline personality traits and in those who have eating disorders. The research on other disorders and symptoms is quite contradictory.

One criticism of the research is also obvious. Too often, it would appear, psychiatrists happen to have a data base available for a sample of psychiatric patients and decided to compare those with and without suicidal behavior. Thus the studies are often without any theoretical basis or theoretical importance.

Furthermore, psychiatric research into suicide is usually completely dependent on the diagnostic system of the American Psychiatric Association, the latest version of which made great efforts to remove any etiological basis for the classification of psychiatric disorders. Thus, the research fails to come to grips with the *causes* of the behavior under investigation. The research can easily degenerate into studies of the diagnostic system rather than of suicidal behavior.

REFERENCES

Achimovich, L. Suicidal scripting in the families of anorectics. *Transactional Analysis Journal,* 1985, 15(1), 21–29.

Achte, K. Depression and suicide. *Psychopathology,* 1986, 19, supplement 2, 210–214.

Adam, K. S., Bouckoms, A., & Scarr, G. Attempted suicide in Christchurch. *Australian & New Zealand Journal of Psychiatry,* 1980, 14, 305–314.

Agren, G., & Jakobsson, S. W. Validation of diagnosis on death certificates for male alcoholics in Stockholm *Forensic Science International,* 1987, 33, 231–241.

Alessi, N., McManus, M., Brickman, A., & Grapentine, L. Suicidal behavior among serious juvenile offenders. *American Journal of Psychiatry,* 1984, 141, 286–287.

Allebeck, P., Allgulander, C., & Fisher, L. D. Predictors of completed suicide in a cohort of 50,465 young men. *British Medical Journal,* 1988, 297, 176–178.

Allebeck, P., Varla, A., Kristjansson, E., & Wistedt, B. Risk factors for suicide among patients with schizophrenia. *Acta Psychiatrica Scandinavica,* 1987, 76, 414–419.

Allebeck, P., Varla, A., & Wistedt, B. Suicide and violent death among patients with schizophrenia. *Acta Psychiatrica Scandinavica,* 1986, 74, 43–49.

Allebeck, P., & Wistedt, B. Mortality in schizophrenia. *Archives of General Psychiatry,* 1986, 43, 650–653.

Altman, H., Sletten, I. V., Eaton, M. E., & Ulett, G. A. Demographic and mental status profiles. *Psychiatric Quarterly,* 1971, 45, 57–64.

Angst, J., & Clayton, P. Premorbid personality of depressive, bipolar and schizophrenic patients with special reference to suicidal issues. *Comprehensive Psychiatry,* 1986, 27, 511–532.

Angst, J., & Dobler-Mikola, A. The Zurich study. *European Archives of Psychiatry & Neurological Sciences,* 1985, 234, 408–416.

Angst, J., Felder, W., & Lohmeyer, B. Schizoaffective disorder. *Journal of Affective Disorders,* 1979, 1, 139–153.

Apter, A., Bleich, A., Plutchik, R., Mendelsohn, S., & Tyano, S. Suicidal behavior, depression and conduct disorder in hospitalized adolescents. *Journal of the American Academy of Child & Adolescent Psychiatry,* 1988, 27, 696–699.

Arroyoa, D., & Tonkin, R. Adolescents with bulimic and non-bulimic eating disorders. *Journal of Adolescent Health Care,* 1985, 6(1), 21–24.

Asarnow, J. R., Carlson, G. Suicide attempts in preadolescent child psychiatric inpatients. *Suicide & Life-Threatening Behavior,* 1988, 18, 129–136.

Asarnow, J. R., Carlson, G. A., & Guthrie, D. Coping strategies, self-perceptions, hopelessness, and perceived family environments in depressed and suicidal children. *Journal of Consulting & Clinical Psychology,* 1987, 55, 361–366.

Asarnow, J. R., & Guthrie, D. Suicidal behavior, depression and hopelessness in child psychiatric patients. *Journal of Clinical Child Psychology,* 1989, 18, 129–136.

Asscheman, H., Gooren, L. J., & Eklund, P. L. Mortality and morbidity in transsexual patients with cross-gender hormone treatment. *Metabolism: Clinical & Experimental,* 1989, 38, 869–873.

Babigan, H. M., Lehman, A. F., & Reed, S. K. Suicide epidemiology and psychiatric care. In R. Cohen-Sandler (ed.) *Proceedings of the 18th Annual Meeting.* Denver: AAS, 1985, 73–74.

Babigan, H. M., Lehman, A. F., & Reed, S. K. Suicide in psychiatric and non-psychiatric populations. *Acta Psychiatrica Belgica,* 1986, 85, 528–532.

Bagley, C. Psychosocial correlates of suicidal behaviors in an urban population. *Crisis,* 1985, 6(2), 63–77.

Bagley, C. Profiles of youthful suicide. *Psychological Reports,* 1989, 65, 234.

Barner-Rasmussen, P., Dupont, A., & Bille, H. Suicide in psychiatric patients in Denmark, 1971–1981. *Acta Psychiatrica Scandinavica,* 1986, 73, 441–455.

Barr, H. L., Antes, D., Ottenberg, D. J., & Rosen, A. Mortality of treated alcoholic and drug addicts. *Journal of Studies on Alcohol,* 1984, 45, 440–452.

Bascue, L., & Epstein, L. Suicide attempts and experiences of hospitalized alcoholics. *Psychological Reports,* 1980, 47, 1233–1234.

Battegay, R., & Haenel, T. Confrontation with suicide. *Crisis,* 1985, 6(2), 78–88.

Batten, P. J. The descriptive epidemiology of unnatural deaths in Oregon's state institutions. *American Journal of Forensic Medicine & Pathology,* 1989, 10, 310–314.

Battle, A. O., & Battle, M. N. Caretakers' attitudes toward suicidal acting-out in three adolescent populations. In R. F. Diekstra, R. Maris, S. Platt, A. Schmidtke, & G. Sonneck (Eds.) *Suicide and its prevention.* Leiden: Brill, 1989, 167–185.

Beck, A. T., Brown, G., & Steer, R. A. Prediction of eventual suicide in psychiatric inpatients by clinical ratings of hopelessness. *Journal of Consulting & Clinical Psychology,* 1989a, 57, 309–310.

Beck, A. T., Brown, G., & Stewart, B. L. Cognitive predictors of eventual suicide. In D. Lester (Ed.) *Suicide '89.* Denver: AAS, 1989, 284–285.

Beck, A. T., & Steer, R. A. Clinical predictors of eventual suicide. *Journal of Affective Disorders,* 1989, 17, 203–209.

Beck, A. T., Steer, R., Kovacs, M., & Garrison, B. Hopelessness and eventual suicide. *American Journal of Psychiatry,* 1985, 142, 559–563.

Beck, A. T., Steer, R., & McElroy, M. Relationships of hopelessness, depression and previous suicide attempts to suicidal ideation in alcoholics. *Journal of Studies on Alcohol,* 1982a, 43, 1042–1046.

Beck, A. T., Steer, R. A., & McElroy, M. G. Self-reported precedence of depression in alcoholism. *Drug & Alcohol Dependency* 1982b, 10, 185–190.

Beck, A. T., Steer, R. A., & Trexler, L. D. Alcohol abuse and eventual suicide. *Journal of Studies on Alcohol,* 1989c, 50, 202–209.

Benson, B. A., & Laman, D. S. Suicidal tendencies of mentally retarded adults in community settings. *Australian & New Zealand Journal of Development Disabilities,* 1988, 14(1), 49–54.

Berglund, M. Suicide in alcoholism. *Archives of General Psychiatry,* 1984, 41, 888–891.

Berglund, M., & Nilsson, K. Mortality in severe depression. *Acta Psychiatrica Scandinavica,* 1987, 76, 372–380.

Berglund, M, & Smith, G. J. Postdiction of suicide in a group of depressive patients. *Acta Psychiatrica Scandinavica,* 1988, 77, 504–510.

Berk, N. A personality study of suicidal schizophrenics. Doctoral dissertation, New York University, 1949.

Berman, A. L., & Schwartz, R. Suicide attempts among adolescent drug users. In D. Lester (Ed.) *Suicide '89.* Denver: AAS, 1989, 64–66.

Bettes, B. A., & Walker, E. Symptoms associated with suicidal behavior in childhood and adolescence. *Journal of Abnormal Child Psychology,* 1986, 14, 591–604.

Bianchi, G. N. Origins of disease phobia. *Australian & New Zealand Journal of Psychiatry,* 1971, 5, 241–257.

Biro, M., & Lazic, P. Methodological problems of suicide prediction. *European Journal of Psychiatry,* 1988, 2, 233–240.

Black, D. W. The Iowa record-linkage experience. *Suicide & Life-Threatening Behavior,* 1989, 19, 78–89.

Black, D. W., Warrack, G., & Winokur, G. The Iowa record-linkage study. *Archives of General Psychiatry,* 1985a, 42, 71–75.

Black, D. W., & Winokur, G. Age, mortality and chronic schizophrenia. *Schizophrenia Research,* 1988, 1, 267–272.

Black, D. W., Winokur, G., Bell, S., Nasrallah, A., & Hulbert, J. Complicated mania. *Archives of General Psychiatry,* 1988a, 45, 232–236.

Black, D. W., Winokur, G., Hulbert, J., & Nasrallah, A. Predictors of immediate response in the treatment of mania. *Biological Psychiatry,* 1988b, 24, 191–198.

Black, D. W., Winokur, G., & Nasrallah, A. Suicide in subtypes of major affective disorders. *Archives of General Psychiatry,* 1987a, 44, 878–880.

Black, D. W., Winokur, G., & Nasrallah, A. The validity of secondary depression. *Psychiatria Fennica,* 1987b, 97–102.

Black, D. W., Winokur, G., & Nasrallah, A. Effect of psychosis on suicide risk in 1593 patients with unipolar and bipolar affective disorder. *American Journal of Psychiatry,* 1988c, 145, 849–852.

Black, D. W., Winokur, G., & Warrack, G. Suicide in schizophrenia. *Journal of Clinical Psychiatry,* 1985b, 46(11 part 2), 14–17.

Black, D. W., Yates, W., Petty, F., Noyes, R., & Brown, K. Suicidal behavior in alcoholic males. *Comprehensive Psychiatry,* 1986, 27, 227–233.

Blankfield, A. Female alcoholics. *Acta Psychiatrica Scandinavica,* 1989, 79, 355–362.

Blumenthal, S., Bell, V., Neumann, N. U., Schutter, R., & Vogel, R. Mortality and rate of suicide among first admission patients. In S. D. Platt & N. Kreitman (Eds.) *Current Research on Suicide and Parasuicide.* Edinburgh: University of Edinburgh, 1989, 58–66.

Bonner, R. L., & Rich, A. R. Toward a predictive model of suicidal ideation. *Suicide & Life-Threatening Behavior,* 1987, 17, 50–63.

Bonner, R. L., & Rich, A. R. A prospective investigation of suicidal ideation in college students. *Suicide & Life-Threatening Behavior*, 1988, 18, 245–258.

Bonner, R. L., & Rich, A. R. Risk factors of suicide intention in a jail population. In D. Lester (Ed.) *Suicide '89*. Denver: AAS, 1989, 233–234.

Book, J. A., & Modrzewska, K. Schizophrenia and suicide in a north Swedish isolate. *Clinical Genetics*, 1982, 22, 280–283.

Bornstein, R. F., Klein, D. N., Mallon, J. C., & Slater, J. F. Schizotypal personality disorder in an outpatient population. *Journal of Clinical Psychology*, 1988, 44, 322–325.

Borst, S. R., & Noam, G. G. Suicidality and psychopathology in hospitalized children and adolescents. *Acta Paedopsychiatrica*, 1989, 52, 163–175.

Breier, A., & Astrachan, B. Characterization of schizophrenic patients who completed suicide. *American Journal of Psychiatry*, 1984, 141, 206–209.

Brenner, M. H. Mortality and economic instability. *International Journal of Health Services*, 1983, 13, 563–620.

Brent, D. A. Correlates of the medical lethality of suicide attempts in children and adolescents. *Journal of the American Academy of Child & Adolescent Psychiatry*, 1987, 26, 87–91.

Brent, D. A., Kalas, R., Edelbrock, C., Costello, A. J., Dulcan, M. K., & Conover, N. Psychopathology and its relationship to suicidal ideation in childhood and adolescence. *Journal of the American Academy of Child Psychiatry*, 1986, 25, 666–673.

Brent, D. A., Perper, J. A., Goldstein, C. E., Kolko, D. J., Allan, M. J., Allman, C. J., & Zelenak, J. P. Risk factors for adolescent suicide. *Archives of General Psychiatry*, 1988, 45, 581–588.

Briere, J., & Corne, S. Previous psychiatric hospitalization and current suicidal behavior in crisis-line callers. *Crisis Intervention*, 1985, 14(1), 3–10.

Brim, J., Wetzel, R., Reich, T., Wood, D., Viesselman, J., & Rutt, C. Primary and secondary affective disorder. *Journal of Clinical Psychiatry*, 1984, 45, 64–69.

Bronisch, T., & Hecht, H. Comparison of depressed patients with and without suicide attempts in their past history. *Acta Psychiatrica Scandinavica*, 1987, 76, 438–449.

Brower, K. J., Blow, F. C., Eliopulos, G. A., & Beresford, T. P. Anabolic androgenic steroids and suicide. *American Journal of Psychiatry*, 1989, 146, 1075.

Brown, R. P., Sweeney, J., Loutsch, E., Kocsis, J., & Frances, A. Involutional melancholia revisited. *American Journal of Psychiatry*, 1984, 141, 24–28.

Buda, M., Tsuang, M. T., & Fleming, J. A. Causes of death in DSM–III schizophrenics and other psychotics. *Archives of General Psychiatry*, 1988, 45, 282–285.

Burke, A. W. The proportional distribution of suicide among mental hospital deaths and persons in the general population. In J. P. Soubrier & J. Vedrinne (Eds.) *Depression and Suicide*. Paris: Pergamon, 1983, 204–208.

Buydens-Branchey, L., Branchey, M. H., & Noumair, D. Age of alcoholism onset. *Archives of General Psychiatry*, 1989, 46, 225–230.

Cadlouski, G., Tarnik-Mitreva, L., & Aleksievski, S. Suicidal tendencies and a masked depression. In J. P. Soubrier & J. Vedrinne (Eds.) *Depression and Suicide*. Paris: Pergamon, 1983, 227–230.

Carlson, G. A. (1984) More analysis of Eli Robins's data. *American Journal of Psychiatry,* 1984, 141, 323.

Carlson, G. A., & Cantwell, D. Suicidal behavior and depression in children and adolescents. *Journal of the American Academy of Child Psychiatry,* 1982, 21, 361–368.

Casey, P. R. Personality disorder and suicidal intent. *Acta Psychiatrica Scandinavica,* 1989, 79, 290–295.

Cavaiola, A. A. Chemical dependency and adolescent suicide. In D. Lester (Ed.) *Suicide '88.* Denver: AAS, 1988, 167–168.

Cattell, H. R. Elderly suicide in London. *International Journal of Geriatric Psychiatry,* 1988, 3, 251–261.

Chabon, B., & Robins, C. J. Cognitive distortions among depressed and suicidal drug abusers. *International Journal of the Addictions,* 1986, 21, 1313–1329.

Chabrol, H., & Moron, P. Depressive disorders in 100 adolescents who attempted suicide. *American Journal of Psychiatry,* 1988, 145, 379.

Chiu, L. P., & Rimon, R. Interrelationship of hypochondriacal, paranoid, depressive, and suicidal symptoms in Chinese psychiatric patients. *Psychopathology,* 1988, 21(1), 38–43.

Chlewinski, Z. Application of sequential discriminative analysis for differentiation of two populations. *Polish Psychological Bulletin.* 1984, 15(3), 201–210.

Chynoweth, R., Tonge, J., & Armstrong, J. Suicide in Brisbane. *Australian & New Zealand Journal of Psychiatry,* 1980, 14, 37–45.

Clarkin, J. F., Friedman, R., Hurt, S., Corn, R., & Aronoff, M. Affective and character pathology of suicidal adolescents and young adult inpatients. *Journal of Clinical Psychiatry,* 1984, 45, 19–22.

Cole, D. A. Hopelessness, social desirability, depression and parasuicide in two college student samples. *Journal of Consulting & Clinical Psychology,* 1988, 56, 131–136.

Cole, D. A. Psychopathology of adolescent suicide. *Journal of Abnormal Psychology,* 1989, 98, 248–255.

Copas, J. B., & Robin, A. Suicide in psychiatric inpatients. *British Journal of Psychiatry,* 1982, 141, 503–511.

Coryell, W. Diagnosis-specific mortality. *Archives of General Psychiatry,* 1981a, 38, 939–942.

Coryell, W. Obsessive-compulsive disorder and primary unipolar depression. *Journal of Nervous & Mental Disease,* 1981b, 169, 220–224.

Coryell, W. Panic disorder and mortality. *Psychiatric Clinics of North America,* 1988, 11, 433–440.

Coryell, W., Andreasen, N. C., Endicott, J., & Keller, M. The significance of past mania or hypomania in the course and outcome of major depression. *American Journal of Psychiatry,* 1987, 144, 309–315.

Coryell, W., Endicott, J., Andreasen, N., & Keller, M. Bipolar I, bipolar II and nonbipolar major depression among the relatives of affectively ill probands. *American Journal of Psychiatry,* 1985, 142, 817–821.

Coryell, W., Noyes, R., & Clancy, J. Excess mortality in panic disorder. *Archives of General Psychiatry,* 1982, 39, 701–703.

Coryell, W., Noyes, R., & House, J. D. Mortality among outpatients with anxiety disorders. *American Journal of Psychiatry,* 1986, 143, 508–510.

Coryell, W., & Tsuang, M. T. Primary unipolar depression and the prognostic importance of delusions. *Archives of General Psychiatry,* 1982, 39, 1181–1184.

Cosyns, P., Peuskens, J., Pierloot, R., Pieters, G., & Vermote, R. Completed suicide in young schizophrenic patients. In R. Yufit (Ed.) *Proceedings of the 20th Annual Conference.* Denver: AAS, 1987, 360–361.

Cullberg, J., Wasserman, D., & Stefanson, C. G. Who commits suicide after a suicide attempt? *Acta Psychiatrica Scandinavica,* 1988, 77, 598–603.

Czeizel, A., Szentesi, I., & Molnar, G. Self-poisoning as a model for the study of the mutagenicity of chemicals in human beings. *Acta Medica Hungarica,* 1984, 41(2–3), 77–92.

Dahlegren, L., & Myrhed, M. Alcoholic females. *Acta Psychiatrica Scandinavica,* 1977, 56, 81–91.

D'Amanda, C., Plumb, M., & Taintor, Z. Heroin addicts with a history of glue sniffing. *International Journal of the Addictions,* 1977, 12, 255–270.

Davidson, F. Suicide and the abuse of drugs. In H. Z. Winnick & L. Miller (Eds.) *Aspects of Suicide in Modern Civilization.* Jerusalem: Academic, 1978, 220–227.

Davidson, J. R. T., Miller, R. D., Turnbull, C. D., & Sullivan, J. L. Atypical depression. *Archives of General Psychiatry,* 1982, 39, 527–534.

Davis, A. Depression and attempted suicide. *Australian & New Zealand Journal of Psychiatry,* 1989, 23, 59–66.

De Alarcon, R. Hypochondriasis and depression in the aged. *Gerontologia Clinica,* 1964, 6, 266–277.

De Leo, D., Pellegrini, C., & Serraiotto, L. Adjustment disorders and suicidality. *Psychological Reports,* 1986, 59, 355–358.

Delga, I., Heinssen, R. K., Firtsch, R. C., Goodrich, W., & Yates, B. T. Psychosis, aggression, and self-destructive behavior in hospitalized adolescents. *American Journal of Psychiatry,* 1989, 146, 521–525.

Derlet, R. W., Rice, P., Horowitz, B. Z., & Lord, R. V. Amphetamine toxicity. *Journal of Emergency Medicine,* 1989, 7, 157–161.

Dietzfelbiner, T., Kurz, A., Torhorst, A., & Moller, H. J. The prognostic value of hopelessness in patients following a suicide attempt. In S. D. Platt & N. Kreitman (Eds.) *Current Research on Suicide and Parasuicide.* Edinburgh: University of Edinburgh, 1989, 146–152.

Dingman, C. W., & McGlashan, T. H. Discriminating characteristics of suicides. *Acta Psychiatrica Scandinavica,* 1986, 74, 91–97.

Dingman, C. W., & McGlashan, T. H. Characteristics of patients with serious suicidal intentions who ultimately commit suicide. *Hospital & Community Psychiatry,* 1988, 39, 295–299.

Drake, R. E., Gates, C., Cotton, P., & Whitaker, A. Suicide among schizophrenics. *Journal of Nervous & Mental Disease,* 1984, 172, 613–617.

Drake, R. E., Gates, C., & Cotton, P. Suicide among schizophrenics. *British Journal of Psychiatry,* 1986, 149, 784–787.

Drake, R. E., Gates, C., Whitaker, A., & Cotton, P. Suicide among schizophrenics. *Comprehensive Psychiatry*, 1985, 26, 90–100.

Dukes, R. L., & Lorch, B. D. The effects of school, family, self-concept, and deviant behavior on adolescent suicide. *Journal of Adolescence*, 1989, 12, 239–251.

Dunner, D., Gershon, E., & Goodwin, F. Heritable factors in the severity of mental illness. *Biological Psychiatry*, 1976, 11, 31–42.

Dyer, J., & Kreitman, N. Hopelessness, depression and suicidal intent in parasuicide. *British Journal of Psychiatry*, 1984, 144, 127–133.

Eaton, P., & Reynolds, P. A comparison of adolescent and adult suicide attempters. In D. Lester (Ed.) *Suicide '89*. Denver: AAS, 1989, 80–82.

Ellis, T. E. The hopelessness scale and social desirability. *Journal of Clinical Psychology*, 1985, 41, 634–639.

Ellis, T. E., Berg, R., & Franzen, M. Organic and cognitive deficits in suicidal patients. In D. Lester (Ed.) *Suicide '89*. Denver: AAS, 1989, 291–293.

Ellis, T. E., & Ratliff, K. G. Cognitive characteristics of suicidal and nonsuicidal psychiatric inpatients. *Cognitive Therapy & Research*, 1986, 10, 625–634.

Emery, G., Steer, R., & Beck, A. T. Depression, hopelessness and suicidal intent among heroin addicts. *International Journal of the Addictions*, 1981, 16, 425–429.

Engelbrecht, G. K. Alcohol as a possible variable in suicide. *Humanitas*, 1983, 9(1), 61–68.

Evans, A. L., Williams, J. L., & McKinnon, S. The relationship of hopelessness, depression, and anger to suicidal ideation in Canadian University students. In R. Cohen-Sandler (Ed.) *Proceedings of the 18th Annual Meeting*. Denver: AAS, 1985, 54–56.

Evenson, R. C. Community adjustment of patients who threaten and attempt suicide. *Psychological Reports*, 1983, 52, 127–132.

Evenson, R. C., Wood, J., Nuttall, E., & Cho, D. Suicide rates among public mental health patients. *Acta Psychiatrica Scandinavica*, 1982, 66, 254–264.

Farberow, N. L., Litman, R. E., & Nelson, F. L. A survey of youth suicide in California. In R. Yufit (Ed.) *Proceedings of the 20th Annual Conference*. Denver: AAS, 1987, 298–300.

Fawcett, J. Predictors of early suicide. *Journal of Clinical Psychiatry*, 1988, 49(10), supplement, 7–8.

Fawcett, J., Scheftner, W., Clark, D., Hedeker, D., Gibbons, R., & Coryell, W. Clinical predictors of suicide in patients with major affective disorders. *American Journal of Psychiatry*, 1987, 144, 35–40.

Fernandez-Pol, B. Characteristics of 77 Puerto Ricans who attempted suicide. *American Journal of Psychiatry*, 1986, 143, 1460–1463.

Fernando, S., & Storm, V. Suicide among psychiatric patients of a district general hospital. *Psychological Medicine*, 1984, 14, 661–672.

Flynn, P., & McMahon, R. Indicators of depression and suicidal ideation among drug abusers. *Psychological Reports*, 1983, 52, 784–786.

Fowler, R., Kiskow, B. I., & Tanna, V. L. Alcoholism, depression and life events. *Journal of Affective Disorders*, 1980, 2, 127–135.

Fowler, R., Tsuang, M., & Kronfol, Z. Communication of suicidal intent and suicide in unipolar depression. *Journal of Affective Disorders,* 1979, 1, 219–225.

Friberg, L., Cederlof, R., Lorich, U., Lundman, T., & deFraire, U. Mortality in twins in relation to smoking habits and alcohol problems. *Archives of Environmental Health,* 1973, 27, 294–304.

Friedman, R. C., Aronoff, M., Clarkin, J., Corn, R., & Hurt, S. History of suicidal behavior in depressed borderline inpatients. *American Journal of Psychiatry,* 1983, 140, 1023–1026.

Friedman, R. C., Corn, R., Aronoff, M., Hurt, S., & Clarkin, J. The seriously suicidal adolescent. In H. S. Sudak, A. B. Ford, & N. B. Rushforth (Eds.) *Suicide in the Young.* Boston: John Wright, 1984a, 209–226.

Friedman, R. C., Corn, R., Hurt, S., Fibel, B., Schulick, J., & Swirsky, S. Family history of illness in the seriously suicidal adolescent. *American Journal of Orthopsychiatry,* 1984b, 54, 390–397.

Fyer, M. R., Frances, A. J., Sullivan, T., Hurt, S., & Clarkin, J. Suicide attempts in patients with borderline personality disorder. *American Journal of Psychiatry,* 1988, 145, 737–739.

Gaines, T., & Richmond, L. Assessing suicidal behavior in basic military trainees. *Military Medicine,* 1980, 145, 263–266.

Gale, S. W., Mesnikoff, A., Fine, J., & Talbott, J. A study of suicide in state mental hospitals in New York City. *Psychiatric Quarterly,* 1980, 52, 201–213.

Gardner, A., & Rich, C. L. Eating disorders and suicide. In D. Lester (Ed.) *Suicide '88.* Denver: AAS, 1988, 171–172.

Garfinkel, B. D., Froese, A., & Hood, J. Suicide attempts in children and adolescents. *American Journal of Psychiatry,* 1982, 139, 1257–1261.

Garvey, M. J., Tollefson, G. D., & Tuason, V. B. Is chronic primary major depression a distinct depression subtype? *Comphrensive Psychiatry,* 1986, 27, 446–448.

Garvey, M. J., Tuason, V., Hoffman, N., & Chastek, J. Suicide attempters, nonattempters and neurotransmitters. *Comprehensive Psychiatry,* 1983, 24, 332–336.

Gibbens, T. C. N., & Robertson, G. A survey of the criminal careers of hospital order patients. *British Journal of Psychiatry,* 1983, 143, 362–369.

Gibbs, J. T. Depression and suicidal behavior among delinquent females. *Journal of Youth & Adolescence,* 1981, 10, 159–167.

Gips, C. H. Alcohol, diseases of alcoholics and alcoholic liver disease. *Netherlands Journal of Medicine,* 1978, 21(2), 83–90.

Goldney, R. D., Adam, K. S., O'Brien, J. C., & Termansen, P. Depression in young women who have attempted suicide. *Journal of Affective Disorders,* 1981, 3, 327–337.

Goldney, R. D., Winefield, A. H., Tiggeman, M., Winefield, H., & Smith, S. Suicidal ideation in a young adult population. *Acta Psychiatrica Scandinavica,* 1989, 79, 481–489.

Goldring, N., & Fieve, R. Attempted suicide in manic-depressive disorder. *American Journal of Psychotherapy,* 1984, 38, 373–383.

Gomberg, E. S. Suicide risk among women with alcohol problems. *American Journal of Public Health,* 1989, 79, 1363–1365.

Goodwin, D. W. Alcohol in suicide and homicide. *Quarterly Journal of Studies on Alcohol,* 1973, 34, 144–156.

Gorenc, K. D., Kleff, F., & Welz, R. Intentionality and seriousness of suicide attempts in relation to depression. *Boletin de Estudios Medicos y Biologicos,* 1983, 32, 233–247.

Gulyamov, M. G., & Bessonov, Y. V. Psychological mechanisms of suicidal acts by patients with progressive paranoid schizophrenia compounded by Kandinsky's syndrome. *Soviet Neurology & Psychiatry,* 1986, 19(1), 29–43.

Gutierrez, H. O., Russakof, L. M., & Oldham, J. M. The prediction of suicide. In D. Lester (Ed.) *Suicide '88.* Denver: AAS, 1988, 127–128.

Haberman, P., & Baden, M. Alcoholism and violent death. *Quarterly Journal of Studies on Alcohol,* 1974, 35, 221–231.

Haberman, P., & Baden, M. *Alcohol, Other Drugs and Violent Death.* New York: Oxford University, 1978.

Hagnell, O., Lanke, J., & Rorsman, B. Suicide rates in the Lundby study. *Neuropsychobiology,* 1981, 7, 248–253.

Hagnell, O., & Rorsman, B. Suicide and endogenous depression with somatic symptoms in the Lundby Study. *Neuropsychobiology,* 1978, 4, 180–187.

Hagnell, O., & Rorsman, B. Suicide in the Lundby Study. *Neuropsychobiology,* 1979, 5(2), 61–73.

Halsukami, D., Mitchell, J. E., Eckert, E. D., & Pyle, R. Characteristics of patients with bulimia only, bulimia with affective disorder and bulimia with substance abuse. *Addictive Behaviors,* 1986, 11, 399–406.

Hankoff, L. D., & Einsidler, B. Drug abuse among suicide attempters. *International Journal of Offender Therapy,* 1976, 20, 26–32.

Harris, R., Linn, M. W., & Hunter, K. Suicide attempts among drug abusers. *Suicide & Life-Threatening Behavior,* 1979, 9, 25–32.

Harrison, P. A. Women in treatment. *International Journal of the Addictions,* 1989, 24, 655–673.

Harry, J. Parasuicide, gender and gender deviance. *Journal of Health & Social Behavior,* 1983, 24, 350–361.

Harry, J. Sexual identity issues. In *Report of the Secretary's Task Force on Youth Suicide.* Washington, DC: US Government Printing Office, 1989, 2, 131–142.

Hasin, D., Grant, B., & Endicott, J. Treated and untreated suicide attempts in substance abuse patients. *Journal of Nervous & Mental Disease,* 1988, 176, 289–294.

Hauser, P., Pollock, B., & Voineskos, G. Parasuicide and schizophrenia. In R. Cohen-Sandler (Ed.) *Proceedings of the 18th Annual Meeting.* Denver: AAS, 1985, 51–53.

Hawton, K., Fagg, J., & McKeown, S. P. Alcoholism, alcohol and attempted suicide. *Alcohol & Alcoholism,* 1989, 24(1), 3–9.

Hecht, H., & Bronisch, T. Psychopathological course of depressives with and without a suicide attempt. In H. J. Moller, A. Schmidtke, & R. Welz (Eds.) *Current Issues of Suicidology.* Berlin: Springer Verlag, 1988, 137–143.

Heller, M. S., Ehrlich, S., & Lester, D. Suicidal history of defendants and offenders. *Journal of General Psychology,* 1985, 112, 221–223.

Hesselbrock, M., Hesselbrock, V., Syzmanski, K., & Weidenman, M. Suicide attempts and alcoholism. *Journal of Studies on Alcohol,* 1988, 49, 436–442.

Hill, R. D., Gallagher, D., Thompson, L. W., & Ishida, T. Hopelessness as a measure of suicidal intent in the depressed elderly. *Psychology & Aging,* 1988, 3, 230–232.

Hillard, J. R., Ramm, D., Zung, W., & Holland, J. Suicide in a psychiatric emergency room population. *American Journal of Psychiatry,* 1983, 140, 459–462.

Hoffman, H., & Modestin, J. Completed suicide in discharged psychiatric inpatients. *Social Psychiatry,* 1987, 22, 93–98.

Holden, R. R., Mendonca, J. D., & Mazmanian, D. Relation of response set to observed suicide intent. *Canadian Journal of Behavioral Science,* 1985, 17, 359–368.

Holden, R. R., Mendonca, J. D., & Serin, R. C. Suicide, hopelessness, and social desirability. *Journal of Consulting & Clinical Psychology,* 1989, 57, 500–504.

Inciardi, J. A., McBride, D. C., & Pottieger, A. E. Gambling with death. In D. Lettieri (Ed.) *Drugs and Suicide.* Beverly Hills: Sage, 1978, 47–74.

Jablensky, A., Sartorius, N., Gulbinat, W., & Ernberg, G. Characteristics of depressed patients contacting psychiatric services in four cultures. *Acta Psychiatrica Scandinavica,* 1981, 63, 367–383.

Janofsky, J. S., Spears, S., & Neubauer, D. N. Psychiatrists' accuracy in predicting violent behavior on an inpatient ward. *Hospital & Community Psychiatry,* 1988, 39, 1090–1094.

Joffe, R. T., Offord, D. R., & Boyle, M. H. Ontario Child Health Study. *American Journal of Psychiatry,* 1988, 145, 1420–1423.

Joffe, R. T., & Regan, J. J. Personality and suicidal behavior in depressed patients. *Comprehensive Psychiatry,* 1989, 30, 157–160.

Kapamadzija, B., Biro, M., & Till, E. Alcoholism, depression and suicide. In J. P. Soubrier & J. Vedrinne (Eds.) *Depression and Suicide.* Paris: Pergamon, 1983, 463–466.

Kapamadzija, B., Souljanski, M., & Skendzic, S. Alcoholics and non-alcoholics in committed suicides. In V. Aalberg (Ed.) *Proceedings of the 9th International Congress for Suicide Prevention.* Helsinki: Finnish Association for Mental Health, 1978, 311–315.

Kashani, J. H., Reid, J. C., & Rosenberg, T. K. Levels of hopelessness in children and adolescents. *Journal of Consulting & Clinical Psychology,* 1989, 57, 496–499.

Kazdin, A. E., French, N. H., Unis, A. S., Esveldt-Dawson, K., & Sherick, R. B. Hopelessness, depression and suicidal intent among psychiatrically disturbed inpatient children. *Journal of Consulting & Clinical Psychology,* 1983, 51, 504–510.

Kendall, R. E. Alcohol and suicide. *Substance & Alcohol Actions/Misuse,* 1983, 4, 121–127.

Kerfoot, M. Deliberate self-poisoning in childhood and early adolescence. *Journal of Child Psychology & Psychiatry,* 1988, 29, 335–343.

Kiloh, L. G., Andrews, G., & Neilson, M. The long-term outcome of depressive illness. *British Journal of Psychiatry,* 1988, 153, 752–757.

Kinkel, R. J., Bailey, C. W., & Josef, N. C. Correlates of adolescent suicide attempts. *Journal of Alcohol & Drug Education,* 1989, 34, 85–96.

Kivela, S. L., Pahkala, K., & Eronen, A. Depressive symptoms and signs that differentiate major and atypical depression from dysthymic disorder in elderly Finns. *International Journal of Geriatric Psychiatry*, 1989, 4(2), 79–85.

Kosten, T. R., & Rounsaville, B. J. Suicidality among opoid addicts. *American Journal of Drug Abuse*, 1988, 14, 357–369.

Kotila, L. Age-specific characteristics of attempted suicide in adolescence. *Acta Psychiatrica Scandinavica*, 1989, 79, 436–443.

Kotila, L., & Lonnqvist, J. Suicide and violent death among adolescent suicide attempters. *Acta Psychiatrica Scandinavica*, 1989, 79, 453–459.

Kullgren, G. Factors associated with completed suicide in borderline personality disorder. *Journal of Nervous & Mental Disease*, 1988, 176, 40–44.

Kullgren, G., Renberg, E., & Jacobsson, L. An empirical study of borderline personality and psychiatric suicides. *Journal of Nervous & Mental Disease*, 1986, 174, 328–331.

Kuperman, S., Black, D. W., & Burns, T. L. Excess suicide among formerly hospitalized child psychiatric patients. *Journal of Clinical Psychiatry*, 1988, 49(3), 88–93.

Landmark, J., Cernovsky, Z. Z., & Merskey, H. Correlates of suicide attempts and ideation in schizophrenia. *British Journal of Psychiatry*, 1987, 151, 18–20.

Langevin, R., Paitich, D., & Steiner, B. The clinical profile of male transsexuals living as females. *Archives of Sexual Behavior*, 1977, 6, 143–154.

Leonard, C. V. Depression and suicidality. *Journal of Consulting & Clinical Psychology*, 1974, 42, 98–104.

Lesch, O. M., Walter, H., Mader, R., Musalek, M., & Zeider, K. Chronic alcoholism in relation to attempted or effected suicide. *Psychiatrie et Psychobiologie*, 1988, 3, 181–188.

Lester, D., Beck, A. T., & Steer, R. A. Attempted suicide in those with personality disorders. *European Archives of Psychiatry & Neurological Sciences*, 1989, 239, 109–112.

Lester, D., & Math, Y. S. Drug use and prior suicidal preoccupation in college students. *Psychological Reports*, 1988, 62, 114.

Levy, J. C., & Deykin, E. Y. Suicidality, depression and substance abuse in adolescence. *American Journal of Psychiatry*, 1989, 146, 1462–1467.

Lindberg, S., & Agren, G. Mortality among male and female hospitalized alcoholics in Stockholm 1962–1983. *British Journal of Addiction*, 1988, 83, 1193–1200.

Linehan, M. M., & Laffaw, J. Suicidal behaviors among clients at an outpatient psychological clinic versus the general population. *Suicide & Life-Threatening Behavior*, 1982, 12, 234–239.

Linehan, M., & Nielsen, S. Assessment of suicidal ideation and parasuicide. *Journal of Consulting & Clinical Psychology*, 1981, 49, 773–775.

Linehan, M., & Nielsen, S. Social desirability. *Journal of Consulting & Clinical Psychology*, 1983, 51, 141–143.

Linkowski, P., de Maertelaer, V., & Mendlewicz, J. Suicidal behavior in major depressive illness. *Acta Psychiatrica Scandinavica*, 1985, 72, 233–238.

Lonnqvist, J., Koskenvuo, M., Kaprio, J., & Langinvainio, H. The mortality in psychiatric disorders. In J. P. Soubrier & J. Vedrinne (Eds.) *Depression and Suicide.* Paris: Pergamon, 1983, 198–203.

Marneros, A., Rohde, A., & Deister, A. Unipolar and bipolar schizoaffective disorders. *European Archives of Psychiatry,* 1989, 239, 164–170.

Marneros, A., Rohde, A., Deister, A., Fimmers, R., & Junemann, H. Long-term course of schizoaffective disorders. *European Archives of Psychiatry,* 1988, 237, 283–290.

Martin, R. C., Cloninger, C. R., & Guze, S. B. Alcohol misuse and depression in women criminals. *Journal of Studies on.Alcohol,* 1985, 46, 65–71.

Masterson, E., & O'Shea, B. Smoking and malignancy in schizophrenia. *British Journal of Psychiatry,* 1984, 145, 429–432.

McGlashen, T. M. Borderline personality disorder and unipolar affective disorder. *Journal of Nervous & Mental Disease,* 1987, 175, 467–473.

McKenry, P., Tishler, C., & Kelley, C. The role of drugs in adolescent suicide attempts. *Suicide & Life-Threatening Behavior,* 1983, 13, 166–175.

McLeavey, B. C., Daly, R. J., Murray, C. M., O'Riordan, J., & Taylor, M. Interpersonal problem-solving deficits in self-poisoning patients. *Suicide & Life-Threatening Behavior,* 1987, 17, 33–49.

Mendonca, J., Holden, R. R., Mazmanian, D., & Dolan, J. The influence of response style on the Beck hopelessness scale. *Canadian Journal of Behavioral Science,* 1983, 15, 237–247.

Miller, F. M., & Chabrier, L. A. The relation of delusional content in psychotic depression to life-threatening behavior. *Suicide & Life-Threatening Behavior,* 1987, 17, 13–17.

Miller, M., Chiles, J., & Barnes, V. Suicide attempters within a delinquent population. *Journal of Consulting & Clinical Psychology,* 1982, 50, 491–498.

Mitchell, J. E., Hatsukami, D., Pyle, R. L., Eckert, E. D., & Soll, E. Late onset bulimia. *Comprehensive Psychiatry,* 1987, 28, 323–328.

Mitteraure, B., Leibetseder, M., Pritz, W. F., & Sorgo, G. Comparisons of psychopathological phenomena of 422 manic-depressive patients with suicide-positive and suicide-negative family history. *Acta Psychiatrica Scandinavica,* 1988, 77, 438–442.

Modestin, J. Completed suicide in personality disordered inpatients. *Journal of Personality Disorders,* 1989, 3, 113–121.

Modestin, J., & Emmenegger, P. A. Completed suicide and criminality. *Psychological Medicine,* 1986, 16, 661–669.

Modestin, J., Greube, E., & Brenner, H. D. Problem patients in a psychiatric inpatient setting. *European Archives of Psychiatry,* 1986, 235, 309–314.

Modestin, J., & Hoffman, H. Completed suicide in psychiatric inpatients and former inpatients. *Acta Psychiatrica Scandinavica,* 1989, 79, 229–234.

Modestin, J., & Kopp, W. A study of clinical suicide. *Journal of Nervous & Mental Disease,* 1988a, 176, 668–674.

Modestin, J., & Kopp, W. Study on suicide in depressed inpatients. *Journal of Affective Disorders,* 1988b, 15, 157–162.

Moise, R., Kovach, J., Reed, B. G., & Bellows, N. A comparison of black and white women entering drug abuse treatment programs. *International Journal of the Addictions,* 1982, 17, 35–49.

Montgomery, S. A., Montgomery, D., Baldwin, D., & Green, M. Intermittent 3-day depressions and suicidal behavior. *Neuropsychobiology,* 1989, 22, 128–134.

Moore, J. T., Judd, L., Zung, W., & Alexander, G. Opiate addiction and suicidal behaviors. *American Journal of Psychiatry,* 1979, 136, 1187–1189.

Morrison, J. Suicide in a psychiatric practice population. *Journal of Clinical Psychiatry,* 1982, 43, 348–352.

Morrison, J. Suicide in psychiatric patients. *Suicide & Life-Threatening Behavior,* 1984, 14, 52–58.

Morrison, J., & Herbstein, J. Secondary affective disorder in women with somatization disorder. *Comprehensive Psychiatry,* 1988, 29, 433–440.

Motto, J., Heilbron, D., & Juster, R. Development of a clinical instrument to estimate suicide risk. *American Journal of Psychiatry,* 1985, 142, 680–686.

Munley, P., Devore, N., Einhorn, C., Gash, I., Hyer, L., & Kuhn, K. Demographic and clinical characteristics as predictors of length of hospitalization and re-admission. *Journal of Clinical Psychology,* 1977, 33, 1093–1099.

Murphy, S. L., Rounsaville, B., Eyre, S., & Kleber, H. Suicide attempts in treated opiate addicts. *Comprehensive Psychiatry,* 1983, 24, 79–89.

Nace, E. P., Saxon, J. J., & Shore, N. A comparison of borderline and non-borderline alcoholic patients. *Archives of General Psychiatry,* 1983, 40, 54–56.

Nekanda-Trepka, C. J., Bishop, S., & Blackburn, I. Hopelessness and depression. *British Journal of Clinical Psychology,* 1983, 22, 49–60.

Nicholls, P., Edwards, G., & Kyle, E. Alcoholics admitted to four hospitals in England. *Quarterly Journal of Studies on Alcohol,* 1974, 35, 841–855.

Nicholson, R. A. Correlates of commitment status in psychiatric patients. *Psychological Bulletin,* 1986, 100, 241–250.

Niskanen, P., Rinta-Manty, R., & Oliikainen, L. A comparison of hospitalized suicidal and non-suicidal psychiatric patients with a long-term follow-up. *Psychiatria Fennica,* 1976, supplement, 159–165.

Nurnberger, J., Roose, S. P., Dunner, D. L., & Fieve, R. R. Unipolar mania. *American Journal of Psychiatry,* 1979, 136, 1420–1423.

Nuttall, E. A., Evenson, R., & Cho, D. W. Patients of a public state mental health system who commit suicide. *Journal of Nervous & Mental Disease,* 1980, 168, 424–427.

Nyman, A. K., & Jonsson, H. Patterns of self-destructive behavior in schizophrenia. *Acta Psychiatrica Scandinavica,* 1986, 73, 252–262.

Obayuwana, A., Collins, J., Carter, A., Rao, M., Mathura, C., & Wilson, S. Hope index scale. *Journal of the National Medical Association,* 1982, 74, 761–765.

O'Donnell, J. A. *Narcotic addicts in Kentucky.* Chevy Chase, MD: NIMH, 1969.

Ohara, K., Suzuki, Y., Sugita, T., Kobayashi, K., Tamefusa, K., Hattori, S., & Ohara, K. Mortality among alcoholics discharged from a Japanese hospital. *British Journal of Psychiatry,* 1989, 84, 287–291.

O'Sullivan, G. H., & Kelleher, M. J. A study of firesetters in the South-West of Ireland. *British Journal of Psychiatry,* 1987, 151, 818–823.

Overall, J. E., & Rhoades, H. M. Use of the Hamilton Rating Scale for classification of depressive disorders. *Comprehensive Psychiatry,* 1982, 23, 370–376.

Overholser, J. C., Miller, I. W., & Norman, W. H. The course of depressive symptoms in suicidal versus nonsuicidal depressed inpatients. *Journal of Nervous & Mental Disease,* 1987, 175, 450–456.

Papa, L. Responses to life events as predictors of suicidal behavior. *Nursing Research,* 1980, 29, 362–369.

Paris, J., Brown, R., & Nowlis, D. Long-term follow-up of borderline patients in a general hospital. *Comprehensive Psychiatry,* 1987, 28, 530–535.

Paris, J., Nowlis, D., & Brown, R. Developmental factors in the outcome of borderline personality disorder. *Comprehensive Psychiatry,* 1988, 29, 147–150.

Paris, J., Nowlis, D., & Brown, R. Predictors of suicide in borderline personality disorder. *Canadian Journal of Psychiatry,* 1989, 34, 8–9.

Pattison, E. M., & Kahan, J. The deliberate self-harm syndrome. *American Journal of Psychiatry,* 1983, 140, 867–872.

Perugi, G., Musetti, L., Pezzica, P., Piagentini, F., Cassano, G., & Akiskal, H. Suicide attempts in primary major depressive subtypes. *Psychiatria Fennica,* 1988, 95–102.

Petrie, K., & Chamberlain, K. Hopelessness and social desirability as moderator variables in predicting suicidal behavior. *Journal of Consulting & Clinical Psychology,* 1983, 51, 485–487.

Petrie, K., Chamberlain, K., & Clarke, D. Psychological predictors of future suicidal behavior in hospitalized suicide attempters. *British Journal of Clinical Psychology,* 1988, 27, 247–257.

Pfohl, B., Stangl, D., & Zimmerman, M. The implications of DSM III. *Journal of Affective Disorders,* 1984, 7, 309–318.

Plummer, B., Gispert, M., Hayden, R., Robbins, D., & Seifer, R. Depression, hopelessness, and substance abuse among hospitalized adolescents with suicidal ideation or behavior. Paper presented at the International Association for Suicide Prevention, Brussels, 1989.

Pokorny, A. D. Prediction of suicide in psychiatric patients. *Archives of General Psychiatry,* 1983, 40, 249–257.

Poldinger, W. Suicidal tendencies, anxiety and depression. In P. Kielholz (Ed.) *Depressive Illness.* Baltimore: Williams & Wilkins, 1972, 63–73.

Prasad, A. J. Attempted suicide in hospitalized schizophrenics. *Acta Psychiatrica Scandinavica,* 1986, 74, 41–42.

Prasad, A. J., & Kellner, P. Suicidal behavior in schizophrenic day patients. *Acta Psychiatrica Scandinavica,* 1988, 77, 488–490.

Prasad, A. J., & Kumar, N. Suicidal behavior in hospitalized schizophrenics. *Suicide & Life-Threatening Behavior,* 1988, 18, 265–269.

Putnam, F. W., Guroff, J., Silberman, E., Barban, L., & Post, R. The clinical phenomenology of multiple personality disorder. *Journal of Clinical Psychiatry,* 1986, 47, 285–293.

Raczek, S. W., True, P. K., & Friend, R. C. Suicidal behavior and personality traits. *Journal of Personality Disorders,* 1989, 3, 345–351.

Ramos-Brieva, J. A., & Cordero-Villafafila, A. Aggressiveness or low control of impulsiveness. *Medical Science Research,* 1989, 17, 229–230.

Ranieri, W. F., Steer, R. A., Laurence, T. I., Rissmiller, D. J., Piper, G. E., & Beck, A. T. Relationships of depression, hopelessness and dysfunctional attitudes to suicide ideation in psychiatric patients. *Psychological Reports,* 1987, 61, 967–975.

Reveley, A. M., & Revely, M. A. Distribution of primary and secondary affective disorders. *Journal of Affective Disorders,* 1981, 3, 273–280.

Reynolds, W. M. *Suicidal ideation questionnaire.* Odessa, FL: Psychological Assessment Resources, 1988.

Rich, A. R., & Bonner, R. L. Concurrent validity of a stress-vulnerability model of suicidal ideation and behavior. *Suicide & Life-Threatening Behavior,* 1987, 17, 265–270.

Rich, A., Kirkpatrick-Smith, J., Bonner, R., & Jans, F. Gender and the prediction of suicidal ideation. In D. Lester (Ed.) *Suicide '89.* Denver: AAS, 1989, 28–29.

Rich, C. L., Fowler, R. C., & Young, D. Suicide and psychosis. In R. Cohen-Sandler (Ed.) *Proceedings of the 19th Annual Meeting.* Denver: AAS, 1986b, 94–95.

Rich, C. L., Fowler, R. C., & Young, D. Substance abuse and suicide. *Annals of Clinical Psychiatry,* 1989, 1, 79–85.

Rich, C. L., Fowler, R. C., Young, D., & Blenkush, M. San Diego suicide study. *Suicide & Life-Threatening Behavior,* 1986a, 16, 448–457.

Rich, C. L., Motooka, M. S., Fowler, R. C., & Young, D. Suicide by psychotics. *Biological Psychiatry,* 1988, 24, 595–601.

Rich, C. L., Young, D., & Fowler, R. C. The San Diego suicide study. In R. Cohen-Sandler (Ed.) *Proceedings of the 18th Annual Meeting.* Denver: AAS, 1985, 67–72.

Rippetoe, P. A., Alarcon, R. D., & Walter-Ryan, W. G. Interactions between depression and borderline personality disorder. *Psychopathology,* 1986, 19, 340–346.

Robbins, D., & Alessi, N. Depressive symptoms and suicidal behavior in adolescents. *American Journal of Psychiatry,* 1985, 142, 588–592.

Robertson, G. Mentally abnormal offenders. *British Medical Journal,* 1987, 295, 632–634.

Robinette, C. D., Hrubec, Z., & Fraumeni, J. Chronic alcoholism and subsequent mortality in World War Two veterans. *American Journal of Epidemiology,* 1979, 109, 687–700.

Rohde, A., Marneros, A., & Deister, A. Suicidal behavior in schizophrenic patients. In S. D. Platt & N. Kreitman (Eds.) *Current Research on Suicide and Parasuicide.* Edinburgh: University of Edinburgh, 1989a, 78–87.

Rohde, A., Marneros, A., & Deister, A. Schizoaffective disorders and suicidal behavior. In S. D. Platt & N. Kreitman (Eds.) *Current Research on Suicide and Parasuicide.* Edinburgh: University of Edinburgh, 1989b, 88–97.

Roose, S. P., Glassman, A., Walsh, T., Woodring, S., & Vital-Herne, J. Depression, delusions, and suicide. *American Journal of Psychiatry,* 1983, 140, 1159–1162.

Rorsman, B., Hagnell, O., & Lanke, J. Suicide rates in the Lundby study. In J. P. Soubrier & J. Vedrinne (Eds.) *Depression and Suicide.* Paris: Pergamon, 1983, 300–304.

Rosenberg, M. On accidents and incidents. *Comprehensive Psychiatry,* 1967, 8, 108–118.

Rosenstock, H. Depression, suicidal ideation, and suicide attempts in 90 adolescents. *Crisis,* 1985, 6, 89–105.

Ross, C. Comparison of hospital and prison alcoholics. *British Journal of Psychiatry,* 1971, 118, 75–78.

Ross, C. A., & Norton, G. R. Suicide and parasuicide in multiple personality disorder. *Psychiatry,* 1989, 52, 365–371.

Rotheram-Borus, M. J., & Trautman, P. D. Hopelessness, depression, and suicidal intent among adolescent suicide attempters. *Journal of the American Academy of Child & Adolescent Psychiatry,* 1988, 27, 700–704.

Roy, A. Suicide in chronic schizophrenia. *British Journal of Psychiatry,* 1982a, 141, 171–177.

Roy, A. Risk factors for suicide in psychiatric patients. *Archives of General Psychiatry,* 1982b, 39, 1089–1095.

Roy, A. Suicide in depressives. *Comprehensive Psychiatry,* 1983a, 24, 487–491.

Roy, A. Family history of suicide. *Archives of General Psychiatry,* 1983b, 40, 971–974.

Roy, A. Depression and suicide in psychiatric patients. In J. P. Soubrier & J. Vedrinne (Eds.) *Depression and Suicide.* Paris: Pergamon, 1983, 502–505.

Roy, A. Suicide in recurrent affective disorder patients. *Canadian Journal of Psychiatry,* 1984, 29, 319–322.

Roy, A. Family history of suicide in affective disorder patients. *Journal of Clinical Psychiatry,* 1985a, 46, 317–319.

Roy, A. Family history of suicide in manic-depressive patients. *Journal of Affective Disorders,* 1985b, 8, 187–189.

Roy, A. Depression, attempted suicide and suicide in patients with chronic schizophrenia. *Psychiatric Clinics of North America,* 1986, 9(1), 193–206.

Roy, A., Mazonson, A., & Pickar, D. Attempted suicide in chronic schizophrenia. *British Journal of Psychiatry,* 1984, 144, 303–306.

Roy, A., Schreiber, J., Mazonson, A., & Pickar, D. Suicidal behavior in chronic schizophrenic patients. *Canadian Journal of Psychiatry,* 1986, 31, 737–740.

Roy-Byrne, P. P., Post, R. M., Hambrick, D. D., Liverich, G. S., & Rosoff, A. S. Suicide and course of illness in major affective disorder. *Journal of Affective Disorders,* 1988, 15, 1–8.

Rubenstein, J. L., Heeren, T., Housman, D., Rubin, C., & Stechlet, G. Suicidal behavior in normal adolescents. *American Journal of Orthopsychiatry,* 1989, 59, 59–71.

Ryser, P. E. Sex differences in substance abuse. *International Journal of the Addictions,* 1983, 18, 71–87.

Saunders, J. M., & Valente, S. M. Suicide risk among gay men and lesbians. *Death Studies,* 1987, 11, 1–23.

Saxon, S., Kuncel, E., & Kaufman, E. Self-destructive behavior patterns in male and female drug abusers. *American Journal of Drug & Alcohol Abuse,* 1980, 7(1), 19–29.

Schmidt, W., & De Lint, J. Causes of death of alcoholics. *Quarterly Journal of Studies on Alcohol,* 1972, 33, 171–185.

Schneider, S. G., Farberow, N. L., & Kruks, G. N. Suicidal behavior in adolescent and young adult gay men. *Suicide & Life-Threatening Behavior,* 1989, 19, 381–394.

Schotte, D., Clum, G. Suicidal ideation in a college population. *Journal of Consulting & Clinical Psychology,* 1982, 50, 690–696.

Schotte, D., Clum, G. Problem-solving skills in suicidal psychiatric patients. *Journal of Consulting & Clinical Psychology,* 1987, 55, 49–56.

Schuckit, M. Primary men alcoholics with histories of suicide attempts. *Journal of Studies on Alcohol,* 1986, 47, 78–81.

Schuckit, M., & Gunderson, E. Deaths among young alcoholics in the US Naval Service. *Quarterly Journal of Studies on Alcohol,* 1974, 35, 856–862.

Schwartz, R., & Eisen, S. The risk of suicide in young psychiatric patients hospitalized out-of-state. *Psychiatry,* 1984, 47, 342–350.

Selakovic, S., Kamapadzija, B., & Biro, M. Alcoholics and non-alcoholics in suicide attempters. In J. P. Soubrier & J. Vedrinne (Eds.) *Depression and Suicide.* Paris: Pergamon, 1983, 467–471.

Shachar, S. A., Hagan, B. J., & Evenson, R. C. Diagnosing homosexuality in a state department of mental health. *Psychological Reports,* 1983, 53, 1179–1188.

Shafii, M., Carrigan, S., Whittinghill, J., & Derrick, A. Psychological autopsy of completed suicide in children and adolescents. *American Journal of Psychiatry,* 2985, 142, 1061–1064.

Shafii, M., Steltz-Lenarsky, J., Derick, A., Beckner, C., & Whittinghill, J. Comorbidity of mental disorders in the post-mortem diagnosis of completed suicide in children and adolescents. *Journal of Affective Disorders,* 1988, 125, 227–233.

Shearer, S. L., Peters, C. P., Quaytime, M. S., & Wadman, B. E. Intent and lethality of suicide attempts among female borderline inpatients. *American Journal of Psychiatry,* 1988, 145, 1424–1427.

Snyder, S., Pitts, W., & Pokorny, A. Selected behavioral features with borderline personality traits. *Suicide & Life-Threatening Behavior,* 1986, 16, 28–39.

Spalt, L. Suicidal behavior and depression in university student psychiatric referrals. *Psychiatric Quarterly,* 1980, 52, 235–239.

Spalt, L. Suicide attempts among non-patient college students. In J. P. Soubrier & J. Vedrinne (Eds.) *Depression and Suicide.* Paris: Pergamon, 1983, 627–631

Spirito, A., Stark, L., Fristad, M., Hart, K., & Owens-Stively, J. Adolescent suicide attempters hospitalized on a pediatric unit. *Journal of Pediatric Psychology,* 1987, 12, 171–189.

Spirito, A., Williams, C. A., Stark, L., & Hart, K. The hopelessness scale for children. *Journal of Abnormal Child Psychology,* 1988c, 16, 445–458.

Stallone, F., Dunner, D., Ahearn, J., & Fieve, R. Statistical predictions of suicide in depressives. *Comprehensive Psychiatry,* 1980, 21, 381–387.

Steer, R. A., Beck, A. T., Brown, G., & Berchick, R. J. Self-reported depressive symptoms that differentiate recurrent episode major depression from dysthymic disorders. *Journal of Clinical Psychology,* 1987, 43, 246–250.

Steer, R. A., McElroy, M. G., & Beck, A. T. Correlates of self-reported and clinically assessed depression in outpatient alcoholics. *Journal of Clinical Psychology,* 1983, 39, 144–149.

Sternlicht, M., Pustel, G., & Deutsch, M. Suicidal tendencies among institutionalized retardates. *Journal of Mental Subnormality,* 1970, 16, 93–102.

Strosahl, K. D., Linehan, M., & Chiles, J. Will the real social desirability please stand up? *Journal of Consulting & Clinical Psychology,* 1984, 52, 449–457.

Swart, G. T. Death by suicide at Ontario provincial psychiatric hospitals. In J. Morgan (Ed.) *Suicide.* London, Ontario: King's College, 1987, 161–174.

Tardiff, K., Gross, E., Wu, J., Stajic, M., & Millman, R. Analysis of cocaine-positive fatalities. *Journal of Forensic Sciences,* 1989, 34, 53–63.

Taussigova, D., Vinar, O., Bastecky, J., & Tenkrat, M. A method of predicting suicidal behavior. *Activitas Nervosa Superior,* 1975, 17, 240–241.

Taylor, E., & Stansfeld, S. Children who poison themselves. *British Journal of Psychiatry,* 1984, 145, 127–135.

Tejedor, M. C., Castillon, J., Percay, J., Puigdellivol, M., & Turnes, E. Suicidal behavior in schizophrenics. *Crisis,* 1987, 8, 151–161.

Thorarinsson, A. A. Mortality among men alcoholics in Iceland. *Journal of Studies on Alcohol,* 1979, 40, 704–718.

Till, E., & Kapamadzija, B. Endogenous depressions and suicidal behavior. In J. P. Soubrier & J. Vedrinne (Eds.) *Depression and Suicide.* Paris: Pergamon, 1983, 235–238.

Tolstrup, K., Brinch, M., Isager, T., Nielsen, S., Nystrup, J., Severin, B., & Olesen, N. Long-term outcome of 151 cases of anorexia nervosa. *Acta Psychiatrica Scandinavica,* 1985, 71, 380–387.

Topol, P., & Reznikoff, M. Perceived peer and family relationships, hopelessness and locus of control as factors in adolescent suicide attempts. *Suicide & Life-Threatening Behavior,* 1982, 12, 141–150.

Trenteseau, J. A., Hyer, L., Verenes, D., & Warsaw, J. Hopelessness among later-life patients. *Journal of Applied Gerontology,* 1989, 8, 355–364.

Tsuang, M., & Woolson, R. Excess mortality in schizophrenia and affective disorders. *Archives of General Psychiatry,* 1978, 35, 1181–1185.

Tsuang, M., Woolson, R., & Fleming, J. Premature deaths in schizophrenia and affective disorders. *Archives of General Psychiatry,* 1980, 37, 979–983.

Tunving, K. Fatal outcome in drug addiction. *Acta Psychiatrica Scandinavica,* 1988, 77, 551–566.

Vaglum, S., & Vaglum, P. Differences between alcoholic and non-alcoholic female psychiatric patients. *Acta Psychiatrica Scandinavica,* 1987, 76, 309–316.

Vandivort, D. S., & Locker, B. Z. Suicide ideation. *Suicide & Life-Threatening Behavior,* 1979, 9, 205–218.

Van Praag, H. M., & Plutchik, R. Increased suicidality in depression. *Psychiatry Research,* 1988, 26, 273–278.

Videbech, T. The psychopathology of anancastic endogenous depression. *Acta Psychiatrica Scandinavica,* 1975, 52, 336–373.

Viesselman, J. O., & Roig, M. Depression and suicidality in eating disorders. *Journal of Clinical Psychiatry,* 1985, 46, 118–124.

Virkkunen, M. Suicides among alcoholics on social welfare rolls. *Acta Sociomedica Scandinavia,* 1971, 3, 51–58.

Wade, N. L. Suicide as a resolution of separation-individuation among adolescent girls. *Adolescence,* 1987, 22, 169–177.

Walsh, B. W., & Rosen, P. M. *Self-mutilation.* New York: Guilford, 1988.

Wandrei, K. E. Identifying potential suicides among high-risk women. *Social Work,* 1985, 30, 511–517.

Wandrei, K. E. Lesbians and suicide. In R. Yufit (Ed.) *Proceedings of the 20th Annual Conference.* Denver: AAS, 1987, 104.

Ward, N., & Schuckit, M. Factors associated with suicidal behavior in polydrug abusers. *Journal of Clinical Psychiatry,* 1980, 41, 379–385.

Wasileski, M., & Kelly, D. Characteristics of suicide attempters in a Marine recruit population. *Military Medicine,* 1982, 147, 818–830.

Watterson, O., Simpson, D., & Sells, S. Death rates and causes of death among opoid addicts in community drug treatment programs during 1970–1973. *American Journal of Drug & Alcohol Abuse,* 1975, 2(1), 99–111.

Weeke, A. Causes of death in manic-depressives. In M. Schou & E. Stromgren (Eds.) *Origin, Prevention and Treatment of Affective Disorders.* New York: Academic, 1979, 289–299.

Weeke, A., Joel, K., & Vaeth, M. Cardiovascular death and manic-depressive psychosis. *Journal of Affective Disorders,* 1987, 13, 287–292.

Weeke, A., & Vaeth, M. Excess mortality of bipolar and unipolar manic-depressive patients. *Journal of Affective Disorders,* 1986, 11, 227–234.

Weiner, A. A., & Pfeffer, C. Suicidal status, depression, and intellectual functioning in preadolescent psychiatric inpatients. *Comprehensive Psychiatry,* 1986, 27, 372–380.

Weiss, S. R., & Ebert, M. H. Psychological and behavioral characteristics of normal weight bulimics and normal weight controls. *Psychosomatic Medicine,* 1983, 45, 293–303.

Weissman, M. M., Klerman, G., Markowitz, J., & Ouellette, R. Suicidal ideation and suicide attempts in panic disorder and attacks. *New England Journal of Medicine,* 1989, 321, 1209–1214.

Weissman, M. M., Myers, J., & Harding, P. Prevalence and psychiatric heterogeneity of alcoholism in a US urban community. *Journal of Studies on Alcohol,* 1980, 41, 672–681.

Westefeld, J., & Furr, S. Suicide and depression among college students. *Professional Psychology,* 1987, 18, 119–127.

Wetzel, R. D., Margulies, T., Davis, R., & Karam, E. Hopelessness, depression and suicidal intent. *Journal of Clinical Psychiatry,* 1980, 41, 159–160.

Wetzel, R. D., & Reich, T. The cognitive triad and suicide intent in depressed inpatients. *Psychological Reports,* 1989, 65, 1027–1032.

Whitters, A., Cadoret, R., Troughton, E., & Widmer, R. Suicide attempts in antisocial alcoholics. *Journal of Nervous & Mental Disease,* 1987, 175, 624–626.

Whitters, A., Cadoret, R., & Widmer, R. Factors associated with suicide attempts in alcohol abusers. *Journal of Affective Disorders,* 1985, 9, 19–23.

Wihelmsen, L., Elmfeldt, D., & Wedel, H. Causes of death in relation to social and alcohol problems among Swedish men aged 35–44. *Acta Medica Scandinavica,* 1983, 213, 263–268.

Wilkinson, G., & Bacon, N. A clinical and epidemiological survey of parasuicide and suicide in Edinburgh schizophrenics. *Psychological Medicine,* 1984, 14, 899–912.

Winokur, G., & Black, D. Psychiatric and medical diagnoses as risk factors for mortality in psychiatric patients. *American Journal of Psychiatry,* 1987, 144, 208–211.

Winokur, D., Black, D., & Nasrallah, A. Neurotic depression. *European Archives of Psychiatry,* 1987, 236, 343–348.

Winokur, G., Black, D., & Nasrallah, A. Depression secondary to other psychiatric disorders and medical illnesses. *American Journal of Psychiatry,* 1988, 145, 233–237.

Wold, C. I., & Tabachnick, N. Depression as an indicator of lethality in suicidal patients. In R. J. Friedman & M. Katz (Eds.) *The Psychology of Depression.* New York: Wiley, 1974, 187–196.

Wolfersdorf, M., Bary, P., Steiner, B., Keller, F., Vogel, R., Hole, G., & Schuttler, R. Schizophrenia and suicide in psychiatric inpatients. In S. D. Platt & N. Kreitman (Eds.) *Current Research on Suicide and Parasuicide.* Edinburgh: University of Edinburgh, 1989, 67–77.

Wolfersdorf, M., Keller, F., Steiner, B., & Hole, G. Delusional depression and suicide. *Acta Psychiatrica Scandinavica,* 1987, 76, 359–363.

Wolfersdorf, M., & Vogel, R. Types of hospital suicide and depression. *Crisis,* 1987, 8, 37–48.

Wolk-Wasserman, D. Some problems connected with the treatment of suicide attempt patients. *Crisis,* 1987, 8, 69–82.

Yates, W., Sieleni, B., & Bowers, W. Clinical correlates of personality disorder in bulimia nervosa. *International Journal of Eating Disorders,* 1989, 8, 473–477.

Zetin, M., Sklansky, G., & Cramer, M. Sex differences in inpatients with major depression. *Journal of Clinical Psychiatry,* 1984, 45, 257–259.

Zimmerman, M., Coryell, W., Stangle, D., & Pfohl, B. Validity of an operational definition for neurotic unipolar major depression. *Journal of Affective Disorders,* 1987, 12, 29–40.

Chapter 19

MEDICAL ILLNESS

The relationship between medical illness and suicide has been reviewed earlier by Lester (1988a), and this chapter will update this earlier review.

General Health

Suicidal Preoccupation

Hill et al. (1988) found that general health predicted suicidal preoccupation in a community sample of depressed elderly. Zautra et al. (1989) found that older adults who had suffered an illness or injury in the last year were more depressed and anxious and had more suicidal ideation than those who had not suffered any illness or injury.

Attempted Suicide

Choquet et al. (1980) found that teenage suicide attempters in France were more likely to have poor health (and to be taking sedatives and sleeping tablets) than normal teenagers. Goldney (1981) found that young female suicide attempters had poorer physical health than controls.

Adam et al. (1980) found that attempted suicides were as healthy as general medical patients but had a greater fear of ill health.

In a sample of Hungarian residents, Kopp et al. (1987) found that attempted suicide was rare in diabetics and hypertensives but common in gastric and liver patients, psychiatric patients and neurotics. Kopp et al. also correlated the diseases over regions and found that attempted and completed suicide rates were not associated with high blood pressure or liver disease. (Attempted suicide rates were associated with heavy drinking.)

Kontaxakis et al. (1988) studied attempted suicides who also had psychiatric illnesses and compared those with a physical illness in addition with those who did not. Those who had a physical illness were older, more often married, used violent methods more often (such as jumping and cutting) and overdoses less often, and were more often diagnosed as having organic psychoses and affective disorders and less often with schizophrenia and antisocial personality disorder. The groups did not differ in prior suicide attempts.

Completed Suicide

Barraclough (1971) compared elderly suicides with accidental deaths and found that more of the suicides were medically ill. This illness appeared to be a precipitating cause of the suicide in some cases. (Also, more of the suicides were living alone than in the general population. The suicide rate of the elderly in British boroughs and the frequency of one-person elderly households were positively related.)

As a result of autopsies on suicides in Stockholm, Hjortsjo (1987) found that 30 percent of male and 27 percent of female suicides had known somatic illness. Adding in the suspected illnesses, these percentages rose to 42 percent and 31 percent, respectively.

Barraclough and Hughes (1987) found no excess of illness or handicaps in a sample of suicides as compared to living controls, though they did complain more of pain. Cattell (1988) found that elderly suicides did not differ from those dying of accidental causes in physical health, though the suicides did have more pain. Fernando and Storm (1984) and Gutierrez et al. (1988) both found that psychiatric patients who completed suicide did not differ from those who did not in physical illness. Hawton and Fagg (1988) found that poor physical health predicted subsequent completed suicide in a follow-up study of attempted suicides. Wandrei (1985) found no differences between female suicide attempters who subsequently completed suicide and those who did not in physical health (though the suicides were more psychiatrically disturbed). Kuperman et al. (1988) found that having a medical problem predicted subsequent completed suicide in child psychiatric patients.

Lin et al. (1989) compared suicides from an HMO practice with depressed controls and found no differences in pain symptoms, vegetative symptoms, autonomic symptoms, and gastrointestinal symptoms. (The suicides had more family and interpersonal problems and were more likely to have a psychiatric diagnosis of psychosis, major affective disorder, or personality disorder than depressed and non-depressed controls.)

Biro and Lazic (1988) found that the presence of chronic organic illness differentiated between completed and attempted suicides. Motto (1980) found that poor health (and especially if it was getting worse) predicted subsequent completed suicide in alcohol-abusing depressed inpatients.

In Sweden, Stensman and Sundqvist-Stensman (1988) found that 17 percent of a sample of completed suicides had a somatic disease. As compared to the general population, there was an excess of multiple sclerosis, Parkinson's disorder, sequelae to polio and malignant neoplasms (but not sequelae to stroke, chronic rheumatoid arthritis, diabetes, epilepsy, myocardial infarction, bronchial asthma, or chronic low back and benign pain).

In contrast, Burke (1983) found that psychiatric patients who eventually died of natural deaths were more physically ill than those subsequently completing suicide. Kettl and Bixler (1988) found that Alaskan natives who completed suicide did not differ from controls in fractures, tuberculosis, congenital deformities, or other medical problems (or psychiatric illness), but were more often alcohol abusers and had more often made prior suicide attempts.

In Singapore, Kua and Sim (1982) found that completed suicides more often had physical illness than psychiatric controls. (They were also younger, less often married and had attempted suicide more in the past, but did not differ in psychiatric diagnosis or employment status).

Batten and Hicks (1988) found that mentally ill or depressed suicides had a higher incidence of physical illness than suicides who were not mentally ill. In Singapore, Chia (1984) found that suicides who had physical illness were older and less often Malay than those with physical illness.

Whitlock (1986) reviewed studies of completed suicide (excluding samples solely of psychiatric patients or geriatric patients) and found that about 34 percent of the suicides had a physical illness. In a comparison of 200 completed suicides with 200 accidental deaths in Australia, he found that the female suicides had more physical illness but not the males. In a comparison of one thousand completed suicides in England with the general population, he found significantly more epilepsy, cerebrovascular disorders, dementia, visual defects, multiple sclerosis, head injury, cerebral tumors, peptic ulcer, cancer and cirrhosis of the liver (but not any excess of cardiac disease, hypertension, bronchitis, asthma, arthritis, endocrine disorders, anemia, or surgical operations).

AIDS

The problem of suicide in AIDS patients has been discussed by Lester (1988b). He noted that AIDS is typically a terminal illness. As such AIDS patients may have some similarities to other terminal patients. Second, AIDS affects some groups in our society more than others: homosexuals, minority drug addicts, and those given blood transfusions. Since many AIDS patients are homosexuals and drug addicts, their homosexuality and addiction respectively have implications for their suicidal behavior.

It has probably been true of all patients with chronic, terminal illnesses, but many patients dying from AIDS (and often their relatives) face bankruptcy. This creates additional stress for the AIDS patient. Finally, there is great stigma attached to having AIDS, and AIDS patients often face rejection, both from friends and from professionals, and even physical abuse. This too creates additional stress for the AIDS patient.

Suicide in AIDS patients is, therefore, most often suicide in homosexuals and addicts, dying in poverty and facing rejection and abuse from others.

Fryer (1987) noted that he thought that drug addiction and promiscuous homosexual behavior (especially among those men who desire anal penetration with physical injury) to be a form of self-destructive behavior. Continuing these behaviors after the discovery of AIDS is even more easily viewed as self-destructive behavior. Fryer also expressed the opinion, based on clinical experience only, that suicide is more common among patients with the symptoms of ARC and those who test positive for the syndrome than among patients with AIDS.

Several case reports have appeared of people seeking to contract AIDS as a means of committing suicide (Flavin et al., 1984).

Kiozer et al. (1988) compared the number of completed suicides in AIDS patients with the number of AIDS cases on a register in California and calculated a suicide rate of 463 per 100,000 per year, extremely high. The rate was higher in men aged 20–39 than in those 40–59. In New York City, Marzuk et al. (1988) reported a suicide rate in 1985 of 19 per 100,000 per year for men aged 20–59 without AIDS and 681 for men with AIDS. Plott et al. (1989) identified 2,255 AIDS patients in Texas in one year, and 1,143 died. Of these, five completed suicide. Plott et al. calculated a suicide rate of 222 per 100,000 per year, but this fails to take into account the fact that not all the patients lived the whole year, a factor which would increase the estimated rate.

Rundell et al. (1989) found that US Air Force personnel who found out that they were HIV seropositive were forty times more likely to attempt suicide than the average Air Force personnel. The rate was more common several months later than soon after learning of the diagnosis. Brown and Rundell (1989) found that 21 percent of men and 7 percent of women diagnosed as HIV positive in the Air Force reacted with suicidal ideation.

Amputees

Hrubec and Ryder (1980) found that amputees of limbs had more suicides than those simply disfigured or who lost only a hand or foot. Shukla et al. (1982) found that 29 percent of right-handed amputees had had suicidal ideation (and 3 percent had attempted suicide). Suicidal ideation was more common in those who lost their right arm (who showed more general disturbance, too) than in those who lost their left arm, but there was no difference between those losing right versus left legs. Bakalim (1969) reported an excess of suicides among amputees, but only for those under the age of 65.

Ankylosing Spondylitis

Radford et al. (1977) found that 1.3 percent of deaths in patients with ankylosing spondylitis (not given x-ray therapy) were due to suicide.

Appendectomies

Joyce et al. (1981) found no differences in attempted suicide rates after removal of normal versus inflamed appendices. However, Vassilas (1988) found among women who underwent appendectomies that those who had inflamed appendices were less likely to have shown attempted suicide (either before or after the appendectomy) and less likely to have had psychiatric contacts.

Asthma/Hypertension

Levitan (1983) found suicidal preoccupation to be more common in patients with asthma and hypertension than in patients with chronic obstructive pulmonary disease or cholelithiasis.

Cancer

Allebeck et al. (1989) found an increased rate of suicide in cancer patients of all ages, especially in the first year after discovery. The site of the tumor appeared to be unrelated to the risk of suicide. Fox et al. (1982) found an increased rate of suicide only in male cancer patients, not in females. The risk of suicide was greater soon after the diagnosis. No trends were found by age.

Bolund (1985) reported that 1.4 percent of completed suicides in Sweden had cancer and that 0.1 percent of cancer patients completed suicide. Marshall et al. (1983) found that samples of completed suicides in New York State contained more cancer patients than motor vehicle accident deaths or those dying from a sudden myocardial infarction.

Olafsen (1983) followed up all cancer patients in Norway and found an excess of completed suicides only in those more than 60 years old. The cancer suicides were older than the other suicides in Norway.

Siegel and Tuckel (1984–1985) reviewed five studies on suicide mortality in cancer patients: two found a high rate, one a low rate and two an average/expected rate. They concluded that cancer patients had not reliably been shown to have a high suicide rate.

Teta et al. (1986) followed up children and adolescents who had survived cancer. The incidence of attempted and completed suicide in the group did not differ from the incidence in their siblings.

Corticosteroid-Induced Psychosis

Braunig et al. (1989) reported cases of corticosteroid-induced psychosis some of which resulted in suicidal ideation and attempts. A literature review revealed that about 17 percent of patients given corticosteroids develop suicidal preoccupation.

Crohn's Disease

Prior et al. (1981) found an excess of completed suicide in female patients with Crohn's disease but not in male patients.

Cushing's Syndrome

Cohen (1980) found that most of the patients he studied with Cushing's syndrome were depressed and that there was a family history of depression and/or suicide in 28 percent of the cases.

Dermatitis

Haenel et al. (1984) found that 25 percent of patients making non-lethal skin self-injuries (dermatitis artefacta) had previously attempted suicide.

Diabetes

Foster (1988) found that the suicide rate and the death rate from diabetes were negatively associated over states in the US and over census divisions in Canada. He also reported that in Canada the suicide rate was positively associated with the level of magnesium in the drinking water.

Dialysis Patients and Renal Disease

Goldstein (1980) reviewed research on dialysis patients and concluded that hemodialysis patients do have a high suicide rate. An unpublished study, though, found no differences in suicidal potential between dialysis patients who violate their diet restrictions and non-violators.

Haenel et al. (1980) found that the suicide rate of patients undergoing renal dialysis was very high (232 per 100,000 per year in Switzerland and 102 in Europe in general), and that an additional high rate of patients refuse treatment. Smith et al. (1985) found that 15 percent of patients with chronic renal failure showed signs of suicidal ideation. Kaplan de Nour (1979) found that suicidal ideation was more frequent among older dialysis patients (30–49) than younger patients (14–19).

Disability

Tweed et al. (1988) found that depression and suicidal ideation increased with increasing disability, but that attempted suicide rates peaked for those with mild (versus no, moderate and severe) disability.

Epilepsy

Brent (1986) found more epileptics in a sample of adolescent suicide attempters than expected. He compared adolescent suicide attempters with epilepsy and without and found that the epileptics had better school functioning but made more lethal suicide attempts with greater suicidal intent. The groups did not differ in age, sex, race, whether living with biological parents, family discord, or stress life events.

Hawton et al. (1980) found that a sample of attempted suicides contained a higher proportion of epileptics (3.2 percent) than the general population (0.6 percent), with the proportion higher in male attempters than in females (5.2 percent versus 2.4 percent). The epileptic attempters were more often repeaters, used alcohol during the attempt, were unemployed and had received prior psychiatric treatment than the non-epileptic attempters (but did not differ in age or method for suicide).

Mendez et al. (1989) compared epileptic and non-epileptic suicide attempters. The epileptics more often had a borderline personality disorder (and less often an adjustment disorder) and psychosis and had made more prior suicide attempts. The groups did not differ in depression. Attempting suicide was associated with increased seizure activity in only one of the twenty-two epileptics.

Jensen and Larson (1979) found that nineteen percent of drug-resistant temporal lobe epileptics (who had undergone a unilateral temporal lobe resection) had attempted or completed suicide pre- or post-surgery, but they presented no comparison data.

Zielinski (1974) followed up epileptics in Poland and found that 12 percent of their deaths were from suicide. (Among hospitalized epileptics, 3 percent of the deaths were from suicide.) This excess mortality from suicide was greater in females and in those in whom the epilepsy had began at an earlier age. Iivanainen and Lehtinen (1979) found a higher percentage of deaths from suicide in hospitalized epileptics than in the general population. Whitlock (1986) found an excess of epileptics in a sample of completed suicides in Great Britain as compared to the general population.

Gibbs and Gibbs (1952) found the highest incidence of suicidal tendencies in epileptics with psychomotor disturbances (especially simple, with grand mal and with an anterior temporal lobe focus) than in those with other types of seizures. Roy (1979) found a greater incidence of attempted suicide (and depression and other psychiatric symptoms) in patients with hysterical seizures as compared to patients with epileptic seizures.

Cooper et al. (1974) reported a case of an assaultive and suicidal patient with seizures whose aggression was eliminated by electrical stimulation of the cerebellum. The stimulation of the cerebellum apparently restored its ability to inhibit the aggression.

Matthews and Barabas (1981) reviewed research on suicide in epileptics and estimated that 5.0 percent of the deaths of epileptics were due to suicide versus 1.4 percent in the general population. Whitlock (1982) also reviewed previous research and concluded that both attempted and completed suicide was more common in epileptics (but not in temporal lobe patients).

This research is reasonably consistent in finding an increased risk of suicide in epileptics, a conclusion shared by Barraclough (1981, 1987) in a review of the research. But there are not enough studies to identify whether particular types of epilepsy carry a higher risk of suicide, though Barraclough felt that the risk was higher for temporal lobe epilepsy, severe epilepsy and epilepsy with handicap. The risk may be greater also in the earlier years of the condition. A few studies are now trying to identify differences between suicidal behavior in epileptics and suicidal behavior in non-epileptics. Barraclough suggested that the increased risk of suicide in epileptics might be a result of the accompanying psychiatric disturbance, addiction, or personality disorder caused by the epilepsy.

Headache

Lipton et al. (1989) found that patients withdrawing from cocaine who had accompanying headaches were more likely to become suicidal and depressed. Murphy (1982) found that attempted suicides suffered from headaches more than appendicitis patients (but did not differ in abdominal pain).

Heart Disease Patients

Simon et al. (1980) reported that attempted and completed suicide were rare in patients with pacemakers.

The Homebound

Bushman et al. (1989) found that 19 percent of homebound patients had suicidal ideation, especially if depressed and if there was no organic mental syndrome. Living alone was not related to feeling suicidal.

Huntington's Disease

Farrer (1986) found that 5.7 percent of deaths in Huntington's patients were from suicide. The suicides did not differ in the age of onset of the disorder, but they were younger than patients dying of other causes and had made fewer prior suicide attempts. Farrer found few suicide attempts in Huntington's patients. Schoenfeld et al. (1984) found an increased risk of completed suicide in Huntington's patients, but only for those aged 50–69.

Kessler (1987a) interviewed people with relatives who had Huntington's disease, and 34 percent reported attempted or completed suicides in their families. Five percent said they would commit suicide if they tested positive. Others surveys have obtained even higher percentages. Mastromauro et al. (1987) interviewed people at risk for Huntington's disease and found that 12 percent said that they might kill themselves if they tested positive for the disease. This possibility was greater in those close to the age when their parents showed symptoms and in those who did not want to be tested.

Whitlock (1982) reviewed research and concluded that suicide was more common than expected in patients with Huntington's disease.

Leprosy

Tokudome et al. (1981) found that female (but not male) patients at a leprosarum had a higher than expected suicide rate. This was statistically significant for women with lepromatous disease but not tuberculoid disease.

Pain

Shulman et al. (1982) found that more patients with incurable neuropathic pain completed suicide than those with curable neuropathic pain. Von Knorring (1975) found that depressed psychiatric patients who had recent experience of pain were more likely to have had thoughts of suicide and to be more depressed than those who had not experienced pain.

Parkinsonism

Hoehn and Yahr (1967) found that only 0.9 percent of deaths in Parkinson's patients were from suicide. In a review of research, Whitlock (1982) concluded that suicide was less common than expected in patients with Parkinson's disease.

Psychosomatic Disorders

Levitan (1983) found that suicidal preoccupation was more common in patients with asthma and hypertension than in patients with chronic obstructive pulmonary disease or cholelithiasis.

Spinal Cord Patients

Nyquist and Bors (1967) found that 8 percent of deaths in spinal cord injury patients were from suicide. The incidence was the same for all levels of injury. Wilcox and Stauffer (1972) reported an incidence of 18 percent. Tribe (1963) found only one suicide in 150 deaths of paraplegic patients.

Wilcox and Stauffer (1972) found that 18 percent of the deaths of spinal cord patients were from suicide. Le and Price (1982) found 21 percent of the deaths of spinal cord patients to be from suicide, and the risk was much greater in quadriplegics than in paraplegics.

Devivo et al. (1989) found an excess mortality from suicide in spinal cord patients (only for men), both in paraplegics and quadriplegics and in completely and incompletely injured patients. Nehemkis and Groot (1980) found that suicidal behavior and indirect self-destructive behavior were common in spinal cord patients. Suicidal attempts and ideation were more common in those patients who also showed indirect self-destructive behavior. From their review of previous research, they claimed that the risk of completed suicide was not related to age or the level of injury.

In a review of research, Hopkins (1971) suggested that spinal cord injury patients completed suicide much later after the accident than did amputees.

Terminally Ill

Brown et al. (1986) found that only 10 of 44 terminally ill patients desired death (and all were severely depressed), but only three of these had suicidal ideation.

Transplant Patients

Matas et al. (1976) found that 5 percent of deaths in kidney transplant patients were from suicide. Haenel et al. (1980) found a high rate of suicide in patients with renal transplants (57 per 100,000 per year in Europe). Washer et al. (1983) found that 15 percent of the deaths of patients with kidney transplants were either overt suicides or covert suicides (such as refusing dialysis).

Ulcers

Bonnevie (1977) found no excess mortality from completed suicide in duodenal or gastric ulcer patients. Krause (1963) found no excess mortality from suicide in non-operated and bleeding ulcer, but operated patients did (though the excess was unrelated to the method of operation). In contrast, Westlund (1963) found an excess mortality from suicide for operated and non-operated patients for both ulcer sites.

Berglund (1984, 1986) found that alcoholics who completed suicide were more likely to have peptic ulcers than those who did not kill themselves. Alcoholics with peptic ulcer, however, were not more likely to have attempted suicide in the past. The association between completed suicide and peptic ulcer was not found in non-depressed and non-alcoholic psychiatric patients (Berglund et al., 1987). Eriksson (1983) found an excess of suicide in patients operated on for benign gastroduodenal disease. Suicide was especially common in men operated after the age of 60 for duodenal ulcer and before the age of 30 for gastric ulcer.

In small samples of adolescents, Christodoulou et al. (1979) found that those with peptic ulcer had a higher incidence of attempted suicide than those without.

Knop and Fischer (1981) found a high incidence of suicidal deaths in patients with duodenal ulcers, both for men and women. The suicides were more often alcoholics and older at the time of the operation. Thus, the high rate of suicide in ulcers patients may be a result of the accompanying alcoholism and other psychiatric disturbances.

Correlations Between Illnesses

Karcher and Linden (1982) correlated the death rates from different causes over twelve major industrial categories in the US. Suicide rates were most strongly associated with deaths from stomach ulcer and homicide and less so with deaths from hypertensive heart disease and hypertension.

Discussion

The literature on physical illness and suicide was reviewed by Barraclough (1985) who concluded that the evidence supported a high suicide rate in epilepsy, peptic/gastric ulcer (probably because of the accompanying alcohol addiction), in ulcerative colitis (probably because of the steroid treatments), lupus (probably because of the resulting psychosis), hemodialysis, renal transplants, juvenile diabetes, traumatic brain injury, multiple sclerosis, Huntington's chorea, and spinal cord injury. Barraclough concluded that the suicide rate was probably average for adult diabetes, Parkinson's disease, and colostomy.

The research reviewed above has taken samples of patients with specific diseases (often quite small samples) and estimated the risk of suicide in them. Whitlock (1986) illustrated three different approaches to the study of suicide and medical illness.

First, he reviewed fifteen previous studies of completed suicides and, after excluding the psychiatric and geriatric patients, found the incidence of physical illness in them to be 34 percent.

Second, he compared two hundred suicides with two hundred accidental deaths and found significantly more physical illness in the females (but not in the males).

Third, he studied one thousand completed suicides and found significantly more epilepsy, cerebrovascular disease, dementia, visual defect, multiple sclerosis, head injury, cerebral tumor, peptic ulcer, cancer and cirrhosis of the liver than expected. In contrast, cardiac disease, hypertension, bronchitis, asthma, arthritis, endocrine diseases, anemia and surgical operations were no more frequent than expected.

The general conclusions of the research reviewed in this chapter seem to indicate a high suicide rate in patients with AIDS, limb amputation, epilepsy, Huntington's disease, and spinal cord injuries and in those on dialysis. Low suicide rates have been documented in patients with Parkinson's disease. The suicide rates in patients with other disorders have not yet been reliably documented.

REFERENCES

Adam, K. S., Bouckoms, A., & Scarr, G. Attempted suicide in Christchurch. *Australian & New Zealand Journal of Psychiatry,* 1980, 14, 305–314.

Allebeck, P., Bolund, C., & Ringback, G. Increased suicide rate in cancer patients. *Journal of Clinical Epidemiology,* 1989, 42, 611–616.

Bakalim, G. Causes of death in a series of 4738 Finnish war amputees. *Artificial Limbs,* 1969, 13(1), 27–36.

Barraclough, B. M. Suicide in the elderly. In D. W. P. Kay & A. Walk (Eds.) *Recent Development in Psychogeriatrics.* London: RMPA, 1971, 87–97.

Barraclough, B. Suicide and epilepsy. In E. Reynolds & M. Trimble (Eds.) *Epilepsy and Psychiatry.* Edinburgh: Churchill Livingston, 1981, 72–77.

Barraclough, B. M. Physical illness preceding suicide. In P. Pichot, P. Berner, R. Wolf, & K. Thau (Eds.) *Psychiatry: The State of the Art, volume 1.* New York: Plenum, 1985, 895–900.

Barraclough, B. M. The suicide rate of epilepsy. *Acta Psychiatrica Scandinavica,* 1987, 76, 339–345.

Barraclough, B. M., & Hughes, J. *Suicide.* Beckenham, UK: Croom Helm, 1987.

Batten, P. J., & Hicks, L. J. The use of mental status in death certification of suicide. *American Journal of Forensic Medicine & Pathology,* 1988, 9, 203–206.

Berglund, M. Suicide in alcoholism. *Archives of General Psychiatry,* 1984, 41, 888–891.

Berglund, M. Suicide in male alcoholics with peptic ulcers. *Alcoholism,* 1986, 10, 631–634.

Berglund, M., Krantz, P., Lundqvist, G., & Therup, L. Suicide in psychiatric patients. *Acta Psychiatrica Scandinavica,* 1987, 76, 431–437.

Biro, M., & Lazic, P. Methodological problems of suicide prediction. *European Journal of Psychiatry,* 1988, 2, 233–240.

Bolund, C. Suicide and cancer. *Journal of Psychosocial Oncology,* 1985, 3(1), 17–52.

Bonnevie, O. Causes of death in duodenal and gastric ulcer. *Gastroenterology,* 1977, 73, 1000–1004.

Brent, D. A. Overrepresentation of epileptics in a consecutive series of suicide attempters seen at a children's hospital. *Journal of the American Academy of Child Psychiatry,* 1986, 25, 242–246.

Brown, G. R., & Rundell, J. R. Suicidal tendencies in women with HIV infection. *American Journal of Psychiatry,* 1989, 146, 556–557.

Brown, J. H., Henteleff, P., Barakat, S., & Rowe, C. J. Is it normal for terminal patients to desire death? *American Journal of Psychiatry,* 1986, 143, 208–211.

Burke, A. W. The proportional distribution of suicide among mental hospital deaths and persons in the general population. In J. P. Soubrier & J. Vedrinne (Eds.) *Depression and Suicide.* Paris: Pergamon, 1983, 204–208.

Bushman, K., Schrage, H., & McKegney, F. P. Psychiatric health of the homebound. *Einstein Quarterly Journal of Biological Medicine,* 1989, 7(1), 12–18.

Cattell, H. R. Elderly suicide in London. *International Journal of Geriatric Psychiatry,* 1988, 3, 252–261.

Chia, B. H. Physical illness and suicide. *Singapore Medical Journal,* 1984, 25(1), 30–33.

Choquet, M., Facy, F., & Davidson, F. Suicide and attempted suicide among adolescents in France. In R. F. Farmer & S. Hirsch (Eds.) *The Suicide Syndrome.* London: Croom Helm, 1980, 73–89.

Christodoulou, G. N., Gargoulas, A., Papaloukas, A., Marinopoulou, A., & Rabovilas, A. D. Peptic ulcer in childhood. *Psychotherapy & Psychosomatics,* 1979, 32, 297–301.

Cohen, S. I. Cushing's syndrome. *British Journal of Psychiatry,* 1980, 136, 120–124.

Cooper, I., Amin, I., Gilman, S., & Waltz, J.: The effects of chronic stimulation of cerebellar cortex on epilepsy in man. In I. Cooper, M. Riklan, & Snider, R. (Eds.) *The Cerebellum, Epilepsy and Behavior.* New York: Plenum, 1974.

Devivo, M. J., Kartus, P. L., Stover, S. L., Rutt, R. D., & Fine, P. R. Cause of death for patients with spinal cord injuries. *Archives of Internal Medicine,* 1989, 149, 1761–1766.

Eriksson, S. B. *The Operated Stomach.* Lund: University of Lund, 1981. (Bulletin #36, Department of Surgery)

Farrer, L. A. Suicide and attempted suicide in Huntington's disease. *American Journal of Medical Genetics,* 1986, 24, 305–311.

Fernando, S., & Storm, V. Suicide among psychiatric patients of a district general hospital. *Psychological Medicine,* 1984, 14, 661–672.

Flavin, D. K., Franklin, J. E., & Frances, R. J. The acquired immune deficiency syndrome and suicidal behavior in alcohol-dependent homosexual men. *American Journal of Psychiatry,* 1984, 143, 1440–1442.

Foster, H. D. Suicide and mortality from diabetes. *American Journal of Psychiatry,* 1988, 145, 272.

Fox, B. H., Stanek, E., Boyd, S., & Flannery, J. Suicide rates among cancer patients in Connecticut. *Journal of Chronic Disease,* 1982, 35, 89–100.

Fryer, J. E. AIDS and suicide. In J. Morgan (Ed.) *Suicide: Helping Those At Risk.* London, Ont.: King's College, 1987, 193–200.

Gibbs, F., & Gibbs, E.: *Atlas of Electroencephalography, Volume 2.* Reading: Addison-Wesley, 1952.

Goldney, R. D. Parental loss and reported childhood stress in young women who attempt suicide. *Acta Psychiatrica Scandinavica,* 1981, 64, 34–49.

Goldstein, A. M. The "uncooperative" patient. In N. L. Farberow (Ed.) *The Many Faces of Suicide.* New York: McGraw-Hill, 1980, 89–98.

Gutierrez, H. O., Russakoff, L. M., & Oldham, J. M. The prediction of suicide. In D. Lester (Ed.) *Suicide '88.* Denver: AAS, 1988, 127–128.

Haenel, T., Brunner, F., & Battegay, R. Renal dialysis and suicide. *Comprehensive Psychiatry,* 1980, 21, 140–145.

Haenel, T., Rauchfleisch, U., Schuppli, R., & Battegay, R. The psychiatric significance of dermatitis artefacta. *European Archives of Psychiatry & Neurological Science,* 1984, 234, 38–41.

Hawton, K., & Fagg, J. Suicide and other causes of death following attempted suicide. *British Journal of Psychiatry,* 1988, 152, 359–366.

Hawton, K., Fagg, J., & Marsack, P. Association between epilepsy and attempted suicide. *Journal of Neurology, Neurosurgery & Psychiatry,* 1980, 43, 168–170.

Hill, R. D., Gallagher, D., Thompson, L. W., & Ishida, T. Hopelessness as a measure of suicidal intent in the depressed elderly. *Psychology & Aging,* 1988, 3, 230–232.

Hjortsjo, T. Suicide in relation to somatic illness and complications. *Crisis,* 1987, 8, 125–137.

Hoehn, M., & Yahr, M. Parkinsonism. *Neurology,* 1967, 17, 427–442.

Hopkins, M. T. Patterns of self-destruction among the orthopedically disabled. *Rehabilitation Research & Practice,* 1971, 3(1), 5–16.

Hrubec, Z., & Ryder, R. A. Traumatic limb amputations and subsequent mortality. *Journal of Chronic Diseases,* 1980, 33, 239–250.

Iivanainen, M., & Lehtinen, J. Causes of death in institutionalized epileptics. *Epilepsia,* 1979, 20, 485–492.

Jensen, I., & Larsen, J. Mental aspects of temporal lobe epilepsy. *Journal of Neurology Neurosurgery & Psychiatry,* 1979, 42, 256–265.

Joyce, P. R., Walshe, J. W., Bushnell, J. A., & Morton, J. B. Readmission to hospital after appendectomy for nonspecific abdominal pain. *Australian & New Zealand Journal of Surgery,* 1981, 51, 465–467.

Kaplan de Nour, A. Adolescents' adjustment to chronic hemodialysis. *American Journal of Psychiatry,* 1979, 136, 430–433.

Karcher, C., & Linden, L. Is work conducive to self-destruction? *Suicide & Life-Threatening Behavior,* 1982, 12, 151–175.

Kessler, S. Psychiatric implications of presymptomatic testing for Huntington's disease. *American Journal of Orthopsychiatry,* 1987a, 57, 212–219.

Kessler, S. The dilemma of suicide and Huntington's disease. *American Journal of Medical Genetics,* 1987b, 26, 315–320.

Kettl, P. A., & Bixler, E. O. Suicide in Alaska natives. In D. Lester (Ed.) *Suicide '88.* Denver: AAS, 1988, 175–176.

Kizer, K. W., Green, M., Perkins, C. I., Doebbert, G., & Hughes, M. J. AIDS and suicide in California. *Journal of the American Medical Association,* 1988, 260, 1881.

Knop, J., & Fischer, A. Duodenal ulcer, suicide, psychopathology and alcoholism. *Acta Psychiatrica Scandinavica,* 1981, 63, 346–355.

Kontaxakis, V., Christodoulou, G., Mavreas, V., & Havaki-Kontaxaki, B. Attempted suicide in psychiatric outpatients with concurrent physical illness. *Psychotherapy & Psychosomatics,* 1988, 509, 201–206.

Kopp, M. S., Skrabski, A., & Magyar, I. Neurotics at risk and suicidal behavior in the Hungarian population. *Acta Psychiatrica Scandinavica,* 1987, 76, 406–413.

Krause, U. Long-term results of medical and surgical treatment of peptic ulcer. *Acta Chirurgica Scandinavica,* 1963, 125 (suppl. 310), 1–77.

Kua, E. H., & Sim, L. P. Suicide by psychiatric inpatients in Singapore. *Singapore Medical Journal,* 1982, 23, 252–254.

Kuperman, S., Black, D. W., & Burns, T. L. Excess suicide among formerly hospitalized child psychiatric patients. *Journal of Clinical Psychiatry,* 1988, 49(3), 88–93.

Le, C. T., & Price, M. Survival from spinal cord injuries. *Journal of Chronic Diseases,* 1982, 35, 487–492.

Lester, D. Suicide and disease. *Archives of the Foundation of Thanatology,* 1988a, 14(3), unpaged.

Lester, D. Suicide and AIDS. *Archives of the Foundation of Thanatology,* 1988b, 14(4), unpaged.

Levitan, H. Suicidal trends in patients with asthma and hypertension. *Psychotherapy & Psychosomatics,* 1983, 39, 165–170.

Lin, E. H., Von Korff, M., & Wagner, E. H. Identifying suicide potential in primary care. *Journal of General Internal Medicine,* 1989, 4(1), 1–6.

Lipton, R. B., Choy-Kwong, M., & Solomon, S. Headaches in hospitalized cocaine users. *Headache,* 1989, 29, 225–227.

Marshall, J., Burnett, W., & Brasure, J. On precipitating factors. *Suicide & Life-Threatening Behavior,* 1983, 13, 15–27.

Marzuk, P. M., Tierney, H., Tardiff, K., Gross, E. M., Morgan, E. B., Hsu, M. A., & Mann, J. Increased risk of suicide in persons with AIDS. *Journal of the American Medical Association,* 1988, 259, 1333–1337.

Mastromauro, C., Myers, R. H., & Berkman, B. Attitudes toward presymptomatic testing in Huntington's disease. *American Journal of Medical Genetics,* 1987, 26, 271–282.

Matas, A., Simmons, R., Buselmeier, T., Kjellstrand, C., & Najarian, J. The fate of patients surviving three years after renal transplants. *Surgery,* 1976, 80, 390–395.

Matthews, W., & Barabas, G. Suicide and epilepsy. *Psychosomatics,* 1981, 22, 515–524.

Mendez, M. F., Lanska, D. J., Manon-Espaillat, R., & Burnstone, T. H. Causative factors for suicide attempts by overdose in epileptics. *Archives of Neurology,* 1989, 46, 1065–1068.

Motto, J. Suicide risk factors in alcohol abuse. *Suicide & Life-Threatening Behavior,* 1980, 10, 230–238.

Murphy, D. The self-poisoner. *Public Health,* 1982, 96, 148–154.

Nehemkis, A. M., & Groot, H. Indirect self-destructive behavior in spinal cord injury. In N. L. Farberow (Ed.) *The Many Faces of Suicide.* New York: McGraw-Hill, 1980, 99–115.

Nyquist, R. H., & Bors, E. Mortality and survival in traumatic myelopathy during 19 years from 1946 to 1965. *Paraplegia,* 1967, 5(1), 22–48.

Olafsen, O. Suicide among cancer patients in Norway. In J. P. Soubrier & J. Vedrinne (Eds.) *Depression and Suicide.* Paris: Pergamon, 1983, 587–591.

Plott, R T., Benton, S. D., & Winslade, W. J. Suicide of AIDs patients in Texas. *Texas Medicine,* 1989, 85(8), 40–43.

Prior, P., Gyde, S., Cooke, W., Waterhouse, J., & Allan, R. Mortality in Crohn's disease. *Gastroenterology,* 1981, 80, 307–312.

Radford, E., Doll, R., & Smith, P. Mortality among patients with ankylosing spondylitis not given x-ray therapy. *New England Journal of Medicine,* 1977, 297, 572–576.

Rundell, J. R., Hebert, F. E., & Brown, G. R. Use of home test kits for HIV is bad medicine. *Journal of the American Medical Association,* 1989, 262, 2385–2386.

Schoenfeld, M., Myers, R., Cupples, L., Berkman, B., Sax, D., & Clark, E. Increased rate of suicide among patients with Huntington's disease. *Journal of Neurology, Neurosurgery & Psychiatry,* 1984, 47, 1283–1287.

Shukla, G. D., Sahu, S. C., Tripathi, R. P., & Gupta, D. K. A psychiatric study of amputees. *British Journal of Psychiatry,* 1982, 141, 50–53.

Shulman, R., Turnbull, I. M., & Diewold, P. Psychiatric aspects of thalamic stimulation for neuropathic pain. *Pain,* 1982, 13, 127–135.

Siegel, K., & Tuckel, P. Rational suicide and the terminally ill cancer patient. *Omega,* 1984–1985, 15, 263–269.

Simon, A. B., Kleinman, P., & Janz, N. Suicide attempt by pacemaker abuse. *PACE,* 1980, 3, 224–228.

Smith, M. D., Hong, B., & Robson, A. M. Diagnosis of depression in patients with end-stage renal disease. *American Journal of Medicine,* 1985, 79, 160–166.

Stensman, R., & Sundqvist-Stensman, U. Physical disease and disability among 416 suicide cases in Sweden. *Scandinavian Journal of Social Medicine,* 1988, 16, 149–153.

Teta, M., Del Po, M., Kasl, S., Meigs, J., Myers, M., & Mulvihill, J. Psychosocial consequences of childhood and adolescent cancer survival. *Journal of Chronic Diseases,* 1986, 39, 751–759.

Tokudome, S., Kono, S., Ikeda, M., Kuratsune, M., & Kumamaru, S. Cancer and other causes of death among leprosy patients. *Journal of the National Cancer Institute,* 1981, 67, 285–289.

Tribe, C. R. Causes of death in the early state stages of paraplegia. *Paraplegia,* 1963, 1(1), 19–47.

Tweed, D. L., Shern, D. L., & Ciarlo, J. A. Disability, dependency and demoralization. *Rehabilitation Psychology,* 1988, 33, 143–154.

Vassilas, C. A. Parasuicide and appendectomy. *British Journal of Psychiatry,* 1988, 152, 706–709.

Von Knorring, L. The experience of pain in depressed patients. *Neuropsychobiology,* 1975, 1(3), 155–165.

Wandrei, K. E. Identifying potential suicides among high-risk women. *Social Work,* 1985, 30, 511–517.

Washer, G., Schroter, G., Starzl, T., & Weil, R. Causes of death after kidney transplantation. *Journal of the American Medical Association,* 1983, 250, 49–54.

Westlund, K. Mortality of peptic ulcer patients. *Acta Medica Scandinavica,* 1963, 174 (suppl. 402), 1–99.

Whitlock, F. The neurology of affect disorder and suicide. *Australian & New Zealand Journal of Psychiatry,* 1982, 16, 1–12.

Whitlock, F. Suicide and physical illness. In A. Roy (Ed.) *Suicide.* Baltimore: Williams & Wilkins, 1986, 151–170.

Wilcox, N., & Stauffer, E. Follow-up of 423 consecutive patients admitted to the spinal cord center. *Paraplegia,* 1972, 10, 115–122.

Zautra, A. J., Maxwell, B., & Reich, J. Relationship among physical impairment, distress and well-being in older adults. *Journal of Behavioral Medicine,* 1989, 12, 543–557.

Zielinski, J. Epilepsy and mortality rate and cause of death. *Epilepsia,* 1974, 15, 191–201.

Chapter 20

SUGGESTION AND SUICIDE

There are two main sources of evidence for the impact of suggestion on suicidal behavior: clustering in suicidal actions and the effect of media reporting of suicides on suicidal actions.

Clusters of Suicide

Coleman (1987) documented many suicide clusters in history and in recent years. Several papers have also presented particular clusters of suicide: by burning in England and Wales (Ashton and Donan, 1981), of adolescents in a hospital (Kaminer, 1986), of attempted suicide during cold weather in New Brunswick, Canada (Kubacki et al. 1986), of teenage suicides (Lester, 1987), of adolescents on one native American reservation (Tower, 1989), and of attempted suicide by burning in schizophrenics in a psychiatric hospital (Zemishlany et al., 1987).

Brent et al. (1989) examined the students involved in a cluster of attempted suicide and suicidal ideation after a student completed suicide in one school and found that those involved had been more suicidal in the past and more often had suffered from an episode of a major depressive disorder. Those involved who were close friends of the victim showed less pathology (for example, were less often diagnosed as having had an affective disorder) than those who knew the victim less well. In a cluster of suicides among physicians on probation in Oregon, Crawshaw et al. (1980) found that all were psychiatrically disturbed.

Davidson et al. (1989) examined two clusters of teenage suicides in Texas and found that the suicides had been more suicidal in the past, had recently experienced breakups with girl/boyfriends, had switched schools more often, had been arrested more and had lived with more parental figures. They were not more likely to know someone who had attempted or completed suicide or to be more aware of the suicide cluster.

Epidemics

Although not the same as a cluster, an epidemic of suicide does have some similarities. For example, Rubinstein (1983) documented that, whereas up to 1965 in Micronesia almost no adolescents completed suicide, two adolescent suicides in Ebeye in 1967 were followed by 25 more in the next twelve years.

Statistical Tests of Clustering

Church and Phillips (1984) found nine completed suicides using plastic bags in a town in England and found that there was significant clustering. Davis and Hardy (1986) examined five clusters of teenage suicide in Texas and found that three fitted the mathematical model for an epidemic while two did not. Medestin and Wurmle (1989) examined the suicides in two Swiss psychiatric hospitals and found no evidence for clustering.

Kirch and Lester (1986b) looked at completed suicide by plastic bags in the study by Church and Phillips (1984) and found statistical evidence for clustering if 90-day or 150-day intervals were chosen but not for 30- or 120-day intervals. For suicides from the Golden Gate Bridge, they found no evidence for clustering for any chosen time period (Kirch and Lester, 1987a).

Lewis and Brockett (1980) explored spatial clustering of completed suicides by asphyxiation in Cleveland over a two-year period and found that cases in 1974 were no closer spatially to other cases in 1974 than they were to cases in 1973. Thus, there appeared to be no spatiotemporal clustering. Wallenstein et al. (1989) looked at adolescent suicides in the counties of the USA with large adolescent populations and found that significant time-space clustering occurred, but only for a small number. (1.3% of the adolescent suicides studied clustered beyond the amount predicted by chance.)

The Effects of Publicized Suicides

Television News

Bollen and Phillips (1982) found that national television coverage of suicide stories of specific individuals led to increases in the suicide rate in the following week.

Kessler et al. (1989) studied the effect of television news stories on suicide in the US and found no increase in the total number of completed suicides or in teenage suicides in the following week. (Teenage suicides increased in the following week from 1973–1980 but decreased in the following week for 1981–1984.) Restricting the study to television news stories of teenage suicides produced the same results.

Phillips (1980) found that murder-suicide stories in the US in newspaper or on television were followed by an increase in the next ten days in multi-fatality plane crashes (but not in single-fatality plane crashes). The amount of newspaper publicity was associated with the number of multi-fatality crashes but the amount of television coverage was not. The same phenomenon was found for commercial plane crashes, in terms of an increase in the number of crashes and the number of fatalities per crash, and the increases were proportional to the amount of publicity.

Phillips and Carstensen (1986) found that there was an increase in teenage suicides in the US in the week following a televised news story about suicide. The more networks carrying the story, the larger the increase. The increase was larger in teenagers than in adults, and larger in female teenagers than in male teenagers. There was no increase in undetermined or accidental deaths due to guns or poisons. The authors could find no evidence for a subsequent dip in the suicide rate, and there was no effect from television news stories about other causes of death.

In California, Phillips and Carstensen (1988) found a significant increase in both male and female suicides after a television news story about suicide. Phillips et al. (1989) found no effect from the content of the story, for example, whether a photograph of the suicide was shown, the method reported, or whether the suicide was American or overseas, a celebrity or not, or male versus female.

Horton and Stack (1984) looked at the monthly suicide rate and the seconds of coverage of suicide stories on the national television news each month from 1972–1980. In a multiple regression analysis, the duration of unemployment and spring were significantly associated with suicide rates, but the divorce rate and the television coverage of suicide were not.

Stack (1989) found that television news on mass gangland murder/suicides had an impact on monthly suicide rates, but not news of snipers/suicides, serial murder/suicides or political murder/suicides.

Newsworthy Events

Stack (1983) found that the mass suicide at Jonestown had no impact on the monthly suicide rate in the US. However, a daily analysis showed that the suicide rate dipped during the coverage, but only for females (Stack, 1988).

Television Films

Gould and Shaffer (1986) found that television films about suicide led to an increase in teenage completed and attempted suicide in the two weeks afterwards in the New York City area. Extending the study to four cities, Gould et al. (1988) found increases in New York City and Cleveland, but not in Dallas or Los Angeles. However, trying to replicate these results using the same movies, Phillips and Paight (1987) failed to find an increase in teenage suicides in Pennsylvania or California. Ostroff et al. (1985; Ostroff and Boyd, 1987) found an increase in the number of adolescent suicide attempts to one hospital after a television movie depicting a teenage suicide, and they found that all of the attempters had watched the show.

Kessler and Stipp (1984) examined the daily number of completed suicides and television fictionalized stories about suicide using a multiple regression analysis over days and found no significant effect, overall, for men and women, and for urban and rural areas. They did find some evidence for a drop in fatalities from single motor vehicle crashes.

Berman (1988) examined the effect of three television films about teenage suicide on the suicide rates of adolescents in 21 cities. The suicide rates two weeks before and two weeks after the films were similar. One film, however, did show suicide by carbon monoxide, and there was an increase in carbon monoxide suicides in youths after this film.

In Newcastle (England), Fowler (1986) found an increase in attempted suicides immediately following an attempted suicide depicted on television. Sandler et al. (1986) reported an increase in overdoses in their region too. Williams et al. (1987) found an increase in attempted suicides after the episode in two hospitals but noted that the attempted suicide rate was rising in these hospitals before the episode. Platt (1987) examined more general the impact of this attempted suicide (by an overdose in a London female in a British soap opera) and found an increase in attempted suicides by overdoses in the following days. This increase was found in women only and the increase was greater the further the hospitals were from London. Platt was not, however, convinced of a suggestion effect in his data.

In Germany, Schmidtke and Hafner (1988) found that a suicide of a 19-year-old male in a television film led to an increase in suicides by the same method (jumping in front of a train) for the next 70 days, but only in teenagers and younger adults (and especially in those aged 15–19).

Phillips (1982) found that suicides on soap operas were followed by an increase in suicides in the next week, motor vehicle fatalities and, in California (where data were available), non-fatal car crashes. The increase was stronger in urban areas and for females.

Newspaper Coverage

Littmann (1985) found no impact from newspaper reports of all types of suicides on the frequency of suicides in the Toronto subway in the following 21 days after the newspaper report. In Detroit, Bollen and Phillips (1981) found that newspaper publicity about suicides led to an increase in motor vehicle fatalities on the third day after the publicity, and they suggested that these fatalities may be covert suicides.

In a monthly time-series multiple regression analysis, Stack (1987) found that only suicides by celebrities and American politicians had an impact on the monthly suicide rate in the US. There was no impact for foreigners, villains, or artists. The same difference was found when Stack examined the impact of the number of column inches. Looking at the motives of the suicides, the suggestion effect was found for suicides after divorce and if psychiatrically disturbed but not for suicide as a result of physical illness. Wasserman (1984) looked at newspaper coverage of suicide also in a monthly time-series multiple regression analysis from 1948 to 1977 and found that celebrity suicides had a significant impact on the suicide rate while non-celebrity suicides did not. During the first part of this Century, Stack (1988) found that publicized suicide stories had an impact on monthly suicide rates only during peacetime.

Discussion

There is growing interest in clusters of suicides, and investigators are beginning to develop ways of showing whether suicides close together in time are truly clusters. Research is also beginning to identify the particular characteristics of those suicides which occur in clusters.

The 1980s have witnessed several replications of the suggestion effect

from media coverage of suicide and from fictional suicides presented on
television which David Phillips documented in the 1970s. As yet, however,
little research has appeared to identify the kinds of people whose suicidal behavior is elicited by such media coverage. This would appear to be
a promising area of study for the 1990s.

REFERENCES

Ashton, J., & Donnan, S. Suicide by burning as an epidemic phenomenon. *Psychological Medicine,* 1981, 11, 735–739.

Berman, A. L. Fictional depiction of suicide in television films and imitation effects. *American Journal of Psychiatry,* 1988, 145, 982–986.

Bollen, K., & Phillips, D. P. Suicidal motor vehicle fatalities in Detroit. *American Journal of Sociology,* 1981, 87, 404–412.

Bollen, K., & Phillips, D. P. Imitative suicides. *American Sociological Review,* 1982, 47, 802–809.

Brent, D. A., Kerr, M. M., Goldstein, C., Bozigar, J., Wartella, M., & Allan, M. J. An outbreak of suicide and suicidal behavior in a high school. *Journal of the American Academy of Child & Adolescent Psychiatry,* 1989, 28, 918–924.

Church, I. C., & Phillips, J. P. Suggestion and suicide by plastic bag asphyxia. *British Journal of Psychiatry,* 1984, 144, 100–101.

Coleman, L. *Suicide clusters.* Boston: Faber & Faber, 1987.

Crawshaw, R., Bruce, J., Eraker, P., Greenbaum, M., Lindeman, J., & Schmidt, D. An epidemic of suicide among physicians on probation. *Journal of the American Medical Association,* 1980, 243, 1915–1917.

Davidson, L. E., Rosenberg, M. L., Mercy, J. A., Franklin, J., & Simmons, J. T. An epidemiological study of risk factors in two teenage suicide clusters. *Journal of the American Medical Association,* 1989, 262, 2687–2692.

Davis, B. R., & Hardy, R. J. A suicide epidemic model. *Social Biology,* 1986, 33, 291–300.

Fowler, B. P. Emotional crises imitating television. *Lancet,* 1986, 1, 1036–1037.

Gould, M. S., & Shaffer, D. The impact of suicide in television movies. *New England Journal of Medicine,* 1986, 315, 690–694.

Gould, M. S., Shaffer, D., & Kleinman, M. The impact of suicide in television movies. *Suicide & Life-Threatening Behavior,* 1988, 18, 90–99.

Horton, H., & Stack, S. The effect of television on national suicide rates. *Journal of Social Psychology,* 1984, 123, 141–142.

Kaminer, Y. Suicidal behavior among hospitalized adolescents. *New England Journal of Medicine,* 1986, 315, 1030.

Kessler, R. C., Downey, G., Stipp, H., & Milavsky, J. R. Network television news stories about suicide and short-term changes in the total US suicides. *Journal of Nervous & Mental Disease,* 1989, 177, 551–555.

Kessler, R. C., & Stipp, H. The impact of fictional television suicide stories on US fatalities. *American Journal of Sociology,* 1984, 90, 151–167.

Kirch, M., & Lester, D. Suicide from the Golden Gate Bridge. *Psychological Reports,* 1986a, 59, 1314.

Kirch, M., & Lester, D. Clusters of suicide. *Psychological Reports,* 1986b, 59, 1126.

Kubacki, A., Boyle, B., & Baldwin, J. Suicide weather? *Canadian Journal of Psychiatry,* 1986, 31, 602–604.

Lester, D. A subcultural theory of teenage suicide. *Adolescence,* 1987, 22, 317–320.

Lewis, M., & Brockett, P. Spatial relationships among epidemiological and community populations. *Psychological Bulletin,* 1980, 88, 296–306.

Littmann, S. Suicide epidemics and newspaper reporting. *Suicide & Life-Threatening Behavior,* 1985, 15, 43–50.

Modestin, J., & Wurmle, O. Role of modelling in inpatient suicide. *British Journal of Psychiatry,* 1989, 155, 511–514.

Ostroff, R., Behrends, R., Lee, K., & Oliphant, J. Adolescent suicides modelled after a television movie. *American Journal of Psychiatry,* 1985, 142, 989.

Ostroff, R., & Boyd, J. H. Television and suicide. *New England Journal of Medicine,* 1987, 316, 876–878.

Phillips, D. P. Airplane accidents, murder and the mass media. *Social Forces,* 1980, 58, 1001–1024.

Phillips, D. P. The impact of fictional television stories on US adult fatalities. *American Journal of Sociology,* 1982, 87, 1340–1359.

Phillips, D. P., & Carstensen, L. L. Clustering of teenage suicides after television news stories about suicide. *New England Journal of Medicine,* 1986, 315, 685–689.

Phillips, D. P., & Carstensen, L. L. The effect of suicide stories on various demographic groups, 1968–1985. *Suicide & Life-Threatening Behavior,* 1988, 18, 100–114.

Phillips, D. P., Carstensen, L. L., & Paight, D. J. Effect of mass media news stories on suicide, with new evidence on the role of story content. In C. R. Pfeffer (Ed.) *Suicide Among Youth.* Washington, DC: American Psychiatric Press, 1989, 101–116.

Phillips, D. P., & Paight, D. J. The impact of televised movies about suicide. *New England Journal of Medicine,* 1987, 317, 809–811.

Platt, S. D. The aftermath of Angie's overdose. *British Medical Journal,* 1987, 294, 954–957.

Rubinstein, D. Epidemic suicide among Micronesian adolescents. *Social Science & Medicine,* 1983, 17, 657–665.

Sandler, D. A., Connell, P. A., & Welsh, K. Emotional crises imitating television. *Lancet,* 1986, 1, 856.

Schmidtke, A., & Hafner, H. The Werther effect after television films. *Psychological Medicine,* 1988, 18, 665–676.

Stack, S. The effect of the Jonestown suicides on American suicide rates. *Journal of Social Psychology,* 1983, 119, 145–146.

Stack, S. Celebrities and suicide. *American Sociological Review,* 1987, 52, 401–412.

Stack, S. The effect of Jonestown on suicide perception and behavior. In F. McGehee & R. Moore (Eds.) *Ten Years After Jonestown.* Lewiston, NY: Edwin Mellon Press, 1988, 133–148.

Stack, S. Suicide. *Suicide & Life-Threatening Behavior,* 1988, 18, 342–257.

Stack, S. The effect of publicized mass murder and murder-suicides on lethal violence. *Social Psychiatry*, 1989, 24, 202–208.

Tower, M. A suicide epidemic in an American Indian community. *American Indian and Alaskan Native Mental Health Research*, 1989, 3(1), 34–44.

Wallenstein, S., Gould, M., & Kleinman, M. Use of the scan statistic to detect time-space clustering. *American Journal of Epidemiology*, 1989, 130, 1057–1064.

Wasserman, I. Imitation and suicide. *American Sociological Review*, 1984, 49, 427–436.

Williams, J. M., Lawton, C., Ellis, S., Walsh, S., & Reed, J. Copycat suicide. *Lancet*, 1987, 2, 102–103.

Zemishlany, Z., Weinberger, A., Ben-Bassat, M., & Mell, H. An epidemiology of suicide attempts by burning in a psychiatric hospital. *British Journal of Psychiatry*, 1987, 150, 704–706.

Chapter 21

SUICIDE AND AGGRESSION

The association between suicide and homicide was first explored by Henry and Short (1954) in their theory of suicide, and Lester (1987a) has continued to explore this association.

Anger And Aggression in Suicidal People

Aggression in Completed Suicides

Wandrei (1986) found that female suicide attempters who subsequently completed suicide showed more acting-out of anger than attempters who did not kill themselves, but they were also more psychiatrically disturbed.

Aggression in Suicide Attempters

A number of studies have reported an excess of anger or aggression in suicidal subjects. Drug addicts who had attempted suicide had higher levels of anger than those who had not attempted suicide (Harris et al., 1979). Currently suicidal schizophrenics and those who had previously attempted suicide had been more assaultive than other schizophrenics (Berk, 1949).

Rutstein (1971) compared female attempted suicides and psychiatric patients for their response to subliminal aggressive stimuli. After the subliminal aggressive stimuli, the attempted suicides showed increased depression whereas the controls did not. When the stimuli were shown supraliminally, the attempted suicides showed an increase in outward-aggression scores, whereas the controls did not.

Husain and Vandiver (1984) analyzed case studies of children and adolescents in the literature who had completed, attempted or threatened suicide. Those aged 4–8 were more aggressive than the older children, who showed withdrawal and delinquent behavior more.

Lester (1988) found that college students who had attempted suicide obtained higher indirect hostility scores (but similar assault and verbal hostility scores) to equally depressed non-suicidal students. Lester and Lindsley (1988) found that college students who had attempted suicide had higher inward irritability (but no difference in outward irritability) than equally depressed non-suicidal students. Those who had threatened suicide in the past had high inward and outward irritability.

Bland and Orn (1986) found that attempted suicide in a community sample was associated with family violence in general and with being a child neglector.

In contrast, Ellis et al. (1989) found no differences in hostility between psychiatric inpatients who had attempted suicide and those who had not.

The Direction of Aggression

Waugh (1974) found no differences between attempted suicides and non-suicidal psychiatric patients in their scores on the Rosenzweig Picture-Frustration Test. However, the attempters judged to be dependent-dissatisfied were more extrapunitive, those judged to be satisfied-symbiotic more intropunitive and those judged to be unaccepting were more impunitive. Schwartzburd (1972) found that adolescent suicide attempters (some of whom were delinquents) were more intropunitive and less extrapunitive than assaultive delinquents.

Farmer and Creed (1986) found that attempted suicides scored higher than norms on a test of extrapunition and intropunition. They did not differ from the norms on the direction of their hostility. Depressed suicide attempters were both more extrapunitive and more intropunitive but did not differ in the urge to act out their hostility or the direction of their hostility. Suicidal intent was associated with intropunition but not extrapunition. Repeaters had more intropunition and the urge to act out their hostility but not more extrapunition. Farmer and Creed (1989) found that extrapunitive attempters had experienced more recent legal problems and more severely stressful events, while intropunitive attempters had experienced more recent job loss and less severely stressful events.

Goldberg and Sakinofsky (1988) found that intropunitiveness (but not locus of control scores) predicted improvement in depression as a result of therapy in a sample of attempted suicides.

Suicidal Ideation and Aggression

Suicidal ideation in psychiatric patients was associated with homicidal ideas (Altman et al., 1971). Berger (1987) found that trait anger was associated with suicidal risk in a sample of university counseling students.

Evans et al. (1985) found that scores on a measure of anger were associated with suicidal ideation in college students but only for some groups (females and engineering students, not males and arts students).

Kashani et al. (1989) found that adolescents in the community with current suicidal ideation were more likely to use verbal aggression as a conflict resolution tactic (but did not differ from non-suicidal children in the use of reasoning or violence). They were also more depressed, anxious and impulsive and showed more conduct disorders.

Plutchik and van Praag (1986) found that suicidal risk, impulsivity and scores on a violence-risk scale were all associated in a sample of psychiatric inpatients. Controlling for violence risk, suicide risk was associated with depression, hopelessness, psychiatric symptoms, life problems, and family violence. Controling for suicidal risk, violence risk was associated with impulsivity, menstrual problems, recent stress and legal problems.

Goldberg (1981) found that people in the community aged 18–24 with little or a lot of prior suicidal ideation were more likely to have shown overt aggression in the prior week, while those with no suicidal ideation or a moderate amount showed less overt aggression. (The suicidal young adults also had more symptoms of depression and mild psychiatric disturbance.)

Yesavage (1983a, 1983b) found that the presence of self-destructive behavior in psychiatric patients was positively associated with the indirect aggression, irritability, negativism and verbal assault scores on the Buss and Durkee hostility inventory and negatively with the resentment and suspicion scores. Over an eight-day period, the incidence of self-destructive behavior in patients was positively associated with an overall measure of indirect hostility from the hostility inventory (but not with an overall measure of direct hostility).

In contrast, Myers et al. (1985) compared suicidal children who were psychiatric inpatients with non-suicidal inpatients and found no differences in assaultiveness or a history of conduct disorder. However, the non-assaultive suicidal children were more seriously suicidal than the assaultive suicidal children.

Suicide Attempters Versus Assaultive Persons

Maiuro et al. (1989) compared attempted suicides with assaultive psychiatric patients. The attempters had the higher depression scores. On a direction of hostility test, both groups were high on extrapunition, but the attempters were also high on intropunition. On the Buss and Durkee hostility inventory, the assaultive patients were high on all scales (overt hostility, covert hostility, assault, indirect hostility, resentment, guilt and suspicion, and verbal hostility), while the attempters were high only on covert hostility, indirect hostility, guilt, suspicion, and resentment. After controls for depression, the assaultive patients still scored higher on overt, assaultive and verbal aggression.

Moesler and Weidenhammer (1989) compared completed suicides, attempted suicides and those convicted of assault in Nuremberg. The assaultive individuals and attempted suicides were similar in age, unemployment and the proportion of foreigners, but both of these groups differed from the completed suicides. The three groups, however, had different regional distributions.

Completed Versus Attempted Suicides

Pallis et al. (1982) found that attempted suicides had been more physically violent to other in recent months than had completed suicides, and they had shown more irritability and anger. Biro and Lazic (1988) found that an aggressive personality distinguished between completed and attempted suicides.

Murder and Suicide

The research on the relationship between suicide and murder has been reviewed in depth by Lester (1987a). Here we will examine only the recent research on this issue.

Studies of Murder-Suicide

Wong and Singer (1973) found a lower percentage of murder-suicide in Hong Kong murderers than in Philadelphia or British murderers. Hansen and Bjarneson (1974) reported that, over a 25-year period in Iceland, 16 percent of murderers completed suicide and 11 percent attempted suicide. Berman (1979) found that 1.5 percent of suicides were murder-suicides. These suicides were more often male and used guns than the other suicides. Their victims were more likely to be family members or lovers, female and white, and less likely to have been drinking than were other murder victims.

In a study of prisoners, Hafner and Boker (1973) found murder/suicide to be more common in females with a diagnosis of depression who had typically killed their children or spouse.

In Iceland in this century, Petursson and Gudjonsson (1981) reported that 8.5 percent of murderers completed suicide. Allen (1983a, 1983b) found that 2 percent of homicides in Los Angeles were followed by suicide and 14 percent of these left suicide notes. The offenders were mainly men, over 40 years of age, typically killing women who were wives or girlfriends. There were two major types: (1) after a quarrel with jealousy involved and (2) older men who had physical illnesses and who were depressed.

Copeland (1985) found that murder-suicides included very few double suicides (only 5 percent) and accounted for 2.3 percent of the murders and 3.1 percent of the suicides. The murderers were more often male and the victims females. The men were often intoxicated and killing wives or girlfriends who were younger than them.

Coid (1983) reviewed research by others and found that the percentage of murderers who completed suicide ranged from 3.6 percent (in Philadelphia) to 67.8 percent (in Israel among Western Jews). The rate of murder-suicide ranged from 0.06 (per 100,000 per year) in Iceland to 0.40 in Western Jews in Israel. Coid argued that the higher the rate of homicide, the lower the percentage of murderers who complete suicide (and his data support this). The rate of murder-suicide was not related to either the homicide rate or the abnormal homicide rate.

Fishbain et al. (1985) found that women who perpetrated a murder-suicide differed from female victims of such acts in living more often in mobile homes, more often killing a lover on a weekend, with an accidental discovery, leaving a suicide note, more often depressed and less often killing a spouse. Compared to female suicides, the female perpetrators of murder-suicides were more often living with a lover, with less of a history of depression, and more often living in a mobile home. (They did not differ in age, season of birth, race, religion, marital status, employment status, method for suicide, drugs or alcohol in the blood, previous psychiatric history, or previous police record.)

Gottlieb et al. (1987) found that 30 percent of murderers committed suicide in Denmark (though a far smaller percentage in the capital, Copenhagen). The rate of murder-suicide in Denmark from 1946–1970 was 2.04 per 100,000 per year and the homicide rate 3.72. The murder-suicides were older and more often killing close relatives (men killing wives and women killing children).

Palmer and Humphrey (1980) compared murder-suicides with other murders. The victim of a murder-suicide was more often a family member, white and a woman killed by a man. The murderer was older, more often older than the victim and more often white. The typical murder-suicide was a married white male over the age of 30, killing a wife.

In France, Santoro et al. (1985) identified 18 cases of murder-suicide, comprising 9 percent of the cases of murder and attempted murder. Most murder-suicides were committed by men who committed suicide right after the murder using the same method for killing and who were closely involved or related to the victim.

Lester (1987b) found that murderers of police officers had a very high suicide rate (3,430 per 100,000 per year), and the typical murder-suicide was a young white male.

Murderers Versus Other Offenders

Langevin et al. (1982) found that murderers and non-violent offenders had similar histories of attempted suicide. Having a history of attempted suicide was associated in the murderers with substance abuse, recent frustrations and having a lack of memory for the murder. Attempting suicide after the murder (which occurred in 11 percent of the murderers) was positively related to job strain and negatively to psychiatric diagnosis. Jarvinen (1977) found that murderers had more suicidal ideation than assaulters.

Murderers Versus Suicides

Jarvinen (1977) compared male murderers and assaulters with female attempted suicides, thus confounding sex and type of aggression. The attempted suicides obtained higher outward and inward-directed aggression on the TAT, were more depressed, and were more hostile on the Rorschach inkblot test.

Sociological Studies

De Castro et al. (1986) found no association between suicide and homicide rates in Portugal from 1970–1982. Over time in the US, Holinger (1987) found that suicide rates were positively associated with death rates from homicide, motor vehicle accidents and other accidents. However, the size and the direction of the associations differed by race. Wilbanks (1982) found no association between suicide and homicide rates over SMSAs in the US, but the association was positive over time in Dade

County and in the US as a whole. Over time in Finland, Kivela (1985) found no association between the homicide and suicide rates of the elderly.

Violent Offenders and Patients

Achte et al. (1983) compared chronically suicidal offenders with acutely suicidal violent offenders (all of whom had attempted suicide) seen at a forensic-psychiatric unit. The chronically suicidal offenders reported more chronic violence, excessive use of alcohol, paternal deprivation, violent parents, school problems, and prior suicide attempts. The acutely suicidal offenders had more often experienced the threat of the loss of a close relationship and, though they quarreled less with the victim, had a more intense relationship with the victim.

Barber et al. (1988) looked at the most assaultive patients in a state hospital and found that the non-psychotic patients showed more self-injurious behavior. Berglund and Tunving (1985) found that assaultive and suicidal alcoholics subsequently completed suicide at a slightly higher rate than non-suicidal/non-assaultive alcoholics.

Cairns et al. (1988) found that violent/aggressive youths who had attempted suicide did not differ in the severity of their aggression or the type of victim (parent versus other) from non-suicidal violent youths.

Hafner and Boker (1982) found no differences in prior acts of attempted suicide between mentally abnormal violent offenders and psychiatric patients. The violent offenders had threatened suicide more. After the crime, 10.6 percent of the male violent offenders and 8.5 percent of the women attempted suicide, not a significant difference. Murdering as part of a murder-suicide was more common in the women than in the men. The women were typically depressed and killing their children along with themselves.

Krakowski et al. (1989) found that persistently violent psychiatric inpatients were more likely to have attempted suicide in the past than transiently violent and non-violent inpatients.

Kermani (1981) described two types of violent psychiatric patients. The violent-depressive type, a chronic condition, was more likely to have attempted suicide and, in addition, was more likely to be a drug or alcohol abuser and to be homicidal. The assaultive psychotic type, an acute condition, was delusional but came from a relatively normal home and had no history of suicide.

Myers and Dunner (1984) found that psychiatric patients who assaulted others were older and more often psychotic than those who were violent toward themselves. The self-violent patients more often had depressive and personality disorders. Both groups, however, were more likely to be substance abusers than other patients.

Tardiff (1981) found that 45 percent of psychiatric inpatients who had attempted suicide in the past three months had also assaulted others. The assaulters were younger and had more seizures, but did not differ in sex, race, diagnosis, length of stay, hallucinations or depression. Tardiff and Sweillam (1980a) studied attempters and ideators and found that more of the male patients were also assaultive. The assaultive suicidal patients more often had schizophrenic symptoms, disturbed relationships with family members and others, and more anger/agitation. They did not differ in depression or obsessions. In a study of over nine thousand psychiatric inpatients, Tardiff and Sweillam (1980b) found that suicidality and assaultiveness were associated in the men but not in the women. For the men the assaultive/suicidal patients resembled the suicidal patients more in psychiatric diagnosis than the assaultive patients, whereas for the women the assaultive/suicidal patients resembled the assaultive patients more than the suicidal patients.

However, among psychotic children, Inamdar et al. (1982) found no association between violence and suicidality (attempts or threats).

Discussion

Research in the 1980s continued to show that, on occasions, suicidality is associated with violence. Research is needed to ascertain whether this is a general phenomenon or whether it pertains only to some individuals. In the latter case, we need to know for which individuals the association is found. What role do intrapsychic and situational variables play in this association, and what insights does this give us into the nature of suicide? For example, can suicide be simply a result of poor impulse control in general for some individuals?

REFERENCES

Achte, K., Lonnqvust, J., & Waloranta, O. Suicidal tendencies in violent individuals. In J. P. Soubrier & J. Vedrinne (Eds.) *Depression and Suicide.* Paris: Pergamon, 1983, 245–249.

Allen, N. H. Homicide followed by suicide. In J. P. Soubrier & J. Vedrinne (Ed.) *Depression and Suicide.* Paris: Pergamon, 1983a, 250–254.

Allen, N. H. Homicide followed by suicide. *Suicide & Life-Threatening Behavior,* 1983b, 13, 155–165.

Altman, H., Sletten, I. V., Eaton, M. E., & Ulett, G. A. Demographic and mental status profiles. *Psychiatric Quarterly,* 1971, 45, 57–64.

Barber, J. W., Hundley, P., Kellogg, E., Glick, J. L., Godleski, L., Kerler, R., & Viewey, W. R. Clinical and demographic characteristics of 15 patients with repetitively assaultive behavior. *Psychiatric Quarterly,* 1988, 59, 213–224.

Berger, A. L. Suicide probability, cognitive style and affect in college students. In R. Yufit (Ed.) *Proceedings of the 20th Annual Meeting.* Denver: AAS, 1987, 113–115.

Berk, N. A Personality Study of Suicidal Schizophrenics. Doctoral dissertation, New York University, 1949.

Berman, A. L. Dyadic death. *Suicide & Life-Threatening Behavior,* 1979, 9, 15–23.

Biro, M., & Lazic, P. Methodological problems of suicide prediction. *European Journal of Psychiatry,* 1988, 2, 233–240.

Bland, R., & Orn, H. Family violence and psychiatric disorder. *Canadian Journal of Psychiatry,* 1986, 31, 129–137.

Cairns, R. B., Peterson, G., & Neckerman, H. J. Suicidal behavior in aggressive adolescents. *Journal of Clinical Child Psychology,* 1988, 17, 298–309.

Coid, J. The epidemiology of abnormal homicide and murder followed by suicide. *Psychological Medicine,* 1983, 13, 855–860.

Copeland, A. R. Dyadic death revisited. *Journal of the Forensic Science Society,* 1985, 25, 181–188.

de Castro, E. F., Albino, L., & Martins, I. Relation between suicide and homicide in Portugal from 1970 to 1982. *Acta Psychiatrica Scandinavica,* 1986, 74, 425–432.

Ellis, T. E., Berg, R., & Franzen, M. Organic and cognitive deficits in suicidal patients. In D. Lester (Ed.) *Suicide '89.* Denver: AAS, 1989, 291–293.

Evans, A. L., Williams, J. L., & McKinnon, S. The relationship of hopelessness, depression, and anger to suicidal ideation in Canadian university students. In R. Cohen-Sandler (Ed.) *Proceedings of the 18th Annual Meeting.* Denver: AAS, 1985, 54–56.

Farmer, R. D., & Creed, F. Hostility and deliberate self-poisoning. *British Journal of Medical Psychology,* 1986, 59, 311–316.

Farmer, R. D., & Creed, F. Life events and hostility in self-poisoning. *British Journal of Psychiatry,* 1989, 154, 390–395.

Fishbain, D. A., Rao, V. J., & Aldrich, T. E. Female homicide-suicide perpetrators. *Journal of Forensic Sciences,* 1985, 30, 1148–1156.

Goldberg, E. Depression and suicidal ideation in the young adult. *American Journal of Psychiatry,* 1981, 138, 35–40.

Goldberg, J., & Sakinofsky, I. Intropunitiveness and parasuicide. *British Journal of Psychiatry,* 1988, 153, 801–804.

Gottlieb, P., Kramp, P., & Gabrielsen, G. The practice of forensic psychiatric in cases of homicide in Copenhagen 1959–1983. *Acta Psychiatrica Scandinavica,* 1987, 76, 514–522.

Hafner, H., & Boker, W. Mentally disordered violent offenders. *Social Psychiatry,* 1973, 8, 220–229.

Hafner, H., & Boker, W. *Crimes of Violence by Mentally Abnormal Offenders.* New York: Cambridge University, 1982.

Hansen, J., & Bjarneson, O. Homicide in Iceland. *Forensic Sciences,* 1974, 4, 107–117.

Harris, R., Linn, M. W., & Hunter, K. Suicide attempts among drug abusers. *Suicide & Life-Threatening Behavior,* 1979, 9, 25–32.

Henry, A. F., & Short, J. F. *Suicide and Homicide.* New York: Free Press, 1954.

Holinger, P. C. *Violent Deaths in the United States.* New York: Guilford, 1987.

Husain, S. A., & Vandiver, T. *Suicide in Children and Adolescents.* New York: Spectrum, 1984.

Inamdar, S., Lewis, D., Siomopoulos, G., Shanok, S., & Lamela, M. Violent and suicidal behavior in psychotic adolescents. *American Journal of Psychiatry,* 1982, 139, 932–935.

Jarvinen, L. *Personality Characteristics of Violent Offenders and Suicidal Individuals.* Helsinki: Finnish Academy of Science & Letters, 1977.

Kashani, J. H., Goddard, P., & Reid, J. C. Correlates of suicidal ideation in a community sample of children and adolescents. *Journal of the American Academy of Child & Adolescent Psychiatry,* 1989, 28, 912–917.

Kermani, E. Violent psychiatric patients. *American Journal of Psychotherapy,* 1981, 35, 215–225.

Kivela, S. L. Relationship between, suicide, homicide and accidental deaths among the aged in Finland in 1951–1979. *Acta Psychiatrica Scandinavica,* 1985, 72, 155–160.

Karkowski, M. I., Convit, A., Jaeger, J., Lin, S., & Volavka, J. Inpatient violence. *Journal of Psychiatric Research,* 1989, 23, 57–64.

Langevin, R., Paitich, D., Orchard, B., Handy, L., & Russon, A. The role of alcohol, drugs, suicide attempts and situation strains in homicide committed by offenders seen for psychiatric assessment. *Acta Psychiatrica Scandinavica,* 1982, 66, 229–242.

Lester, D. Murders and suicide. *Behavioral Sciences & the Law,* 1987a, 5, 49–60.

Lester, D. Murder followed by suicide in those who murder police officers. *Psychological Reports,* 1987b, 60, 1130.

Lester, D. Locus of control, anger and suicide. *Activitas Nervosa Superior,* 1988, 30, 315–316.

Lester, D., & Lindsley, L. K. Inward and outward irritability in the suicidally inclined. *Journal of General Psychology,* 1988, 115, 37–39.

Maiuro, R. D., O'Sullivan, M. J., Michael, M. C., & Vitaliano, P. P. Anger, hostility, and depression in assaultive versus suicide-attempting males. *Journal of Clinical Psychology,* 1989, 45, 531–541.

Moesler, T. A., & Weidenhammer, W. Suicide and aggression. In S. D. Platt & N. Kreitman (Eds.) *Current Research on Suicide and Parasuicide.* Edinburgh: University of Edinburgh, 1989, 123–132.

Myers, K. M., Burke, P., & McCauley, E. Suicidal behavior by hospitalized pre-adolescent children on a psychiatric unit. *Journal of the American Academy of Child Psychiatry,* 1985, 24, 474–480.

Myers, K. M., & Dunner, D. L. Self and other directed violence on a closed acute-care ward. *Psychiatric Quarterly,* 1984, 56, 178–188.

Pallis, D. J., Barraclough, B. M., Levey, A., Jenkins, J., & Sainsbury, P. Estimating suicide risk among attempted suicides. *British Journal of Psychiatry,* 1982, 141, 37–44.

Palmer, S., & Humphrey, J. A. Offender-victim relationships in criminal homicide followed by offender's suicide. *Suicide & Life-Threatening Behavior,* 1980, 10, 106–118.

Petursson, H., & Gudjonsson, G. H. Psychiatric aspects of homicide. *Acta Psychiatrica Scandinavica,* 1981, 64, 363–372.

Plutchik, R., & van Praag, H. The measurement of suicidality, aggressivity and impulsivity. *Clinical Neuropharmacology,* 1986, 9, supplement 4, 380–382.

Plutchik, R., van Praag, H., & Conte, H. Correlates of suicide and violence risk. *Psychiatry Research,* 1989, 28, 215–225.

Rutstein, E. H. The effects of aggressive stimulation on suicidal patients. *Dissertation Abstracts International,* 1971, 31B, 7611.

Santoro, J. P., Sawood, A. W., & Atral, G. The murder-suicide. *American Journal of Forensic Medicine & Pathology,* 1985, 6, 222–225.

Schwartzburd, L. Reliability and validity of the timed multiple response method of administering the Rosenzweig Picture-Frustration Study. *Dissertation Abstracts International,* 1972, 32B, 4228.

Tardiff, K. The risk of assaultive behavior in suicidal patients. *Acta Psychiatrica Scandinavica,* 1981, 64, 295–300.

Tardiff, K., & Sweillam, A. Factors related to increased risk of assaultive behavior in suicidal patients. *Acta Psychiatrica Scandinavica,* 1980a, 62, 63–68.

Tardiff, K., & Sweillam, A. Assault, suicide and mental illness. *Archives of General Psychiatry,* 1980b, 37, 164–169.

Wandrei, K. E. Identifying potential suicides among high-risk women. *Social Work,* 1985, 30, 511–517.

Waugh, D. Attempted suicide and aggression. *Dissertation Abstracts International,* 1974, 35B, 1398.

Wilbanks, W. Fatal accidents, suicide and homicide. *Victimology,* 1982, 7, 213–217.

Wong, M., & Singer, K. Abnormal homicide in Hong Kong. *British Journal of Psychiatry,* 1973, 123, 295–298.

Yesavage, J. Relationships between measures of direct and indirect hostility and self-destructive behavior by hospitalized schizophrenics. *British Journal of Psychiatry,* 1983a, 143, 173–176.

Yesavage, J. Direct and indirect hostility and self-destructive behavior by hospitalized depressives. *Acta Psychiatrica Scandinavica,* 1983b, 68, 345–350.

Chapter 22

THE PERSONALITY OF SUICIDAL PEOPLE

A great deal of research has appeared in the 1980s into personality correlates of suicidal behavior. The following review organizes this research by alphabetical order of the traits.

Academic Performance

Garfinkel and Golombek (1983) found that adolescent suicide attempters making severe attempts had more school success while those making moderate or mild attempts had more school failure than emergency room controls. Grossi (1987) found that adolescents in a residential treatment program who had previously attempted suicide had experienced more school failure than the non-attempters. Kosky (1983) found that adolescent attempted suicides were doing less well academically than non-suicidal psychiatric patients. Reynolds (1988) found that suicidal ideation was associated with lower grade point averages in adolescents.

In sixth, seventh and eighth graders, Harter and Marold (1987) found that those with suicidal ideation were more depressed, had less self-esteem, and perceived a greater discrepancy between their achievements and the importance of success to themselves or their parents. They felt as if they had failed themselves and their parents.

Holmstrom and Vauhkonen (1986) found that suicidal ideation predicted which university students dropped out.

Lewis et al. (1988) found that teenage attempted suicides identified in a community sample had lower school achievement (and mothers' educational expectations), lower social class and higher depression scores. The association between attempting suicide and lower achievement survived controls for social class but not for social class and depression. Pettifor et al. (1983) found that poor grades predicted completed suicide in youths.

Pronovost (1987) found that high school students who were suicidal (that is, had a suicide plan or had already attempted suicide) were more often absentee from school, drop-outs and discipline problems. (They were also more often female, confided more in friends and less in parents, and had higher depression scores.)

Slimak (1986) reported conflicting results for the association between SAT scores and suicidal behavior in college students and Coast Guard Academy students. For men, the suicidal ideators had higher SAT mathematics scores and the attempted/completed suicides lower SAT mathematics scores as compared to non-suicidal students. For women, the suicidal ideators and attempted/completed suicides had higher SAT verbal scores; the ideators had lower SAT mathematics scores and the attempted/ completed suicides higher SAT mathematics scores.

In contrast, Khan (1987) found no differences in academic achievement between adolescent suicide attempters and psychiatric controls. Pfeffer (1984) found no differences in school achievement between suicidal children and non-suicidal children in a community sample.

Alexithymia

Haviland et al. (1988) found that alexithymia (lacking words for emotions) was related to depression but not to a history of attempted suicide.

Anhedonia

Watson and Kucala (1978) found that VA patients who later completed suicide had less anhedonia (the ability to experience pleasure) than patients who died of other causes, but they did not differ from living patients.

Anomie

Goldney et al. (1989) found that suicidal ideation was associated with scores on a test of anomie in young adults.

Anxiety

Berger (1987) found that trait anxiety was associated with a rating of suicidal risk in university counseling patients. Goldney et al. (1989) found that anxiety was associated with suicidal ideation in young adults, as did Reynolds (1988) in adolescents.

In contrast, Ellis et al. (1989) found no differences in anxiety between psychiatric inpatients who had attempted suicide and those who had not. Pospizyl (1985) found no differences between prisoners who injured themselves and those who had not on the Taylor Manifest Anxiety Scale, but among non-inmate adolescents, the suicide attempters had higher scores than normal kids.

Attitude Toward Suicide

In a US poll, Johnson et al. (1980) found that suicide when suffering from an incurable disease was approved more by whites, males, younger adults, the more educated, Jews, those with weak religious beliefs, if in good health (males only), and low satisfaction with family life (females only). Sawyer and Sobal (1987) reported from national poll data that those most opposed to suicide were older adults, non-whites, women, the widowed, rural residents, those retired, those with no college education, low income and a low status job, conservatives, Protestants, and those strongly religious. Approval of suicide was related to social participation, civil libertarianism and attitudes toward the sanctity of life but not to life satisfaction or anomie. Hoelker (1979) found that ratings of the acceptability of suicide were negatively related to religiosity and (less consistently) to the fear of death.

Ketelaar and O'Hara (1989) found students with a history of depression and suicidal preoccupation rated suicide as less negative and more potent on the Semantic Differential than did nonsuicidal students.

Limbacher and Domino (1985–1986) gave students a suicide opinion questionnaire and found that those who had thought about or attempted suicide in the past were more accepting of suicide and saw suicide as more impulsive. Attempters saw suicides as less mentally ill and less impulsive than did suicidal ideators.

Linehan et al. (1987) found that psychiatric inpatients who had thought about or attempted suicide viewed suicide as a more effective solution to problems than did non-suicidal patients. Minear and Brush (1980–1981) found that a positive attitude toward suicide was associated in college students with having more suicidal preoccupation in the past, being atheist, agnostic or Jewish, with death anxiety and negatively with belief in life after death.

Stillion et al. (1984a, 1984b, 1986) found that approval of suicide as a solution was stronger in females in some groups (but not in all). Approval was associated with depression and self-esteem. Approval was not associated with androgyny, self-actualization tendencies, death anxiety, church attendance, birth order, religiosity or living in a single parent home. White and Stillion (1988) found that men felt more negative toward male attempted suicides than toward female attempted suicides while women showed no such difference in attitudes.

Parker (1981) found that suicide attempters with low suicidal intent viewed an overdose differently from those with high suicidal intent. For example, they saw the overdose more as a behavior like getting drunk.

Baseball Performance

Lester and Topp (1988, 1989) found that only about 1 percent of the deaths of major league baseball players were from suicide. Those who committed suicide did not differ from those murdered in batting averages (if batters) or the percentage of games won (if pitchers).

Death Concerns

Weis and Seiden (1974) found attempted suicides to be more preoccupied with death, to have more suicidal ideation and more prior attempts than suicide prevention center workers.

McIntire et al. (1972) found that 3 percent of school children frequently wished they were dead (and 40 percent occasionally wished it). The frequent wishers were more often Protestant and had a less naturalistic concept of death (with more belief in reincarnation, death's reversibility and the existence of thought after death).

Firth et al. (1986) found that violent psychiatric inpatients had more death content in their dreams (but not their day dreams) and suicide attempters had more death content in both dreams and day-dreams than depressed but non-suicidal patients. The suicide attempters had more death content in their dreams only if their depression score was high (or if their MMPI impulsivity score was high).

Goldney (1982b) found no association between the lethality of the suicide attempt in young women and death anxiety. However, the higher the suicidal intent, the less death anxiety.

Orbach et al. (1983, 1984) reported that suicidal children had less aversion and more attraction to death than chronically ill children, but the results could not be replicated. Compared to normal children, however, the differences were strong. Pfeffer (1989–1990) found that suicidal children in a community sample were more preoccupied with death than non-suicidal children but did not differ in the concept of death.

Defense Mechanisms

Apter et al. (1989) found that attempted suicides had higher scores on a measure of regression than non-suicidal psychiatric inpatients. Suicidal risk (as measured by a scale) was positively associated with regression and displacement and negatively with denial.

Delayed Auditory Feedback

Basteky et al. (1982) found that suicidal patients resembled neurotics but both groups differed from normal subjects in their task performance under conditions of delayed auditory feedback.

Developmental Maturity

Ball and Chandler (1989) found that adolescent psychiatric inpatient who had a high risk of suicide were more developmentally immature on a test of the continuity of the self assessed by interview than were low-risk patients.

Extraversion

Roy (1978) found that non-psychotic self-mutilators (cutters) were more introverted and neurotic but did not differ in psychoticism on Eysenck's personality inventory as compared to other psychiatric patients. They were more hostile on Fould's inventory, but did not differ in depression or anxiety. Lester (1987) found that college students who had thoughts about suicide in the past or attempted it (but not threatened it) were more introverted than non-suicidal students.

Angst and Clayton (1986) found that psychiatric patients who had attempted suicide had higher extraversion (and aggression) scores on the Freiberg Personality Inventory, but did not differ on the other dimensions.

Among prisoners, Pospizyl (1985) found that self-injurers have higher extraversion scores, but among non-inmate adolescents, the suicide attempters have lower extraversion scores than normal kids.

In contrast, Ross et al. (1983) found no association between suicidal ideation and extraversion.

Handedness

Chyatte and Smith (1981) found a high incidence (30 percent) of left-handedness in Navy recruits making suicidal gestures. The left-handed attempters used alcohol more often and other drugs less often than the right-handed attempters.

Hysteroid-Obsessoid

Goldney (1981) found no differences between female suicide attempters and normal controls on hysteroid-obsessoid scores. Suicidal lethality was also unrelated to the scores.

Impulsivity

Cabiles (1976) found that the incidence of attempted suicide in psychiatric and non-psychiatric patients was positively related to depression scores but was not related to their scores on a measure of impulsivity.

Intelligence

Allebeck et al. (1988) found that Swedish conscripts who later completed suicide had lower intelligence than those who did not. Fourestie et al. (1986) found that women suicide attempters scored below the mean on scale 5 of the WAIS.

Dingman and McGlashan (1986) found that private psychiatric patients who subsequently completed suicide were more intelligent than those who did not. Husain and Vandiver (1984) analyzed case studies in the literature of children and adolescents who were suicidal (completers, attempters or threateners) and found more above average intelligence than below. In a small sample of adolescent suicide attempters, Kosky (1983) found more above average intelligence than below.

Kuperman et al. (1988) found that having an IQ greater than 90 predicted subsequent completed suicide in child psychiatric patients. Motto (1980) found that high intelligence predicted subsequent completed suicide in alcohol-abusing depressed suicidal inpatients. Myers et al. (1985) found that acutely suicidal child psychiatric inpatients had higher IQ scores (verbal and performance) than non-suicidal patients.

Smith (1981) found that the more seriously suicidal psychiatric patients had a larger Vocabulary-minus-Digit Symbol discrepancy than the less suicidal patients.

In contrast, Asarnow and Guthrie (1989) found no differences between adolescent psychiatric inpatients who had attempted suicide and the nonsuicidal group in intelligence. Batzel and Dodrill (1986) found no differences between epileptics who had attempted suicide and those who had not (nor between repeaters and non-repeaters). Ellis et al. (1989) found no differences between psychiatric inpatients who had attempted suicide and those who had not. Gaines and Richmond (1980) found no differences between basic trainees in the military who made suicidal gestures and normal controls. Harder et al. (1980) found no association between intelligence and the severity of the suicidal attempt in psychiatric inpatients. Harkey and Hyer (1986) found no differences between suicidal and/or depressed patients and non-depressed/non-suicidal psychiatric patients in Shipley concept or vocabulary test scores (or Hooper Visual Orientation Test scores). Kazdin et al. (1983) found no differences in intelligence between disturbed inpatient children who had attempted suicide, suicidal ideators and nonsuicidal children. Borst and Noam (1989) found no differences in intelligence between adolescent suicide attempters and psychiatric controls. Linehan et al. (1987) found no differences between non-suicidal psychiatric patients and those who had thought about or attempted suicide. Murphy et al. (1983) found no differences between opiate addicts who attempted suicide and those who did not. Pettifor et al. (1983) found that IQ did not predicted completed suicide in youths. Pfeffer (1984) found no differences in intelligence between suicidal and non-suicidal children in a community sample. Plummer et al. (1989) found that adolescent suicide attempters did not differ from suicidal ideators and nonsuicidal adolescents in WISC scores. Predescu and Grigoroiu (1976) found that IQ scores of a sample of attempted suicides did not differ from chance expectations. Weiner and Pfeffer (1986) found that suicidal ideation was not associated with intelligence in a sample of preadolescent psychiatric inpatients.

Terman and Oden (1947) followed up a sample of gifted children and found that by age 30 about 17 percent of the male deaths and 4 percent of the female deaths were suicidal.

Jungian Personality Traits

Lester (1989d) found that suicidal students (currently and in the past) tended to have lower sensing, thinking and judging scores (but did not differ on extraversion) than nonsuicidal students, even after controls for current depression.

Learned Helplessness

Reynolds (1988) found that suicidal ideation and a measure of learned helplessness were associated in some samples of adolescents.

Learning Disability

Myers et al. (1985) found no differences between acutely suicidal child psychiatric inpatients and non-suicidal patients in the incidence of learning disabilities.

Locus of Control

Budner and Kumler (1973) found that college students with a high degree of suicidal ideation were more external in their belief in locus of control. They were also more anxious, more moody, less happy and less able to control their anger. Froyd and Perry (1985) found that suicidal ideation and an external locus of control were positively associated in college students (significant for males only). Goldney (1982a) found that young women who had attempted suicide were more external than non-suicidal patients. The lethality of the attempt was not related to locus of control scores. The external scores of the attempters were related to depression, hopelessness and perceived childhood stress. Goldney et al. (1989) found that young adults with suicidal ideation were more external than those without such ideation. Topol and Reznikoff (1982) found that adolescent suicide attempters were more external than normals (but not psychiatric controls).

Lester (1988) found that college students who had attempted suicide obtained lower powerful others scores (but similar internal and chance scores) compared to equally depressed non-suicidal students. In contrast, Lester (1989c) found that students who were currently thinking of suicide or who had in the past obtained higher chance and powerful others scores (that is, were more external). Similarly, Sidrow and Lester (1988) in a study of psychiatric patients found that those who had suicidal ideation were less internal and had higher scores for external control by chance. The lower internal scores remained even after controls for depression.

However, Luscomb et al. (1980) and McLeavey et al. (1987) found no differences between attempted suicides and psychiatric controls on locus of control scores. Papa (1980) found no association between suicidal intent and locus of control in a sample of attempted suicides. Plummer et al. (1989) found no differences in locus of control scores between adolescent suicide attempters, suicidal ideators and nonsuicidal adolescents.

Loneliness

Kirkpatrick-Smith et al. (1989) found that loneliness scores predicted suicidal ideation in high school students.

Memory

Williams and Broadbent (1986b) found no differences between suicide attempters and patients with physical illnesses in semantic memory, but the attempters took longer to retrieve positive (but not negative) autobiographical memories. Williams and Dritschel (1988) also found that suicide attempters recalled more general personal memories to stimulus words whereas control patients recalled more specific memories. The attempters recalled more specific memories when asked for negative (rather than positive) memories.

Mood

Neuringer (1982; Neuringer and Lettieri, 1982) found that highly suicidal callers to a suicide prevention center were more perturbed than other callers (and this did not decline over three weeks), more angry, anxious, and depressed and felt more that life was empty and they were inadequate.

Nervous Habits

Thomas and McCabe (1980) compared medical students who later completed suicide with healthy controls. The suicides as medical students had more habits of nervous tension (such as urinary frequency, difficulties sleeping, loss of appetite, urge to be alone, and irritability).

Neuroticism And Psychoticism

De Man et al. (1987a) found that neuroticism, anxiety, depression and self-esteem (but not extraversion) were all related to suicidal ideation in a mixed sample of students and patients. In a multiple regression analysis, depression and self-esteem were the strongest predictors of suicidal ideation. In a sample of community residents, suicidal ideation was related to life stress, self-esteem, and neuroticism, depression, and extraversion but not to the degree of social support (De Man, 1988; De Man et al., 1987b).

Dietzfelbinger et al. (1988) found that attempted suicides were more neurotic than normal people but less neurotic than neurotic depressives. Subsequent repeated suicide attempts were predicted by tests of social disintegration and compulsive orderliness.

Lester (1987) found that college students who had thought about suicide in the past and threatened it (but not attempted it) had higher neuroticism and psychoticism scores than non-suicidal college students.

Simons and Murphy (1985) found that suicidal ideation in high school students was associated with emotional problems (and for both sexes self-esteem, hope for the future and absence of parental support; for males employment and interpersonal problems at school; and for females delinquent behavior).

Pospizyl (1985) found that self-injuring prisoners had higher neuroticism scores than prisoners who did not injure themselves and also that adolescent non-inmate suicide attempters had higher scores than normal kids. Ross et al. (1983) found that suicidal ideators had higher neuroticism and psychoticism scores than nonideators.

Tishler and McKenry (1983) compared adolescent suicide attempters to adolescents with minor injuries. The attempters had more overall psychiatric symptoms, anxiety, obsessive-compulsive symptoms, depression, hostility, and psychoticism (but not somatic symptoms, phobias, or paranoid ideation), and lower self-esteem.

Purpose In Life

Using a path analysis, Harlow et al. (1986, 1987) found that suicidal ideation in men and in the total pool of subjects was related to purpose in life scores (as well as depression). Feifel and Nagy (1981) found that prior suicidal ideation was associated with scores on tests of the meaningfulness of life, the value of oneself as a person and life satisfaction, but not with the fear of death.

Reasons for Living and Dying

Linehan et al. (1983) devised an inventory for measuring different reasons for not committing suicide. Scores on the test were associated with suicidal preoccupation, including prior attempts. Scores on the reasons for living test were associated with suicidality, depression and hopelessness in both school students and juvenile delinquents (Cole, 1989a; Kirkpatrick-Smith et al., 1989) and androgyny (Ellis and Range, 1988). Ellis and Range (1989) found that increases in depression were associated with decreased scores on the inventory while increases in elation were associated with increased scores in a set of students.

Williams (1986) found that more hopeless suicide attempters gave similar reasons for taking overdoses as the less hopeless patients except for the reasons of dying and getting relief which they gave more often.

Religiosity

Bagley and Ramsay (1989) found that various aspects of religiosity were associated with a history of suicide in a community sample, with secure religiosity reducing the likelihood of suicidal involvement. Best and Kirk (1982) found that religiosity was associated with students being less accepting of suicide.

Risk-Taking

Spittle et al. (1976) found that psychiatric patients who had attempted suicide were more likely to be risk-takers (with respect to money, driving, drugs, etc.) than other psychiatric patients, but similar in depression.

Silberfeld et al. (1985) found no differences between suicidal attempters and ideators and non-suicidal patients on a choice-dilemma test which permitted risky versus safe choices.

Self-Concept

Clifton and Lee (1976) found that college student who were more preoccupied with suicide viewed themselves less favorably but did not differ in self-confidence. Neuringer (1974) found that attempted suicides rated themselves more negatively and others more positively than did psychosomatic and medical patients. Bagley (1975) found that self-depreciation and suicidal ideation were associated in 14-year-olds. Suicidal ideation was also associated with neuroticism and social isolation (a feeling that there was no one to help them).

Kaplan (1978) gave all seventh grade children in Houston a test of "self-derogation." A year later he asked them about their suicidal preoccupation in the last year. Those with higher self-derogation scores were more likely to attempt suicide in that year (and to show other deviant behaviors), and this was found for all groups except lower class white boys.

Beck et al. (1989) found that a low self-concept predicted subsequent completed suicide in a sample of psychiatric outpatients. Duke and Lorch (1989) found that suicidal ideation in school children was associated with self-confidence, self-concept, and purpose-in-life scores as well as closeness to parents and the disparity between actual and rated importance of academic achievement. Goldney et al. (1989) found that suicidal ideation was associated with self-esteem in young adults as did Reynolds (1988). Kazdin et al. (1983) found that disturbed inpatient children who had attempted suicide had lower self-esteem than those who had not.

Ellis et al. (1989) found that psychiatric inpatients who had attempted suicide had more self-blame for bad events than non-suicidal patients. In a path analysis, Harlow et al. (1986) found that suicidal ideation was related to self-derogation in women (as well as depression).

Nichols and Fasko (1988) found that scores on a suicide risk scale and the Tennessee self-concept scale were negatively correlated in both a sample of disadvantaged teenagers and in a sample of musically gifted teenagers. The two groups did not differ in suicidal risk or self-concept. Sreenan-Auger (1989) also found that scores on the Tennessee self-concept scale were related to suicidal ideation in adolescents.

Petrie et al. (1988) found that self-esteem predicted prior and future suicide attempts and future (but not current) suicidal ideation in a sample of attempted suicides when placed in a multiple regression analysis with other psychological test scores.

Schmidtke and Schaller (1985) found that in teenage suicide attempters, the similarity between their ratings of self and self-as-perceived-by-family was less than in non-suicidal psychiatric controls. Furthermore, the self-as-perceived-by-family was rated more negatively by the suicide attempters. Similar results were found for the similarity between the ideal self and the self-as-perceived-by-family. In a sample of prisoners, the results were less clear, but both suicide attempters and self-mutilators had less similarity between the ideal self and the self-as-perceived-by-family than non-suicidal/nonmutilating prisoners.

In contrast, Plummer et al. (1989) found no differences in self-esteem between adolescents who had attempted suicide, had thought about suicide or were non-suicidal.

Separation Anxiety

Wade (1987) found that adolescent girls who had attempted suicide showed more symbiotic-attachment and hostility and less individuation on a test of separation-anxiety (but only for mild separation experiences). Thus, the attempters were judged to have greater separation-anxiety.

Smoking And Recreation

Friberg et al. (1973) found that suicide rates were higher in smokers than in non-smokers. Ishii (1973, 1978) found that completed suicides at Kyoto University (Japan) had obtained better grades at high school but had been absent more. They were less likely to have participated in extra-curricular activities, drank and smoked more, but did not differ in hobbies and recreational behavior).

Abane et al. (1978) compared young suicide attempters with non-psychiatric controls and found the attempters to have had poorer school and work performance, less social, political and cultural activities and to use medication and tobacco more (but not alcohol).

Social Dysfunction

Goldney et al. (1989) found that suicidal ideation was associated with scores on a test of social dysfunction in young adults. Petrie et al. (1988) found that social anxiety (but not social skills) predicted prior suicidal attempts (but not future attempts) in a sample of suicide attempters. Spirito et al. (1988b) found no differences between adolescent suicide attempters and medical controls in socializing activities.

Thinking

Berger (1987) found that a rating of suicidal risk was associated with irrational thinking in university counseling patients. Bonner and Rich (1987, 1988) found that suicidal preoccupation in college students was associated with irrational thinking. Ellis and Ratliff (1986) found that suicidal psychiatric inpatients (attempters and ideators) had more dysfunctional attitudes than non-suicidal patients.

Lester (1989e) found that students who were currently thinking about suicide obtained higher scores on a test of general irrational thinking. However, those who had previously attempted suicide did not differ from equally depressed but non-suicidal students in rational thinking. Woods and Muller (1988) found that current suicidal ideation in therapy clients was related to irrational thinking, but also to state anxiety and depression, and the authors failed to control for these latter variables.

Chabon and Robins (1986) found that cognitive bias (choosing distorted solutions to problems) in depressed drug abusers was not related to suicidal intent (though it was related to depression and hopelessness). Ellis et al. (1989) found no differences between psychiatric inpatients who had attempted suicide and non-suicidal patients in irrational thinking. Ranieri et al. (1987) found that irrational thinking was associated with suicidal ideation in a sample of psychiatric patients, even after controls for depression and hopelessness in an inpatient sample.

Neuringer and Lettieri (1982) compared women who called a suicide prevention center who differed in suicidal potential. Those with the higher potential rated life as less valuable but death and suicide as more active. They also showed more dichotomous thinking (making extreme ratings). Their evaluations of life, death and suicide also varied with their self-rated daily suicidal potential and, for the most suicidal women, with their dichotomous thinking. Schmidtke et al. (1989) found no differences, however, between attempted suicides and psychiatric controls in embedded figures, progressive matrices and semantic differential tasks, that is, on tests presumably measuring field-dependence and dichotomous thinking.

Perrah and Wichman (1987) found no differences between attempted suicides (after their crisis) and normal individuals in rigidity on the Rorschach map test or on an alternative uses test. Petrie et al. (1988) found that flexibility scale scores were not associated with past, present or future suicidal attempts or ideation when placed in a multiple regression analysis with other psychological test scores.

In a sample of unipolar depressed patients, Prezant and Neimeyer (1988) found that suicidal ideation was associated with distorted performance on some tests of thinking, including selective abstraction, overgeneralization, and stable attribution style, but only after controls for the level of depression.

Problem-Solving Skills

Bonner and Rich (1987) found that students with suicidal preoccupation had worse problem-solving skills than non-suicidal students. They were also more cognitively rigid (using the F-scale).

Carson and Johnson (1985) found that college students with suicidal ideation had lower GPAs and less knowledge about how to solve their problems or handle their emotions than non-suicidal students.

Kirsch (1982) found that suicidal patients (attempters and ideators), when given tasks at which they failed and when accused of having negative personality traits, were less able to negotiate a better self-description than were non-suicidal psychiatric patients. However, depression scores were also associated with the response to this task, and the authors did not control for this.

Linehan et al. (1987) found that suicidal ideators and attempters did not differ from non-suicidal patients in interpersonal skills (assertiveness), but the attempters chose more passive solutions in a means-end problem-solving task. (The ideators chose the most active solutions and the non-suicidal patients intermediate solutions.)

McLeavey et al. (1987) found that self-poisoners performed worse on a cognitive problem-solving test concerned with interpersonal problems than psychiatric patients and normal controls. Orbach et al. (1987) found that suicidal children generated fewer solutions to problems presented to them and chose death-oriented solutions more than chronically ill and normal children.

Scholz and Pfeffer (1987) found no differences between attempted suicides and psychiatric patients on whether they used problem-focussed, wishful-thinking or seeking-support tactics as coping behaviors. Thomssen and Moller (1988) found that suicide attempters used emotion-focussed ways of coping more often than did surgical patients as well as resigned/ wishful thinking, self-blame and denial/avoidance and used problem-focussed ways of coping less often.

Schotte and Clum (1982) found that interpersonal problem-solving skills contributed, along with stressful life events to the prediction on suicidal ideation in college students, but that depression and hopelessness (and sex) were the strongest predictors. In psychiatric patients, Schotte and Clum (1987) found that those with suicidal ideation were differentiated from the non-suicidal patients by cognitive skills (using an alternative-uses test and a means-end problem-solving test), but the means-end problem-solving test and hopelessness did predict suicidal intent for the attempters.

Spirito et al. (1989) found that adolescent suicide attempters had experienced more recent problems with parents (and less with school) than normal adolescents, but they resembled the normal students in coping strategies. They were similar on many strategies (including self-blame, cognitive restructuring and seeking social support) but used wishful thinking and social withdrawal more often.

Time Perception

Barnes (1977) compared suicide attempters with other psychiatric patients and found no differences in the ability to estimate time intervals ranging from one second to 64 seconds. The serious attempters, however, had more negative attitudes toward the future, but not on a scale of "projection into the future."

Neuringer and Harris (1974) found that attempted suicides over-estimated time as compared to terminal, geriatric and medical patients. In a time opinion survey, the attempters did not differ in the quickness of time passage or delay of gratification. However, the attempters (and the geriatric patients) had lower scores for future time orientation.

Barnes (1977) found that highly lethal suicide attempters had a more negative view of the past, present and future but did not differ from less lethal attempters on the Yufit time questionnaire or on time estimations up to one minute. Donovan et al. (1987) found that suicidal attempters and ideators saw the past and the future more positively and the present less positively than normal controls. The suicidal people projected into the future for a shorter time period.

Type A Personality

Froyd and Perry (1985) and Lester (1989a) found no association between suicidal ideation and Type A personality in college students.

Understanding of Suicide

Dobert and Nunner-Winkler (1985) found that adolescents who had attempted suicide were more likely to see suicide as a result of deep motives and multifactorial causes (rather than as a momentary response to an external incident) than were non-suicidal adolescents.

Domino (1981) found that Mexican-American high school students were less in favor of suicide as a solution to life problems than were Anglo-Americans.

Durocher et al. (1989) found that people who had thought about suicide had more accurate information about suicide on a test of facts and fables about suicide. Lester and Nivison (1988) found that having accurate information about suicide was not associated with either depression or prior suicidal behavior.

Withdrawal

Fry and Smith (1984) found that those making suicide attempts in the hospital participated less in hospital activities prior to their attempts, the more so if their attempts were serious. In general in five hospitals, the greater the attendance at activities, the lower the completed and the attempted suicide rates. Del Gaudio et al. (1977) found that attempted suicides were less likely to get involved with a treatment agency than other patients.

Personality in General

Motanky (1971) found that suicidal adolescents had lower scores on scales for nervous symptoms, anti-social tendencies, belonging and personal adjustment than normal adolescents and adolescents in crisis. On a test of defense mechanisms, the suicidal adolescents used denial less, while both the suicidal and in-crisis adolescents used projection more than the normal adolescents.

Wilson et al. (1971) compared attempted suicides (tested prior to their attempt), psychiatric patients and normals. The attempted suicides had goals which were the most inconsistent with society. (Wilson believed that this scale measured anxiety.) The attempters felt that others viewed them more negatively. Three scales showed no differences, but overall the attempters showed most maladjustment.

Scholz (1972) compared attempted suicides with psychiatric patients and found no differences in their use of defense mechanisms. On an adjective checklist the groups did not differ in "lability" (flexibility). Classifying the attempters, Scholtz found that the dependent-dissatisfied type was more aggressive and autonomous, showed less self-control and poorer personal judgment, and more likely to have a psychotic profile on the MMPI. The satisfied-symbiotic type was more deferent. The groups did not differ in succorance, abasement, achievement or self-confidence.

Diamond (1978) compared women professionals who had previously attempted suicide with those who had not and found no differences on some scales of the California Psychological Inventory, on the Bem Androgyny Scale, or on a role-conflict questionnaire. However, in an interview the attempters did report more role conflict.

Sonneck et al. (1976) compared attempted suicide and depressed patients on the Freiburger Personality Inventory. Non-suicidal patients were more nervous, inhibited and tense; suicidal depressed patients were more depressed, excitable and inhibited; attempters were more open, extraverted and aggressive than the non-suicidal depressed patients and more sociable and feminine than the suicidal depressed patients. In symptoms, the attempted suicides were less restless, the suicidal depressed patients had stronger feelings of inferiority, and the non-suicidal depressed patients were less hopeless. (They did not differ in guilt, fear and tension.)

Iga (1986) found that suicidal Japanese college students (completers, attempters and threateners) were more dependent, rigid, suspicious, and unrealistic, had weaker egos and poorer physical and mental health, and more often had family problems, school work problems, family economic insecurity and financial worries.

On the Psychological Screening Inventory, Larsen et al. (1983) found that female psychiatric patients with suicidal ideation had higher discomfort scores while the males had lower discomfort (and alienation scores) than the non-suicidal patients. Thus, sex differences in the predictors of suicidal risk seemed to be quite strong.

On the Jackson Personality Inventory, Silberfeld et al. (1985) found that suicide attempters obtained the lowest responsibility scores and suicidal ideators the lowest self-esteem scores as compared to non-suicidal patients.

Range and Goggin (1989) found that suicidal ideators in a college sample scored lower on the scales of dominance, social presence, responsibility, intellectual efficiency, and psychological mindedness on the California Psychological Inventory than non-ideators.

Mehrabian and Weinstein (1985) compared attempted suicides with norms for a temperament inventory he devised and found them to be unpleasant (versus pleasant), arousable (versus unarousable) and submissive (versus dominant). The lethality of the attempt was associated only with arousability.

On the 16PF, Singh et al. (1987) found that a sample of attempted suicides scored lower on intelligent, venturesome, shrewd and controlled and higher on apprehensive, tense and anxious than normal individuals. On the California Test of Personality, Wilder (1986) found a negative association between suicide potential and general adjustment in a group of high school students.

Papa (1980) found no association between suicidal intent and scores on the FIRO B scale in a sample of attempted suicides. Slimak (1986) found no differences between college and Coast Guard Academy students who were suicidal ideators or attempters/completers and nonsuicidal students on the Strong Vocational Interest Blank, except that the suicidal students had higher occupational introversion.

On the Profile of Mood States, Williams and Broadbent (1986a) found that suicide attempters obtained higher scores on depression, anxiety, confusion, fatigue, anger, preoccupation, and rumination and lower scores on vigor. On the Stroop Interference Test, the attempters showed most interference for emotional words, but depression scores in the attempters were correlated with interference scores, and Williams did not control for depression scores.

Predicting Suicidal Risk with Psychological Tests

The 1980s witnessed a loss of interest in using the standard psychological tests for predicting suicidal risk. A few studies, however, appeared.

MMPI

Tarter et al. (1975) found that female attempted suicides did not differ from psychiatric patients on MMPI scores or on an inventory of social role orientation. For males, the attempted suicides were more disturbed on the MMPI (with higher scores on F, Hs, Pd, and Pa and lower scores on K). The male attempters also got higher scores for "turning against the self" on the social roles inventory (but not on "avoidance of others" or turning against others"). The risk-rescue scores of the attempters were not related either to MMPI scores or social role orientation scores.

Peniston (1978) found that the number of suicide attempts in a sample of Ute Indians was associated with their ego-strength scores on the MMPI but not their D scores. The number of alcohol-related attempts was not related to either score.

Leonard (1977) compared male and female completed suicides who had taken the MMPI. The females obtained lower scores on F and Pt scales and higher scores on Si, Pa, Ma, and an alcoholism scale and on the Goldberg Index. (The sex differences for highly suicidal but living patients differed from these above.) Both the male and female completed suicides differed from non-suicidal psychiatric patients in their MMPI scores, and the female completers differed from alive highly suicidal females.

Sendbuehler et al. (1978a, 1978b) found that Mf scores correlated with the seriousness of the suicide attempt, positively in men and negatively in women. They also found different profiles for suicidal men and women (824 and 482, respectively). Compared to controls, male attempters had higher Mf scores and the females lower scores.

Batzel and Dodrill (1986) found that epileptics who had attempted suicide had lower F scale, Welsh A and Manifest Anxiety scores on the MMPI and higher K and Ego Strength scale scores than nonattempters. The attempters appeared, therefore, to have higher anxiety and decreased ego strength. Repeaters and non-repeaters did not differ in scale scores.

Chlewinski (1984) found that suicide attempters were less disturbed on the MMPI than non-suicidal psychiatric patients, less anxious on the IPAT test of anxiety and less depressed. On the Adjective Check List, the attempters scored higher on exhibitionism, aggression, heterosexuality and changeability and lower on abasement and deference. Cole (1989b) found that K scale scores were associated with previous suicidal preoccupation in juvenile delinquents. Gaines and Richmond (1980) found that basic trainees in the military who made suicidal gestures obtained higher D scale scores than normal controls.

Franco (1986) found that female attempted suicides scored higher on the Pd scale than non-suicidal psychiatric patients on the Minimult, while male attempters scored lower on the F scale. For all attempters combined, no scale significantly differentiated suicidal from non-suicidal patients.

Kincel (1983) found that suicide attempters obtained higher Pd and Mf scores than non-suicidal psychiatric patients. (All subjects had D scores greater than 70.) The male attempters also differed on Hs, Ma, Sc and F scores.

Clopton et al. (1983), however, found no MMPI profile differences between suicide attempters and non-suicidal psychiatric patients or between repeaters and non-repeaters. Harkey and Hyer (1986) found significantly lower scores in depressed and/or suicidal patients as compared to non-depressed/non-suicidal psychiatric patients on scales Pd and Ma.

Pilecka (1985) found that youthful suicide attempters with high Hy scores were more likely to repeat their suicide attempts subsequently (but they were also more likely to have elevated scores on other MMPI scales). In contrast, Plummer et al. (1989) found no differences in Hy scores between adolescent suicide attempters, suicidal ideators and non-suicidal adolescents.

Spirito et al. (1988a) found no differences between adolescent female suicide attempters and non-suicidal psychiatric patients on MMPI scales or profiles, except for lower K scores for the attempters.

Stancak et al. (1983) found that male attempted suicides had higher scores on scales D, Pd and Pa than normal controls, while female attempted suicides had higher scores on scales D, Pd, Mf, Pa, Pt, and Sc than normal controls.

Waters et al. (1982) found that male suicide attempters had higher scores than non-suicidal patients on scales F, Pd, Mf, Sc, and Hs. Female attempters showed fewer differences, with only lower Mf scores and higher Pd scores.

Watson et al. (1983, 1984) found only one difference between completed suicides and psychiatric patients on the standard and experimental scales: the suicides had higher Mf scores. No differences in the MMPI profiles could be identified, and the authors concluded that the MMPI did not differentiate completed suicides from non-suicidal patients. Comparing those who completed suicide soon after MMPI testing with those completing suicide later, only one significant difference was identified: the recent completers had higher Pa scores. However, the recent completers had higher (but not significantly so) scores also on scales Hs, Sc, Ma and F, suggesting slightly greater disturbance.

Rorschach

Arffa (1982) identified ten Rorschach signs which differentiated attempted suicides from non-suicidal adolescent psychiatric patients. Hansell et al. (1988) found that the color-shading and transparency responses were not associated with the number of prior suicide attempts in a sample of depressed patients. During the depressive episode, the suicide risk was negatively associated with the color/shading response (opposite to the predicted finding).

Lester (1989d) found that Sylvia Plath's poems showed an increase in dark-shading just before her suicide, consistent with the imminent acting-out of her self-destructive desires.

Santostefano et al. (1984) explored movement responses on the Rorschach by adolescent suicide attempters and psychiatric controls. Although there was no difference in overall movement, the movement in the attempters' responses was less vigorous, and more often inanimate objects were the recipients of the motion. Comparing the pre-adolescent and adolescent suicidal children, the movement responses of the preadolescents were more often vigorous, had the self as agent, and were completed.

Smith (1981) found some differences on the Rorschach between seriously suicidal psychiatric patients and less suicidal patients, with the more suicidal patients giving more responses, more movement responses and more FC responses. Smith also validated the suicide signs proposed for the Rorschach. In contrast, responses to the Thematic Apperception Test and the word association response time to the word "suicide" did not differentiate the groups.

Thomas and Duzynski (1985) found that medical students who later completed suicide gave more whirling responses on the Rorschach taken in medical school than did other students.

Suicide Prediction Scales

Motto has worked on devising predictive scales for suicide. He has used over one hundred patient variables to predict suicide in alcoholics (Motto, 1980) and in adolescents (Motto, 1984), for short-term suicidal risk (Motto, 1988) and long-term risk (Motto et al., 1985). Similarly, Pallis et al. (1984) have devised a scale which predicts subsequent completed suicide in the long-term in attempted suicides.

Stanley et al. (1986) devised a 22-item scale for suicidal assessment. Scores on the scale were associated with depression, anxiety and prior attempted suicide but not with a history of aggression.

Discussion

Although much of the research reviewed here is methodologically unsound (for example, very few of the studies controlled for the level of psychiatric disturbance and, in particular, depression), several consistent findings have emerged. Suicidal individuals have more academic failure, higher levels of anxiety, an external locus of control, higher neuroticism scores, lower self-esteem, more irrational thinking, and worse problem-solving skills. They may also smoke more and have higher IQ scores.

Future research must control for psychiatric disturbance, so that correlates of suicidal behavior per se may be ascertained, and must also explore the ways in which these personality traits combine and interact to produce suicidal behavior.

REFERENCES

Abane, M., Buffard, G., Dussuyer, I., Morel, J., Quenard, O., & Vedrinne, J. Some comparative factors of suicidal behavior in young civilians and servicemen. In V. Aalberg (Ed.) *Proceedings of the 9th International Congress for Suicide Prevention & Crisis Intervention.* Helsinki: Finnish Association for Mental Health, 1978, 422–428.

Allebeck, P., Allgulander, C., & Fisher, L. D. Predictors of completed suicide in a cohort of 50,465 young men. *British Medical Journal,* 1988, 297, 176–178.

Angst, J., & Clayton, P. Premorbid personality of depressive, bipolar and schizophrenic patients with special reference to suicidal issues. *Comprehensive Psychiatry,* 1986, 27, 511–532.

Apter, A., Plutchik, R., Sevy, S., Korn, M., Brown, S., & van Praag, H. Defense mechanisms in risk of suicide and risk of violence. *American Journal of Psychiatry,* 1989, 146, 1027–1031.

Arffa, S. Predicting adolescent suicidal behavior and the order of Rorschach measurement. *Journal of Personality Assessment,* 1982, 46, 563–568.

Asarnow, J. R., & Guthrie, D. Suicidal behavior, depression and hopelessness in child psychiatric patients. *Journal of Clinical Child Psychology,* 1989, 18, 129–136.

Bagley, C. Suicidal behavior and suicidal ideation in adolescents. *British Journal of Guidance & Counseling,* 1975, 3, 190–208.

Bagley, C., & Ramsay, R. Attitudes toward suicide, religious values and suicidal behavior. In R. F. Diekstra, R. Maris, S. Platt, A. Schmidtke, & G. Sonneck (Eds.) *Suicide and Its Prevention.* Leiden: Brill, 1989, 78–90.

Ball, L., & Chandler, M. Identity formation in suicidal and nonsuicidal youth. *Development & Psychopathology,* 1989, 1, 257–275.

Barnes, T. Time perception and time orientation as assessment devices of suicidal potential *Dissertation Abstracts International,* 1977, 38B, 343–344.

Basteky, J., Kozeny, J., & Brichacek, V. DAF method in the diagnosis of neuroses. *Activitas Nervosa Superior,* 1982, 24(3), 176–178.

Batzel, L. W., & Dodrill, C. B. Emotional and intellectual correlates of unsuccessful suicide attempts in people with epilepsy. *Journal of Clinical Psychology,* 1986, 42, 699–702.

Beck, A. T., Brown, G., & Stewart, B. L. Cognitive predictors of eventual suicide. In D. Lester (Ed.) *Suicide '89.* Denver: AAS, 1989, 284–295.

Berger, A. L. Suicide probability, cognitive style and affect in college students. In R. Yufit (Ed.) *Proceedings of the 20th Annual Meeting.* Denver: AAS, 1987, 113–115.

Best, J., & Kirk, W. Religiosity and self-destruction. *Psychological Record,* 1982, 32, 35–39.

Bonner, R. L., & Rich, A. R. Toward a predictive model of suicidal ideation and behavior. *Suicide & Life-Threatening Behavior,* 1987, 17, 50–63.

Bonner, R. L., & Rich, A. R. A prospective investigation of suicidal ideation in college students. *Suicide & Life-Threatening Behavior,* 1988, 18, 245–258.

Borst, S. R., & Noam, G. G. Suicidality and psychopathology in hospitalized children and adolescents. *Acta Paedopsychiatrica,* 1989, 52, 163–175.

Budner, S., & Kumler, F. Correlates of suicidal ideation. American Association of Suicidology, Houston, 1973.

Cabiles, P. Impulsivity and depression as factors in suicidal males. *Dissertation Abstracts International,* 1976, 37B, 1890.

Carson, N. D., & Johnson, R. E. Suicidal thoughts and problem-solving preparation among college students. *Journal of College Student Personnel,* 1985, 26, 484–487.

Chabron, B., & Robins, C. J. Cognitive distortions among depressed and suicidal drug abusers. *International Journal of the Addictions,* 1986, 21, 1313–1329.

Chlewinski, Z. Application of sequential discriminative analysis for differentiation of two populations. *Polish Psychological Bulletin,* 1984, 15(3), 201–210.

Chyatte, C., & Smith, V. Brain asymmetry predicts suicide among Navy alcohol abusers. *Military Medicine,* 1981, 146, 277–278.

Clifton, A. K., & Lee, D. E. Self-destructive consequences of sex-role socialization. *Suicide & Life-Threatening Behavior,* 1976, 6, 11–22.

Clopton, J. R., Post, R. D., & Larde, J. Identification of suicide attempters by means of MMPI profiles. *Journal of Clinical Psychology,* 1983, 39, 868–871.

Cole, D. A. Validation of the reasons for living inventory in general and delinquent adolescent samples. *Journal of Abnormal Child Psychology,* 1989a, 17, 13–27.

Cole, D. A. Psychopathology of adolescent suicide. *Journal of Abnormal Psychology,* 1989, 98, 248–255.

Del Gaudio, A., Carpenter, P., Stein, L., & Morrow, G. Characteristics of patients completing referals from an emergency department to a psychiatric outpatient clinic. *Comprehensive Psychiatry,* 1977, 18, 301–307.

De Man, A. F. Suicidal ideation, stress, social support, and personal variables in French Canadians. *Journal of Social Behavior & Personality,* 1988, 3, 127–134.

De Man, A. F., Balkou, S., & Iglesias, R. I. A French-born adaptation of the scale for suicide ideation. *Canadian Journal of Behavioral Sciences,* 1987a, 19, 50–55.

De Man, A. F., Balkou, S., & Iglesias, R. I. Social support and suicidal ideation in French-Canadians. *Canadian Journal of Behavioral Sciences,* 1987b, 19, 342–346.

Diamond, H. A. Suicide by women professionals. *Dissertation Abstracts International,* 1978, 38B, 5009.

Dietzfelbinger, T., Kurz, A., Torhorst, A., & Moller, H. J. Description and prognostic value of standardized procedures for determining remarkable personality traits in patients following a suicide attempt. In H. J. Moller, A. Schmidtke, & R. Welz, (Eds.) *Current issues of suicidology.* Berlin: Springer-Verlag, 1988, 328–340.

Dingman, C. W., & McGlashan, T. H. Discriminating characteristics of suicides. *Acta Psychiatrica Scandinavica,* 1986, 74, 91–97.

Dobert, R., & Nunner-Winkler, G. Interplay of formal and material role-taking in the understanding of suicide among adolescents and young adults. *Human Development,* 1985, 28, 225–239, 313–330.

Domino, G. Attitudes toward suicide among Mexican-Americans and Anglo youth. *Hispanic Journal of Behavioral Science,* 1981, 3, 385–395.

Donovan, M. J., Fitzpatrick, J. J., Reed, P., & Johnston, R. L. Experience of time during suicidal crises. In R. Yufit (Ed.) *Proceedings of the 20th Annual Conference,* Denver: AAS, 1987, 166–167.

Dukes, R. L., & Lorch, B. D. The effects of school, family, self-concept, and deviant behavior on adolescent suicide. *Journal of Adolescence,* 1989, 12, 239–251.

Durocher, G. J., Leenaars, A. A., & Balance, W. D. Knowledge about suicide as a function of experience. *Perceptual & Motor Skills,* 1989, 68, 26.

Ellis, J. B., & Range, L. M. Femininity and reasons for living. *Educational & Psychological Measurement,* 1988, 8(1), 19–24.

Ellis, J. B., & Range, L. M. Does mood affect reasons for living? *Journal of Cognitive Psychotherapy,* 1989, 3, 223–232.

Ellis, T., Berg, R., & Franzen, M. Organic and cognitive deficits in suicidal patients. In D. Lester (Ed.) *Suicide '89.* Denver: AAS, 1989, 292–293.

Ellis, T. E., & Ratliff, K. G. Cognitive characteristics of suicidal and non-suicidal psychiatric inpatients. *Cognitive Therapy & Research,* 1986, 10, 625–634.

Feifel, H., & Nagy, V. Another look at fear of death. *Journal of Consulting & Clinical Psychology*, 1981, 49, 278–286.

Firth, S. T., Blouin, J., Natarajan, C., & Blouin, A. A comparison of the manifest content in dreams and suicidal, depressed and violent patients. *Canadian Journal of Psychiatry*, 1986, 31, 48–53.

Fourestie, V., de Lignieres, B., Roudot-Thoraval, F., Fulli-Lemaire, I., Cremniter, D., Nahoul, K., Fournier, S., & Lejonc, J. L. Suicide attempts in hypo-oestrogenic phases of the menstrual cycle. *Lancet*, 1986, 2, 1357–1360.

Franco, J. N. Utility of the mini-mult in a community mental health setting. *Psychological Reports*, 1986, 59, 959–962.

Friberg, L., Cederlof, R., Lorich, U., Lundman, T., & deFaire, U. Mortality in twins in relation to smoking habits and alcohol problems. *Archives of Environmental Health*, 1973, 27, 294–304.

Froyd, J., & Perry, N. Relationships among locus of control, coronary-prone behavior and suicidal ideation. *Psychological Reports*, 1985, 57, 1155–1158.

Fry, B., & Smith, K. Activity attendance, hospital expectations and suicide. *Psychiatric Quarterly*, 1984, 56, 270–275.

Gaines, T., & Richmond, L. Assessing suicidal behavior in basic military trainees. *Military Medicine*, 1980, 145, 263–266.

Garfinkel, B., & Golombek, H. Suicidal behavior in adolescence. In H. Golombek & B. Garfinkel (Eds.) *The Adolescent and Mood Disturbance*. New York: International Universities Press, 1983, 189–217.

Goldney, R. Are young women who attempt suicide hysterical? *British Journal of Psychiatry*, 1981, 138, 141–146.

Goldney, R. Locus of control in young women who have attempted suicide. *Journal of Nervous & Mental Disease*, 1982a, 170, 198–201.

Goldney, R. Attempted suicide and death anxiety. *Journal of Clinical Psychiatry*, 1982b, 43, 159.

Goldney, R. D., Winefield, A. H., Tiggeman, M., Winefield, H., & Smith, S. Suicidal ideation in a young adult population. *Acta Psychiatrica Scandinavica*, 1989, 79, 481–489.

Gross, V. Deliberate self-harm among adolescents in residential treatment centers. In R. Yufit (Ed.) *Proceedings of the 20th Annual Conference*. Denver: AAS, 1987, 276–277.

Hansell, A. G., Lerner, H. D., Milden, R. S., & Ludolph, P. S. Single-sign Rorschach suicide indicators. *Journal of Personality Assessment*, 1988, 52, 658–669.

Harder, D. W., Strauss, J. S., Kokes, R. F., Ritiler, B. A., & Gift, T. E. Life events and psychopathology severity among first psychiatric admissions. *Journal of Abnormal Psychology*, 1980, 89, 165–180.

Harker, B., & Hyer, L. Suicide among psychiatric inpatients of older ages. *Psychological Reports*, 1986, 58, 775–782.

Harlow, L. L., Newcomb, M. D., & Bentler, P. M. Depression, self-derogation, substance use and suicidal ideation. *Journal of Clinical Psychology*, 1986, 42, 5–21.

Harlow, L. L., Newcomb, M. D., & Bentler, P. M. Purpose in life test assessment using latent variables. *British Journal of Clinical Psychology*, 1987, 26, 235–236.

Harter, S., & Marold, D. Familial values and adolescent suicidal ideation. In R. Yufit (Ed.) *Proceedings of the 20th Annual Conference.* Denver: AAS, 1987, 288–290.

Haviland, M. G., Shaw, D. G., MacMurray, J. P., & Cummings, M. A. Validation of the Toronto Alexithymia Scale with substance abusers. *Psychotherapy and Psychosomatics,* 1988, 50(2), 81–87.

Hoelker, J. W. Religiosity, fear of death and suicide acceptability. *Suicide & Life-Threatening Behavior,* 1979, 9, 163–172.

Holmstrom, R., & Vauhkonen, K. University studies and academic performance. *Psychiatria Fennica,* 1986, 17, 17–27.

Husain, S. A., & Vandiver, T. *Suicide in Children.* New York: Spectrum, 1984.

Iga, M. *The Thorn in the Chrysanthemum.* Berkeley: University of California Press, 1986.

Ishii, K. Backgrounds and suicidal behaviors of committed suicides among Kyoto University students. *Psychologia,* 1973, 16, 85–97.

Ishii, K. Backgrounds and suicidal behaviors of committed suicides among Kyoto University students. *Psychologia,* 1977, 20, 191–205.

Johnson, D., Fitch, S., Alston, J., & McIntosh, W. Acceptance of conditional suicide and euthanasia among adult Americans. *Suicide & Life-Threatening Behavior,* 1980, 10, 157–166.

Kaplan, H. B. Self-attitudes and multiple modes of deviance. In D. Lettieri (Ed.) *Drugs and Suicide.* Beverly Hills: Sage, 1978, 75–116.

Kazdin, A. E., French, N. H., Unis, A. S., Esveldt-Dawson, K., & Sherick, R. B. Hopelessness, depression and suicidal intent among psychiatrically disturbed inpatient children. *Journal of Consulting & Clinical Psychology,* 1983, 51, 504–510.

Ketelaar, T., & O'Hara, M. W. Meaning of the concept of suicide and risk for attempting suicide. *Journal of Social & Clinical Psychology,* 1989, 8, 393–399.

Khan, A. U. Heterogeneity of suicidal adolescents. *Journal of the American Academy of Child & Adolescent Psychiatry,* 1987, 26, 92–96.

Kincel, R. MMPI indicators of the suicide attempt. In J. P. Soubrier & J. Vedrinne (Eds.) *Depression and Suicide.* Paris: Pergamon, 1983, 847–850.

Kirkpatrick-Smith, K., Rich, A., Bonner, R., & Jans, F. Substance abuse and suicidal ideation among adolescents. In D. Lester (Ed.) *Suicide '89.* Denver: AAS, 1989, 90–91.

Kirsch, N. L. Attempted suicide and restrictions in the eligibility to negotiate personal characteristics. *Advances in Descriptive Psychology,* 1982, 2, 249–274.

Kosky, R. Childhood suicidal behavior. *Journal of Child Psychology & Psychiatry,* 1983, 24, 457–468.

Kuperman, S., Black, D. W., & Burns, T. L. Excess suicide among formerly hospitalized child psychiatric patients. *Journal of Clinical Psychiatry,* 1988, 49(3), 88–93.

Larsen, K. S., Garcia, D., Langenberg, D., & Leroux, J. The Psychological Screening Inventory as a predictor of predisposition to suicide among patients at the Oregon State Hospital. *Journal of Clinical Psychology,* 1983, 39, 100–103.

Leonard, C. V. The MMPI as a suicide predictor. *Journal of Consulting & Clinical Psychology,* 1977, 45, 367–377.

Lester, D. Suicidal preoccupation and dysthymia in college students. *Psychological Reports,* 1987, 61, 762.

Lester, D. Locus of control anger and suicide. *Activitas Nervosa Superior,* 1988, 30, 315–316.

Lester, D. Type A behavior, depression and suicidal ideation. *Psychological Reports,* 1989a, 65, 1234.

Lester, D. Jungian dimensions of personality, subclinical depression and suicidal ideation. *Personality & Individual Differences,* 1989b, 10, 1009.

Lester, D. Locus of control, depression and suicidal ideation. *Perceptual & Motor Skills,* 1989c, 69, 1158.

Lester, D. Application of Piotrowski's dark shading hypothesis to Sylvia Plath's poems written before her suicide. *Perceptual & Motor Skills,* 1989d, 68, 122.

Lester, D. Depression, suicidal preoccupation and rational thinking. *Journal of General Psychology,* 1989e, 116, 221–223.

Lester, D., & Nivison, B. Depression as a correlate of believing in myths about suicide. *Psychological Reports,* 1988, 63, 562.

Lester, D., & Topp, R. Suicide in the major leagues. *Perceptual & Motor Skills,* 1988, 67, 934.

Lester, D., & Topp, R. Major league baseball performances of players who were later suicides and homicide victims. *Perceptual & Motor Skills,* 1989, 69, 272.

Lewis, S. A., Johnson, J., Cohen, P., Garcia, M., & Velez, C. N. Attempted suicide in youth. *Journal of Abnormal Child Psychology,* 1988, 16, 459–471.

Limbacher, M., & Domino, G. Attitudes toward suicide among attempters, contemplators and non-attempters. *Omega,* 1985–1986, 16, 325–334.

Linehan, M. M., Camper, P., Chiles, J. A., Strosahl, K., & Shearin, E. Interpersonal problem solving and parasuicide. *Cognitive Therapy & Research,* 1987, 11, 1–12.

Linehan, M., Goodstein, J., Nielsen, S., & Chiles, J. Reasons for staying alive when you're thinking of killing yourself. *Journal of Consulting & Clinical Psychology,* 1983, 51, 276–286.

Luscomb, R., Clum, G., & Patsiokas, A. Mediating factors in the relationship between life stress and suicide attempting. *Journal of Nervous & Mental Disease,* 1980, 168, 644–650.

McIntire, M. S., Angle, C. R., & Struempler, L. J. The concept of death in midwestern children and youth. *American Journal of Diseases in Children,* 1972, 123, 527–532.

McLeavey, B. C., Daly, R. J., Murray, C. M., O'Riordan, J., & Taylor, M. Interpersonal problem-solving deficits in self-poisoning patients. *Suicide & Life-Threatening Behavior,* 1987, 17, 33–49.

Mehrabian, A., & Weinstein, L. Temperament characteristics of suicide attempters. *Journal of Consulting & Clinical Psychology,* 1985, 53, 544–546.

Minear, J., & Brush, L. The correlation of attitudes toward suicide with death anxiety. *Omega,* 1980–1981, 11, 317–324.

Motanky, C. S. The role of acting-out and identification in adolescent suicidal behavior. *Dissertation Abstracts International,* 1971, 31B, 7106.

Motto, J. Suicide risk factors in alcohol abuse. *Suicide & Life-Threatening Behavior,* 1980, 10, 230–238.

Motto, J. Suicide in male adolescents. In H. S. Sudak, A. B. Ford, & N. B. Rushforth (Eds.) *Suicide in the Young.* Boston: John Wright, 1984, 227–244.

Motto, J. Empirical indicators of near term suicide risk. In D. Lester (Ed.) *Suicide '88.* Denver: AAS, 1988, 131–132.

Motto, J., Heilbron, D., & Juster, R. Development of a clinical instrument to estimate suicide risk. *American Journal of Psychiatry,* 1985, 142, 680–686.

Murphy, S. L., Rounsaville, B., Eyre, S., & Kleber, H. Suicide attempts in treated opiate addicts. *Comprehensive Psychiatry,* 1983, 24, 79–89.

Myers, K. M., Burke, P., & McCauley, E. Suicidal behavior by hospitalized pre-adolescent children on a psychiatric unit. *Journal of the American Academy of Child Psychiatry,* 1985, 24, 474–480.

Neuringer, C. Self and other-appraisals by suicidal, psychosomatic and normal hospital patients. *Journal of Consulting & Clinical Psychology,* 1974, 42, 306.

Neuringer, C. Affect configurations and changes in women who threaten suicide following a crisis. *Journal of Consulting & Clinical Psychology,* 1982, 50, 182–186.

Neuringer, C., & Harris, R. M. The perception of the passage of time among death-involved hospital patients. *Life-Threatening Behavior,* 1974, 4, 240–254.

Neuringer, C., & Lettieri, D. *Suicidal Women.* New York: Gardner, 1982.

Nichols, S. P., & Fasko, D. Personality variables. In D. Capuzzi & L. Golden (Eds.) *Preventing Adolescent Suicide.* Muncie, IN: Accelerated Development, 1988, 87–109.

Orbach, I., Feshbach, S., Carlson, G., & Ellenberg, L. Attitudes toward life and death in suicidal, normal and chronically ill children. *Journal of Consulting & Clinical Psychology,* 1984, 52, 1020–1027.

Orbach, I., Feshbach, S., Carlson, G., Glaubman, H., & Gross, Y. Attraction and repulsion by life and death in suicidal and normal children. *Journal of Consulting & Clinical Psychology,* 1983, 51, 661–670.

Orbach, I., Rosenheim, E., & Hary, E. Some aspects of cognitive functioning in suicidal children. *Journal of the American Academy of Child & Adolescent Psychiatry,* 1987, 26, 181–185.

Pallis, D., Gibbons, J., & Pierce, D. Estimating suicide risk among attempted suicides. *British Journal of Psychiatry,* 1984, 144, 139–148.

Papa, L. Responses to life events as predictors of suicidal behavior. *Nursing Research,* 1980, 29, 362–369.

Parker, A. The meaning of attempted suicide to young parasuicides. *British Journal of Psychiatry,* 1981, 139, 306–312.

Peniston, E. G. The ego strength scale as a predictor of Ute Indian suicide risk. *White Cloud Journal,* 1978, 1(2), 17–19.

Perrah, M., & Wichman, H. Cognitive rigidity in suicide attempters. *Suicide & Life-Threatening Behavior,* 1987, 17, 251–255.

Petrie, K., Chamberlain, K., & Clarke, D. Psychological predictors of future suicidal behavior in hospitalized suicide attempters. *British Journal of Clinical Psychology,* 1988, 27, 247–257.

Pettifor, J., Perry, D., Plowman, B., & Pitcher, S. Risk factors predicting childhood and adolescent suicides. *Journal of Child Care,* 1983, 1(3), 17–49.

Pfeffer, C. Suicidal impulses of normal children. *International Journal of Family Psychiatry,* 1984, 5(2), 139–150.

Pfeffer, C. Preoccupations with death in "normal" children. *Omega,* 1989–1990, 20, 205–212.

Pilecka, B. Selected personality predictors of renewed suicide attempts in young people. *Polish Psychological Bulletin,* 1985, 16(2), 99–108.

Plummer, B. A., Gispert, M., Hayden, R. M., Robbins, D., & Seifer, R. Depression, hopelessness, and substance abuse among hospitalized adolescents with suicidal ideation or behavior. Paper presented at the International Association for Suicide Prevention, Brussels, 1989.

Pospizyl, K. Extraversion, neuroticism and anxiety in self-injurers and suicide attempters. *Polish Psychological Bulletin,* 1985, 16, 109–112.

Predescu, V., & Grigoroiu, M. Aspects of the personality of young suicide attempters. *Neurologie & Psychiatrie (Bucuresti),* 1976, 14(3), 203–209.

Prezant, D. W., & Neimeyer, R. A. Cognitive predictors of depression and suicidal ideation. *Suicide & Life-Threatening Behavior,* 1988, 18, 259–164.

Pronovost, Y. Adaptive profile of adolescents with suicidal tendencies in the Quebec school system. In R. Yufit (Ed.) *Proceedings of the 20th Annual Conference.* Denver: AAS, 1987, 394–396.

Range, L. M., & Goggin, W. C. California Psychological Inventory differences between undergraduate suicide ideators and nonideators. *Personality & Individual Differences,* 1989, 10, 1193–1194.

Ranieri, W. F., Steer, R. A., Laurence, T. I., Rissmiller, D. J., Piper, G. E., & Beck, A. T. Relationships of depression, hopelessness and dysfunctional attitudes to suicide ideation in psychiatric patients. *Psychological Reports,* 1987, 61, 967–975.

Reynolds, W. M. *Suicidal Ideation Questionnaire.* Odessa, FL: Psychological Assessment Resources, 1988.

Ross, M. W., Clayer, J., & Campbell, R. Parental rearing patterns and suicidal thoughts. *Acta Psychiatrica Scandinavica,* 1983, 67, 429–433.

Roy, A. Self-mutilation. *British Journal of Medical Psychology,* 1978, 51, 201–203.

Santostefano, S., Rieder, C., & Berk, S. The structure of fantasied movement in suicidal children and adolescents. *Suicide & Life-Threatening Behavior,* 1984, 14, 3–16.

Sawyer, D., & Sobal, J. Public attitudes toward suicide. *Public Opinion Quarterly,* 1987, 51, 92–101.

Schmidtke, A., & Schaller, S. Looking-glass self as a suicide predictor. In P. Pichot, P. Berner, R. Wolf, & K. Thau (Eds.) *Psychiatry: The State of the Art.* New York: Plenum, 1985, 1, 987–991.

Schmidtke, A., Schaller, S. Flurschutz, E., & Meier, G. Field dependence and dichotomous thinking in patients who have attempted suicide. In S. D. Platt & N. Kreitman (Eds.) *Current Research on Suicide and Parasuicide.* Edinburgh: University of Edinburgh, 1989, 110–122.

Scholz, J. A. Defense styles in suicide attempters. *Dissertation Abstracts International,* 1972, 33B, 452–453.

Scholz, O. B., & Pfeffer, M. On the relation between depression, coping behavior and suicide. *Crisis*, 1987, 8, 138–150.

Schotte, D., & Clum, G. Suicidal ideation in a college population. *Journal of Consulting & Clinical Psychology*, 1982, 50, 690–696.

Schotte, D., & Clum, G. Problem-solving skills in a suicidal population. *Journal of Consulting & Clinical Psychology*, 1987, 55, 49–56.

Sendbuehler, J. M., Kincel, R. L., Beausejour, P., & Nemeth, G. Attempted suicide. *Psychiatric Journal of the University of Ottawa*, 1978a, 3(2), 87–94.

Sendbuehler, J. M., Kincel, R. L., Nemeth, G., & Oertel, J. Dimensions of seriousness in attempted suicide. In V. Aalberg (Ed.) *Proceedings of the 9th International Congress for Suicide Prevention & Crisis Intervention*. Helsinki: Finnish Association for Mental Health, 1978b, 506–522.

Sidrow, N. E., & Lester, D. Locus of control and suicidal ideation. *Perceptual & Motor Skills*, 1988, 67, 576.

Silberfeld, M., Steiner, B., & Ciampi, A. Suicide attempters, ideators and risk-taking propensity. *Canadian Journal of Psychiatry*, 1985, 30, 274–277.

Simons, R. L., & Murphy, P. I. Sex differences in the causes of adolescent suicide ideation. *Journal of Youth & Adolescence*, 1985, 14, 423–434.

Singh, S. B., Nigam, A., Gahlaut, D. S., & Sinha, G. C. Attempted suicide. *Journal of Personality & Clinical Studies*, 1987, 3, 117–121.

Slimak, R. E. Prediction of suicidal ideation in higher education. In R. Cohen-Sandler (Ed.) *Proceedings of the 19th Annual Meeting*, Denver: AAS, 1986, 111–113.

Smith, K. Using a battery of tests to predict suicide in a long-term hospital. *Journal of Clinical Psychology*, 1981, 37, 555–563.

Sonneck, G., Grunberger, J., & Ringel, E. Experimental contribution to the evaluation of the suicidal risk of depressive patients. *Psychiatria Clinica*, 1976, 9(2), 84–96.

Spirito, A., Faust, D., Myers, B., & Bechtel, D. Clinical utility of the MMPI in the evaluation of adolescent suicide attempters. *Journal of Personality Assessment*, 1988a, 52, 204–211.

Spirito, A., Overholser, J., & Stark, L. J. Common problems and coping strategies. *Journal of Abnormal Child Psychology*, 1989, 17, 213–221.

Spirito, A., Stark, L. J., Hart, K. J., & Fristad, M. Overt behavior of adolescent suicide attempters hospitalized on a general pediatrics floor. *Journal of Adolescent Health Care*, 1988b, 9, 491–494.

Spittle, B., Bragan, K., & Jame, B. Risk-taking propensity, depression and parasuicide. *Australian & New Zealand Journal of Psychiatry*, 1976, 10, 269–273.

Sreenan-Auger, M. Adolescent male self-concept and suicide ideation. In D. Lester (Ed.) *Suicide '89*. Denver: AAS, 1989, 93–94.

Stancak, A., Fraenkel, E., & Jassova, Z. Suicidal types according to MMPI. *Studia Psychologia*, 1983, 25(2), 151–157.

Stanley, B., Traskman-Bendz, L., & Stanley, M. The suicidal assessment scale. *Psychopharmocology Bulletin*, 1986, 22(1), 200–205.

Stillion, J., McDowell, E., & May, J. Development trends and sex differences in adolescent attitudes toward suicide. *Death Education*, 1984a, 8, supplement, 81–90.

Stillion, J., McDowell, E., & Shamblin, J. The suicide attitude vignette experience. *Death Education*, 1984b, 8, supplement, 65–79.

Stillion, J., McDowell, E., Smith, R., & McCoy, P. Relationships between suicide attitudes and indicators of mental health among adolescents. *Death Studies*, 1986, 10, 289–296.

Tarter, R. E., Templer, D. I., & Perley, R. L. Social role orientation and pathological factors in suicide attempts of varying lethality. *Journal of Community Psychology*, 1975, 3, 295–299.

Terman, L. M., & Oden, H. H. *The Gifted Child Grows Up.* Palo Alto: Stanford University, 1947.

Thomas, C. B., & Duzynski, K. Are the words of the Rorschach predictors of disease and death? *Psychosomatic Medicine*, 1985, 47, 201–211.

Thomas, C. B., & McCabe, O. Precursors of premature disease and death. *Johns Hopkins Medical Journal*, 1980, 147, 137–145.

Thomssen, C., & Moller, H. J. A description of behavioral patterns of coping with life events in suicidal patients. In H. J. Moller, A. Schmidtke, & R. Welz (Eds.) *Current Issues of Suicidology.* Berlin: Springer-Verlag, 1988, 316–321.

Tishler, C. L., & McKenry, P. Intrapsychic symptom dimensions of adolescent suicide attempters. *Journal of Family Practice*, 1983, 16, 731–734.

Topol, P., & Reznikoff, M. Perceived peer and family relationships, hopelessness and locus of control as factors in adolescent suicide attempts. *Suicide & Life-Threatening Behavior*, 1982, 12, 141–150.

Wade, N. L. Suicide as a resolution of separation-individuation among adolescent girls. *Adolescence*, 1987, 22, 169–177.

Waters, B., Sendbuehler, J., Kincel, R., Boodoosingh, L., & Marchenko, I. The use of the MMPI for the differentiation of suicidal and non-suicidal depressions. *Canadian Journal of Psychiatry*, 1982, 27, 663–667.

Watson, C., Klett, W., Walters, C., & Laughlin, P. Identification of suicidal episodes with the MMPI. *Psychological Reports*, 1983, 53, 919–922.

Watson, C., Klett, W., Walters, C., & Vassar, P. Suicide and the MMPI. *Journal of Clinical Psychology*, 1984, 40, 115–119.

Watson, C., & Kucala, T. Anhedonia and death. *Psychological Reports*, 12978, 43, 1120–1122.

Weiner, A. S., & Pfeffer, C. R. Suicidal status, depression, and intellectual functioning in preadolescent psychiatric inpatients. *Comprehensive Psychiatry*, 1986, 27, 372–380.

Weis, S., & Seiden, R. H. Rescuers and the rescued. *Life-Threatening Behavior*, 1974, 4, 118–130.

White, H., & Stillion, J. M. Sex difference in attitudes toward suicide. *Psychology of Women Quarterly*, 1988, 12, 357–366.

Wilder, M. A. Identifying patterns of self-injurious behavior in youths. In R. Cohen-Sandler (Ed.) *Proceedings of the 19th Annual Meeting.* Denver: AAS, 1986, 103–104.

Williams, J. M. Differences in reasons for taking overdoses in high and low hopelessness groups. *British Journal of Medical Psychology*, 1986, 59, 269–277.

Williams, J. M., & Broadbent, K. Distraction by emotional stimuli. *British Journal of Clinical Psychology*, 1986a, 25, 101–110.

Williams, J. M., & Broadbent, K. Autobiographical memory in suicide attempters. *Journal of Abnormal Psychology*, 1986b, 95, 144–149.

Williams, J. M., & Dritschel, B. H. Emotional disturbance and the specificity of autobiographical memory. *Cognition & Emotion*, 1988, 2, 221–234.

Wilson, L. T., Braucht, G. N., Miskimins, R. W., & Berry, K. L. The severe suicide attempter and self-concept. *Journal of Clinical Psychology*, 1971, 27, 307–209.

Woods, P. J., & Muller, G. E. The contemplation of suicide. *Journal of Rational Emotive & Cognitive Behavioral Therapy*, 1988, 6, 236–258.

Chapter 23

SUICIDAL TYPES

The analysis of many behaviors has been facilitated by the identification of different *types* of the behavior. In previous decades little research appeared on identifying reliable and general types of suicides, and psychiatric diagnosis remained the most common way of classifying suicides. The 1980s witnessed little progress in this regard.

Robertson (1977) suggested three types of suicide attempters: (1) exhibitionists who were usually single, adolescent and female, (2) pseudocides who were usually middle-aged, unstable, uncertain about dying and repeaters, and (3) malignant who were usually elderly with a recent loss.

Motto (1977) distinguished between stable suicidal people who have changes forced upon them and alienated suicidal people. He found that the items predicting later suicide differed for these two types of people.

Empirical Analyses

Adolescents

Several studies have examined the associations of a number of variables to identify clusters of patients. Bagley (1989) examined 23 variables in a sample of adolescent suicides and identified six clusters. However, he did not name these clusters. Biro (1987) found seven clusters of variables in a sample of completed suicides in Yugoslavia.

In France, Choquet et al. (1980) distinguished four types of teenage suicide attempters: (1) serious repeaters, from disturbed families and disturbed themselves, (2) serious first-timers, from disturbed families and with behavior problems, (3) not lethal, with little psychiatric disturbance but from disturbed families, and (4) not serious with little disturbance and from families with little pathology.

Hawton et al. (1982) identified three types of adolescent self-poisoners: acute, chronic, and chronic plus behavior disturbance. This latter group came from large and more psychiatrically disturbed families, and were less often living at home with their families. Their attempts were more impulsive, they were more often drug and alcohol abusers, they had more problems, and they were more likely to repeat their attempts in the next year. Both chronic types had received more prior psychiatric treatment and tended to have worse relationships with their parents. The acute group had the fewest problems and were more likely to be reacting to problems in current relationships.

In the Netherlands, Kienhorst et al. (1987) identified three types of attempted suicides in children: (1) boys aged 9–11 who used active methods, (2) only children from disturbed families, and (3) girls aged 12–14 from intact homes, with no prior attempts, who used passive methods.

Kowalski et al. (1986) identified two types of serious suicide attempters among teenagers: (1) with an intense reaction to loss and (2) after a failure to fulfill high self-expectations or some ideal.

Adults

In a study of attempted suicides, Katschnig and Fuchs-Robetin (1985) identified six clusters, two of which had a high subsequent completed suicide rate (the failed suicide and the chronic type) while one had a low rate (the cry for help). Paykel (1980) found three types of suicide attempters which he labelled recurrent, overdosers and non-overdosers.

Kurz et al. (1987) identified three groups of suicide attempters from a cluster analysis: (1) young males, with prior attempts, hostility, personality disorder and substance abuse, with premeditation, (2) older males, severely intoxicated, taking precautions against discovery, highly dependent, with little hostility, and with a neurotic/addictive/reactive disorder, and (3) younger females, with few previous attempts and rarely intoxicated, with little concealment, interpersonally motivated, and with a reactive disorder.

Stephens (1985) described four types of female suicide attempters on the basis of their relationship with men: smothering love from her to him, infidelity by him, brutality and battering by him, and denial of affection by him.

Studies of Different Types

Bourque et al. (1983) compared female suicides whose precipitants were physical illness, family loss, with prior psychiatric treatment, and others. They found that those with physical illness and family loss were the most despondent, while the "others" had less prior suicidal behavior. There were no differences in alcohol abuse, recent arrests, method for the suicide, or committing suicide at home.

Modestin (1986) simply classified ex-psychiatric patients who completed suicides by diagnosis and compared the schizophrenics, depressives and alcoholics. For example, the alcoholic suicides had experienced more recent stress, the depressives had a better adjustment at admission and were more suicidal, while the schizophrenics were more disturbed early in life. The groups did not differ in the family history of suicide, but the schizophrenics had made fewer prior suicide attempts.

Cultural Differences

One study compared suicides in different nations. Chinese suicidal patients, as compared to Americans, were older, with less prior suicidal behavior, less communication of suicidal intent and more physical problems (Chiles et al., 1989). The groups did not differ in suicidal intent or hopelessness. However, the comparison did not extend to types.

Abstract Typologies

Lester (1988) drew on Phillips (1989) distinction between research paradigms of suicide as a chronic process and suicide as an acute process to suggest that there were two types of suicidal individuals, the one in an acute crisis and the other who has shown a chronic lifelong pattern of depression and suicide. Lester and Yang (1991) have also drawn an analogy between these two types of suicidal people and Becker's (1962) two types of irrational behavior as viewed from an economic perspective — decisions which are simply a repetition of choices made in the past and decisions which are made from a random choice of the alternatives.

Baechler (1979) proposed a classification of types of suicide, and Smith and Bloom (1985) found that all of a sample of attempters, completers and ideators could be classified into the categories, 22 percent into one single category and 78 percent into more than one category.

Taylor (1982) proposed a classification for the social context of suicide. Taylor used two dimensions: whether the action is inner-directed (ectopic) or other-directed (symphysic) and whether it is purposive in seeking death (certainty) or merely an ordeal (uncertainty). These two dimensions provide four types: thanation (ectopic/uncertain), submissive (ectopic/certain), appeal (symphysic/uncertain) and sacrifice (symphysic/certain).

Discussion

As in the 1970s, little was written in the 1980s on the taxonomy of suicide. This remains a puzzle since an adequate taxonomy is often the first step in the study of a phenomenon. It is unlikely that all suicides are alike, and a taxonomy of types of suicide would seem to promise an advance in our understanding of suicidal behavior.

REFERENCES

Baechler, J. *Suicides.* New York: Basic Books, 1979.

Bagley, C. Taxonomy of 130 cases of youth suicide. *Perceptual & Motor Skills,* 1989, 69, 318.

Becker, G. S. Irrational behavior and economic theory. *Journal of Political Economy,* 1962, 70, 1–13.

Biro, M. Factor analytic study of suicidal behavior. *Crisis,* 1987, 8, 62–68.

Bourque, L., Kraus, J., & Cosand, B. Attributes of suicide in females. *Suicide & Life-Threatening Behavior,* 1983, 13, 123–138.

Chiles, J. A., Strosahl, K. D., Ping, Z. Y., Michael, M. C., Hall, K., Jemelka, R., Senn, B., & Reto, C. Depression, hopelessness and suicidal behavior in Chinese and American psychiatric patients. *American Journal of Psychiatry,* 1989, 146, 339–344.

Choquet, M., Facy, F., & Davidson, F. Suicide and attempted suicide among adolescents in France. In R. F. Farmer & S. Hirsch (Eds.) *The Suicide Syndrome.* London: Croom Helm, 1980, 73–89.

Hawton, K., Osborn, M., O'Grady, J., & Cole, D. Classification of adolescents who take overdoses. *British Journal of Psychiatry,* 1982, 140, 124–131.

Katschnig, H., & Fuchs-Robetin, G. A typology of attempted suicide. In P. Pichot, P. Berner, R. Wolf, & K. Thau (Eds.) *Psychiatry: the State of the Art, Volume 1.* New York: Plenum, 1985, 945–950.

Kienhorst, C. W., Wolters, W. H. G., Diekstra, R. F. W., & Otte, E. A study of the frequency of suicidal behavior in children aged 5 to 14. *Journal of Child Psychology & Psychiatry,* 1987, 28, 153–165.

Kowalski, P., Crawford, S., & Smith, K. Comparison of mild versus serious adolescent attempters. In R. Cohen-Sandler (Ed.) *Proceedings of the 19th Annual Meeting.* Denver: AAS, 1986, 63–65.

Kurz, A., Moller, H. J., Baindl, G., Burk, F., Torhorst, A., Wachter, C., & Lauter, H. Classification of parasuicide by cluster analysis. *British Journal of Psychiatry,* 1987, 150, 520–525.

Lester, D. Suicidal individuals. *Crisis,* 1988, 9, 130–134.

Lester, D., & Yang, B. Suicidal behavior and Becker's definition of irrationality. *Psychological Reports,* 1991, 68, 655–656.

Modestin, J. Three different types of clinical suicide. *European Archives of Psychiatry,* 1986, 236, 148–153.

Motto, J. A. Estimation of suicide risk by the use of clinical models. *Suicide & Life-Threatening Behavior,* 1977, 7, 234–245.

Paykel, E. S. A classification of suicide attempters by cluster analysis. In R. Farmer & S. Hirsch (eds.) *The Suicide Syndrome.* London: Croom Helm, 1980, 144–153.

Phillips, D. P. Recent advances in suicidology. In R. F. Diekstra, R. F., Maris, R., Platt, S., Schmidtke, A., & G. Sonneck, (Eds.) *Suicide and Its Prevention.* Leiden: Brill, 1989, 299–312.

Robertson, J. The epidemiology of self-poisoning. *Public Health,* 1977, 91(2), 75–82.

Smith, G., & Bloom, I. A study of the personal meaning of suicide in the context of Baechler's typology. *Suicide & Life-Threatening Behavior,* 1985, 15, 3–13.

Stephens, B. J. Suicidal women and their relationships with husbands, boyfriends and lovers. *Suicide & Life-Threatening Behavior,* 1985, 15, 77–89.

Taylor, S. *Durkheim and the Study of Suicide.* London: Macmillan, 1982.

Chapter 24

OTHER SELF-DESTRUCTIVE BEHAVIORS

Farberow (1980) has sought to include the study of indirect self-destructive behaviors in the realm of suicidology. He classified indirect self-destructive behaviors according to whether a prior physical condition exists which the person's behavior makes worse or whether no prior physical condition exists.

In this latter situation, the person may cause his body or his mind damage actually (by smoking, overeating, and self-mutilation or by severe sexual disorders and asceticism), potentially (by violent crime and repeated accidents or by compulsive gambling and delinquency), and by stress-seeking and risk-taking (by mountain climbing and hang-gliding or by games of risk and stock market speculation). Where a prior physical condition already exists, the person may also harm his body or his mind (by polysurgery and psychosomatic disorders or by loss of function as in sensory loss from blindness).

Farberow suggested that those who engage in indirect self-destructive behavior differ from those who engage in direct self-destructive behaviors in symptoms, cognition, affect, dynamics, futurity, risk-taking, communication, relationships and coping mechanisms.

Nelson and Farberow (1976, 1980) devised a measure of indirect self-destructive behavior and gave this, along with an MMPI scale of suicidal potential, to a group of chronically ill, elderly patients. Indirect self-destructive behavior scores were positively associated with suicidal potential, risk-taking, manipulativeness, hopelessness, no prospect of going home, and personal losses and negatively with life satisfaction and an internal locus of control.

Farberow and Williams (1983) compared a group of hyperobese patients with attempted suicides and found no differences in manipulativeness, risk-taking, locus of control or recent losses. The hyperobese were more assertive, aggressive, self-reliant and tough-minded on the 16 PF inventory while the attempted suicides were less emotionally stable, more insecure, more tense and more sensitive.

408

General Self-Destructiveness

Borst and Noam (1989) found an association between attempting suicide and general self-destructive behavior in a sample of adolescent psychiatric patients. Lee (1985, 1987) used a suicide proneness scale in which he asked college students questions such as "How likely would you be to take your own life?" and found that scores on the scale were associated with scores on a measure of involvement in generally self-destructive behaviors. On some personality tests, suicide proneness and self-destructive behavior had similar associations (such as religiosity, self-liking, value of life, and the acceptability of suicide). However, when he looked at the extremely suicide prone and the extremely self-destructive students, he found differences in personality. The highly self-destructive, for example, scored high on dogmatism and religiosity. The highly suicide prone scored high on the acceptability of suicide and low on self-evaluation.

Cantor (1976) found that students who had attempted suicide showed much more self-destructive behavior than non-suicidal students, including drinking, drug use, and reckless driving. Clifton and Lee (1976) found that students preoccupied with suicide showed more self-destructive behaviors, including drinking a lot and overeating.

Lester and Gatto (1989) found that a measure of general self-destructiveness was associated with current suicidal ideation in male high school students, even after controls for depression. In the females, controls for depression eliminated the association.

Mehr et al. (1981), however, found no differences between small samples of adolescent suicide attempters, accident victims and other patients on an inventory of general self-destructiveness.

Indirect Life-Threatening Behavior

Osgood et al. (1988–1989) has studied indirect life-threatening behavior (such as refusal to eat or to take medication) in elderly patients in nursing homes. They found that about 0.97 percent of patients engaged in some form of life-threatening behavior. Of these, 15 percent showed overt suicidal behavior while the rest showed only indirect behaviors. Females were more likely to engage in the indirect forms as were those over the age of 75. Those over the age of 75 were more likely to engage in passive forms of indirect behaviors, but they were more likely to die.

Reynolds and Nelson (1981) studied chronically ill male patients and found that those who engaged in more indirect-self-destructive behavior were more likely to die in the following year.

Car Crashes

Schmidt et al. (1978) investigated car fatalities and estimated that 2.7 percent of single car crash fatalities were suicide as compared to zero percent of the multicar fatalities. Two percent of the fatalities of these crashes had attempted suicide in the prior six months. In non-fatal accidents, fewer of the accidents were judged to be suicidal and a history of prior suicide attempts was less common. Pokorny et al. (1972) compared auto fatalities where the deceased was responsible (and so, possibly suicidal) with ordinary drivers. The fatalities were more often depressed or suicidal prior to the accident, had experienced more recent stress (in the past six months and in the last 24 hours), were more often alcoholics and had more traffic convictions. Comparing the depressed and suicidal fatalities with the other fatalities revealed no differences in psychiatric symptoms or psychosis, intoxication, anger, traffic convictions, poor impulse control or precipitating stresses. The depressed fatalities were, however, more often alcoholics. Four of the 28 fatalities were judged to be suicides.

Edland (1972) studied 112 traffic fatalities of which 63 involved single vehicles. Nineteen of the fatalities were judged to be homicides, three were clear suicides, three were probable suicides, and two more may have been suicides.

Isherwood et al. (1982a, 1982b) found that attempted suicides had experienced more recent stressful events (of all kinds) than people who had been in car crashes. The suicide attempters were more depressed, neurotic, with low sports participation, and more often taking prescribed medication. Tattoos, smoking, drug or alcohol abuse, psychiatric history, loss in childhood, psychoticism, extraversion or financial/physical risk-taking did not discriminate between the two groups.

Jenkins and Sainsbury (1980) looked at single car crash deaths in England. The distributions by month and age were different from those for completed suicides. Comparing single occupant crash deaths with multiple occupants revealed no differences in age or weather/road conditions. The authors concluded that car crashes were not disguised suicides.

Sociological Studies

Kivela (1985) found a positive association between the suicide rate of elderly Finnish males over time (but not elderly Finnish females) and accidental deaths from motor vehicle crashes and all accidental causes (but not falls). In England, Tweedie (1980) found the monthly suicide rates and the monthly single-car/single-occupant road death rates were negatively associated. In the US, Wilbanks (1982) found that the suicide rate was positively associated with deaths for motor vehicle accidents (and all other accidents as well) over SMSAs but not with motor vehicle accidents over time from 1960–1975.

Self-Mutilation

Carr (1977) reviewed theories of self-injurious behaviors (primarily occurring in animals, the mentally retarded and those severely psychiatrically disturbed). He found five major theories. Two theories focussed on extrinsic motivation. The positive reinforcement hypothesis asserts that self-injurious behavior is a learned behavior reinforced by social rewards such as attention or social interaction. The negative reinforcement hypothesis asserts that self-injurious behavior is engaged in to terminate aversive conditions, such as demands being made on the person or to escape from confinement or the dark.

Two theories have focussed on intrinsic motivation. The self-stimulation hypothesis asserts that self-injurious behavior has the purpose of producing a certain level of stimulation in the tactile, vestibular and kinesthetic modalities. The organic hypothesis asserts that the problem has an organic basis. Genetically produced syndromes (such as the Lesch-Nyhan syndrome and the de Lang syndrome) are often accompanied by self-injurious behaviors. Middle-ear infections or elevated pain thresholds may induce or facilitate self-injurious behaviors. Finally, psychodynamic theories focus on the role of self-injurious behaviors in establishing body reality or tracing ego boundaries or reducing guilt.

Walsh and Rosen (1988) have also discussed the relationship between self-mutilation and suicidal behavior. They felt that the two behaviors were quite different. Self-mutilation more often has the goal of releasing tension. It is less lethal, more repetitive and more chronic. Self-mutilators also tend to use multiple methods more and to switch methods more.

Jones (1986) found that prisoners who self-mutilated attempted suicide in prison more than did non-mutilators. The self-mutilators were more often white, had discipline problems in prison, felons, assaultive in prison, and with arm and wrist scars on admission. Walsh and Rosen (1988) noted that from 28 percent to 40 percent of self-mutilators have suicidal ideation. In a study of adolescent self-mutilators, they found that 13 percent had suicidal thoughts at the time when they self-mutilated and 31 percent had previously attempted suicide. The suicide attempters did not differ from the non-attempters in the characteristics of their self-mutilating behavior. In a study of a small sample of adolescent inpatients, Walsh and Rosen found that incidents of self-mutilation clustered over time whereas talk of suicide did not.

Alcoholism

Although the association between alcoholism and suicide is covered elsewhere (Chapter 18), Burns (1980) has suggested that alcoholism might be viewed as a suicidal behavior. A review of studies of female suicides and female alcoholics revealed many similarities, such as childhood loss, interpersonal disharmony, depression and disorganized lives.

Faking Suicide

Weitzman (1974) studied a sample of husbands who faked their own death (primarily by suicide) and then went off to another part of the country to start a new life—people she called *social suicides.* She noted that the disappearance was well planned, and there was typically no dramatic precipitating crisis. Their wives were often ignorant of their husband's financial affairs and were surprised by his disappearance. The men took nothing personal with them, leaving behind even their credentials.

Suicides Versus Accidental Deaths

Howard (1984) found that suicides from overdoses were older, more often white and female, more often residents from outside the county and more often married/widowed/divorced than those dying from accidental overdoses. Jacobsen et al. (1984) found that attempted suicides by self-poisoning had a higher level of coma than accidental poisonings.

Discussion

The relationship between suicidal behavior and other forms of indirect self-destructive behavior is an interesting issue, not simply for empirical reasons, but because any similarity has implications for our conception of suicide. Is suicide a behavior completely different from other forms of self-destructive behavior, or it merely at one extreme of a general continuum? Previous research does not permit us to answer this question, but perhaps future research will move us toward an answer.

REFERENCES

Borst, S. R., & Noam, G. G. Suicidality and psychopathology in hospitalized children and adolescents. *Acta Paedopsychiatrica,* 1989, 52, 163–175.

Burns, M. M. Alcohol abuse among women as indirect self-destructive behavior. In N. L. Farberow (Ed.) *The Many Faces of Suicide.* New York: McGraw-Hill, 1980, 220–231.

Cantor, P. Frequency of suicidal thoughts and self-destructive behaviors among females. *Suicide & Life-Threatening Behavior,* 1976, 6, 92–100.

Carr, E. G. The motivation of self-injurious behavior. *Psychological Bulletin,* 1977, 84, 800–816.

Clifton, A. K., & Lee, D. E. Self-destructive consequences of sex-role socialization. *Suicide & Life-Threatening Behavior,* 1976, 6, 11–22.

Edland, J. Suicide by automobile. *Albany Law Review,* 1972, 36, 536–542.

Farberow, N. L. *The Many Faces of Suicide.* New York: McGraw-Hill, 1980.

Farberow, N. L., & Williams, J. L. Indirect self-destructive behavior and the hyperobese. *Psychiatria Fennica,* 1983, supplement, 21–39.

Howard, D. J. Drug-related deaths in a major metropolitan area. *Journal of Applied Social Sciences,* 1984, 8, 235–248.

Isherwood, J., Adam, K. S., & Hornblow, A. Life event stress, psychosocial factors, suicide attempts and auto-accident proclivity. *Journal of Psychosomatic Research,* 1982a, 26, 371–383.

Isherwood, J., Adam, K. S., & Hornblow, A. Readjustment, desirability, expectedness, mastery and outcome dimensions of life stress, suicide attempts and auto accidents. *Journal of Human Stress,* 1982b, 8(1), 11–18.

Jacobsen, D., Frederichsen, P., Knutsen, K., Sorum, Y., Talseth, T., & Odegaard, O. Clinical course in acute self-poisonings. *Human Toxicology,* 1984, 3, 107–116.

Jenkins, J., & Sainsbury, P. Single-car road deaths. *British Medical Journal,* 1980, 281, 1041.

Jones, A. Self-mutilation in prison. *Criminal Justice & Behavior,* 1986, 13, 286–296.

Kivela, S. L. Relationship between suicide, homicide and accidental deaths among the aged in Finland in 1951–1979. *Acta Psychiatrica Scandinavica,* 1985, 72, 155–160.

Lee, D. E. Alternative self-destruction. *Perceptual & Motor Skills,* 1985, 61, 1065–1066.

Lee, D. E. The self-deception of the self-destructive. *Perceptual & Motor Skills*, 1987, 65, 975–989.

Lester, D., & Gatto, J. L. Self-destructive tendencies and depression as predictors of suicidal ideation in teenagers. *Journal of Adolescence*, 1989, 12, 221–223.

Mehr, M., Zeltzer, L., & Robinson, R. Continued self-destructive behaviors in adolescent suicide attempters. *Journal of Adolescent Health Care*, 1981, 1, 269–274; 1982, 2, 183–187.

Nelson, F. L., & Faberow, N. L. Indirect suicide in the elderly, chronically ill patient. *Psychiatria Fennica*, 1976, supplement, 125–139.

Nelson, F., & Farberow, N. L. Indirect self-destructive behavior in the elderly nursing home patients. *Journal of Gerontology*, 1980, 35, 949–957.

Osgood, N. J., Brant, B. A., & Lipman, A. A. Patterns of suicidal behavior in long-term care facilities. *Omega*, 1988–1989, 19, 69–78.

Pokorny, A. D., Smith, J. P., & Finch, J. R. Vehicular suicides. *Life-Threatening Behavior*, 1972, 2, 105–119.

Reynolds, D., & Nelson, F. Personality, life situation, and life expectancy. *Suicide & Life-Threatening Behavior*, 1981, 11, 99–110.

Schmidt, C. W., Shaffer, J. W., Banks, W., Zlotwitz, H. I., Masemore, W. C., & Fisher, R. S. Suicide by vehicular crash. In V. Aalberg (Ed.) *Proceedings of the 9th International Congress for Suicide Prevention*. Helsinki: Finnish Association for Mental Health, 1978, 322–329.

Tweedie, M. C. Single-car road deaths. *British Medical Journal*, 1980, 281, 1288.

Walsh, B. W., & Rosen, P. M. *Self-Mutilation*. New York: Guilford, 1988.

Weitzman, L. J. Social suicide. *Dissertation Abstracts International*, 1974, 34A, 5356.

Wilbanks, W. Fatal accident, suicide and homicide. *Victimology*, 1982, 7, 213–217.

Chapter 25

SUICIDAL BEHAVIOR IN LOWER ANIMALS

The term *suicide* is being increasingly applied to the behaviors of biochemicals, microorganisms, and lower animals. A few examples of these applications are described briefly below.

Completed Suicide

McConkey et al. (1989) described the process *apoptosis* in which the glucocorticoids in the body activate a suicide process in immature thymocites (lymphocytes arising in the thymus gland) by causing an elevation of the cytosolic Ca^{2+} concentration.

Namdari and Cabelli (1989) noted that motile aeromonads (bacteria which are pathogenic to marine and fresh water animals), when grown in the presence of glucose and in the temperature range of 30°C to 37°C, produce high levels of acetic acid which kills them. They called this process suicide.

Bariola (1978) observed that pink bollworm moths occasionally emerge from hibernation before the appropriate time, and he considered this behavior to be suicidal.

Trail (1980) described a process in which some organisms infected by parasites show aberrant behavior and increase their probability of death, for example, death from predators. Trail gave examples from butterflies and called the process host-suicide. In a similar fashion McAllister and Roitberg (1987) noted that pea aphids which are parasitized by the braconid wasp (Aphidius erri), are more likely to choose behaviors which increase their risk of death (such as dropping off the plant and dying). This suicide in the host, therefore, damages the parasite too, and the suicidal behavior was considered adaptive by the authors.

O'Connor (1978) noted that, as starvation mortality increases in bird populations, the birds differentially feed their young (infanticide), intrasibling rivalry increases (fratricide), and some appear to give up living (suicide).

Self-Mutilation

Jones (1982, 1983) noted that animals self-mutilate when agitated, when their aggression is blocked or frustrated, and when socially isolated (though the self-mutilation is less severe in this latter situation). Thus, self-mutilation appears to reduce arousal, to release aggression and to be aberrant self-grooming. Self-mutilation is made more likely by brain damage, rearing in isolation, and irritative lesions.

Similar situations may arise for humans, for whom self-mutilation may also be aberrant grooming (to reduce arousal), or stimulated by rage and isolation. Mild self-mutilation may increase arousal while severe self-mutilation may decrease arousal. Thus, Jones argued that self-mutilation has a phylogenetic basis.

Crawley et al. (1985) noted that self-mutilation is common among zoo animals and resembles the self-mutilation found in penal and mental institutions. Monkeys commonly self-mutilate after separation from their mother or their peers.

Discussion

This application of word *suicide* to biochemicals and lower animals is a new etymological phenomenon and may raise interesting conceptual issues for the definition of suicide in the 1990s.

REFERENCES

Bariola, L. A. Suicidal emergence and reproduction by overwintered pink bollworm moths. *Environmental Entomology*, 1978, 7, 189–192.

Crawley, J., Sutton, M., & Pickar, D. Animal models of self-destructive behavior and suicide. *Psychiatric Clinics of North America*, 1985, 8, 299–310.

Jones, I. H. Self-injury. *Perspectives in Biology & Medicine*, 1982, 26, 137–150.

Jones, I. H. An animal model of self-injury and its use in human states. In J. P. Soubrier & J. Vedrinne (Eds.) *Depression and Suicide*. Paris: Pergamon, 1983, 221–226.

McAllister, M. K., & Roitberg, B. D. Adaptive suicidal behavior in pea aphids. *Nature*, 1987, 328, 797–799.

McConkey, D. J., Nicotera, P., Hartzell, P., Bellono, G., Wyllie, A. H., & Orrenius, S. Glucocorticoids activate a suicide process in thymocytes through an elevation of cytosolic calcium concentration. *Archives of Biochemistry & Biophysics*, 1989, 269, 365–370.

Namdari, H., & Cabelli, V. J. The suicide phenomenon in motile aeromonads. *Applied & Environmental Microbiology,* 1989, 55, 543–547.

O'Connor, R. J. Brood reduction in birds. *Animal Behavior,* 1978, 26, 79–96.

Trail, D. R. Behavioral interactions between parasites and hosts. *American Naturalist,* 1980, 116(1), 77–91.

Chapter 26

PSYCHOLOGICAL THEORIES OF SUICIDE

T he 1980s witnessed the initial presentation of a variety of psychological theories of suicide, few of which have yet been subjected to
empirical testing. In this chapter, we will briefly review these theories
and hope that the 1990s will bring research to test them.

Lester's Social Learning Theory of Suicide

Lester (1987a, 1987b) proposed a social learning theory of completed
and attempted suicide. He reviewed the literature on viewing depression
from a learning theory perspective and then explored such topics as:
suicide as a manipulative behavior, childhood experiences leading to
later suicide, suicide as a failure of socialization, societal shaping of
suicide, an economic cost-benefit analysis of suicide, subcultural factors,
the role of suggestion, learning influences in the methods chosen for
suicide, suicide in significant others, the role of the family, and cultural
patterns. Lester concluded that a strong case could be made for viewing
suicide as a learned behavior.

Classic Theories of Personality and Suicide

Lester (1988b) considered some of the major theories of personality
and reviewed how research into suicide was consistent with them. The
theories he found research support for included Sigmund Freud, George
Kelly, Alfred Adler, Carl Rogers, Henry Murray, William Sheldon,
Hans Eysenck and social learning theory. Lester concluded that three of
theories appeared to contribute to the understanding of suicide, explaining
many of the research findings of suicidal individuals: Freud, Eysenck
and social learning theory. Neimeyer (1983) has also examined suicide
from the viewpoint of George Kelly's theory of personality suggesting
the following elements: constriction in contruct content and application,
breakdown in anticipation of future events, a disorganized construct

418

system, negative self-construing, polarized or dichotomous thinking, and perceived interpersonal isolation.

Maris's Pathways Theory

Maris (1981) proposed a theory of suicide which stemmed from his study of completed suicides, natural deaths and attempted suicides. The results of the study are complex. For example, Maris found that the completed suicides had experienced different recent stresses than had the natural deaths, were less devout, were more psychiatrically disturbed, were less often physically ill, were more often upward mobile, but also more often unemployed and with blocked aspirations. They did not differ in substance abuse, social relations, or early trauma and problems.

For his theory Maris took a developmental approach and proposed that completed and attempted suicides have failed to master the developmental tasks of life. This leads to a greater likelihood of failure, abortive transitions and developmental stagnation. For both attempted and completed suicides there is evidence of repeated depression, repeated life failure, and prolonged negative interactions and social isolation, and Maris proposed possible pathways for the appearance of completed and attempted suicide (Maris, 1981, pp. 324, 328).

New Psychological Theories of Suicide

Lester (1988b) proposed several new theories of suicide.

Lester's Physiological Theory of Suicide

It seems quite unlikely that a specific genetic factor will be found for suicide. Suicide is typically associated with psychiatric illness, and studies to explore the inheritance of suicidal tendencies have always failed to tease out the confounding effect of psychiatric illness. For example, twin studies of suicide have not assessed the role of psychiatric disturbance in the completed suicides (Lester, 1985).

Research into the brains of suicides also runs up against the same problem. Those physiological features identified for suicidal people are typically characteristic depressives in general (Lester, 1983).

Thus, what is critical for an organic model of suicide is to suggest factors that may be unique to the suicidal individual rather than characteristic of psychiatrically disturbed people in general. It is possible to suggest several factors that might be relevant.

First, the act of suicide requires courage, inhibition of fear and anxiety, and the suppression of guilt (if the act is against one's moral philosophy). Those about to complete suicide may fear the pain of the act of dying or the consequences should there be a life after death. Jacobs (1967) has noted that suicide notes often include content to deal with the problem of life after death. The note writer may ask the survivors to pray for them, or he may indicate that he knows that God will understand his act.

What would facilitate suppression of emotions? The psychopath, by definition, experiences less shame, guilt and remorse. Thus, we might expect to find psychopathic traits in suicidal individuals, and there are several organic theories of psychopathy (see, for example, Lester, 1974). In addition, it may be that suicidal individuals (especially those who repeat suicidal acts) are less sensitive to pain. Such people have been called reducers (Petrie, 1967) or extraverts (Eysenck, 1967). Spiegel and Neuringer (1963) have argued that those about to complete suicide will avoid thinking about the imminent action and so their suicide notes will have less mention of suicide. The personality style of repression (Bryne, 1961) would facilitate such a tactic.

Second, there may be physiological factors that resist succumbing to the mode chosen for suicide. It has been suggested that females are physiologically more resistant than males to physical trauma, a factor which may in part account for the fact that more females survive suicidal actions (Lester, 1984a). For example, in falls, females are more likely to survive (Robertson et al., 1978).

Other similar factors may include an "allergic" reaction to drugs, so that the person is more likely to vomit after an ingestion. Or perhaps a higher threshold for succumbing to their effects. (Sheldon [1942], for example, argued that cerebrotonics were more resistant to the effects of various drugs such as sedatives and hypnotics.)

Lester's Existential Theory of Suicide

Often people have difficulty meeting the demands or expectations placed upon them by society (or by themselves). This can result in conflict, and the resulting emotion from this conflict may be anxiety. If this anxiety is accompanied by a belief that one is powerless to affect one's environment (a feeling of helplessness) and thereby to eliminate the source of the stress, then the person will probably experience low self-esteem. Not many options remain open for such an individual.

As Gold (1980) has pointed out, such an individual may turn to drug use as a means of reducing their anxiety. However, other tension-relieving tactics exist. Those who have talked to wrist-cutters, for example, have reported how the feelings of tension build up in the patient until, on cutting the wrists and seeing the blood flow, the tension drains away (Graff and Mallin, 1967). Often the patient reports an absence of pain under this state of intense tension.

The existential position sees suicide as a tactic in which the person assumes control of his or her life. By the act of the suicide, the individual responds, behaves, becomes fully human. Indeed, Binswanger (1958), in discussing the case of Ellen West, an anorexic female, concluded that "only in her decision for death did she find herself and choose herself. The festival of death was the festival of the birth of her existence" (p. 298).

Thus, under conditions of external demands and a feeling of powerlessness, suicide may be a behavior that resolves the conflict, reduces the anxiety and relieves the feelings to powerlessness. Such a theory may explain why some people make repeated attempts at suicide. (These repeaters appear to differ in personality from one-time attempters [Lester, 1983].)

A Personality Factor Relevant for Suicide

Many personality factors have been suggested as being particularly relevant to suicide. Lester (1983), for example, has noted depression and a sense of hopelessness, belief in an external locus of control, neuroticism, alienation, low self-esteem, and a propensity for risk taking as traits likely to be found in the suicidal individual.

These traits are all easily measured by psychological inventories currently available. An interesting personality variable that may also be associated with the suicidal personality (through less easily measured) has been suggested by Khantzian (1978). Khantzian has described an ego-function which he has called self-care and self-regulation. These ego-functions include signal-anxiety, reality-testing, good judgment, and adequate self-control. It is possible that the suicidal individual has a defect in these self-care functions. The suicidal person may not anticipate, perceive or appreciate the danger in the things that he does and in the life-style he chooses. This is especially true of the suicide attempter, who may repeatedly make life-threatening gestures which are harmful (though not lethal) to himself. Suicidal people are frequently found to be violent and assaultive, more likely to abuse drugs and alcohol, and more likely to have committed crimes than non-suicidal people (Lester, 1983). They show a general tendency to harm themselves, indicating a chronic failure in self-care and self-regulation.

Why have these people failed to develop these important ego-functions? Khantzian saw the cause to be a failure to adopt and internalize these functions from caring parents in early and subsequent phases of development, most likely because the parents overly deprived (frustrated) or indulged the child.

If the infant, on the other hand, experiences good mothering, then he can internalize these qualities and functions from the parents, thereby developing an ability to care for himself. (Incidentally, he will probably also develop an ability to relate more intimately with others and a secure sense of his own value, both of which will make suicide less likely in later life.)

Psychotherapists frequently focus on this issue with their patients. However, caring for oneself has been typically defined narrowly by psychological researchers to mean valuing oneself, or having high self-esteem. Caring for oneself can also mean taking care of oneself, however, and this has been ignored on the whole by researchers.

Lester's Deindividuation Theory of Suicide

There are two conceptual approaches to the concept of deindividuation (Dipboye, 1977). Deindividuation refers to the process of losing one's distinctiveness or individuality. According to the first viewpoint, deindividuation reduces moral constraints, thereby releasing random, irrational and destructive behavior. Such an experience may not be undesirable, for the person may enjoy engaging in these new behaviors. The second approach proposes that people actively seek a separate and unique identity. A loss of identity arouses negative affect and a renewed search for an individual identity. Dipboye compares these two views with the invisible man of H. G. Wells (whose invisible man sought the anonymity of the mass movement) and of Ralph Ellison (whose invisible man searched for an identity that a racist society had denied him).

The notion of deindividuation leading to a loss of restraint stems from the ideas of Freud (1960) and Jung (1946) and has been developed by

Zimbardo (1969). This conception, however, appears to have little usefulness for a theory of suicide.

The notion of deindividuation as an unpleasant experience that
motivates a search for identity has more potential as an explanation
for suicide. Dipboye defines identity seeking as a set of behaviors that
are instrumental in affirming the identity of a person who has been
deindividuated.

Fromm (1956) has pointed out the dilemma here. People want both a
separate identity while also escaping from the feeling of separateness. It
is important to belong while feeling unique. Dipboye noted that one
consequence of deindividuation can be aggression, aggression whose
aim is to achieve reindividuation.

If an external source is seen as responsible for the person's deindividuation, then the aggression may well be directed outward, as assaultive
or murderous acts. The assassination of John Kennedy by Lee Harvey
Oswald can perhaps be viewed in this light (Progoff, 1967). However, if
the person feels that he is mainly responsible for the deindividuation,
then the aggression may well be directed inward, resulting in suicidal
behavior.

Klapp (1969) has described a process which he names "ego screaming"
in which the person seeks an audience and tries to draw attention to
himself. The critical goal may be attention rather than approval. This
process seems applicable to suicides which take place in public places
and which may involve city officials (such as police officers) and the news
media, such as Japanese seppuku or some jumpers from bridges and
buildings, and some murder-suicide incidents.

Dipboye noted that the search for an identity may lead to anticonformity
(rather than more passive non-conformity) and risk-taking. Both of these
consequences may facilitate suicidal behavior.

Lester's Depression Paradox Theory of Suicide

Among the many theories of depression, two are the focus for this
theory of suicide. First, depression is often characterized by a sense of
hopelessness, powerlessness and futility. Seligman (1975) proposed a
learned helplessness model of depression, in which he asserted that the
component symptoms of depression are consequences of the person
having learned that outcomes are uncontrollable. If you learn that there
is no relationship between what you do and the outcomes, then you give
up responding because you feel helpless.

Second, Beck (1967) proposed a model of depression in which a salient feature is that depressed people tend to accept personal responsibility for failures and negative outcomes. Such beliefs may in some cases approach delusional proportions. This self-blame often leads to desires for self-punishment. Beck has shown that these symptoms of depression increase with the depth (severity) of the depression.

Abramson and Sackeim (1977) have pointed out that these two models, if combined, constitute a paradox. The paradoxical situation is that individuals who are depressed are blaming themselves for outcomes that they believe they neither caused nor controlled.

Abramson and Sackeim explored various possible resolutions of this paradox. Two are of interest to a theory of suicide. One possible resolution is that there are two groups of depressives. Each group could be characterized by one of the opponent features of the paradox. They noted that no single study has examined the covariation of the two kinds of symptoms in a single sample of clinically depressed patients.

A second possible resolution is that, indeed, people do exist with internal inconsistencies (of which they may or may not be aware). The externally perceived (by others) paradox is a result of an internal inconsistency in the patient.

This leaves us with four possible types of depressives: those with only one of the two component symptoms of the paradox, those with neither, and those with both. When we turn to the issue of suicide, it can be seen that patients with both component symptoms of the paradox may be especially likely to contemplate suicide. Patients who feel both blameworthy and who simultaneously feel helpless may be especially prone to see suicide as the only response in the life situation. Patients with only one of the component symptoms still have other options. Those feeling blameworthy but who feel in control have the option of considering possible non-suicidal effective tacts. Those feeling helpless but not blameworthy have an external source to blame for their misery and so may be expected to feel angry at others, thereby reducing the desire to harm themselves.

Other writers have seen the suicidal person as thinking rigidly, in either-or dichotomies, and irrationally (Neuringer, 1964; Shneidman and Farberow, 1957). These thinking characteristics may increase the dangerousness of the depression paradox for the potentially suicidal person with both component symptoms.

Thus, the depression paradox theory of suicide proposes that suicidal behavior will be especially likely in those depressed individuals who show both components of the paradox.

Lester (1989) confirmed this theory, showing that students who had both high depression scores and external locus of control scores had the greatest amount of suicidal ideation.

Lester's Family Process Theory

A theory of suicide could focus on the family from which the suicidal individual comes, rather than the individual himself. In this perspective the family becomes the patient. In proposing a family process theory of juvenile drug addiction, Coleman (1980) suggested that the families experience a high incidence of traumatic events connected with premature deaths, losses and separations which are not effectively mourned or otherwise resolved. The death or loss is not in itself the critical event, but rather the family interactions that result in unsuccessful mourning.

A review of the literature on loss in suicides revealed some inconsistencies (Lester, 1983). About half of the studies find no excess of loss in the childhoods of suicides as compared to other pathological groups, while the remaining studies find an excess. It is reasonable, therefore, to assume that loss is a problem for some families with potentially suicidal children.

Coleman did not explain how an incomplete mourning process leads to drug addiction in a child, but she did point to parallels between drug addiction and death: early drug use symbolizes imminent death, removal from the home to a treatment facility symbolizes the funeral, and family treatment symbolizes resurrection. Attempted suicide in an adolescent produces a much closer parallel to death. When the adolescent in a family attempts suicide, the family can re-experience and work through an event very similar to previous losses in the family. The ineffectiveness of the family in working through such losses adequately may result in the adolescent making repeated suicide attempts, and the family shows what might be called a repetition compulsion. The suicidal adolescent member of the family perhaps martyrs him/herself in order to fulfill the family's need for a death (see Stanton [1977] for this view of the juvenile drug addict).

Again, in discussing the juvenile addict, Coleman pointed to the likelihood that adolescent drug use is facilitated by the conflicts over separation that are intensified during adolescence. A similar problem can be seen in the suicidal family, especially since the suicide attempt threatens death (a separation), but results in the family showing concern about the problem adolescent (reunion). It is likely that adolescent suicide attempts are intimately related to the issue of separation from the parents. Separation at this time may be especially difficult if earlier losses were incompletely or ineffectively mourned.

Coleman suggested that the absence of religious orientation in a family may increase the likelihood of an adolescent becoming an addict. The absence of a religious orientation makes mourning more difficult. A sense of family hopelessness and lack of purpose or meaning in the family philosophy may similarly contribute to suicidal behavior in adolescent members of problem families, particularly since depression and hopelessness are so closely related to an increased risk of suicide.

Thus, it can be seen that Coleman's theory of adolescent drug use can be easily applied to adolescent suicide attempts.

Lester's Predispositional and Situational Factors Theory

This theory proposes an interactional view of the causation of suicide. An important predisposing factor in suicide is the degree of access to the methods for suicide (see Chapter 15). For example, research by Lester (1984) showed that states with the strictest handgun control laws had lower suicide rates by firearms and, indeed, lower suicide rates overall. Experience in Australia has shown that reducing the size of prescriptions for drugs and enclosing the pills in plastic blisters has dramatically reduced the incidence of self-poisoning with these drugs (Stoller, 1969).

This factor of access has been used to account for the overwhelming use of guns by police officers who complete suicide (Danto, 1978) and their high suicide rate (since guns are a more lethal method for suicide than other methods) and the use by doctors and nurses of medications.

A second important predisposing factor for suicide is the prevailing degree of tolerance toward suicide in the culture. Dublin and Bunzel (1933) first suggested this factor, but it has often been proposed as an etiological factor since then, for example, by Farber (1968) and by Henderson and Williams (1974).

To some extent this factor feeds into a cycle. If a society has a tolerant attitude toward suicide, then suicide may well become more common. But then as suicide becomes more common, the society becomes used to, familiar with and accepting of suicide.

The crucial predisposing factor for suicide, however, is the possession of particular personality traits. This factor is critical, for many people in a society have access to the means for suicide, and almost all are aware of the attitude of the society toward suicide. The fact that only a few of the members of the society complete suicide suggests that the individual personality traits must play the critical role.

What are these personality traits? First the presence of psychiatric disorders, in particular depression, seems to be important. The evidence appears to indicate that the presence of a psychiatric depression increases the likelihood of suicide as the cause of death by a factor of fifteen (Lester, 1983).

Secondly, there appear to be particular personality traits that may predispose a person to complete suicide. A recent review of research pointed to low self-esteem, neuroticism, introversion, a belief in an external locus of control, alienation and a risk-taking propensity (Lester, 1983).

The theory has been applied so far to completed suicide, but it can also be applied to attempted suicide. The access to the means for suicide is no different for completed and attempted suicide. However, societal attitudes may affect the choice of behaviors. For example, society perceives attempted suicide as a "feminine" behavior and completed suicide as a "masculine" behavior (Linehan, 1973), and this has been used to account for the sex difference in the outcome of suicidal actions (Lester, 1979). Furthermore, the personality traits of completed suicides and attempted suicides may be different. Several authors have noted that those who make repeated suicide attempts are more likely to have personality disorders than other suicidal groups (Lester, 1983).

Shneidman's Commonalities of Suicide

Shneidman has proposed ten common elements in or characteristics of completed suicides: (1) situational/common stimulus (unendurable psychological pain), (2) situational/common stressor (frustrated psychological needs), (3) conative/common purpose (to seek a solution), (4) conative/common goal (cessation of consciousnessness), (5) affective/common emotion (hopelessness-helplessness), (6) affective/common internal attitude toward suicide (ambivalence), (7) cognitive/common cognitive state (constriction), (8) relational/common interpersonal act (communication of intention), (9) relational/common action (aggression/leaving), and (10) serial/common consistency (lifelong coping patterns).

Shneidman saw ten similar commonalities for attempted suicides but the particular content (the item in parentheses in the paragraph above) differed: (1) situational/common stimulus (intense but bearable psychological pain), (2) situational/common stressor (frustrated psychological needs), (3) conative/common purpose (to reduce tension and elicit a response, (4) conative/common goal (to reorder the life space), (5) affective/common emotion (disconnectedness and disenfranchisement), (6) affective/common internal attitude toward suicide (ambivalence), (7) cognitive/common cognitive state (obsessional and planfulness), (8) relational/common interpersonal act (communication, cry for help), (9) relational/common action (communication), and (10) serial/common consistency (lifelong adjustment patterns).

The Rationality of Suicide

Several people have explored the rationality of suicide by viewing suicide from the perspective of rational choice theory (Lester, 1988a) or an economic cost-benefit analysis (Yeh and Lester, 1987). These approaches have provided a very different view of suicide than those stemming from the view of human behavior as pathological.

Lester's Early Events Theory

Lester (1991) proposed a theory of suicide based on early events in the infant's life drawing from elements in psychoanalysis, transactional analysis and primal scream theory.

Suicide in transactional analysis is seen as deriving from an injunction given to the child (Woollams et al., 1977). Infants need permission to exist and to belong in the world. From the moment of birth, infants receive messages, both verbal and non-verbal, from parents and significant others about whether they really want him around. The infant or child can receive a "Don't be" message at any age and in various ways. Perhaps the infant is handled stiffly or with distaste. Perhaps a parent actually says "I wish you'd never been born."

These "Don't exist" injunctions can come from the mother's or father's Parent ego state (You are bad! Go away!) or from their Child ego state (I hate you! You are a nuisance!) If several significant others make such "Don't exist" injunctions, then the injunction will be stronger than when only one significant other makes the injunction.

This injunction becomes part of the individual's script. Since these injunctions are made to the child, they become part of the Child ego state. Thus, in later life, even though the individual's Adult ego state may make a decision not to commit suicide, the individual's Child ego state must also accept this decision for the individual to be free of suicidal impulses.

Stewart and Joines (1987) felt that these "Don't exist" injunctions are most likely to come from the Child ego states of the parents. The father may be jealous of the attention his wife gives to the newborn. The mother may resent having the family pressure of raising children. It is the Child of these parents that covertly or overtly conveys the "Don't exist" injunction to their infant.

Children may also perceive "Don't exist" injunctions where there are in fact none. Hearing that his birth was a difficult one may lead the child to think, "Just by being born, I hurt Mommy. Therefore, I am dangerous and so I deserve to be hurt or killed."

Arthur Janov's (1972) theory of how disturbed behavior develops is in some respects similar to psychoanalytic theory. Janov believes that babies have important psychological and physiological needs which have to be gratified. These needs include being fed, kept warm, held, stimulated, and so forth. These needs are the *primal needs.* Babies often have their needs ignored, and parents sometimes fail to gratify them. Some babies suffer more frustration of their needs than do other babies. If the needs are consistently frustrated, the baby will learn to block out of his awareness the emotions that accompany the deprivations. With continued severe deprivation, the baby will also learn to repress the needs themselves, and he will pursue substitute gratifications instead. Satisfying these substitute needs satisfies the primal needs symbolically, and this is the essence of neurotic behavior.

Janov (1974) locates the source of the problems for suicidal persons in the birth process. Seeking suicide as a solution for ending current pain stems from a prototypic trauma, usually around the time of birth, when death was perceived as the *only* solution. This notion (of death as the only way out) becomes fixated in the mind as an unconscious memory shaping the way the person thinks about solving overwhelming problems later in life. Pain during or soon after birth almost always involves near-death situations, and death is nearly always the result if that pain is carried to its extreme. Being left totally alone without warmth or human touch immediately after birth or being almost strangled at birth are examples of such sources of pain.

Trauma occurring in the first few years of life can also set up a death-thought syndrome, but these trauma are usually *possible*-death events. Janov gives the case of a woman who had attempted suicide on several occasions who had been raped by her father when she was three years old. Such a catastrophic trauma happened at an age when there was no other way to end the pain but through death. Later, any stress or hurt reactivated the earlier pain and the suicidal thoughts would reoccur.

The method chosen for suicide may be related to the primal pain experienced. One suicidal woman slashed her wrists with razor blades in order to see the blood ooze out. In the course of primal scream therapy, she recalled an incident when she was six years old when her father smashed her in the face. She smeared the blood from her nose on walls to show her parents how much she hurt. Blood became the symbol for making her hurt known to others. Another patient thought of hanging himself whenever he was upset, and during his primal re-encounters he lived through the experience of being strangled at birth.

Suicide is made more likely if, in addition to the primal trauma, there is a very repressive atmosphere in the home which stifles the outward expression of pain. The person can only turn inward to experience the pain, and the crushing weight of this inverted pain can eventually lead to suicide.

More recently, Grof (1985) in a speculative vein has suggested that the choice of method for suicide is based upon one's earliest memories, particularly during the birth process. Those who choose non-violent methods for suicide, particularly medications, have inhibited depressions and are seeking a return to a uterine existence in order to escape physical and psychological pain. In contrast, those choosing violent methods for suicide have agitated depressions and are seeking to intensify their suffering in order to reach liberation, as in the birth process.

Speculative though such views may be, Salk et al. (1985) found that adolescents' suicides as compared to non-suicidal adolescents were more likely to have suffered respiratory distress at birth. Jacobson and his colleagues (1987) found that the choice of method for suicide in adults was associated with birth conditions. For example, those who committed suicide in a way that involved asphyxia (hanging, strangulation, drowning or gas) were more likely to have experienced asphyxia at birth. Those who chose violent methods for suicide (such as hanging, jumping and firearms) had experienced more mechanical birth trauma.

Draper (1976), writing from a psychoanalytic perspective, has also suggested that suicidal behavior may be a result of early trauma. He speculated that attachment to the mother in the late oral stage is critical for the development of later suicidal behavior. If loss occurs during this phase, later losses cause regression to the loss of this first relationship. Suicide is then a relief from abandonment. People who never achieve this object differentiation and cathexis (such as schizophrenics) are less likely to complete suicide.

It may not be, of course, that the speculations and research mentioned above will necessarily withstand further empirical testing. However, it is interesting to consider the possibility that the seeds for suicide may be sown much earlier in life than we had hitherto suspected.

This idea would further our understanding of suicide. Freud's view of suicide was that it was result of the loss of someone with whom the child had closely identified, and the anger once directed toward the loved one is now redirected inward toward oneself (Litman, 1967). The speculations presented above amplify this formulation by suggesting that this process is more likely to occur when the loved one with whom the child identified harbored hostile wishes toward the child and, in particular, conscious or unconscious desires for the child's non-existence. Then, not only will such a child feel anger toward a lost significant other with whom he or she identified but also, by identifying with this hostile loved one, the child will have introjected the other's hostile wishes toward itself. In this situation, then, the child is programmed for eventual self-destruction.

Discussion

The 1990s have seen two developments in psychological theorizing about suicide. First, the classic theories of psychology, which have hitherto ignored suicide, have been applied to suicide by Leenaars (see Chapter 17) and by Lester. Second, Lester, in particular, has proposed several new preliminary theories of suicide, one or two of which may stimulate theory and research in the 1990s.

REFERENCES

Abramson, L., & Sackheim, H. A paradox in depression. *Psychological Bulletin,* 1977, 84, 838–851.

Beck, A. T. *Depression.* New York: Harper & Row, 1967.

Binswanger, L. The case of Ellen West. In R. May, E. Angel & H. Ellenberger (Eds.) *Existence.* New York: Basic, 1958, 237–364.

Byrne, D. The repression-sensitization scale. *Journal of Personality,* 1961, 29, 334–349.

Coleman, S. Incomplete mourning and addict/family transactions. In D. Lettieri, M. Sayers, & H. Pearson (Eds.) *Theories On Drug Abuse.* Washington, DC: NIDA, 1980, 83–89.

Danto, B. Police suicide. *Police Stress,* 1978, 1(1), 32–40.

Dipboye, R. Alternative approaches to deindividuation. *Psychological Bulletin,* 1977, 84, 1057–1075.

Draper, E. A developmental theory of suicide. *Comprehensive Psychiatry,* 1976, 17, 63–80.

Dublin, L. I., & Bunzel, B. *To Be Or Not to Be.* New York: Harrison Smith, 1933.

Eysenck, H. J. *The Biological Basis of Personality.* Springfield: Charles C Thomas, 1967.

Farberow, N. *The Many Faces of Suicide.* New York: McGraw-Hill, 1980.

Freud, S. *Group Psychology and the Analysis of the Ego.* New York: Bantam, 1960.

Fromm, E. *The Art of Loving.* New York: Harper & Row, 1956.

Gold, S. The CAP control theory of drug abuse. In D. Lettieri, M. Sayers & H. Pearson (Eds.) *Theories On Drug Abuse.* Washington, DC: NIDA, 1980, 8–11.

Goldstein, K. *Human Nature in the Light of Psychopathology.* Cambridge: Harvard University Press, 1940.

Graff, H., & Mallin, R. The syndrome of the wrist cutter. *American Journal of Psychiatry,* 1967, 124, 36–42.

Grof, S. *Beyond the Brain.* Albany: New York University Press, 1985.

Henderson, S., & Williams, C. On the prevention of suicide. *Australian & New Zealand Journal of Psychiatry,* 1974, 8, 237–240.

Jacobs, J. A phenomenological study of suicide notes. *Social Problems,* 1067, 15, 60–72.

Jacobson, B., Eklund, G., Hamberger, L., Linnarson, D., Sedvall, G., & Valverius, M. Perinatal origin of adult self-destructive behavior. *Acta Psychiatrica Scandinavica,* 1987, 76, 364–371.

Janov, A. *The Primal Scream.* New York: Dell, 1972.

Janov, A. Further implications of "levels of consciousness." *Journal of Primal Therapy,* 1974, 1(3), 193–212.

Jung, C. *Psychological Types Or the Psychology of Individuation.* New York: Harcourt Brace, 1946.

Khantzian, E. The ego, the self and opiate addiction. *International Review of Psychoanalysis,* 1978, 5, 189–198.

Klapp, P. *Collective Search For Identity.* New York: Holt, Rinehart & Winston, 1969.

Lester, D. *A Physiological Basis For Personality Traits.* Springfield: Charles C Thomas, 1974.

Lester, D. Sex differences in suicidal behavior. In E. Gomberg & V. Franks (Eds.) *Gender and Disordered Behavior.* New York: Brunner/Mazel, 1979, 287–300.

Lester, D. *Why People Kill Themselves,* 2nd Ed. Springfield: Charles C Thomas, 1983.

Lester, D. Suicide. In C. S. Widom (Ed.) *Sex Roles and Psychopathology.* New York: Plenum, 1984a, 145–150.

Lester, D. *Gun Control.* Springfield, IL: Charles C Thomas, 1984b.

Lester, D. Genetics, twin studies and suicide. *Suicide & Life-Threatening Behavior,* 1986, 16, 274–285.

Lester, D. Suicide as a failure in socialization. *Corrective & Social Psychiatry,* 1987a, 33, 199–200.

Lester, D. *Suicide As a Learned Behavior.* Springfield: Charles C Thomas, 1987b.

Lester, D. Rational choice theory and suicide. *Activitas Nervosa Superior,* 1988a, 30, 309–312.

Lester, D. *Suicide From a Psychological Perspective.* Springfield: Charles C Thomas, 1988b.

Lester, D. A depression paradox theory of suicide. *Personality & Individual Differences,* 1989, 10, 1103–1104.

Lester, D. *Psychotherapy for Suicidal Clients.* Springfield, IL: Charles C Thomas, 1991.

Litman, R. Sigmund Freud on suicide. In E. Shneidman (Ed.) *Essays in Self-Destruction.* New York: Science House, 1967, 324–344.

Maris, R. *Pathways to Suicide.* Baltimore: Johns Hopkins University Press, 1981.

Neimeyer, R. A. Toward a personal construct conceptualization of depression and suicide. *Death Education,* 1983, 7, 127–173.

Neuringer, C. Rigid thinking in suicidal individuals. *Journal of Consulting Psychology,* 1964, 28, 54–58.

Petrie, A. *Individuality in Pain and Suffering.* Chicago: University of Chicago Press, 1967.

Progoff, I. The psychology of Lee Harvey Oswald. *Journal of Individual Psychology,* 1967, 23, 37–47.

Robertson, H., Lakshminargan, S., & Hudson, L. Lung injury following a 50 meter fall into water. *Thorax,* 1978, 33, 175–180.

Salk, L., Lipsitt, L., Sturner, W., Reilly, B., & Levat, R. Relationship of maternal and perinatal conditions to eventual adolescent suicide. *Lancet,* 1985, 1, 624–627.

Seligman, M. *Helplessness.* San Francisco: Freeman, 1975.

Sheldon, W. *The Varieties of Temperament.* New York: Harper, 1942.

Shneidman, E. S., & Farberow, N. L. The logic of suicide. In E. S. Shneidman & N. L. Farberow (Eds.) *Clues to Suicide.* New York: McGraw-Hill, 1957, 31–40.

Shneidman, E. S. *Definition of Suicide.* New York: Wiley, 1985.

Spiegel, D., & Neuringer, C. Role of dread in suicidal behavior. *Journal of Abnormal & Social Psychology,* 1963, 66, 507–511.

Stanton, M. The addict as savior. *Family Process,* 1977, 16, 191–197.

Stewart, I., & Joines, V. *TA today.* Chapel Hill, NC: Lifespace, 1987.

Stoller, A. Suicide and attempted suicides in Australia. *Proceedings of the 5th International Conference on Suicide Prevention.* London: IASP, 1969.

Woollams, S., Brown, M., & Huige, K. What transactional analysts want their clients to know. In G. Barnes (Ed.) *Transactional Analysis after Eric Berne.* New York: Harper's College Press, 1977, 487–525.

Yeh, B. Y., & Lester, D. An economic model for suicide. In D. Lester, *Suicide As a Learned Behavior.* Springfield: Charles C Thomas, 1987, 51–57.

Zimbardo, P. The human choice. In W. Arnold & D. Levine (Eds.) *17th Nebraska Symposium on Motivation.* Lincoln: University of Nebraska, 1969.

Chapter 27

CONCLUSIONS

In this chapter I will draw a few conclusions from the body of research into suicide which has appeared in the 1980s, focussing on trends in the research which are apparent. I will also choose what appear to me to be the major contributions made during this decade.

Trends in the 1980s

Genetics

Although studies of suicide in twins have appeared, no methodologically sound study (using monozygotic twins separated at birth or cross-fostering) has appeared. In addition, researchers have failed to take into account the inheritance of suicide *apart from* the inheritance of psychiatric disturbance. Thus, no conclusions can be drawn.

Biochemistry

The 1980s witnessed a tremendous growth in the number of physiological studies of suicide. This research has been marked by inconsistent results. Trends which seemed to be apparent early in the 1980s have been reversed by later research results, leaving us with few conclusions.

The research has also been remarkably poor. There is typically a failure to control for psychiatric disturbance, so that the biochemical difference identified may simply be due to a difference in the type or the severity of psychiatric disorder. The research has also been marked by multiple publication by researchers so that it is often hard to know whether a paper is reporting data on new subjects or updating a previous study conducted on the first few subjects of the present sample. The sample sizes have been grossly inadequate, given the variety of factors which can affect the biochemical measures made. Samples in the hundreds would be required to tease out the effects of suicide and other variables, but samples are often only in the tens.

Medical school education is incredibly intense, with students required to learn massive amounts of information in a brief period of time. There is hardly any study of research methodology, statistics or the philosophy of science. If psychiatrists are going to become researchers, it is imperative that they acquire this information or work with skilled researchers. A reading of the psychiatric and medical research on suicide indicates that these steps are rarely taken.

Sex Differences

Virtually no progress has been made in the 1980s toward understanding the sex difference in the lethality of suicidal behavior.

Childhood Experiences

The 1980s has seen a growing interest in the role of sexual and physical abuse in increasing the risk of suicidal behavior. The research has been quite poor, again failing to control for the type and severity of psychiatric disturbance. Perhaps abuse increases the risk of psychiatric disturbance which incidentally increases the risk of suicide? The 1990s will, hopefully, witness a more methodologically sound investigation of this topic.

Sociological Approaches

Research in the 1980s began to test the classic sociological theories of suicide and, furthermore, witnessed the proposal of several new sociological theories of suicide, particularly by Lester. The sociological research into suicide has been, on the whole, methodologically sound and open to far fewer criticisms than the psychiatric research.

Social Relationships

As was mentioned at the end of the chapter on the social relationships of suicidal individuals (Chapter 11), this area has great potential for increasing our understanding of suicide, but the difficulties in conducting good research into this area (the time and effort involved) has deterred suicidologists from meaningful research in this area.

Methods for Suicide

The 1980s witnessed a growth in interest given to the methods used for suicide. Lester and his colleagues explored to the fullest earlier suggestions about the role of the availability of lethal methods for suicide on the incidence of suicide. In addition, the method chosen for suicide began to appear more often as a variable in studies of suicide (including, incidentally, even biochemical research).

Suicide Notes

The verbal communication of suicidal intent was ignored in the 1980s, but research on the suicide note has been built upon findings from the 1970s and earlier. In particular, Leenaars' attempts to test psychological theories of suicide, using the content of suicide notes, was a creative innovation in the field.

Suggestion and Clusters

The rise in teenage suicide rates resulted in a concern with imitative suicide, often occurring in clusters in communities. In the 1980s, clusters were identified and described and beginning attempts made to understand this phenomenon. Research also continued on the effect of media presentations of suicide (news and fictional) on precipitating suicides in the community, building on the research of Phillips in the 1970s. Phillips continued to study the phenomenon, Stack contributed some excellent research, and others also contributed to the field.

Personality

Although large numbers of studies continue to appear on the personality of suicides, the research seems to be stuck on the task of exploring new psychological correlates of suicidality. Thus, the number of possible correlates of suicidality has increased, but the ways in which personality traits might interact with one another and with other variables (such as the social milieu and biochemistry) has not been explored.

Animals

There has a been a growth in the use of the word "suicide" by those in biology and microbiology, applying it to phenomenon not hitherto seen as suicidal. This is of interest, but it is unlikely to have any impact on our understanding of suicide.

Indirect Self-Destructive Behavior

There has been a moderate growth in interest in the relationship between suicide and other self-destructive behaviors, stimulated in part by Farberow's work. This may prove of importance in changing our conceptualization of suicide, placing it on other behavioral continua besides those of depression and aggression.

Psychological Theory

The 1980s witnessed attempts to tie suicide into the framework of classic psychological theory which for too long has ignored the topic. Leenaars sought to find elements derived from some classic theories of personality in suicide notes, and Lester explored whether hypotheses about suicide derived from classic theories of personality had been confirmed by research. The 1980s also witnessed the proposal of a few new embryonic psychological theories of suicide whose potential is yet to be explored.

Noteworthy Contributions

In my volume reviewing the research into suicide during the 1970s, I identified two major contributions. In this volume, I will give my personal opinion of the major contributions, not only for the 1980s, but for each recent period of research.

The criteria for a major contribution include being a substantial contribution (that is, several research studies or a complex theory), greatly increasing our knowledge of the field, and having relevance in succeeding decades. The following is my judgment about the major contributions to the field of suicidology:

1800s: Emile Durkheim—sociological theory
1950s: Andrew Henry/James Short—sociological/psychological theory
1960s: Edwin Shneidman/Norman Farberow—psychological studies
       Charles Neuringer—the thought processes of the suicidal individual
       Alex Pokorny—the role of climate
1970s: Aaron Beck—hopelessness in suicidal individuals
       David Phillips—imitation effects
1980s: Antoon Leenaars—the study of suicide notes
       Steven Stack—sociological studies of suicide/imitation effects
       David Lester—availability of methods/theories of suicide/sociological studies of suicide